THE MAMMOTH BOOK OF

CRIME SCENE INVESTIGATION

D0769782

THE MAMMOTH BOOK OF

CRIME SCENE INVESTIGATION

Edited by Roger Wilkes

CARROLL & GRAF PUBLISHERS
NEW YORK

Carroll & Graf Publishers
An imprint of Avalon Publishing Group, Inc.
245 W. 17th Street, 11th Floor
New York, NY 10011-5300
www.carrollandgraf.com

AVALON
publishing group incorporated

Originally published in the UK as *The Mammoth Book of Murder and Science* by Robinson, an imprint of Constable & Robinson Ltd, 2000

This amended and updated edition published in the UK by Robinson, an imprint of Constable & Robinson Ltd 2007

First Carroll & Graf edition 2000
Amended and updated edition 2007

ISBN-13: 978-0-78671-898-6
ISBN-10: 0-7867-1898-6

Printed and bound in the EU

CONTENTS

CONTENTS VII

INTRODUCTION

In the 1930s, when the mass-circulation Sunday newspapers still savoured faintly of brown stout and chitterlings, a headline in the old *Empire News* proclaimed: TWO HAIRS HANGED THIS MAN! The story beneath was a startling example of how modern forensic science was finally getting the better of criminals like William Podmore, hanged (it seemed) on the evidence of two tiny hairs. Like most murderers, Podmore was a stupid and unattractive man who mistakenly believed he could get away with it. He had tried to swindle a man called Messiter, who'd given him a job not knowing his history as a fraudster. When Messiter realized he was being duped, he confronted Podmore who seized a heavy hammer and smashed it down on Messiter's face, killing him. Not two hairs but one, a single wiry hair from Messiter's eyebrow, was later found on the hammer, but what landed Podmore on the hangman's trap was not a hair at all but a stubby, grubby pencil. A receipt book was also recovered containing records of Podmore's fraudulent dealings with Messiter. The top copies had been torn out, but the pencil used to write up these transactions had left tell-tale indentations on the pages beneath. The appliance of science came when the police photographed these indented pages using special lighting. The wretched Podmore was hanged, not on the strength of microscopic hairs but by the ghosts of a few hastily jotted names, dates and places. What helped to propel the case to public notice was the appearance at Podmore's trial of the celebrated pathologist Sir Bernard Spilsbury. Ever since his spectacular debut at the Crippen trial in 1910, Spilsbury's name had made news. Revered by Bench and Bar, lionized by the public, Spilsbury had earned a reputation for infallibility. His evidence, low-key and matter-of-fact, had helped convict the likes of the poisonous Major Armstrong, Norman Thorne, the chicken-run killer and Patrick Mahon, the Crumbles murderer, whose case features here. Although Spilsbury played only a small part in the case against Podmore, his appearance in the witness box sowed the seed of the legend about a man hanged on the strength of two hairs. "The revealing lens," confided the *Empire News*, "had focused on two tiny hairs on the weapon. Sir Bernard made up his mind very quickly. Hair . . . human . . . male . . . eyebrow . . . These two hairs pointed the killer to the police." The story had a fine Holmesian ring to it, but nothing else. As Spilsbury's biographers pointed out: "There was one hair, not two, on the hammer, and since it was Messiter's, not Podmore's and the hammer was never traced to Podmore, a whole scalp would not have pointed the killer to the police." And while it was the kind of story that appealed to a sensation-loving public, to the dour Spilsbury it was an irritating folderol. He detested personal publicity, and when he saw his carefully weighed testimony reduced to a Sunday newspaper sideshow he was angry and ashamed. Shortly after the Podmore trial, Spilsbury got wind of a forthcoming book dealing with his career and cases. He was mortified and complained that it gave the impression of having been compiled from his personal case-notes. Spilsbury never understood the public fascination with the way in which science wages war on crime.

Criminals and scientists are old adversaries. For centuries, men of science peered through a glass darkly at the debris of murder. In the mid-18th century, long before the modern tests devised by Marsh, Reinsch and Gutzeit, the detection of arsenic was a mightily inexact science. "Why do you believe it to be white arsenic?" Dr Anthony Addington was asked at the trial of Mary Blandy in 1752, (the first recorded case of murder in which scientific evidence was adduced). Addington held aloft a parcel of powder, described it as milky white, like arsenic, gritty and almost insipid, and explained that although part of it floated on cold water, most sank to the bottom undissolved, again like arsenic. "This thrown on red-hot iron," Dr Addington added, "does not flame, but rises entirely in thick white fumes . . . white arsenic does the same." It was another hundred years before investigators in cases of suspected arsenic poisoning discarded their red-hot irons, for the mid-point of the Victorian age marked the dawn of the Age of Detection. The cases collected here spin a scarlet thread running all the way to our own computer and digital age. Many tell of tremendous forensic triumphs, but others serve as a warning against trusting blindly to science.

The ancient Romans knew a surprising amount about crime and medicine. The physician Antistius examined the assassinated Julius Caesar and concluded that of the twenty-three stab wounds, only the chest wound had been mortal. The French surgeon Ambroise Pare (c.1510–90), the father of modern surgery, studied the effects of violence on the vital human organs. In Palermo, Fortunato Fidelis discovered how to tell an accidental drowning from one caused deliberately. In Rome Paolo Zacchia studied bullet wounds, cuts and stab wounds, stranglings and infanticide, and understood how to tell suicide from murder. In the late 17th century, the Italian anatomist Morgagni compared changes in the organs of the dead with the symptoms of the diseases that had killed them, so laying the foundations of the science of pathology. The microscope, invented around this time, enjoyed a forensic flowering in the 19th century although the medical establishment took a sceptical view of such pioneers as Johann Ludwig Casper who produced his practical handbook of forensic medicine in 1856. Yet despite huge strides in the progress of Victorian medicine, the profession itself seemed dogged by taint. The public, marvelling at such achievements as the steam engine and electric telegraph, was impatient for similar life enhancements from the men of medicine. By mid-century, the doctors had yet to produce any. Their ranking in public esteem declined. To make matters worse, a celebrated few featured in notorious murder cases of the day, either as defendants or "expert" witnesses. At the trial of Dr Smethurst, the judge ticked off Crown counsel for baffling the jury with detailed medical evidence. The distinguished medical expert recruited by the Crown made such a hash of his tests for arsenic that he had to admit that none was present in the body of Smethurst's late lamented wife. Public confidence vanished. Professional reforms ensued.

Towards the century's end, a young assistant in the French Sureté, Alphonse Bertillon, developed a system of identification that classified various characteristics – size of head, fingers and so on – and codified them in an accessible way. His anthropometric system became known as Bertillonage and although it was widely adopted in Europe, the authorities in England, particularly Scotland Yard, remained sceptical. They pointed out that Bertillon's system was far from infallible because it failed to produce a unique set of data for each individual criminal. Something was needed that defined such an individual absolutely and uniquely. The answer was the fingerprint.

The ancient Chinese had recognized the potential of fingerprints, sealing their documents with thumbprints by way of a "signature". An English naturalist, Thomas Bewick, used woodblock engravings of his own fingerprints as an imprint on the books he published. In the early 19th century, a Czech physiologist called Purkinje set out a description of the nature of fingerprints and classified various kinds. But it wasn't until 1880 that an expatriate Scottish physician, Dr Henry Faulds, living in Japan, first recognized their forensic potential, suggesting that fingerprints found at the scene of a crime could lead to the conclusive identification of the culprit. His idea led to the publication in 1892 of the scientific exploration of fingerprints by Dr (later Sir) Francis Galton. This in turn prompted Edward Henry (later head of Scotland Yard) and an Argentinian researcher Juan Vucetich to develop more sophisticated classification systems for fingerprints. By the early 1900s, fingerprinting had become a front-line weapon in the fight against crime. In London in 1905 two brothers were convicted of murder on fingerprint evidence. How they earned their unique place in criminal annals is related here. So is the case of Emile Gourbin. He was caught out thanks to a breakthrough accomplished in 1910 by the French criminologist Edmond Locard of the University of Lyon who formulated his famous principle of interchange. This held that every criminal leaves something at a crime scene that wasn't there before and takes away something that he didn't have when he arrived. Locard's theory laid the cornerstone of modern criminal investigation, and became the basis of the "clue" in crime stories. It was applied with dramatic results as early as 1912 in the Gourbin case. Gourbin had murdered his mistress. Her face powder was analyzed under a microscope that by today's standards would seem clumsy and crude. Modern electron microscopes can magnify up to 150,000 times, making it possible to analyze the tiniest fragments of debris such as paint flakes, fibres, hairs, wood and paper and use them as evidence. Such technology, harnessed to revolutionary changes in police methods, has dramatically shortened the odds in their favour. In almost every country of the world, police forces became more effective during the course of the twentieth century because they came to terms with science and stood ready and equipped to use it in the fight against crime. The discovery of DNA fingerprinting in the 1980s placed an awesome weapon at the disposal of crime investigators. With the Pitchfork case in the English Midlands, the new technique achieved early success (as the American writer Joseph Wambaugh recounts in these pages), but the full potential of genetic typing for crime fighters is still imperfectly understood.

This selection of cases – some famous, a few infamous and one or two, perhaps, less well-known – represents a series of milestones on the long haul from the forensic dark ages to the dawn of the new millennium. Some of the most high-profile cases of recent years are featured, among them that of the Liverpool toddler James Bulger, the enduring mystery of Lord Lucan, and the troubling case of Barry George, convicted on the strength of what many consider extremely flimsy forensic evidence of the murder of the television presenter Jill Dando in 1999. With only a few exceptions, I have chosen accounts by established writers in the true-crime field. The cases have all been written for the general reader, and no specialist or technical knowledge is needed to understand in each case how science proved decisive in the outcome. We meet murderers like the acid-bath monster Haigh, whose vats of sulphuric acid consumed almost (but not quite)

enough of Mrs Durand-Deacon to cost him the distinction of
being ranked among those convicted of murder without the
victim's body being wholly present. Haigh reckoned without
the enduring properties of false teeth, fragments of which, when
recovered from the murderous residuum, bit back from beyond
the grave. For in death, nothing outlasts teeth, especially syn-
thetic ones, and this durability makes them ideal as a means of
identification. There are the riddles, written in scarlet, of Dr Sam
Sheppard and Jeremy Bamber, both convicted on blood evidence, and the mystery, wrapped in an enigma, of the Australian
dingo baby case, where blood and bite-marks combine. The great
forensic breakthroughs of the twentieth century are charted, with
landmark cases such as those of Dr Crippen (whose wife was
identified because he'd unwittingly preserved the poison that had
killed her) and another deadly doctor, Buck Ruxton (whose
victims were identified by the superimposition of photographs).
Also included are cases in which forensic science has been less
footsure, as the Lindbergh baby kidnap case (the great American
cause célèbre of the 1930s) and the saga of the Birmingham Six,
whose conviction and imprisonment for murderous IRA atro-
cities in the mid-1970s was shown to be demonstrably unsafe
when, some twenty years later, the original forensic evidence was
discredited.

An early American case involving questioned documents, cases
in which dentists were able to identify murder victims from
surgery records, and others in which the time of death – often
a vital factor in assigning guilt – was fixed by examining stomach
contents and even the pupation cycle of maggots: the stories that
follow range across the entire spectrum of forensic science.
Ballistics and bacteria, blood, teeth and hair all leave their traces
on these pages. As the frontiers of forensic knowledge and
expertise are pushed ever outwards, this is the kaleidoscopic
story of how science and scientists have tried to meet the changing demands of crime investigators in their unending crusade
against the complexities of murder.

SWEET BABY JAMES

(Robert Thompson and Jon Venables, 1993)

Winifred Robinson

The killing of two-year-old James Bulger in Liverpool in 1993 made headlines around the world. CCTV footage taken at a shopping centre where James was abducted showed him placing a trusting hand into that of an older boy while another boy walked a short distance ahead. James's body was found on a railway track two days later. He had been battered to death. The sustained ferocity of the assault inflicted on such a small child by strangers makes this case unique in crime history. Two boys – both aged 10 – were soon arrested, but while Jon Venables confessed to taking part in the fatal attack on James, Robert Thompson blamed everything on his friend. Because they were so young the accused boys were never cross-questioned and challenged in police interviews in the way an adult suspect would have been. The officer who headed the inquiry, Detective Superintendent Albert Kirby, realized immediately that two 10-year-olds had to be dealt with gently and ordered that no officer must ever be ill-tempered, harsh or impatient with them, there must be no leading questions, and that any information must come from the boys and be freely given. He chose four detectives from among his team who had been trained in, and had experience of, interviewing children; until that moment their skills had been put to use in drawing out child victims of crime rather than child perpetrators. It proved a daunting task since both Thompson and Venables were streetwise children, cunning beyond their years. Both told a stream of lies, and the full truth of what they did to James, and why, has never fully emerged. A distinctive pattern of bruising on the dead child's face initially baffled forensic scientists, but would ultimately prove that, despite what he said, Robert Thompson was no innocent onlooker. Both boys were convicted of murder. Winifred Robinson (b. 1957) is a BBC reporter who worked closely with the police for a television documentary about the crime and its investigation.

When Jon Venables' taped police confession was played out before an ashen-faced jury, his great heaving sobs and wails of anguish echoed around the vast Victorian court room. Here was a child of 10 recounting his part in a crime so terrible it would separate him from home and family and set him apart for the rest of his life.

In initial interviews with detectives, supported by his parents, Jon Venables had sought to deny any part in the killing of James Bulger even though he could be identified from CCTV images leading the small boy away by the hand. The turning point came during a break in the questioning when his mother Susan Venables told Jon that he must tell the detectives the truth and that his parents would always love and support him, no matter what he had done. It was then that Jon blurted out: "I did kill James. Tell his mum I'm sorry." When the interview resumed some of the truth began to emerge.

On the day that James Bulger was abducted and killed, Jon Venables and his friend Robert Thompson should have been at school. Instead they were playing truant, hanging around the Bootle Strand shopping centre in north Liverpool. They were shoplifting and had stolen a packet of batteries and a pot of blue enamel modelling paint.

The CCTV footage recovered from the mall that day shows James Bulger walking with his mother Denise towards a butcher's shop on the ground floor. Once inside, James had strayed briefly from her side to stand at the doorway. The camera's field of vision is narrow and incomplete. It does not cover the doorway from where James was led away. But seconds later it records Denise frantically running up and down the aisles searching for her son.

As Denise Bulger searches, another camera records Thompson and Venables leading James away toward an exit on the upper floor. They had taken him through the ground floor entrance of T.J. Hughes's department store, up an escalator inside and then out of the store through a first floor doorway. As the time codes on the pictures attest, they had abducted James and taken him out of the shopping precinct in the space of just three minutes.

In his confession, Jon Venables told police that the pair came across James and that his friend Robert Thompson had suggested: "Let's get this kid lost." As they walked through the department store with James following, Thompson had said: "Come on, mate." Venables went on: "The boy followed us downstairs and Robert Thompson said: 'Let's get him lost outside so when he goes in the road he will get knocked over.' I said that was a very bad thing to do."

He admitted holding James by the hand as they left the shopping precinct.

On the banks of the nearby Leeds–Liverpool canal, he went on, Robert Thompson "picked him up and slammed him down and put a bump on his head".

He described how the pair had half-carried, half-dragged James to a railway line two and a half miles from the shopping precinct. There they "started throwing bricks at him". The attack allegedly began with Robert Thompson throwing a brick in James's face and challenging Jon Venables to do the same. Venables claimed he only "picked up little stones" because he did not want to hurt James but "Robert Thompson did".

James, he added, "fell over and kept getting up again. He wouldn't stay down."

Jon Venables then admitted "hitting James about two times in the arm before Robert Thompson hit him with a steel bar". Robert Thompson, he said, had pulled James's pants off "at the end when he was knocked out. He kicked his underpants up and put them on his face, then threw them back again, where there was all blood."

Finally as James's life ebbed away, they placed bricks over his face to cover it.

"I think he was moving because the bricks were moving about," Jon Venables said.

Although Jon Venables' account sought to place most of the blame on his co-accused, his admission that he threw small stones made him a party to murder.

As police recorded Jon Venables' statement, Robert Thompson, in the company of his mother and solicitor, was being questioned at another police station a few miles away. Like Jon Venables, Robert Thompson initially denied all knowledge of James Bulger and the circumstances of his death. He only gradually changed his story as the detectives questioning him revealed more of the evidence they had amassed.

Much of it came from the people who recalled seeing Thompson, Venables and James at various points on the route they walked from the shopping centre to the railway track where James's battered body was later found. They made a strange trio – two older boys with a two-year-old who had a fresh graze on his forehead and was visibly distressed. Some witnesses had been so concerned they had stopped to question the boys but each time they were challenged Robert Thompson and Jon Venables made a convincing excuse: James was their little brother, he had fallen and hurt himself and they were hurrying him home. Their victim looked on in mute suffering, too young to frame the words that would have secured his deliverance.

The last witness, a man, reported seeing two boys with James near a bridge where a steep slope led up to the railway track.

Clothes recovered by police from the homes of Thompson and Venables were marked with the blue modelling paint they had stolen earlier that day. It was on James Bulger's body, smeared on his cheek, ear and neck. Officers found the empty paint tin on the railway track at the bridge so they knew the small child had suffered the pain and fright of having paint thrown in his eyes before they walked him further along the line to the spot where he was killed. Extensive blood staining at the scene and brick dust recovered from James's clothes and underpants suggested that he had first been taken to one side of the railway track and stripped from the waist down, then attacked with the bricks and the steel bar. He was afterwards dragged to the other side where his body was placed across the rails and the bricks piled on his face. It was Friday evening and James's body remained undisturbed until 6am the next day when a goods train passed over – cutting it in two; the driver didn't notice. On Sunday afternoon at 3.15 some children playing saw what they thought was a doll on the track. When they moved closer they realized it was a body and ran to a nearby police station.

Denise Bulger and her husband Ralph were waiting for news at another station – Marsh Lane, about three miles away. James was their second and only surviving child; a daughter had been stillborn. Because of this earlier loss James was especially loved and cherished, not only by his parents but by everyone within their large extended family. There were a great many older cousins who all made a big fuss of James. As his mother would later tell the police, James had no experience of other children ever being unkind. He would have trusted Robert Thompson and Jon Venables because, until they chanced upon him, in all his short life James Bulger had known only love. When police told Denise that a child's body had been found she responded with what one officer who heard it later described as "a great heart-breaking wail of grief, a sound of sorrow and anguish, impossible to forget."

It was a week later that detectives at Marsh Lane – selected for their training and experience in dealing with children – began to question Robert Thompson. Both boys had been identified when the CCTV pictures, initially blurred and grainy were technically enhanced.

It was only when Robert Thompson realized that witnesses had seen him with James right to the point where they climbed up to the railway track that he admitted he was there. But where Venables had sought to lessen his role, Thompson placed all of the blame on his friend. He told detectives: "Jon might have hit him sly because Jon is sly." Asked when James had started crying he replied: "When Jon threw paint in his eye."

Later he added that "Jon threw a brick in his face and he just fell on the floor." Why had he not stopped the other boy? "I was trying and he just threw it. When the brick hit him in the face he started bleeding. I would not hit the baby."

Thompson continued his account by referring to his co-defendant throwing another brick. "Then he hit him again. He picked up a big metal thing that had holes in it and hit him on the head. Then he hit him again with a stick."

In the eighth interview on the third day of questioning Robert Thompson finally admitted: "I did touch the baby. I tried to get him off the track . . . James was knocked out and he wasn't moving. He was lying on his back over the railway track. I was trying to see if the baby was alive and he would not move. I got my ear against his belly and he wasn't breathing. I lifted him up by the belly. Then I put him back because I was going to get full of blood." He went on: "I never touched him except for getting him under the fence (to the railway track) and seeing if he was breathing. So I've nothing to bother about."

Young as he was, Robert Thompson had framed a version of events making his friend wholly responsible for the killing while at the same time providing an innocent explanation for any tell-tale staining on his own clothes: he had touched James only when the fatal assault was finished and the child was already dead.

By way of persuasion he had added: "If I wanted to kill a baby I would kill my own wouldn't I?" He was referring to the youngest member of his family, a baby boy 10 months old. In contrast to Jon Venables who had wept throughout his confession, Robert Thompson's voice cracked only once very briefly when he protested that he had done nothing but was going to take all the blame.

Police knew that both boys were lying to try to minimize what they had done because neither of their accounts gave any indication of the sustained ferocity of the final assault on James. The child had suffered so many injuries it was impossible for the Home Office pathologist, Dr Alan Williams, to determine which of at least 30 blows to the head was the one that had proved fatal.

These blows had been inflicted using bricks and stones found at the murder scene and a steel plate two-and-a-half feet long used for bolting together the railway lines, known as a fishplate. This was the "big metal thing" Thompson referred to in his interviews; it weighed 22 lbs. In all Dr Williams found 42 wounds from head to toe on James Bulger's body. His lower lip had been ripped from the jawbone with a blow to the mouth, one star shaped cut to his forehead exposed the skull. He had been kicked so savagely in the groin that his penis was damaged. And although, in their interviews, the accused boys had talked of the bricks being thrown at James, the evidence suggested that rather than being hurled, the bricks had been used to bludgeon him and had been smashed into his skull.

As the CCTV video confirmed, the abduction of James had begun as a joint endeavour. Detectives believed that the intention from the outset had been to kill him. He had been taken immediately to the canal side in what may have been a failed attempt at drowning. Several opportunities to release James had been passed up when adults who intervened were fobbed off with lies. Detectives thought it highly unlikely that Robert Thompson switched from active participant to innocent onlooker in the final assault on James.

As the man who led the murder inquiry, Detective Superintendent Albert Kirby, recalls, their age and stature was so at odds with the magnitude of what they had done it was hard to take in: "I was absolutely amazed at how small they were. When I saw them in court they had great difficulty in actually sitting on the chairs and had to swing themselves on and their legs were swinging clear of the floor and that is a picture which I found very hard to reconcile myself with, having seen the end product of their activities. There is no doubt though that these boys were wicked beyond anyone's expectations and they had a high degree of cunning. The evidence shows two boys of different character but when they joined together there was no difference between them."

Further proof that the abduction was a calculated joint endeavour was provided by a young mother who contacted police in the days after the killing. Three hours before James was abducted, she had been waiting at a till in T.J. Hughes's department store near the door on the upper floor that would later be used to take James out. Her two children, a girl of three and a boy aged two, kept running away from her. The mother saw Robert Thompson and Jon Venables watching them and overheard Robert Thompson say, "We will take one of these". At the time she thought he was referring to a display of ladies bags and purses right by the door. Twice she went after her children and brought them back but when they ran off a third time only the little girl returned.

As the woman later told the murder trial she could see her son on the concourse outside the shop doorway with Thompson and Venables who were "running and stopping, running and stopping towards him, then running away". Her son was following them. "He was happy and giggling, having fun. They were enticing him." When Jon Venables saw her she heard him say, "Go back to your mum."

In his taped police interviews Venables admitted what they were doing. "We were going to take a kid earlier in the day," he said, "and push him under a bus."

Of the two accused, Robert Thompson had the more troubled background. The fifth in a family of six brothers, his life had been relatively stable until he was six when his father – also named Robert – left his mother, Ann, for another woman. He had no further contact with his children. Ann Thompson found the betrayal hard to bear and the misery was compounded soon afterwards when the family returned from a visit to their grandmother to find their home had burned down. For a time they lived in a hostel for the homeless until another house was found. According to neighbours Ann buckled under the strain of raising her large family, single-handed, in reduced circumstances. She started to drink heavily.

The Thompson boys were often left to fend for themselves and a pattern of bullying was established where the physically strong preyed on the weaker siblings. One of the older boys went into voluntary care in a children's home after telling social workers that a brother had threatened him with a knife.

Robert, too, drew the attention of the authorities because of his poor record of attendance at school. In one half term he was absent for 37 out of a possible 60 half days. In the year or so leading up to the killing the Thompsons' family life had begun to improve. Ann Thompson had met a new man and had a seventh child, another boy. Even though the relationship soon foundered, she had sobered up and was making an effort to regain control of her boys, sometimes delivering Robert to the school gates and meeting him in the afternoon to try to prevent him playing truant.

Forensic psychiatrists consulted about the case have suggested that Robert Thompson would have resented the new baby in the family who was receiving the attention from his mother that he had been denied. His statement to police: "If I wanted to kill a baby I would kill my own", betrays the source of his murderous anger just as the rough handling, the dragging and pulling of James, mirrored the way the older boys treated the younger brothers in his family.

Jon Venables was another boy who probably missed out on attention, not because his parents were neglectful but because their two other children, an older boy and a younger girl, had learning difficulties and attended special schools. Neil and Susan Venables were divorced but remained friends and shared the care of the children. Jon lived with his mother mid-week in Norris Green and stayed with his father in Walton at weekends. At his first school Jon Venables was unruly and disruptive. He would act in bizarre ways to draw attention to himself, rocking backwards and forwards in class, moaning and making strange noises. He would attack other pupils, poking them with sharp pencils and once grabbed another boy from behind holding a ruler to his throat.

Venables was suspended but never expelled from school and in 1992 – hoping for a fresh start – his parents moved him to St Mary's in Walton where he met Robert Thompson. The two immediately struck up a friendship. Because of his academic record Jon, like Robert, had been held back for a year and, as the oldest there, he and Thompson gravitated towards one another. Before they met, Jon Venables had no history of truancy but after a year together both frequently went off together. On the day James was killed Mr Venables had gone to school to collect Jon, only to discover he had truanted. He and his wife reported Jon missing to police and then scoured the local area until dark. Susan Venables finally spotted the two boys going into a video shop and took Jon to the local police station and asked a police officer to give him "a good telling off".

The Venables insisted that Jon had been led into trouble by

Robert Thompson. His mother would attest: "He is one of those children who if you told him to put his hand in the fire he would. He didn't want to hurt him (James) but he was weak and he was provoked."

Yet despite extensive blood-staining all around the railway track there was, initially at least, nothing to link Robert Thompson to any blow that had been struck. And while Jon Venables had James's blood on one of his shoes, a tiny particle of blood on Robert Thompson's shoe proved insufficient to generate a DNA match: a single hair from James's head was retrieved tangled in the laces.

Detectives were concerned that, in the absence of any confession from Robert Thompson, they would be unable to prove beyond reasonable doubt that he had been a party to the murder.

In the aftermath of the killing as police built their case, Albert Kirby and the forensic scientists met at laboratories at Chorley in Lancashire to review the evidence. The scientists were puzzling over a pattern on bruising on James's face. The marks ran in parallel lines forming a series of loops and crosses across the soft contours of his right cheek. They could find nothing among the piles of bloodied debris retrieved from the railway track that could account for these marks.

"Are we missing something here?" they asked Albert Kirby. "Did James have a necklace that might have caused these bruises, might a zip on his anorak have been pulled up roughly over his face?"

As the group pored over the post mortem photograph showing the bruising on the dead child's face, a visiting forensic scientist happened to be walking past. He had recently been involved in a murder inquiry where a youth had been kicked to death and he instantly recognized the pattern of bruising from this earlier case. "You'll find," he explained, "it comes from a shoe with raised metal eyelets where the laces thread through." The visiting scientist demonstrated how the eyelets made the loops across James's cheekbone while the laces had caused the straight lines running down.

Robert Thompson's shoes were black brogues with just this raised metal trim.

Scientists hadn't recognized the pattern the shoes had imprinted because the bruising to James's face had formed not at the point of impact as they would normally expect but around the point of impact, creating a series of parallel lines. Pathologists now call this the "tramline bruising phenomenon", but at the time of James Bulger's killing, although it had been observed in one or two cases, little about it was known or understood. Dr Alan Williams, the pathologist in the case, then set out to investigate why the bruise marks had formed in these parallel lines. He was able to demonstrate to the court that tramline bruising occurs where tissue is soft with little or no muscle to support it. The blow compresses the blood vessels in the skin, forcing the blood to the margins of the impact area so the bruise reflects the outline of the object which caused it, rather than the shape of the object itself.

When the case came to court jurors were given the photograph of James, his face in profile, the pattern of bruising clearly visible on the babyish curve of his right cheek. The forensic scientist Philip Rydeard explained how he had traced these marks, then overlaid them on to a photograph of the brogues worn by Robert Thompson on the day of the killing. The marks were a perfect fit and all of the measurements tallied. In another exhibit, the prominent D-shaped rings and laces had been drawn over the photograph of the dead child's face.

Photographs of mannequins employed to recreate the point of contact between shoe and cheek provided further evidence. They suggested that Robert Thompson had approached his victim from behind to deliver a kick as James was in a prone or semi-prone position, either kneeling or stumbling down. To Detective Superintendent Albert Kirby this was the crucial piece of evidence against Robert Thompson: "It showed the violence he had used towards James. To make those marks the foot had to wrap around the face, it had to be a strong kick, and that was the damning part and he couldn't get away with it. Those bruises proved he wasn't an innocent onlooker but an active participant."

During the trial it was suggested by the defence that the tramline bruises could have been caused if Robert Thompson had tripped over James' body in an effort to get away, but Dr

Williams replied that the force used to create the pattern of marks had to be "considerable."

In lectures to senior detectives at the Police Staff College at Bramshill in Hampshire, Albert Kirby has highlighted how the bruising to James's face was caused. As a result, the marks on other murder victims have been identified and evidence of the "tramline bruising phenomenon" has been brought in at least two other murder trials where the victims had been kicked to death. In his lectures Detective Superintendent Kirby also draws attention to the lack of blood evidence on Thompson and Venables. As he explains: "I have found through investigating the death of James and other killings that you can be close, or even in direct contact with a victim and get little blood on your clothing. This can be due to the position you are standing in, the direction of the blows, and the wind."

The jury found both Robert Thompson and Jon Venables guilty of the murder of James Bulger, and they were detained in separate secure children's units for eight years until their release in June 2001. Both have been given new identities and any reporting of their whereabouts is banned by order of the court. No motive for the killing was ever given by either boy in the course of the investigation or the month-long trial; what drove them to abduct, torture and murder James remains a mystery to this day.

As Jon Venables' lawyer Lawrence Lee put it on the day the trial concluded: "We still haven't got the full story of what happened on that railway line and we may never get from them the truth of who did what." Both boys, though, were – as police suspected – guilty of the killing of James, and the marks on his poor battered little face were an indelible testimony.

DEATH OF A PAGEANT QUEEN

(JonBenet Ramsey, 1996)

Gaby Wood

No witnesses, no OJ-style bloody glove, no confession: just a small girl's body covered by a blanket in the basement of her family's home, a bizarre handwritten ransom note and an extraordinary cast of suspects. The savage killing of JonBenet Ramsey in Boulder, Colorado, at Christmas 1996, was only ever going be solved by the most careful forensic examination, but even now – more than 10 years on – experts are unsure whether enough physical evidence, including body fluids, fingerprints, hair, fibres and handwriting, survives to determine conclusively who sexually assaulted and strangled the six-year-old beauty queen, the youngest child of John and Patsy Ramsey. The case fascinates from the forensic science perspective because so many basic questions remain unanswered and so many possibilities still exist about what really happened in the Ramsey house that Christmas night. Ten years on, the killing continues to grip America. The British journalist Gaby Wood (b. 1971) read French at Cambridge University and is now based in New York, from where she contributes to the Observer *and* Guardian *newspapers in London. In the summer of 2006 she visited Colorado to meet the investigators still trying to solve one of the most notorious US murders of the 20th century.*

The house on 15th Street isn't quite the house it used to be. Indeed, some effort has been made to claim that it no longer exists at all. Five years ago, the number was officially changed from 755 15th Street to 749. There is no 755 any more. "The owners are anxious to sell it," says the estate agent in charge of the empty mansion. "It's been on the market for a while." The house has five bedrooms and seven bathrooms. It's in a wealthy part of what is often referred to as a "perfect town", just by the university campus and near the foot of the Rocky Mountains. The views are breathtaking. Nevertheless, I suggest, perhaps at $1.5m it's too expensive. "Oh, it's worth the money by far," says the estate agent. "It's worth $2m. It's just that there's some history that has to be sorted out by whoever buys it . . ." He tapers off, then adds: "But I mean, it's been sold three times since the event."

At 1.05 p.m. on Boxing Day 1996, the body of six-year-old beauty queen JonBenet Ramsey was found by her father in the basement of this house in Boulder, Colorado. Her arms had been pulled up over her head and tied together at the wrists. A broken paintbrush had been used to tighten a garrotte around her neck. Her skull was severely fractured, but there was no blood. Her mouth was covered with duct tape. Her body showed signs of sexual abuse. She was blue, rigid, half-wrapped in a blanket, and stuck to the blanket was a pink Barbie doll nightie. John Ramsey pulled off the duct tape, untied some of the cord, picked up his daughter and ran, screaming, up the stairs. He put her down in the front hallway, at the base of the Christmas tree. His wife, Patsy, threw herself over the child's body and cried: "Jesus, you raised Lazarus from the dead, please raise my baby!"

The police had arrived early that morning. They had been called at 5.52 a.m., 20 minutes after Patsy had woken up and found a three-page hand written ransom note at the foot of the stairs (the Ramseys were up early; they were due to leave for Michigan in their private plane at 7 am). Strange as the ransom note was – long, literate, over-familiar, written with a pen and paper found in the kitchen and demanding a ransom that was the exact amount of John Ramsey's Christmas bonus – it was taken at face value. The case was treated as a kidnapping. Police searched the house and found nothing. At 10 a.m., John went down to the basement: he found a window open and broken. Beneath it stood a suitcase on the floor. He closed the window and went back upstairs.

People were anxiously milling about, waiting for the kidnappers to call. Along with police officers, John and Patsy Ramsey had been joined by two sets of friends – the Whites and the Fernies – and Reverend Hoverstock, the Ramseys' pastor. Their nine-year-old son, Burke, was taken to a friend's house. Priscilla White started cleaning the kitchen, not thinking she might be destroying evidence. Just before one o'clock Detective Linda Arndt dispatched John Ramsey and his friend Fleet White to search the house again. And that was when, in the labyrinthine basement, behind a door that had been bolted shut, John found his daughter. White, who was a few feet behind him and claimed to have searched that room earlier, felt sure Ramsey had shouted, "Oh my God!" before turning on the light.

Linda Arndt called headquarters and revised the initial report. It was not a kidnapping. It was a homicide. And the evidence had been smeared and left lying all over the place.

JonBenet Ramsey's was the only murder in Boulder that year. None of the Boulder police detectives who went on to investigate the case had ever dealt with a murder before, and this was the day after Christmas. The coroner didn't get there until after 8 p.m., and by the time he performed the autopsy the following morning, he was unable to determine the time of death. Within days, this was to become one of the most infamous murders of the 20th century. Pandemonium descended on the house, and on Boulder. One TV channel alone sent 20 people. Money started flying around – supermarket tabloids were offering to hire informants for vast sums and trying to buy copies of the ransom note for tens of thousands of dollars. A photo-lab technician stole autopsy photographs and sold them to *The Globe* newspaper. In 1996, 804 children were murdered in America. But the country didn't care about any of them as much as it cared about JonBenet.

A high metal fence now cuts across the front lawn of 749 15th Street, and fortifies the entire property. Recently planted trees shade the mock-Tudor building from potential voyeurs. At the back of the house is a public alleyway that runs the length of the block. Local kids used to ride their bikes here, and if you look up you'll see a sign, a little obscured by overgrown branches: "Children At Play". Ten years ago, you used to be able to walk right into the Ramseys' back yard. Now, where the fence has been erected, a large, indelible letter has been carved deep into the bark of a big old tree. A capital letter for the capital crime that refuses to be forgotten: "M".

"I'll always remember that day. Shortly after dinner I got a call from my office saying that there was this kidnapping situation at a home in Boulder, nearby, and could I get over there." Charlie Brennan is a reporter for the *Rocky Mountain News*. He was the first journalist to arrive at the Ramsey home on December 26, and he is perhaps the only one who has followed the story consistently for the past 10 years. In 1997, Brennan teamed up with Lawrence Schiller, who had written a bestseller about O.J. Simpson, and conducted almost 600 interviews for a book that was to become the most authoritative on the Ramsey case, *Perfect Murder, Perfect Town*. Over breakfast in downtown Denver, he recalls those first days.

"Before I left home I called one source I had at the DA's office, and I was told that yes, it's a kidnapping, and the child is inside the home. And I thought, these facts do not belong in the same sentence. It sounded like the craziest kidnapping I'd ever heard of, and my source agreed, and said it did not add up."

Statistically speaking, in cases where a child's body is found in the family home, the culprit is almost always a "family member perpetrator". Early on the morning of the 26th, when the Ramsey case was thought to be a kidnapping in a wealthy neighbourhood, the Ramseys were treated as victims. As soon as the body was found, they became prime suspects. Except that they were never exactly declared to be suspects – the foggy phrase "under the umbrella of suspicion" was used. Police, however, appeared to have made up their minds. They thought, in the words of one ex-officer, that "it was a slam-dunk case, and they would question people with the opening line: 'The Ramseys say you did it'. You don't say that to someone who could possibly be a suspect! When you focus on the Ramseys, you taint whatever you're going to get from other people."

But the press went with them. It wasn't long before the police leaked the following: there were no footprints in the snow, and no signs of forced entry. The garrotte was an unusual method of strangulation, though one which was common in the Philippines, where John Ramsey had once been stationed at a naval base. The geography of the house was so complicated you'd have to be extremely familiar with it to know which was JonBenet's room and how to get to the basement. Both John and Patsy Ramsey told police that Burke was not awake when they called 911, but when the tape was analyzed a third voice was heard in the background, and it sounded like Burke. Midway through the afternoon, John Ramsey insisted that he had to catch a plane. The ransom note, with its mysteriously precise sum and in-joke about John Ramsey's "good southern common sense" (Ramsey was not from the south, Patsy was; that he had a more "southern" character than she had was a family joke), was so long it was referred to by one FBI profiler as "the War and Peace of ransom notes". Clearly, whoever had written it on the Ramseys' notepaper had no fear of being caught in the act.

Charlie Brennan arrived to find a macabre scene. Patsy Ramsey's over-the-top Christmas decorations were still in place – red and white striped candy canes dotted along the walkway, white lights around the doorframe, an illuminated Santa in a sled on the snow-strewn front lawn. And all around the house, crime scene investigation tape, investigators' vans, police cars. There was only one other reporter there that night and Brennan thought: "Where is everyone?" When the body was brought out, he remembers thinking, "That's the most bizarre name. And I thought: this is going to be an unusual case".

Eventually, other details emerged which competed with the original picture. Though there was no sign of forced entry, there was that small broken window into the basement that had been left open. Though there were no footprints in the snow, there was no snow on the part of the lawn that would need to be crossed to get in through the window. There was a footprint near the body left by a Hi-Tec boot. There was a latent handprint on the doorframe that didn't match any of the Ramseys'. If you looked closely, there were marks on the child's back and neck that were consistent with the use of a stun gun. The garrotte was viciously tightened: would a parent kill their child that way?

"When I had just come to Boulder," says Brennan, "my editors explained to me that it's an unusual community – it's described as 27 square miles surrounded by reality. They said, 'We want you to look into the "only in Boulder" story. The kind of story that couldn't happen anywhere else.' Well, this is the 'only in Boulder' murder. We're talking about a murder that occurred on Christmas night in which Santa Claus is actually a suspect. You can't make that up."

For those committed to the intruder theory, there was no shortage of strange characters, though none was ever charged. Bill McReynolds had played Santa at the Ramseys' Christmas party three days earlier, for the third year in a row. He had been given a tour of the house, so he would have been familiar with its complicated geography, and he had written JonBenet a Christmas card saying that Santa would be giving her a "special present" after Christmas. It was found in her rubbish bin after her death. On the very same day in 1974 – Boxing Day – McReynolds's nine-year-old daughter had been abducted with a friend, and had witnessed the sexual molestation of her friend. No suspects were ever found. In 1976, McReynold's wife Janet had written a play in which a young girl is molested, tortured, murdered and left in a basement. Bill McReynolds died in 2002.

Other suspects cropped up: there was Gary Oliva, a convicted sex offender who had been seen hanging around the alleyway at the back of the house. He had spent time in prison for raping a seven-year-old girl in Oregon, and talked about making bacon out of a little girl's skin. In March 1997, a tip came in about Oliva: he had called a friend on 26 December and sobbed hysterically, saying he had done something terrible to a little girl. A year later, he attended JonBenet's memorial service. Four years later, two weeks before Christmas, he was arrested on the Colorado University campus for trespassing. The policeman who made the arrest searched his backpack and found a stun gun, a photo of JonBenet and an ode to her.

Chris Wolf, a freelance journalist, became a suspect when his girlfriend called the police and said he had stormed out of the house on Christmas night and come back the following morning, with muddy clothes. He became furious when he saw news reports of JonBenet's death on TV. The ransom note was signed "S.B.T.C"; Wolf had a sweatshirt bearing those initials – they stood for Santa Barbara Tennis Club. He had written an article about John Ramsey's company, Access Graphics, and may have had access to information about his bonus. He was a friend of Bill McReynolds. The theory that there was more than one intruder has been seriously considered.

But the suspect who looked most likely was dead within two months of the murder. Michael Helgoth seemed to have shot himself the day after District Attorney Alex Hunter announced they were closing in on the killer. But this, too, began to look like murder. Helgoth was right-handed, but the trajectory of the fatal bullet went from left to right. In Helgoth's apartment were found a pair of Hi-Tec boots, a stun gun, a baseball cap with the letters "SBTC" on it, and a videotape of a news story about the unsolved kidnap and murder of a six-year-old girl. If there were two assailants, could the other have silenced this one?

On New Year's Day 1997, Patsy Ramsey went on CNN. "Hold your babies close," she said. "There's a killer out there."

Ten years on, the case is still open.

Judith Phillips had known the Ramseys since before they moved to Boulder. They had lived in Atlanta together, Patsy had been a colleague of Judith's then husband, the two women had been pregnant at the same time. Burke Ramsey and Lindsey Phillips were born a month apart.

Judith, a photographer, now lives in Denver with Tom "Doc" Miller, a wild-eyed, electric-haired lawyer, private investigator and handwriting expert who she met through the Ramsey case. Miller is trying to find a publisher for his book about JonBenet's death. By way of introductory warning, he tells me that everyone who has written about JonBenet has profited from her death. "Every drop of her blood has been sold! There's not enough blood in that girl's body to pay for all the ink that's been spent on her."

Judith brings down a black and white photo she took of Patsy, Burke and JonBenet in the year before the murder. "It haunts a lot of people," she says. "A lot of people have said they see a lot of evil in Patsy's eyes." She pauses and fiddles with that opinion for a second. "I'm too close to it, I don't know."

In the photograph, Patsy is wearing a dramatically ruffled cream blouse; Burke is seated on her right; JonBenet is draped over her left shoulder, looking at the camera with hooded, seductive, melancholic eyes. It is the pose of a much older woman, a worn-out temptress, and she is heavily made-up with great sweeps of powder and shadow and dark, Fifties eyeliner. Later, when pictures of JonBenet as a miniature prom queen began to circulate in the supermarket tabloids, John Ramsey would say that they had been retouched. Yet here was the black and white truth of how Patsy wanted her children to be seen.

In the year of her death, JonBenet Ramsey had been crowned Little Miss Colorado. She had also been America's Royale Little Miss, National Tiny Miss Beauty, and Colorado State All-Star Kids Cover Girl, among others. In her youth, Patsy had been crowned Miss West Virginia, and so had her sister Pam. A special display case was made to house JonBenet's pageant trophies. Once, when Judith's daughter Lindsey Phillips asked JonBenet about these, she said: "They're not really mine. They're more my mom's trophies." JonBenet was dressed in outfits reminiscent of a Vegas showgirl; she wore tiaras and lipstick; her hair was lightened and curled; she was taught to dance provocatively. She was an icon of cross-dressing – crossing from girl to woman, from child to plaything. The month after her death, a photographer named Randy Simons, who had been hired by the Ramseys in June 1996 to take photographs of JonBenet in her pageant clothes, sold his JonBenet portfolio to Sygma Photo Agency for $7,500. A year later, he was arrested for walking naked in the street, crying, "I didn't kill JonBenet!" He was hospitalized, and not considered a suspect.

Judith was out of town when the murder took place – which was just as well, she now says, "because I would have been blamed. They blamed everybody. They blamed Fleet White – their best friend! When we came back to Boulder, nobody was talking to each other – everybody was afraid to discuss anything with anybody. I felt like I was in a Robert Ludlum novel."

Gradually, many of the Ramseys' friends fell away in the swell of suspicion. The Ramseys fought with the Whites at JonBenet's funeral; the Whites urged the governor to appoint an independent prosecutor.

"It's a sickening, sickening, sickening thing!" Doc Miller starts to shout. "That little girl was murdered. And billions of dollars have been spent covering up her murder, unfortunately, by the press. You're as guilty as that woman if you print the goddam intruder theory. You're just taking more blood out of her. You'll come out of here with blood on your hands, Gaby!"

Judith gives me a copy of her latest coffee-table book, uncannily entitled *Scream, Baby, Scream*, and takes me into every room of the house but one. Glancing into this last, I see two rows of Sig-Sauer rifles, laid side by side on a double bed. There are so many guns that not an inch of bedspread is visible beneath.

One of the most immediately striking aspects of the Ramsey investigation was the dispute that broke out between the police department and the DA's office. The police detectives were led by Steve Thomas, who believed that Patsy had accidentally killed JonBenet in a bedwetting incident, and that the Ramseys had then staged it to look like a murder. The DA's office called out of retirement a legendary investigator from Colorado Springs, who had solved over 200 homicide cases: Lou Smit. Smit believed the Ramseys were innocent, that an intruder had entered the house and lain in wait in a nearby bedroom. He could be found, Smit thought, if DNA evidence was carefully considered. Foreign DNA was found under JonBenet's fingernails: "I think she got a piece of her killer," Smit said.

Two weeks after the murder, the results of a DNA test came back to the police. A drop of JonBenet's blood found in her underpants was mixed with the DNA of a Caucasian male, and no member of the Ramsey family was a match. It was six months before that report reached the DA's office. In August 1998, Steve Thomas resigned from the police department over the way the Ramsey case had been handled. In September 1998, Lou Smit resigned from the DA's office on the same grounds.

In 1999, just before the grand jury was about to be sworn in, the internationally recognized forensic expert Henry Lee was brought in. Yes, he suggested, the DNA in the underpants was not the Ramseys', but who was to say it was the murderer's? It could have been left there at any time, from the point of manufacture onwards.

"They were going to test all the Bloomingdales factory workers in Hong Kong, until they realized it wouldn't have made any difference," says Bob Grant, former District Attorney for Adams County and adviser to the grand jury. "I can make the whole argument – it came from the factory, it came from the cleaners, it came from the pants being placed in a hamper with other clothes that had other foreign DNA on them – it could have come from any number of places. But as a prosecutor, I've got to prove beyond a reasonable doubt. And foreign male DNA mixed with her blood in her underpants: that's reasonable doubt, by definition."

The grand jury voted not to indict the Ramseys. At this point, for the prosecutors, the case was over – it was, as Grant realized early on, an "unprosecutable case". But the public battles continued. Steve Thomas wrote a book that laid the blame squarely on Patsy, and the Ramseys wrote a book listing other suspects. Both came out in 2000. The Ramseys sued Thomas, and settled. That year, Chris Wolf, one of the suspects listed in the Ramseys' book, sued them for defamation. But in order to prove his own innocence, he had to prove Patsy's guilt. In dismissing the case, federal judge Julie Carnes said that the evidence presented in that civil case suggested an intruder was more likely to have committed the crime than Patsy. In the Ramsey camp, it was widely thought this meant they had been cleared.

It has been pointed out even by those who once suspected them that in the past 10 years the Ramseys have not behaved as guilty people might. They wrote a book, which locked them into a version of the story; they sued Steve Thomas, which could have brought them into a courtroom; in 2004, John Ramsey ran for the state legislature in Michigan, where they now live – why would a guilty man do that knowing the scrutiny to which politicians are routinely subjected? And from time to time, when they pass through Boulder, the Ramseys meet with the DA to find out how the investigation is coming along. Those who have been in touch with them recently say the Ramseys are devastated and broke. "They've been badgered and kicked and everything else," said one acquaintance. They were contacted for this story, but remained silent.

I meet Michael Tracey in a place he refers to as his "downtown office" – a bar called the Hungry Toad, which is owned by a Brit and is the only place in Boulder where you can buy a pint of bitter. Tracey is a professor of journalism at the University of Colorado; he has made three documentaries about the Ramsey case, is currently at work on a book about it, and has the ear of John and Patsy Ramsey, in whose innocence he firmly believes. He arrives with a manila envelope and tells me knowingly that he feels very close to solving the case. He can't say why, but he tells me that the DNA from JonBenet's underpants has now been tested accurately enough to be logged in the FBI system. Which means that anyone in any part of the country who has committed any crime for which a DNA sample is taken will automatically be cross-checked. Any day now, the FBI may find a match.

"This was not a staging," Tracey says, pulling a photograph of JonBenet's neck out of his envelope. "This was a vicious attack. There's no question in my mind now that someone came in who kind of knew them, who got off on little girls, extremely violent. She was asphyxiated – that begins to explain why there's no blood in the head – and he's getting off on this. I think they wanted to play with her. I think it was a very sick game by a very sick person."

JonBenet's death gripped America, Tracey suggests, because it had everything going for it: "Sex, sleaze, the rich father, the American dream gone bad . . . It was a combination of voyeurism, resentment, anger, irrationality, a cultural viciousness. It was Greek – a lot of people focused on it as a kind of catharsis."

Where is the catharsis, I ask, if the case is unsolved?

"It's in the hate. Hate the Ramseys, you feel better. This was pretty close to a conspiracy."

When Tracey pulled the image out of the manila envelope, I thought it was one I had already seen – a close-up of JonBenet's neck, designed to show the garrotte and the marks thought to have been made by a stun gun. But I noticed Tracey only pulled half the picture out of the envelope. The photographs I had seen were not close-ups but crops of this one. On instinct, I reached for the photo and pulled it out a little further. JonBenet's face came into view. She was lying down, and shot in profile. Her mouth was slightly open, her eyes were closed. If the photo had been in black and white, so that her skin's bluish tinge was invisible, you might have thought that she was merely asleep – until your eyes were drawn down to the fine blonde hair trapped under the cord with which she had been strangled.

I looked at this photograph only briefly; in an unforeseeable split second I felt suddenly, swimmingly sick. Tracey's voice became background noise. Come on, I told myself, you're not squeamish. But back she came, the seemingly sleeping child. I started to sweat.

Later, I realized what it was about the photo that had haunted me: it was so ordinary. Over the course of many conversations, I'd become accustomed to hearing of "the garrotted neck", "the fingernails", "the blood in the underpants"; these things were never hers. And the infamous pageant photos, haunting in their own perverse, made-up way, put her at several removes from herself. So in our minds she seems to have gone from icon to crime-lab fodder without passing through the most obvious and fundamental incarnation. I expected her body to look unrecognizable in some way, to be bloody or obscured or overly clinical. The last thing I expected it to be was what she was: a little girl.

The sign on Frank Coffman's door reads: "The Crypt. Ring twice for best results." Coffman makes horror masks for a living. He lives a few blocks away from the Ramseys' old house, and first became interested in the case because he lived nearby. Ten years ago, he was a regular Columbo, bumbling around, discovering where the cord and duct tape had been bought, befriending every nanny and cleaning person who had ever worked for the Ramseys. He has photographs and floor plans of the house. He has samples of Patsy's handwriting. "A lot of people thought I had a kind of encyclopedic knowledge of the case," he says, on the phone.

Later, as he leads me into his apartment, Coffman tells me he likes murder mysteries. "I like books about the Lindbergh case, things like that. I know everything about the Kennedy assassination – that's pretty obvious really, when you look at the evidence. The Ramsey case has a lot of curlicues – it's still puzzling, even if you think you know who did it."

As we wander down Boulder's central shopping street towards a coffee shop, Coffman tells me of a parade JonBenet took part in here just before the murder. She was dressed up "as Little Miss Christmas, or something like that". It was a tradition – the previous year she had sailed down the high street as Shirley Temple, singing "The Good Ship Lollipop". Then Coffman stops and tells me something that became lost as soon as the media frenzy began. "She wasn't famous in Boulder, you know," he says. "I never heard of her before the murder. You get the impression that she was some kind of celebrity here. She was totally just another kid. Even though she was in that parade, nobody knew her. It's not like she was a target for a stranger. Her name never appeared in the newspaper before her murder. Her mother maybe wanted her to become famous, and maybe she was famous on the pageant circuit, but who the hell even was aware of that? Well," he adds more slowly, "she's famous now."

I come back to my hotel and leave a message for Lou Smit. I've tried him through the DA's office for months without success, but now I have a number for his home in Colorado Springs and, although it's late, I can't get out of my mind the idea that so much of this hangs on him, whichever way you look at it.

If some of Smit's former colleagues are to be believed, he was swayed by his own religious convictions into believing the Ramseys were innocent. District Attorney Alex Hunter later said Smit got too close. Bob Grant, who had worked with Smit on a number of difficult homicide cases in Colorado Springs, says that in the Ramsey case "people thought Lou was set up. The first time he met the Ramseys there was some kind of prayer group or something, and Lou's a very religious man. He got more so during his employment in Boulder. Patsy asked him to pray with them at the house – it felt natural to Lou. It should not have. I'm not saying it coloured his objectivity, but it certainly lends itself to that appearance."

On the other hand, here was a man who had solved over 200

homicide cases, while the detectives in Boulder had not even investigated one. By the time he was called out of retirement to work on it, the evidence gathered was not as he would have wanted it. He told Michael Tracey, for instance, that had he been the first detective on the scene, he would have brought a dog in, which would have found the body in 30 seconds; he would have separated the Ramseys, asked them to come down to the station to give hair samples and blood samples; he would have taken their clothes and conducted initial interviews. Had they refused, he told Tracey, he would have arrested them. This from the man who believes most strongly in their innocence: an arrest would at least have given them the chance to clear their names.

There was another detail. In 1996, the year of JonBenet's death, Smit had solved one of Colorado's most puzzling crimes – the kidnap and murder of a 13-year-old girl called Heather Church. The trail had gone cold, Smit had been brought in and he'd solved the case on the basis of a latent fingerprint submitted to the FBI – years after the crime had taken place. Now he was suggesting that the Ramsey case could still be solved, 10 years on, using DNA evidence. Maybe he knew something others didn't.

Last year, Patsy's cancer recurred so aggressively that it was assumed she would die. Smit drove up to Michigan to visit her. Tracey speculates: "I think he went to see her just in case." In case of a confession? I asked. But why? He's on their side. "No," said Tracey, "he's on the side of JonBenet. Now, does Lou Smit think the Ramseys killed JonBenet? No. But, would he just . . . a final . . . you know, just in case? Sure. That's how good he is." In the letter of resignation he sent to Alex Hunter in September 1998, Smit wrote: "Shoes, shoes, the victim's shoes, who will stand in the victim's shoes?"

The following morning, Lou Smit rings while I'm having breakfast. With direct, old-fashioned charm, he tells me he can't talk about the case because he is officially back inside it, and wants to remain that way in order to solve it. The DA, who has rehired him, has a strict policy of no publicity. But he does say he's hopeful, and tells me of others who are working on the case separately.

Ollie Gray and John San Augustin were hired by John and

Patsy Ramsey in 1999. When the Ramseys ran out of money to pay them, the private eyes kept going. But it's hard. They needed the police to co-operate, and now that the police files have been handed over to the DA's office, they need the DA to co-operate. "If they had put as much energy into investigating the crime itself as they did in trying to persecute the Ramseys, this thing would already have been put to bed," says Ollie Gray. "I'll bet you a nice steak dinner and a good bottle of wine that they have a bunch of evidence they have never processed. I think they have reports that basically prove that the Ramseys are innocent."

On my last morning in Colorado, I go to meet Bill Wise, Alex Hunter's former deputy district attorney, at his home. His big white husky greets me at the door. Wise tells me that he was taken off the case for complaining about the police department's incompetence. I ask him why he thinks Smit has always believed in the Ramseys' innocence. "I don't know," he says, taking a deep drag on his cigarette. "It would be because he is a much better investigator than me, and he sees things I don't see. He's a hell of an investigator. And if you can get a match anytime – murder has no statute of limitations . . . with all these databases that have been put together, there's a pretty good chance that DNA's gonna turn up sometime."

In a corner of Wise's house is a framed Victorian picture. On the frame, it says it's a puzzle picture but, try as I might, I can't see the image two ways – all I can see is a pleasant pastoral scene. Eventually, I give up, and ask Wise to show me how it works. He laughs, and points a smoky finger at various details. "There, see? That's a cat in the shrubbery," he says, "and there's a face there, and a crocodile down there." Gradually, the whole hidden flip side comes into view – the English country scene is replaced by a fleeting kind of zoo.

"You can find them," Wise says with a smile. "You just have to look hard enough."

WHO KILLED BAMBI?

(Jeremy Bamber, UK 1985)

Jim Shelley

Jeremy Bamber was convicted of murdering five of his own family in cold blood. At first detectives believed him when he blamed the killings on his deranged sister. But Bamber's jilted girlfriend denounced him to the police, and he was arrested a few weeks later. At his trial, the judge told Bamber that his conduct had been "evil beyond belief" and that for all his glamorous image and playboy lifestyle, the young farmer's son had "a warped, callous and evil mind." Bamber himself has always maintained his innocence. He says that when the killer rampaged through White House Farm on that dreadful harvest night, he was several miles away at home, in bed, alone, asleep. He insists it was his drug-fuelled sister Sheila who shot her sleeping twin sons and gunned down her adoptive parents before turning the gun on herself. The complex forensic evidence in this case principally concerned blood found in the silencer fitted to the murder weapon. Bamber and his lawyers challenge this evidence. The facts are examined here by the journalist Jim Shelley (b.1963) who wrote for The Guardian *for ten years. He now freelances and contributes a weekly TV column to* The Guardian Guide.

This is a story about a silencer, a telephone call, an ex-girlfriend and a schizophrenic. It's a story about mass murder and the massive uncertainties surrounding it, involving two potential culprits but offering no obvious explanation. One of the suspects,

Sheila Caffell, is dead. The other, Jeremy Bamber, is serving five life sentences for something he says he didn't do. Bamber was found guilty in 1986 of killing his adoptive father and mother, his step-sister and her twin sons. The jury which convicted him had been divided, and after nine and a half hours of deliberation still couldn't reach a unanimous verdict. The judge eventually settled for a majority verdict of 10:2. So it's not surprising that every scenario that can be thrown up by the crime remains so clouded by inconclusive or questionable evidence. The press and the public, however, were in no doubt that Bamber was guilty.

In the early hours of Wednesday 7 August 1985, the bodies of Nevill and June Bamber, their adopted daughter Sheila "Bambi" Caffell and her two young children Daniel and Nicholas were found dead from multiple gunshot wounds at their home in Essex. In the mire of possibilities surrounding the events that night, one thing, at least, is certain: the killer was either Jeremy Bamber or his schizophrenic step-sister Sheila Caffell. The Bambers' son, Jeremy, had alerted police at about 3.30 a.m. and told them his father had just phoned him saying: "Please come over . . . Your sister has gone crazy and has got a gun."

This phone call ensured that the possibility of the perpetrator being some sort of deranged drifter or burglar or jealous ex-lover could be discounted, and fixed the possibility that Bamber himself was responsible for the killings at precisely 50 per cent. Either he was telling the truth, and "Bambi" had shot her family before turning the gun on herself, or he was lying in which case he was almost certainly responsible for the slaughter himself.

The bodies were found at the Bambers' farm in Tolleshunt D'Arcy, Essex, five miles from Jeremy Bamber's cottage, from where he phoned the police. Between them, the five victims had been shot twenty-five times by a .22 Anschutz semi-automatic rifle, mostly at extremely close range.

Sheila's six-year-old twins were found in their beds and were probably shot first in their sleep. Daniel had been shot five times through the back of the head and was found curled up in a foetal position, sucking his thumb. Nicholas had been shot three times, through the nose, cheek and eyebrow. Nevill and June were also shot in bed but had not died instantaneously. June had crawled across the bedroom, but died having been shot seven times, in the ear, neck, arm, chest, the right knee and, point blank, between the eyes.

Despite being shot twice in the bedroom, Nevill Bamber made it to the kitchen where, after what looked like a violent struggle, he was found dead slumped on a stool having received a further six shots to the head and neck. The kitchen phone was found off the hook. Finally, Sheila Caffell was found dead by her parents' bed from two gunshot wounds to her chin and throat. Her right hand was lying across the butt of a .22 rifle, which was across her chest, pointed upwards towards her head.

That Thursday's *Daily Mail* was in no doubt – "Drugs Probe After Massacre By Mother of Twins" – and certainly Sheila's wounds, together with Bamber's phone call, led police to treat the case as if only she could have committed the murders and had then committed suicide. The police were so certain at this stage about the case that shortly afterwards, many items from the crime scene, including bloodstained bedding and carpets, were destroyed.

But the 50 per cent chance that Bamber was the killer endured. There were two sets of fingerprints on the gun – Sheila's and Jeremy's. As the days passed, police suspicions changed. Fifty-three days after the bodies were found, Jeremy Bamber was charged with murder. He pleaded not guilty but a year later, on 28 October 1986, he was convicted of all five murders.

Sentencing him to life imprisonment, Mr Justice Drake described him as having "a warped, callous and evil mind . . ." and condemned his conduct as "evil beyond belief". But the uncertainties about the entire series of events on the murder night and the three days that followed remained. Bamber has always protested his innocence and in September 1993 made a second application for his case to be referred back to the Court of Appeal, an application that supporters of the campaign for his eventual release were confident he would win.

The campaign has raised serious doubts about the validity of his conviction, focusing on questionable forensic evidence, the judge's guidance to the jury, police incompetence and even possible fabrication of evidence.

Such are the circumstances of this case that neither Jeremy Bamber's guilt or his innocence has ever really been certain. Nevertheless the announcement that Bamber's solicitors had asked the Home Secretary to refer his case back to the Court of Appeal was greeted with a certain amount of disbelief: Jeremy Bamber was one of the most reviled criminals of the 1980s. The murders, if he committed them, were planned, pre-meditated and callous. And his motives seemed obvious.

Bamber was said to have actively disliked his adoptive family, and he stood to inherit an estate of 300 acres and over £430,000 from his parents' wills. He had already admitted stealing £980 in cash from the family's caravan site five months before the murders, offering the court a blunt explanation for the theft: "greed". But it was Bamber's conduct before and after the killings that really turned the tide of public opinion against him.

In the press and in court, Bamber was portrayed as appallingly arrogant and pompous. In an early exchange with the prosecution, when the QC accused him of not telling the truth, Bamber loftily replied: "That is what you have got to establish." It emerged in court that Bamber often complained to the family about not being made a company director and evidently aspired to a more glamorous lifestyle than his £100 a week farming job afforded him. He had celebrated the caravan burglary by drinking pink champagne and was generally portrayed as someone who longed for the good life. Much was made of his sun bed and his plan to buy a kit car.

It was said Bamber detested his parents because, having adopted him and Sheila as babies, they had then sent them to boarding school. It was alleged that he disliked Sheila and resented her success in London as a model, and the allowances made for her illnesses while he was stuck working on a farm in the sticks.

Even though Bamber was photographed weeping at the family's funeral, in the days immediately following the discovery of the bodies, relatives reported that he had showed little distress and seemed interested only in his parents' financial assets.

During the fifty-three days between the massacre and being charged, he was said to have spent freely and generally enjoyed himself, even travelling to Amsterdam. Immediately after the funeral he went on holiday to the south of France.

"He wanted to sell everything," said his ex-girlfriend. Through Sotheby's, he sold an antique clock, three paintings and some of the silver bequeathed to him, claiming later that he wanted to pay death duties without breaking up the farm. It was reported that before the funeral, he bought a Hugo Boss suit and a Rolex watch. His relative David Boutflour, who was involved in the discovery of the silencer which eventually helped convict Bamber, said he noticed Bamber looking at his watch at the funeral and remarking: "Come on, let's get out of here. Time's up."

The tabloids crucified him, particularly with the story that he had approached them with soft porn pictures of "Bambi" from her modelling days for which he wanted £100,000. In court, although the police doctor described how, when told of the deaths, Bamber broke down and cried and then vomited, other officers described him as "unusually cool" and "very calm", and even that he had told them he was "starving" and cooked himself breakfast.

But other than this emotive testimony, the evidence was slim. Bamber's fingerprints had been found on the murder weapon. But so had Sheila Caffell's. So, incidentally, had the prints of the police officer who picked up the gun with his bare hands. Bamber had explained how his prints had come to be on the murder weapon, telling police that on the day before the murders, he had taken the gun out to shoot rabbits.

The prosecution provided no other forensic evidence against Bamber from the scene, from his clothes or his person – no hairs, blood or bruising, no incriminating fibres and no gunshot residues – partly because police procedure had been so inadequate. (The police had destroyed the bedding and carpets from the bedrooms at Bamber's request – he said they were too upsetting – and left other examinations too late to be meaningful.) After an inquiry by the Chief Inspector of Constabulary in March 1989, the then Home Secretary, Douglas Hurd, endorsed eighteen recommendations to all police forces for future investigations. But a nineteen month inquiry by the Police Complaints Authority decided that no action was to be taken against officers, despite twenty-six specific complaints by Bamber – including thirteen allegations of tampering with evidence and perjury.

After the trial, Essex's deputy chief constable, Ronald Stone, admitted: "We were duped by a very clever young man". However, the prosecution's case had rested on three pieces of bizarre circumstantial evidence, all of which had been needlessly provided by the "very clever young man" himself.

According to the prosecution, the phone call that Bamber claimed to have received from his father had clearly been intended to establish Bamber's whereabouts at the time of the crime, placing him away from the scene and also placing the blame firmly with Sheila. Yet if it was intended as an alibi, the phone call – besides narrowing possible guilt to either himself or Sheila – actually left Bamber open to several difficult questions.

If Sheila had indeed gone berserk with a gun, wounding Nevill and June Bamber in bed, why had Nevill Bamber left his wife alone, at Sheila Caffell's mercy, to go to the kitchen and telephone Jeremy? And why, having made it downstairs to the phone, would he call Jeremy instead of dialling 999? It was suggested that Nevill Bamber would not have wanted to involve the police with the family's problems, though this might seem unlikely, especially as Jeremy was not close enough to Sheila to be the best person to pacify her.

Furthermore, Jeremy Bamber told the police that his father's call had ended abruptly ("the line went dead") and that when he phoned his father back "it was engaged each time". Would it technically have been possible for Jeremy Bamber to dial out and call the police if his phone was still connected to his father's line? And, if the telephone was, as Bamber said, engaged, who else did his father phone?

According to a police statement, the British Telecom telephonist on duty that night said that when she was asked by the police to check the line, she could "tell that the receiver was off the hook . . . I could hear a dog barking."

Shortly before police entered the house, the telephonist was asked to check again. "The line was still open. The only thing I could hear was a very slight moving sound." In order for this statement to be true, Nevill Bamber must have abuptly ended his call to his son, and called someone else, who never came forward. If he simply dropped the receiver while talking to his son, Bamber would not have been able to get a line and phone the police.

But simply because Bamber could not explain his father's actions, it did not necessarily follow that he had not received that call. The prosecution could not prove that he had not.

The most vital piece of evidence against Bamber was a silencer found in the Bambers' farmhouse several days after the murders.

It was discovered in the gun cupboard on 10 August by relatives of the deceased – June Bamber's niece, Christine Ann Eaton, and her brother, David Boutflour – who had gone to the farm to secure and remove the remaining firearms. They admitted they were "looking for clues", but emphasized "it was quite a surprise for us to find such particular essential pieces of gun lying in the cupboard".

Various members of the family saw it, and in their statements reported seeing a grey hair, traces of red paint, a large scratch and a dot of blood the size of a match-head.

According to Bamber's campaigners, of the thirty or forty police officers who had searched the farmhouse, at least three had searched the gun cupboard, even removing items (such as ammunition) from the very box that contained the silencer. Yet none of them came across it. The relatives took the silencer to Ann Eaton's house, but it was not collected by police until the evening of 12 August five days after the killings. It was examined on 13 August at the Home Office's forensic science laboratory at Huntingdon, and returned to Essex police the same day.

Thirty-six days after the killings, forensic scientist John Hayward examined the *inside* of the silencer and found blood that, he concluded, was of the same type as Sheila Caffell's, in an example of what is known as "backspatter". If the blood in the silencer *was* Sheila Caffell's, she plainly had not committed suicide. First, with the silencer attached, the gun would have become too long for her to have shot herself in the chin with it. Second, she could not, of course, have returned it to the gun cupboard after using it.

The prosecution's logic dictated that if Sheila Caffell could not have committed suicide, then she was murdered. If she was murdered, then Jeremy Bamber's story about the phone call was a lie. And if Jeremy Bamber was lying, then it could only have been for one reason. He was guilty.

Like the police with the gun, the Boutflours and the Eatons had omitted to wear gloves when handling the silencer, even though they had realized its importance. And they had kept it at their house from Saturday until Monday evening, before it was collected by the police for examination.

At the trial the family's version of events surrounding the silencer did not entirely tally, perhaps not surprisingly, as a year had passed since its discovery.

Some of them asserted that they had seen a grey hair on the silencer (similar to Nevill Bamber's), something the Judge brought up later (telling the jury that Hayward "was then asked about the grey hair that had been seen") even though this grey hair had never been produced in court. (It was said to have been lost by the police in transit.) David Boutflour was asked if the silencer was in the same box as "an ABU carrier bag". "I do not recall," he replied. "It may well have been in the second box."

Ann Eaton could not remember who had contacted the police ("probably me") and who had moved it: "I could have taken it upstairs, or my husband . . ." But, as she pointed out: "I never knew we were going to be put through all this."

In the end, it was a remarkable coincidence that the family's discovery proved so important, and that Bamber the adoptive son, was thus prevented from claiming the family inheritance.

Apart from the traces of blood, there was nothing to indicate that the silencer had been used. Malcolm Fletcher, a firearms expert for the prosecution, said: "I have been unable to establish whether any of these bullets or bullet fragments have been fired through a sound moderator [silencer]."

He admitted under cross-examination that a .22 calibre weapon was "the least likely" weapon to produce "backspatter", and that a silencer made it less likely still.

The jury were clearly troubled by the silencer, and even sent out a question to the judge during their deliberations, asking:

"What was the chance of the blood group being Mr and Mrs Bamber's?"

Smears of blood were found all over the rifle, particularly on the broken butt used to beat Nevill Bamber, but forensic scientists were not able to identify any of it, not even to group it. Yet the prosecution forensic expert, John Hayward, *was* able to state that blood found *inside* the silencer was group A,1 and conclude that it was Sheila Caffell's. Bamber's campaign says that Hayward now accepts that the blood could be a mixture of Nevill Bamber's (O,1) and/or June Bamber's blood (A, 2–1). In his statement of 13 October, Hayward also noted that the blood group of prosecution witness Robert Boutflour, who was at the farmhouse when his son, David, found the silencer, was identical to Sheila Caffell's.

Forensics and ballistics experts, including a senior lecturer at London Medical College, support the campaign's view that "the possibility remains that there was blood from more than one source inside the silencer" and that "the way the blood tests were carried out could have resulted in an error in interpretation".

At the trial, the judge emphasized to the jury how, from experience, Hayward could judge the possibility of a mixture by appearance. Hayward had said the opposite and, in fact, under cross-examination, admitted he had never in all his experience seen "backspatter" before.

The campaign says he now admitted the judge "did not direct the jury accurately regarding his evidence." In his summing up, Mr Justice Drake said: "The sound moderator is clearly of very great importance and the evidence relating to the sound moderator could, on its own, lead you to the conclusion that the defendant is guilty."

He also floated two possibilities about the sequence of deaths that not even the prosecution had sought to prove: that June Bamber had been shot first, and also that Sheila Caffell had died before June Bamber. June Bamber's bloodtrails (which were under the body of Sheila Caffell) showed this was the one thing that had not happened.

Freddie Mead, an expert in forensic ballistics and a specialist in the investigation of accidents involving firearms for the army, says: "The speculation in the learned judge's summing-up is totally wrong." Mead's conclusion is that "there aren't any grounds to believe a silencer was involved, apart from that the silencer was found."

According to the police and the prosecution, Jeremy Bamber's carefully devised plan to murder his family and fake Sheila Caffell's suicide was undone largely by one minor detail: he had told his girlfriend about it. He not only told her about it; after he had murdered them, he dumped her. And thirty-one days after the murders she went to the police.

According to Julie Mugford, Bamber had been talking about "the perfect murder" the previous summer. He had talked of sedating his parents and burning the farm down, but had then learnt that the insurance on the house and some of the antiques (including, interestingly, the clock) wasn't high enough. She claimed Bamber had been "killing rats with his bare hands" to steel himself for the attack. Bamber denied this.

She also said he had bragged about hiring a mercenary to kill them for £2,000. In court, she testified that hours before the murder, Jeremy Bamber had called her and said: "It's tonight or never." She claimed she told him not to be a fool, and he hung up. She did not phone the Bambers to warn them. Later that night (around the same time he called the police), Bamber called her again. "He said: 'Everything is going well. Don't worry, something is wrong at the farm. I love you lots.'" When Mugford arrived at the scene, she said that she and Bamber "went into the dining room for a cuddle and he said to me: 'I should have been an actor', and just laughed."

Mugford claimed that hours after the bodies were discovered, with the house still full of police, he had told her a man called Matthew had carried out the killings, and that Matthew had instructed Sheila Caffell to shoot herself.

The jury (presumably) believed her, but didn't believe Bamber's story about the hitman. (In court a Mr Matthew MacDonald denied that he was a hitman, or that he had been offered £2,000, saying that he was "a plumber". No charges were ever brought against him, and police did not pursue this line of inquiry.) And yet a month after the murders, Julie Mugford had still done nothing. She escorted Bamber to, and comforted him at, the family funeral.

"I was scared to believe it," she testified. "He said that if I said anything that I could be implicated in the crime as well because I knew about it."

Although some of her testimony was detailed enough to be convincing, it was mostly uncorroborated – virtually hearsay. Julie Mugford was openly besotted with Bamber, and only went to the police after she discovered he had cheated on her, and finished their relationship. Bamber said in evidence that he attributed her testimony to jealousy, bitterness, and believing what the tabloids had been writing about him. He said: "There are two people I think who are lying; Julie – she is the main one who is making up stories – and Robert Boutflour (Bamber's uncle and a witness for the prosecution), who could not have been mistaken."

Most of the crucial questions at the heart of this case revolve, not around Jeremy Bamber, but around one of the victims, Sheila Caffell. Several people who knew Sheila testified that she did not have the necessary expertise to have fired twenty-three shots, killing four people, without any "wasted" bullets.

June Bamber's niece, Ann Eaton, said that as soon as she heard the weapon had been reloaded, she realized Sheila could not possibly have done it. "She would not know one end of the barrel of a gun to another." Peter Eaton told the police: "Sheila, I would have said, was definitely frightened of guns. I had never seen Sheila hold a gun or fire one."

David Boutflour said: "I do not think I can recall seeing her with a gun." He added, "though I have seen a photograph of her holding a gun . . ."

However, nothing from Sheila Caffell's actual person supported the possibility that she had perpetrated this violent and bloody massacre. Her nightdress revealed no traces of cartridge oil or blood from the other victims, and it had no pockets, posing doubts about how she would have reloaded. (A box of cartridges for a .22 was found on the kitchen sideboard and Sheila could, arguably, have carried the box around with her.) What's more, Sheila's fingernails were described as "long and painted with red varnish", and not at all damaged by having (inexpertly) fired and re-loaded a .22 rifle.

As "a mere slip of a girl", doubts were also expressed that she could not possibly have been involved in the fight with Nevill Bamber, a fight in which stools were upturned, crockery broken, and in which he received lacerations and bruising to his nose, forehead, cheekbones, temples, wrists, forearms and chest, having been battered with the butt of a rifle. And yet Sheila showed no sign of a struggle at all.

The judge felt compelled to remark that these things pointed to it "being very, very unlikely indeed that she fought and overcame that tough farmer . . ." In fact, the palms of Sheila's hands and the soles of her feet were clean; no blood, no sugar (spilt during the fight with Nevill Bamber), no incriminating substances of any kind. Added to this, Sheila's psychiatrist, Dr Hugh Ferguson, stated that he "did not see Sheila as a violent person, and certainly not as a patient who would have committed suicide."

From the tracks of the bullets, and the entry wounds, a post-mortem concluded that Sheila was shot at point-blank range "from right under the throat, pointing up". The tracks of the wounds had gone "upwards and backwards" through the chin and throat and the blood had run "down her face in a vertical direction", suggesting that she was seated when she was shot. But could she have shot herself twice?

Although the post-mortem said the first wound would have caused "substantial" haemorrhaging, it also reported that Sheila could have been "stunned" and "not necessarily rapidly lose consciousness", thus making the second shot, which was fatal "virtually instantaneously", quite feasible.

However, the possibility remained that this was exactly what Jeremy Bamber had intended, and that he had murdered Sheila Caffell and made it look like suicide. The problem was how? How did Bamber get close enough to shoot her, and to shoot her from that angle, with Sheila showing no signs of struggle or resistance?

Certainly the coroner, influenced by the police at the scene, believed that Sheila Caffell had committed suicide. Exactly a week after the killings, at the inquest, the coroner gave permission for the family to bury her body, and returned it to the authority of Jeremy Bamber, who decided to have it cremated.

David Boutflour had said in court that when police suggested Sheila had been the culprit, he told them: "Let's see the forensics." He said: "I wanted them to show me her fingerprints on the cartridges."

He could have made the same demands in Bamber's case. No blood or dust or incriminating fibres were ever found. Bamber's clothing was not taken for forensic tests until after he came back from holiday, nor was he examined for bruising or cartridge residues until a month after the event. As for the question of how Jeremy Bamber had managed to murder Sheila Caffell and fake her suicide, be it by lying on the floor below her, drugging her or threatening her, the prosecution never offered any explanation. It is true that traces of the tranquilliser drug, Halo-peridol (used to treat schizophrenia) were found in Sheila's blood, and Sheila's psychiatrist, Hugh Ferguson, told the court that if Sheila had been over-sedated, "it is quite possible she would have slept quite soundly and deeply". In fact, her own doctor, Dr Angeloglou, had requested her dosage be reduced for this reason.

A statement by one of Bamber's relatives suggested Sheila was on medication, and that Bamber told him (correctly) that even if Sheila had taken the drugs a considerable time before, they would still be detected. But then Sheila had been on medication for years.

Just as Julie Mugford told the court that Jeremy Bamber had threatened to kill his family, so, according to other witnesses, had Sheila Caffell.

When she got divorced from her husband, Colin Caffell, the twins had been put into his custody because of her mental instability. Her cousin testified that Sheila had asked her whether she ever had thoughts of killing herself; and that she had contemplated suicide on more than one occasion. It was said she had "expressed morbid thoughts about killing herself or the boys".

Sheila's doctor, Hugh Ferguson, from St Andrew's Hospital, Northampton, told the court that Sheila had "bizarre delusions about possession by the devil". She had told him she hated her mother and, in the past, she had seen herself as both Joan of Arc and the Virgin Mary.

Sheila had been discharged as recently as 29 March 1985 (four months before the murders), and Dr Ferguson wrote he "was not happy about her leaving so soon."

We get a glimpse of the extent of Sheila's illness from a letter she had written to Ann Eaton. "The reason I'm here . . . I asked God into my life so that I can understand mum's moods more and became completely high on his love, so much so that I wanted to join CND, thinking I had a calling from God to sort the world's problems out myself. Then I got a thing about the CIA following me. I finally thought a friend saw the devil, so I went through a tough time of unreality . . . I'm missing the boys. Love Sheila."

According to Jeremy and June Bamber's sister, on the night of the murders, Nevill and June Bamber had talked to Sheila about putting her children in foster homes. Bamber said Sheila had become upset. Ferguson had confirmed in court: "She had complex ideas about having sex with her twin sons. She thought her sons would seduce her and saw evil in both of them. In particular, she thought Nicholas was a woman-hater and a potential murderer."

Although her husband Colin Caffell said that "over the years I have known Sheila, she has never used or had any involvement with guns", he also said that if she had used firearms, he would have been "concerned, bearing in mind her violent outbursts".

He justified this by saying "her outbursts have always been towards property rather than people – pots and pans etc. Apart from the odd occasion when she struck me in temper, she has, to my knowledge, never struck anyone."

In his report for the defence, Major Mead points out: "The actual facts of the shooting make accuracy an irrelevancy . . . the distances were so close as to make the question of hitting academic." He goes on to add: "A degree of familiarity would be needed." But, as Jim Stephenson maintains: "She'd been on farms, and around shoots, all her life – twenty-seven years. She couldn't have done that without knowing something about shotguns."

The prosecution argued that the fight with Nevill Bamber pointed to someone other than Sheila, but the opposite could also be true. As Nevill Bamber was badly wounded from the shots he had received in bed (probably to the arm and lower jaw), it is quite possible that it was Sheila, not Jeremy, who had followed, him downstairs and battered him with the butt of the rifle before shooting him a further six times.

As for an explanation as to why Sheila's hands or feet bore no forensic evidence. Home Office pathologist and Professor of Forensic Pathology at the University of Wales, Professor Bernard Knight, testified that it was quite normal and common for suicide victims to wash themselves. A religious fanatic such as Sheila could well have done this. Suicide victims, said Professor Knight, performed all sorts of "mundane" and "ritualistic tasks". Sheila could have put the silencer away in the gun cupboard before shooting herself. Knight also testified that "women almost never commit suicide by shooting", especially in this manner (to the neck; the mouth being more common). At the same time he also expressed the opinion that "for a third party to do this seems rather extraordinary . . . I think it would be difficult for someone else to do this without her objecting." As the post-mortem said: "One cannot say with any degree of certainty whether the injuries were produced by another party."

And that uncertainty remains. The new evidence collected by Bamber's campaigners does not resolve the crucial question: Who killed Bambi? If the blood in the silencer could indeed be Nevill or June Bamber's, as expert witnesses now claim, it remains feasible that either Bamber or Caffell could have killed their family. So although this evidence throws considerable doubt over the prosecution's case, it does not establish Bamber's innocence either. If it were possible that Bamber's conviction had left a killer at large, the Home Secretary would be compelled to look more carefully at Bamber's grounds for appeal. There can be little doubt that the case needs to be very seriously looked at again. But whether any Home Secretary will take the chance or whether the Court of Appeal would recommend a new trial is another matter. Whether a new trial would find Jeremy Bamber innocent or guilty remains the final question of all.

THE MEDEA OF KEW GARDENS HILLS

(Alice Crimmins, USA 1965)

Albert Borowitz

Stomach contents often enable murder investigators to fix the time at which a victim died. In the case of the raunchy American housewife Alice Crimmins, time of death proved critical. Mrs Crimmins' two children had been the subject of a tug-of-love contest between their mother and her estranged husband. The children were reported missing, and found strangled. Mrs Crimmins claimed they'd been abducted, and described making them a meal of manicotti (noodles) and beans at about 7.30 p.m. on the night she said they'd been taken. She put them to bed at 9 p.m. and last saw them alive at midnight when she looked in on them. But her daughter's stomach contained that last meal virtually undigested, indicating that the child died within two hours of eating it. "It was evident to me," declared Milton Helpern, who was present at the autopsy, "that somebody was lying." Albert Borowitz (b.1930) is a retired Cleveland attorney and the author of several true-crime books.

On the morning of 14 July 1965, Eddie Crimmins received a telephone call from his estranged wife Alice, accusing him of having taken the children. When she had opened their bedroom door, which she kept locked by a hook-and-eye on the outside, she had seen that the beds had been slept in but Eddie Jr, aged five, and his four-year-old sister Alice (nicknamed Missy) were gone. The casement window was cranked open about 75 degrees; Alice remembered having closed it the night before because there was a hole in the screen and she wanted to keep the bugs out. The screen was later found outside, leaning against the wall beneath the window, and nearby was a "porter's stroller" – a converted baby-carriage with a box on it.

Alice's husband, an aeroplane mechanic who worked nights, protested that he knew nothing of the children's whereabouts and, alarmed by the message, said he would come right over to see her. Alice and the children lived in a dispiriting redbrick apartment complex flatteringly named Regal Gardens, located near the campus of Queens College in the Kew Gardens Hills section of the New York City borough of Queens. Shortly after joining his wife, Eddie called the police, and the first contingent of patrolmen were on the scene in a matter of minutes. By 11 a.m. precinct cars were parked all around the grassy mall adjoining Alice's apartment building at 150–22 72nd Drive.

Jerry Piering, who was the first detective to arrive, quickly made the case his own. Hoping for a promotion to second grade on the Queens' detective command, he immediately sensed that he had stepped into an important investigation. It took only one glance at Alice for him to decide that she did not look the picture of the anxious mother, this striking redhead in her twenties, with thick make-up, hip-hugging toreador slacks, flowered blouse and white high-heeled shoes. Patrolman Michael Clifford had already filled Piering in on the background – the Crimminses were separated and in the middle of a custody fight, but the role that the vanished children might have played in their skirmishing was still obscure.

The first fruits of Piering's look around the premises confirmed the unfavourable impression Alice had made. In the garbage cans there were about a dozen empty liquor bottles that Alice later attributed to good housekeeping rather than overindulgence, explaining that she had been cleaning the apartment in anticipation of an inspection visit from a city agency in connection with the custody suit. Still more revealing to Piering was a proverbial "little black book" that Alice had dropped outside; the men listed outnumbered women four to one. While Piering was making his rounds, Detective George Martin found trophies of Alice's active social life in a pastel-coloured overnight bag stowed under her bed. The greetings and dinner programmes that filled the bag documented her relationship with Anthony (Tony) Grace, a fifty-two-year-old highway contractor with ties to important Democratic politicians. Alice's souvenirs showed that Tony Grace had introduced her to such party stalwarts as Mayor Robert Wagner and Senator Robert Kennedy; messages from Grace and important city officials addressed her as "Rusty".

Piering took Alice into her bedroom and questioned her about her activities on 13 July. Between 2.30 and 4.30 in the afternoon she and the children had picnicked in Kissena Park, six blocks from the apartment. They came home after stopping to pick up some food for dinner; at Sever's delicatessen in the neighbour-hood she had bought a package of frozen veal, a can of string beans and a bottle of soda. When she arrived home she called her attorney, Michael LaPenna (recommended to her by Grace), to discuss the custody case which was scheduled for a hearing in a week. She was concerned about a former maid, Evelyn Linder Atkins, who claimed that Alice owed her $600 and, according to Alice, had hinted that if she were paid she would not testify against her in the proceedings. Evelyn had a worrisome story to tell the judge if she decided to do so, for Alice had without warning abandoned the children one weekend while she took a boat trip to the Bahamas with Tony Grace and his friends. Alice told Piering that it was not her fault; she had thought she was aboard only for a *bon voyage* party but the men had playfully locked her and a girlfriend in a washroom and carried them off to sea. Perhaps LaPenna shared her concern about the maid, because the lawyer did not seem as optimistic about her chances of retaining custody as he usually did.

After dinner, Alice took the children for a ride in the direction of Main Street, wanting to find out the location of a furnished apartment to which her husband had recently moved. Knowing that Eddie had planted a crude "bug" on her telephone, she was hoping to retaliate by finding him to be living with a woman. She drove around for more than an hour until it was almost dark and then gave up the search.

Upon returning home, Alice prepared the children for bed about 9 p.m. (Theresa Costello, aged fourteen, Alice's former babysitter, later told the police that it was at this very moment that, passing below the bedroom window on her way to a babysitting job, she heard the Crimmins children saying their prayers.) Alice brought a replacement screen from her room to the children's bedroom but noticed that it had been fouled by her dog, Brandy. She therefore reset the children's punctured screen in the window without bothering to bolt it into place. Mindful of the coming agency visit, she disposed of wine and liquor bottles and made a pile of old clothing; by 10.30 p.m. she was tired, and collapsed on the living-room couch to watch *The Defenders* on TV. The programme did not make her forget that Tony Grace had not returned the call she had made earlier in the day. She reached him at a Bronx bar and to her jealous questions he responded that he was alone. After she hung up, Alice received a call from a man Grace had apparently replaced in her favour, a house renovator named Joe Rorech. Alice had met Rorech in January 1964 when she was working as a cocktail waitress at the Bourbon House in Syosset, Long Island. After Eddie had moved out of the Crimmins apartment, another Bourbon House waitress, Anita ("Tiger") Ellis, had come to live with Alice. For a while they had shared the favours of Joe Rorech, but "Tiger" had soon moved on to new attachments. In their conversation last night, Joe Rorech asked Alice to join him at a bar in Huntington, Long Island, but she evaded the invitation, pleading the unavailability of a babysitter.

After talking to Joe, Alice returned to her television set. At midnight she took little Eddie to the bathroom but could not wake Missy; she thought she had re-latched the bedroom door. (The door was kept locked, she explained, to keep Eddie from raiding the refrigerator.) Afterwards, Alice took the dog Brandy for a walk, then sat on the front stoop for a while. She told Piering that she may not have bolted the front door at the time. When at last she was getting ready for bed, her husband called and angered her by repeating the maid's claim that Alice owed her money.

Alice calmed down by taking the dog out again and, after a bath, went to sleep between 3.30 and 4 a.m.

Alice and Eddie, childhood sweethearts, had been married seven years. They were reasonably happy for a while but, soon after the birth of their son, they quarrelled frequently about Eddie's staying out late working or drinking with friends. After Missy was born, Alice decided to have no more children and Eddie, brought up a good Catholic (as was she) never forgave her after he found birth control devices in her purse. Their relationship went from bad to worse until, on 22 June 1965, he went to the Family Court to seek custody of the two children. By then, the couple were already separated, the children living on with Alice at the Regal Gardens. The custody petition charged that, immediately after the separation, Alice "began to indulge herself openly and brazenly in sex as she had done furtively before the separation". It was further detailed in the petition that Alice "entertains, one at a time, a stream of men sharing herself and her bedroom, until she and her paramour of the evening are completely spent. The following morning, the children awake to see a strange man in the house."

Combining a high degree of jealousy with a flair for the technology of snooping, Eddie had devoted many of his leisure hours to surveillance of her relations with men. He had much to observe, for when Alice gave up her secretarial work to become a waitress at a series of Long Island restaurants and bars, her opportunities for male acquaintance multiplied. To keep his compulsive watch, Eddie bugged her telephone and installed a microphone in her bedroom which he could monitor from a listening-post he had established in the basement below. Once he had burst in on Alice and a usually overdressed waiter named Carl Andrade, who had fled naked out of the window to his car.

Eddie liked to think that the purpose of his spying was to gather evidence for the custody case, but he ultimately admitted that he had often invaded Alice's apartment when she was out just to be near her "personal things". During their separation, so Alice said, Eddie told her that he had exposed himself to little girls in a park, but Alice disbelieved him, thinking that he was trying to play on her sympathy for his loneliness and distress.

Eddie's preoccupation with his wife's love life dominated his activities on 13 July, as he recounted them to the police. At 7 a.m. he had played a poor round of golf at a public course at Bethpage in Nassau County. Afterwards he drank three beers in the clubhouse with a friend and watched the New York Mets baseball game on television, leaving around 2 p.m. before the game ended. He then drove to Huntington to see whether Alice was visiting Joe Rorech but was disappointed to find no sign of her four-year-old Mercury convertible there. He arrived home at 5 p.m. and spent the evening watching television. Then, about 11 p.m., he drove along Union Turnpike to a small fast food stand near St John's University, bought a pizza and a large bottle of Pepsi Cola, and returned home. Alice, though, was still very much on his mind. After driving back to the Union Turnpike and drinking gin and tonic at a bar until 2.45 a.m., he drove into the parking lot behind his wife's bedroom window; he thought he saw a light there and in her living-room. He went home and called up Alice to talk about the maid. When Alice hung up, he watched a movie on television, read briefly and fell asleep by 4 a.m. A detective who checked out Eddie's story found that the movie he claimed to have seen on the CBS channel had actually been on much earlier.

In addition to questioning Alice, Jerry Piering, a fledgling in his job, directed the police inspection and photographing of the apartment, apparently with more enthusiasm than expertise. Piering later claimed that when he first came into the children's room, he observed a thin layer of dust on the bureau-top, which in his mind eliminated the possibility that the children had left the room through the window since they would have had to cross over the bureau. However, technicians had covered the top of the bureau with powder for detecting fingerprints before the bureau could be photographed in its original condition. It was Piering's further recollection that when he had moved a lamp on the bureau, it had left a circle in the layer of dust. This story was later disputed by Alice's brother, John Burke, and others, who agreed that the lamp on the bureau had tripod legs. Also, many people had come into the room before Piering arrived; Eddie Crimmins had leaned out of the window to look for the missing children, and, of course, Alice on the previous evening had removed and replaced the screen; it seemed unlikely that Piering's dust-film would have remained undisturbed amid all this activity. In any event, neither the layer of dust nor the impression left by the lamp base was noted in Piering's first reports.

In the early afternoon of 14 July 1965, the Crimmins case was transformed from mysterious disappearance into homicide. A nine-year-old boy, Jay Silverman, found Missy's body in an open lot on 162nd Street, about eight blocks from the Regal Gardens. A pyjama-top, knotted into two ligatures, was loosely tied around her bruised neck. An autopsy, performed with the participation of Dr Milton Helpern, New York City's distinguished Chief Medical Examiner, found no evidence of sexual assault; haemorrhages in the mucous membrances in the throat and vocal cords confirmed that Missy had been asphyxiated. The contents of the stomach were sent to an expert, who reported finding, among other things, a macaroni-like substance. This discovery rang a bell with Detective Piering, who recalled that on the morning of 14 July he had seen in Alice's trash can a package that had held frozen manicotti and had also noticed a plate of leftover manicotti in her refrigerator. However, none of this evidence had been preserved – nor had Piering's discoveries been referred to in his contemporaneous reports.

Following the discovery of Missy's body, the search for young Eddie intensified. A false alarm was raised in Cunningham Park when what looked like a blond-headed body turned out to be a discarded doll. On Monday morning, 19 July, Vernon Warnecke and his son, walking together to look at a treehouse used by the children in the neighbourhood, found Eddie Crimmins on an embankment overlooking the Van Wyck Expressway. The boy's body was eaten away by rats and insects and in an advanced state of decay. The site was about a mile from Alice Crimmins' apartment and close to the grounds of the New York World's Fair that was then in progress.

After the children were buried, Alice and her husband, reunited by their tragedy, faced a relentless police investigation which explored many trails, always only to return to Alice. Detectives pursued reports of strange intruders in the Crimmins' neighbourhood, including a so-called "pants burglar" who broke

into homes only to steal men's trousers. A closer look was taken at
the boyfriends whose names filled Alice's black book. Anthony
Grace admitted in a second interview that he had lied when he
told the police he had never left the Bronx on the night of 13/14
July. He now stated that he had driven over the Whitestone
Bridge to a restaurant called Ripples on the Water with a group of
"bowling girls", young married women who partied around town
under the pretext that they were going bowling. Grace maintained that he had stayed away from Alice during the period of
the custody battle and had not seen her much recently. She had
called him several times on 13 July but he was preoccupied with
business and had taken his wife to dinner without remembering
to call Alice back. At 11 p.m. she phoned him again at the Capri
Bar, telling him that she wanted to join him for a drink. He had
put her off by telling her that he was about to leave and had
denied her well-founded suspicion that he was with the bowling
girls.

Joe Rorech told Detective Phil Brady that he had called Alice
twice on the night of the disappearance, first after 10 p.m., when
she declined his invitation to the Bourbon House bar, and then at
2 a.m., when there had been no answer. Rorech had been
drinking all night and admitted he might have misdialled the
number. On 6 December 1965 the police administered the first of
two sodium pentothal "truth tests" to Rorech. Satisfied with the
results, and finding Rorech's self-confidence weakened by business reverses, they conscripted him as a spy. Joe took Alice to
motel rooms where recorders had been planted, but their conversations contained nothing of interest.

At first Eddie Crimmins had been more inclined to co-operate
with the police than Alice. He submitted to a session with the lie
detector, and persuaded Alice to take the test. However, after she
agreed and the preliminary questions were completed, she refused to continue. With the exception of Detective Brady, the
police now decided to forget about Eddie and concentrate on
Alice. Before the Crimminses moved into a new three-room
apartment in Queens to avoid the eyes of their unwanted public,
the police, succeeding to the role long played by Alice's jealous
husband, planted ultrasensitive microphones and tapped the

telephone wires. Detectives monitored the apartment around the clock from the third floor pharmacy of a neighbouring hospital, but could not pick up a single incriminating statement. Their failure was not remarkable since Alice seemed well aware of the police presence, beginning many of her conversations, "Drop dead, you guys!" Unable to overhear a confession, the secret listeners were tuned into the sounds of Alice's sexual encounters, which resumed shortly after she took up her new residence. As their high-tech recording devices picked up Alice's cries of physical need, her pursuers became more certain of her guilt, convinced as they were that grief for the dead children would demand an adjournment of the flesh.

According to reporter Kenneth Gross, who has written the principal account of the case, police investigators vented their hostility against Alice by interfering with the love affairs that they were recording so assiduously. When the tireless eavesdroppers overheard Joe Rorech and Alice making love, they informed Eddie Crimmins, who promptly called and was assured by Alice that she was alone. The police, hoping for a confrontation between lover and outraged husband, flattened Rorech's tyres, but he managed to have his car towed safely out of the neighbourhood before Eddie got home. When Alice moved out of the apartment to live with an Atlanta man for whom she was working as a secretary, the police thoughtfully advised the man's wife, and when she came to New York, helped her destroy Alice's clothing. Undaunted by this harassment, Alice reappeared in her familiar nightspots, now as a customer instead of cocktail waitress.

The investigation dragged on for a year and a half without result, and meanwhile there was a growing public clamour for action. At this point New York politics intervened to step up the pace of events: Nat Hentel, an interim Republican appointment as Queens District Attorney, was soundly defeated for re-election and decided to convene a grand jury before his term of office expired. The grand jury failed to return an indictment, and a second grand jury impanelled under Hentel's Democratic successor "Tough Tommy" Mackell also disbanded without indictment in May of the following year. Then, on 1 September 1967, Assistant District Attorney James Mosley went before still an-

other grand jury to present the testimony of a "mystery witness",
who was soon identified as Sophie Earomirski.

Sophie's original entrance into the case had been anonymous.
On 30 November 1966, she had written to then District Attorney
Hentel telling him how happy she was to read that he was
bringing the Crimmins case to a grand jury. She reported an
"incident" she had witnessed while looking out of her living-
room window on the early morning of 14 July 1965. Shortly after
2 a.m., a man and woman came walking down the street towards
72nd Road in Queens. The woman, who was lagging about five
feet behind the man, was holding what appeared to be a bundle of
blankets shining white under her left arm, and with her right
hand led a little boy walking at her side. The man shouted at her
to hurry up and she told him "to be quiet or someone will see us".
The man took the blanket-like white bundle and heaved it onto
the back seat of the nondescript automobile. The woman picked
up the little boy and sat with him on the back seat; she had dark
hair, and her companion was tall, not heavy, with dark hair and a
large nose. Sophie apologised for signing merely as "A Reader".

Shortly after he was entrusted with the Crimmins case by
Mackell, Mosley came across Sophie's letter, and the hunt for her
began. The police obtained samples of the handwriting of tenants
living in garden apartments from which the scene described in
the letter could have been viewed, and they identified Sophie,
who recognized Alice's photograph as resembling the woman she
had seen. Sophie's testimony before the third grand jury was
decisive, and Queens County finally had its long-coveted indictment, charging Alice Crimmins with the murder of Missy. The
prosecution had persuaded the grand jury that there was reasonable cause to believe that the bundle of blankets Sophie had seen
contained the little girl's dead body.

On 9 May 1968, the trial began in the ground floor courtroom
of the Queens County Criminal Court Building amid widely
varying perceptions of the defendant. To the sensationalist press,
Alice was a "modern-day Medea" who had sacrificed her children to a deadly hatred for her husband, and the pulp magazine
Front Page Detective, invoking another witch from antiquity,
called her an "erring wife, a Circe, an amoral woman whose many

affairs appeared symptomatic of America's Sex Revolution". A group of radical feminists offered to identify Alice's cause with their own, but she declined their help. Between these two wings of public opinion there was a dominant vision of Alice as a manhunting cocktail waitress, and her longer years as housewife, mother and secretary receded into the background.

The prosecution case was presented for the most part by James Mosley's aspiring young assistant, Anthony Lombardino, but Mosley himself scored the first important point while questioning Dr Milton Helpern. The forensic expert testified that the discovery of as much food as was found in Missy's stomach was consistent with a post-ingestion period of less than two hours. If Helpern was right, then assuming that Alice had been the last to feed the children, she could not have seen them alive at midnight, as she claimed.

Lombardino insisted that the prize job of examining the prosecution's star witness was his – his alone. Since the police had first enlisted Joe Rorech's aid, Joe's difficulties had continued to mount; his marriage was in trouble and he had been upset by a brief period of arrest as a material witness. In his testimony he made it plain that he had lost any vestige of loyalty to his former mistress.

The defence, led by Harold Harrison, was unmoved when Rorech indirectly quoted Alice, "She did not want Eddie to have the children. She would rather see the children dead than Eddie have them." Harrison had not heard this before, but he did not regard the statement as damaging; surely the jury would understand that it was just the kind of thing that a divorcing spouse was likely to say in the heat of a custody battle. Rorech, though, had something more to disclose that would change the course of the trial. Though the police had learned nothing incriminating from electronic eavesdropping, Joe testified to a long conversation with Alice at a motel in Nassau County. After weeping inconsolably, she had said again and again that the children "will understand, they know it was for the best". At last she had added, "Joseph, please forgive me, I killed her."

Stung by the witness's words, Alice jumped out of her chair and banged her fists on the defence table, crying, "Joseph! How could you do this? This is not true! Joseph . . . you, of all people! Oh, my God!" Harrison was unable to follow Alice's outburst with telling cross-examination for he had no effective means of rebutting Rorech's quotes. In fact, he may have been preoccupied by a dilemma of his own: the next morning he went before Judge Peter Farrell and unsuccessfully sought to withdraw from the case on the grounds that prior to the trial he had represented Joe Rorech as well as Alice, to whom Joe had introduced him.

After Rorech's damning testimony, the appearance of Sophie Earomirski, The Woman in the Window, came as an anticlimax. Sophie elaborated the scene she had recalled in her anonymous letter by adding a pregnant dog. She told the jury that the woman had responded to her male companion's order to hurry by explaining that she was waiting for the dog. She had said, "The dog is pregnant," and the man had grumbled, "Did you have to bring it?" In fact, Brandy *was* pregnant that night, but several witnesses swore that nobody had recognized the pregnancy – that when the dog produced a single puppy the week after the killing, Alice and the neighbours were surprised.

The defence tried to destroy Sophie's credibility, but the scope of the attack was narrowly limited by Judge Farrell. The judge excluded an affidavit of Dr Louis Berg to the effect that a head injury suffered by Mrs Earomirski at the World's Fair had resulted in "permanent brain damage". Defence lawyer Marty Baron questioned her about two suicide attempts, but to no avail: the courtroom spectators cheered her recital that she had placed her head in an oven to see how dinner was coming along. A press photograph records Sophie's exit from the courthouse, her hand raised in triumph like a triumphant boxer, still champion, on whom the challenger could not lay a glove.

The principal strategy of the defence was to put Alice on the stand to deny the murder charge and to show that she was not made of granite, as portrayed by certain sections of the media. When Baron's questioning turned to the children, Alice began to tremble and whispered to Judge Farrell that she could not continue. Farrell declared a recess. When the trial resumed, Alice concluded her testimony with a strong denial of Rorech's account of her confession.

The decision to permit Alice to testify gave prosecutor Lombardino the opportunity he had been waiting for: to question her closely about her love life. All the most titillating incidents were brought out: the night Eddie had caught her in bed with the amorous waiter Carl Andrade, an afternoon tryst with a buyer at the World's Fair, a 1964 cruise with Tony Grace to the Democratic National Convention in Atlantic City, and nude swimming at Joe Rorech's home when, Lombardino was careful to stress, the children were dead. To reporter Kenneth Gross it seemed that Lombardino had torn away the last shred of Alice's dignity when he enquired whether she remembered making love with her children's barber in the back of a car behind the barbershop; Alice admitted having had ten dates with the barber, but, straining at a gnat, couldn't recall the incident in the car. Lombardino continued the catalogue of Alice's conquests with obvious relish until the judge ordered him to conclude.

The trial ended after thirteen days on Monday 27 May, and early the next morning the jury returned a verdict of guilty of manslaughter in the first degree; one of the jurors said that a large majority had voted for conviction on the first ballot, but that he had doubts about the proof and did not regard her as a danger to society. At her sentencing hearing, Alice protested her innocence and angrily told Judge Farrell, "You don't care who killed my children, you want to close your books. You don't give a damn who killed my kids." The judge sentenced her to be confined in the New York State prison for women at Westfield State Farms, Bedford Hills, New York, for a term of not less than five nor more than twenty years.

Alice's conviction was far from the last chapter of the case. In December 1969 the Appellate Division of the New York Supreme Court, an intermediate appeals court, ordered a new trial because three of the jurors had secretly visited the scene of Sophie Earomirski's identification of Alice. One of the jurors had made his visit alone at about two in the morning, hoping to verify what Sophie could have seen at that hour. The court reasoned that "the net effect of the jurors' visits was that they made themselves secret, untested witnesses not subject to any cross-examination". The State's highest court, the Court of Appeals, agreed, ruling in

April 1970 that the unauthorized visits were inherently prejudicial to the defendant, and adding, in a significant aside, that the
evidence of guilt "was not so overwhelming that we can say, as a
matter of law, that the error could not have influenced the
verdict". The Court noted that only two witnesses, Sophie
Earomirski and Joe Rorech, had directly implicated Alice, and
that Rorech's testimony "was seriously challenged, and the
witness was subjected to searching cross-examination".

When the case was retried in 1971, a change in counsel and the
presiding judge and the cooling of community passions resulted
in a more restrained courtroom atmosphere. Gone from the
prosecution team was Tony Lombardino, replaced by Thomas
Demakos, the experienced chief of the District Attorney's trial
bureau. The judge to whom the second trial was assigned, George
Balbach, planted court attendants in the courtroom and adjacent
corridors to assure better order. Perhaps the most significant
change was at the defence table, where Herbert Lyon, a leader of
the Queens trial bar, now sat in the first chair. Lyon had devised a
more conservative defence plan, intended to place greater stress
on Alice's grief and loss, and to keep her off the witness stand so
that the prejudicial parade of her love affairs could not be
repeated.

The stakes had been raised in the second trial, which began on
Monday, 15 March 1971. As Alice's first jury had found her
guilty of manslaughter in the death of Missy, principles of double
jeopardy prohibited her from being charged with a greater
offence against her daughter, but the prosecution had compen-
sated for that limitation by obtaining an additional indictment for
the murder of young Eddie. Though the state of his remains ruled
out proof of cause of death, Demakos offered the evidence of Dr
Milton Helpern that murder could be "inferred" because of the
circumstances of his sister's death. Joe Rorech, obliging as ever,
adapted his testimony to the new prosecution design; according
to his revised story, Alice had told him that she had killed Missy
and "consented" to the murder of her son.

The presentation of defence evidence was already in progress
when Demakos, over vigorous objection by Lyon, was permitted
to bring a surprise witness to the stand. Mrs Tina DeVita, a

resident of the Kew Gardens Hills development at the time of the crime, testified that on the night of 13/14 July, while driving home with her husband, she had looked out of the driver's window from the passenger's side and seen "people walking, a man carrying a bundle, a woman, a dog, and a boy". The angry Lyon could not shake Mrs DeVita's story but did much to neutralize its impact by introducing an unheralded witness of his own, Marvin Weinstein, a young salesman from Massapequa, Long Island. Weinstein swore that on the morning of 14 July he, together with his wife, son and daughter, had passed below Sophie Earomirski's window on the way to his car; he had carried his daughter under his arm "like a sack" and they were accompanied by their dog – who might well have looked pregnant for she had long ago lost her figure. As a final jab at the State's case, Lyon called Vincent Colabella, a jailed gangster who had reportedly admitted to a fellow prisoner that he had been Eddie's executioner, only to deny that report when questioned by the police. On the stand Colabella chuckled as he disowned any knowledge of the crime; he said that he had never seen Alice Crimmins before.

In his closing argument, Lyon cited Sophie Earomirski's testimony that she had been led to tell her story by the voices of the children crying from the grave; if they were crying, Alice's defence lawyer suggested, they were saying, "Let my mother go; you have had her long enough!" Demakos had harsher words, reminding the jury of Alice's failure to take the stand, "She doesn't have the courage to stand up here and tell the world she killed her daughter." Alice interrupted to protest, "Because I didn't!" but the prosecutor went on without being put off his stroke, "And the shame and pity of it is that this little boy had to die too."

The jury deliberations began after lunch on Thursday 23 April and ended at 5.45 p.m. on the following day. Alice was found guilty of murder in the first degree in the death of her son and of manslaughter in the strangling of Missy.

On 13 May 1971 Alice Crimmins was remanded to Bedford Hills prison, and there she stayed for two years while her lawyers continued the battle for her freedom in the appellate courts. In

May 1973 the Appellate Division ruled for a second time in her favour. The court threw out the murder conviction on the grounds that the State had not proved beyond reasonable doubt that young Eddie's death had resulted from a criminal act. With respect to the manslaughter count relating to Missy, the court ordered a new trial on the basis of a number of errors and improprieties, including the prosecutor's comment that Alice lacked the courage to admit the killing of Missy: this argument amounted to an improper assertion that the prosecutor knew her to be guilty and, in addition, was an improper attack on her refusal to testify. Alice was freed from prison following this ruling, but the rejoicing in her camp was premature. The tortuous path of the judicial proceedings had two more dangerous corners.

The first setback was suffered when the Court of Appeals in February 1975 announced its final decision in the appeals relating to the verdicts in the second trial. The court sustained the decision of the Appellate Division only in part: it agreed with the dismissal of the murder charge but reversed the grant of a new trial in the manslaughter conviction for the killing of Missy, returning that issue to the Appellate Division for reconsideration. Explaining the latter ruling, the Court of Appeals conceded that Demakos's comment on Alice's refusal to testify violated her constitutional privilege against self-incrimination. However, in seeming contradiction of its sceptical view of the prosecution case in the first trial, the court decided that the constitutional error was harmless in view of the weighty evidence of Alice's guilt.

The Appellate Division confirmed the manslaughter conviction in May 1975, and Alice was once again sent back to prison to continue serving her sentence of from five to twenty years. Persevering in his efforts for her vindication, Lyon still had one card to play, an appeal from the denial of his motion for retrial, based on newly discovered evidence. A would-be witness, an electronics scientist named F. Sutherland Macklem, had given the defence an affidavit to the effect that, shortly after one o'clock on the morning of 14 July 1965, he had picked up two small children, a boy and a girl, hitchhiking in Queens County. The boy had told him he knew where his home was, and Macklem had let them out, safe and sound, at the corner of 162nd Street and 71st Avenue. The affiant did not learn the children's names, but stated that the boy could well have identified his companion as "Missy" instead of "my sister", as he had first thought. He admitted that he had identified his passengers as the Crimmins children only after reading newspaper accounts of the first trial, three years after the incident.

On 22 December 1975, the New York Court of Appeals affirmed the trial court's rejection of this defence initiative. The court was influenced by the affiant's seven year delay in coming forward, and commented scathingly that the affidavit "offers an imaginative alternative hypothetical explanation [of the crime], worthy of concoction by an A. Conan Doyle".

In January 1976 Alice Crimmins became eligible for a work-release programme and was permitted to leave prison on week days to work as a secretary. In August 1977 the New York *Post* reported that Alice had spent the previous Sunday "as she has spent many balmy summer Sundays of her prison-term – on a luxury cruiser at City Island". (Under the work-release programme, participants were allowed every other weekend at liberty.) In July 1977, Alice married the proprietor of the luxury cruiser, her contractor boyfriend, Anthony Grace. The *Post* was indignant over the nuptials, furnishing telephoto shots of Alice in a bikini and T-shirt, and headlining a follow-up story with a comment of the Queens District Attorney, "Alice should be behind bars!"

On 7 September 1977, Alice Crimmins was granted parole, after thirty months in prison and nine months in the work-release programme. When a new petition for retrial was denied in November, she slipped into what must have been welcome obscurity; she had become that stalest of all commodities, old news.

The Crimmins case remains an intractable puzzle. In his opening argument in the second trial, Herbert Lyon invited the jury to regard the case as a troubling mystery that had not been solved. It is always difficult to persuade the community to live at ease with an unknown murderer, but never more so than when a child or spouse has been killed and the evidence suggests that the household was the scene of the crime or of the victim's disappearance. As in the Lindbergh kidnapping or the murder of Julia Wallace, there is a strong tendency to suspect an "inside job". Alice Crimmins, who slept close by but claimed to have heard nothing out of the ordinary during the murder night, naturally came under suspicion. She was a mother (perhaps harbouring the nameless daily hostilities familiar to the annals of family murder) and the only adult living in the Kew Gardens Hills apartment, and she had the opportunity to commit the crime – but can anything more be said to justify the certainty the investigators showed from the start that she was guilty? If we reject the equation that the State of New York made between sexuality and murderousness, it appears that Alice displayed only one suspicious trait: despite her avowed grief over her lost children, she does not seem to have shown much interest in helping the authorities to identify the killer. Even this curious passivity may have been due to the defensive posture into which she was immediately thrust by police antagonism and surveillance, and she may also have genuinely believed that the murderer was not to be found in her circle of acquaintances, however wide and casual.

The prosecution never attributed a plausible motive to Alice. The presence of Missy and young Eddie in the apartment does not seem to have inhibited Alice's amorous adventures, but if she found the children to be under foot, she could easily have surrendered custody to her husband. It was rumoured that she had never liked Missy much, that she had killed her in anger and then called for underworld help to dispose of her son as an inconvenient witness. Under those circumstances it is hard to visualize the boy going willingly to his doom, a docile figure in the peaceful domestic procession belatedly recalled by Sophie Earomirski in which the murderers and their future victim were accompanied by a pregnant dog. If the theory of sudden anger did not sell, the police investigators were likely to fall back on Alice's own words, that she would rather see her children dead than lose them to Eddie in the pending custody battle. Alice enjoyed a tactical advantage as a mother in possession of the children, and there is no reason to conclude that, despite the lessened optimism she detected in her lawyer's voice during their conversation before the children's disappearance, the prospect was hopeless or that she thought so. If the uncertainty of the divorce court's ruling provided a viable motive, the police had as good a reason to charge Eddie with the crime, but they never took him seriously as a suspect.

In the mind of Joe Rorech, the theory of underworld involvement in the murder of Alice's son took on an even more sinister tone. After the second trial he told New York *Post* reporter George Carpozi Jr that Alice "had to have those children out of the way to avoid the custody proceedings" that were to have been held on 21 July 1965. He spelled out his belief that Alice had arranged for three of her girlfriends to sleep with a prominent New York politician, who was afraid that the details of his indiscretion would come out at the custody hearing. Therefore, the man, who was "deeply involved in New York politics and relied almost solely on the Democratic organisation for his bread and butter", had called on his gangland connections to eliminate the children, thereby averting the hearing. Rorech had no satisfactory answer when Carpozi asked him why the same objective could not have been accomplished with less pain to Alice by the murder of her estranged husband. Rorech's theory also fails to explain why the politician's scandal was deemed more likely to be publicised in a custody hearing than in the course of a murder investigation that was bound to focus on Alice Crimmins and her florid love life.

If Alice was in fact guilty, the reason for her crime must, despite the best surmises of the police and Joe Rorech, remain wrapped in mystery. Even more puzzling, though, is the autopsy evidence regarding Missy's last meal, which raises doubts concerning the time and place of the child's murder. This strange facet of the case was prominently featured in the dissenting opinion rendered by Justice Fuchsberg when the New York State Court of Appeals rejected Alice's motion for a new trial in 1975. Justice Fuchsberg noted that the testimony of the Queens medical examiner, Dr Richard Grimes, indicated that Missy had died shortly after ingesting a meal including a macaroni-like substance that differed substantially from the last dinner that Alice had told the police she served the children. This evidence suggested to the judge that "the child might have had another meal at some unknown time and unknown place considerably after the one taken at home".

Could Alice Crimmins have been so cunning a criminal planner as to have created this enigma by lying to the police about the food she had served on the night of the crime? Apart from the difficulty of finding traits of calculation and foresight in her character, many circumstances militate against the inference that the veal dinner was a fabrication intended by Alice to mislead the investigation. When she first mentioned the purchase of the frozen veal to Detective Piering, neither of the children's bodies had been found. If she was the murderer and had hidden the corpses, she had reason to hope that they would long remain undiscovered. Even if she feared the worst – that the victims would soon be found – it seems doubtful that she was so familiar with the capabilities of forensic medicine that she decided to turn to her own account the possibility that an autopsy might be performed in time to analyses the contents of the last meal.

There would have been a powerful deterrent to Alice's lying about the veal dinner. She told Piering that she had purchased the veal on the afternoon of 13 July in a neighbourhood delicatessen; she was presumably well known there, and the grocer who had waited on her could very likely have contradicted her story. As events turned out, the grocer did not remember what she had purchased, but she could not have counted on that in advance.

If the Crimmins case is viewed with the hindsight of the 1980s – when a young mother with a strong sexual appetite is less likely to be pronounced a Medea – it seems that Alice is entitled to the benefit of the Scottish verdict: Not Proven.

THE HILLDROP CRESCENT MYSTERY

(Hawley Harvey Crippen, UK 1910)

Philip Willcox

Everybody knows the Crippen case. Poisoned his wife, thinking hyoscine – a rare and deadly alkaloid – was undetectable. Chopped her up and hid her remains under the cellar. Fled with his mistress, but got caught by wireless. The very name Crippen is the epitome of the classic British murder (although not everyone realizes that Crippen himself was an American). The case was a landmark in the history of forensic medicine, and the first in a long series of sensational murder trials in which the great pathologist Bernard Spilsbury was to play a leading role. Indeed, it was Spilsbury's appearance that established his name with the general public. Spilsbury, at thirty-three, was the junior of the four pathologists who gave evidence for the Crown, but he made by far the biggest impact. But the case was important in the development of modern forensic science, which had lain largely in the doldrums following the fiasco of the Smethurst trial more than half a century before. Crippen's guilt turned almost entirely on the identification of a piece of skin which was found buried in the cellar of his house in Hilldrop Crescent, Camden Town. It was essential that the scientific witnesses at Crippen's trial were able to convince the jury that the flesh in question came from the body of Crippen's wife Cora. The responsibility for this vital aspect of the case rested with Richard Muir, the junior Crown counsel, and number two to the attorney-general, Sir Rufus Isaacs. Working under Muir's direction, Spilsbury – a man of

whom the public had hitherto never heard – conclusively demon-
strated that the human remains found in Crippen's cellar were those
of Cora Crippen and no one else. Crippen's own precautions proved
to be his downfall. He buried his wife's body in lime, hoping it would
be destroyed. Not only did this fail, but the lime actually preserved
the hyoscine Crippen used to kill her. Without the lime, it would have
been impossible to definitely fix the cause of Mrs Crippen's death. In
court, Dr (later Sir) William Willcox described how he had detected
the poison as being alkaloidal, first a mydriatic and then a vegetable
mydriatic alkaloid. Final tests showed the alkaloid to be hyoscine.
The Crippen case was a triumph for the science of toxicology, and
Willcox's son, Dr Philip Willcox (1910–2000) focuses on this aspect
in his reconstruction of the story using his father's unpublished case
notes and papers.

In the history of crime in Britain probably no other mystery has
attracted more profound fascination than the disappearance of
Mrs Cora Crippen on January 31st, 1910. This, and the events
which followed, notably the trial and conviction of Dr Crippen on
a charge of wife-murder, have provided useful and profitable
material for plays and articles in the press. Certainly no other
crime has been more frequently discussed or debated for so long a
period, and the name of Crippen has become almost a household
word. Even when the case was finished, the secret of the true
course of events surrounding his wife's death was never revealed
but died with Crippen at Pentonville. The police investigations,
and the inquiries at the inquest and at Bow Street and the Old
Bailey were headline news in the press for almost the whole
period from July until the end of that year.

In the trial of Crippen, so fully described in Filson Young's
book (*Notable English Trials*) written ten years later, the medical
evidence was of paramount importance; that of Willcox was
second only to that of Augustus Pepper in length and authority.
At no stage in his career did Willcox describe in any kind of detail
the role he played in the corroborative evidence of identification
of the remains, and the cause of death.

Hawley Harvey Crippen was born in Michigan in 1862. He was reasonably well educated and studied medicine at Cleveland Homoeopathic Hospital, becoming a doctor of medicine there in 1885. This qualification did not enable him to practise in this country on the medical register. He was interested in the ear, nose and throat speciality. He first married at the age of twenty-five, and had one son. After his wife died in 1891 his son was brought up by his grandmother. Dr Crippen worked in New York for a time and the following year married an attractive blonde Russian Pole, by whom he had no children. For a time they lived in St Louis, but came to London in 1900 when Crippen became manager of Munyon's advertising business for homoeopathic remedies, established in Shaftesbury Avenue. According to Crippen and other witnesses at the trial, Mrs Crippen had had an abdominal operation for the removal of an ovary. In 1902 Crippen returned to New York on business for his firm. During this period of six months, Mrs Crippen was said to have become friendly with Bruce Miller, but he had returned to America before Crippen's return to London and he never met Cora Crippen again. At this stage, according to Crippen, their marriage began to disintegrate and she became irritable, bad tempered and impossible to live with as a wife. In 1905 they took up residence at 39 Hilldrop Crescent off the Camden Road and near Holloway prison – a rented semi-detached house which was too large for them and gave them the opportunity to supplement his income by taking in paying guests. In 1909 Munyon's offices were in Albion House, New Oxford Street, but Crippen resigned his position in order to join a dental surgeon in a business known as the Yale Tooth Specialists in the same building as Munyon's. His position as medical adviser to several other firms dealing with drugs and an aural clinic ceased when they were shut down in 1909.

Mrs Crippen was apparently a vain, flamboyant and selfish woman who lost her affection for her husband several years before her mysterious "disappearance". She was also extravagant and resented her duties as a lodging-house keeper, fancying herself as an actress, with an ambition for operatic work. Styling herself Belle Elmore, she was scarcely a success even as a music hall actress with a moderately good singing voice, though she did acquire periodic engagements in this role. Mixing with the stage fraternity, she became treasurer of the Ladies' Music Hall Guild whose meetings were held at Albion House.

In 1909 Crippen's affections had drifted towards a young typist, Ethel Le Neve, who was in his employment. His finances were in a precarious state, maybe on account of his wife's extravagance rather than his own. At the time of Mrs Crippen's disappearance his current banking account was overdrawn.

Their friends Mr and Mrs Martinetti dined at Hilldrop Crescent on January 31st – "quite a nice evening" as Mrs Martinetti described it at the trial. But they had accepted the invitation under pressure from Crippen. They left the house at 1.30 a.m. Mrs Crippen was never seen alive again. Crippen's explanation of her disappearance, which he later confessed was false, was that she had been summoned to go immediately to America to care for a sick relative. The secretary of the Music Hall Guild received this news and notification of her resignation as treasurer in a letter written by hand, but not by Mrs Crippen's.

On February 9th Crippen pawned her brooch and rings for £115 and on the same day visited the Martinetti's to let them know that Cora had preferred to go to America herself rather than let him go. Had Crippen played his cards well he would probably have succeeded in evading undue suspicion. He had merely to play the part of a lonely husband awaiting the return of his wife, but like so many criminals he blundered on several occasions, no doubt losing his head.

On February 20th in company with Miss Le Neve wearing several pieces of his wife's jewellery, Crippen attended a dinner and ball of the Ladies' Music Hall Guild, meeting several of his wife's friends. By March 12th Ethel Le Neve was openly living at Hilldrop Crescent, and about this time he gave three months' notice to terminate the lease of his house. Before Easter he told the Martinetti's that Cora had developed pneumonia. Two days later he departed with Ethel to Dieppe for an Easter holiday but sent a telegram to the Martinetti's informing them of Cora's death at Los Angeles. Unfortunately for Crippen, it so happened that a Mr Nash, whose wife was one of Cora's friends, was on business in California in May. While visiting Los Angeles he had been unable to obtain any news of Cora's illness or any record of her death. Returning to England, he visited Scotland Yard without delay on June 30th, being dissatisfied with Crippen's explanation of his wife's disappearance and death.

Chief Inspector Dew was detailed to launch an inquiry into the disappearance of Mrs Crippen. When he visited Hilldrop Crescent on July 6th, he found Ethel Le Neve already running the house with the help of a French maid. Crippen gladly conducted him over the house, displaying his wife's furs, clothes, and the unpawned jewellery. But by then his nerve began to fail him. Confessing that his story of her death was a complete fabrication he explained that he had said this in order to cover up the "scandal" of her sudden departure to rejoin her ex-lover Bruce Miller; for all he knew his wife was still alive and well in America, but he did not know where. Crippen promised Dew that he would write a description of his wife to be published in the American press in order to solve the mystery of her disappearance – a step that was never fulfilled. When Dew returned the next day, he found that Crippen and Ethel Le Neve had gone. Crippen had notified Albion House of his resignation as assistant to his employer, the dental surgeon. Dew and his assistants then made a most exhaustive search of the house. Noticing several loose bricks on the floor of the coal cellar he explored further and found human remains caked with soil and lime, wrapped in a pyjama jacket corresponding in pattern to Crippen's pyjama trousers found in the bedroom. The police then circulated descriptions of the missing couple and issued a warrant for their arrest.

On Friday, July 29th, the missing couple became headline news when their identity by the captain of S.S. *Montrose* was first made known. Captain Randall had been given details of the missing couple. After the departure of his ship from Antwerp bound for Quebec on July 20th he kept his passengers under close observation. Being himself interested in crime, he used his powers of detection with unusual effect. He noticed that "Mr Robinson" and his son were an unusually devoted couple. Not only so, but "Master" Robinson was a girl disguised as a boy, wearing trousers with hair cut short. Two days after sailing, he ordered his wireless operator to tap out a message to Scotland Yard – the first time wireless telegraphy was used to assist in the arrest of a criminal at sea.

Dew wasted no time. Leaving Liverpool the next day on the *Laurentic*, which was a faster ship, they overtook the *Montrose* on the St Lawrence River at Father Point on July 31st. The Robinsons were arrested, taken into custody and, after extradition formalities at Quebec, were brought back to England, arriving at Liverpool on August 28th.

Pepper was the first scientific expert summoned by the police to inspect the remains *in situ* in the excavated cellar. Piece by piece he conveyed them to Islington mortuary for detailed inspection on July 14th. It was on July 22nd at the end of the day's work that Willcox himself received specimens at his laboratory at St Mary's Hospital from the coroner's officer of Holloway. His extensive examination and description was made on the following day, a Saturday afternoon.

Five stoppered glass jars were properly sealed but not labelled as usual, for Pepper had already told him the news. He first labelled the jars and systematically examined the contents of each in turn. The first jar contained the stomach, heart, one kidney and part of the liver. No organ showed signs of disease, but there was some putrefaction. The second contained a pair of combinations coated with lime, blood-stained in places; the third, brown human hair in a hair curler with the name of the maker inscribed, a tattered handkerchief, a cotton camisole with six pearl buttons; the fourth, the armpiece of a flannelette pyjama jacket with brown and green stripes, caked with blood and lime; the fifth contained another piece of the same bloodstained jacket labelled "Jones Bros. Ltd. Holloway, Shirt Makers".

Willcox was eager to obtain as much as was possible of the human remains from the grave, for analysis for poisons, in order to be able to calculate as accurately as possible the amount of any discoverable poison in the body as a whole. He requested further supplies, preferably whole organs if possible. Further samples of human hair varying from 2 ins. to 6 ins. in length, a hair curler and another piece of liver were brought by the police surgeon, Dr

Marshall, on July 25th. On August 8th Pepper himself delivered the piece of skin which was to supply the chief evidence of identification at the trial in October. At the end of the portion of skin human hairs were growing, resembling pubic hair. After writing a careful description of it he put the skin in a special fluid designed to prevent further changes of putrefaction and handed it to Dr Bernard Spilsbury on the same day for pathological study.

On August 2nd Pepper informed Willcox that the police had discovered that Crippen had purchased five grains of hyoscine on January 1st, 1910, from a chemist in Oxford Street. By that time the analysis was well under way. On August 13th Pepper witnessed Willcox's experiments on the alkaloid extracted from the liver and stomach contents. The effect on the cat's eye of a few drops of the extract was to dilate the pupils widely, thus showing the presence of a mydriatic alkaloid, one of a group of drugs of which hyoscine was a member.

Further specimens were brought to him by Marshall on August 14th, another hair curler, the lungs, intestines, portions of muscle and more hair. Soil from the grave in a separate jar was found to contain traces of an alkaloid.

When Willcox visited Hilldrop Crescent on August 23rd with Inspector Cornish, his purpose was not merely idle curiosity. He wanted to satisfy himself that all possible contents were investigated, and also to take samples of soil. He took three separate specimens away. Not content with his discovery of a mydriatic alkaloid, he was intent on investigating for arsenic as well. But his analysis showed that the soil was free of all poison and could not have been the source of the alkaloid already found in the remains.

He next set out to identify the individual alkaloids by chemical tests and microscopical examination of the crystals, the brown spheres characteristic of hyoscine.

By the time-honoured method of extraction devised by Stas, the pure alkaloid obtained from all the organs amounted to .43 of a grain. But it must be remembered that the head, neck and limbs with their muscles were never recovered from the cellar. Willcox's calculation that there was probably half a grain in the whole body was perhaps an understatement clearly on the cautious side, as the content in the brain and muscles must have been con-

siderable. In his final report of September 2nd he commented
that the relatively large amount found in the stomach (1/30 grain)
and intestines (1/7 grain) showed that the poison was taken by
mouth. The liver (1/10 grain) and kidney (1/40 grain) content
suggested that the deceased probably lived for an hour or more
after the poison was taken.

Earlier the inquest had opened on July 18th at Holloway. But
the unexpected death of Mr Danford Thomas, the coroner,
rendered it invalid. It was accordingly re-opened by Mr (later
Sir) Walter Schroder, on August 16th when formal evidence was
submitted. On September 12th Willcox presented the results of
his investigations and his opinion on the cause of death. The
Crippen case was unusual in that the inquest proceedings termi-
nated several days after the end of the Magistrates' Court inquiry
at Bow Street, the former proceedings being held up by the
prolonged police inquiries and the necessity to call many witnesses. The opinion of Pepper and Willcox was that the remains
had been buried for a period between four and eight months. The
jury returned a verdict of wilful murder against Crippen. But on
the coroner's advice the jury made no reference to Miss Le Neve
as an "accessory after the fact".

Crippen and Ethel Le Neve appeared before the magistrates on
August 29th, the former charged with the wilful murder of his wife,
and the latter with being an accessory after the fact. Presided over
by Sir Albert de Rutzen the hearing was attended by many notable
people connected with the stage, including Sir W. S. Gilbert and
H. B. Irving on all six days. The court was fully packed.

Travers Humphreys appeared for the prosecution and Arthur
Newton for the two prisoners. The evidence of Pepper lasted for
most of the morning of the fourth day, and was supported by that
of Spilsbury for a period of forty minutes on the fifth day. Their
evidence was mainly concerned with the skin of the abdominal
wall and the scars on it – the most important part of the remains
used for identification.

Willcox was in the box for three hours. He agreed with the
previous experts that the piece of skin was from the abdominal
wall and that the scar was identifiable.

He had never before given evidence in a case of alleged murder by hyoscine, this being the first case of its kind in Britain. The isolation of a mydriatic alkaloid meant that it was either hyoscine, atropine or hyoscyamine, confirmed by Vitali's test. The differentiation by the bromine test and the nature of the residue – a gummy mass – pointed to hyoscine, the typical brown spheres being seen under the microscope. His evidence was of great technical interest as it illustrated the difficulty that faces the analyst working on contaminated specimens sent for analysis. He had been puzzled by finding traces of cresol in the stomach, and arsenic in the intestines and liver, but not in other organs. On inquiry, he found that the mortuary attendant had sprinkled liberal amounts of cresol on the specimens in the mortuary. The solution and powders at the mortuary were also analyzed and found to contain a small percentage of arsenic. The presence of arsenic in some organs, and none in others, indicated that it was due to contamination in this way, as he had informed Travers Humphreys three days earlier. He regarded a fatal dose of hyoscine to be half a grain, the medicinal dose being 1/100th of a grain or less. The poison could have been taken in a drink such as sweetened tea or coffee without altering the flavour. Putrefaction of the remains would be delayed by the presence of lime in the grave – but adipocere formation would be accelerated by it. The remains had been buried for less than a year; in that period some of the hyoscine would have been destroyed. In cross-examination he denied the possibility that alkaloids produced by the changes of putrefaction could have been confused with hyoscine.

At the trial, it was said that there were over four thousand applications for seats at the Old Bailey, so great was the interest attached to the case. Half-day tickets were accordingly issued. At Crippen's entry into a packed court on October 18th, a hushed silence suddenly prevailed. The case was tried before the Lord Chief Justice, Lord Alverstone, and lasted five days. Counsel for the Crown were Mr Richard Muir and Mr Travers Humphreys and Mr Ingleby Oddie, later well known as a London coroner. Appearing for Crippen were Mr A. Tobin, KC, Mr Huntly Jenkins and Mr H. D. Roome. Thirty-six witnesses gave evidence, two of whom came specially from America – Mr Bruce Miller who had been friendly with Mrs Crippen several years previously, and Mrs Hunn, Mrs Crippen's sister.

The evidence of the scientific experts occupied close on half the time taken up by all thirty-six witnesses; the testimony of Augustus Pepper lasted nearly twice as long as that of Willcox and was heard for the greater part of the second day.

The main scientific evidence expected from the experts concerned the identification of the remains, the approximate time of their burial and the cause of death. All were interrogated about the all important exhibit of skin and muscle, but for Pepper and his young colleague Spilsbury, then aged thirty-seven, this was the main object of their attention in their evidence concerning the identification of the remains. Willcox's main concern was the cause of death – poisoning by hyoscine, as he had already indicated at Bow Street.

Muir and Humphreys had been coached in the subject of the chemical and medical properties of hyoscine before they appeared at Bow Street; and Willcox had loaned them a well-known text book of toxicology.

When Willcox entered the box on October 20th, it was almost a repetition of his evidence at Bow Street, but the audience was a new one. By the Stas technique of extraction he had obtained a gummy substance, the mydriatic alkaloid which dilated the cat's pupil. Applying the bromine test he had found typical brown spheres of hyoscine under the microscope; the first occasion in which this drug had been used in alleged criminal poisoning. The well-established Vitali test yielded the typical change of colour to violet, thus confirming that it was a vegetable alkaloid distinct from certain alkaloids sometimes produced by bacteria in putrefaction of animal flesh.

Willcox had been disappointed to be unable to estimate the melting point of his alkaloid. It was a method which served to differentiate not only alkaloids from one another but the individual members of the mydriatic group, hyoscine, hyoscyamine and atropine. Cross-examined by Tobin, he explained that the melting point of hyoscine treated with gold chloride was 190°C, at least thirty degrees higher than the other two. In the Crippen case he had less than half a grain at his disposal, whereas he needed at least two grains to carry out this test along with the other investigations; and he had failed to find any further supplies in his personal search of the soil from the grave. Nevertheless, the fact remained that the method offered a new line of advance in the identification of alkaloids in courts of law.

Recent technical advances have now enabled scientists to estimate the melting point of alkaloids by micro-physical methods whereby minute amounts can be melted under the microscope while a special thermometer is read. Not only so, but many new techniques of analysis can now be used, such as paper chromatography and ultra-violet and infra-red spectroscopy. But the Stas process of extraction, though further elaborated, still remains in use today. Police inquiries revealed that Crippen had purchased five grains of hyoscine from an Oxford Street chemist on January 1st. It was perhaps unfortunate that Pepper communicated the information to Willcox about two weeks before the analysis was completed. Willcox was thus exposed to the suggestion by defence counsel that hyoscine was discovered as an afterthought – a cruel and unkind inference which was not used by Tobin in the later stages of the trial, to his own advantage in view of the fact that Willcox claimed a period of three weeks to complete extraction and analysis of the alkaloid.

Willcox's evidence was supported by that of A. P. Luff who had been junior Home Office analyst until succeeded by Willcox in 1904. Luff's experience of cadaveric alkaloids had been greater than his successor's, and his reliance on Vitali's test was equally firmly held.

The scientific experts for the Crown were all from St Mary's Hospital; Pepper supported by Spilsbury, and Willcox by Luff. It seemed that the case might lead to a battle between teams from two London hospitals, for the three experts for the defence were G. M. Turnbull (pathologist), R. C. Wall (physician and pathologist) and A. W. Blyth, all from the London Hospital. But try as they did, their evidence lent feeble support to the defence counsel. Turnbull and Wall had previously formed the opinion that the exhibited piece of skin had come from the thigh and that the supposed scar was merely a fold in the skin. But during their

testimony in the box they were forced to change their minds and
agree that it was more probably part of the abdominal wall. Blyth
was equally unable to counter the firmly held view of Willcox and
Luff about the nature of the alkaloid. He had to admit compara-
tive ignorance of cadaveric alkaloids in putrefaction and was
merely able to quote from an obscure Italian text-book which
was critical of the value of the Vitali test.

The jury was left in little doubt that the Crown experts were
right; death had been caused by hyoscine, the remains had been
buried for a period between two and four months, and the
exhibited skin with its scar of the old operation was in fact from
the abdominal wall of Mrs Crippen.

Richard Muir enhanced his reputation by his masterly conduct
of the case as prosecuting counsel.

After retiring for half an hour the jury found the prisoner guilty
at 2.45 p.m. on the fifth day of the trial, after a strictly impartial
summing-up by the Lord Chief Justice.

The trial of Ethel Le Neve at the Old Bailey on October 25th
was completed in one day. The same three counsel appeared for
the Crown. She was defended by F. E. Smith (later Lord Birkenhead), who had earlier refused the more difficult brief for the
defence of Crippen, supported by Mr Barrington Ward. Only
nine witnesses were called; Pepper and Willcox gave formal
evidence each for only a few minutes. She was found not guilty
and acquitted.

Crippen appealed against his verdict. The case came before the
Court of Criminal Appeal on November 5th, before Mr Justice
Darling, Mr Justice Channell and Mr Justice Pickford, but was
unsuccessful. Crippen was executed at Pentonville on November
23rd, 1910.

As a criminal, Crippen was notable for his strangely attractive
qualities of character, his courtesy and unselfishness, and the
calmness with which he faced up to his succession of misfortunes.
He certainly faced his trial and death with courage, and earned
the sympathy of a wide circle of people who appreciated the
horrors of a selfish, nagging and overbearing wife. Even Inspector Dew liked him, and enjoyed his company at lunch at the
Holborn Restaurant after the first unproductive search of his

house. None of the witnesses at the three court inquiries described him as other than a pleasant man; and one described him as one of the nicest men she had ever met. His affection for Ethel never wavered and in his last letters he did his best to protect her from any accusation of guilt.

For close on sixty years, the case has been the subject of frequent debate. Having poisoned his wife with hyoscine, why did Crippen need to dispose of her remains in the way he did? Why did he not call a doctor and claim that she had poisoned herself with the drug he had left lying about the house? Doubtless the ruse would have been successful and would have saved him the need for the hasty flight and the ghastly task of disposal. And how did he dispose of the head and limbs? Only Crippen knew the answers and the secrets died with him.

Willcox resented being referred to as "the man who hanged Crippen", and rightly so. He would have been far happier if it had been shown that Mrs Crippen had committed suicide. In spite of his acute sense of right and wrong, he felt sorrow and compassion for Crippen as did many people. Nevertheless, the case established certain records. It was the first case of alleged murder by hyoscine in British legal history and the first case in which wireless telegraphy was used to arrest a criminal on ship at sea.

Willcox alluded to the case in various lectures on toxicology in later years, and a quotation from his Harveian Lecture to the Harveian Society on March 15th, 1928, refers to Crippen's purchase of poison in relation to the Poisons Register:

"The numerous Acts and Regulations governing the sale of poisons in this country have served as a great protection to the public. In many noted trials the purchase of poison by the accused has been revealed by the record of the register of the sale kept by the vendors. This happened in the Crippen case, where the purchase of hyoscine had been recorded in the poison register of the chemist."

The liberal sprinkling of quicklime on the remains in the cellar was a fatal mistake referred to in a lecture to the Society of Dyers, and to the Literary and Philosophical Society of Manchester in 1924:

"Before the Crippen case it had been stated that hyoscine was a very decomposable alkaloid that no one could detect a few days or weeks after death . . . To make assurance doubly sure Crippen buried the viscera in quicklime which was just what the expert wanted, for it helped to preserve the viscera, and without it I doubt whether the hyoscine would ever have been discovered. Crippen possessed the little knowledge that is dangerous."

Willcox was asked by a barrister interested in forensic chemistry about the mode of action of quicklime as a preservative, as it had been understood that executed criminals had customarily been buried in quicklime to destroy the body rapidly. The answer lay in the rapid hydration of quicklime yielding calcium hydrate, a fairly efficient alkaline antiseptic, but in addition calcium hydrate combines with the fat of viscera to form a calcium soap called adipocere, which forms a protective covering round buried remains.

The cat used in his experiment at the laboratory was subsequently named "Crippen" and was cared for by one of the students. It lived for several years, produced a family of kittens. But the name of Crippen must have carried a curse, for it was later unfortunately killed by a dog.

Miss Ethel Le Neve escaped the publicity that often pursues acquitted prisoners by emigrating to Canada soon after the trial. There she married and had children. She returned to Britain after many years and lived to a ripe old age, dying in obscurity in 1965.

Postscript

There is a curious sequel. Nearly twenty years after Ethel's death, the author Jonathan Goodman was researching a book on the Crippen case and traced her two children, a son and a daughter, who were living in southern England. His letter seeking an interview was received with astonishment and some consternation, since it transpired that Ethel Smith (as she had become) had never told her children who she really was. In their mother's lifetime, neither knew that she had been Ethel Le Neve, Crippen's mistress, who in the autumn of 1910 had been the most infamous woman in England.

THE DINGO BABY CASE

(Lindy Chamberlain, Australia 1980)

Colin Wilson

"We are not treading in the ground of unequivocal, unchallenged scientific opinion," declared the judge in the Chamberlain case. "To the contrary, the scientific opinion on these vital issues is divided." But after a seven-week trial, the jury's verdict was unanimous: Lindy Chamberlain was guilty of murdering her baby daughter Azaria, and her pastor husband guilty of being an accessory after the fact. Mrs Chamberlain, thirty-four at the time of her trial and heavily pregnant with her fourth child, had claimed a dingo had carried Azaria into the Australian bush from the family tent. The child's clothing was recovered, and it was forensic evidence uncovered during exhaustive tests on the bloodstained jump-suit and singlet that eventually led to one of Australia's most sensational trials. According to the prosecution, this evidence showed that Lindy Chamberlain had murdered Azaria by slitting the baby's throat in the family car. Other forensic experts called by the defence said it was possible for a dingo to take a small child. Some of the forensic evidence, gathered more than a year after Azaria's disappearance, showed traces of blood in the car, inside the tent and in a camera bag. But pathologists disputed whether the traces were foetal blood. Moreover, dental and forensic experts gave conflicting evidence about the marks found in the dead child's clothing. Mrs Chamberlain's appeal failed, but the doubts in the case persisted and she was released from prison early in 1986, having served just over two years of her life sentence. One of Britain's most prolific chroniclers of crime, Colin Wilson (b. 1931) examines the evidence

and concludes that Lindy Chamberlain was the victim of a mis-
carriage of justice.

It was 8 o'clock on a warm August evening, and most of the
occupants of the camping site below Ayers Rock, the mammoth
red-stone landmark that rises out of the desert of central Australia, were engaged in preparing supper. This included thirty-
two-year-old Alice Lynne ("Lindy") Chamberlain and her
thirty-six-year-old husband Michael, a minister in the Seventh
Day Adventist Church. Their elder son, seven-year-old Aidan,
was still awake; the other two children, Reagan, four, and Azaria
("Blessed of God"), nine weeks old, were already asleep in the
tent.

It was Michael Chamberlain who asked, "Is that Bubby crying?", and Lindy Chamberlain returned to the tent. A moment
later she shouted, "My God, the dingo's got my baby!" Michael
rushed to the tent. The baby's blankets were scattered round the
empty carrycot.

Within minutes most of the campers on the site were rushing
into the darkness with torches. Lindy explained that, as she
approached the tent, she had seen a dingo – a wild dog – walking
away from it, with its rear towards her. It had been moving its
head from side to side, although she had been unable to see
whether it was carrying anything. The night was pitch black,
without a breath of wind; although 300 searchers scoured
through the scrub, they found nothing. Back in the camp, some
women were praying. Lindy Chamberlain was trying to quieten
Aidan, who was crying, "Don't let the dingo eat our baby."
Frank Morris, the local police officer, arrived to organize the
search. But he suspected that Azaria Chamberlain was already
dead.

By dawn, it was obvious that he was right. Lindy Chamberlain
had also come to accept it. Over the radio telephone she told her
parents, "Our baby was killed by a dingo last night." Then she
sobbed.

By mid-morning, the Chamberlains had another problem:

their story had caused a nationwide sensation – Baby Stolen by Dingo at Ayers Rock – and press and television reporters were beginning to arrive. Michael Chamberlain agreed to talk to them – a decision that was later to arouse some criticism. Meanwhile, Lindy told her story to the police: how her elder son had been in bed when he said he was still hungry. Instead of fetching him some food as he lay in bed, she made the fatal mistake of telling him to come with her; and, since he would be returning in a few minutes, she left the tent flap unzipped. Before the day was out, Michael Chamberlain had already noticed that some people were asking questions in an oddly suspicious way, as if they felt that the idea of a baby being stolen by a dingo was preposterous.

This was not the view of the police. The day after Azaria's disappearance, they began shooting dingos and wild dogs in the area of Ayers Rock, hoping to find the child's remains in the stomach of one of them. They shot several dingos but their search was unsuccessful. On Tuesday, the Chamberlains returned to their home in Mount Isa, Queensland. Their religious faith had given them the strength to accept the tragedy. But there were many people who felt they had accepted it a little too stoically.

In fact, they might have received far more sympathy if they had been less religious. As Seventh Day Adventists, they were regarded as a little "odd". Seventh Day Adventists have been described as "Fundamentalists of Fundamentalists". Like the Jehovah's Witnesses, they believe in the literal truth of every word of the Bible, and in an imminent return of Christ to earth. Their movement was founded in the first half of the nineteenth century by an American, William Miller, who announced that the end of the world would occur in 1843 or 1844. On 22 October 1844, twenty families sat out all night in Phoenixville, Pennsylvania, waiting for the end, and two children froze to death. That night was known as the Great Disappointment. But the Adventists declared that the Second Coming had been delayed by their failure to recognize Saturday as the Sabbath, and that it could be expected fairly soon. In spite of the Great Disappointment, the sect continued to prosper.

Modern Seventh Day Adventists disapprove of alcohol, gambling, jewelry, cosmetics, cinema and television, with the inevitable consequence that there is a tendency among the worldly to regard them as cranks and "killjoys". This helps explain why, instead of receiving universal sympathy and commiseration, the Chamberlains found themselves confronted by a curious hostility after the loss of their baby.

Eight days after Azaria's disappearance, a tourist on the west side of Ayers Rock noticed some clothing; it proved to be a bloodstained stretchsuit, napkin, singlet and booties. Yet there was not the slightest trace of flesh. It looked as if the dingo had removed the baby from the stretchsuit and taken it to its lair. Oddly enough, the singlet was inside out. How could a dingo do that? One local theory was that the dingo had dropped the baby, which had then been taken home by a camp dog, and that the owner of the camp dog, worried about being implicated, had removed the clothes and buried the body. But that still failed to explain why such a person had not simply buried the baby with her clothes on.

The Chamberlains were questioned several times by the police. A rumour began to circulate that she had fallen from a supermarket trolley and become spastic, and that her parents had decided to kill her for this reason. Another rumour was that Azaria meant "the sacrifice", and that she had been sacrificed on top of Ayers Rock in some gruesome ceremony.

Forensic evidence seemed to throw some doubt on the story about the dingo. A stuffed stretchsuit was dragged across the ground from the camp site to the base of Ayers Rock, then examined by botanists. There were fragments of charcoal in the experimental stretchsuit, as might have been expected, since there had been bush fires in the area. Yet there was no charcoal on Azaria's suit. Forensic tests seemed to indicate that Azaria's clothes had been rubbed in the dust at the base of the rock. A dead goat was put into baby clothes and thrown into the dingo pen at Adelaide Zoo. The dingo buried the carcass and clothes in various parts of the pen. Forensic experts concluded that the damage caused to the clothing – particularly the teeth-marks – was quite unlike the damage to Azaria's stretchsuit. Moreover, the blood that soaked the stretchsuit seemed to suggest that the baby had been in an upright position during the bleeding.

Michael Chamberlain, pursued by journalists who wanted to know what he thought about this suggestion that his baby had not been taken by a dingo, admitted that it was possible that a human being had carried Azaria off, "but he or she would have been a maniac". But where was the baby? It seemed unlikely that a dingo had eaten every morsel of a 9 lb baby.

The inquest opened in Alice Springs in December, and moved to Ayers Rock. By that time, the Chamberlains were living in an atmosphere of continual hostility – there were even death threats. Many people simply doubted that a small wild dog would steal a nine-week-old baby. And when the police forensic laboratory announced that the holes in the garment had been made with an instrument like a pair of scissors, the Australian public began to feel that there was more in this case than met the eye. On Wednesday, 18 February 1981 Coroner Barritt startled everyone by announcing that because of the widespread interest in the case, he had granted permission for television to film the findings of the inquest. But Australians who hoped for some sensational revelation, or accusation, were disappointed when the coroner found that Azaria Chamberlain had met her death through a wild dingo. He added that it was untrue that Azaria meant "sacrifice in the wilderness".

The debate continued. In September that year the police were ordered to reopen their investigations. In November, a supreme court judge ordered a new inquest. It opened on 14 December 1981. Just before the inquest, the police received a letter from an anonymous couple who claimed that they had seen a dingo carrying what they thought was a doll, and that when one of them threw a stone at the dog, it dropped its burden, which they found to be a badly mutilated child. The couple decided to bury the baby, so the parents would not see it in this condition; they undressed it, and later got rid of the clothes at Ayers Rock. But the writers could not be located.

At the inquest, Michael Chamberlain was asked whether he had cleaned blood out of the car. He agreed that he may have cleaned "some blood", but insisted that it was not much. Lindy was asked why she had sent a bloodstained tracksuit – which she had worn on the night of the baby's disappearance – to the cleaners. When a policeman told how he had unbolted the front seats of the car and found bloodstains on the cross section, the court sensed that this inquest was, in fact, a trial of the Chamberlains. This became even clearer when Joy Kuhl, a forensic biologist, told how she had discovered foetal bloodstains on a pair of nail scissors, and on the inside of a yellow container found in the car. But the most sensational evidence came from a British expert in legal medicine, Professor James Cameron. He had been sent the baby's clothing at the London Hospital Medical College, and his examination had led him to conclude that the blood on the stretchsuit suggested that it had flowed down from above. He also commented that the holes in the stretchsuit had been made with scissors, and that he had been surprised at the absence of teethmarks or of animal saliva around the neck of the suit. And when he added that ultra violet light had revealed a bloodstained handprint on the stretchsuit – a print too large to be a child's but too small for a man – it was obvious that the finger of guilt was now pointing at Lindy Chamberlain.

When the inquest resumed after Christmas 1981, Mr Desmond Sturgess, the barrister appointed to help the coroner, finally made the accusation that everyone was expecting. He believed that Azaria had been killed in the family car, and her body concealed in a camera bag. The coroner then committed Lindy Chamberlain for trial on a murder charge, and Michael Chamberlain was charged as an accessory after the fact.

The trial of Lindy Chamberlain began on 13 September 1982, and the prosecuting counsel, Ian Barker QC, announced that he would attempt to prove that Azaria Chamberlain died of a cut throat while Lindy Chamberlain was in the front passenger seat of the car. The prosecution case was that Lindy Chamberlain had taken the baby from the tent and into the front seat of the car, where she had cut Azaria's throat. The case depended largely on forensic evidence. It lacked one vitally important element – a reason why Lindy Chamberlain, mother of a happy family, should have murdered her own baby.

The defence called experts who disagreed that the stains found in the car were foetal haemoglobin, and a dental expert argued that the holes found in the stretchsuit were caused by an animal's teeth. Lindy Chamberlain's doctor testified that she was not suffering from post-natal depression after the birth of Azaria. A mother testified that a dingo had tried to grab her twelve-year-old child by the elbow at Ayers Rock on the evening before Azaria disappeared. A Geelong pathologist flatly denied that the blood-stains on the tracksuit could have been caused by a head injury or a cut to the throat. And he denied that there was a bloodstained handprint on the suit.

The one point that emerged very clearly from the trial was that the evidence of the various experts could not be accepted as scientifically unshakeable. The defence made the telling point that if Lindy Chamberlain had murdered her baby, surely she would have claimed that the child had been carried off in the dingo's mouth? From the beginning she had stuck to her story of only seeing the dingo moving away into the darkness.

The trial lasted for seven weeks. When the jury returned from six and a half hours of deliberation, the foreman announced that their verdict was unanimous: the Chamberlains were guilty as charged. Thereupon the judge, Mr Justice Muirhead, told Lindy Chamberlain, "There is only one sentence I can pass upon you – hard labour for life." She was taken away to Berrimah Jail where, within a few days, she would give birth to another daughter. Michael Chamberlain was sentenced to an eighteen-month sus-pended sentence.

When, in April 1983, the Federal Court rejected Lindy Cham-berlain's appeal, it seemed that the Dingo Baby Case was finally over. But soon Lindy Chamberlain support groups were formed all over the country. In February 1984 the High Court of Australia rejected Lindy Chamberlain's appeal. But soon after that a family described how, eight weeks before the disappearance of Azaria, a dingo at Ayers Rock had dragged their child from the car. The chief ranger from the Ayers Rock district, Derek Roff, wrote to the *National Times* saying he was convinced the dingoes might well attack a child. Thirty-one scientists signed an open letter protesting about the conclusions drawn from Joy Kuhl's evidence. A psychologist who had examined Lindy Chamberlain in prison stated on television that he was unable to account for criminal behaviour on her part, and affirmed his conviction that she was totally innocent.

Although these pleas had no effect on the authorities, Lindy Chamberlain was released from prison on 7 February 1986 on the grounds that she had paid her debt to society. She had served just over two years of her life sentence. After her release, she announced that she and her husband would continue the fight to establish their innocence. Part of that campaign was a long television interview with reporter Ray Martin, in which she spoke frankly about the charges against her, and of the reasons why so many had felt her to be guilty – her apparently cool demeanour during the inquests and in television appearances. She pointed out the obvious – that if a mother who has lost her baby is then faced with a campaign of rumour and innuendo, her reaction is bound to be one of anger, and she is not likely to look bereaved and miserable. During the course of the programme, one of the jurors who had been responsible for the guilty verdict announced that she had since become convinced that Lindy Chamberlain was innocent. She went on to admit that many of the other jurors had felt doubts but said that the forensic evidence had seemed conclusive.

In retrospect, it is difficult to see why Lindy Chamberlain was ever suspected of murder. No one disputed that the Chamberlains were a happy and affectionate family unit, and no one was ever able to allege any kind of motive. It seems fairly certain that the Lindy Chamberlain case will be regarded as Australia's most tragic miscarriage of justice.

BLOOD IN THE BASEMENT

(Lord Lucan, 1974)

Linda Stratmann

Officially the Lucan case remains one of the great unsolved murder mysteries of the 20th century, but few doubt that the killer was, indeed, the 7th Earl of Lucan; modern DNA techniques would almost certainly have put the issue beyond doubt. Analysis of the blood, hair and fibres found at Lucan's London town house and in the car he used to flee the murder scene told their own story. The victim, Sandra Rivett, the Lucans' nanny, was blood type B, and her blood type was concentrated mostly in the basement of the house, where her body was found. Lady Lucan's blood (type A), on the other hand, was found mostly in the hallway at the top of the basement stairs but also, intriguingly, on the canvas mailbag containing Sandra Rivett's body. Further bloodstains, on the envelopes addressed by Lord Lucan to his friend Bill Shand Kydd, were of type AB, the result perhaps of mixing two separate blood types, type A and type B, pointing to the possibility that it could have been a mixture of the blood of Lady Lucan and Sandra Rivett. This account of one of the most celebrated crimes of modern times is by the British crime writer Linda Stratmann (b. 1948), a true crime aficionado since watching Edgar Lustgarten on television in the 1950s. She spent 27 years in the civil service, writing novels and plays in her spare time, but success eluded her until she finally turned to non-fiction crime. Her first book, Chloroform: the quest for oblivion *(2003) was followed by* Essex Murders, Whiteley's Folly, Gloucestershire Murders *and* The Crooks Who Conned Millions. *Linda Stratmann shows how the forensic evidence in the case supports the contention that Lucan – and no one else – must have been the killer.*

At 9.45 p.m. on the night of November 7 1974, a distressed and bloodstained woman burst into the bar of The Plumber's Arms pub in Lower Belgrave Street, in London's Belgravia, crying out "Help me, help me, help me. I've just escaped from being murdered. He's in the house. He's murdered the nanny!" She was the Countess of Lucan, who had fled from her home at number 46, leaving behind her three children. She was obviously the victim of a serious assault, and the police and an ambulance were called to the scene. The Lucans' home was a substantial house with a ground floor, a basement and four upper floors. Forcing open the front door, the police searched the premises, and found the children in their bedrooms, unharmed. The door to the basement was open. There was no light in the hall, so using a flashlight, the police descended the stairs to the breakfast room, where they found the walls splashed with blood, a pool of blood on the floor, with some male footprints in it, and, near the door connecting the breakfast room to the kitchen, a bloodstained sack. The top of the sack was folded over but not fastened. Inside was the corpse of Sandra Rivett, the children's' nanny. She had been battered to death with a blunt instrument. In the hallway was a length of lead piping, covered in surgical tape, very bent out of shape and heavily bloodstained. The back door was unlocked.

When Lady Lucan was able to make a statement to the police she named her husband both as her attacker and the murderer of Sandra Rivett. Of Lord Lucan, there was no sign.

Shortly after 10 p.m. on the fatal night, Mrs Madeleine Floorman, a friend of the Lucans, who lived a short distance away, was dozing in front of the television after a tiring day when she was awoken by someone pressing the doorbell insistently. Assuming it was a local youth, who had done this kind of thing before, she ignored it and went back to sleep. Some time later, the telephone rang. The caller, she felt sure, was Lord Lucan, but he sounded distressed and became incoherent. She put the phone down and went back to sleep.

At approximately 10.30 that evening, Lord Lucan telephoned his mother, who lived in St John's Wood, telling her there had been a catastrophe at the house, and he wanted her to collect the children. She went straight there, found the place occupied by police, and informed them that the Lucans were separated, the children were wards of court, and that Lord Lucan currently resided at a nearby flat. She then took the children to her home. The police searched Lord Lucan's flat. He was not there, but they found his car keys, passport, chequebook, driving licence, wallet and glasses. His blue Mercedes car, which had been suffering from battery trouble for some time, was parked outside. The battery was flat.

Lord Lucan was driving another car that night, a Ford Corsair he had borrowed from a friend some two or three weeks previously, insisting that he wanted the car for that particular evening. At about 11.30 p.m. he arrived in Uckfield, Sussex, at the home of his friends Ian and Susan Maxwell-Scott. The house was forty-two miles from Lower Belgrave Street, a journey of about an hour at average speed, though he was a fast driver and might have taken less time. Ian Maxwell-Scott was away, but his wife admitted Lord Lucan and was surprised to see him in dishevelled daytime clothing. His flannel trousers looked as though they had been stained and something sponged off.

Lord Lucan told Susan Maxwell-Scott that earlier that evening he had been walking past the Lower Belgrave Street house and, peeping in through the basement window, saw someone struggling with Lady Lucan in the kitchen. Letting himself in through the front door he ran down the stairs, but in the kitchen he slipped and fell in a pool of blood. The man had run off. Lord Lucan said he had tried to calm his wife, and taken her upstairs to try and clean her up, but while he was in the bathroom she had run out of the house shouting "Murder!" Realizing that things looked very bad for him, he panicked, and decided to get out.

He mentioned the two phone calls, to Mrs Floorman and his mother, and said he had also tried to telephone Bill Shand Kydd, who was married to Lady Lucan's sister, but there was no reply. He did not say where he made these calls from, but Mrs Maxwell-Scott got the impression they had been made after he left the house. At 12.15 a.m. he rang his mother from the Maxwell-Scotts' house to check that she had the children, and rang Bill Shand Kydd again, but there was no reply.

Lord Lucan then wrote two letters, both addressed to Bill

Shand Kydd at his home in Bayswater. They were posted the
following day. When recovered, the envelopes were found to have
smears of blood on them. Mrs Maxwell-Scott tried to persuade
him to remain so they could go to the local police the next
morning, but he said he had to "get back". He drove away.
There has been no validated sighting of him since.

Three days after the murder, the Ford Corsair was found
abandoned at Newhaven. Bloodstains were found inside of both
type A and type B; also, a piece of bandaged lead piping,
unstained, but very similar to the one found in the murder house.
Of Lord Lucan, there was no sign.

Richard John Bingham – usually known as "John" – the future
7th Earl of Lucan was born on 18 December 1934. He went to
Eton where he discovered the great passion of his life – gambling.
In 1953 he joined the Coldstream Guards, and spent much of his
off-duty time playing poker or visiting casinos. After leaving the
Army he joined a merchant bank, but one night, after a substantial win at chemin-de-fer he decided to quit his job and
become a professional gambler. His gambling nickname was
"Lucky".

In March 1963 he was introduced to Veronica Duncan, whose
sister was the wife of Bill Shand Kydd. They were married the
following November. Two months later, John Bingham's father
died, and the couple became the 7th Earl and Countess of Lucan.
In October 1964 their first child, Lady Frances, was born. By
then, they were living at the Lower Belgrave Street house.

Lord Lucan's usual routine was to spend his nights at the
gaming tables, and return home in the early hours of the morning,
to sleep. Rising late, he would go out to lunch at his club, the
Clermont. Lady Lucan would join him there at 9 p.m.

In September 1967 their son George was born, followed by
another daughter, Camilla, in June 1970. Lady Lucan suffered
from post-natal depression after the birth of her children, and in
1968 her husband encouraged her to have treatment. She agreed,
provided it could be based at home. He took an interest in her
condition, and studied books on psychiatry. By the early 1970s,
however, the relationship was breaking down. Lady Lucan
became increasingly concerned about her husband's continued

heavy losses at the gaming tables. She felt that he was danger-ously addicted to gambling, and should have treatment for it. He had also refused to put money aside for the children's education.

Shortly after Christmas 1972 the couple separated, and from then on, Lord Lucan was determined to gain custody of his children. In March 1973 he obtained a court order and took the two younger children while they were out with their nanny, then collected Frances from school. For the next three months Lady Lucan was cared for by hired nurses and during this time voluntarily went into a psychiatric clinic for a week. Lady Lucan, who had no prior history of mental illness, has always believed that when suffering from post-natal depression she was pre-scribed drugs which were inappropriate and that this was re-sponsible for her continuing illness. Lucan, she believed, had been hoping that the medical reports would show that she was not fit to have custody of the children, but in June, to his surprise and mortification, the Court ordered that the children be returned to their mother.

By now, with the family to support, a nanny to pay, houses to maintain, and legal bills from the custody case, Lucan was deeply in debt. He was also continuing to lose at the tables. He kept a constant watch on the house, and still entertained hopes that he could go back to court and regain custody. He also tried to arrange for Lady Lucan to be bought off with a sum of money, but this came to nothing. He hired private detectives to watch the house and, when he went there to collect the children for his access visits, made secret tape recordings. When he could no longer afford to pay private detectives, he did the snooping himself.

At 6.30 p.m. on the night of the murder, Lord Lucan was at his flat in Elizabeth Street, where he had been visited by a friend. At about 7.45 he drove the friend home to Chelsea, dropping him off and leaving at about 8 p.m. He was not using the Mercedes. During that evening he telephoned the Clermont Club to book a restaurant table for a late meal with friends. The assistant manager recalled the conversation to have taken place at 8.30 whereas Lucan's visitor thought it happened before 7.45. It is an unimportant point, but it does illustrate how two witnesses to the same event can disagree considerably about the time at which it occurred.

At about 8.30 p.m., in 46 Lower Belgrave Street, the Lucans' nanny, Sandra Rivett, put the two younger children to bed. Sandra, a 29-year-old redhead, was 5ft 2in in height, the same as Lady Lucan, and was one dress size fuller in figure. It was a Thursday, which was Sandra's usual night off, something of which Lucan was aware, but unknown to him, that week she had changed her free night to Wednesday. Lady Frances was in her room, playing a game. At approximately 8.40 she went to her mother's bedroom and asked where Sandra was. Lady Lucan said she had gone downstairs to make tea. This was another departure from normal routine, as it was usual for Lady Lucan to make tea at about 9 p.m. About twenty minutes or so after Sandra had gone downstairs, Lady Lucan began to wonder why she hadn't returned. There are two reported sightings of Lord Lucan near that time. The linkman at the Clermont said he saw Lucan drive up at 8.45 p.m. to ask if any of the usual crowd was there. He said he felt sure Lucan was driving the Mercedes. According to him, Lucan said he would be back later. Another employee believes he saw Lucan standing on the step of the club at about 9 p.m.

Lady Lucan's account of events, as related at the inquest, is that at about 9.15 p.m. she descended the stairs to the ground floor, and peered down into the basement, calling Sandra's name. It was dark, and she assumed that Sandra was not there. She was standing at the top of the basement stairs when someone rushed out of the ground floor cloakroom and hit her on the front of the head several times with a weapon that felt as though it had been bandaged. When the person told her to "shut up" she recognized her husband's voice. He thrust three gloved fingers down her throat, and they struggled. He tried to strangle her and gouge her eye, and she grabbed him by the testicles. The attack suddenly ceased and they both ended up on the floor with her sitting between his legs. After a time, they went upstairs to assess her injuries, sending Frances up to her room, and it was while Lucan was in the bathroom getting a wet cloth that Lady Lucan had jumped up and run out of the house.

Lady Lucan confirmed that she had not seen anyone else at the house, and that she did not recognize the sack in which Sandra's body had been found.

The first letter to Bill Shand Kydd was read out in court. In it Lucan referred to interrupting a fight between his wife and an unknown man, and said that she had accused him of hiring a hitman, a comment that Lady Lucan has always denied making. Evidence about the Lucans' relationship was not permitted at the inquest – an inquest, after all, is not a trial, but an examination into how someone died – but the letter clearly implied that Lady Lucan was mentally ill and hated her husband, and that her accusations were not to be believed.

Lady Frances had made a statement to a WPC some days after November 7, and this was read out in court. She said that on the murder evening she had been in the second-floor bedroom watching television. She had heard her mother scream but had assumed the cat had scratched her. Later, her parents had walked in together. Frances was sent up to bed, and later heard her father calling for her mother, and saw him searching, then going downstairs. She confirmed that during the last weekend the children had spent with their father they had told him that Sandra went out with her boyfriend on Thursdays. Lady Frances believed that her mother went to look for Sandra before the *9 o'Clock News* started. The differences between the timings given by Lady Lucan and Lady Frances are critical only in relation to the reported sightings at the Clermont.

Lady Lucan's description of the bandaged weapon and the darkness on the basement stairs was supported by the evidence. The weapon, found by the police near the door leading to the basement, was a length of lead piping wrapped with tape. A light bulb had been found on a chair by the stairway in the basement. It had been removed from the light at the bottom of the stairs – the only one which could be controlled by a switch at the top of the stairs.

A casualty officer testified to Lady Lucan's injuries – seven large lacerations on her scalp, bruising to her eye and injuries to the palate and on the back of her throat, all completely in keeping with her description of the attack. Pathologist Professor Keith

Simpson testified that the injuries to the two women were similar in nature.

The second letter to Bill Shand Kydd was read out, and this mentioned an upcoming sale at Christie's which would satisfy bank overdrafts. It was signed "Lucky". Lord Lucan's overdrafts exceeded £14,000, although his total debts were far greater.

Lucan's mother Kait, the Dowager Countess of Lucan, denied the suggestion that Lucan had told her he was driving past the house. This was important, as it was possible to see into the basement if on foot, but not from a car.

After Susan Maxwell-Scott's testimony, a third letter from Lucan was read out. This had been sent to the friend who had lent him the Corsair, and referred to "a traumatic night of unbelievable coincidences", and asked that his children should know that all he cared about was them. A writing pad found in the car had had a piece torn roughly out. This matched the piece used to write the note.

The evidence on bloodstaining needs careful examination. Sandra's blood group was B and Lady Lucan's is group A. The area around the top of the hall stairs leading to the basement was an obvious site of attack, since a pattern of radiating blood splashes showed that a victim had been battered. These bloodstains were group A, and sticking to some of them were hairs of a type similar to Lady Lucan's. One stain appeared to be group AB, but it was thought that this could have been the result of A and B types mixing. There were also a great many greyish blue textile fibres. Some were on a bloodstained towel, some were stuck to the bloodstained lead pipe, and still more, together with some of Lady Lucan's hair and blood, were in the Ford Corsair. This was extensively stained with both A and B type blood, with some areas of mixed types.

At the bottom of the stairs, in the breakfast room, was another attack site with numerous blood splashes. There was a large area of bloodstaining near the piano, and some bloodstained footprints of a man's shoes. These stains were all group B. One small spot of blood on the floor was group A, and the sack was heavily stained with group B blood but with some indications of group A. Lady Lucan's clothes were heavily stained with her own blood, but there was a small amount of group B staining on her dress, some group B spots on her shoes with staining on the soles and arches. There was some question as to whether this staining meant that Lady Lucan had been in the basement after the murder, although it was thought that the staining could also have happened through contact with the stained clothing of her attacker.

The smears of blood on the letter to Bill Shand Kydd gave an AB reaction. There were also some bloodstains on leaves in the garden, and these were group B. The piece of lead piping was "grossly distorted" and was stained with both group A and group B blood, suggesting that the weapon had been used both for Sandra's murder and the attack on Lady Lucan.

Expert evidence suggested that the attacker would have been spattered with blood, although that might not have been obvious, and when the body was put in the sack his clothes could have become saturated.

The inquest jury was out for only 31 minutes and their verdict was "Murder by Lord Lucan". It was the last time that an inquest jury exercised its right to name a murderer. As a direct result of this case, the right was abolished by the Criminal Law Act of 1977.

Published works on the case suggest three main scenarios. Sally Moore in *Lucan: Not Guilty* (1987) suggests that the murderer was an unknown assailant. Lord Lucan is cast as the hero saving his wife from an attacker then fleeing because he will not be believed. Ms Moore consulted with Lord Lucan's family (though not Lady Lucan) in her research for the book, and she attaches considerable importance to the random blood drips. Patrick Marnham in *Trail of Havoc* (1987) and James Ruddick in *Lord Lucan: What Really Happened* (1994) both suggest that although Lord Lucan did not murder Sandra Rivett, he hired a hit man to murder his wife. Arriving later to dispose of the body, he discovered the mistake and attacked his wife. Lady Lucan has never believed that her husband hired a hit man to kill her and, contrary to what he wrote in his letters after the murder, never accused him of having done so. The simplest explanation, and the one most consistent with the facts, is that Lord Lucan is guilty and no one else was involved.

Theories that do not cite Lucan as the murderer are partly based on two ideas, first, that an attack with a blunt instrument was simply "not like him" – certainly his friends refused to believe it. There was also the fact that the murderer had mistaken Sandra for Lady Lucan, which it is suggested is unlikely unless the murderer was a stranger. But people tend to see what they expect to see, and Lord Lucan could have made that mistake. Sandra was the same height as Lady Lucan, and not a great deal different in build. It was dark, and he did not expect the nanny to be in the house that night.

My starting point in analyzing any case where there are conflicting stories is to look at the hard evidence and see which of the stories it supports. So let us compare the accounts of the physical attacks as told by Lord Lucan and his wife.

Lucan stated that on the night of the murder, he was passing the house of his wife and children, and saw through the basement window his wife struggling with an assailant. He entered the house, using his key, and rushed down to the basement where he slipped in some blood on the floor. The unknown assailant ran off.

Lady Lucan's account is that after Sandra went downstairs to the basement kitchen to make tea, she became concerned about the long absence and went to the head of the stairs down to the basement and called her name. She was attacked by someone wielding a blunt instrument, and grappled with her attacker. She screamed and her attacker told her to shut up. She recognized the voice as her husband's. He forced his gloved fingers down her throat and she fought back, squeezing his testicles. At this he drew back and the attack ended.

Now let us compare the two accounts. There are two very important differences. In Lucan's account, Lady Lucan was attacked in the basement, and in hers, she did not enter the basement at all, but was attacked at the head of the stairs. Secondly, although it is clear that both Lucan and his wife knew that the nanny had been killed, Lucan said that he knew because his wife told him, while she said that he had told her.

Forensic evidence can answer a number of questions. Where was Lady Lucan attacked? Did Lord Lucan rush in and slip on the blood?

There is no doubt that the presence of group A (Lady Lucan's) blood splashes at the top of the stairs, making it an obvious attack site, is powerful evidence that Lucan's story cannot be true. Sally Moore hypothesizes that Lady Lucan was first attacked in the basement with blows that did not create splashes, then ran up the stairs to be struck again, while Lucan ran down into the basement to chase the man, where he slipped in Sandra's blood. The difficulty about this story is that *neither* Lady Lucan nor Lord Lucan suggested that this was what had happened. Lucan's story as told to Susan Maxwell-Scott was that he had run into the basement and found Lady Lucan there, covered in blood. If Lady Lucan had been in the basement covered with blood after being attacked there, then there would have been splashes of her blood on the walls – but there were none. This story, hastily concocted by Lucan in a panic to explain his presence in the house, does not fit the facts.

Did Lucan slip in the blood in the basement? No, he did not. The blood was in a pool, and foot prints showed that a man had stepped in it, but there were no signs of anyone slipping. The purpose of this concoction is obvious – the story would explain to friends how the "intruder" got away and also the presence of blood on Lord Lucan's clothing.

How did both Lady Lucan and her husband know of Sandra's death before the body was discovered? For Lucan to have told Lady Lucan, the obvious and simple answer is that he knew because he was the murderer. In Lady Lucan's account, she did not enter the basement at all. She only knew Sandra was dead because Lucan had told her. Although she had some group B stains on her shoes, there were no bloody footprints of a woman's shoes in the basement. Lady Lucan confirms that during the struggle with her husband, she kicked him, which accounts for the staining of group B blood. Once again, the forensic evidence supports Lady Lucan's story.

A suggestion has occasionally been made that the murder was a burglary gone wrong. A burglar might certainly have come to the house carrying a large sack but, once he had killed, why would he stuff the body in the sack? A burglar who had committed a murder after being surprised would have run off immediately,

not waited 20 minutes. Whoever came to the house with that sack
came to commit murder, and dispose of the body.

Both Patrick Marnham and James Ruddick make strong cases
for the more complicated scenario, that Lord Lucan hired a man
to kill his wife, the hitman killed Sandra, then Lord Lucan,
arriving to clear up and dispose of the body, discovered the
mistake and attacked his wife. I will look at this in more detail
later, but first there are some specific questions I would like to
ask.

1. What happened between 9.45 and 10.30? If Lord Lucan had
left the house at about 9.45, it would have taken no more than a
few minutes to go round and bang on Mrs Floorman's door.
Spots of what appeared to be blood were later found on her
doorstep. If his call to his mother was at about 10.30, which seems
likely, judging by the time she arrived at the house, he would have
had to leave for Uckfield immediately afterwards to get there by
11.15. Between about 9.50 and 10.30 pm he not only made several
phone calls which were not from a coin box, he also had the
facilities to sponge down his clothing. Where did he do this? Did
he ask help of a friend – or was there somewhere empty to which
he had a key? There was a mews cottage, 5 Eaton Row, immediately behind No. 5 Eaton Square which Lucan leased to a
friend whom he knew was out that evening, but the police had
already broken in and searched it, and presumably there was no
evidence of Lucan's presence.

The nearest and most obvious place was his own flat in
Elizabeth Street, only minutes away. There are a few problems
associated with this idea. First of all there was no physical sign
that he had been there but, according to Lady Lucan, corroborated by the evidence of Susan Maxwell-Scott, he was not heavily
bloodstained. It was also a dangerous place to be, as the police
would look there for him first. If he had gone there then it seems
logical that he would have taken items such as his passport and
wallet, and also changed into fresh clothes rather than sponge
down the stained ones. With no evidence of blood smears, it is
impossible to conclude from where the phone calls were made.
Either way, the fact that he had not collected his passport and

other essentials strengthens the suggestion that he had already decided to kill himself. Where he was bound, no passport was required. Everything he did after leaving the house was intended to do two things, first, to ensure that the children were being looked after, and secondly to protect his family from the stain of his guilt. His unsuccessful attempts to get in touch with Mrs Floorman were probably because she lived nearby and he wanted her to take care of the children.

2. Could anyone have escaped over the back wall? This is extremely unlikely. The wall was very high and overgrown. There was no sign of anyone having clambered over it, or even making the attempt. (Some years later a burglar was surprised on the premises, and he was unable to escape over the garden wall.)

3. Why was there group B (Sandra's) blood on the leaves in the garden? This evidence has been used to support the anonymous intruder theory, but there are less complicated explanations. The police had made extensive searches of the premises, and there were two pet cats roaming freely. There was ample opportunity for transference of staining.

4. Why was the back door unlocked? Sally Moore has suggested that some unknown person might have had a key to the house without anyone's knowledge. One plank of her argument is that in December 1964 some jewellery worth £2,000 was stolen from a second floor bedroom of number 46, with no signs of forced entry. In the very same paragraph, however, she mentions that Lucan had received a letter the previous month pressing him for payment of £1,400 in gambling debts. This leads to the strong suspicion that Lucan may have used the jewellery to pay his debts. Regarding the unlocked door, Lady Lucan has stated that they often left the back door unlocked to allow free access to the two cats.

5. How come Lady Lucan was struck several times with the pipe and did not lose consciousness, whereas Sandra died after being hit four times? This has led to the speculation that Sandra and

Lady Lucan were attacked by different people, but there are a
number of facts to take into consideration. Sandra was hit from
behind, while Lady Lucan was hit on the forehead where the
bones are thicker. The weapon when found was very distorted. It
had originally been a straight length of pipe. At the inquest Lady
Lucan described it as a curved object. If it had been straight when
used on Sandra and was distorted by the first attack, then it
would have been a much less effective weapon for the second.
Lady Lucan also described her husband as emotionally exhausted
after his attack on her. His emotional state could have reduced the
effectiveness of the second attack.

6. What about the statements that Lord Lucan had been seen
outside the Clermont at 8.45 p.m. and then at 9 p.m.? Marnham,
who believes that Lord Lucan hired a hitman, suggests that the
8.45 visit was made to establish an alibi. If so, it was a pretty
flimsy alibi, when one considers the likely margin of error in
memory of time, and the fact that the distance between the club
and the house could be covered in a few minutes. It should also be
noted that, according to the linkman, Lucan was in the Mercedes.
Certainly, if he had wanted to establish an alibi, this was the car to
do it in – the one people would have been familiar with – but that
car was found with a flat battery outside Lucan's flat at 11.50,
some two hours after the sighting. Was the car even driveable that
night? If it was not, then the linkman cannot have seen Lucan in
the Mercedes that evening at all.

Was Lord Lucan, as has been suggested, standing on the steps
of the Club at 9 p.m.? This approximates either to the time of the
murder (Lady Lucan's timing) or the attack on Lady Lucan
(Lady Frances' timing). Looking at the times, it must be remembered that all the three theories (guilty, innocent, hitman)
place Lord Lucan at 46 Lower Belgrave Street at the time of the
attack on Lady Lucan. Let us look at Lady Frances' timing first.
She states that Lady Lucan went downstairs just before the *9
o'Clock News*, and we know that Lady Lucan was attacked very
soon after reaching the basement stairs, so this times the attack at
the very time when Lord Lucan is said to have been standing
outside the Clermont. In none of the three scenarios is this

possible. Lady Lucan's timings place the attack on herself at about 9.15. It could be suggested that Lord Lucan was establishing an alibi before going to the house, either to commit murder or to clear up after the hitman; but, as already stated, this is not much of an alibi. Surely he would not have wanted anyone to know he was even in the area. If the sighting is accurate, then it can only fit with Lord Lucan's story, which has already been discredited by forensic evidence. The conclusion can only be that Lord Lucan was not standing on the steps of the Clermont at 9 p.m. on the evening of the murder, though he may well have been there at another time that day, and had certainly been there at just that time on numerous other occasions.

7. Why was there a single spot of type A blood in the basement? Lady Lucan has confirmed that she did not set foot in the basement after the murder and never saw the mail bag. The simplest explanation is accidental transference as mentioned at point 3 above.

8. How did smears of blood type A get on the outside of the murder sack? It has been suggested that the blood got on the sack as it brushed against the walls while being carried up, but the sack was seen by reporters being removed from the house wrapped in plastic. Was it wrapped before or after it went up the stairs? The evidence as published does not make this clear. Again, accidental transference is the theory that makes most sense.

9. Why was there no type B blood in the ground floor cloakroom where Lord Lucan was supposed to have lain in wait for Lady Lucan, and none upstairs where he went to tend her wounds? There was a great deal of speculation about the likely amount of staining on the murderer, but Lady Frances did not observe any blood on her father though she was near enough to notice the blood on her mother. Once again, the evidence of Lady Lucan and Susan Maxwell-Scott suggests that Lord Lucan was not as heavily stained as has been supposed. Lady Lucan has also pointed out that the blood splashes in the house were not as extensive as has been often reported.

10. What happened in the gap of time between Sandra's death and the attack on Lady Lucan? Lady Lucan has suggested that Sandra went to make the tea at about 8.55 and she went to look for her at 9.15. Lady Frances believes that Sandra went down to make the tea at about 8.40 to 8.45. Sandra would have been killed almost immediately – the tray of dirty crockery she was taking down to the kitchen was found scattered on the floor at the bottom of the stairs, but whatever the time Sandra went to make tea, Lady Lucan didn't go to look for her for about 20 minutes. This makes sense – after all, ten minutes to make tea and do some washing up is reasonable, so she would not have started wondering where Sandra was until about twenty minutes had passed. But what was the killer doing during that time? Assuming the killer was Lord Lucan, he had discovered his mistake, and was putting the body in the sack. He knew that his wife would soon be coming downstairs and he was waiting for her to arrive. As already observed, the theoretical burglar would probably have run off immediately.

11. What happened between the attack on Lady Lucan and her running from the house? The gap is about 35 minutes and in many ways is the key to the mystery. I will return to this point later.

12. Why was Lord Lucan not heavily bloodstained? When an attack is made with a blunt instrument, the result is often a fine spray of blood, not immediately visible to the eye, but obvious to detailed forensic examination. The main areas of heavy staining, if Lord Lucan had put the body in the sack, were his hands and possibly the lower part of his clothing; also the soles of his shoes, from stepping into the spreading pool of blood. (He had in any case admitted to stepping in the blood.) His hands were stained with both type and A and B, as the smears on the letters and in the car show. Susan Maxwell-Scott has given evidence that his trousers looked as though they had recently been sponged.

   Some friends of Lord Lucan's tell very interesting stories. One was Greville Howard, the lessee of the mews cottage, and one of the people who had waited at the Clermont that night at the table

Lucan had booked. One week after the murder he went voluntarily to the police and told them that a fortnight before the murder he had had a conversation with Lucan in which his friend had suggested that a way out of his troubles was to kill Lady Lucan, and had even discussed the idea of dumping her body in the Solent. He knew that he was about to go bankrupt, and he needed to get possession of the house in order to clear his debts and save the reputation of the family. Bankruptcy was for him a public humiliation he did not think he could stand.

The writer Taki Theodoracopoulos is reported to have said (in *Trail of Havoc*) that Lucan bought a 20 ft speedboat in the year before he disappeared. The boat, he stated, was kept moored on the South Coast, and in 1974 Lucan made two dummy runs from Belgravia to the South Coast with a sack weighing 8 stone. The sack was then loaded into the boat and he headed out into the Channel. Lord Lucan certainly knew about power-boats, having competed in the Cowes–Torquay race in 1964, though there is no evidence that he ever owned a boat, and Lady Lucan is certain that he did not. Taki also said that Lord Lucan had borrowed £5,000 from him shortly before the murder, having already borrowed £3,000 from a moneylender at a high rate of interest the previous September. Patrick Marnham suggests that the money was to pay a hitman but, bearing in mind Lucan's heavy debts, there are numerous other reasons why he might have required such sums.

Patrick Marnham and James Ruddick both believe that, unable to commit the crime himself, Lord Lucan hired someone to do it for him. A professional, however, bringing a sack in which the body was to be disposed of neatly, would hardly have used a bludgeon, which anyone but an amateur would have known would spray blood all over the place. Marnham suggests that Lucan hired a good hitman who was unable to come that night and sent a bungling associate! This is rather straining credulity. A simpler explanation is that the bungling amateur was Lord Lucan himself.

Marnham believes that Lord Lucan's part in the affair was to dispose of the body. In his scenario, the hired man kills Sandra, but does not put the body in the sack. He reports success to

Lucan who is nearby, and Lucan goes round to the house to discover, to his horror, that the wrong woman has been killed and the cellar is in a mess. Checking to see if Sandra is dead, he gets some smears of blood on his clothing. The problem with this theory – apart from lack of any evidence that another person was present – is that if Lord Lucan was too squeamish to commit the murder why would be volunteer to come and dispose of the body? The "hitman" theory is altogether too complicated, and it fails to take one very important fact into account.

Lord Lucan confessed to his wife that he had murdered Sandra Rivett.

Even without the confession, the overwhelming weight of the evidence points clearly to Lord Lucan alone being both the murderer of Sandra Rivett and the attacker of Lady Lucan.

Lord Lucan assumed that Sandra would be out that night, and that Lady Lucan would come down at about 9 p.m. to make the tea. Removing the light bulb, he hid in the darkness. A petite woman descended the stairs with a tea tray and he bludgeoned her to death, the blows distorting the lead piping into a curved shape. As he put the body into the sack, he realized his error, but decided to go ahead with the murder of his wife and lay in wait at the top of the stairs. Lady Lucan survived the less effective attack and, with the shock of pain when she squeezed his testicles, and his emotional exhaustion he could not go on. They sat on the stairs and talked.

Lady Lucan asked her husband where Sandra was. At first he said that she had gone out, but when she insisted that Sandra would never have done this without telling her, he admitted that he had killed her. In the next half hour the badly injured Lady Lucan found the resources she needed to save her own life. The front door was just too far for her to be able to make a break for it and run. She played for time, calming her husband, persuading him that Sandra would not be missed, that they could dispose of the body together, that he could go out and meet his friends while she told the police she had been attacked by a burglar, that she would do whatever he asked.

Lucan thought about this, and said, "I must make a decision." He then asked his wife if she had any sleeping tablets. She said yes, that they were upstairs. He asked her if she would take an overdose, and to placate him she agreed to do so, if he would just permit her to lie down and rest. He pulled her to her feet and said that they would leave together and she would take her pills. He hustled her upstairs and she lay down on the bed while he went to the bathroom to wet some cloths. As the taps started to run Lady Lucan knew that she had only seconds to get away, the noise of the water covering the sound of her footsteps. Quietly, she got up, crept downstairs, and ran. She did not, as Lord Lucan suggested, scream, "Murder!" as she ran down the street. With the terrible injuries to her head and the lacerations to her palate and throat caused by Lord Lucan's gloved fingers, she saved every scrap of her energy and voice for when she burst into the Plumber's Arms.

Once we know that Lord Lucan confessed to the murder of Sandra Rivett, everything that happened subsequently falls into place. Once he had made the confession he must have determined that his wife must die, although not as originally planned. When he came out of the bathroom and found that she had run from the house, carrying with her the knowledge of his guilt, he knew he was a dead man. From that moment on, all his actions were aimed at one thing: protecting the family reputation. He first made sure that the children were being looked after, but he also wanted them to be free from the shame and scandal of their father in the dock accused of a crime. The other great scandal he wanted to avoid was bankruptcy. The only way he could do that was to disappear. The only way he could be absolutely certain that he would never have to face the consequences of his actions was to die.

The odds are that Lord Lucan is dead. Many of his friends believe that he simply took a speedboat or ferry out into the Channel, and leaped over the side. Gamblers do not often give up, but English gentlemen have been known to do the decent thing. The shame of appearing in the dock accused of murder, and of financial ruin, was something he did not want to face, both on a personal level, and also for his family's sake.

Had Lady Lucan wished to remarry she could have sought a decree of presumption of death seven years after her husband's disappearance, but chose not to do so as she felt it would not have been in the best interests of her family. The 7th Earl of Lucan was officially presumed dead on 11 December 1992, at which time his son George became the 8th Earl, although he prefers not to use the title. Probate was granted on 11 August 1999, with the Countess of Lucan the sole beneficiary of her late husband's residuary estate.

The Letters

1. 7 Nov 1974
Dear Bill,
   The most ghastly circumstances arose tonight which I briefly described to my mother. When I interrupted the fight at Lower Belgrave St and the man left Lady Lucan accused me of having hired him. I took her upstairs and sent Frances up to bed and tried to clean her up. She lay doggo for a bit and when I was in the bathroom left the house. The circumstantial evidence against me is strong in that V will say it was all my doing. I also will lie doggo for a bit but I am only concerned for the children. If you can manage it I want them to live with you – Coutts (trustees) St Martins Lane (Mr Wall) will handle school fees. V. has demonstrated her hatred of me in the past and would do anything to see me accused. For George & Frances to go through life knowing their father had stood in the dock for attempted murder would be too much. When they are old enough to understand, explain to them the dream[1] of paranoia, and look after them
   Yours ever,
   John.

1. The word "dream" has been the subject of much speculation. The writing is very sprawling and hard to read accurately. My own opinion is that "disease" gives the most logical reading of the sentence, but Lady Lucan, familiar with her husband's handwriting, is certain that the word is "dream". The meaning of this sentence has never been clear.

2. Financial Matters

There is a sale coming up at Christies Nov 27th which will satisfy bank overdrafts. Please agree reserves with Tom Craig.
Proceeds to go to:
Lloyds, 6 Pall Mall
Coutts, 59 Strand
Nat West, Bloomsbury Branch
Who also hold an
Eq. and Law Life Policy.
The other creditors can get lost for the time being.
Lucky

3.

My dear Michael,

I have had a traumatic night of unbelievable coincidences. However I won't bore you with anything or involve you except to say that when you come across my children, which I hope you will, please tell them that you knew me and that all I cared about was them.

The fact that a crooked solicitor and a rotten psychiatrist destroyed me between them will be of no importance to the children.

I gave Bill Shand Kydd an account of what actually happened but judging by my last effort in court no-one, let alone a 67-year-old judge, would believe – and I no longer care except that my children should be protected.

Yours ever,
John

DID THE EVIDENCE FIT THE CRIME?

(Bruno Hauptmann, USA 1936)

Tom Zito

The kidnap and murder of the Lindbergh baby in 1932 was among the first to earn the accolade "Crime of the Century". On the wild night of 1 March, a ramshackle ladder was placed up against the first-floor nursery window of the Lindbergh country home in New Jersey. Someone stole the sleeping child from his cot and left a ransom note demanding $50,000. Colonel Charles Lindbergh, whose solo transatlantic flight in 1927 had made him a world hero, was a wealthy man; the money in marked bills was delivered, by arrangement, to a cemetery in New York's Bronx. Waiting in his car, Colonel Lindbergh heard one of the kidnap gang shout just two words: "Hey, Doc". Six weeks later, the kidnapped baby was found dead, buried in a shallow grave. It was another two and a half years before the breakthrough in the case. One of the marked bills was traced to Bruno Hauptmann, an immigrant carpenter who lived in the Bronx. Hauptmann was tried for kidnap and murder. Evidence was lost, other evidence invented. A timesheet giving Hauptmann a perfect alibi for the day of the kidnapping went missing (it has never been found). Forensic evidence fuelled further controversy, particularly that of a detective and wood expert who, in order to link Hauptmann to the kidnapping, said that one of the rails of the ladder had come from the attic floor of Hauptmann's landlord. Hauptmann was convicted and sent to the electric chair, still protesting his innocence, in 1936. In the early 1980s, shortly after the Freedom

*of Information Act became law in the United States, the journalist
Tom Zito (b.1948) re-examined Hauptmann's case for* Life *magazine. He received a tip from someone at the FBI that there were
reams of evidence vindicating Hauptmann sitting in its vaults.
Although he has since quit journalism to run his own multi-million
dollar software company, Zito vividly remembers the Lindbergh
assignment. "Little did I know what a journey it would become,"
he wrote. "The eeriest part of the reporting was meeting with
Wilentz, the prosecutor, who was still in legal practice fifty years
later, still in New Jersey. His self-righteous attitude was that he had
performed a public service to close a long national disgrace (namely
having the murder be unsolved)."*

Just hours before he was scheduled for execution in the electric
chair to atone for "the Crime of the Century" – kidnapping and
murdering the son of Charles and Anne Morrow Lindbergh –
Bruno Richard Hauptmann had scrawled a letter to New Jersey
Governor Harold Hoffman and, indirectly, to the prosecutor in
the case, New Jersey Attorney General David Wilentz. "My
writing is not in fear of losing my life, this is in the hands of God,
it is His will," Hauptmann wrote.

I will go gladly, it means the end of my tremendous
suffering. Only in thinking of my dear wife and my little
boy, that is breaking my heart . . . Mr Wilentz, with my
dying breath I swear by God that you convicted an innocent
man. Once you will stand before the same Judge to whom I
go in a few hours. You know you have done wrong on me
. . . I beg you, Attorney General, believe at least a dying
man. Please investigate because this case is not solved, it
only adds another dead to the Lindbergh case.

Hauptmann's execution was in fact, delayed for three days
because another man had confessed to the crime. But that man
recanted, and notwithstanding a grand jury investigation into the
matter, the execution went ahead. On the evening of April 3,

1936, with crowds ringing the New Jersey State Prison in Trenton shouting for his death, the thirty-six- year-old carpenter from Kamenz, Germany, was led to the electric chair and strapped into place. "Here was Hauptmann's chance to talk," wrote Edward Folliard for the next morning's *Washington Post*. "It was the moment when he was expected to talk – when reporters had their pencils poised to catch his words, words that would end forever the controversy as to whether he snatched that little child from his crib in the Sourland Mountains.

"No words came. There was only that dazed look – that look of the soldier about to get the bayonet and knowing that nothing could save him . . . There was now a steady whine in the death chamber, the death song of the dynamo. It continued for what seemed an eternity . . ."

A few minutes later, six physicians, one after the other, laid their stethoscopes to Hauptmann's chest and pronounced him dead.

When word reached Hauptmann's wife, Anna, in her hotel room across town, she threw her hands up to her face and cried, "Ach, Gott! Mein Richard!" The words were immediately scribbled by hordes of reporters who had broken down her door. When asked for his reaction, Lloyd Fisher, the Hauptmann defence attorney who had filed and lost the appeals, said to reporters in the warden's office, "This is the greatest tragedy in the history of New Jersey. Time will never wash it out."

Tragedy or not, time still has not washed out the questions in the Lindbergh case. A half century after the March 1, 1932, kidnapping, the mysteries have only grown. In 1977, under the Freedom of Information Act, San Francisco attorney Robert Bryan reviewed the FBI's voluminous files on the case. In the fall of 1981, Anna Hauptmann herself, with the help of Bryan, forced open the records of the New Jersey State Police. Armed with the federal documents, she filed a civil suit against the State of New Jersey, former Attorney General David Wilentz (still practising law in Woodbridge, NJ), the Hearst Corporation and others for "wrongfully, corruptly and unjustly" trying and executing Hauptmann.

The new evidence strongly suggests that witnesses were coached and even coerced, evidence was tampered with or suppressed and testimony by key witnesses was altered between the crime itself and the trial – a period of two years and 10 months – to fit the suspect. There is an excellent chance that a competent defense attorney, in possession of these documents and operating under today's more stringent legal proceedings, could have gotten Hauptmann off on technical grounds, arguing a mis-trial or "reasonable doubt." Far more disturbing, however, is another possibility these dusty files raise: that Bruno Richard Hauptmann might have been telling the truth.

Clearly that thought did not seriously occur to the eight men and four women who found Hauptmann guilty of murder in the first degree. And who could blame them? The outlines of the case, as presented by Wilentz in his brilliant prosecution, are remembered by millions of Americans, as well as by more recent readers of George Waller's best-selling book, *Kidnap*. The case seemed airtight. Indeed, one of the chief arguments of Hauptmann's defense attorney at the time was that Wilentz's case was "too perfect."

According to Wilentz, on the night of March 1, 1932, Bruno Richard Hauptmann, an illegal immigrant with a prison record back in Germany, placed a crudely built wood ladder against the wall of the Lindberghs' Hopewell, NJ, country home, pried open the nursery window and grabbed twenty-month-old Charles Lindbergh Jr in his sleep. He escaped the way he came, after leaving behind the ladder and a ransom note demanding $50,000. At some point during the kidnapping, the child had been killed and buried about five miles from his home under a pile of leaves. Before his body had been found, the ransom money had been turned over in St Raymond's Cemetery in the Bronx to a man called "John" – a man later identified by America's greatest living hero, Charles Lindbergh, as well as by his go-between, as Bruno Richard Hauptmann.

As presented during the trial, the case against Hauptmann seemed overwhelming. Over $14,000 of the $50,000 ransom money had been found hidden in his garage; eyewitnesses had placed the Bronx carpenter near the scene of the crime; a

Forestry Department expert had traced to Hauptmann's attic a board used in fashioning the kidnap ladder; handwriting experts had testified that Hauptmann had written all the ransom notes.

Wilentz's presentation of the evidence was so dramatic, so thorough, that at one point he suggested that the unusual geometric symbols used to sign the ransom notes spelled out Hauptmann's guilt. The blue intersecting circles, with a center filled with red and punched with three holes, Wilentz argued, spelled, "*b* in blue for Bruno; *r* in red for Hauptmann!"

The entire nation hungered for the verdict that the jury so swiftly rendered. On the streets near the Hunterdon County Courthouse in Flemington, where the trial was held, a crowd of 10,000 screamed, "Kill Hauptmann! Kill the German!!" Indeed, who better than the man who had faced the Allies from the wrong end of a machine gun in World War I, who had gone on to become a convicted thief and second-story man and who had arrived in America as a fugitive from justice? Hauptmann seemed to symbolize not only the once and future German menace abroad but also the larger "alien" threat back home. "What type of man would murder the child of Colonel Charles A. Lindbergh and Anne Morrow . . ." Wilentz asked rhetorically during his summation. "He wouldn't be an American. No American gangster . . . ever sank to the level of killing babies. Ah, no! An American gangster that did want to participate in a kidnapping wouldn't pick out Colonel Lindbergh." Just years before, in 1927, "Lucky Lindy," having made his historic solo fight across the Atlantic, had become, in Wilentz's words, "the most popular and the most glorious man in this world." His family was the true first family of the country, and his son was, according to a periodical of the time, "the most famous child on earth." The murder of that child had been more than a personal loss; it was a national tragedy.

President Herbert Hoover immediately announced, "We will move heaven and earth to find out who is this criminal that had the audacity to commit a crime like this." There ensued one of the greatest criminal investigations ever mounted, one that finally, on September 19, 1934, ensnared its first indictable suspect. The trial of Bruno Richard Hauptmann was, in the words of

H. L. Mencken, "the biggest story since the Resurrection," and its outcome a national catharsis. But even at the time, a few questions could be heard through the cries for revenge.

The trial judge, Thomas Trenchard, had admitted in his charge to the jury that "the evidence produced by the state is largely circumstantial in character." Said famed trial lawyer Clarence Darrow, "No man should be executed on such flimsy evidence." "The entire trial left me with a question in my mind," said Eleanor Roosevelt.

Far more substantive, however, was a confidential memo that came to rest on the desk of J. Edgar Hoover, the director of the FBI. Since kidnapping did not become a federal crime until after the passage of the so-called Lindbergh law, the FBI had not controlled the investigation but had nonetheless participated throughout, observing as a silent witness from the day of the kidnapping until after Hauptmann's arrest. This memo – one of thousands on the case sent by Hoover's agents – suggested that the investigative agencies were playing free and loose with the case against Hauptmann. Just days before the trial began, an FBI agent wrote that the "questionable tactics of all the other governmental agencies would probably come to light in a new trial." That memorandum, along with many other mitigating documents, remained sealed away in federal and state labyrinths until Anna Hauptmann sued to reopen the case.

"The questionable tactics," FBI memos make clear, extended to virtually every aspect of the state's case, including virtually every piece of evidence. Nowhere was that case more flawed than in the witnesses it produced to place Hauptmann, who lived a two-hour drive away, near the Lindbergh home in Hopewell, NJ. An October 1934 FBI memo stated that the New Jersey police "did not have one single reliable witness who could place Hauptmann in the vicinity of Hopewell prior to or on the date of the crime." Yet witness after witness did just that.

Millard Whited, for instance, testified at the trial that he had seen Hauptmann near the Lindbergh home on two occasions; yet state records of his initial interrogation shortly after the crime reveal that he saw no one suspicious. In a New Jersey State Police report of April 26, 1932, Whited is asked, "Is there any informa-

tion that you can give us that would assist us in this investigation
. . ." He answers, "No." Only after Hauptmann was arrested,
and it was suggested that Whited might share in some of the
bounty for capturing the Lindbergh kidnapper, did he change his
testimony. (Whited eventually received $1,000 of the $25,000.)
In another 1934 FBI memo, an agent reported: "Mr Wilentz . . .
stated that he had run into a little difficulty over the witness,
Millard Whited . . . Mr Wilentz stated that several neighbours of
the Whiteds, as well as the brother of this witness, had given
affidavits to the effect that he was a confirmed liar, and totally
unreliable."

In court, witness Amandus Hochmuth placed Hauptmann in
Hopewell on the very day of the crime and said that Hauptmann
had glared "at me as if he saw a ghost." A Public Welfare record
at the time, in fact, listed Hochmuth as "partly blind" and
mentions his "failing eyesight due to cataracts." When Hochmuth was called into Governor Hoffman's office in 1937 in an
effort to determine who should receive the reward money for
Hauptmann's arrest, Hoffman asked Hochmuth to identify an
object ten feet away – a file cabinet, topped by a silver cup filled
with flowers. Hochmuth said it was a woman wearing a hat; when
people in the room laughed, he changed his description to a bowl
of fruit sitting on a piece of furniture.

Other identifications of Hauptmann also are suspect in light of
these newly released documents. Joseph Perrone, a cab driver,
testified during the trial that Hauptmann had handed him one of
the ransom notes to deliver to go-between Dr John F. Condon.
Yet just six weeks after the delivery, he had told police that he
could not remember details of what the man who handed him the
ransom note had looked like. After Hauptmann's arrest, Perrone's memory was refreshed by police, according to FBI documents, with "what might be termed a 'pep talk': 'Now, Joe, we've
got the right man at last. There isn't a man in this room who isn't
convinced that he is the man who kidnapped that baby . . . Now
we're depending on you, Joe. Take a good look at him when we
bring him in but don't say anything until I ask you if he is the man
. . .'" Hauptmann, rather than being placed in a lineup as is
customary, was flanked by only two men, one in a police uniform.

In a subsequent memo an FBI agent wrote, "I informed Mr Lanigan [New Jersey assistant attorney general] that several of us were present when Inspector Lyons practically coerced Joseph Perrone into identifying Hauptmann."

As important as anything at the trial was the courtroom identification of Hauptmann by the prosecution's two star witnesses, Charles Lindbergh himself and go-between Condon. Both Lindbergh and Dr Condon had gone to St Raymond's Cemetery to deliver the ransom money to the man who called himself John. Condon, who had spent considerable time talking face to face to "John" during the ransom negotiations, was positive that "John" was indeed Hauptmann. Lindbergh's identification, coupled with Condon's, proved decisive. Writing for the Hearst newspapers, Adela Rogers St Johns seemed to speak for the jurors, if not for the entire country, when she reported: "Watching Lindbergh today in this ordeal I cannot believe he would swear away the life of any man unless he was sure."

Yet just how sure was Lindbergh? An FBI agent wrote a memo before the trial, saying, "I am somewhat skeptical of some of the evidence now being produced in New Jersey, particularly some of the identifications and the testimony of Lindbergh relative to recognizing the voice, etc."

Several months before the trial, Lindbergh had testified before a Bronx grand jury that he could not positively identify the voice, which he had heard say only two words ("Hey, Doc") from more than 200 feet away over two and a half years earlier. Yet at the trial Lindbergh was positive. And the words he had heard were. "In a foreign accent: 'Hey, Doctor.'"

The identification by Dr John F. Condon was even more puzzling. A highly eccentric seventy-two-year-old retired schoolteacher, Condon had placed an advertisement in the Bronx *Home News* a week after the kidnapping, offering his services as an intermediary between the Lindberghs and the kidnappers. Condon had spent considerable time conversing with "John"; he told police and friends he "could pick him out of a thousand." When asked by Wilentz who "John" was during the trial, Condon had announced in a strong, deliberate voice, separating each syllable for dramatic effect: "John is Bru–no Rich–ard Haupt–mann!"

When first shown Hauptmann in a police lineup, however, Condon had acted very confused. He talked to Hauptmann; asked him to repeat something he, Condon, wrote on a piece of paper; looked for a growth he remembered on his right thumb. Said the FBI memo describing the meeting: "Finally, after a totally lapsed time of approximately 10 minutes, Inspector Lyons asked Dr Condon if Hauptmann was the man and Dr Condon replied, I would not say he was the man. I am not sure." Another memo says, "He [Condon] remarked on one occasion that Hauptmann is not the man because he appears to be much heavier, has different eyes, different hair, etc. . . ." When Hauptmann left the police lineup, reported an FBI agent, the following exchange took place: Q. "Have you seen him before, Doctor?" A. "No, he is not the man."

Before the trial, Condon went to visit Hauptmann in jail. Describing that visit, a recently discovered New Jersey State Police report quotes Condon saying to Hauptmann, "I believe you, but the evidence is against you." In fact, documents reveal that Condon not only was unsure about Hauptmann but also was unsure that the kidnapper was German. A much earlier New Jersey police file quotes Condon as saying, "I figure he [the kidnapper] was not a German, from the way he spoke to me."

If the testimony of "eyewitnesses" was suspect, the testimony of the so-called experts seems more so in retrospect. Wilentz's case rested heavily on the testimony of a handwriting expert and a wood expert. One of Wilentz's tasks in the courtroom was to establish that the kidnapper and the extortionist were one and the same. It had been considered highly possible during the investigation of the crime that the original note – left by the kidnapper – had been seen by so many people that it could have been copied, and subsequent notes could have been written by people totally unconnected with the kidnapping.

Such possibilities were dismissed authoritatively by Albert S. Osborn and his son Albert D. Osborn, two of the nation's best-known handwriting analysts. The Osborns and other handwriting experts brought in to testify against Hauptmann claimed that all the ransom notes were written by Hauptmann. There could be no doubt. Yet a 1934 FBI memo discovered only recently describes a conversation between the younger Osborn and Colonel

Schwarzkopf, who led the investigation for the New Jersey State Police. After talking to Osborn, Schwarzkopf hung up the phone, turned to the other officers present and said, " 'It doesn't look so good. He [Osborn] says that when he first looked at the specimens he thought they were the same, and that there were some striking similarities, but after examining them for a while he found a lot of dissimilarities, which outweighed the similarities, and is convinced he [Hauptmann] did not write the ransom notes.' " It was only after the ransom money was found in Hauptmann's garage that Osborn reversed his opinion. The same FBI memo reports: "Within an hour [of being informed that the money had been found] Mr Osborn called the Undercover Squad headquarters . . . and advised that he and his son had positively decided that Hauptmann wrote the ransom letters." The report concludes, "There was . . . laughing [among police officers present] as to the ability of handwriting experts, it being pointed out that the Osborns did not make the identification until after the money was found."

In a trial filled with high drama, there was perhaps no more dramatic testimony than that of Arthur Koehler, a scholarly Forestry Department wood expert who at one point clamped a vice on one end of the judge's bench and planed down a piece of ponderosa pine. Koehler testified that there was overwhelming proof that one of the boards used in the ladder had actually come from Hauptmann's attic. The ladder rail was almost the same length as a gap in the flooring on one side of the attic, and square nail holes in the board exactly fit the pattern of nail holes in the floor joist running below the gap. Even the most skeptical juror had to be impressed by the evidence. Lindbergh might have been wrong. Condon might have been wrong, but what were the odds that four square nail holes would line up perfectly with four other square nail holes – so perfectly that four square-cut nails could be tapped into place with a finger!

Yet here again the FBI had its doubts. Several FBI memos from the fall of 1934 note that there had been numerous searches of the attic and that no evidence had been found. No less than thirty-seven police officers – directed to look specifically for boards that might match a rail of the ladder – had conducted

nine searches of the attic, to no avail. It was not until the FBI was
denied access to the attic that the gap was found. The gap was
discovered by New Jersey State Police Detective Lewis J. Bornmann on September 26, 1934 – seven days after Hauptmann's
arrest. Bornmann had actually moved into the Hauptmann house
after the arrest and had participated in several of the previous
fruitless searches. And even on the 26th, Bornmann had filed this
report: "This date detailed by Captain Lamb to continue the
search on the above-captioned home. Meeting Detective Tobin,
two police carpenters, and Supt. Wilson on the premises at 9
a.m., we immediately proceeded to make a thorough search of the
attic. Nothing of value was found." Yet in another report bearing
the same date, Bornmann disclosed his important discovery in the
attic. The following day the FBI requested access to the Hauptmann house but were denied entry by the New Jersey State
Police. Why?

The FBI's collective eyebrows, often raised during the Lindbergh kidnapping investigation, seemed particularly arched in
respect to Koehler's testimony. A review of the FBI's own files,
conducted a month after Hauptmann's execution, notes that
Hauptmann's defence lawyers had been expected during the
1935 trial to subpoena FBI records to prove the ladder-rail
identification was "fabricated by the joint efforts of the New
Jersey State Police and the New Jersey prosecutor's office in co-
operation with Arthur Koehler; however, this request was not
received by the bureau from the defense attorneys."

The ladder was not the only physical piece of evidence that
might have been tampered with by the police. In his book
Scapegoat, author Anthony Scaduto makes a persuasive case that
the police also may have tampered with the payroll books from
Hauptmann's job at the Majestic Apartments in Manhattan –
books that could have backed up his alibis for both the day of the
kidnapping (March 1) and the day that the ransom money was
passed by Dr Condon (April 2).

Hauptmann first told police that he had worked all day on
March 1; and the supervisor from the Majestic Apartments gave
an affidavit to that effect shortly after the hearings on Hauptmann's extradition from New York to New Jersey. Yet the

payroll books that would have proved the matter one way or another were missing – missing, even though the New York City police files bore receipts indicating that they had at one point received them. Without those records, Hauptmann's supervisor felt obliged to soften his own affidavit to "I am not positive . . . I do not know," and Hauptmann had lost one of his best defences.

The payroll records covering April 2, the day of the ransom pass, do exist, but they, too, may have been tampered with. Where there should be a check opposite Hauptmann's name for April 2, there is, instead, a large ink blob, a blob big enough to cover the check mark that would have been there if Hauptmann was telling the truth. All the other circles in the book that mark someone's absence from work are neat and small.

If there was a smoking gun in the case, it was the ransom money. Hauptmann had been arrested after cashing a $10 Lindbergh ransom bill at a Manhattan gas station two years and seven months after the kidnapping. After many days of searching, police found $14,600 more in ransom bills hidden in Hauptmann's garage. Almost as incriminating was the incredible tale Hauptmann told to explain the money. A friend and business partner, Hauptmann said, a man named Isidor Fisch, had left a shoe box in his care before returning to Germany for a visit, without telling him its contents. Hauptmann had stuck it on a kitchen closet shelf and forgotten about it. Even after relatives wrote from Germany that the tubercular Fisch had died, Hauptmann did not remember. Finally, a few weeks before his arrest, he had poked the decomposing box accidently with a broom and noticed the money (the closet had a leak, and the water had partially destroyed the box). He had buried the money in his garage, intending to spend the few thousand dollars Fisch owed him and to keep the rest for Fisch's relatives who were coming to the US to settle the estate.

A tall tale – or so Wilentz made it sound in court. He called it Hauptmann's "Fisch story." But now, almost 50 years later, documents suggest that the "Fisch story" was not so fishy after all. Business ledgers confiscated by the police and never introduced in court established that Fisch and Hauptmann were indeed business partners. Further supporting evidence could have been supplied by police files – references to letters written by Isidor Fisch's friend and room-mate, Henry Uhlig, that were also confiscated by the police and never introduced in court. A rediscovered New Jersey State Police file refers to a letter Uhlig wrote to a friend in Germany the day *before* Hauptmann's arrest, in which he claims that Hauptmann had loaned Fisch $7,500 and states that Fisch "had been swindling people." After Uhlig learned of Hauptmann's arrest, according to another state police document, he wrote a letter stating that Fisch had "bought some hot money and gave it to Hauptmann." Uhlig added, "Now the poor man is going to have to pay."

Also unavailable for Hauptmann's defence was a letter written to the carpenter by Isidor's brother from Germany shortly after Isidor's death and later confiscated from Hauptmann's home by police. Pinkus Fisch wrote to Hauptmann of his brother's death: "I feel it is my duty to let you know about it in America as my brother has often talked about you and your business connections with him . . . In his last few hours he mentioned your name and I suppose he wanted to say something to us about you, or something for us to tell you, but he did not have the strength . . ."

Hauptmann well understood the importance of this letter as evidence to support his case. A New Jersey State Police report on the secret and illegal surveillance of Hauptmann in his jail cell has the prisoner saying to his wife, "If Isidor Fisch had not died in Germany, I would not be here behind bars. Have you the letter from Fisch's brother?" Anna Hauptmann responds that the police have taken it.

Other documents also support Hauptmann's contention that he had not known about the ransom money, let alone spent any, until shortly before his arrest. Lindbergh ransom bills discovered between 1932 and the summer of 1934 almost all shared similar characteristics. New York police files contain lab reports of all known ransom money passed in the city, showing that most of those bills bore traces of lipstick and mascara, not to mention microscopic traces of gold or brass particles. Moreover, the bills were folded repeatedly so as to fit into a small watch or vest pocket. The half dozen or so ransom bills known to be passed by Hauptmann bore no resemblance to bills passed earlier. No lipstick traces. No gold or brass particles. No folds of any kind. Furthermore, they all showed evidence of being waterlogged, consistent with his testimony of the saturated shoe box.

Perhaps even more interesting, a magazine report published shortly after Hauptmann's arrest refers to Lindbergh ransom money cashed in by Isidor Fisch to buy his boat ticket to Germany. In its December 31, 1934, issue, *Time* magazine, summarizing evidence that would be brought forward by the prosecution against Hauptmann in his trial, wrote, "Isidor Fisch, Hauptmann's partner in random business ventures, used ransom money to pay for his passage back to Germany, where Fisch died of tuberculosis in 1933." Yet this fact was never mentioned by the prosecution during the trial.

The reason: police evidently believed at the time that the $2,000 in Lindbergh bills cashed by Fisch was the same $2,000 that Hauptmann had told them he had loaned to Fisch the day he sailed for Germany. The money seemed to constitute important evidence against Hauptmann. Only later was it discovered that Fisch had cashed the ransom money several hours *before* Hauptmann withdrew $2,000 from his bank account to give to his friend. The implication is clear: either Hauptmann had been telling the truth, and it was Fisch, not Hauptmann, who had the ransom money in 1933, or they were partners in the crime as well as in stocks and furs.

From the very beginning of the Lindbergh case, police believed that more than one person was involved in the kidnapping and extortion. Even more important, they were very suspicious that at least someone in the kidnapping group had come from, or had friends inside, the Lindbergh household.

An FBI report, quoting state police, put it bluntly: "At least two persons perpetrated the kidnapping." According to state records, one of the first police officers to arrive at the Lindbergh home found two sets of footprints leading from the road near the house to the nursery and back. But the trooper, Joseph Wolf, was not called to testify. In his reports on his contacts with the kidnapper, Dr Condon mentioned other people – people he had heard over the telephone, speaking Italian in the background . . . a small, dark-skinned woman who had approached him at a charity bazaar in the Bronx to say that her accomplices were nervous but that she would be in touch. And both Condon and Lindbergh reported seeing a second man – a lookout – at their cemetery rendezvous with the kidnapper.

Yet Hauptmann was electrocuted on the theory that he was the "lone-wolf" kidnapper and murderer. What had happened in between to all the other suspected accomplices? What had happened to the story of Violet Sharpe?

A young serving maid, Violet Sharpe, who worked in the household of Anne Morrow Lindbergh's mother, had become a suspect shortly after the kidnapping when she gave vague and conflicting testimony about what she had done the night of the kidnapping. Under further questioning about a telephone call she had received the afternoon of the crime, Sharpe remembered that her mystery caller had been a man named Ernie, a petty thief whose business cards were found in Sharpe's room. Yes, she admitted, Ernie had called in time to have learned that the baby would remain in Hopewell that night. The following day, the police told Violet Sharpe to get ready to go to the police barracks for additional questioning. Highly distraught, she ran upstairs to her room, choked down the cyanide chloride she had stored in a tin can on her shelf, and was dead within minutes. Colonel Norman Schwarzkopf hastened to tell reporters that "the suicide of Violet Sharpe strongly tends to confirm the suspicions of the investigating authorities concerning her guilty knowledge of the crime against Charles Lindbergh Jr." Yet, when the trial finally took place, the prosecution not only forgot about Violet Sharpe but about the possibility of a conspiracy as well.

Of all the things that weighed against Hauptmann at his trial, few undermined him as much as the incompetence of his own chief defence lawyer. Once a brilliant criminal attorney in New York, Edward Reilly clearly was approaching the end of his career when he reached the Lindbergh trial; two years later he would have a nervous breakdown.

Reilly was hired to defend Hauptmann by none other than William Randolph Hearst, who was anxious in return to have exclusive access to the defendant and his wife for his newspapers.

Hearst passionately believed in Hauptmann's guilt. He told one reporter, "In this trial, I am sure we can produce a flame of nationwide indignation which will deter other criminals." Hearst's control over Reilly raised conflict of interest questions unknown to the jurors and never properly understood by the Hauptmanns themselves.

A heavy drinker, Reilly had little interest in talking to Hauptmann before the trial and revealed his own prejudices by having stationery down one side of which was printed a blood-red ladder, the prosecution's main piece of evidence. A recently discovered 1936 FBI memo notes that during the course of the trial, Reilly had told T.H. Sisk, the top FBI agent assigned to the Lindbergh case, that "he knew Hauptmann was guilty, didn't like him, and was anxious to see him get the chair."

Nowhere was Reilly's incompetence more apparent than in the matter of the *corpus delicti*. In order to convict Hauptmann for murder as well as extortion, it was essential to establish that Lindbergh's son was dead. The prosecution argued that of course he was, and that the proof was the body found about five miles from the Lindbergh home in the Sourland Mountains, a body that had been identified by the baby's governess as well as by his father. Reilly was all too happy to concede the point. Yet the body had been so horribly decomposed that its sex, let alone its identity, could not be firmly established. The pediatrician to Charles Lindbergh Jr summoned to the funeral home just before the corpse was cremated, was quoted as saying, "If you were to lay ten million dollars on that table and tell me it was mine if I said positively this was the Colonel's son, I'd have to refuse the money." When Reilly failed to challenge the body's identity, his assistant counsel, Lloyd Fisher, stalked out of the courtroom shouting, "You are conceding Hauptmann to the electric chair!"

In addition to being represented by such feeble counsel, Hauptmann was tried in a courtroom atmosphere as chaotic and biased as almost any in the history of American jurisprudence. The courtroom was not just crowded; it was jammed. On a particularly titillating day, some 20,000 people showed up in Flemington, NJ, to gain entrance. Spectators sneaked in on phone passes, even came through the windows. The jurors

themselves had to enter and exit the courthouse through pha-
lanxes of onlookers and journalists, all rendering their soapbox
judgments at will. Merchants peddling miniature 10-cent repli-
cas of the kidnap ladder could barely keep up with the demand;
many spectators entered the courtroom with their ladders pinned
on, literally wearing their verdicts on their lapels.

While Hauptmann was in jail awaiting trial, he was severely
beaten by the police – a fact established by FBI documents. His
treatment inside the courtroom was not much better. Judge
Thomas Whitaker Trenchard allowed prosecutor Wilentz to
shake his fist at Hauptmann, to shout at him without interruption, often calling him "a snake." "Since I am a foreigner and
besides an irregular immigrant," Hauptmann wrote to his mother
in Germany while on death row, "I was a person on whom they
could vent everything . ... The prosecutor addressed me [as] wild
animal, snake, tiger, lowest being on the animal kingdom. You
can hardly conceive how I felt . . ."

That Hauptmann felt anything would have come as a surprise to
most Americans, much less to the jury. Wilentz portrayed him not
only as a snake but also as a man with "ice water in his veins" – a
humourless, bloodless unreformed criminal capable of perpetrat-
ing any crime, however heinous. It was an image that Reilly himself
scarcely tried to counter. Yet there was evidence, in the form of
pictures and the testimony of friends, that might have been introduced to show a very different Hauptmann – a sometime musician, a
gregarious and curious traveller, an amateur photographer who
took warm and witty portraits of himself and his friends.

When Hauptmann first met Anna, his bride to be, he confessed
his life of crime back in Germany and said he had changed his
ways. And so it seemed. The New Jersey police never found so
much as a traffic violation against him in the nine years he had
lived in the United States.

In his cell immediately after hearing the verdict, Bruno Richard Hauptmann muttered, "Little men, little pieces of wood,
little scraps of paper." A guilty man cursing the various witnesses
and pieces of evidence that finally forced a harsh justice upon
him? Perhaps. However much the FBI's memorandums cast
doubt upon the case against Hauptmann, they never argue his

innocence, and the man who received them all, J. Edgar Hoover, claimed years later that he had never doubted Hauptmann's guilt. But it now seems at least possible that Hauptmann was innocent as claimed, and that he was ruminating on the brittleness of justice, hanging as it so often does on "little men, little pieces of wood, little scraps of paper."

When New Jersey Governor Harold Hoffman received word of Hauptmann's execution, he sat alone at his desk in the state house in Trenton and reread the impassioned letter Hauptmann had sent him just days before. Hoffman wondered anew, he wrote years later in his memoirs, "if the almost friendless alien who became the focal point of one of the world's bitterest controversies" had, in fact, been innocent "of the crime that for over two years baffled the high command and the brainiest sleuths in the country."

Certainly there is no doubt about his innocence in the mind of his widow. The wedding band that Richard Hauptmann gave Anna Hauptmann 56 years ago still remains on her hand, now gnarled by arthritis: on her coffee table once again rests the leather-bound album of pictures her husband had taken on their three-month trip across the United States in 1931, an album the police finally returned to her years after the trial, tattered, with many of the pictures missing. At eighty-three, Anna Hauptmann is still committed to carrying the case forward. "You ask me why I am so sharp and so agile?" she says. "I tell you that I had to stay like this so I can clear the good name of my husband."

Bruno Richard Hauptmann on death row in 1936:
"The poor child has been kidnapped and murdered, so somebody must die for it. For is the parent not the great flier? And if someone does not die for the death of the child, then always the police will be monkeys. So I am the one who is picked to die."

Former New Jersey Attorney General David Wilentz, in an interview with *The New York Times*, March 28, 1977:
"If you disbelieve Lindbergh, disbelieve the handwriting experts, the government expert on wood – if you believe District Attorney Foley suppressed evidence, and I suppressed evidence – then of course you have a different story."

A WELSH MUMMY

(Sarah Jane Harvey, UK 1960)

Robert Jackson

The best-known case in Britain involving mummified remains is that of Mrs Sarah Harvey, tried for the murder of her lodger, Mrs Frances Knight, but acquitted. Mrs Knight's doubled-up body, shrouded in the mouldering remnants of her night-dress and dressing gown, was discovered in a locked cupboard at Mrs Harvey's house in Rhyl, North Wales, in 1960. Mrs Harvey said that she'd put Mrs Knight there after finding her dead in her room in April 1940. The skin was shrunken and leathery, and the corpse had been mummified by the natural process of warm, dry air rising and circulating in the cupboard, slowly drying out the body tissues. But suspicion arose during a post-mortem examination, prompted by a groove on the neck associated with the disintegrating vestige of a knotted stocking. The pathologist concluded that Mrs Knight had been strangled, and Mrs Harvey was charged with murder. She denied the charge, and it was not supported by the physical evidence. Neither the hyoid bone nor thyroid cartilage was fractured, as would be expected in a case of strangulation. Cleared of murder, Mrs Harvey was nevertheless convicted of fraud, because for twenty years she had drawn a special pension to which her dead lodger had been entitled. Robert Jackson (1911–77), a Yorkshireman, was a journalist who worked as a foreign and war correspondent before turning to authorship with a series of biographies of twentieth century legal luminaries including the former Lord Chief Justice, Lord Hewart. Surprisingly, perhaps, he was also editor of Gardening Illustrated.

Of all the people who took part in the trial in October, 1960, of Mrs Sarah Jane Harvey, a sixty-five-year-old Rhyl, North Wales, landlady for murder, the most unremarkable was the woman in the dock.

The Solicitor-General, Sir Jocelyn Simon, QC, who prosecuted, was to become President of the Probate, Divorce and Admiralty Division of the High Court. Mr Elwyn Jones, QC his chief assistant, was picked by the Labour Prime Minister in 1964 to be Attorney-General. Professor Sir Sydney Smith, called the "patriarch" of all forensic experts, and Dr (later Professor) Francis E. Camps, one of the leading Home Office pathologists for a quarter of a century, attended to give advice to the defence on matters about which not more than a dozen men in the world could have spoken with authority. Sir Francis Walshe, the great neurological specialist was present, as was Lord Cohen of Birkenhead, the famous physician. Dr Edward Gerald Evans, Home Office pathologist for North Wales and West Midlands, was the chief prosecution witness and although the defence experts disagreed with his conclusions, they openly expressed admiration for his work. Not the least remarkable man in court was the defence counsel, Mr Andrew Rankin, a rugged figure, an expert in both Scottish and English law and a triple Blue (hockey, swimming and water-polo) of both Edinburgh and Cambridge universities who, at thirty-six, took on a formidable team of prosecutors.

Yet the frail, ailing, drab little woman in the court had done something which extraordinary and ordinary people could not think of without revulsion. For twenty years, she had kept the mummified body of Mrs Frances Alice Knight, her lodger, in a locked cupboard at the top of the bedroom stairs. She was suspected of murder, accused of it, and acquitted. As her counsel said, she must have gone through hell, knowing the body was there and that, having put it there, she could not turn back. With her secret always in danger of exploding, she walked the streets of the holiday town of Rhyl and except for her few friends nobody gave her a second look.

The case of the Mummy in the Cupboard, as it came to be called, was followed by the public for a number of reasons. To begin with, mummies are not found in cupboards every day of the week in Britain. The trial when it was held at Ruthin, the little assize town in Denbighshire, came to an end immediately after exhaustive cross-examination of the Crown's two principal witnesses, but particularly of the pathologist, Dr Evans. The two defence crime doctors, Sir Sydney Smith and Dr Camps, were present throughout. They did not give evidence but the knowledge that they were there – and what they would say if they were called – had a profound effect. There was another fact which made the trial interesting, although it was not revealed at the time. Barristers in murder trials have been experts on guns, poisons and other technical matters but the defence counsel, Mr Rankin, had an unusual qualification. For two years, he had studied medicine at Edinburgh University under one of his own forensic experts, Sir Sydney Smith.

To a large extent, Mrs Sarah Jane Harvey was responsible for her own predicament. Mrs Knight, the estranged wife of a Rhyl dentist who had gone in 1936 to live in Hove, Sussex, took a 30s. a week bed-sitting room in Mrs Harvey's house in West Kinmel Street early in 1940. The exact date she went there was not certain but a policeman handed her personally on February 27, 1940, the magistrates' order awarding her £2 a week for maintenance at the time she was living in another Rhyl boarding house. Mrs Knight found difficulty in walking from what was first thought to be rheumatism but turned out later to be disseminated sclerosis, a deadly crippling disease. She managed to get to the magistrates' office to collect the first payment. The second payment was made to Mrs Harvey, who showed the clerk's experienced assistant, Mr Albert Reveley, a chit signed by Mrs Knight authorizing her to collect the money. She continued to do so until she went into hospital herself with suspected cancer in April, 1960.

The death of Mrs Knight came to light in an unusual way, too. While Mrs Harvey was undergoing treatment in hospital her son Leslie, a taxi-driver, decided to do his mother a good turn. Mrs Harvey had no lodger but as she had given Leslie the key he began to redecorate the house. Leslie had lived in the house all his life until two years after he married, when he found a place of his own. It had often puzzled him why his mother had never allowed the cupboard built on to the wall at the top of the stairs to be opened but he accepted her story that it contained various articles belonging to a former lodger who one day would want them back. Leslie Harvey decided to make a good job of decorating the top landing and deal with the cupboard inside and out. He forced one of the doors with a screw-driver and peered through the dark, musty-smelling cobwebby interior with the aid of a torch. It was a severe shock when he saw what seemed to be a human foot. His wife was downstairs and he hurried her off to her father's house. The two men returned together to the house and immediately they had made certain that what was inside the cupboard was a body, they sensibly hurried to the police station for help.

A local doctor was called but realized that the task of examining a mummified body would have to be undertaken by a highly-skilled pathologist and within a few hours Dr Evans and Dr Alan Clift, a biologist from the Home Office Forensic Laboratory at Preston, had begun to unravel the mystery of the mummy in the cupboard.

Bodies do not become mummies in a day or two in cold, damp climates and the obvious person to question first was Mrs Harvey, who had lived in the house for over forty years. Mrs Harvey was naturally shocked to hear of the mummy in the cupboard. She was a respectable as well as a sick woman and the only blemish on her character was a conviction for the theft of £10 in 1942.

Her first reaction when the police called to see her was to feign surprise and say she knew nothing about the mummy. No doubt with thoughts of her own illness uppermost in her mind she forgot any prepared story – if in the course of twenty years living with the mummy she had ever had one clearly mapped out.

But Mrs Harvey was sharp and knew her way about. She must have realized quickly that the police would not shrug off the finding of the mummy as one of those inexplicable things that happen. They had already questioned Leslie about the lodgers he remembered and the name of Mrs Knight, a lodger in his boyhood days, had cropped up. Yes, Mrs Harvey told the police, she knew Mrs Knight, a crippled lady, who had lived with her until the end of the war. She now lived in Penymaes, Llandudno, with a Mrs Collins. Mrs Harvey said she was sure of that because every week, she still collected £2 due to Mrs Knight under a maintenance order and posted it on, either in cash or as a postal order.

The police made a note to look up Mrs Knight in Penymaes and asked her about other lodgers who might know something about the mummy in the cupboard. Mrs Harvey took her time to answer but eventually she said she did remember a couple, named White or Wright. They had come to Rhyl at the time the bombing started in the South of England. Mrs Harvey said they wanted to store "stuff and foodstuff" and she had let them use the landing cupboard. They had the key and went off with it about the end of the war. For two Christmases in succession she had had cards from the couple but they never returned to collect whatever it was they had left in the cupboard.

Mrs Harvey had furnished streets, places and names so that the police could trace Mrs Knight but they were unsuccessful. Mrs Harvey was being discharged from hospital temporarily but instead of going home she went, by invitation, to the police station.

She now decided that the time for fencing was over. The police had held her on a charge of obtaining one of Mrs Knight's weekly instalments of £2 by false pretences and in the cells she began to unburden herself. "Mrs Knight is in the cupboard," she informed Chief Inspector H. I. Williams. "I will tell you what happened. She died in the bedroom and I put her in the cupboard."

Bit by bit, the secret she had bottled up for twenty years came out. She said that soon after coming to lodge with her, Mrs Knight became very frail and weak and developed great pains in her knees. Four or five weeks after she arrived, Mrs Harvey was getting ready for bed in the back bedroom, when she heard Mrs Knight screaming in her own bedroom. "I went into the bedroom and saw her lying on the floor in her night-dress and coat. I asked her what had happened and she said 'I am in an awful lot of pain and would rather be dead'."

Mrs Harvey said she tried to pick her distressed lodger up but could not manage it. She dressed herself and went downstairs to make tea but when she returned, Mrs Knight was still lying on the floor and was dead. "I was on my own in the house and was scared stiff, so I pulled her along the landing and put her into the empty cupboard," she said. "I put fly-papers in the cupboard and then locked it. I didn't tell anyone she had died – but I kept trying to keep things covered up. I have gone through hell ever since. I have told you everything now and that is the truth."

The Rhyl detectives now had plenty of clues to follow up – apart from what the work of the pathologists would yield – since it was clear that Mrs Harvey's story would have to undergo the most stringent tests. Sudden death in a quiet house to a woman on her own can be a frightening experience but the question in the minds of the police and lawyers was simple: which was the more frightening thing to do – run into the house of a friendly neighbour and get help, or drag a freshly-dead body out on the landing, somehow – remembering that Mrs Harvey had said she could not lift Mrs Knight from the floor into bed – get her into the cupboard and wedge a bedspread between her thighs to prevent pollution.

A first thought was that Mrs Harvey, seeing Mrs Knight dead on the floor, suddenly realized that if only she could conceal the body she would in effect have inherited a pension of £2 a week. The prosecution at her trial went further and suggested that Mrs Harvey had done more than that – she had actually strangled Mrs Knight herself with a stocking so that she could continue to draw the money. The court did not accept the view but over the years, Mrs Harvey *did* collect £2,098 paid over by Mr Knight from Hove.

Mrs Harvey had also taken good care to see that the arrangement was not disturbed. The clerks in the magistrates' office showed an interest in their "clients" and often asked how Mrs Knight, whom they never saw, was getting on. Mrs Harvey's replies varied week by week, from "about the same" to "a little better" or "not too good". Occasionally at Christmas, Mrs Harvey negotiated for the money to be paid in advance and when it did not turn up, the clerks were surprised to hear that the invalid would be in a "bloody bad temper" or would "play hell" in consequence.

When the trial took place, Mr Reveley, one of the senior clerks, was questioned closely by Mr Rankin about the office system which had allowed Mrs Harvey to draw the money for so long. Mrs Harvey's signed authority could not be found in the files but Mr Reveley remembered that she had handed it over. It had never occurred to him to doubt her honesty. "I have known her forty or forty-five years and have always found her perfectly straightforward," he said.

In 1949, the dead woman in the cupboard must have been very much on Mrs Harvey's conscience because she sold a black trunk which had belonged to Mrs Knight and had her initials stamped on it. She remarked to the buyer that she did not think Mrs Knight would ever come back for it.

Mrs Harvey had undoubtedly taken trouble to keep inquisitive lodgers away from the cupboard. A miner who lodged with Mrs Harvey when he worked at a Rhyl colliery was traced to Newark. He said he and his wife were "a bit nosey" when they lived in the house for periods in 1950 and 1951 and had tried to open the cupboard. He lost interest in it when Mrs Harvey told him that it contained her best linen.

But the most significant discovery which the police thought cast great doubt on Mrs Harvey's story was a fly-paper found hanging from the roof of the cupboard. Mrs Harvey said that from the day Mrs Knight was put in the cupboard in the early spring of 1940, the door had remained locked. This could not have been true. The fly-paper bore a code number and the name of the manufacturer at Derby. That particular batch of fly-papers, the manager said, could not have been on sale before the early spring of 1942 – a whole year after Mrs Knight's death.

Some of these matters could be drowned or at least obscured by the vigorous cross-examination to which Mr Rankin subjected every witness. But in the end, the case against Mrs Harvey depended on the evidence given – or to be given – by the doctors who had treated Mrs Knight in life and those who had known her as what Dr Camps called "a shell of dried skin and bones".

Mrs Harvey, even twenty years before her trial, had not been particularly robust and part of the Crown case was that she was able to kill because Mrs Knight was "vulnerable". "You may think that the fact that Mrs Knight was a cripple is significant in considering whether she would not be an easy victim of attack," said the Solicitor-General, in opening the case.

Mrs Knight's friend, Mrs Phyllis Rogers, partially upset the idea that Mrs Knight was always miserable, complaining, and by inference, almost helpless. She produced a holiday snapshot which showed Mrs Knight looking quite happy, though admittedly she walked with a stick. "She was cheerful with a keen sense of humour," said Mrs Rogers. "She never complained of pain." Mrs Rogers maintained that though her condition was slowly deteriorating, Mrs Knight was chiefly worried because she was losing her sense of balance.

Mrs Rogers had taken Mrs Knight to Liverpool to see the famous consultant physician, Lord Cohen of Birkenhead, who had diagnosed disseminated sclerosis but anticipated that there would be some improvement in her condition. Mrs Knight's medical records showed that she was slightly overweight and there was nothing in them to suggest that she would die from natural causes within a short period.

But Sir Francis Walshe, the neurologist, advised the defence on a point in Mrs Harvey's favour. Her counsel took it up with Lord Cohen, who agreed that Mrs Knight had been suffering from a kidney infection which, in an acute form, might lead to death. He said anyone predisposed to the infection might fall dangerously ill suddenly and die within a fortnight. So, one of the most distinguished physicians went on the court record with the view that it was *possible* for Mrs Harvey's account of Mrs Knight's death to be correct.

The case reached the beginning of its crucial stage when crime doctor Gerald Evans stepped into the witness box to tell of the discovery and detailed examination of the mummy. There is a great deal of *camaraderie* among crime doctors, though they often speak in slighting terms of each other's work when talking privately. But there is no tendency for them to hang together and in most cases the cross-examination of counsel, usually based on the opinions of other crime doctors, are as a rule searching and prolonged. In the mummy case, Dr Evans was to be put to the fiercest test.

The mummy, it turned out, was not a "true" mummy, though the difference between "true" and "false" could be appreciated only by crime doctors. Mummification was drying until the moisture was removed from the tissues, said Dr Evans. The passage of a current of dry air over the body, day and night, led to mummification and the preservation of the features and contours of the body. It was well known in Egypt.

In the case of the Rhyl mummy, mummification might have occurred because of a freak of chance. For many weeks and months, warm, dry air had circulated up the stairs into the landing and cupboard where the body lay. A small trap door above the cupboard may have helped the draughts. Dr Camps said later that the explanation was over-simplified but he admitted that it seemed to satisfy the jury. Gruesome photographs of the body were handed up to Mr Justice Davies, who seemed to approve of them on the principle that one picture is worth a thousand words.

It had been late at night when Dr Evans climbed the carpeted stairs of Mrs Harvey's house and in the light of police torches began to make clinical observations on the contents of the cupboard. Laymen in the old courthouse at Ruthin listened in a kind of awed wonder.

The sight he saw was not pretty – the fly-paper saturated with flies, the thick cobwebs on the walls to which dead spiders clung in grotesque masses, and the object on the floor that had been a woman. Here the lacey cobwebs were several inches deep. He could also make out the shape of a mound of mould and literally many hundreds of pupa cases from which maggots had emerged as flies. They told their own story of what had happened when the natural putrefaction of the body set in.

A foot was visible, brown and skinny, as Leslie Harvey had seen it. Moving closer into the smell of decay, Dr Evans gently began to brush aside the cobwebs, mould and dust. He uncovered what had been a human face with nostrils dilated and lips stretched and distorted. But immediately he had had to retreat on to the landing to cough out the dust that rose in clouds and choked him.

The greatest care was obviously necessary in recovering the

mummy and Dr Evans examined the cupboard to see whether he
could unscrew it to take it away. But the cupboard had been built
on to the wall and it could not be done. So he began again to stir
the dust as gently as possible and after a time he saw the outline of
the mummy under a crumbling blue dressing gown and blanket.
He had to remove two more types of material before the mummy
was completely exposed – the bedspread, which had been packed
between the legs, and a long-sleeved night-dress, the V-shaped
neck of which could be traced.

The mummy under the touch of his fingers was rock hard – an
absolute statue, Dr Evans said in court. It was lying on its back
with the thighs bent backwards towards the abdomen and the legs
bent or flexed at the knees. The left arm was extended down the
side of the body and the right forearm, with a claw-like hand, lay
across the chest. The whole of the skin from the neck to the feet
was peppered with maggot holes.

Dr Evans's experience in removing the crumbling matter other
than the body had made him apprehensive about what would
happen when he attempted to take the mummy out of the cupboard but he need not have worried. Far from disintegrating, he
could not budge the mummy. Finally, he saw only one solution.
He would have to lever it from the cupboard floor. "Get me a
spade," he said to the police.

In his own mortuary, Dr Evans made a detailed examination of
the mummy before he put it in a bath containing a solution of
glycerine to soften it. The mummy's head was turned to the right
and when the dust had been brushed from the neck, he saw a
distinct groove with a localized depression at the front. A great
deal was to be heard at the trial about the groove. He tilted the
mummy to see whether the groove ran all the way round the neck.
It did, and what appeared to have caused the groove – a piece of
tape-like material – fell away. A further piece of the same material
was still embedded in the groove and when Dr Evans had eased it
out he saw that it was part of a stocking. There was only a few
inches of it altogether – the fragments were exhibited in a test-
tube in court – but it contained an undoubted reef knot.

As Dr Evans said in court, the body was in a "deplorable"
condition but the post-mortem on the mummy, and later the

examination of the skeleton, produced a very adequate build-up of the sort of person the mummy had been in life. She was a European woman between forty and sixty, nearly 5 ft, 4 ins, tall with shapely ears. She was married – her ring finger was grooved but – another minor mystery – the ring was not in the cupboard.

She could not have had children without a Caesarian operation. She was right-handed and dragged her left foot when she walked. In her early teens, she had had an illness which had been cured by medicine containing arsenic, lead or iron. All her teeth had been extracted but her dentures were missing. Many of the internal organs had been eaten away over the years but the crime doctors did not think she had been poisoned. They had even been able to find her blood group. They compared it with blood groups of Mrs Knight's close relatives and, if they had been called to give an opinion in court, would have said that Mrs Knight's group might well have been that of the mummy's.

The defence discussed the possibility of trying to prove that the mummy in the cupboard was not that of Mrs Knight, relying on a legal objection to Mrs Harvey's own admission. The idea was quickly abandoned and the line they were to take became apparent soon after the cross-examination of Dr Evans began.

Dr Evans had been taken through his evidence-in-chief by the Solicitor-General and had told the court how he had seen the groove around the neck and retrieved the piece of stocking, with the tightly tied reef knot. When he put the stocking on the postmortem bench, it remained in a curve and this suggested that at one time it had encircled the neck. "If you tie a stocking tightly round a person and knot it and take the stocking off fairly soon after, you will get no depression. But if that stocking is left in contact with the skin over a period of time, then, especially after mummification starts, I think it is more than probable that an indentation would remain," he said.

There had been a depression on the side of the thyroid cartilage and he had found a knot in the stocking, but not where the depression was. Dr Evans found the groove on the left side difficult to associate with a natural fold of the neck and there was nothing in the cupboard which would account for the external pressure.

"Are you able on medical grounds, excluding the fact that you found a stocking, to state what was the cause of death?" asked Sir Jocelyn. "No," was the reply, "I am afraid I cannot do that to help the court."

"So that within your province as an expert, there is nothing to indicate what had happened?" The answer was "No".

Mr Rankin, impressive and confident, plunged into battle and Dr Evans told him that it was quite impossible to determine whether the stocking had been put round Mrs Knight's neck before or after death.

The judge intervened. "That is your opinion now?" "Yes."

"In your opinion now, was there or was there not a ligature?" pursued the judge. "Yes, there was a ligature."

Dr Evans explained that if there was a collar round the neck of a dead man and the skin became swollen, there would be a groove.

Said Mr Rankin: "Sir Sydney Smith and Dr Camps, whose experience is unrivalled, say that this was never a homicidal ligature." "I could well understand that," came the wry answer.

"They say that what you saw on the neck was caused by postmortem changes in the body, there having been before death what I have described as a natural ligature round the neck," said Mr Rankin. "That is an opinion I cannot agree with," answered Dr Evans.

"Could a groove made by a collar be mistaken for a homicidal groove?" "Not by a forensic pathologist."

Mr Rankin commented that, "We will see what another forensic expert will say" and Dr Evans thereupon amplified his answer. "If this body does not disrupt but goes on to a more drying process, I think this groove would disappear and the skin flatten out again."

"You think it disappears but leaves a mark?" queried Mr Rankin. "Yes."

Mr Rankin's comment that, "the difficulty you are labouring under is lack of experience of this kind of case" brought from Dr Evans the complaint: "I think you are putting it rather hardly."

It was, as Dr Evans had admitted, only the second case of a mummy he had dealt with but he had been in no way put out when Mr Rankin told him that every year Dr Camps, whose opinion differed from his on several aspects of the case, saw about four cases a year. "Four mummies twenty years old?" exclaimed Dr Evans, incredulously. "I am only sorry he has not written up his experiences."

Mr Rankin justifiably made all the capital he could from the fact that the thyroid cartilage had been accidentally fractured by an ear, nose and throat specialist to whom it had been sent for an opinion on possible abnormalities – Dr Evans had made it clear that when he first saw the cartilage, it was not fractured – and also because the neck skin had been cut up into many pieces during Dr Evans's investigation. Why had this been done, asked Mr Rankin.

"I thought it was necessary so as to identify any haemorrhages under the skin. But I found none. Laboriously I went on," said Dr Evans.

"You went on cutting it up into small pieces?" asked Mr Rankin. "You were doing away with what is regarded as a very important piece from the neck. This very important exhibit, which contains what is said to be a tightly-tied knot, was sent by registered post to the forensic laboratory, and in the post things could happen?" "I agree," said Dr Evans.

Mr Rankin returned later to the question of the skin collar. "My experts find it difficult to understand why in this case the skin collar does not show a groove running right round the neck." said Mr Rankin. Retorted Dr Evans: "Your experts – and I am sorry this has to be – have not seen the skin collar as a whole, but only a portion of it."

There was whispering between counsel and the defence pathologists. "I am informed by them that they saw a major part of the collar," said Mr Rankin. "Do you agree?" "No."

"If it had been preserved, there would have been some degree of certainty?" Countered Dr Evans: "Your experts could have had a much better chance of seeing what I saw."

"They have seen enough to be exceedingly puzzled why it is that some of the skin shows no groove marks at all," said Mr Rankin. "Would you agree that it would be reasonable to conclude from that, that there was post-mortem change with swelling which caused the mark you saw on the neck at the post-mortem?"

Dr Evans would not agree. "I would rather expect Sir Sydney Smith and Dr Camps to see the difficulty of this particular case, with glycerine as an additive," he said. A few questions later, he did not conceal his exasperation. "I am trying to be completely scientific and I am not prepared to be dogmatic, as apparently some are," he said.

There was little wonder that after nearly twelve hours in the witness box, Dr Evans became annoyed at the tone of some of the questions, in spite of honeyed words about his fairness. "You do twist things, don't you," he exclaimed to Mr Rankin at one point. "It's very difficult for me to put anything across."

The ligature had been put round Mrs Knight's neck either by Mrs Knight herself or by someone else and the defence developed an ingenious theory that Mrs Knight was wearing the stocking as a cure for a cold. It was no more than an idea which, according to some observers, made the court murmur in surprise. No doubt. Perhaps the surprise was felt at the idea of the wife of a professional man believing in such an old-fashioned remedy, quite apart from the fact that there was no evidence whatever that Mrs Knight had had a cold.

Dr Evans had not excluded the possibility that Mrs Knight had died naturally for the simple reason that he had very little tissue to work on. He was asked whether she could have died from a heart attack, lung infection like lobar pneumonia, bladder, kidney, or other infection. The answer in each case was "yes" because Dr Evans had already said that he did not know the cause of death. Why then, he was asked, was it suggested that Mrs Knight was strangled with a stocking? He replied that there were six reasons – the neck groove, the depression on the neck, the depression on the thyroid cartilage, the ligature itself, the tightness of the ligature and finally, the evidence as a whole.

After much sound, fury and wind, Dr Evans had conceded little at the end of his cross-examination and the only important point for the Solicitor-General to re-emphasize was how the distortion of the thyroid cartilage had occurred. "Is there any question of it taking place as a result of dissection?" he asked.

"In my opinion, no, or I would readily say so," affirmed Dr Evans.

The case for the prosecution was concluded with the evidence given by Dr Alan Clift, the biologist who had gone to Rhyl on the night of the discovery of the mummy. The fragments of stocking round Mrs Knight's neck were not much to go on but he said they showed that originally the stocking had been stretched tightly round her neck. Not only had the stocking been stretched but the fragment was the typical shape of a ligature. He was emphatic that the stretching had not occurred by the natural process of the swelling of the neck. He was asked whether the stretching of the stocking was of a homicidal character and his reply was "yes", with the surprise proviso that he could not rule out suicide.

Mr Rankin challenged the evidence of Dr Clift as vigorously as he had done that of Dr Evans. The late Lord Birkett in the Rouse case had confounded an engineering expert because he did not know the co-efficient of the expansion of brass and Mr Rankin attempted a similar manœuvre. He drew from Dr Clift an admission that he did not know how to distinguish between American, Egyptian and Indian cotton. Nevertheless Dr Clift answered firmly "I do", when he was asked whether he considered himself an expert on fabrics. Dr Clift agreed that he could find no other evidence on the stocking breaking under tension except that of insect attack.

At this point, Mr Justice Davies interrupted counsel's cross-examination. "The allegation here is that this stocking was used by the prisoner to strangle this woman. The vital question is 'Has it been unduly stretched?' That is the first question to my mind that should have been asked."

Mr Rankin bowed to the judge and asked Dr Clift whether he would be interested to learn that the defence had been to the Manchester Chamber of Commerce Commercial Testing House and their conclusion was that the stocking had not been abnormally stretched. "I don't agree," said Dr Clift.

It was clear that not only did the crime doctors disagree about the conclusions to be drawn from the marks on the body but that the fabric experts on both sides would be diametrically opposed.

Mr Eric Jones, director of the Testing House, had carried out a number of tests at the request of Mrs Harvey's advisers on how much tension would have been required to strangle Mrs Knight with a stocking. His conclusion, stripped of its technical terms, was that there was no evidence that the stocking round the mummy's neck had been under any abnormal tension, although the experts would not go as far as to say that the stocking had never been under an abnormal stretching force.

Dr Clift, before his evidence was complete, had fainted in the witness box and while the court waited for him to recover counsel for both sides talked the case over informally outside. The weakness of the prosecution case had been exposed and the Solicitor-General took the decision not to pursue it further.

The Judge was informed in his private room and later, in open court, Sir Jocelyn said that after considering his duty, the state of the case and the evidence so far, it would not be right to invite the jury to find a verdict of guilty.

For once in the case, the experts – this time on law – agreed. "There seemed to be manifold circumstances of suspicion in the case," said Mr Justice Davies. "But when one considers the evidence of Dr Evans, which was given with conspicuous skill, fairness and moderation, it comes to this: he cannot say whether the ligature was put on before or after death and he cannot say that the ligature caused death. If it cannot be proved that the stocking stretched, then the prosecution fails. Without saying any more; because we have not heard the defence evidence, it does appear that the prosecution are in no position to prove that the stocking was stretched."

The money to defend Mrs Harvey had been raised privately and Mr Graham Roberts, the young defence solicitor – like Mr Rankin, engaged on his first murder case – said that the considerable sum of £3,000 had been spent. When the jury had found Mrs Harvey not guilty of murder, Mr Rankin applied for costs. "I appreciate that it could be said that this lady left herself open to this kind of charge," observed Mr Rankin. "But whatever lies she may have told, or cold, cool, calculating woman she may have been, in the end the prosecution case came down to two witnesses, Dr Evans and Dr Clift." The heavy costs incurred by the defence, he said, had been in respect of those witnesses.

The Solicitor-General rose to his feet to resist the application but the judge stopped him. "I don't think I need trouble you, Mr

Solicitor," he said. "No, Mr Rankin," he added, dismissing the application.

Two token charges of fraud concerning Mr Knight's maintenance payments remained to be dealt with and Mr Justice Davies rejected Mr Rankin's suggestion that Mrs Harvey should be allowed to go free after her years of terrible strain. The judge said the medical evidence before him showed that Mrs Harvey was a very sick woman. But taking into account the frightful anxiety she had undergone, the fact that she had been on trial for murder and had been imprisoned for four months awaiting trial, it was still impossible to overlook the case. The sentence was fifteen months' imprisonment.

Sniffing smelling salts, supported by a nurse and a wardress, the inconspicuous figure of Mrs Harvey passed from the dock, without having said a word about her long and extraordinary ordeal. Nor were the comments of Mr Knight, the loser almost by chance of more than £2,000, ever made available.

THE MAN WHO COULD READ THOUGHTS

(Vernon Booher, Canada 1928)

Mike Gier

When conventional science fails, perhaps it's time to try the unconventional. This is the curious case of Vernon Booher, the first recorded murder case solved by psychic detection. A Viennese doctor claiming to have special powers led police to the weapon used to murder two members of the Booher family and two of their farmhands. The killings took place in a remote area of Edmonton, Alberta, and there were no surviving witnesses. Yet the little white-haired doctor was able to tell officers how the murder was committed, and by whom. Hitherto unsuspected, Vernon Booher was confronted, broke down and confessed. The Booher investigation was headed by police chief Mike Gier, who recalled the case some thirty years later in this short memoir.

To recognize a killer and know that you will never be able to put him where he belongs is infuriating enough, but to be faced with a murder whose very simplicity presages defeat . . . well, that is just humiliating.

As a matter of fact the Booher case involved the slaying of not one but four persons; the tracks led everywhere and nowhere, and since the department of which I was the head was under heavy fire from various quarters, I decided that the situation called for unorthodox measures.

I knew already what people were saying about police methods, and I could guess what some of my officers were thinking when I told them what I proposed to do. Particularly Detective Jim Leslie, who was to meet the train in at Edmonton and bring Dr Maximilian Langsner, late of Vienna, to my office.

Leslie was an astute investigator with a good record, but the Booher case had him foxed, and he had not been able to uncover a single lead that offered any hope of a solution. The slaying of four people appeared as mad and motiveless now as it did when the crime was discovered.

Let me say that I knew I might be leading with my chin in introducing Dr Langsner to the problem. He could be a mountebank rather than the marvel some people claimed him to be.

Nevertheless, I knew of his successes elsewhere. There was, for instance, the episode at Vancouver when he had walked into police headquarters and announced that he could put the finger on the missing jewels in a robbery case which was baffling the authorities, despite the fact that they had managed to pick up a suspect.

Dr Langsner undoubtedly had a way with him, for the police, at his suggestion, had allowed him to enter the cell of the suspect. He stood stiffly in a corner for half an hour without saying a word and then signalled to the jailer that he had finished.

To the detective in charge of the case Dr Langsner had said: "You'll find the stolen jewels hidden behind a picture in a room whose walls are yellow."

The description did not fit the suspect's apartment, but that of his girl friend, and the detective found the jewels exactly as Dr Langsner had depicted.

The Vancouver affair was one of three cases in which Dr Langsner had displayed his extraordinary powers. As far as I could understand it, he had the ability to read the thoughts of others and was demonstrating this long before studies in extrasensory perception were introduced at various universities. When asked to explain his ability to tune in to another's mind he said: "It is not easy to say what happens, but there are some people who can do it."

To get back to the Booher case, Detective Leslie was hopping mad as he waited at the railway station. I know all this, because he told me everything that happened that day – later, of course, and when he was calmer. In fact, Jim Leslie never forgot the little doctor from Vienna, and he had good reason not to, as you will see.

Dr Langsner got off the train with an umbrella and a battered piece of luggage. Leslie stepped forward, introduced himself, and said: "Welcome to Edmonton. I am happy to meet you, and all of us are looking forward to the help we know you can give us."

There was not much of Dr Langsner, and he appeared even smaller when he took off his hat and his hair popped out all over the place. He looked at Leslie for a moment, tapped his umbrella, and replied: "I don't believe a word you say. You would rather I hadn't come, and I know you are sure that I shall accomplish nothing. I hope, though, that we shall become friends and that I can help."

Leslie crimsoned, knowing that the doctor had read his mind. He was a good loser, though, and shrewd enough to realize at once that Dr Langsner was no ordinary person. He asked the doctor to talk about himself, and it was not just out of politeness.

Langsner smiled and said: "I was born and educated in Vienna, and it was my good fortune to study under Freud. During the First World War I saw a lot of shell-shocked cases, and, more than ever, became interested in the mind and its functioning. In 1926 I went to India and stayed longer than I intended. I found much that surprised me in the field of intuitive control of the mind.

"It was from this experience that I learned much of what I now know. People are sceptical about my powers, but it is not my wish to be a bloodhound. I help the police whenever they ask me, or when I have a strong pull, such as I felt in the Vancouver case."

Leslie asked Langsner what had brought him to Canada, and he explained that he wanted to study the minds of the Eskimos. The Melanesians and Polynesians of the South Pacific had become indoctrinated and corrupted by Western influences, but the intuitive abilities of the Eskimos had remained unimpaired. "They sense weather changes," said Dr Langsner with enthusiasm. "They are able to sense danger long before its appearance and they have their minds, so to speak, at their fingertips. I want to live with them and communicate with them through the channels of thought."

When Detective Leslie walked into my office with our visitor I could see that he had had a change of heart and mind. I had the feeling that Langsner did not need briefing, but I had prepared a report and began to read it and he listened without interrupting.

"On July 9th," I said, "the police at Mannville, eighty miles from here, were notified by a Dr Heaslip that half the members of the Booher ranch had been murdered. It was evening, but the summer nights in the Arctic regions are bright and glowing and Constable Olson drove over from Mannville and found Dr Heaslip waiting for him at the ranch house, together with the survivors, Henry Booher, his youngest son Vernon, and a neighbour, Charles Stevenson.

"Booher, middle-aged and still greatly shocked, led the way into the house. In the kitchen the body of Mrs Booher was slumped over the table. She had died from three bullets in the back of the neck. In the next room Fred, another of the Booher sons, was sprawled on the floor. He had been shot through the mouth. A third victim was Gabriel Cromby, one of the hired hands. He was an Austrian immigrant and his body was found in the bunkhouse. Two shots had found their mark, one in the head and the other in the chest.

"Olson was unaccustomed to dealing with this type of crime, but he had the good sense to get everybody out on the porch for questioning. Vernon Booher said he had found the bodies about eight o'clock that evening. He had been working in the fields for a couple of hours and heard the shots. They seemed to come from the house, and he hurried over and found the body of his mother first. He then saw his dead brother, and when he ran over to the bunkhouse for help he discovered what had happened to Cromby. There was no telephone in the house and he got a neighbour to call Dr Heaslip.

"The constable wanted to know if anything was missing, and Henry Booher said he thought not. His wife had a diamond ring, and it had not been taken. Vernon then remembered the other cowhand, a man named Rosyk. He had not been seen and Vernon asked if he might not be the murderer.

"The little party began to search the outhouses, and in one of the barns they found the missing man . . . Rosyk was dead from a couple of bullets. Henry Booher was asked what he had been doing at the time and if he had not heard the shots. He said: 'No, I wish to God I had heard them, but I was working too far away. There is a lot of acreage to this farm and the sounds did not carry that far.' Stevenson, the neighbour, explained his presence. He had stopped at the house to look at a farming catalogue Henry Booher had told him about. They were thinking of buying a harvester together.

"Booher corroborated this, and when asked if he had any idea who might be responsible for the murders replied: 'No. As far as I can tell we have no enemies anywhere. Rose, my wife, was a well-loved woman among our community. She was always ready to help any of our neighbours.'"

I explained to Dr Langsner that when the crime was notified to Edmonton I had sent Detective Leslie and Inspector Longacre out to the farm. "Tell the doctor what you found," I said to Leslie.

He looked a bit uncomfortable and glanced at Langsner, who was sitting very upright in his chair and grasping his umbrella.

"We carried out a routine examination, but found no strange fingerprints; just those of the Booher family and hired help. The murder weapon was a .303 rifle, but we were unable to find it. There was a .22 rifle and an old shotgun in the house, but neither had been fired for some time. One thing that interested us was the absence of rifle shells. Whoever had done the killing had picked them up, except one, which we found in a pan of water.

"We organized a search of the countryside with the help of neighbours, but it was no good. The murder weapon is still missing, and at the moment we are stuck without a clue."

Dr Langsner nodded sympathetically. "I can see how difficult everything is. Perhaps I shall be able to help you a little."

The inquest took place that afternoon, and Dr Langsner occupied a seat at the Press table. Everyone wondered who he was. The inquiry did not yield much more than we knew already.

Mrs Booher was the first victim and she was killed at the table as she was preparing a dish of strawberries. Fred died next, Rosyk a little later and Cromby last of all – about two hours after the first murder.

The time factor was testified to by neighbours and other witnesses and the shots were heard between half-past six and eight o'clock in the evening. They did not arouse any concern, because around Mannville it is hunting country and almost everybody keeps a gun.

One important piece of evidence was that provided by Councilman Robert Scott, who said he had driven down the farm road about six-thirty and had stopped to talk with Vernon Booher. Rosyk put in an appearance and asked Vernon what remained to be done around the house. Vernon told him to feed the stock in the barn.

Vernon gave evidence and was asked how it was that he had not heard those shots which occurred earlier in the evening. He said that since thinking the events over he must have heard them, but had paid no attention. He knew there was a fox in the neighbourhood and that Charles Stevenson had told him that he meant bagging it.

Charles Stevenson, somewhat nervous, had not long been sworn when he was asked if he owned a gun.

"Yes, I do, but I haven't it at the moment," he said. "It has been troubling me and I want to tell you about it. My gun is a .303 and the same calibre as the murder weapon. It was in my closet, but it is not there now and I think somebody must have stolen it."

"Can you tell the court when the gun was stolen?"

"Yes. It was taken last Sunday during the time I left home to go to church. I know it was there before I left because I saw it."

"Why didn't you report the theft?"

"Aw, shucks, you know how it is round here. Neighbours just come over and borrow things if you don't happen to be around. If I wanted a gun I wouldn't think twice of taking one from the Boohers."

Henry Booher and Vernon, too, were at the church service and said that they knew nothing about the missing rifle.

Following the inquest we had a conference in my office to

decide our next step, but neither Detective Leslie nor Inspector Longacre looked very happy, and that was understandable, for we had not much to work on. Nobody seemed very talkative, so to get the ball rolling I said: "It seems to me that three people could have done these murders . . . Henry Booher or Vernon or Charles Stevenson. What puzzles me most is the motive, and maybe we shall find the killing was done by a lunatic. Our first and most important task is to find the gun. It may tell us all we want to know."

Dr Langsner was looking at me steadily and I must confess that I was half joking when I asked him: "You look as if you know something. Could it be the name of the killer?"

He was not in the mood for badinage, and like a professor addressing an inattentive class he said in a clipped voice: "The rifle is not important. There are no suspects in this case, only the murderer, and I have already recognized him."

Detective Leslie leaned forward, prepared to listen. I was not at all certain if the little doctor was not now paying me back in my own coin. Nevertheless, I asked him to name the person he thought was the killer. "Vernon Booher," he said quite simply.

"Have you any proof?" asked Inspector Longacre.

Dr Langsner was surprised by the question. "Of course I have no proof. How is that possible? I am sure, though, and yet I cannot tell you why I am sure. I can tell you, though, that I knew what one or two people were thinking about in court today."

"Do you mean to say you could read the minds of the witnesses as they were giving evidence?"

"I do not know if I was reading their minds, as you say, but I knew what they were thinking about."

Inspector Longacre looked very puzzled, and Dr Langsner began to develop his theory.

"When a man commits a crime, and it may not necessarily be murder, he knows he has offended against the social code. Nevertheless, he seeks for ways to protect himself and his mind plays with the details of the crime so that he can have an explanation prepared, should it be necessary to defend himself. The problem is much more acute, naturally, when he has killed somebody, and often the persistency of thought becomes too great to bear and the criminal confesses, because only by so doing can he find relief from an intolerable burden. For instance, I know that Vernon is terribly worried by something that may prove his guilt."

"You mean the discovery of the missing rifle?" I asked. "If you know where it is, why not say so?"

Dr Langsner sighed as if he somehow regretted our persistence. "Yes, I know where it is. When Mr Stevenson told the court of finding that it had been taken from his home, Vernon began to think intently about the weapon. I could see where he had put it."

"And I'll bet he could, too," said Leslie quietly.

We waited for Dr Langsner to continue. He closed his eyes and quietly said: "It is in a clump of prairie grass beyond the back of the house. It is to the west, because I can now see the sun in that direction."

Inspector Longacre gave him a hard look. He was by no means convinced that he was not a charlatan.

"I am willing to go out to the farm with you," continued Langsner. "But let us go tomorrow and I will find the rifle for you. I am very tired now."

By noon next day the four of us arrived at the Booher farm. It commanded a lot of land, and the house, timbered and two-storey, was well constructed with a large veranda which the family must have used on many a summer evening when they had visitors. Everything looked well kept and spruce, and the various farm buildings stood under the shadow of some great linden trees.

I glanced once more at Dr Langsner, and could hardly repress a chuckle. He was still carrying his umbrella on this hot day and wore the black suit he had arrived in. I was certain it was the only one he possessed. His bangs of white hair were imprisoned by his black hat, except, of course, the thick fringe that lay on the back of his neck. The Booher farm had never seen a stranger figure than Dr Langsner.

Despite the heat of the day and his unsuitable clothes, he appeared quite cool and composed, and we followed him as he walked slowly to the back of the house. He reminded me of the old water-diviners who used a hazel twig to discover a hidden well, except that he had nothing in his hand.

For twenty minutes or so he quartered the ground and then, apparently, got the scent and hurried ahead. We followed, and he stopped somewhere between the bunkhouse and one of the linden trees. His eyes were closed and he drew his hand over his brow.

"*Ja, ja! Ach Gott!*" he exclaimed. "I have it now. If you will take about ten big steps forward."

Leslie was the nearest to him and began to count the steps. At the ninth he stumbled and bent down. We hurried over, and there was the rifle lying in the grass.

"Oh no," said Inspector Longacre as if he could not believe what he saw. It was the murder weapon right enough, and it was lifted and wrapped very carefully. When we got back to Edmonton it would be examined for finger-prints.

"You will not find any," warned Dr Langsner. "Vernon wiped the rifle very carefully and kept thinking of what he had done."

And so it turned out. In the meantime, though, I booked Vernon, not on suspicion of murder, but as a material witness, and he was placed in the jail at Edmonton, "for his own protection."

"Would it be impertinent for me to tell you what I think should now be done?" asked Dr Langsner.

We were only too willing to hear his opinion. It certainly appeared as if Vernon was the murderer, but we had to prove it, and at the moment we had not the semblance of a case against him. It would need much more conclusive evidence than Dr Langsner's ability to read thoughts to convince any jury.

The little doctor then outlined his plan, and to meet his wishes we placed a chair outside Vernon's cell and saw to it that there was no unnecessary noise or interruption.

Dr Langsner seated himself and then leaned forward to stare at Vernon through the bars. At first the young man appeared quite pleasant and tried to make conversation, but later he became angry and turned his back on the doctor. Dr Langsner just sat there and stared. He was there for about an hour and then got up and said "Goodbye" to Vernon, but got no reply.

We were waiting for him in my office, and he said: "Vernon is guilty, there is not a shadow of a doubt about it. He killed his mother because he had come to hate her. I don't know the reason, but he has no regret. He walked into the kitchen to kill her, and she spoke to him without turning round. In his fury he fired three shots, and Fred, his brother, heard them. Vernon knew he had to kill him, although he did not want to, and he is sorry for it.

"When he ran out to hide the gun, he saw Rosyk and Cromby in the fields; he was sure Rosyk had seen him, and killed him when he had the chance. Two hours later he decided that it was unsafe to allow Cromby to live. He felt he had to eliminate every possible witness."

I told the doctor that I thought his reconstruction of the murders was correct. "How can we prove it?" I asked.

"Find the woman," he said quickly, and when he saw he had us puzzled he explained:

"I do not know her name. Vernon stole the gun on the Sunday that Stevenson missed his weapon. He sneaked out of church, took it away and then returned. The woman who saw him leave was wearing a poke-bonnet. She has small eyes and a long jaw and she was sitting at the back of the church, to the left of the aisle. She saw him leave and watched to see if he would return."

"Find her," I said to Leslie, and he got up and went out immediately.

At noon the following day Leslie brought Erma Higgins to police headquarters. She was exactly as Langsner had described her and looked like an ancient pixie. She was a spinster and very much alert to what was going on around her, especially the flirtations between young people. Yes, she had seen Vernon leave and return later.

Now was the time to put the pressure on Vernon, but before he was brought into my room we set up the "scene." I sat at my desk and I had Erma Higgins and Dr Langsner placed in the centre of the room facing the door, on either side of which stood Detective Leslie and Inspector Longacre. A chair was so placed that Vernon would face Miss Higgins and the doctor.

As soon as Vernon came in and sat down Miss Higgins said to him as she had been instructed: "Vernon, I saw you leave the church the day Charlie's rifle was stolen."

Vernon looked at her and then stared at the doctor.

"I know you did," he said heavily, "I know you did."

I heard the clock on the wall tick away the lost seconds and began to watch the gentle swing of the brass pendulum. Then Vernon turned a desperate face towards me and said pleadingly: "Let me confess. I killed them. Let me confess to you."

He began to sob, and his story was a broken account of a quartet of killings that had happened in the way Langsner had said. The motive was his rage against his mother. She was a woman of good deeds, but she ruled the home and she ruled Vernon, who was her favourite son. He had brought a girl to the house, the daughter of a farm worker, one Sunday whom Mrs Booher had ordered out. Vernon believed he loved the girl and not only did his mother ridicule the attachment but she wounded him even more cruelly by telling him what she thought of his choice. He began to hate his mother, and when his talk of an elopement made no impression on her his resentment became murderous.

On April 26th, 1929, Vernon Booher was hanged for his fourfold murders.

Some months before, however, Detective Leslie and I drove Dr Langsner to the station. He was leaving Edmonton and going north to Eskimo territory. I think he realized how grateful we were to him, even though we expressed our thanks so clumsily. Against his wishes he had accepted a small cheque, which, as I told him, was only a token tribute to his invaluable help.

As he left us he said with a rueful smile: "It is fine to make friends, but rather sad to leave them."

We shook hands and that was the last we saw of him. Time went by and then one day Detective Leslie laid a news clipping on my desk. It read:

Maximilian Langsner, PhD. (University of Calcutta), was found dead yesterday in a small hut on the outskirts of Fairbanks, Alaska. Dr Langsner was known for his theory on "brain waves" and for his ability, often demonstrated, in reading the thoughts of other people. He was engaged in research on this subject at the time of his death.

Dr Langsner was widely known, and his undoubted gifts had been made use of by Royalty. He had solved mysteries for the Shah of Persia, the King of Egypt and had helped the British Government in Asia. He will remembered, too, for the assistance he gave to many police departments faced with difficult cases.

When I looked up from reading the news clipping Detective Leslie had left the room.

UNGUARDED MOMENT

(Colin Pitchfork, UK 1986)

Joseph Wambaugh

DNA is the master molecule of life, carrying coded messages of heredity, governing everything from eye colour to allergies. It is present in trillions of cells in the human body. The structure of the DNA molecule was solved in the early 1950s by James Watson and Francis Crick, but the technique of so-called DNA fingerprinting is comparatively new. At first it was used to establish genetic relationships in paternity and immigration cases. It was based on a method developed in 1984 by a British geneticist, Dr Alec Jeffreys, in an attempt to identify genetic markers for disease. Jeffreys and his colleagues at Leicester University found a way of extracting DNA from a specimen of blood or other bodily fluid or tissue, slicing it into fragments and tagging them with a radioactive probe so that they would expose a piece of X-ray film. The resulting pattern of stripes on the film, resembling a supermarket barcode, is a DNA "fingerprint". In Britain in 1986, the technique resulted in a forensic triumph. Police had been searching for a man who'd been preying on girls in the East Midlands, raping and killing two fifteen-year-olds, Lynda Mann in 1983 and Dawn Ashworth in July 1986. At first, a seventeen-year-old kitchen porter was suspected of both murders, but he was released after DNA tests showed he could not have been the killer of Lynda Mann. Detectives knew that Lynda's killer was a Group A secretor, PGM 1 + . Moreover, Dr Jeffreys' tests on the murdered girls had shown that the same man had killed both of them. There were few leads, only reports of a motorcycle seen near one of the murder sites, and an unknown man

*running along a footpath. The inquiry seemed stalled. So in early
1987, detectives announced "a revolutionary step", the mass screening of all young males living in the Leicestershire villages of Narborough, Littlethorpe and Enderby. Nevertheless the real killer,
Colin Pitchfork, nearly managed to fool the police. He bribed a
workmate to take his place at the screening. The friend, Ian Kelly,
posed as Pitchfork with a passport altered to carry his photograph.
The best-selling American crime writer Joseph Wambaugh (b.
1937), in his book* The Blooding, *described how Pitchfork might
have foiled the scientists, but for an unguarded remark in a Leicester
pub.*

As the summer of 1987 began to burn itself out, the murder squad
had some of their most difficult times. They drove blood buses to
housing estates and factories in order to call people out. In larger
work places they even took a doctor with them: a daunting display
of mobile blooding. But they were exhausting their bloodlust.

They tried other tacks. They raided a travelling fair in Blaby
with two dozen officers, searching the caravans of carnival workers. And they caught a flasher on a village footpath, a professional
tennis player who was a psychiatric patient at Carlton Hayes. But
he was good only for a few lame jokes about flashing and tennis
balls. Always they returned to blooding for the answer.

The DI's, Pearce and Thomas, often went to the blooding.
Those were long nights when they bloodied, and sometimes the
doctors treated them to dinner. The DI's had to keep it light-
hearted for nervous donors as well as weary cops. One night they
conducted a lottery where everyone tossed in fifty pence and
guessed how many they'd bloody by evening's end. Some of the
frightened donors, many of whom had never been in contact with
police before, wanted in.

Then one of them said, "Wait a minute! If I win, how will I
know?"

"We'll drop the money in your letter box," Pearce told him.
"If you can't trust us, who *can* you trust?"

"Okay, I'll have a go!" he said.

Then they planned a prank in which one of the local bobbies, himself scheduled for a blooding, was to pose as a civilian and come in protesting furiously, whereupon four of them were to pounce on him, snap on the handcuffs and carry him to whichever doctor looked most horrified. Superintendent Tony Painter got wind of it and stopped that one.

There was a travelling construction worker from Nottinghamshire whom they particularly wanted to bloody, but he was a fugitive on an assault charge and kept avoiding them. The best they could do after much effort was to leave a message for him to ring the incident room.

He complied, demanding to speak to a superior officer. Pearce handled the telephone call, and after a long conversation they struck a bargain. The fugitive agreed to be bloodied if Pearce would give his word of honour not to arrest him on the warrant.

Not only did the fugitive show up on schedule, he brought with him another travelling worker they'd been seeking. Both men were bloodied, and when they were finished and walking out the door, Pearce suddenly appeared and yelled, "Hold on! You can't just walk out!"

The fugitive crouched, ready to run or fight, or both, but he didn't know about the inspector's offbeat sense of humour.

Pearce grinned and said, "Fancy a pint or two?"

He took both men to a pub and stood them some drinks, after which it was discovered they didn't have bus fare. Pearce had to give them five pounds to get back home.

It was like that: trying to keep everybody interested, entertained and, above all, dedicated. Pearce's own dedication had gotten a boost just before the Ashworths left on their Australian holiday. When he'd taken a can of soda to gardener/cop Phil Beeken at the cemetery, he'd found Barbara Ashworth tending Dawn's grave. Pearce had met her on only one other occasion, but Barbara talked to him in the graveyard for thirty minutes.

When Pearce returned to the incident room he commented that whenever someone's killed you *always* hear that the victim was a nice person, but in this case it was true. "Lynda and Dawn were lovely, bubbly girls," he said to his detectives. "Pleasant, helpful, and *ever* so well liked, weren't they?"

He really didn't have to arouse any member of the small group that was left. The hunt for the footpath killer had consumed them all. They were becoming more fearful of the rumours that they were going to be closed down.

The squad held a meeting where everyone put forth arguments to be taken to Chief Superintendent David Baker and beyond. They wanted it noted that Dawn Ashworth II had been opened on a restricted budget because the first Dawn Ashworth inquiry had eaten up so much of the budgetary allowance. They pointed out that the reopening should have been treated as a *new* murder inquiry and budgeted accordingly. They promised not to drag in donors so indiscriminately, but said that in the long run it was still cheaper than a time-consuming verification of alibis. It wasn't their fault, they argued, that the laboratory was months behind in analyzing the blood, perhaps even the blood of the murderer, for all they knew.

They'd begun getting time-and-a-third pay for working more than eight hours in a day, as well as £5.54 for a meal allowance. They offered to give it up, as long as the inquiry was kept open.

They began a renewed search into computer print-outs of everyone in Britain who'd been imprisoned in the interim between the murders of Lynda Mann and Dawn Ashworth. It seemed a long time between murders for a serial sex killer, at least according to the psychiatric profile.

There had always been speculation that the kitchen porter, who seemed to know too much, could have had something to do with Dawn Ashworth's murder after all. There were bizarre theories about why samples taken from the vaginal and anal cavities had not shown a transfer of fluid back and forth, the implication being that perhaps two men had raped Dawn Ashworth, front and back, with only one leaving a sample. Perhaps one of them was a voyeur who had assaulted the dead body *after* the murderer was gone! There were macabre theories like that, because that's the way a murder cop's mind works after he's been in the business awhile.

Each of the sixteen officers still on the inquiry reiterated that morale was high, and that there was no doubt they'd flush him out sooner or later, one way or the other. They debated as to how the footpath phantom might try, or perhaps had *already* tried, to beat their system. The consensus was that he would induce a brother or close relative to take the test for him. A few thought he might be gambler enough to take it himself and hope that Jeffreys' system was not foolproof, and who among them could say it was?

Sergeant Mick Mason, like Inspector Mick Thomas, had been on the Lynda Mann inquiry as well as Dawn Ashworth I and II. Only the "two Micks," DC John Reid and Detective Policewoman Tracy Hitchcox had been on all three. Tracy Hitchcox worked with DC Roger Lattimore, who lived in the village and harboured personal fears for his own teenage daughter. Lattimore never forgot to ring the Ashworths or to stop by with hopeful reports as the hopeless months dragged on.

Mick Mason was the CID opposite of Derek Pearce. Where Pearce was fiery, the kind to shoot from the hip (sometimes hitting his own foot), Mason was deliberate, methodical, with a completeness compulsion. He didn't just dot his *i*'s and cross his *t*'s. They said he duplicated every bleedin *i* and every ruddy *t*. He was the kind to stress over the menu at a sandwich shop: Swiss or cheddar? Swiss or cheddar? Swiss or bloody cheddar! But when he finally made up his mind he was implacable.

Mick Mason would come to work fifteen minutes before he had to and might stay hours after he could have gone home. He was one of the first that Pearce and Mick Thomas had chosen when Superintendent Tony Painter wanted a squad on Dawn Ashworth II "to sort out the business once and for all."

Until you got to know the big middle-aged cop, he was the last you would imagine in a pub after an evening of blooding – after they got the music going and had a few pints – doing his version of Tom Jones doing "Delilah," complete with bumps and grinds! Mick Mason, "the pub singer," had that other side. But he'd been devoted to Kath Eastwood, Lynda Mann's mother, from the day her daughter had been murdered, and always promised her that he'd never forget Lynda, that they'd *get* the killer. The pub singer was, by his own admission, obsessed with this murder hunt. Possibly, he wanted the killer more than any of the rest of them.

When frustrated voices were raised in the incident room, when the possibility of closure loomed, nobody even looked up if it was Derek Pearce's voice; they were used to that. But when Mick Thomas started raising his voice, as one later put it, "We'd think, 'Blimey! Maybe something *is* wrong!'"

The three-month duty charts had been changed to one-month duty charts. As far as the top brass was concerned, the end was near, and *that* was obvious to the two inspectors. The remaining sixteen held a very tense meeting with Superintendent Tony Painter. He informed them that Chief Superintendent David Baker was getting great pressure from the chief constable who in turn was being pressured by the Home Office. The inquiry could not stay open indefinitely.

There was an extraordinary clamour at that meeting. People wondered aloud what the Press would make of a surrender after four years of hunting the footpath killer. Sergeant Mick Mason openly suggested they should have the courage to begin blooding other places. Like Whetstone, for instance.

Tony Painter became annoyed. He said, "You will not mention Whetstone. We will not bloody Whetstone!" Of course, he didn't know that Mick Mason was *already* blooding Whetstone.

Derek Pearce jumped in to say, "All right, let's pack it up and go home!"

Painter rebuked Pearce about the need for a DI to control himself, but the clamour persisted. Somebody actually said that if the inquiry was closed, the Police Complaints Board should bring a complaint against the chief constable himself!

Baker and Painter and their superiors were facing kamikaze dedication here. Maybe they realized that these last sixteen were foundering in a bloodlust frenzy. They might bloody every goddamn mammal in Leicestershire!

A new television story was aired that didn't exude confidence. Chief Superintendent David Baker, Superintendent Tony Painter, DI's Derek Pearce and Mick Thomas were all videotaped by a news team during a blooding session. Baker made another appeal. He said, "We have not got that vital piece of information which allows us to put the jigsaw together completely."

When he was finished, newsmen made *sotto voce* comments about whether or not the squad had *any* puzzle pieces. The announcer called Baker's statement "a painful admission."

More painful to the murder squad was a visit by an inspection team from the deputy chief constable and the high sheriff of Leicester, who, after being given a brief summary of the mountain of work accomplished by the inquiry, had only one comment: the sign they'd posted for civilians that said, COFFEE 10P, TEA 5P, was "unprofessional."

Such is the policeman's lot, as Gilbert and Sullivan had long ago observed.

On a more upbeat note, a Midlands newscaster said, "As more men come forward the net slowly closes on the killer. If the police hunch is right, and he *is* a local man, he dare not run the risk of giving blood."

On the day of that newscast, David Baker offered a statement to the print media – a prayer almost – that proved to be prophetic. He said, "Somebody's *bound* to say something in an unguarded moment. Now *that's* the kind of information we need!"

The beginning of an answer to Baker's prayer had already taken place on the 1st of August, one year after Dawn Ashworth's murder. It happened in a pub.

The Clarendon Pub in Leicester was a pub for locals: students, university people, journalists. It was a bit Bohemian in an area that had become trendy. A nice pub, the Clarendon had salmon-coloured drapes and valances, co-ordinated wallpaper, and plush banquettes. It was near one of the Hampshires Bakery outlet shops, off Queens Road.

During the lunch break on that Saturday afternoon Ian Kelly went to the Clarendon, along with a twenty-six-year-old woman who managed one of the bakery outlets. Another woman and a young man, both Hampshires employees, tagged along.

They sat in the busy pub having a "cob," a Leicester snack consisting of a roll filled with meat, cheese or anything you fancy. The talk turned to bakery tittle-tattle, centering on Colin Pitchfork, whom the manager of the outlet shop knew by sight and reputation.

They gossiped about Pitchfork's girlfriends, Brown Eyes and her stillborn, and the fact that Colin couldn't stay away from women. As Ian Kelly sipped his drink, a bemused smile crossed his face and he blurted, "Colin had me take that blood test for him."

The bakery manager said, "*What* test?"

"For the murder inquiry?" the male companion asked. "That one, Ian?"

Ian Kelly got up and went to the bar for another pint. When he was gone the bakery manager turned to the other young man and said, "What's that all about?"

"It's odd," the young baker said. "Colin asked *me* to do it too. Offered me two hundred quid to take the blood test. He's just scared of coppers. A weird bloke, that Colin."

The shop manager was deeply disturbed. She tried to broach another question, but it was lightly dismissed as though the implication was preposterous.

Still she couldn't get it off her mind. A week passed, and she took aside the young baker who'd been offered the money and said, "What are we going to *do* about Colin Pitchfork?"

He said, "Leave it. He's a friend. You don't even know him."

She *couldn't* leave it, but she was fearful of involving someone in a double murder – someone who might be innocent – not to mention getting Ian Kelly into police trouble.

Three days later while the bakery manager stewed, history was made in London at the Old Bailey. Genetic fingerprinting was used in a criminal court for the first time in the case of a man accused of unlawful intercourse with a fourteen-year-old mentally handicapped girl who'd given birth to his baby.

Dr Alec Jeffreys was quoted as saying, "The use of the test in a court case is exciting for us. It is an historic occasion."

The bakery manager knew that the owner of the Clarendon Pub had a son who was a police constable. She inquired but found that the bobby was on holiday. It was six weeks before she rang him up.

It had been a good summer for Carole Pitchfork. She'd been

noticing a marked improvement in her husband's attitude since she had allowed him to return home in March. She felt that he was trying very hard to make a go of their marriage. He seemed to be maturing and accepting responsibility for his past actions. She didn't even have to nag him to change clothes anymore. He was dressing better, as beffitted a budding entrepreneur.

His scheme for opening the cake-decorating studio was beginning to jell at last. Colin had been to a banker, and was discussing things like cash flow with an accountant. He'd even accepted a small commission to make a birthday cake for a policeman's twenty-first birthday. It was cleverly conceived and skilfully executed. The policeman loved it. Colin had done an icing sculpture of a bobby's helmet, alongside a set of steel handcuffs.

Friday, the 18th of September, started off in a river of blood like all the others. Derek Pearce and Gwynne Chambers were on a London run to pick up four blood samples and to interview one man. Whenever they took trips like that they'd call in several times a day. But they got caught in motorway traffic coming back and it was some time before they could get to a phone box. They found one occupied by a girl who had about three pounds, all in tenpence coins, spread out in front of her.

She gave the impatient detectives a glance or two but wasn't about to give up the phone. They jumped back in the CID car and kept going.

When they got to the office at 9.00 p.m. there were messages all over the door. One said, "Don't go home!" Another said, "Got a job on!" A third said, "Don't go home. Got a job on!"

When Pearce got to his desk he found a huge one saying, "DON'T GO HOME!"

Phil Beeken had taken a telephone message that afternoon from a bobby whose father owned a pub near the Queens Road outlet shop of Hampshires Bakery. Beeky relayed the information from that telephone call directly to Inspector Mick Thomas and they pulled an old house-to-house *pro forma* from the Lynda Mann inquiry. They compared the signature of the resident of a semi-detached house in Littlethorpe with the *pro forma* from his blooding in January. The two signatures of Colin Pitchfork didn't match.

Mick Thomas and Phil Beeken tried to keep each other from getting too excited. After all, signatures can change over a period of three years, particularly with young people. But Pitchfork wasn't a kid. Then they looked at each other and decided, The hell with it! They were over the moon and rising!

Mick Mason was telephoned at home and given the job of immediately contacting the others from the bakery, who'd been present in the Clarendon Pub when Ian Kelly blurted an admission during an unguarded moment. Thomas and Beeken went to the manager's house and took her written statement.

She began by saying, "This is probably a waste of your time, but my conscience *forced* me to ring the police." She kept apologizing until they reassured her.

By the time Mick Thomas and Phil Beeken hooked up with Derek Pearce and Gwynne Chambers later that evening they were practically hyperventilating.

Mick Thomas said to Pearce, "Roger and Tracy are still in Yorkshire trying to bloody some bloke! You and Gwynne were in London! Everybody else had gone home! I was going crazy with no one to tell!"

One of them noticed something very peculiar. The conversation in the Clarendon Pub, that unguarded moment, had occurred exactly one year after the day that Dawn Ashworth's body lay undetected in a field by Ten Pound Lane. It seemed to be an omen.

They unanimously elected to go immediately to a pub, and they did. While drinking his second pint Pearce said that going to bed was out of the question. He wanted morning to come without having to sleep through the interim. Mick Thomas suggested that they'd better not get drunk because of the importance of the following day. But they didn't have to worry – the booze couldn't compete with the adrenaline rush.

Each man later reported that he spent a near-sleepless night. Each later reported that he felt he was facing the most important day in his police career.

As far as Pearce was concerned: "It was the most important day of our *lives*."

Ian Kelly had not been having an easy time at the bakery since he'd given blood for Colin Pitchfork. It seemed as though too many things were going wrong, and Colin Pitchfork was always around to "help" him. Once when they were making buns, Ian burned them. Colin observed the error and told Ian not to worry, he'd take care of it. Ian later heard that Colin "took care of it" by informing the foreman.

There was a more serious incident when Ian was making buns with another baker. A huge steel machine cover was propped against a wall. Ian pushed a baking trolley past it and was absolutely sure he had sufficient clearance, but somehow the heavy metal cover fell over and crashed into his partner's legs.

The man bellowed and swore and accused Ian of crippling him. It turned into such a row that the gaffer came out and shouted, "Stop behaving like kids, the two of you!"

The injured baker was so outraged he told the boss to stuff it. The baker quit his job that day, saying that Ian Kelly was the one who should've been sacked.

Ian went back to work, absolutely baffled as to how the machine cover could've fallen. Until he later learned that Colin Pitchfork had been standing nearby when it happened. It was *beginning* to look like somebody wanted him out of Hampshires Bakery.

On the morning of Saturday, September 19th, it was decided that Pearce and Chambers would arrest Ian Kelly. And they might arrest the young baker who'd been offered £200 by Colin Pitchfork, depending on his answers. Mick Thomas and Mick Mason were to call on that young man. Even though they were off duty, DC Brian Fentum and Phil Beeken insisted on being there. Nothing could've kept them away.

Ian Kelly opened his door that morning to a pair of visitors he knew weren't selling magazines. Derek Pearce showed his warrant card and said, "We're from the murder enquiry incident room at Narborough, investigating the murders of Lynda Mann and Dawn Ashworth. Have you given a blood sample regarding those enquiries?"

"No, not me!" Ian said.

"I don't believe you," Pearce said. "I have reason to believe you've given a blood sample."

"No, I haven't!" Ian said.

"We've talked to other people at the bakery," Pearce said. "I believe you *have*."

"Yes, you're right," Ian said. "I did it for another lad at work."

"Who's that?" Gwynne Chambers asked.

"Colin Pitchfork," Ian Kelly answered.

Pearce said, "I'm arresting you for conspiracy to pervert the course of justice and we're taking you to Wigston Police Station."

"Yes," said Ian Kelly. "I'll just put me shoes on."

They took Ian Kelly to the station, which was already humming, and put him into an interview room where his statement was recorded.

Pearce said, "I must tell you, you do not have to say anything unless you wish to do so, but anything you say may be given in evidence. Do you understand that?"

Ian began by saying, "Yes, well, the gentleman in question, Colin Pitchfork, he come up to me and asked if I'd do him a favour. I didn't know it were for them murders. I didn't know what it were really for cause he didn't explain what it were for. He just had to give a thingybob cause he got a letter from the police station."

Then Ian related the story that Colin Pitchfork had told him about giving a sample for the other bloke, and Ian told about the photo strip and altering the passport. But he stuck to his claim that he didn't know that the blooding was for anything as serious as murder.

Derek Pearce didn't look *quite* as dangerous as a Shi'ite with an AK-47 when he said, "Yeah, you're Mister Muggins. And you've just gone along and given the sample. And he got what he wanted: full protection. *You've delayed us eight months!*"

Ian started to understand what was facing him. He said, "Well, when I went to his house, more or less . . . well, the day before, he *told* me it were a murder enquiry. But I didn't know *which* murder it was at the time!"

And he admitted to having been given a little schooling on the dates of birth of the children and other personal information. He said, "I knew it were for a murder but I didn't know whose it were for, cause at the time when I walked in I were *that* sick. I'd got a temperature. I was feeling really low. I mean, when I began writing his signature I got shaking like a leaf!"

Supt. Tony Painter was called in that afternoon and found Derek Pearce bobbing and bouncing like a dinghy in a storm.

"Let's go nick him!" Pearce said to their commander.

"No, take it all down on paper," Painter said. "And *then* go get him."

Pearce said, "We want him *now*!"

"I'm the boss and I say paper first," Painter said.

"Quite right," Pearce said. "Paper first."

So they had to wait another two hours until all statements were transcribed and put in some semblance of order. By the time six of them got to the house in Haybarn Close, the blue Fiat was gone. There was nobody at the Pitchfork home. One stayed; the rest returned to the station, *trying* to be philosophical. After all, they'd waited four years.

PICKING UP THE PIECES

(Patrick Mahon, 1924)

James McClure

The great British pathologist Sir Bernard Spilsbury, asked which of his famous cases he considered the most difficult, said he thought the Mahon case had been the most interesting. "It gradually took shape," he added, "as in building up a jigsaw puzzle." It began with the disappearance of a young woman called Emily Beilby Kaye and the discovery, in the cloakroom at Waterloo Station, of a locked Gladstone bag which, when forced open, was found to contain a number of bloodstained articles, including a cook's knife and a racquet-case marked EBK, all sprinkled with disinfectant. When the bag's owner, Patrick Mahon, was questioned, his story about cutting up dog meat failed to account for the blood, which was human; Mahon changed his tale, but the truth was only established through the painstaking work of Spilsbury in what, technically speaking, has been hailed as one of the masterpieces of his long and varied professional career. The story of how he did it is told here by James McClure (1939–2006), a journalist who also produced a series of successful crime novels set in South Africa featuring a white detective called Kramer and his black assistant Zondi. Later he became a newspaper editor in Oxford.

Animal magnetism is common among lady-killers, or so the more gallant Press would have us believe – while overlooking how unflattering the corollary must be for the ladies it defends.

But this does seem to have been literally true of Patrick Herbert Mahon: all sorts of creatures were drawn to him in a most unusual way. Frequently he would arrive back at his boarding house with other people's loyal pets, which had tagged along uninvited, and he would delight his friends by whistling wild birds down out of the trees. Perhaps it was simply that animals could recognize the beast in him.

Which isn't as fanciful or as forgiving as it might sound. There is, however, something ridiculous about the repeated gasps over how "callous" he was in committing a particularly revolting murder and, in the same bated breath, bedding a new woman with only his selfish needs in view. One might as well start calling any domesticated predator, which mixes gruesome acts of survival with moments of sexual frolic, an unfeeling son of a bitch – and very few dog-lovers would take kindly to that.

Plain Herbert Mahon was born to a large Liverpool-Irish family in 1890; a family which kept its grip on the lower rung of the middle class by placing its faith in diligence, sportsmanship and God. He appeared to respond well to the demands made upon him, and soon endeared himself in every quarter with his puppy-like energy, appealing looks and eagerness to please.

After leaving school, where his brightness and athletic prowess earned special mention, he was first an office boy and soon a junior clerk. He maintained an interest in French (which he spoke fluently) and in Latin (which he liked to quote), attended worship regularly, and played football in the local church league.

But he was not altogether the conformist that these rather superficial facts would seem to indicate.

This first became apparent when Herbert, as his frugal parents had him christened, helped himself to a second name. Patrick, he felt, went much better with Mahon; it also allowed him to encourage his acquaintances to call him Pat, which was undoubtedly a more short caressing form than Herb or Bert.

Clearly, Mahon himself decided what sort of man he wanted to be, and altered things accordingly. For a foretaste of that cultivated image at its prime, there's the blarney-laden entry he made beside his name in a bowls club register: "A Broth of a Bhoy, who deserved to be born at sea."

His early independence showed itself in other ways as well. The most startling for his parents was the proposal of marriage he put to his school-days sweetheart when she was only sixteen. This didn't much amuse her parents either, and both families opposed the match on the grounds of the couple's extreme youth.

Two years later, however, the persuasive Mahon and his dark-haired, very capable bride were setting up home in Liverpool. He had needed her, and having got her, the long chase down the straight and narrow had ended.

And so, within a matter of months, he decided to go in pursuit of someone else. He and the girl ran away together to the Isle of Man, but there Mahon was arrested for financing the flight by forging and uttering cheques worth £123 of his firm's money.

Back in Liverpool, the first offender's luck improved. He was merely bound over, and Mrs Mahon, believing he had come to heel, forgave him. They then agreed to start all over again from the beginning, preferably somewhere else.

The Mahons settled in Wiltshire. He found a job with a dairy, and all went well for a time. Mahon's business acumen was considerable, his colleagues liked him, and his skill as a footballer won him general popularity.

However, shortly after Mrs Mahon had given birth to a daughter, the new father was jailed for a year, having embezzled £60 belonging to the dairy.

That was a formative year for Mahon: he made a number of unusual friends, and learned a thing or two, behind those prison walls.

Burglary could have been one of them. There was a series of unsolved raids round about Calne in Wiltshire after his release. And Mahon, who had been living there, moved on.

Surrey was his next stop. He started working for a dairy at Sunningdale and, possibly with fresh resolve, kept his fingers out of the till. But he couldn't keep his hands off the women.

Fired for scandalous behaviour and thrown back on his own resources, Mahon tried to scrape a living from odd jobs at race meetings, helped by the contacts he'd made in prison. On really good days, he'd act as a bookmaker's clerk. On bad days, he'd have the law after him or not make a thing.

Mahon had experienced quite a few of those bad days by the beginning of 1916, and this drove him to commit his first major crime.

He bungled it in an extraordinary fashion.

His target was the Sunningdale branch of the National Provincial Bank. He managed to break in successfully after dark, but was surprised by a maidservant from the floor above. Mahon reacted instinctively, attacking her with a hammer so that she fell stunned.

When the maid recovered her senses, Mahon was still there. He had her in his arms, and was kissing and stroking her gently, while reassuring her most charmingly that he'd never meant her any real harm. He was so anxious she should think no ill of him, that it didn't occur to her that his attentions were anything other than honourable; it was, in fact, rather like being licked by a penitent big dog.

Whatever the lasting impression he made on her, it was certainly a vivid one. Assisted by an excellent description, the police arrested Mahon in another town, and he appeared for trial at Guildford Assizes.

Sweet talk was wasted on Mr Justice Darling, as Mahon – with his sensitivity for names – should have guessed.

He tried it all the same. And when the jury returned their verdict of "guilty", the prisoner begged to be allowed to join the army and do his stuff for dear old England.

The army had no need of hypocrites, he was told, before being sent down for five years.

But what irony there was in that mawkish little scene: asking to serve at the Front in 1916 was tantamount to inviting a death sentence, and that was something Mahon would try anything to avoid when next he faced a judge.

The Crumbles says it all. Two miles of unlovely shingle, stretching from Eastbourne to Wallsend on Pevensey Bay, a mile across at its widest point, skirted by a road and some coarse, dusty undergrowth, and valued only as a source of railway ballast in the year 1920.

Except by humble young holidaymakers like Irene Munro, a poorly-dressed typist of 17 down from London, for whom the uninterrupted vista it provided must have been "heaven" – as, no doubt, some of them wrote on their postcards home. One hopes Miss Munro didn't: that would have been altogether too horribly apt.

Her body was found on the Crumbles five days after her arrival in Eastbourne. A blood-stained stone lay nearby, and her head had also been struck by a stick which had left the imprint of a carved bulldog. Her handbag, which her landlady had seen to contain holiday money, was empty.

A murder hunt began.

Other visitors remembered seeing a girl in green walking with two youngish men, one of whom had been wearing a herring-bone suit.

So the Eastbourne police stopped and questioned anyone in a herring-bone suit. William Gray, 29, answered the description, and he was taken into custody for two days with his companion, 19-year-old Jack Field, another idler. But they were released for want of any evidence against them, and were able to return to their life of leisure.

Until the investigating officers received an odd piece of information from the recruiting station in the town. It then appeared that, within minutes of the grim discovery on the shingle, both men had made urgent applications to join the army.

From there on, the rest was fairly simple: a barmaid recalled the pair being penniless on the morning of the murder, but flush in the evening; and a labourer, who knew Gray, said he'd seen him walking with a young couple towards the Crumbles on the same day.

Gray and Field were tried before Mr Justice Avory at Lewes Assizes on December 13, where they denied having any part in the murder. The jury thought otherwise, and the executions were carried out at Wandsworth, with each man finally blaming the other for the killing before the gallows cut short their argument.

The trial was memorable in itself for Gray's nonchalance. After being advised against giving evidence by his eminent counsel, Mr Edward Marshall-Hall, the accused dozed off. This was not mistaken for the sound sleep of the just, however, and the judge reprimanded him severely.

But there were other reasons the trial was to be remembered when, some four years later, Mr Justice Avory again presided over a murder trial at Lewes.

One reason was that the Irene Munro case introduced Sir Bernard Spilsbury, the Home Office Pathologist, to the Crumbles. He was called in only to verify the findings of two postmortems on the body, and did not give evidence at the trial himself. (Spilsbury's conclusions were that Miss Munro had probably taken 30 minutes to die, through the combined effects of shock, loss of blood, and asphyxia caused by the weight of shingle on her chest.) Yet this brief visit did establish for him a link with the scene of what he would come to regard as his greatest triumph.

And then there was the remark made on Gray's behalf by Marshall-Hall. "I am not suggesting that murders go on there," he told a witness, after asking if the Crumbles wasn't held to be a sinister sort of place.

These can't be called prophetic words exactly. Neither can they be dismissed as having nothing to do with the really uncanny elements in the downfall of Patrick Herbert Mahon.

Who was about to be released again.

Many people would have given up the struggle long before Mrs Mahon first showed any sign of weakening. That five-year sentence must have been a dreadful jolt for her, but there was worse to follow. The son she had in 1916 died without living long enough to see his father.

Mother and daughter moved to London, not expecting much, although willing to believe that their fortune might still change for the better. And it did.

Not long after Mrs Mahon succeeded in securing a lowly position with Consols Automatic Aerators Ltd., which had a factory at Sunbury-on-Thames, her exceptional effciency caught

the management's attention. They were so impressed by her that
she was promoted to company secretary.

This meant that when Mahon came out of prison, as contrite as
ever, and promising to mend his ways for good, his wife was able
to use her influence in getting him on to the staff. It was a
calculated risk – nobody was informed of his criminal record –
but one which seemed more than likely to come off.

Mahon made the most of this opportunity, and rapidly earned
the reputation of being one of the firm's best travelling salesmen.
He doesn't appear to have neglected the domestic side of his life
either; the family settled into a flat in Kew, built up a new circle
of friends, and prospered.

Then in May, 1922, came a threat to everything Mrs Mahon
had worked for: the soda-fountain company was placed in the
hands of a receiver, because of some action taken by a debenture
holder, and their jobs seemed suddenly in jeopardy. Her relief
can be imagined when she found out that not only was she to
carry on her normal duties, but that her husband had actually
been promoted to sales manager at £750 a year.

And yet, tragically, that receivership did in fact signal the end
of her hard-won happiness – if in a somewhat roundabout way.

A year passed. Mr Hobbins, the chartered accountant appointed
as receiver in control of Consols Automatic, and the man who'd
chosen Mahon to be his deputy now, as manager, engaged a new
shorthand-typist.

Miss Emily Beilby Kaye was 37 years old, and lived at the
Green Cross Club for "bachelor girls" in Guilford Street,
Bloomsbury. Like Irene Munro, she'd herself been a typist at
17, having lost the security of a comfortably-off middle-class
home when both her parents died suddenly. This early and
traumatic change in her circumstances probably accounted for
her thriftiness, and by 1923 she had accumulated a reasonable
nest egg. Miss Kaye was bright, practical and even-tempered,
and consequently fitted in well at the club. But Miss Kaye wasn't
much to look at. She was tall, according to some descriptions,
with the big build of a hearty woman athlete. Her face was sweet
enough and her chin firm, only her nose was so noticeably large

that unkind comparisons with party novelties become almost unavoidable. She wore her fair hair bobbed, and used a string of beads to accentuate her very long neck.

A neck she laid on the block the day a handsome young businessman came to call on Mr Hobbins. The visitor was expensively dressed and possessed of a charming manner. He had deep-set, merry eyes, a wide dimpled smile, neat pointed ears, a high forehead, and curly fair hair with a natural quiff. A face one might find today in the stills from an old pot-boiler Western, or fronting an evangelical mission on the doorsteps of suburbia.

Miss Kaye fell in love with this man, who called on Mr Hobbins fairly often, and sometimes she discussed business matters on the telephone with his wife.

The Mahons moved to a boarding house in Pagoda Road, Richmond, during January, 1924. An expedient move, it would seem, because Mrs Mahon was now beginning to find her high standards as a company secretary took their toll, and this at least spared her the problems of running a home. She and her husband continued to be a much-sought-after couple at various functions, and, to her delight, he was elected honorary secretary of the bowls club. All was still going just as she'd hoped and prayed.

Mrs Mahon did, however, begin to wonder about this as spring approached and her husband seemed to be away on business rather a lot. Her uneasiness turned to nagging worry, and, when added to the burden of pressure under which she'd worked for so long, it made Mrs Mahon ill. She didn't leave Consols Automatic though; that job was far too precious to her and her picturebook daughter.

April brought a really bewildering sequence of appearances and disappearances. Over two weekends, Mahon sent his wife telegrams from three different places, each with a message intended to explain his absence, but only making it more puzzling.

And then Mrs Mahon, who'd presumably asked around to see if anyone knew what was happening, heard something that made her despair: her husband had been seen on Easter Saturday at the Plumpton races.

She did nothing until Mahon went off for the third weekend running. Then, almost certain he was up to his old Sunningdale tricks again, she started to search through his large wardrobe of clothes for some clue to the reason for his mysterious behaviour. A betting stub would have confirmed her worst suspicions, but all she could come up with was a cloakroom ticket from Waterloo Station.

Mrs Mahon clutched at this straw. On the following Thursday – which was also May Day – she went to ask a friend's help. The former railway policeman took the ticket and promised to make a discreet inquiry.

A promise he found impossible to keep, once he'd claimed the locked Gladstone bag and had taken a look inside it, by pulling open the ends.

Scotland Yard took over. A detective was placed on watch at the cloakroom counter, and the ticket was returned to Mrs Mahon. Reassured to hear that the bag's contents had no connection with bookmaking – which is all that was said to her – she replaced the ticket in Mahon's coat pocket, and made no mention of the incident when he came home that night.

The next morning Mrs Mahon went to hospital, and learned that she'd have to undergo surgery.

At about 6.15 that evening, Mahon went to Waterloo Station, collected his bag, and was stopped on his way out by a detective.

"Rubbish!" snapped Mahon, on being warned that he was to be taken to Kennington Road police station.

Chief Inspector Percy Savage interviewed him there briefly at 8.30 p.m. and, after hearing that the key to the bag had been "lost", suggested a move to his own offices at Scotland Yard.

"All right," said Mahon, more amenably.

An hour later, the contents of the bag were placed before him: two pieces of new silk, a pair of torn twill bloomers, a towel, a silk scarf, a cook's knife, and a tennis racquet cover with the initials *E.B.K.* on it. All these items were covered in blood, and the inside of the bag was heavily sprinkled with Sanitas disinfectant.

Mahon was asked how they had come into his possession.

"I am fond of dogs – I must have carried meat for the dogs in it."

"That will not do," said Chief Inspector Savage. "These stains are of human blood."

"You seem to know all about it!" Mahon retorted.

Then followed a very curious confrontation: for a whole quarter of an hour, nobody said a word.

"I wonder," the prisoner asked, "if you can realize how terrible a thing it is for one's body to be active and one's mind fail to act."

That was all. He fell silent again for 30 minutes.

"I am considering my position," he informed his interrogators.

They made no response, and another quarter of an hour dragged by. The tension was now close to being unbearable.

"I suppose you know everything," he said at last. "I will tell you the truth."

And, having been cautioned, he began to make the first of three statements. It took him until 2.30 on Saturday morning; he collapsed once and had to be revived with a stimulant. At 4 a.m. he started talking again, but by then Chief Inspector Savage was already on his way to the Crumbles – and to the most dreadful sight he'd ever seen.

The whole story of Mahon's secret affair with Miss Emily Bealby Kaye – whom he called "Peter" – was supposedly revealed in those three horrifying statements.

He had met Miss Kaye, Mahon said, about ten months earlier while she was working for Mr Hobbins. They had also often spoken on the telephone together. One day, towards the end of summer, she'd suggested a day on the river.

". . . as I was anxious to gain some impartial knowledge of the legal proceedings in connection with the litigation in which the company was concerned, I accepted.

"We spent the afternoon at Staines, and Miss Kaye was extremely affectionate, and among other things, told me she was particularly fond of me and wished to be friendly.

"Intimacy (friendliness indeed) took place on that occasion; as a result I realized she was a woman of the world, which knowledge came as rather a surprise to me.

"Subsequently I met Miss Kaye, of course, from time to time in the course of my duties, and by her request met her on many occasions by appointment when we had lunch etc. Intimacy took place on several other occasions."

Just before Christmas, Miss Kaye had been dismissed by Mr Hobbins because of some staff rearrangements and this had left her with time on her hands – time to become more demanding.

"I felt sorry for the fact she had been dismissed and did, as a result, meet her a bit more frequently.

"I temporized in the hope of gaining time, but from that moment I felt more or less at the mercy of a strong-minded woman whom, although I liked her in many ways, I did not tremendously care for."

Miss Kaye's next job had been with a financier in Bond Street. This had encouraged her to speculate in francs, and to have Mahon take a fifty-fifty share in the gamble. Miss Kaye had handed him £100 notes to be cashed and shared at various times; he had signed these with false names for fear "she might have some ulterior motive" in not going to the bank herself.

"After losing her job with the financier in Bond Street (Miss Kaye had been filling in for someone away ill), she became thoroughly unsettled and begged me to give up everything and go abroad with her. She informed me of her great love and affection for me, but I plainly told her I could not agree to such a course."

Then Miss Kaye had outlined what they were to call their "love experiment":

". . . she suggested I should take a holiday and go away with her for a week or two, and take a bungalow where we could be alone together, and where she would convince me with her love that I could be perfectly happy with her."

Mahon had resisted this idea until the last day in March, when he met Miss Kaye for tea at Waterloo Station after her return from Bournemouth, where she had been recuperating from a bout of 'flu.

"She startled me with the information that she had written to the club secretary giving up her rooms, and that she was determined to force an issue somehow.

"She suggested plans I did agree with, and I reminded her of the fact that I could not in decency break the pledge I had given

Barry George, convicted of shooting dead Jill Dando

Jon Venables *(left)* and
Robert Thompson,
captured on CCTV in
the James Bulger case

Lord Lucan outside his London home in 1963

Coastguards Cottage on The Crumbles where
Patrick Mahon dismembered Emily Kaye

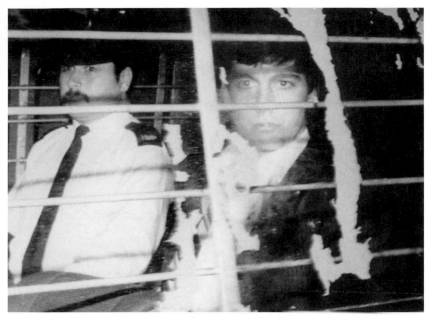

Jeremy Bamber is driven from court after being sentenced to life imprisonment for murdering five members of his family

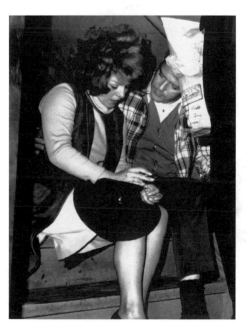

Alice Crimmins slips on the court steps in New York where she was arraigned on a charge of the first-degree murder of her four-year-old daughter

The Crippen case: the remains of Belle Elmore
in the cellar at 39 Hilldrop Crescent

The Crippen case: first use of wireless telegraphy to catch a murder suspect

THE WESTERN UNION TELEGRAPH COMPANY.
THE LARGEST TELEGRAPHIC SYSTEM IN EXISTENCE.
DIRECT ROUTE FOR ALL PARTS OF THE UNITED STAT
CANADA, CENTRAL AMERICA, WEST INDIES
OUTH AMERICA, & VIA THE PACIFIC CABLE TO AUSTRAL
NEW ZEALAND, FANNING, FIJI AND NORFOLK ISLANDS
ATLANTIC CABLES direct to CANADA and to NEW YORK CITY.
DIRECT WIRES TO ALL THE PRINCIPAL CITIES.

Montrose

CABLE OFFICE: EFFINGHAM HOUSE, ARUNDEL ST.
STRAND.

To   Handcuffs Ldn Eng

Crippen and leneve arrested wire later Dew

CABLE ADDRESSES ARE REGISTERED FREE OF CHARGE.
No inquiry respecting this Message can be attended to without the production of this Paper

Crippen (*right*) and Ethel le Neve (*rear*) arrive
back in England after their arrest

Lindy Chamberlain, who claimed a wild
Australian dingo dragged her baby away

Bruno Hauptmann takes the stand in the Lindbergh kidnap case

Investigators display the baby clothing of
Charles Lindbergh Jr at Hauptmann's trial

Dr Sam Sheppard
wearing an
orthopaedic collar
for an injury he
said he received
while grappling with
his wife's killer

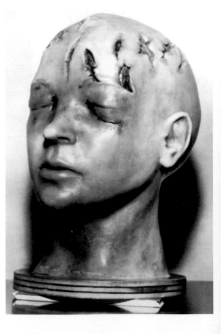

The Sheppard case:
model of victim
Marilyn Sheppard's
head

my business friends to keep things going at the works until the litigation was finally settled."

(That sentence appears to contain a Freudian error in the first line, and the copies of this statement used in court read: "She suggested plans I did *not* agree with . . ." But, as Mahon had signed the original, after checking it, the phrasing had to stand, much to the embarrassment of the defence, which was caught unawares by the typist's mistake.)

. "She however persisted, and ultimately I agreed, feeling it was my best course if only to gain time to consider the suggestion."

On the Friday Miss Kaye had telephoned Mahon and drawn his attention to an advertisement for a bungalow at Langney, near Eastbourne. He'd gone down there the following morning, seen a Mr Muir, and had taken the bungalow for two months.

Mahon's reasons for the long tenancy varied. In one place he said: "I felt convinced that the experiment which Miss Kaye had suggested – that is a few days alone in which to gain my affection – would not succeed." In another he stated, after a reference to his wife's pending operation: "I thought if I took the bungalow it would be a nice surprise for her."

Miss Kaye had been "roused to fury" over the two-month let – the implication being that she'd expected to snare him far sooner – but she had gone down to inspect the property for herself all the same.

This visit had changed everything, and she had enthused over his choice from her hotel in Eastbourne.

"Her last words to me on the phone were: 'Pat, old boy, you'll never regret it, as I can make up fully for all you may have to give up'."

"I felt in myself very depressed and miserable, and did not want to spend the three or four days together as she desired, but as I had given my word, and as I felt that I could definitely prove during that time to Miss Kaye how foolish the hope it was on her part to expect to keep my affection, even if she could gain it, I thought I had better go through with it.

"I travelled down to Eastbourne on the Friday, 11th (of April), saw Mr Muir at the bungalow and obtained the keys, informing him my wife (Miss Kaye) would be down the next day."

Mahon had then gone back to London, where he was needed at the Sunbury factory to deal with some problem, and had returned on Saturday morning with his kitbag.

"Miss Kaye was charmed with the place and told me again that she knew she was going to succeed in her object. To my mind this object was now an idea fixed, almost an obsession in her mind."

Her last weekend had been spent very quietly. Miss Kaye had done some cooking and cleaning, and Monday had passed in much the same way.

But Tuesday had begun with a row at the breakfast table; she had wanted to discuss their "immediate plans" and he hadn't. A little later on, however, he had promised to apply for a passport, and they'd gone up to London. There she had gone off alone to see some friends.

Miss Kaye now had only hours to live.

"We travelled back to Eastbourne and, on the way, the whole question was re-opened and I informed her that I had not been for the passport, and did not intend to do so.

"We quarrelled and had heated words, but eventually arrived at the bungalow more or less in calm mood.

"Soon after arrival, Miss Kaye – having taken off her coat and hat – suddenly startled me with the expression on her face, which appeared to be extremely determined."

Her next move had been to sit down and start writing letters which would commit them both to a "definite line of action".

"She also asked me to write to the Assistant Secretary of a function (the Richmond bowls tournament) of which I am Honorary Secretary, stating that I was giving up the work, and stating also that we were going overland to Paris for a time, and then on to South Africa.

"I refused absolutely to write such a letter, and felt that matters had come by now to a crisis. She, however, fumed and raged and finally wrote the note herself and begged me to sign it; again I refused."

Mahon had not agreed to the next demand she made, which concerned writing a letter of a similar nature to his friends.

"This appeared to anger Miss Kaye beyond endurance and she suddenly picked up a weapon – an axe – a coal axe – and threw it at me; it struck me on the shoulder and glanced off and hit the door, breaking the shaft.

"Then I saw red," Mahon said in his first statement. "We fought and struggled. She was a very big strong girl. She appeared to be quite mad with anger and rage."

In his second statement Mahon said: "I felt appalled at the fury she showed and realized suddenly how strong the girl was. She followed up the throw by dashing at me and clutching at my face and neck.

"In sheer desperation and fright, I closed with her, doing my best to fight back and loosen her hold. We struggled and eventually, in the course of the struggle, we fell over an easy chair and Miss Kaye's head came into violent contact with the round coal cauldron . . .

"My body of course being on top when she fell, her hold relaxed a bit and she lay apparently stunned or dead.

"The events of the next few seconds I cannot remember except as a nightmare of horror, for I saw blood beginning to ooze from Miss Kaye's head where she had struck the cauldron.

"I did my utmost to revive her, and I simply could not at the time say whether I strangled her or whether she died of the fall; but from the moment she fell and struck her head, she did not move.

"By this time, the excitement of the struggle and the fright and the blows I had received, had reduced me to a condition of nervous exhaustion."

Mahon had gone into the garden in "a state bordering on madness", but had returned later to place her body "gently" in the second bedroom before spending the night in Eastbourne.

Two days later – Thursday, April 17 – he had gone to London, where he'd bought a knife and a saw from a "Staines" shop in Victoria Street.

"When I got back to Langney I was still so upset and worried that I could not then carry out my intention to decapitate the body.

"I did so on Good Friday. I severed the legs from the hips, the head, and left the arms on. I then put the various parts in a trunk which I locked up. I left the trunk in the bedroom and locked the door."

Mahon had locked the door because he was expecting a guest to arrive at about lunch-time. She was a Miss Duncan whom he'd met some six weeks before in Richmond – "a woman down on her luck, not a prostitute".

His explanation for this was that when "the realization of the whole thing dawned on me", it had struck him that the "damn place" was haunted.

"I thought: I can't get the wife down – if I do, she will find the body. I got this girl, the one I met at Richmond – I thought I was doing her a good turn – down to the bungalow."

And he added: "I should have gone stark raving mad if I had not had her with me. It was ghastly."

Miss Duncan, who'd received £4 wired to her by Mahon on the Thursday, had done some cleaning for him.

"She came down on Good Friday and went back on Easter Monday (accompanied by Mahon). I never confided in her as to what had happened. She saw feminine articles about, and I told her my wife was down."

Mahon had treated Miss Duncan to dinner in London, and then had taken her home. On Tuesday he'd been able to return to the bungalow as the works at Sunbury were still closed.

"I burnt the head in an ordinary fire; it was finished in three hours. The poker went through the head when I poked it. The next day I broke the skull and put the pieces in the dustbin. The thigh bone I burned. It is surprising what a room fire will burn."

After dealing with the skull, he had been obliged to make an appearance at work.

"I went down to Langney again on Friday night, 25th April, and stayed at the "Sussex" or "Clifton" Hotel that night, going over to the bungalow about 10 o'clock on Saturday morning, the 26th April.

"I had to cut up the trunk, I also cut off the arms. I burned portions of them, the smell was appalling, and I had to think of some other method of disposing of the portions.

"I then boiled some portions in a large pot in the bungalow, cut up the portions small, packed them in the brown bag, and I threw them out of the train whilst I was travelling between Waterloo

and Richmond; these portions were not wrapped in anything; this
was about 10 o'clock on Sunday, 27th April."

Then Mahon corrected himself: he'd actually been compelled
to journey on to Reading, "as I could not dispose of all the
portions between Waterloo and Richmond."

He had stayed overnight at a Reading hotel, and the bag had
been left at Waterloo Station to await his planned return on
Friday night to "get some more flesh".

For the dogs and other scavengers which were helping him
remove every trace of his crime.

There was a ring of truth about much of what Mahon said in
those statements. And the one obvious lie wasn't his own: this
was when he gave Miss Kaye's age as 29 – she was, in fact, in her
39th year.

The nearest thing to a written record of her side of the story
was the small number of letters she sent friends and relatives
about this time.

Her married sister, who'd had her to stay at the New Year, had
received a note during Miss Kaye's convalescence in Bournemouth. The note had told her that Emily was now engaged to
"Pat Derek Patterson", and that he wanted his fiancé to go with
him to South Africa, where he had a "good post" in Cape Town.

Miss Kaye had also written to her again on April 5 (immediately after Mahon had first contacted Mr Muir about the bungalow), to say that they would be off in ten days.

According to Mahon, exactly ten days later Miss Kaye had
departed this life.

A similar irony was to be found in the letter which she'd
written to a former room-mate of hers at the Green Cross Club;
it had been dated the day before her death, and was on notepaper
taken from the Kenilworth Court Hotel in Eastbourne:

Dear Old Phiz:

Very many thanks for sending on the parcel. Apparently
you're up in Town this weekend. I wonder if Fred is up
with you. Pat arrived intact, but his arm in a sling, on
Saturday and we are having a very nice time; quiet, but a

nice change from Town. He particularly wants to get to
Paris for Easter and would like you and Fred to come and
have dinner with us when we return to Town, which we
shall have to do in about a fortnight before setting out on
our final journey. This will probably suit you both better
too, at any rate I hope so and shall look forward to seeing
you then. Any news? We are returning from here Wednesday and go straight over to Paris. Gay old Paris. All news
when we meet. Love to all my pals at the Club and lots to
yourself, old thing.

    Yours ever,
    Peter

P.S. If any more letters or anything should come will you
send them to me c/o Poste Restante, G.P.O. Paris? Hope
you have a good Easter.

Obviously, Miss Kaye was confident of her relationship with
Mahon at this stage, whatever his own reservations or deceits.
And the fact that she told her sister his name was "Pat Derek
Patterson" underlines her willingness to lie in order to achieve
her end. There can be little doubt that this ageing and not very
appetizing spinster wasn't going to give up her "handsome brute
of a man" without a fight.

Neither was she going to suffer any scruples about absconding
with Mrs Mahon's husband – nor, indeed, with Miss Mahon's
father, which means she was prepared to consider two lives as less
important than her own. It wasn't as if she'd never come in
contact with Mrs Mahon; a few casual inquiries, to check out any
sob story Mahon might have told her, could have been fairly
easily made.

Miss Kaye had the benefit of a good deal of posthumous
sympathy, which cast her as an innocent maid betrayed by the
wiles of an Irish charmer. This is a lot of nonsense. She deserves
sympathy simply as the sad, silly, slightly desperate figure so
often found at the lonely point on a triangle. The rare and really
loving disengage themselves before anyone else gets hurt. The
rest have to cope with varying degrees of self-interest, and with

fantasies which can all too readily deny reality – along with all the danger signals only reality can present.

This denial of the *real* situation is evident in Mahon's references to their quarrels. In one place he says he can't run away with her because of a promise he made to his business colleagues to see Consols through its troubles – a fatuous excuse, but quite in keeping with the classical pattern. In another, their elopement is to be announced to a bowls tournament organizer – an obvious choice as the next most important person in his life, yet just as absurd.

On top of this, Miss Kaye was described by her former roommate as being "a strong-minded woman and capable of very deep feeling" – a combination which Mahon, accustomed to easy prey, very likely found surprisingly difficult to handle. And one must always remember that he hated anyone to think ill of him.

His claim that intimacy took place on their first outing has a strong whiff of character assassination about it. But this just could have been true. Miss Kaye hadn't always lived cloistered in the Green Cross Club, but had moved there from a flat in Soho. Perhaps she had been a "woman of the world" for long enough to miss all the eligible young men, who insisted on virtue in their wives, if not in themselves. Instant intimacy does have a way of making up for lost time, lost youth and lost opportunity.

So much for conjecture – well, almost. Because there is still the question of her confidence: on what was it based?

Superintendent Carlin of Scotland Yard, who made a study of Mahon, once said: "He was keenly disposed to philandering or having affairs with this or that woman casually as they attracted him. But he never, I am convinced, wished to sever [*sic*] his connection with the domestic hearth.

"He felt in his own mind that the woman he had married was his sheet anchor; that, if he cast off from her, he would be adrift."

From that one can assume Mahon either told some terrible lies – or that he just went along with things, as he said – and she was stupid enough to believe in his words.

Yet this begs another question: what sort of attraction *did* Miss Kaye have for him? Or was it something far more than that which locked them into a prolonged and calamitous liaison?

It could have been her £700 nest egg – although there were plenty of other susceptible women about, much better off.

It could have been sexual – the jaded Mahon may have become kinky, but nothing is novel forever.

It could have been the child beginning to grow in Miss Kaye's womb – but this would surely have been a source of acute anxiety, rather than of buoyant confidence, until he had actually "married" her. (And besides, there is no positive proof that either of them knew about this pregnancy, which was still in its very early stages.)

It might have been the first of those three strange coincidences which contributed to his damnation. This was when, according to Edgar Wallace at his most responsible, Miss Kaye chanced across a court report while clearing out a drawer – presumably at the Green Cross Club – lined with an old newspaper. From it she had learned Mahon's closely-kept secret: that five-year sentence for the Sunningdale bank fiasco. Just a word or two in the ear of Mr Hobbins at the office and . . .

There is something about this particular coincidence which worries one a bit – the other two being authenticated beyond dispute. It does, however, suggest a most plausible answer to the question.

Such knowledge could, if used to unfair advantage, inspire confidence in someone with designs like Miss Kaye; just as it could inspire someone else to cut them up into very small pieces.

One piece of large intestine found on Sunday, May 4, was eight inches long.

Once, while Sir Bernard Spilsbury was giving a talk to the Cambridge University Medical Society, what he said made a listener scream, throw a fit and bite the chairman's thumb. Others fainted.

So when he described the remains of Miss Kaye as being the most gruesome he'd ever encountered, that was saying something.

It was also paying an oblique compliment to the widow in a fur coat who accompanied him to Eastbourne that weekend. Mrs Bainbridge had applied for a job at his hospital after her husband, a former professor there and a friend of Spilsbury's, had died. She had been appointed to help in the pathology museum but, much as in Mrs Mahon's case, her intelligence and efficiency, coupled with an interest in post-mortem work, had led to rapid promotion as the great man's first secretary. Although her nerve had already been tested in the mortuary, this – her début in a major investigation – could have proved somewhat overwhelming. Yet Mrs Bainbridge stayed at Spilsbury's side, imperturbably taking down his observations, for the whole eight hours they were there.

The bungalow, Spilsbury discovered, was very near to where Irene Munro's foot had been seen sticking out of the shingle by a 13-year-old boy.

It was called the "Officer's House", having once been part of the defunct Langney Coastguard Station, and there was a wall around the property and the adjoining row of smaller quarters. The bungalow had nine rooms, and was a simple, square structure, with a chimney at each of the four corners of its lopped-off, pitched roof, and postage-stamp windows. Looking at a picture of it today, one is immediately reminded of the easier models that can be made in Lego – except that nothing in Lego could look quite so gloomily functional or drab.

A considerable crowd of sightseers was waiting in the spring sunshine when Spilsbury and Mrs Bainbridge arrived and went in through the front entrance.

This brought them immediately into the best-furnished of the nine rooms: a lounge papered with a pattern of potted plants. The walls were also decorated with ornamental plates and a great number of pictures in heavy, wooden frames. There was a mirror over the fireplace, and to the right of the grate stood two coal scuttles, one of which was a tinny replica of a cauldron. A settee and assortment of chairs – ranging from cane to Windsor to plain ordinary – provided enough seating for more than half a dozen people, and beneath the window, with its drawn curtains of a floral design, was a small writing desk. Most poignant, though, was a vase of wilting flowers that had been left on a circular, three-legged table almost in the centre of the carpet.

At a glance, everything looked orderly and neat.

Then the police began to show them around. Spilsbury, who had put on his long white apron and rubber gloves, was shocked to see Chief Inspector Savage handling the grisly evidence with his bare hands, and this was to lead to the introduction of the "murder bag" every force uses today.

The grisly evidence being, in the first instance, a tenon saw which had flesh and human grease on it. There was more of this grease on the metal fender of the fireplace, in a saucepan, in a bath and in a basin. A saucer of solidified fat lay near the cauldron.

In the fireplace was a two-gallon saucepan; beneath its scum of fat was some reddish fluid and a piece of boiled flesh with skin attached to it.

The large fibre trunk in one of the bedrooms had the initials *E.B.K.* on its lid, a fair indication of the contents: the torso of Emily Beilby Kaye, sawn across at the waist and down the middle, making four parts in all. In among them was a biscuit tin filled with various organs – including that length of intestine. And in a hat-box were thirty-seven pieces of flesh, some wrapped in blood-soaked clothing.

Spilsbury had the police move the kitchen table out into the walled yard, and worked there for three hours on the remains. Most probably this was because the light was better – it it could hardly have been anything to do with the dreadful odours. Much to his dismay, Spilsbury's sense of smell, upon which he relied heavily, had begun to fade about four years before. Often, in order to detect a particular odour by contrast, so to speak, he would put down his instruments, go out into the open air, and then rush back into the mortuary to see what difference this made. His handicap was also a source of dismay to others, who had to remain attentive in almost unendurable conditions, while he worked on quite happily, never suggesting a break. Nor would he allow anyone to seek comfort in a cigarette, as one CID officer had cause to remember after an exhumation: Spilsbury politely asked him to refrain, adding, "I can't smell the smells I want to smell", and then bent down to sniff at the corpse as if it were a "rose-garden". His eye-sight, however, was quite extraordinary, and allowed him to make do without a microscope on occasion. He was able to spot the mark of an abortionist's instrument that no one else could see without a lens, and once he correctly diagnosed a spinal disease which was virtually invisible – his finding being checked by someone else using a slide. Not one of his opinions made in this way was ever squashed in court by evidence based on microscopic examination, but, of course, the slightest doubt would have had him at his microscope, too. The instrument was what had given him his initial interest in medical jurisprudence.

This gift of good vision was employed extensively that afternoon. Spilsbury spent almost all of the time on collecting more than 900 fragments of bone from the ashes found in a dustpan and in the bungalow's fireplaces. Many of these fragments were so tiny and dry that they would have turned to dust in less careful fingers.

Outside the garden, the crowd grew to a tremendous size, and the road became jammed with cars. There wasn't much for these spectators to watch, apart from the activities of the police who were searching for skull bones, but the children enjoyed themselves on the shingle. Then, just as the light was fading, a quick glimpse was caught of Spilsbury and Mrs Bainbridge leaving for London, followed by a variety of sinister containers.

Late that night, when Spilsbury had his top-floor mortuary suite at St Bartholomew's Hospital to himself, he went into the preparation room and began what has been called his masterpiece.

A headless corpse had first brought him into the limelight; it had been that of Mrs Crippen, who'd lived for a time in Guilford Street, where the Green Cross Club stood. His own part in the case, important though he made it, had been limited to a section of scar tissue smaller than a matchbox top. Now he was confronted by hundreds of bits and pieces, many a great deal even smaller than that; some cooked, some raw and some pulverized. All of which, theoretically, would go to make up one body.

Spilsbury worked until 6.30 a.m. He attended to his normal duties during the day, and then carried straight on from where he'd left off. He was not simply a pathologist, but a born detective who couldn't read a book on holiday without noting down his medical deductions in the margin. By Tuesday morning, his work was done.

The torso had been reassembled, and the organs were all back in their proper places. Three leg bones had been restored from the pile of brittle bone fragments, one leg had been confirmed missing, and parts of both hands had been juxtaposed. And, apart from the rest of the bone, there was nothing left over.

With the completion of this astounding reconstruction, Spilsbury was not, as one might suppose, then able to state the cause of Miss Kaye's death. But he was able to say how she *hadn't* died — and that was the important thing.

The dogs encouraged to find the missing limb were no help to the police. A leg was discovered on Wimbledon Common, but it wasn't Miss Kaye's. As a matter of dubious interest, unexplained parts of people crop up surprisingly often; Spilsbury examined scores of them during his career, including a mysterious pair of legs abandoned under a train seat at Waterloo Station in 1935.

Not that the missing leg was going to make much difference to the case anyway, and the head had obviously vanished. What the police, who didn't themselves accept Mahon's story for a minute, wanted most was some means of eliminating the "reasonable doubt" that a jury might find in his version of the death struggle. This was a very real anxiety on their part at the time, even after all the evidence had been carefully reviewed, and they went ahead with the trial only because there didn't seem any likelihood of the position changing.

This led to J.D. "Jimmy" Cassels (later Sir James), the former newspaper reporter who had defended Field in the Irene Munro case, being briefed to appear for Mahon. Mr Cassels saw his client at Brixton Prison on several occasions, and on one of them he was told a story which had a most unnerving sequel.

On the Tuesday after escorting Miss Duncan back to London, said Mahon, his return to the bungalow had been made under a stormy sky. As his intention was to destroy the severed head, he built a fierce fire in one of the grates. Then, when the fire was at its hottest, he placed the head upright on the coals. The fair hair lifted in the updraught and burst into flame. And the heat opened those dead eyes to stare at him, just as there was a tremendous thunderclap overhead, followed immediately by lightning that filled the room. This was too much for Mahon: he fled in terror, out into the rain and away across the Crumbles. When he eventually summoned enough courage to return, about three hours later, the head had turned to a skull of ash.

Mr Cassels repeated this tale with caution but, in the event, suffered no embarrassment for having believed it. He also worked very hard and long on his strategy, which included finding an appropriate quotation from William Congreve:

> *Heav'n has no rage, like love to hatred turn'd,*
> *Nor Hell a fury, like a woman scorn'd*

While Mahon prepared himself with confidence for his appearance on Tuesday, July 15, in the County Hall at Lewes, a sleepy little town that came to life only when the Assizes were held.

As has been already remarked, he had a large wardrobe of expensive clothes – they were his chief extravagance – but he still felt the need for a brand-new suit costing nine guineas. The prison pallor of his face troubled him, particularly as a healthy tan had now become the vogue, and he asked for some artificial tanning agent to be bought. This request went unheeded, and so he did what he could with some tobacco juice.

"The bronzed hue of his fine features," wrote a reporter on the opening day of the trial, "was a tribute to the extent to which prisoners are now allowed open-air exercise."

Others went further in their observations, nothing that Mahon's delicate hands were curiously white, and that he'd put on weight since the police court hearing.

An American judge sitting beside Mr Justice Avory also caused some interest, as did the exhibits arrayed before the prosecution: a tenon saw, a cook's knife, a flimsy coal scuttle, and a scale model of the bungalow.

For those who had attended the trial of Field and Gray in the same courtroom, it seemed Marshall-Hall's remark about the Crumbles had indeed been prophetic; not only was Mr Justice Avory there, and Mr Cassels, but Sir Henry Curtis-Bennett was again leading for the Crown.

This imposing, portly and brilliant man, with a passion for motor cars, had, in fact, nearly been briefed to represent the accused. He much preferred defending to prosecuting, and had by then fought the death sentence on behalf of more than fifty defendants – taking his failures to achieve an acquittal very hard. "We are men of the world," he would often say to a jury; a clever ploy, but they'd know he meant it. His obvious empathy was directed not only at the virtuous either; he became very angry when the Bywaters-Thompson love affair was labelled "tawdry", and his fondness for Major Herbert Rowse Armstrong, the poisoner, was no secret, however sinister he found him.

But Mahon had an unprecedented effect upon Curtis-Bennett, who said that, after taking one look at him in court, he'd never disliked a prisoner as much. And when Mahon later inspected the grim relics of his crime with the alert interest of an Alsatian being shown a chewed slipper, this dislike was to turn to loathing. Well disguised, of course, but formidable.

The trial began twice. This was again a matter of history repeating itself, because the illness of a juror had halted the proceedings while Gray and Field were in the dock. At the start of the second day a juror fainted, recovered to hear a little more of the evidence about Miss Kaye's past, and suffered another collapse. Then, just as a fresh juror was about to be sworn in, another of the original twelve was taken ill. A second substitute was found and the jury were finally resworn – after a delay which had also lasted five hours.

Nonetheless, despite the fact Curtis-Bennett had to restate his case for the Crown, twenty-eight witnesses gave their evidence before the overnight adjournment.

Third on the list was Chief Inspector Savage. He said that two minute spots of blood had been found on the cauldron, and it was handed to the jury for examination. The cauldron was light and so unsubstantial that the bottom had worn out once already. Its legs were thin and hollow, and one of them was bent.

The chief inspector hadn't been able to find a mark on the door to show where, according to Mahon's statement, the axe had hit it.

But he agreed with Mr Cassels that the accused had volunteered a great deal of information, most of which had proved to be correct. The knife had, for example, been bought at a shop called Staines.

Mrs Elizabeth Beilby Harrison said she was Miss Kaye's sister, and identified a number of her belongings. She spoke about the letters she'd received.

"My sister was very athletic," Mrs Harrison said. "I just knew what my sister told me about the man she said she was engaged to (that he was taking her to South Africa), nothing more than I have already said. My sister told me nothing more."

The judge asked after the deceased's temperament.

"Quiet and rather placid. She did not get into a temper."

All of her evidence had a strangely flat, noncommital sound to it.

She was followed into the witness box by Miss Ada Constance Smith, the club secretary, who could add little to the picture of the dead woman. "She told me she was engaged to a man whose name I took to be 'Peterson'. I knew the name of 'Pat'; some man having given me that name on the telephone who wanted to speak to Miss Kaye."

Miss Edith Mary Warren, a Green Cross Club resident known as "Phiz", wanted to set the record straight.

"I gave evidence at the police court," she said, "[but I] did not say there that Miss Kaye was well above the average height of a woman and was physically strong, or anything like it. I said she was shorter than I am, and I said I was 5ft. 9 in., which is not exceptional."

Miss Warren had met Mahon at the club, and knew he was the manager of a soda-fountain company. She'd also been shown a diamond and sapphire engagement ring on "Peter's" return from Bournemouth.

"She asked me to call her Pat by another name because one of the girls at the club knew some business acquaintances of Pat, so she asked me to call him in front of the girls at the club 'Derek Patterson'."

If this seemed innocuous enough, the next witness was to produce a very nasty surprise, which incorporated one of those shattering coincidences and a damning lie on Mahon's part.

Mr George Bell Muir began with the evidence expected of him: he explained how he'd acted as an agent for a friend in letting the bungalow, and described arranging the let with a man who called himself "Waller".

Then came the crunch. Mr Muir also stated that on April 12, the Saturday Mahon had gone down to live with Miss Kaye at the bungalow, he'd bumped into "Mr Waller" in Victoria Street, London. And he had noticed that Mr Waller was carrying a bag.

A bag containing a tenon saw, cook's knife and a knife cleaner, according to the evidence of Mr Frederick Charles Stoner, of the Staines Kitchen Equipment Company in Victoria Street. He dithered over the knife cleaner, but had no doubt about selling the prisoner the two other items at around one p.m. Mr Stoner had an invoice carton to prove it.

So Mahon had this equipment before the "accident", and he hadn't bought it, as his statement claimed, the following Thursday.

Jewellers, chambermaids, hotel receptionists and taxi drivers then did their best to recall – often very vaguely – the movements and purchases of "Mr and Mrs P. H. Mahon", "Miss Kaye" and "Mr J. Waller".

The second day of the trial ended with two pieces of testimony which were remarkable for their whimsy.

Mrs Florence Amy Gertrude Tate, of 6 Langney Bungalows, described how she had watched the couple walking arm in arm towards the sea.

And a butcher, Mr Frank Francis, told the court of the difficulty he'd experienced in having them open up and take delivery of some parcels of meat.

The first witness on that heavy, sultry Thursday morning was Mr Reginald Day Finch Hill, who supplied dry details of Miss Kaye's employment as an assistant to Mr Hobbins. She had plainly made no impression on the firm worth mentioning. She had come and she had gone. That was all.

His evidence did, however, contain one piece of information that was worth revealing.

Mrs Mahon was still employed by Consols Automatic Aerators, he said. Most people were pleased to hear that the deception over Mahon's record had not cost her the job she valued so highly.

Even Mahon himself appeared to nod approval. He was as calm and confident as ever, and listened to two more witnesses, both in the hotel trade, without batting an eyelid. They were, after all, saying nothing about his movements he hadn't told the police already.

Then the second of three very imprudent lies caught up with him. This was held to have been the one which made the greatest impression on the jury, although, in actual substance, it lacked the direct relevance of the third.

Miss Ethel Primrose Duncan, who was described as a "tall, well-built, dark woman", nervously took the oath.

"Do you know the prisoner?" asked Sir Henry.

"Please," she begged softly, "do not ask me too many questions."

"Do you know a man of the name of Patrick Mahon?"

"I do."

"When did you first meet him?"

"On the tenth of April."

"Do you remember where?"

"In Richmond."

Mahon had said in his informal statement that this chance encounter had occurred six weeks before Miss Kaye's death, the jury recalled – not a mere five days. It also meant he had been sniffing about the streets on the eve of his trip to the Crumbles to pick up the keys.

Miss Duncan had been told that his marriage was a "tragedy" (how true) and that his name was Pat. This had been enough for her to give him her address in Isleworth – or so she implied. Some form of strong attraction must have also played its part.

At this point, Mr Justice Avory interrupted to say: "I do not gather that the witness has identified the prisoner. You have seen the prisoner, have you not?"

"No, I haven't in court."

"Let him stand up," ordered the judge.

"Oh, please don't!"

Miss Duncan broke down as Mahon rose, and there was a short interval before she could carry on again.

"When you gave him your address," asked Curtis-Bennett, "did he say anything to you?"

"Asked me if I would dine with him the following week," answered Miss Duncan, adding that Mahon had made a tentative date for the Wednesday night.

On the Tuesday Miss Kaye met her death, a telegram had arrived from Mahon late in the afternoon: "Charing Cross 7 tomorrow sure Pat."

They had dined on Wednesday night at Victoria Station, where Mahon had invited her down to Eastbourne for the Easter weekend. He'd said he was staying there in a friend's bungalow – "rather a charming place".

Next day Miss Duncan had received £4 telegraphed to her from Eastbourne, and had used some of it to catch a train down there on Good Friday. After being met at the station, she had lunched and dined in the resort town, before going to the bungalow at about ten in a taxi. There Miss Duncan had spent the night in the bedroom adjoining the one containing the trunk. The court took it for granted that Mahon had shared the same bed.

Miss Duncan had been left in Eastbourne on Easter Saturday while Mahon went to the Plumpton races. They had met up again at the end of the day, dined in an hotel, and had gone back to the bungalow.

On Easter Sunday Mahon had cut his finger on the screw of a lock he was trying to fit to the adjoining bedroom – he had told her that valuable books were stored in there.

"Whilst the prisoner was doing something to the lock, did you see into that room – just a glance?"

"Yes," sighed Miss Duncan.

"Did you notice anything particular in the room?"

"Yes, I did see the trunk; I was not struck by anything; I saw a trunk and a bed, but it did not interest me at all."

Later on Mahon had said to her: "I have locked it up."

Something which, according to his statements, he'd done before leaving the bungalow to meet her at the station.

Mahon had received a telegram that Sunday, signed by someone called "Lees" and summoning him to a business meeting.
This was to cut short her visit by a day, and Mahon had taken her
back to London on Easter Monday, where, after spending the
evening together, they had parted at midnight.

"Did the prisoner make any remark to you as to the work that
you did in the bungalow?" Sir Henry wanted to know.

"I do not remember now. I think he said he wished – he did not
want me to clean to the extent I did."

"Did he say anything else about it; why he did not want you to
do so?"

"Because his wife was coming down the following week, and he
did not know what she would say, because –"

Miss Duncan broke down again.

"I'm sorry; she had been down the previous week."

Mr Cassels began his cross-examination by telling her: "I do
not want to distress you, I only want to ask you one or two
questions."

The first dozen of these were clearly intended to confirm that
Mahon's approach to Miss Duncan had been prompted by
chivalry. They resulted instead in a fragmentary account so
baffling that the jury were left to ponder the strangeness of
human nature.

Miss Duncan said that she'd been walking the considerable
distance from Kensington to Isleworth when Mahon had spoken
to her near a bridge in Richmond. She was very wet at the time.

"Did he offer you a share of his umbrella?" asked Mr Cassels.

"He offered to drive me home."

"At any rate, did you have the shelter of his umbrella?"

"No."

"Had he got one?"

"No," said Miss Duncan.

"Did you tell him you were . . .?"

The unspoken words brought a deep hush.

"I told him some untruths, I admit."

An admission that could have been made by Miss Kaye, and
one which by now seemed characteristic of the world of Patrick
Herbert Mahon. A world of unreality ad-libbed to suit the desires

of the weak and pathetic creatures who lived in it – and who could so easily be manipulated by the strong. By predators like Mahon, whose own fantasies were the more convincing – both to themselves and to others – because of being perversions of what they recognized to be the truth.

And this blurring was what had so troubled the police: would the jury be able to tell where the dividing line lay – beyond any reasonable doubt? The trial, however, was now giving everyone present something to *feel*, as well as to see and hear.

Many winced when they heard how close Miss Duncan had come to escaping her nightmare that rainy night.

"I said: 'I am sorry, because I do not do things like this,' and he said: 'Well, it is a tragedy, we will both go our own way.'"

But just why she had gone on walking home with Mahon after this exchange wasn't explained; she was probably still searching in herself for the reason.

Before Miss Duncan stepped down, Mr Cassels ended a question with: "That means you saw no sign of blood about the place?"

"None whatever," whispered the woman whose body Mahon had also touched on Good Friday.

A refuse collector told the court how he had pointed out where he'd dumped ashes collected at the "Officer's House". Bankers gave details of Miss Kaye's transactions, and a stockbroker recalled selling shares on her behalf during February and early April. A ledger keeper said that Mahon's account at Barclay's Bank, Richmond, stood at £40.

All this could have appeared rather dull stuff to the sensation-seekers in the public gallery. Yet several snippets yielded dividends after a moment's reflection. That bank account, for example, was barely a year old, and it wasn't a joint account. From this one might assume that Mrs Mahon had kept control of her share of their double income – if, indeed, she hadn't done more than that, and had kept Mahon fairly short so he couldn't start gambling . . .

Then Mr John Webster, Home Office Analyst, began to formally identify one blood-stained exhibit after another.

Exhibit 87 was a section of carpet which had been scrubbed clean – but Exhibit 86, a corresponding piece of under-felt, had a large stain soaked into it, and even the floorboards below this had been discoloured. The very act of cleaning the carpet had assisted in the spread of this stain, Mr Webster said, because of the additional moisture.

His evidence should have formed an introduction to the Crown's star witness and the climax of its case, but before Sir Bernard Spilsbury could be called, Mr Cassels begged leave to have Miss Duncan return to the box. It was clear that something important to the defence case had just reached his ear.

Miss Duncan's further ordeal, made worse by the intimacy it implied, did not cause much of a delay. She had remembered seeing four bruises, set close together, on one or other of Mahon's shoulders.

Hindsight would suggest that the defence then erred unwittingly in asking her to point out their approximate position; the bruising did, after all, go some way towards supporting the claim that Mahon had been struck by an axe.

"Where your fingers are?" Mr Cassels asked.

"Just about *there*," Miss Duncan replied, touching her own shoulder.

Which could possibly have prompted the jury to suppose that the pattern of marks might well have been made by four fingertips.

A recent bruise on the back was given some attention in the early part of Sir Bernard's testimony as an expert witness.

He stood tall and elegant in the box, as immaculate as the rotund fellow-knight examining him, and there was, as always, a red carnation in the lapel of his morning coat.

"The Handsomest Man in London", in the opinion of one newspaper, spoke with simplicity and detachment about the handiwork of the prisoner, a man who regarded himself among the most handsome in the world.

"The breast bone was attached to this piece, and the portions of most of the left ribs."

"Was the right breast on that piece?" inquired Sir Henry.

"Yes, it was."

"Is there anything you want to tell us about that?"

"When I pressed it milky fluid escaped from the nipple."

"You had better say at once," the judge broke in, "what that indicates."

"May I deal with the other piece first, my lord?" said Spilsbury.

"Yes."

"The fourth piece formed the left side of the chest and on the back of this piece I found an area two inches long over the shoulder-blade which had a recent bruise."

Sir Henry returned to this injury shortly afterwards: "Are you able to say at all, from your examination of that bruise, whether it was inflicted shortly before death?"

"Yes, it was certainly inflicted before death. It might have been only a few minutes before death – if it was a very serious blow which had been struck. Or it might have been inflicted a few hours before death, if it had been of a less serious character."

There had been no sign of any skull or neck bones whatsoever.

"Can you tell us what your opinion is after your examination?"

"As to what?" Mr Justice Avory interjected.

"As to first of all," Curtis-Bennett explained, "was this the body of a woman, what size woman, and so on."

Spilsbury began his methodical but fluent summary, which was to have something of a twist ending:

"All the material I have examined, portions of the trunk, the organs, pieces of boiled flesh, and those fragments of bone which I have been able to identify, are all of them human, and correspond with parts of a single body – no duplicates at all.

"The four pieces of chest and abdominal wall fit accurately to form one trunk, and the organs in the tin box, together with the fragments of organs attached to the four pieces of trunk, form a complete set of human organs – with the exception of certain missing portions, of which the uterus and one ovary are the most important."

That answered the first question.

"The body was that of an adult female of big build and fair hair."

That the second; now for what could be deduced.

"She was pregnant, in my opinion, at the time of her death, and at an early period, probably between one and three months. (So, in fact, two lives *had* gone into the balance against those of Mrs Mahon and her daughter.)

"There was no indication of any previous pregnancy, or of pregnancy which had run its full term. The organs were those of a healthy person, and the adhesions round the right lung were the only indication of previous disease."

Then came the "catch" conclusion.

"No disease was found to account for natural death – and no condition which would account for unnatural death."

"I do not follow what that means," said the judge.

"The head and neck being missing, there was no evidence of the cause of death being some unnatural cause."

Now the pathologist's careful insinuation was obvious: he couldn't give an opinion about something that wasn't there, so perhaps this was the very reason it wasn't there. Irene Munro's battered skull had allowed for no persuasive stories about an accidental fall. Or, very simply: no head, no evidence – either way.

Mr Justice Avory's response was a striking reminder to every layman of the law's precise use of language, particularly after such a catalogue of hacked-about human tissue.

"In other words," he said to Spilsbury, "you found *no evidence of violence* – except the bruise on the back?"

"Except the bruise," concurred Sir Bernard.

The Crown's case was almost complete. The head had been shown to hold the key to what had really happened, and Curtis-Bennett focused the jury's attention upon it.

"You have seen the coal cauldron, Exhibit 15, which has been produced?" he said to Spilsbury.

"Yes."

"You have heard, have you not, the statements of the prisoner which have been read?"

"Yes."

"In your opinion, could Miss Kaye have received *rapidly* fatal injuries from falling on that coal cauldron?"

The stress placed on that word wasn't lost on Mahon – or so it would seem presently – and he looked across intently to hear the reply.

"No, in my opinion, she could not."

More than one eminent barrister had said that Spilsbury was an ideal but deadly witness. There was considerable sympathy for Mr Cassels when he stood up to challenge the expert's views under cross-examination.

"You told us that you found a clean cut of one of the organs, the uterus?"

"Yes."

"I suppose you found other cuts which were clean, of the internal organs; so far as there were any cuts at all, were they all clean cuts?"

"All except possibly one, they were nearly all clean cuts."

A small victory for Mr Cassels; this had at least removed any undue significance as to how the uterus – a potent symbol of guilt – had been removed. It could well have become lost, or destroyed with other less emotive organs.

He made this his next point, and Spilsbury confirmed that parts of the stomach, a small gland, and possibly a portion of the intestines were unaccounted for.

But from there on, the defence was checked at every turn.

Brain injuries and compression of the spinal cord were suggested as reasons for Miss Kaye's demise – these failed, because of the circumstances described by Mahon, to secure a satisfactory answer.

"Then there is fracture of the bones of the skull," said Mr Cassels. "Does that produce rapid death?"

"Very occasionally; it is not usually rapidly fatal, but certainly fatal in many cases."

Mr Cassels put that one question too many: "When you say 'not rapidly fatal', do you mean not fatal within an hour?"

Mahon could have sat stunned in the garden for two, three, even four hours, nobody could disprove that.

"Yes, usually not within 24 or 48 hours," said Spilsbury.

Status lymphaticus was the defence's next hope, and a definition of it was requested.

"That is a condition in which there is a liability to sudden death owing to certain changes in the organs. There may be no violence at all, or it might be very slight violence." (Status lymphaticus, once an explanation for any seemingly inexplicable death, is today the subject of much controversy; one thing is agreed, however, it can never be a *cause* of death.)

But that idea was totally rejected.

Stabbing, strangulation, throat-slitting . . . and back to the original and most reasonable of suggestions. Miss Kaye had fallen under Mahon's weight and had suffered a mortal head wound when she landed on the cauldron.

"Why not?" Mr Cassels demanded.

"Because no fall on the coal cauldron, such as you have described, would be capable of inflicting such injuries to the head as to cause rapidly fatal results," said Spilsbury. "If that particular cauldron, filled with coal, were the one referred to, a sufficiently severe blow to produce such an injury would have crumpled up the cauldron."

This left the hypothesis of Miss Kaye's neck having been twisted slightly – which could be rapidly fatal in someone with a spinal disease, such as tuberculosis.

"I suppose," Mr Cassels said finally, "we need not go so far as to say that *only* diseased persons die from compression of the spinal cord?"

First came the good news.

"Oh, no," Sir Bernard agreed wholeheartedly.

Then he added: "It requires extreme violence."

The jury's verdict now seemed inevitable to many. Mahon had begun his affair with Miss Kaye with a clandestine meeting at a place called Staines, and he had ended it, to all intents and purposes, with a purchase made at a kitchen equipment shop also called Staines. The grim brackets of coincidence . . .

But the man had still to be allowed his own say, and nobody would have wished the trial to end until he'd done so. There was an intense interest in how he would react in the witness box (if ever a monster should be made to squirm it was he, the whispers went), and in the prospect of experiencing something of his

personality at first hand (some people being very partial to an
attack of the goose pimples). It also had to be conceded that,
somehow or other, he might yet be able to induce enough doubt
in the jury's mind to escape the hangman.

Mahon, it is said, never doubted this at the outset.

The Crown's case had ended most satisfactorily, from his point
of view, with an additional statement he'd made being read out by
the Clerk of Assize. This document had begun: "I have already
made a full statement of the facts in this case, but I wish to add
some details which may save waste of time and money in calling
unnecessary witnesses." Although these details were little more
than a timetable of events, there was an undeniable magnanimity
in their provision. Pat, they declared, is an extremely considerate
fellow.

And when he took the oath, jaunty in his plum-coloured suit,
with its mauve kerchief in the breast pocket, his pleasant, level
voice indicated a surprising degree of quiet confidence. A poise
which, in fact, looked impossible to shake.

Not that Mahon needed to fear any question put to him that hot
afternoon because Mr Cassels was, whether he liked it or not,
duty-bound to present his case in the best possible light. Nor
could any man have expected him to foresee the shattering
phenomenon that Fate had in store.

The prisoner said he was 34 and a married man. A status he had
often impressed on Miss Kaye.

His replies were, for the most part, succinct and clearly stated,
except for when his gift of the gab got the better of him. The
judge said more than once: "You are asked what you did, not all
this imagination." Mahon took little notice of this – his life
depended on the jury's imagination.

He and Miss Kaye had often conversed in French, he said. Her
pretentiousness – and his own – were transparent in an answer he
gave to a question concerning Miss Kaye's job at the Bond Street
financier's.

"Miss Kaye was employed as – I suppose an amanuensis is the
real term, that is what she described it as."

An amanuensis, according to *Cassells New English Dictionary*, is: "A person employed to write what another dictates; a secretary." And a Latin word, too.

Name-dropping came into his next reply.

"When was it?" asked Mr Cassels.

"Before Christmas, 1923," said Mahon, ready with his translation. "She was temporary secretary, and she had inside information from, I think, Colonel Mayes and also, I think it is, Sir William Crossfield, I am not sure."

Inside information concerning the exchange rate of the franc. Mahon was questioned at length about this joint speculation, towards which he'd allegedly contributed £125 before Christmas. He had been handed the first of the three £100 notes in February, and had cashed it under a false name.

"I was not altogether satisfied about the transaction," he said, adding for the judge's benefit: "I mean this: at this period Miss Kaye had not only shown and expressed her love and desire for me, she was not only jealous of my wife, but she was endeavouring, as I thought, to drive a wedge between us, and I wondered if this was part of a plan which I could not see . . . I signed a false name simply so that the note could not be traced back to me."

Mahon had recovered his capital and had made a small profit. The last of the £100 notes had been given to him on the day before Miss Kaye died.

Mr Cassels then had him recall Miss Kaye's repeated efforts to win him over, and his stubborn refusal to leave his wife. This part of his evidence had that old convincing ring of truth to it – even when he said Miss Kaye must have bought the engagement ring for herself. The two-month let of the bungalow was, however, a puzzling factor.

Taking the bull by the horns, Mr Cassels invited the use of an equally unfortunate expression (even for 1924) when he asked Mahon to state his reason for this.

". . . it would kill two birds with one stone, if I took the bungalow for that period, and after Miss Kaye had finished down there, and we returned –"

"After Miss Kaye had *finished*?" Mr Justice Avory echoed.

"After we had finished our love experiment, and she returned and I returned, my wife and I could use the bungalow."

Not a very comfortable sentence.

But Mahon dealt smoothly with the purchases made at Staines Kitchen Equipment Company. He had intended buying a Yale lock to fit to the bungalow's front door – the key he'd been given was too cumbersome – and then had been told by an assistant that the shop was closing. This had happened on the pavement outside, and Mahon had made two impulse-buys from a tray of bargain offers: a knife and a saw, which might turn out to be useful at the Crumbles.

The reconstruction of that fateful evening began.

While Miss Kaye had been writing her letters on their return from London, Mahon had made a fire and heated some milk for them. He had used the axe to break up large lumps of coal.

"I laid the axe carelessly down," said Mahon, choosing his adverb rather too carefully.

"Tell us where?"

"On one of the tables in the sitting-room."

There was the row over the letters, and then Mahon had announced he was going to bed. He'd reached the door when Miss Kaye flung the axe at him.

"I was astounded by the suddenness, by the attack altogether, and in a second Miss Kaye followed up the throw. She leaped across the room, clutching at my face –"

Mahon broke down. He didn't touch the neatly-folded mauve kerchief, but dragged a linen square from his trouser pocket and wiped the tears from his eyes.

"We have got as far as she was clutching at your face," said Mr Justice Avory.

They had fallen after a struggle and Mahon had lost consciousness: "I think I must have fainted with the fear and with the shock. I do not remember when I did become conscious of what was happening or had happened."

After dashing water into her face, and having elicited no response, he'd stumbled "crazy" with fear and fright into the night. He had returned to find her still lying there.

"Can you give us any idea as to what time it would be then?"

"It would be *hours* later, I think; it would be either towards day-break or day-break."

Mahon recovered his composure with little obvious effort and went on earnestly answering the questions put to him by both his counsel and, less to his liking, the judge. At times he veered too close to the dramatic, but became more sure of himself the longer he spoke.

All sorts of loose ends were tied up. The letter to the club room-mate had been posted posthumously to give him time to think – he'd realized what a fool he had been in not summoning help immediately. Keeping his dinner date with Miss Duncan had been "a definite thing in my mind to do" amid the confusion, and he had brought her down for "human companionship" – they'd shared Miss Kaye's vacated bed. The telegram cutting short the weekend he'd sent himself.

Mr Justice Avory balked at the idea of going through the details of the disposal of the body again.

Mahon stood relaxed, waiting his turn to speak quite calmly, while Mr Cassels attempted to justify this line of questioning. The courtroom was stuffy and the late afternoon sunlight very dim. Mr Cassels won his argument.

He turned back to Mahon and said: "On Tuesday you burned the head – and some portions of the body?"

A deafening clap of thunder shook the building, coming so unexpectedly that it made everyone start. In the flash of lightning which followed, Mahon was seen gripping the edge of the witness box and cowering back, his eyes wide with fright and his face a most perplexing off-white.

The court adjourned a few minutes later; Mr Cassels's quick stream of questions having received, in most cases, a faint "yes".

Next morning Mahon looked again a picture of health, and he cocked his head attentively when Sir Henry Curtis-Bennett began the cross-examination. By the end of it, he was not a pretty sight.

The first questions allowed him to repeat answers he'd given several times already, and to his own counsel's apparent satisfaction. Gradually his attitude became less tense as much familiar ground was covered.

The alleged speculation in francs took up some time, without establishing anything other than Mahon's lack of information about it: an ignorance based on trust.

His illicit relationships with both Miss Kaye and Miss Duncan were also examined at length, and Mahon explained them in terms of his lamp-post philosophy, often appearing surprised that some points weren't patently obvious. His continued allegiance to Mrs Mahon being one of them; he clearly felt he belonged to her, whatever he might do when roaming abroad on his own, and would always return to her side.

The thickets of his deceits were explored. Mahon had used some enormously complicated ruses to keep potentially troublesome people like Mr Muir at bay. Several of his plans, such as the one for retrieving a letter sent to an imaginary referee in the Midlands, were really quite ingenious, and he outlined them with due modesty.

"Pure invention?" Sir Henry suggested.

"Pure invention," Mahon affirmed.

And found himself suddenly in the open, twisting from one side to another to fend off attack.

"When did you remember that you had bought that knife and saw on the 12th of April?" asked Sir Henry.

"Not until my statement was read out at Hailsham police court."

"Did you make up your mind to say that you had bought the knife and saw upon the 12th of April after you had heard evidence which was called at Hailsham police court from the Staines equipment company?"

"I don't quite follow," said Mahon.

Making him about the only person in the room who didn't: the revised date of purchase was the soft underbelly of his evidence. Sir Henry pursued the point relentlessly.

"There were mistakes regarding the dates," Mahon said in exasperation.

"I am going to draw your attention to one or two."

"Mistakes regarding one or two things which could only have been made by someone in mental agony at the time!"

But Mahon had made a number of alterations to the statement

in question. Surely the inference had been that he'd bought the tools for the purpose of getting rid of the body.

"It's all so futile, when you come to think of it," whimpered Mahon, losing control of himself. "This is the position: the knife and saw were bought by me for an innocent object! The name was on the knife. I told them the name of the shop and I told them I bought the saw. It's utterly absurd for a man to try and confuse the dates!"

He was reminded that it had been a cash sale, and so his identity had not been required for the invoice.

"Kenilworth Court Hotel, Eastbourne, Monday: 'Dear Old Fizzy' – you knew who that was, did you?"

"I never heard Miss Warren called 'Phiz'."

That was a feint – and Sir Henry would return to "Phiz" with devastating effect. He asked Mahon to define the expression "seeing red".

"One gets angry."

"Would it be right to say you saw red during this struggle with Miss Kaye?"

"I saw many things besides red."

"I dare say."

Back to the knife again. Mahon was asked why he had used the carving knife provided by his landlord, and not the new knife, for cutting up his lover's body.

The day before Mahon had told Mr Cassels that he'd worn a sling because his wrist had been injured in preventing an old lady from falling off a bus. If that had been the sort of thing which made Mr Justice Darling wince, then the prisoner was about to go one better.

"For the reasons perhaps you know, Sir Henry," replied Mahon.

"I should like to hear it."

"It is this," he said, pointing to the carving knife, "Miss Kaye had used with me the other knife, the chef's knife, the cook's knife, and I picked *that* knife."

In short: for sentimental reasons.

But Mahon wasn't as confident as he'd sounded then: he was shivering. Soon he would again protest the futility of trying to give an honest answer to the Crown's questions – he even complained to the judge about the "unfair" tactics being used on him. His whines went ignored.

Sir Henry pointed out that the words "she was in trouble" had been deleted from the first statement made at Scotland Yard. Aggrieved to find this counted as evidence, Mahon offered an involved explanation.

"You did use the expression 'she was in trouble'," Sir Henry summed up for him, "but you meant she was in trouble with someone at the club?"

"That is what I meant."

"You've heard Sir Bernard Spilsbury's evidence?"

"Yes."

"That at the mouth of the uterus there was a clean cut and that the uterus itself is missing?"

"Yes."

"Is that pure coincidence?"

"Pure coincidence," said Mahon, who'd already sworn he wouldn't know a uterus if he saw one.

And probably it was: *none* of that body was meant to have been discovered.

The missing head came next. Sir Henry tried without success to have him give the time that it had been in the fire.

"Are you not clear about the time? This was a terrible thing you were doing. Did you not realize how long it took?"

Mahon paused before answering.

"If you knew the circumstances in which this head was burned – I can only say burned," he began, faltered, and went on, "I could not even stay in the room while it was burning."

When it was implied that this wasn't what had happened to the head – because no trace of its incineration had been found – Mahon looked hurt.

"Where did you throw the bones of this most important part of the body, the skull?"

"I threw them over the garden wall. They were tremendously small bones."

They had landed on the shingle.

"What did you break them with?"

"I broke them in my hands like this," said Mahon, innocent of the effect of his demonstration. "After they came out of the fire, they would break just like *that*."

The gesture chilled; and a few seconds later Curtis-Bennett was sickened into a moment's heavy sarcasm.

"I suggest to you that would be impossible."

"Your suggestion is entirely wrong, Sir Henry."

"I may have leave to call Sir Bernard about it?"

"That," growled Mahon, a bone expert in his own right, "is a thing I know."

And was caught off-guard as Curtis-Bennett closed for the kill. This time the evidence about Miss "Phiz" Warren would drive him back, craven and casting desperate looks of appeal at the jury.

The attack was based on the letter which, in Mahon's own words, had precipitated Miss Kaye's assault on his person. The letter she'd tossed across to him and told him to sign "Pat". A letter she'd actually begun to sign herself . . .

"It starts 'Dear Old Phiz'?"

"I know."

"Do you really mean that Miss Kaye that night, besides being in this paroxysm of rage, was also in the sort of mood she was writing a letter to a strange *man* beginning 'Dear Old Phiz'?"

"It may sound strange to you," said Mahon, "but that is what happened."

Mr Justice Avory asked who the man was.

"I mentioned yesterday he was the assistant secretary of the Richmond bowls tournament of which I was the honorary secretary."

"Was he ever called by this nickname?" asked the judge.

"No, my lord. I think I commented that it was so absurd to address him as 'Dear Old Phiz', because he is a solemn sort of individual."

"It was an extraordinary thing for a lady like Miss Kaye to do, was it not?" said Sir Henry, raising his brows.

"Yes, I know."

"Just let us read what you refused to sign . . ."

And Sir Henry Curtis-Bennett drew particular attention to the first sentence.

Dear Old Phiz,

I am sorry I shall not after all be able to see you before my departure.

You can imagine there has been a lot to do and I have not been able to see quite a lot of people before packing up. We shall be travelling overland through France and Italy en route for the Cape.

On our arrival there I will write to you fully regarding prospects and other matters in general, but I really wish to thank you in this letter for all the kindness and good fellowship you have shown me in the past. One cannot put into words just what one feels, but I am sure if I say just this, that you will understand and appreciate just what is in my mind.

Any letter addressed to me c/o The Standard Bank, Cape Town, will find me, but as I said in an earlier part of my letter, I will write to you fully on my arrival.

With every good wish, believe me,

Yours P

And there it stopped. At *P*.

Cut short by the guile of a woman called Peter.

Or, perhaps, at that very second, by a murderous blow from behind.

The American judge watched the closing stages of the trial with awed solemnity, and then admitted to being utterly astonished by what happened at the end of it.

After commenting on Mahon's behaviour following the dismemberment on the Crumbles, Sir Henry completed his speech for the Crown with these words:

"Nobody noticed anything untoward about him at all, and you may have your opinion as to whether the feeling he showed in the witness box was real or not."

Mr Cassels quoted William Congreve, and then added his own touch of poetic imagery:

"Can you conceive that, possibly on the threshold of eternity, you would get play-acting from a man in such a grave position?"

The jury slept on it. They had also to consider a piece of additional evidence which had brought Sir Bernard Spilsbury back to the box. There he'd stated emphatically that the carving knife could not have made the clean cuts he had found – whereas the cook's knife, which was designed for dividing raw meat, could have.

On Saturday morning, Mr Justice Avory referred to the choice of three verdicts which Mr Cassels had placed before them: guilty of murder, guilty of manslaughter – or not guilty at all. For Mahon to be found not guilty, the judge cautioned, the jury would have to conclude that he'd had to kill in order to save his own life.

They retired to consider their verdict at 12.7 p.m. They were back in 45 minutes.

The prisoner was to die for the crime of wilful murder.

Mahon's face went that odd colour again; his tobacco-juice tan making visible a mask of sham which so many had, to their cost, failed to see.

Shaking, he gripped the edge of the box.

"I feel too conscious of the bitterness and unfairness of the summing-up which you have uttered," he told the judge, "to say anything except I am not guilty of murder."

The black cap was placed on the judge's wig.

Mr Justice Avory prefaced his dread words by reminding Mahon that, in mercy to him, the jury had not known of his Guildford conviction. And after passing the death sentence, he made these the final words of the trial:

"It may perhaps interest the jury to know that the reference I made to the prisoner's previous history was a conviction for an assault upon a woman . . ."

That this information should be revealed, when all was said and done, was what so astonished the American guest sitting beside him.

On the threshold of eternity, Mahon confessed – but asked that this shouldn't be publicized for fear of the "bad impression it might make".

And then he did something equally in character, if paradoxical, which horrified the witnesses to his execution.

Man has the unique capacity to suppress his instincts even in situations where his whole being shrieks out against this. He can be expected to go to his certain death with dignity, knowing that resistance would be pointless, and hoping only that it will be said he died like a man.

Mahon's death had no dignity; he died like a dog.

Everyone entering the execution chamber could see at once that there was no escape from the position chalked on the wide trap.

Tom Pierrepoint worked swiftly; he dropped the hood over the prisoner's head and stepped back to pull the lever. As he did so, Mahon, pinioned hand and foot, made a desperate, instinctive leap forward to save himself somehow. But the trap crashed open beneath him, and he swung back, striking the base of his spine against the scaffold's edge. Then the thread, which held the rope's slack in a coil, snapped – and Mahon plunged out of sight.

"That blow killed him," said Roland Wild and Derek Curtis-Bennett, in their 1937 biography of Sir Henry, and they further described Mahon as "doubly hanged". Which could be interpreted as meaning that Mahon had finally cheated the law by taking the initiative and committing suicide, in a manner of speaking.

The evidence, however, suggests differently. It also provides what some may find a more apposite ending to the story of Patrick Herbert Mahon and the men who hunted him down.

Every execution was followed almost immediately by a post-mortem and a formal inquest in the prison where it had taken place. The one at Wandsworth on September 9, 1924, was the first of fifty or more such inquests for which that most meticulous of men, Sir Bernard Spilsbury, received a small fee.

The customary procedure was for the prison doctor to open the neck and leave it at that. When the coroner saw the body stripped of its suit and being opened right up, he dropped a hint or two, mindful of the jury waiting to hear the inquest. Only his tact was appreciated.

Spilsbury, who performed a thousand autopsies a year, examining each body minutely, even if it had come from under a bus, politely insisted on doing things his way.

He spent an hour on the body, but his case card, headed *Judicial Hanging*, makes no mention of a bruise on the back, self-inflicted or otherwise. Then he spent another hour on. Mahon's brain alone, and took away a piece of it in his own black bag.

THE BIRMINGHAM SIX

(Paddy Hill and others, UK 1974)

Ludovic Kennedy

Most of the cases in this book show how forensic science was harnessed by the prosecution to prove guilt, but there are occasions where it has been used to establish innocence. In the 1990s, some twenty years after the original trial, the case against the Birmingham Six finally crumbled when the defence exposed weaknesses in the original forensic evidence. The story opens in November 1974. The bombing of two crowded pubs in Birmingham, in which 21 people were murdered and 162 wounded, was the worst IRA atrocity on the British mainland since the "Troubles" began in 1969. Most of the victims were young people thronging the city centre on what should have been a carefree night out. Public anger and outrage at the carnage put pressure on the police to track down the culprits. Later the same evening, six Irishmen booked on the boat to Belfast were arrested at the ferry port of Heysham in Lancashire. Traces of nitroglycerine were found on their hands. They were beaten, tortured and threatened by detectives. At the end of this violent intimidation, four of the suspects signed written "confessions" while the other two made oral ones. All six were convicted of murder at their Old Bailey trial the following year and sentenced to life imprisonment. But there were doubts in the case. Twelve years later, in 1987, following an inquiry by the Devon and Cornwall police, the case of the Birmingham Six was referred back to the Court of Appeal. The appeal judges heard fresh evidence. Part of this new evidence concerned the "confessions" and part concerned the tell-tale chemical traces on the Irishmen's hands found when they were picked up at Heysham. The men's lawyers claimed that it could no longer be concluded that any of the six had been in contact with explosives. All six appeals were dismissed, however, and it seemed that the convictions would stand. But the campaigning author and journalist Ludovic Kennedy (b. 1919) took up the case, convinced that a gross miscarriage of justice had occurred. Over the winter of 1989–90 he examined the documents in the case and set out his findings and conclusions in an article for The Sunday Times. *This expanded version appeared the following year.*

Just over two years ago the Court of Appeal in the shape of Lord Lane the Lord Chief Justice, Lord Justice O'Connor and Lord Justice Stephen Brown heard fresh evidence in the case of the six Irish drinking companions, convicted in 1975 for the murder of those killed in the IRA bombing of two Birmingham pubs. Evidence was led on the two heads that had resulted in the men's convictions: firstly that it could no longer be concluded that any of them had been in contact with explosives, and secondly that their alleged "confessions" had been obtained by threats and violence (as in the case of the Guildford Four). The court rejected both submissions. "The longer this case has gone on", they said, "the more convinced this court has become that the verdict of the jury was correct." The appeals would be dismissed.

Yet the case refuses to die . . . which in itself and like so many other cases, indicates that whatever the opinions of judges may be, there are others no less worthy of belief who continue to assert that justice has miscarried. So were the judges in the recent appeal of the Birmingham Six right in their judgement or wrong?

Whenever in the past I have looked into a case of an alleged miscarriage of justice, I have always gone first to the convicted men's solicitors because they are least likely to be conned by the guilty proclaiming innocence. Ivan Geffen has been solicitor of two of the six for twelve years and Gareth Peirce of the other four for nine years. Neither has the slightest doubt about their innocence. Peirce has called the findings of the Court "disgraceful", Geffen says, "It's only what one has come to expect from this Court of Appeal."

The three counsel for the men take a broadly similar view.
Lord Gifford, QC, told me, "The judges had no business dismissing the evidence of police malpractice and violence. To come
to the conclusions they did on evidence which was 90 per cent
written and only 5 per cent oral is to assume powers of divination
which no-one should arrogate to themselves," Richard Ferguson,
QC, said the findings had sickened him. "The whole demeanour
of the judges was not to find the truth but how to counter the
good arguments of our side. They were also gratuitously offensive. Coming as I do from Northern Ireland, I find it particularly
distressing when justice fails to live up to the high standards we
were brought up to believe in." And Michael Mansfield, QC,
who thinks there should have been a retrial, most of the participants being still alive, said that the judgement had left him
angry and upset. "I think it did incomparable damage to people's
concept of justice."

It was the same with the three distinguished scientists whose
evidence clashed with that of Dr Frank Skuse, the forensic
scientist who had appeared for the prosecution and was later
dismissed on the grounds of limited efficiency. David Baldock, a
former senior scientific officer at the Home Office Laboratories,
told me, "When I turned up at the Old Bailey to give evidence,
Michael Mansfield said, 'We're wasting our time. They're not
listening. I think the judges quite failed to grasp the nettle of the
scientific evidence.' Dr Brian Caddy, head of the University of
Strathclyde's Forensic Science Unit agreed, and Dr Hugh Black,
former Chief Inspector of Explosives at the Home Office, went
further. "Their decision", he wrote to me, "was an outrage."

Having myself read the Court's judgement and the evidence
presented to it; having spoken personally to some of the new
witnesses; having visited Birmingham's Queens Road Police
Station where the alleged beatings of the prisoners and the
"confessions" that followed took place; and having also read
Chris Mullin MP's well-documented book on the case, I am
led inexorably to the same conclusions. So if we are all right in
our views, how was it that the Court's findings came to be so at
variance with the evidence presented?

In many murder cases where justice is later found to have

miscarried, it often happens that quite early in their investigations the police light on some small but seemingly convincing piece of evidence that leads them to draw the wrong conclusions; and which, if pursued tenaciously, leads in turn to wrongful prosecution, conviction and sentence. In the 10 Rillington Place case they assumed that Timothy Evans would not have sold his furniture and fled to Wales had he not murdered his wife and child whose bodies they had discovered in the ground-floor wash-house; and from there it was a short step to their manufacturing a false confession which led to his conviction and hanging. In the Ayr murder case Patrick Meehan's life sentence originated from his admission to the police that he and his friend Jim Griffiths had been engaged on a criminal enterprise near the scene of the crime when the only firm evidence the police then had was that the two intruders had called each other "Pat" and "Jim"; and to make certain of a conviction the police planted false evidence in Jim Griffiths's coat pocket. Similarly in the Lindbergh baby kidnapping case the discovery of $14,000 of marked ransom money under the floorboards of Hauptmann's garage in the Bronx was enough to convince New York and New Jersey police of his guilt, and with a wealth of fabricated evidence to railroad him to the electric chair.

In the case of the Birmingham Six their undoing was their association with an IRA bomber named James McDade who on 14 November 1974 blew himself up while planting a bomb in the Coventry Telephone Exchange. Five of the six (Gerry Hunter, Paddy Hill, Richard McIlkenny, Billy Power and Hughie Callaghan) had grown up with McDade in the small Roman Catholic enclave of the Ardoyne in West Belfast, where as children they had suffered abuse and discrimination from the surrounding Protestant majority. All had come to Birmingham to seek work, mostly in the 1960s, and it was there that the sixth member of the group, Johnny Walker from Londonderry, came to know McDade and the others. Until McDade blew himself up, only one of the six, Walker, suspected that McDade was an IRA activist. They themselves were not members of the IRA, or even of Sinn Fein. But they were staunch supporters of the Republican cause and its belief in a United Ireland, and they all helped to raise money to send to dependants of Ulster fellow Catholics who had been imprisoned or interned.

On 21 November 1974 the body of James McDade was to be flown from Birmingham to Belfast, and to show Ardoyne solidarity five of the six agreed to combine attendance at his funeral with a visit to their families. Their friend Hughie Callaghan saw them off at Birmingham's New Street Station on the 7.55 p.m. train which would connect with the night boat from Heysham. At 8.17 p.m. the first bomb went off in the Mulberry Bush pub and a few minutes later the second in the Tavern in the Town, both near to the station, and resulting in the horrific casualties of 21 dead and 162 injured. Ports and airports were immediately alerted, and when the booking clerk at New Street reported that he had sold consecutive numbered tickets to a group of Irishmen travelling to Belfast, the Lancashire Police were asked to interview them at Heysham.

The five reached Heysham at 10.45, having spent most of the journey smoking and playing cards and having been observed by a British Rail guard as being in good humour. Paddy Hill was out first, and after showing the contents of his luggage to the waiting police and told them he was going to see his grandmother and aunt in Belfast, he was allowed through to the boat where he settled himself in the bar to wait for the others. They also were interrogated and had their luggage examined. If they were innocent, they knew nothing of the explosions in the two Birmingham pubs; but because of the IRA bombs that had gone off in the Birmingham area in recent months, they said nothing about going to McDade's funeral. Then their clothing was searched, and in Walker's coat were found Roman Catholic mass cards for the funeral of McDade. The local police called up the head of Lancashire CID who ordered the men to be taken to Morecambe police station for further interrogation, and for Dr Frank Skuse to be there with his equipment for detecting traces of explosive. As the four men were being taken away, they asked what had happened to their mate. They were asked what mate, and when they said Paddy Hill, he was taken off the ferry to join them.

If the six were guilty, there are already two things wrong with this scenario. Firstly, as Lord Scarman has pointed out to me, as trained IRA men they would hardly have been so foolish as to set the bombs to explode at a time which they knew would give the police two and a half hours to alert the Lancashire Police to their arrival at Heysham. And secondly, they would not have called the police's attention to the missing Paddy Hill; they would have been glad that at least one of their number looked like getting away.

There is evidence that on the journey to Morecambe all five of the group appeared relaxed which, if innocent, they had every reason to be. On arrival they were put in different cells. In the small hours of the morning Dr Skuse arrived, also Superintendent George Reade from Birmingham and detectives from the West Midland Serious Crime Squad, now disbanded because of misconduct of many of its officers. One by one the five men were escorted in to Dr Skuse to have their hands swabbed in what was called the Griess test, then regarded as a reliable method of detecting nitroglycerine but now, like Dr Skuse himself, considered unreliable. McIlkenny's, Hunter's and Walker's hands proved negative, as did the left hands of Power and Hill. But the right hands of Power and Hill proved positive. This, said Frank Skuse, made him 99 per cent certain that both Power and Hill had recently been in contact with explosives.

Before considering the "confessions" that followed, let us follow the forensic evidence which began with Dr Skuse's findings at Morecambe right through to the final verdict on them at the 1987–8 Court of Appeal. At the trial of the six in Lancaster, Mr Justice Bridge said that the forensic test was one of two "absolutely critical" chapters in the prosecution's case. Yet Skuse in evidence had to admit that when he subjected the traces of Power's and Hill's right hands to two further tests, one of which, the GCMS at Aldermaston, was said to be a hundred times more sensitive than Griess, both registered negative. But he stuck to his 99 per cent certainty of the tests at Morecambe, and added that in the GCMS test a trace from Hill's *left* hand (which was found negative at Morecambe) had also proved positive. However, Dr Hugh Black for the defence said he had seen a print-out of this GCMS test and that it had *not* proved positive.

Nor was that all. In May 1985 the Granada television programme, *World In Action*, invited Mr David Baldock and Dr
Brian Caddy, the two forensic scientists referred to earlier, to
carry out the Griess test on a variety of common substances.
Between them they found that items containing nitro-cellulose,
such as lacquer, aerosol spray, cigarette packets and old playing
cards, all gave Griess positive. It will be remembered that the
men were smoking and playing cards on their journey to Heysham. Asked later if he was surprised that Dr Skuse had been so
certain of his findings at Morecambe, Mr Baldock said he was
amazed. Also asked to comment on Skuse's findings of nitro-
glycerine on the GCMS on Hill's left hand, both he and Dr Black
said that the test had not been properly carried out. "What Skuse
should have told the Court," said Baldock, "was that it did *not*
confirm the presence of nitro-glycerine." This was also the view
of Mr R.A. Hall, Director of the Northern Ireland Forensic
Laboratory and vastly experienced in the science of detecting
explosives.

In the appeal of the Birmingham Six, the evidence of Mr
Baldock and Drs Black and Caddy again clashed head on with
that of Dr Skuse; with the result that the judges found themselves
obliged to admit that "in our judgement the Griess test at
Morecambe *should not be regarded as specific for nitro-glycerine*."
One would have thought that that left all of Dr Skuse's evidence
in ruins. But like shipwrecked sailors on a spar, the judges clung
to Dr Skuse's positive finding on Hill's left hand in the GCMS
test, and indeed found another spar in the evidence of a Dr Janet
Drayton who had conducted the GCMS test with Skuse. But she
would go no further than to say of Hill's left hand, "*possible* ng
present, very small increase".

So on this flimsy edifice and disregarding the evidence of Mr
Baldock and Dr Black that the test had not been properly carried
out, and of Dr Black that when he had seen the GCMS print-out
thirteen years before it had not registered positive, the Court
came up with this:

So far from creating any doubt the fresh evidence on this
topic [Dr Drayton's] makes us sure that Hill's left hand is

proven to have nitro-glycerine upon it, for which there is, and can be no innocent explanation. That conclusion is fatal to the appellants.

Some conclusion!

I should say here that some months after this article was published, I succeeded in tracking down Dr Janet Drayton at her home in Woking with the help of Heather Mills, home affairs correspondent of the *Independent*. I showed her the above extract from the Court's judgment which she had not seen before. She told us that the Court had no business in saying that Hill's left hand was *proved* to have nitro-glycerine on it when she had gone no further than to say it was *possible* (She even thought her findings could have been "a rogue result".) She also said that she could not see how any findings about Hill could have any bearing on the guilt or innocence of the other five. Nor could we. But that is the sort of perverse reasoning we have come to expect from senior judges in recent times.

Let us now turn to the "confessions", the first of which (that of Billy Power) was obtained at Morccambe at about lunchtime on the Friday, and a further three (those of McIlkenny, Walker and Callaghan) on the Saturday after the return of the prisoners to Birmingham. But first it is necessary to look at the background circumstances in which the "confessions" were obtained.

When the news of the pub bombings with their appalling casualties became known, there was hardly a man in Birmingham who would not have been ready and willing, such was their anger, personally to lynch any of those responsible. When the six arrived at Winson Green Prison on remand only three days later, they were beaten up mercilessly both by prison staff and inmates. Even the wives suffered. Sandra Hunter experienced paint and beer glasses being thrown at her house, bangings on the door in the middle of the night, nooses left hanging on the front gate and daubed on the walls the words HANG IRA BASTARDS. And after Theresa Walker had taken her children to Londonderry, their house was broken into and vandalized, the television set and coins from the gas meter stolen.

It would have been extraordinary if the Birmingham police at Morecambe, once the Griess test had shown positive on Power and Hill, had not also felt, and to some degree shown, their sense of outrage and anger. It is well known that when routinely interrogating suspects police invariably simulate belief in their guilt so that, if guilty, the suspects will be encouraged to admit to it. "They have to be certain," Lord Devlin once wrote of police attitudes, "they are no use if they aren't." On this occasion they did not have to simulate certainty: they *were* certain. The scum of the earth, those who had killed and mutilated nearly two hundred people, many of them young girls and boys, had been delivered into their hands; and they had the power to do to them what they wanted.

Yet if we are to believe those who interrogated the Birmingham Six, they did not so much as lay a finger on them. Reading their evidence, one would be entitled to assume that they never even raised their voices, and that all the "confessions" were given freely and voluntarily.

But those arrested told a different story. This is part of Power's, taken from evidence at his trial and after his right hand was proved Griess positive. Two officers called Watson and French led him to an upstairs room.

> As I walked through the door French punched me on the back of the head. I stumbled forward and they both set about me. I was pushed into a chair. They were shouting, "You dirty, murdering IRA bastard. You got gelly on your hands."

They and another officer, said Power, beat him up again, and then French said they would throw him out of the car on the way back to Birmingham, and explain it by saying he was trying to escape.

> Then they started telling me there was a mob outside my home ready to lynch my wife and children. All that was

saving them was the police who were searching it. The only way to save my wife and children was to tell them what they wanted to know.

He was taken to another room where, he said, several more officers set on him:

From all sides I was punched, hit and kicked. When I slid down the wall, I was dragged up by the hair. This was repeated three or four times.

It was at this stage, said Power, that he fouled his trousers. Then one officer said, "Stretch his balls", and another bellowed into his ear, "You'll never have sex with your wife again." "I screamed 'OK OK.' I had to say something to stop them. I couldn't take any more."

Yet even then they hadn't done with him. When he stalled over answering a question, someone shouted, "Throw him out of the fucking window." Power was not to know that the window was sealed. They dragged him over to it, and another officer said, "If the fall doesn't kill him, the crowd will."

Power screamed, "I'll tell you anything you want me to say," and they prepared to write his confession.

The others told broadly similar stories: of being slapped and punched and kicked, and hearing the screams of their friends as they were punched and kicked in other rooms. Hill said he was dragged round the room by his hair, told he would be shot and his body dumped on the motorway, but that if he signed a statement saying he'd planted the bombs, they would stop beating him. Walker said he was punched repeatedly on an operation scar on his stomach, was also told he would be shot and had a gun pressed against his head and the trigger pulled, had a cigarette stubbed out on a blister on his toe. "In the end I became completely deranged."

In the late afternoon the five men, without shoes and socks, were bundled into police cars. Hunter said that as soon as he got in Superintendent Reade, who was smelling of drink, started slapping and punching him. In another car, Walker said that an officer called Kelly who also smelt of drink, head-butted him. In a third car, Hill complained that a Sergeant Bennett whipped his testicles with the leather thong of his truncheon. Later, he said, an Inspector Moore put a revolver into his mouth, "said he was going to blow my fucking head off", pulled the trigger so that it clicked, then laughed.

Although the prisoners were all kept segregated from each other the police maintained that all these stories, so similar in what they claimed, were total inventions; that they did not assault any of them.

Yet worse was to come. Late that Friday night the five were taken to Birmingham's Queens Road police station where they were joined by Hugh Callaghan, and kept there until the Sunday afternoon. During this time they claimed that they were further savagely assaulted, that they were kept awake all Friday night by the bangings of the cell-door hatches and by an Alsatian dog that was made repeatedly to bark at them, that they were continually made to stand up or sit down and that they were continually abused; and that it was this sustained intimidation and violence that led all but Hill and Hunter to sign written "confessions". (These two allegedly gave oral ones.)

The "confessions" themselves were a mass of contradictions and untruths. Three of the four referred to the bombs being carried in plastic bags (in which, only the police knew, previous unexploded bombs had been found). In fact they had no plastic bags with them, and forensic examination of the remains showed that the bombs had been carried in holdalls or briefcases. Callaghan said he put his bomb *outside* the Mulberry Bush on one side and that Hunter had put his *outside* on the other. Forensic evidence showed that the bomb or bombs had been placed *inside* the pub. Despite Callaghan's claim that he and Hunter had bombed the Mulberry Bush, Walker claimed that Hunter had been with him bombing the Tavern. Callaghan said there were six bombs, Walker and McIlkenny said three.

Subsequently all six denied the voluntariness of the confessions. Callaghan said, "I was in a state of shock. I do not know what I said. They said things to me. I agreed. At the end one of the officers put a pen in my right hand, placed it over the paper

and guided my hand as I signed." Similar assertions were made
by the Guildford Four.

At their trial neither judge nor jury believed the allegations of
beatings or disbelieved the "confessions". With amazing naivety
Mr Justice Bridge spoke of the allegations against the police as
being "of the most bizarre and grotesque character". If the
defendants were telling the truth, he said, "I would have to
suppose that a team of fifteen officers had conspired among
themselves to use violence on the prisoners and to fabricate
evidence." Poor innocent, he did not seem the least aware that
when the police feel sure they have the right man or men, this sort
of conduct is not unusual: there was no need for a conspiracy
because everyone reacted spontaneously. He concluded, "All the
police officers who gave their evidence of the circumstances in
which the statements were taken, impressed me as being straightforward and honest witnesses." But this is how they are trained to
appear; that is how they were with the Guildford Four; that is
why they lie and lie and know they will be believed.

In November 1977 the six men brought a civil action against
the police and the Home Office for injuries they had received
while in police custody; for fresh evidence they were relying on
the findings of a Dr David Paul, a former police surgeon and City
of London coroner, and a specialist in the interpretation of
injuries from photographs. Shown enlarged photographs of the
six taken while they were in custody at Queens Road, he found
signs of injuries on all.

The action was allowed and application made for legal aid. But
the police appealed and in an uncharacteristically depraved
judgement Lord Denning upheld them. If the action were to
succeed, he said, it would show evidence of police perjury and
violence, and the six might have to be pardoned; this was such an
appalling vista that the action could not be allowed to proceed; ie
better that the six rot in jail than to find there had been police
wrongdoing.

But the supporters of the six, including some of the media,
continued to press their case; and in December 1986 a retired
police officer by the name of Tom Clarke, who had been at
Queens Road at the material time, appeared on Granada Tele-

vision to say what he had seen and heard there. Seven weeks later
the Home Secretary announced that he was sending the case back
to the Court of Appeal and was ordering an inquiry into it by the
Devon and Cornwall Police.

At the Appeal hearing Clarke confirmed the prisoners' claims
of police intimidation and ill-treatment, even admitting that he
himself had joined in verbal abuse of the prisoners ('I was thrilled
to know we had got the right people"). He supported what they
had said about being kept awake all night, the dog barking at
them, the cell-door hatches being banged up and down, their
being made to stand up or sit down. He described one prisoner,
whose blanket had slipped from him, as having on his stomach a
red weal turning bluish and measuring about six inches by four.
"He had been hit so badly that, although I wanted to see him
dead, I was worried about him. He had had the hell of a hefty
thump." When he went off duty at 5.30 a.m. on the Saturday
morning he said, the prisoners were "scared out of their wits";
and when he came back on duty that night, he observed puffiness
over and under their eyes and red faces. "They had", he told the
Court, "been hammered." By the time he left on the Sunday
morning, the prisoners were "all in a petrified state, all physical
wrecks" . . . an observation which the photographs of them taken
at Queens Road tend to confirm.

Tom Clarke knew when he came to give evidence that he would
be discredited as a witness for having been dismissed from the
police force for having stolen £5 from a prisoner. He contests that
verdict, and having read his papers on the case and spoken to him,
I would say there could be a doubt in the matter (it was his word
against another's). But he was supported in his Appeal Court
evidence by a former member of his first-aid team, a Sergeant
Brierley, who said that Clarke had told him within weeks or
months of the bombings that cell doors had been banged, the
prisoners had been kept standing up and that police dogs had
been let into the cell block to bark at them. Another former
policeman, Paul Berry, also told the Court of having called in at
Queens Road at this time on a routine matter and seeing in the
cell block a prisoner "whose left eye and lip were puffed and
swollen".

Yet the most impressive witness for the appellants was Joyce Lynas, who was on duty at Queens Road as a police cadet. She gave evidence to the Court on two occasions. On the first she said that on arrival the prisoners were pushed through her office to the cells fairly roughly and had been called "fucking bastards" and "murdering bastards". She also remembered the dog inside the cell block and the cell-door hatches being banged up and down. But she denied having witnessed any prisoners being assaulted.

But a few days later she was back in court to say that she *had* witnessed a prisoner being assaulted. Asked why she had not said so at her first appearance, she said that she had been frightened off by two telephone conversations: the first in the summer when she rang Queens Road to enquire about the *bona fides* of the Devon and Cornwall inquiry and was told by an officer to whom she was put through, "You know what you saw and heard, but remember we have families", and the second, an anonymous call to her home before the hearing began, "Don't forget that you have children." However on the Saturday after her first appearance, she had seen a television programme about bullying in the army and people not reporting it, and after talking to her husband and her minister, she volunteered to return to court, even though it meant having to admit to perjury. This required the same sort of courage as I had witnessed at the trial of Stephen Ward when Ronna Ricardo, having been blackmailed by the police into saying at the Magistrates' Court that Ward had procured clients for her, refused to substantiate it at his trial.

And what new evidence did Joyce Lynas have to offer? Quite simply that when she took tea to officers who were interviewing the prisoners in a room upstairs, she saw two officers holding one by the arms while a third kneed him in the groin. As she entered she heard the third man say, "This is what we do to fucking, murdering bastards," and what she called "other vile words". In court she declined to say what these were, but when I asked her, she told me: "You won't be having sex with your wife again because I'm going to put your balls where your brains are." I asked if she was certain about this, and she said that it was not the kind of thing you could forget.

There was other confirmatory evidence of the prisoners having been beaten up. Prison officer Brian Sharp of Winson Green was on duty when they arrived at the prison on the Monday morning. He said that when Walker undressed, "his torso from the neck to the middle had numerous amounts of bruising, purple, blackish, some had tinges of yellow", which he thought were a day or two old. At the trial of the six, another officer called Murtagh confirmed this, speaking of "a long yellowing bruise" running from Walker's waist up across the front of his ribs, and which he thought was two or three days old. Sharp thought the injuries so bad that he telephoned for a hospital officer to come down and examine them.

And then the former Superintendent Reade appeared, the man who had arrested the six at Morecambe and claimed never to have touched them, and had to admit that later in his career he had led a party of officers on a raid in a house at Walsall at which a Mr Buckley had, in Reade's presence, been punched, kicked and thrown down the stairs; and Mr Reade had to admit that later Mr Buckley had sued the police and been awarded £800. Mr Reade was also found to have altered a document relating to interviews with the six; and Dr Skuse, too, admitted to altering certain timings at the police's request.

And how did the three Appeal Court judges respond to the overwhelming evidence that over a period of three days the appellants had been assaulted and intimidated by the police and that their "confessions" were therefore no longer tenable? Until 1966 it was obligatory on the Court of Appeal when reaching a decision about new evidence, to put themselves in the minds of the original trial jury and say what verdict they might have given in the light of the totality of all the evidence, old and new. This is the course which Lord Devlin thinks should have been taken; and had the three judges done so, they must surely have said that doubts in the minds of the jury would have led to acquittals for all six. But the judges, as they are now entitled to, took it on themselves to decide the truth of the facts – an unfortunate decision for, as lawyers and others have pointed out, judges are notoriously shaky when it comes to assessing the facts.

Those who attended the court, and in particular the appellants' counsel, said it was clear from the start that the judges had made up their minds that the appeals were not going to succeed, although even they had not bargained for the manner in which their witnesses would be rubbished. This is what the judges said of them:

Tom Clarke: "a most unconvincing witness and an embittered man. His motive was . . . at first at least to make money and secondly to blacken the reputation of the West Midlands Police Force." (A year later the reputation of the West Midlands Serious Crime Squad had become so blackened that it had to be disbanded.) Whatever Mr Clarke's motives, the judges did not seem to have asked themselves the only question that mattered: were his observations, corroborated by the appellants, true?

Paul Berry: who had glimpsed a prisoner with a puffed and swollen face, was "mistaken". But how could he have been mistaken? All the cells in the cell blocks were occupied by the appellants: there were no other prisoners there.

Brian Sharp: who had said that Walker's body was covered with bruises on his arrival at Winson Green, was, the judges said, trying to conceal or minimize the violence that prison staff and inmates had inflicted on the prisoners and so "forfeited any credibility that he might otherwise have had". But Sharp had no motive to conceal anything: he had been tried for assaulting the appellants and been acquitted. And again, was his evidence true? If the bruises he and Murtagh saw were coloured yellow, purple and black, they must have been a day or two old and therefore incurred at Queens Road rather than Winson Green.

Joyce Lynas: the writer Robert Kee was in court on the day of her second appearance. He wrote in *The Times* that the way in which she gave her evidence "was so totally convincing that had I been a member of a jury asked to judge her credibility there would have been no question in my mind that she was speaking anything but the truth, or that in consequence very considerable doubt attached to the validity of the men's confessions." Richard Ferguson, QC, agreed: "Anyone who heard her give evidence must have known she was speaking the truth." But the judges described her as "a witness not worthy of belief" and her reasons for changing her story "not acceptable". Mrs Lynas is a committed Christian whose character while in the police force was assessed as "Exemplary" and she was upset and angered by these attacks on her integrity. "I did not have to go back," she told me. "I went because I felt I ought to, and I told the absolute truth."

For the judges to declare, in the light of all they had heard, that the original verdicts were *safe* and *satisfactory* seems to me both an abuse of the English language and an insult to anyone's intelligence. So why did they do it? The harsh truth is that just as the CID have corrupted themselves by their readiness to fabricate evidence against those who they have wrongly convinced themselves are guilty, so the judges, otherwise honourable men, have also corrupted themselves by refusing to recognize police fabrication, even when it is staring them in the face.

All that is new about this is that cases like the Guildford Four and the Maguire Seven and the disbandment of the West Midlands Serious Crimes Squad have brought the corruption to the surface. But it is an old story. "British justice is in ruins," said Lord Denning after the release of the Guildford Four. But it had been in ruins for a long time. Judges at trials of first instance, as well as judges in the Appeal Court, have consistently refused to entertain the ideas of police fabrication unless it is so clear cut that they have no alternative. And every judicial inquiry into miscarriages of justice in recent years – Scott Henderson and Brabin in the two Evans inquiries, Fisher in the Confait inquiry, Hawser in the Hanratty inquiry, Hunter in the Meehan inquiry, as well as Lawton and Roskill in the fourth Luton appeal, Roskill at the appeal of the Guildford Four and again of the Maguire Seven – all have preferred to accept dubious police evidence rather than give the people concerned a clean bill of health; and in so doing they have done both themselves and British justice a grave disservice. Lord Hunter spoke for them all when he wrote, "Reliance is rightly placed on the integrity and competence of police officers." He could not bring himself to believe that the police in question had planted incriminating evidence in a dead man's pocket.

It can, I think, only be a matter of time before the Home Secretary decides that it is time for the ordeal of the Birmingham Six to end and for them to receive proper compensation for all their years inside. And when that has happened, the three judges who had the evidence and power to open the prison gates for them and yet failed to do so, and in whose judgment not only the public but some members of their own profession have lost faith, might care, as honourable men, to consider their position. For collectively they have gravely undermined confidence in British justice.

Towards the end of 1990 and as a result of fresh evidence obtained by the Devon and Cornwall Police, the case was once again referred back to the Court of Appeal. As with the appeal of the Guildford Four, the Director of Public Prosecutions [DPP] announced that he would not contest the case, but unlike that of the Guildford Four, the three judges appointed to hear the case decided that they wished to hear the new evidence which, according to the DPP, made the convictions unsafe.

The appeal was heard at the Old Bailey between 4 and 14 March 1991, and was based on two grounds, both forensic. The first was the final discrediting of Dr Skuse's Griess test which expert evidence said was not and never had been specific for nitro-glycerine. When writing my *Sunday Times* piece I had omitted to say that Dr Hugh Black, the former Chief Explosives officer for the Home Office had in fact said this for the defence at the trial. But Mr Justice Bridge had clung to Dr Skuse's findings as though they were holy writ and told Dr Black in no uncertain terms that his opinions were worthless and he was wasting the court's time. Further expert evidence at the appeal supported Dr Black's trial evidence that Dr Drayton's findings on the GCMS test had not proved positive, and in the witness-box she herself confirmed what she had said to me about her findings possibly being "a rogue result".

The second piece of new forensic evidence concerned what has been called the Electrostatic Document Analysis test, or ESDA, which showed that some police officers' statements of interviews with the accused were not contemporaneous as they had claimed at the trial but had been written at different times on different pads with different pens, and that some parts had been added to or altered afterwards; and an interview which the police claimed to have had with McIlkenny was denied by McIlkenny as ever having taken place. Faced with both these heads of new evidence, the judges concluded that had they been available to the trial jury, they must have made a considerable impact. The convictions therefore were unsafe and unsatisfactory, and the appeals would be allowed.

For me one of the most refreshing aspects of the appeal was that, with the Crown having conceded defeat, this was the nearest I had seen in a British court to the inquisitorial system as practised on the continent. In contrast to the impatience and hostility displayed by Lord Lane at the previous appeal, the three judges here (Lloyd, Mustill, Far-quharson) really did want to understand what was being put to them, and for the appellants Mr Michael Mansfield, QC, guided them most skilfully through the maze of highly tech-nical forensic evidence. The only sour note came at the end of the submissions when Mr Graham Boal, QC for the Crown, powerless to challenge the new forensic evidence, solemnly told the judges that *circumstantial evidence alone* would have been sufficient to secure convictions against all six. This was not only dotty and untrue but, said in the presence of six men who he knew had just endured sixteen years of wrongful imprisonment, extremely distasteful. But that is the adversar-ial system for you: in an inquisitorial system such a submis-sion would not be made.

I was sorry that Mr Mansfield did not raise the matter of the Six's allegations that their "confessions" had been beaten out of them by the police, as this partly enabled the judges to belittle the claim by saying there was no evidence that they had suffered any injuries before their first appearance in court, and then to join with Lord Lane's rubbishing of the witnesses at the 1987 appeal who said they *had* seen evidence of injuries inflicted on the Six when they were at Birmingham's Queens Road police station. The new evidence had shown that the Six were not guilty as charged, and if they were not guilty as charged, what other explanation could there be of their "confessions" – which were detailed, varied and contradictory – than that they were beaten out of them by the police?

Afterwards the judgement of Lord Lane and his colleagues in the 1987 appeal was seen to have been so crass and to have so undermined public confidence in the administration of criminal justice that there were many calls for his resignation. *The Times* urged him to take early retirement and more than 140 MPs signed a motion calling on the Queen to remove him from office; but he gave not the slightest indication that he intended to do other than remain where he was; and he would presumably have considered any sort of apology for his ineptitude, *infra dig*. Yet one cannot think of any other profession or business where had the managing director been guilty of similar incompetence (in this instance a further three years incarceration for six innocent men) he would not have been faced with a call for his immediate resignation or dismissal.

Predictably the legal establishment closed ranks. The Lord Chancellor, who had earlier described my *Sunday Times* article as "clamour", made soothing noises about judicial integrity. The Attorney-General said that all judges do is to see that the rules are kept, while former judges such as Sir Frederick Lawton were quick to point out that it is not they but juries who reach verdicts and judges can only be as good as the evidence put before them – conveniently forgetting that judges do not hesitate to discount good evidence they don't agree with, as Bridge did at the trial of the Birmingham Six, as Lane did at their appeal, and as Lawton himself did at one of the Luton appeals. The *Independent* summed it up:

> Instead of taking a hard look at its own failings, the Court of Appeal has sought to exculpate itself. There could be no clearer evidence that judges are temperamentally inclined to protect the legal system rather than the lives of those with

whom it deals. To them the dignity of the law too often
seems to be more important than justice itself.

Thankfully the Home Secretary realized that after the cases of the
Guildford Four, the Maguire Seven and the Birmingham Six,
things could not be allowed to continue as before and announced
the appointment of a Royal Commission under Lord Runciman
to inquire into the whole criminal justice system; and to make
every effort to report within two years.

I cannot think of any public pronouncement in recent times
which has given me so much satisfaction. Indeed, with the real
possibility it brings of change, I see it as a justification of part of
my life's work.

*The Birmingham Six were released in March 1991 by the Court of
Appeal, which concluded that the prosecution's scientific evidence
and confessions taken under duress failed to meet British legal
standards. Two years later, the Royal Commission on Criminal
Justice under Lord Runciman produced a long string of recommended
reforms. But critics complained that subsequent legislation put into
effect proposals favourable to the prosecution, and largely ignored
those that favoured the defence. Furthermore, it was argued, the new
measures seriously encroached on the defendant's right to silence.*

THE MYSTERY OF THE FLYING BLOOD

(Dr Sam Sheppard, USA 1954)

Leo Grex

The questions and curiosities in the Sheppard affair have established it as one of the most celebrated murder cases in American history. Dr Sam Sheppard was accused of killing his wife Marilyn, apparently striking her twenty-seven times on the head with a blunt surgical instrument while she was asleep. Sheppard himself blamed the murder on a "bushy-haired intruder" who knocked him unconscious at their home in suburban Cleveland. The bedroom was ransacked and steeped in blood. Sheppard was an immediate suspect and soon arrested. At his trial, an affair with another woman (which he had denied at first) was suggested as the motive for murdering his wife. He was convicted of second-degree murder and sentenced to life imprisonment. But in 1966, aided by his lawyer F. Lee Bailey, Dr Sheppard secured a retrial. Bailey dismissed the prosecution case as "ten pounds of hogwash in a five pound bag". This time, the jury was persuaded of Sheppard's innocence and acquitted him, after an expert reassessed the blood evidence. The case of Dr Sheppard inspired the 1960s TV series The Fugitive. *The author here is Leo Grex, one of several aliases used by Leonard Gribble (1908–86), one of the most prolific British crime writers of all time. As well as producing a torrent of detective fiction, Leonard Gribble wrote nearly seventy factual books on crime and detection, invariably collections of cases with such gung-ho titles as* Famous Stories of Scientific Detection *and* They Had A Way With Women. *"The*

*most appropriate description of Gribble's non-fiction," declared one
critic, "would be that it is enthralling and entertaining; concentrat-
ing as he often does upon the stranger aspects of crime and the more
bizarre cases of murder, they certainly hold the imagination."*

One of the strangest mysteries of America in the fifties was
undoubtedly that of the man most Americans thought of as Dr
Sam after his incredible story had received coast-to-coast publicity. It had resulted in two widely reported trials of sensational
interest for the murder of his wife Marilyn. At least one major
film had been made of the story and several books written about
the mystery, and today, years after Sam Sheppard's death, there
are many who feel that the last word has not been said on the
subject of what happened on a very windy day in July 1954.

It was July 3rd when Dr Sheppard, a popular man of considerable personal charm as well as professional standing as an
osteopath among the people of Bay Village, a small community on
the shores of Lake Erie, decided to mark the forthcoming 4th of
July celebrations with a party for his friends the Aherns. The
visitors consisted of Don Ahern and his wife Nancy and their
children. Like the Sheppards they lived only a short distance
away in West Lake Road, where their garden plot ran down to a
private beach.

It was decided that the Aherns should come to the Sheppards
as Dr Sam, as everyone called him familiarly, had to attend a call
at the local hospital and couldn't get away again for about an
hour. The womenfolk elected to get dinner and wait for him.

The Aherns arrived at about six o'clock, when Marilyn told
Chip, the Sheppards' young son of six, to go out and play with the
Ahern children, leaving the adults to their drinks and gossip.

They all seemed relaxed. Later the two women finished preparing a summer meal while their husbands sauntered down to
the nearby beach after Sam had returned from his hospital visit.

"These white-caps won't make it very smooth for skiing across
the lake," Sam Sheppard mused, watching curling breakers
washing the sand bordering a steep embankment. "There's

another hospital picnic fixed for tomorrow, and if this wind keeps up I don't fancy their chances for a ski run."

Ahern agreed.

"That's the best of sticking to golf," he grinned. "At least you can't drown."

When dinner was announced Don Ahern collected his children and took them home to put them to bed. Then he returned to the women and Dr Sam and the two couples settled down in the comfortable lounge. Chip had already been put to bed. Sheppard switched on the television and tuned to a film, but his eyes drooped. He had performed a tricky operation earlier and felt sleepy. His head slipped back on the couch. The film ended at twelve-thirty and Marilyn, who was four months pregnant, felt as tired as Sam looked.

"I can hardly keep my eyes open," she apologized to the Aherns.

"Well, it's high time we were making tracks," said Nancy. "I'll just look in on the children – oh, and that reminds me, Marilyn," – she went on. "Make sure you latch and chain the front door. One can't be too careful about taking precautions, as I keep telling Don."

Marilyn nodded and said goodnight to her guests, patted her mouth to smother a yawn, and then stood waving to them as she closed the front door. The latch clicked and she switched off the light.

Five hours later a 'phone rang in the home of Bay Village's mayor, Spencer Houk, which was only three houses away from the Sheppard residence.

He woke and scowled at the insistent instrument and threw back the bedclothes.

"Who the devil is it at this hour?" he demanded irritably.

A voice he could only with difficulty recognize as Sam Sheppard's called urgently, "Get over here quick, Spence. My God, they've killed Marilyn!"

"Who – what –" the roused mayor stammered and broke off, for Sheppard had already slammed down the receiver and the only sound was the broken bleeping of the familiar dialling tone.

His wife had already been roused, and the pair, now wide

awake, hurriedly scrambled into their clothes and in little more than ten minutes arrived at the Sheppards' front door, which they found unlocked and wide. It was first light, and on the floor of the hall the mayor saw a doctor's bag which had been up-ended with its contents spilled across the carpet. Sam Sheppard was slumped down in an easy chair by a desk in his den.

"What's this all about, Sam?" inquired the mayor, looking at his wife in puzzlement.

Sheppard groaned, shaking his head.

"I don't know," he said, the words clearing. "But someone ought to look at Marilyn."

Esther Houk climbed the stairs to the first floor, while her husband was taking stock of observable details. Three drawers from the desk had been stacked on the floor and Sam Sheppard was clad only in socks, shoes, and slacks. His torso was bare. As he stepped into the living-room Houk glimpsed a tan corduroy jacket on a settee or couch and saw that the drawers of another desk had been pulled out and a pile of papers was strewn across the floor.

He was interrupted by his wife's hurrying feet on the stairs.

"Get the police!" she called. "And get an ambulance – only hurry!"

The mayor snatched up the 'phone and alerted the police. He then rang Dr Richard Sheppard, Sam's eldest brother, who lived only a short distance away. Uniformed officers were quickly at the scene, and the mayor accompanied them to the bedroom at the top of the stairs, where they found Marilyn lying battered in a blood-soaked bed. More than a dozen heavy blows had smashed her skull, destroying her head. Her face, arms, and upper body had also been bludgeoned. She was sprawled on her back, with her legs dangling over the bed's foot. A stained sheet partly covered the remains. The body was clad in pyjamas, one leg free of the trousers and the top tugged down. There was a copious amount of blood. The brother of Dr Sam took only a few moments to inform the police that his sister-in-law was dead. He was clearly shocked by the brutality of the crime, which was destined to become one of the most notorious mysteries of the age.

Meantime, Dr Sam had collapsed and was removed to hospital, while young Chip, who had slept through his mother's murder, was dressed and hurriedly taken to the home of another of the Sheppard brothers, Dr Stephen Sheppard.

Then the police began their questioning. They heard from the Aherns of the informal party which continued until after midnight, when Nancy Ahern herself secured the door into the yard on the Lake Erie side of the house.

"Marilyn was asleep on her feet. In fact, they both were," she admitted. "I believe Sam went to sleep on the couch, which was why Marilyn didn't waken him. He was bushed after a long day at the hospital."

Dr Sam, the Aherns said, had gone home wearing a white T-shirt, slacks, and the corduroy jacket. They said he was frequently sleepy and given to dozing because of his long hours in the hospital. To the police, after listening to the Aherns' story, it seemed a case of a burglar being disturbed by Marilyn Sheppard and being viciously struck down to prevent an alarm being raised. But a rational enlargement suggested that Dr Sam had been awakened by his wife. He then ran to her aid and was struck down by the intruder, who was by then anxious only to escape.

The coroner agreed with the enlargement when the husband explained that he had been awakened by his wife's cries of "Sam! Sam!" He had rushed upstairs and was met by a blow on the back of the head.

"I was rendered unconscious," he told Dr Samuel Gerber.

He had no idea how long he remained unconscious, but it could not have been long for he came to when he heard a noise in the living-room and ran back downstairs in time to see what he said was "a form" running towards the disturbed waters of the lake. He gave chase to a beach hut where he confronted the mystery man. They struggled and he was knocked down, losing consciousness again and coming to with his face in the lake and his legs in deeper water. When he collected his scattered wits he groped his way back to the house, climbed the stairs, and discovered the horror of the battered Marilyn.

He could hardly credit what had happened and he was incoherent when he rang Houk, but he could not say how long had

passed in that wild interval. Later he varied his dramatic story.
He told a couple of Cleveland detectives from his hospital bed on
the Sunday morning that he now thought there had been two
intruders, one who attacked Marilyn Sheppard and a second man
who had hammered himself. While recovering consciousness at
the head of the stairs he saw his wallet on the floor. In it were
three dollar bills and three twenty-dollar notes. When the detectives withdrew he lay listening to the noises of a typical Fourth
of July Sunday when everyone seemed to be *en fête*, except the
doctor who had lost a wife. His head ached and he fell asleep.

It was Larry Houk, the mayor's son, who made an early find.
In some scrub not far from the lake he came upon a green bag
containing Dr Sam's automatic winding watch. There were
several water drops under the wrist-watch's glass and several
dried spots of blood on the band. The green bag, which usually
held tools for the doctor's outboard motor, also contained his
key-chain and signet ring. The contents of this bag had been
spilled on to the floor of the den in the Sheppards' home, and
among them lay Marilyn's watch, stained with blood. There was
more money in the den and other sums in an upstairs room.

But one seeming discrepancy puzzled the police. The Aherns
had reported that Sam Sheppard had gone to sleep wearing a T-
shirt under his tan jacket. But when he summoned the Houks he
had been stripped naked from the waist up. The corduroy jacket
had been neatly folded on the couch.

The detectives broadened their inquiries, but did so discreetly.
They had learned that Sam and Marilyn Sheppard had been
childhood sweethearts, but that a red-headed hospital technician
called Susan Hayes had attracted the doctor's roving eye until she
had left Bay Village in February to secure a post in Los Angeles.
A month later the Sheppards journeyed to California to attend an
osteopathic convention Dr Sam felt was important to his career.
But when Sheppard said he had not indulged in an affair with the
redhead, it was Susan Hayes who revealed that she had spent a
week with him in Los Angeles while Marilyn was staying with
another doctor's family near Oakland, some four hundred miles
away. Sheppard had bought a watch for the redhead to replace
one she had lost at a wedding party attended by both of them. He

had also bought her a ring, and she said she had been Dr Sam's lover for more than a year.

While the threads of the Sheppard episode in California were being woven and taking shape Detectives Schottke and Careau in Cleveland were getting down to further details. They asked Sheppard how badly he had been hurt.

"My brother can tell you," said the man whose wife had been murdered brutally. "I'm told that my neck is broken."

Stephen Sheppard said that an X-ray plate revealed that a vertebrae joint in his brother's neck was chipped and that he was suffering from shock and bruises.

"It is possible," he told the police, "that he has suffered brain injury."

At the best it wasn't conclusive.

The post-mortem had given the time of death as somewhere between three and four in the morning, and Sheppard's self-winding watch had stopped at four-fifteen. On the Monday the Cleveland pair returned to ask the man in the hospital bed if he could recall any further details of the man he had chased towards the lake.

Sheppard shook his head and said, "Only that he was a biggish man with bushy hair."

Stephen Sheppard came into the room at this point. He looked serious as he informed his listeners that he had retained counsel for his brother.

"So I can't allow you to ask any further questions," he told the detectives, who shared a glance and withdrew in silence.

A few days later Sheppard, wearing a surgical collar, left the hospital to attend his wife's funeral; he avoided both Press and police. In fact his avoidance of anything in the nature of news or publicity so annoyed the coroner that Gerber threatened him with a subpoena. Possibly due to this on July 10th Sam Sheppard signed a nine-page formal statement in which he stated that his wife "may have tried to awaken him and get him to go to bed." But he was not sure, he said, for he remained on the couch, until he was roused by her cries and heard her moaning. He ran upstairs, sure that she was suffering from a convulsion of the sort she had had in the early days of her pregnancy. But then he was given a blow on the head, which rendered him unconscious until he came to beside Marilyn's bed.

"I looked at my wife," he related. "I believe I felt her pulse and felt that she was gone."

He looked into Chip's room and found him still sleeping, but when he heard a noise downstairs he turned and gave chase. However, the man landed a blow that knocked the doctor out.

Probed about the Sheppards' home life, he claimed it was ideal and firmly denied ever becoming enraged and angry with Marilyn when discussing what he called marital problems. All the same, it was obvious that the questions were becoming more pointed and penetrating the longer the process of asking and answering continued.

"Do you know of any reason why someone else would take her life?" was one rapier-like thrust from which Sheppard flinched visibly.

He wiped his mouth.

"Possibly," he said uncertainly. "I have heard of individuals who are maniacal enough that when they start something, an act like that, it becomes a compulsion." Then more certainly he added, "She has spurned lovers, potential lovers."

There was sudden silence while the coroner considered what had been said.

"How many of these potential lovers did she have?"

"Three I know of, and I am pretty sure more. I am certain that there were more."

While notes were being transcribed he suddenly seemed to take a mental plunge. He named three men. One was Spencer Houk, a second was Dr Hoversten, and the third a distant relative of Marilyn Sheppard. The unravelling threads explained, at least partially, several new facts. For instance, on the 3rd of July it was established that Sam Sheppard had been both preoccupied and morose, but on the 4th, the day of the murder, Dr Hoversten had hastened to Bay Village to express his commiseration with the appalling news of the tragedy. The police had quietly checked his alibi. It could not be faulted. Nor could the alibis of both Houk and Marilyn's relative.

By this time the police were indulging in fresh thoughts about the crime, and a growing query was expressed by them about the possible motive of a husband who could have slaughtered his wife so brutally. For one thing was not explained away. Why had someone apparently taken the trouble to remove so many smudged fingerprints in the Sheppards' home? Who was incriminated and why was a trail of blood cleaned up, howbeit not very thoroughly?

After a further discussion with the police and Dr Gerber the latter announced that a formal inquest would be heard on the 22nd of July. By this time the case was accumulating vast public interest throughout the Middle West, and Sam Sheppard swore on oath that he had not been guilty of murdering his wife nor had he indulged in a love affair with Susan Hayes.

But there was, the police learned, evidence to refute this latter claim and the story of Sheppard's week spent in Susan Hayes's company and the watch lost at a wedding party became current news. The case widened into the dimensions of a *cause célébre* when Sam Sheppard was arrested for murder and charged. Then began a three-month period before the hearing of the trial in October 1954. The police were busy checking on likely clues, "To sew up the case," as the District Attorney explained to impatient newsmen.

However, there was a good deal of speculation about the merits of the case, and a good many people believed that the popular Dr Sam would be able to clear his name of all imputation in the sordid crime, and as month followed month into the autumn the arguments as to the complicity or otherwise of the doctor grew more voluble and heated.

At last, with the concentrated and riveted gaze of America on the figure of Dr Sam seated at his counsel's table, the trial opened on the 18th of October. The court was crowded to hear the opening words by Judge Edward Blythin, but it did not take long for the first dramatic development. It was provided by the prosecution's first witness, who was Dr Lester Adelson, the deputy coroner. He began by showing a series of colour slides on a screen, including photographs of the terrible wounds inflicted on the victim's smashed head.

They brought an audible gasp from the persons in court, who after showing their revulsion turned to stare at the defendant. Sam Sheppard's shoulders were seen to quiver and tremble beneath the fabric of his neat blue serge. He resolutely turned his gaze away from the slides. Seconds later he broke into convulsive sobbing. But Dr Adelson continued and paid no attention to the side-drama. Using a ruler, he pointed out the thirty-five wounds for the jurors' benefit as he admitted there had been no sex attack on the victim, but turned to declare that "the cause of death is plain enough".

There was utter silence in the court.

Sheppard's counsel, Attorney William J. Corrigan, rose to cross-examine the witness and a wrangle ensued. Adelson admitted that there had been no microscopic study of the various wounds, neither had there been a toxicologist's examination of the victim's internal organs. He made the point that seven gashes in her forehead were just one inch apart and parallel, and he developed the argument that death had been caused by a seven-pronged instrument, and then he insinuated that Marilyn could have been poisoned, and even that she might have drowned in her own blood.

By this time the court was sitting erect.

"It's all circumstantial," he declared waspishly, and said he intended to question every statement made by the prosecution.

The spectators settled down for an intensive session.

Attorney Corrigan claimed he knew what the murder weapon was, but was careful not to define it; he said that a four-month-old male foetus taken from Marilyn's body was not buried with her, but possibly it was for further use in the examination. The cross-examination ground on.

So did the arguments.

For instance, the prosecution insisted that if Sheppard had indeed been knocked out and left unconscious on the beach on a night of growing storm conditions, he would have drowned. But it was Spencer Houk's telling of the 'phone call that produced a real surprise. He claimed that when Richard Sheppard first told Sam that Marilyn was dead the elder brother asked a curious question.

"He said either, 'Did you do this?' or 'Did you have anything to do with this?' and Sam replied, 'Hell, no!'" Houk told the court.

He also claimed that on the day before the inquest he said to Sheppard, "If you did this crime come out and say you did. If it was done by you, it was done in a fit of rage. If you did it, all your family and friends will be behind you."

Sheppard's reply was a dogged, "I couldn't have done it."

However, the defence attorney mounted a special attack on the coroner, whom he claimed had disregarded many clues pointing to Sheppard's innocence. But Dr Gerber came up with a surprise of his own and produced a ghoulish exhibit, a bloodstained pillow removed from the slain woman's bed. He said he had found an impression of a two-bladed instrument, which he said must have been the murder weapon. But the surgical instrument, or whatever it was, had been removed and the pillow turned over. But in contrast, Marilyn's wrist-watch had not been taken off until the blood had dried. In view of Sheppard's claim to have followed the intruder to the beach it seemed extremely unlikely that he would in the circumstances have removed his wife's watch and left it in the den. The case was assuming improbables. Also some snide remarks.

For instance, when Corrigan had asked of the coroner whether there had at any time been a projected divorce and he had replied, "Yes, sir," he had rejoined, "Well, you're divorced, aren't you?"

There had been instant objection by the prosecutor.

"He was asking about divorce," said Corrigan with mock-mildness.

"But his wife wasn't killed," snapped the prosecutor.

"And Dr Sam didn't kill his wife," shouted the defence attorney.

It was a ding-dong legal battle until Susan Hayes appeared, dressed demurely, and related events that occurred in California. She stated in a low voice that she had never seen Sheppard lose his temper, that she had always been aware that he was a married man, and that he only used the word "love" in signing her letters, when he inscribed them, "Love, Sam". Corrigan took the legal bull by the horns and moved for a direct acquittal. But the motion was denied by the judge, and so Dr Stephen Sheppard took the stand as the first of the defence's witnesses, and said, "Sam is the most level-headed one in our family. I have never seen him rise in anger. I have never seen him speak in any way to indicate that he had lost his head. As a child, when he got into arguments, he always refrained from fighting."

He contested the prosecution's evidence at almost every turn, flatly denying that his brother's jacket had been carefully folded and placed on the couch. It had been flung down on the floor. He contended also that his brother had suffered a spinal contusion in his grappling with the intruder, and insisted that police photographs of his sister-in-law's body while on the bed showed both her clothing and an arm in postures and positions different from those he noted upon first seeing her and when he saw her a short time later.

However, on the following day he wavered in cross-examination. Thomas Parrino, the assistant prosecutor, forced him to admit that he had "erred somewhat" in his testimony about the position of the body, but he hedged about the photographs and their actual position. His defensive stand was a prelude to the defendant taking the stand to give his own testimony, which the assembled court awaited with bated breath.

For here was the crux of mystery.

Would the defendant's testimony prove him to be innocent or otherwise?

Garbed in a dark grey suit with a white shirt, and wearing a sober-hued knitted tie, Dr Sam Sheppard turned and addressed his words to the jury. He spoke in a sequence of what many felt were stilted sentences and phrases interspersed with hesitant pauses, so that he cannot be said to have made the best impression on his listeners.

An example was when he referred to his hurry to bring help to his calling wife. The words he chose in such a threatening and dramatic moment fraught with danger sounded contrived and not spontaneous.

"I initiated an attempt," he said, wiping dry lips, "to gather enough senses to navigate the stairs."

Small wonder the jury and other members of the court stared at him with a frown. It was as though he was speaking of a stranger. He told the court that his marriage had always been an ideal one and that he was a man who had welcomed his wife's second pregnancy, refuting all suggestion that he had not wanted the baby.

He was given some help at times by Attorney Corrigan in painting a glowing and warm picture of his marital life with a loving son and contented wife, whom he had no reason to harm. But Parrino, the assistant prosecutor, spoiled the effect of this picture. He asked a number of questions all directed to get Sheppard to admit that it was Marilyn's attacker whom he chased down the stairs and out of the house.

"I had that sensation," was the way Sam Sheppard put it.

But Parrino wanted more than a sensation.

"Did you make any effort to get a weapon?" he demanded.

"No, sir."

"Did you make an outcry?"

"I may have," said Sheppard, hedging again. "I don't know. I have never gone after anyone with a weapon."

Suddenly Parrino changed direction.

"Isn't it a fact that you slapped your wife that morning?"

Again came the flat negative. "No, sir."

The assistant prosecutor slyly posed the next question to inquire expansively, "After you killed her, Doctor, you rushed down those stairs, jumped from the platform on to the beach and fell and injured yourself?"

Sheppard reacted sharply.

"That is absolutely untrue and unfair!"

The needling went on, with the court seemingly mesmerized as were the jury, with the assistant prosecutor listing various items underlining the weaknesses in Sheppard's testimony, including the woman witness who had seen two lights on in the Sheppard home at a quarter past two in the morning of the crime. In rebuttal the defence stressed the defendant's injuries received during the struggle with the intruder, and eventually Judge Blythin summed up a difficult case and the jury filed out to consider their verdict.

They remained debating all aspects of it for a week before the foreman handed a folded paper to a court bailiff who duly offered

it to the judge. All eyes were fixed on Edward Blythin as he read
the slip of paper and started to read aloud: "We, the jury, find the
defendant not guilty of murder—"

There was a stir in court and Dr Sam was suddenly smiling.
But the stirring was quelled and the smiling withered as the judge
continued – "in the first degree, but guilty of murder in the
second degree."

There was a sound like an exhaled overcharged sigh.

Sam Sheppard's eyes went curiously blank, as though actual
sight had left them as well as awareness. He made a choking
sound, but no words came to his lips. A fearful anti-climax had
already begun to set in. It was as though he was seeing a re-run of
a secret truth that was not to be shared and must remain a
mystery for all time.

Then the judge was speaking again, sentencing Sam Sheppard
to imprisonment for life in the Ohio Penitentiary. There was a
scramble and the reporters were suddenly busy at a line of
telephones, for the trial had been snowballing in mounting
interest.

But at last the longest-run trial in US legal history was over.
The decision was to be argued to and fro, pro and con, for years,
for whatever else the trial had proved it was to be considered
inconclusive. But tragedy came to persons concerned with it. A
month after Dr Sam was sentenced came the news that his mother
had committed suicide. Shortly afterwards his father died. Death
followed several other people connected with the case, and a
member of the trial jury committed suicide, while until his death
in 1961 William J. Corrigan maintained a legal fight to obtain his
client's release.

The famous trial lawyer F. Lee Bailey stepped into the dead
Corrigan's shoes, and in typical fighting form and fettle vowed he
would earn for Sheppard a retrial, and his efforts were successful
when the Supreme Court decided that such a hearing should take
place as the previous trial had been prejudiced by an hysterical
Press campaign.

It was on 24th October, 1966, almost a dozen years later, that
Dr Sam arrived in court for yet another hearing to clear his name,
and straight away the militant Lee Bailey went into the attack,

claiming that there had never been an opportunity for finger-prints to be taken from the various items listed in the defendant's possession. But it was a medical technologist whose evidence gave Bailey pause for special consideration. She was Mary Cowan, who had examined the contents of the green bag at the time of the murder. She showed colour photographs to the court of the contents, and these photographs revealed Sheppard's watch as it was originally found, spotted with blood. Such spots, she informed the court, were made by "flying blood". Lee Bailey had a real task explaining the spots, especially when the prose-cutor claimed that they must have got on to the watch while Sheppard was beating his wife to death.

Bailey spent days trying to overcome this evidence of "flying blood". He finally claimed there was further evidence of similar particles on the inside of the watch strap, which meant that they had got on to it after it had been removed from Sheppard's wrist. It was a clever legal interpretation and on November 16th, 1966, the fresh jury accepted his words, and Dr Sam Sheppard was duly found not guilty.

But by this time he was a broken man, both rejected and dejected in his former profession, and his marriage to his second wife, a divorcee, did not last long. He died in 1970.

For years after Dr Sheppard's death his son Sam Reese Sheppard campaigned to have his father's name cleared. In 1997 he exhumed his father's body to get genetic material to support his $2 million lawsuit against the State of Ohio for wrongful imprisonment. DNA tests on four bloodstains from the 1954 crime scene showed they did not belong to Dr Sheppard, but did match the genetic make-up of an odd-job man, Richard Eberling, serving a life term for the murder of a widow in 1984. As we have seen, Dr Sheppard consistently blamed a "bushy-haired intruder" who knocked him unconscious during the attack on his wife.

MURDER IN DEPTFORD

(The Stratton Brothers, UK 1905)

Jurgen Thorwald

Fingerprinting was used as a weapon of detection as early as 1890, but it was some years before the science of dactyloscopy became accepted in a court of law. In 1902, following the theft of billiard balls in Denmark Hill, south London, the culprit was identified from the print of his left thumb and was convicted largely on this evidence. The first murder trial to turn on fingerprints was in 1905, when a couple named Farrow were found brutally murdered at their shop in Deptford. The investigation was personally supervised by Scotland Yard's CID chief Melville Macnaghten. Beyond two black stocking masks, the only clue was a cash box made of black tin, which had been broken open. On it was a single mark which looked like that of a finger or thumb. Two brothers called Stratton were arrested and fingerprinted: the mark on the cash box exactly matched the print of the right thumb of the elder brother. But the judge at their trial urged caution. He pointed out that the fingerprint evidence was the strongest point in the prosecution's case. The resemblance between the two prints was certainly remarkable, but he warned the jury to take the whole of the evidence together in reaching a verdict. They did, and the Strattons were convicted. They were hanged together, blaming each other. Jurgen Thorwald (b. 1916) has written several award-winning books on the history of crime and science. Born Heinz Bongartz, he adopted the pseudonym Jurgen Thorwald to avoid harassment in Soviet-occupied Germany while researching a book after World War II; the book did so well that he took it as his legal name in 1949. Thorwald now lives in Switzerland.

The streets of Deptford, a drab borough of south-eastern London on the south bank of the Thames, were still almost empty at 7.15 a.m. on 27 March 1905. A milkman saw two young men rush out of a small paint shop at 34 High Street and vanish around a corner. They were in such a hurry that they did not close the shop door behind them.

The milkman paid little attention. Life in Deptford was rough and ready; people did not meddle with each other more than they could help.

About ten minutes later a little girl came walking along the High Street. She saw a man with blood all over his clothes who thrust his head out the door of the paint shop, but immediately withdrew and locked the door from inside. The child was not particularly surprised by this sight. Blood flowed in streams in the slaughter-houses of Deptford – bloody faces and smocks were a commonplace in these streets.

It was not until 7.30 a.m. that a boy sounded the alarm. He worked as an apprentice in the paint shop. When he went to work he found the door locked – an unusual circumstance. His employer, Mr Farrow, a kindly old man past seventy, always rose very early to serve the painters who stopped in on their way to their jobs to buy paint or tools. So the door was always open when the apprentice arrived. But this morning it was locked, and there was no response when the apprentice rang the bell. Finally he climbed over the wall of the adjacent property into the courtyard. He glanced through the rear window – and ran screaming for help into the nearest store.

Detective Inspector Fox, accompanied by several detectives, arrived at the High Street within twenty minutes. Shortly afterwards Melville Macnaghten in person appeared.

The small room behind the shop, which served as office and storage space, presented a picture of total devastation. All the furniture had been overturned. Drawers were pulled out, blood was everywhere. Old Farrow lay on the floor in a crumpled heap, barely recognizable as a human being. His bloody head rested on the hob of the fireplace. Under his trousers and jacket the old man was still wearing his nightshirt. From the numerous traces of blood in the shop and on the narrow staircase that led to the upper floor, Fox concluded that Farrow had come down from his bedroom to serve what he must have assumed to be an early customer. He must have been attacked and knocked down in the shop. Apparently the old man had succeeded in pulling himself to his feet and had attempted to keep the murderer (or murderers?) from going upstairs, where Mrs Farrow was asleep. A large pool of blood on the stairs plainly indicated where he had collapsed for the second time. Yet, incredibly, he seemed to have got up again, this time after the assailants had fled. He had crawled to the still open door and looked out. Perhaps he had wanted to call for help. But then, since there was no one in sight, he had bolted the door from inside – perhaps fearing another attack. Then he must have dragged himself into the back room, where death had overtaken him.

In the bedroom upstairs lay Mrs Farrow, a feeble old woman, her head crushed. She was still breathing and was taken to the Greenwich hospital, where she died four days later, without having been able to say a word.

Meanwhile, Fox had discovered two masks made out of women's black stockings. He concluded from this that there must have been two assailants. At first it seemed that they had left no other clues. But then a small money-box was found under Mrs Farrow's bed. It had been broken open and everything but a sixpenny piece taken. From an account slip in the box the detectives concluded that the loot had amounted to no more than £9. Macnaghten, who was closely connected with the development of dactyloscopy, at once examined the money-box for fingerprints. Sure enough, there was a significant smudge on its smoothly varnished inner surface. He promptly ordered Fox and his men, as well as Farrow's distraught apprentice, who were waiting in the shop, to come upstairs. He asked whether any of them had touched the money-box. A young sergeant spoke up with some embarrassment. He had pushed the box further under the bed, so that the stretcher-bearers who had carried Mrs Farrow out would not stumble over it.

Macnaghten had the box carefully wrapped and taken at once to Chief Inspector Collins. The young sergeant was also sent to the fingerprinting division. To make perfectly sure, Macnaghten also had the fingerprints of the apprentice and the two victims taken. (This was the first time that the fingerprints of a corpse had ever been taken in London.) Then Macnaghten informed his superior, Edward Henry, of his actions. Both men tensely awaited the results of the investigation.

Collins reported the following morning. The smudge on the money-box was a thumbprint. It did not correspond with the prints of the apprentice, the victims, or any of the police officers at the scene. Its mate had not been found among the 80,000 fingerprints so far on record. Collins' report concluded with the statement that the print on the money-box proved to be, when photographically enlarged, unusually clear. Should the person who had made this print be arrested, he could be identified without the slightest difficulty.

Meanwhile Fox had begun a house-by-house investigation of the neighbourhood. In the course of it he spoke with a young woman named Ethel Stanton. At approximately the same time as the milkman, she had seen two young men running up the High Street, one of them wearing a brown overcoat. And one of Fox's detectives, eavesdropping in a Deptford pub, overheard a discussion of the murder, in which the names of two brothers, Alfred and Albert Stratton, were mentioned as being "capable of it".

Alfred and Albert Stratton were not altogether unknown to Scotland Yard, although as yet they had never been arrested. Respectively twenty-two and twenty, they were considered good-for-nothings who had never found employment but lived off various girls and women. They had no regular address. Nevertheless, within a few days Fox learned that Albert Stratton had taken lodgings in a shabby house on Knott Street. His landlady, Mrs Kate Wade, was thoroughly afraid of her lodger: that came to light when the detectives questioned her. Once, in cleaning Stratton's room she had come upon several masks made of black stockings hidden under the mattress. Fox also learned that Albert Stratton's brother Alfred had a mistress named Hannah Cromarty. He found the girl living in a wretched room on the ground floor of a house in Brookmill Road. The room's single window gave on to the street. The girl showed traces of a recent beating. Sure enough, Alfred Stratton had beaten her, and she was furious enough to "squeal". He came whenever he felt like it, she said, and she had to do as he said. He had slept with her on Sunday night. Late in the evening a man had come to the window, and Alfred had talked with him. Later, towards morning, there had been a knock at the window, and Alfred had dressed. Then she had fallen asleep. When she awoke, it was broad daylight, and Alfred was standing in the room, fully dressed. He had done this often before, she said, departing through the window at night and coming back the same way. This time he had warned her that if anyone asked she must say that he had spent the entire night with her and had not left until Monday morning, after nine o'clock.

Hannah Cromarty added one significant detail. Since that night, Alfred no longer had his brown coat. When she asked where it was, he had told her harshly that he had given it to a friend. Also, he had dyed his brown shoes black.

Macnaghten issued orders for the arrest of the Stratton brothers, wherever they were found. A first attempt to surprise them at a soccer match in the Crystal Palace failed. Meanwhile Hannah Cromarty vanished from her room. But on the following Sunday Alfred was captured in a pub, and his brother was caught the next day. Both of them were strapping young men with brutal faces. They made a great ruckus when they were brought into the Tower Bridge police station. Macnaghten was well aware that the evidence Fox had gathered would never suffice to secure an indictment. But he wanted to have their fingerprints.

The old police magistrate who had to decide whether the Strattons were to be held proved, in fact, to be scarcely impressed by Fox's arguments. How much evidence did he have? The gossip-mongering of a landlady and a loose woman! But after a good deal of argument back and forth, he agreed to let the suspects be held for a week, and fingerprinted. He had heard only the vaguest rumours about dactyloscopy, and was curious to see it in action. Collins came forward with his apparatus. The Stratton brothers were highly amused when their fingers were blackened and pressed against the filing cards. It "tickled", they innocently blustered.

Macnaghten recorded in his memoirs: "I had returned to the office in the forenoon, and shall never forget the dramatic entry made into my room by the expert an hour or two later. 'Good God, sir,' he exclaimed, with pardonable excitement, 'I have found that the mark on the cash-box tray is in exact correspondence with the print of the right thumb of the elder prisoner.'"

Alfred was the elder of the brothers. Henry, who had since become Police Commissioner of London, was informed immediately. He at once got in touch with the prosecutor, Richard Muir. For he saw that this case was as if made to order to dramatize the usefulness of fingerprinting. The eyes of all England would be upon the trial of the Stratton brothers – for the whole country had been shocked by the brutal murder.

Richard Muir went to Scotland Yard for a lesson in fingerprinting by Macnaghten and Collins. He arrived just in time to learn that the Stratton brothers had been shown to the milkman who had seen two men running out of Farrow's shop on the day of the murder. The milkman had failed to recognize them. Ethel Stanton, however, was prepared to swear that Alfred Stratton had been one of the two running men. Thus the one witness weakened the case, the other reinforced it. The only tangible evidence was the thumbprint on the money-box.

Muir realized fully how frail his case was. Everything would stand or fall on the fingerprint question. Would the jury accept a fingerprint as conclusive evidence, or as any kind of evidence at all? Muir mulled over the problem for two days before he made his decision. Then he announced his willingness to prosecute Alfred and Albert Stratton.

The arraignment took place in the Tower Bridge police court on 18 April. Two policemen stood guard over Muir's table, on which stood the money-box. Muir himself watched that money-box like a hawk. He knew that the judge and jurymen knew too little about the whole procedure of fingerprinting to accept a mere photograph of the thumbprint. He needed the original. "Careful, don't touch," he warned everyone who came near. "There are fingerprints on it."

Collins waited beside Muir, prepared to expound on the science of fingerprinting. The Strattons' lawyer let it be known that if the case were brought to trial, he would call two experts to the witness stand to prove that Henry's fingerprint system was

undependable. He did not give the names of his experts. Muir
and Collins racked their brains wondering who these mysterious
experts could be. How many persons in England had the faintest
knowledge of the subject?

They obtained their indictment, and on 5 May Alfred and
Albert Stratton appeared in the dock at the Old Bailey, with
Judge Channell on the bench. This was the judge's first experience with dactyloscopy; the jurymen had also never heard of the
technique. Booth, the defendants' lawyer, had selected two
barristers to plead the case, Curtis Bennett and Harold Morris,
the former of whom was to reach the front ranks of British
jurisprudence during the next few decades. It was not they,
however, who presented any particular threat. Muir kept glancing at two other persons who had taken seats beside them. The
secret of the counter-experts was out. The first of the men was Dr
Garson, who had so long argued the cause of *bertillonage* and had
then developed his own, quite inadequate fingerprinting system.
He had been worsted in the rivalry with Henry. Did he mean to
discredit the system which had proved better than his own?

Beside Garson, however, sat Dr Henry Faulds! Through a
chain of unlucky accidents, the name of this man, who had first
solved a crime by means of fingerprints found at the scene, had
been overshadowed by the names of Herschel, Galton, and
Henry. Ever since Galton had hailed Herschel as the discoverer
of fingerprinting, Faulds had been bitterly fighting to wrest from
the other man the fame he felt was rightly his. He had grown
more and more paranoiac about the whole situation and by now
believed there had been a conspiracy to deprive him of his
priority. Over the years he had abandoned all moderation; in
articles, open letters, and pamphlets he not only tried to prove his
priority in on-the-scene fingerprints – for which he undoubtedly
deserved the credit – but also for the discovery of finger-printing
in general. Was he going to testify against fingerprinting out of
blind spite – and thus, at bottom, repudiate his own discovery?

Muir glared at his antagonists. When he stood up to speak, a
hush fell over the courtroom. As Muir's biographer, Felstead,
later wrote:

In the hundreds of murder cases in which he prosecuted for the Crown, Muir never revealed such animosity towards prisoners in the dock as he did towards the two Strattons. He looked upon it as the most brutal crime he had ever come across, saying that the manner in which the faces of the poor old couple had been battered about made it quite impossible to extend the slightest human consideration towards the murderers. He spoke perhaps even more slowly and deliberately than usual, but with a deadly effect which made the men in the dock look at him as though he, and not the judge, might at any moment order their execution.

And a Sunday newspaper wrote: "His words rang out as though it was the execution bell at Newgate prison tolling."

Muir called up his parade of witnesses, such as Kate Wade and Ethel Stanton. From their testimony, he constructed a complete picture of the murder, even to the preparations for the alibi. Only after he had presented the whole picture did he bring up the fingerprint. He pointed to the money-box and declared: "There is not the shadow of a doubt that the thumbprint on this money-box, which once belonged to the murdered Mr Farrow, comes from the right thumb of the defendant Alfred Stratton."

Then he called Collins to the witness stand. Behind Collins was a large blackboard, so that Collins could clarify some of his points by means of sketches. Collins gave an even more convincing exposition than he had done three years earlier in the case of the burglar Jackson. He displayed the greatly enlarged photographs of the thumbprint on the box, and set beside it the print which had been taken of Alfred Stratton's thumb. He pointed out that the two prints were identical on at least eleven counts. There was a deep hush over the court while Collins spoke.

The cross-examination by Booth and Bennett quickly exposed the weakness of their position. They themselves were totally without experience in the field of dactyloscopy, and had leaned upon Faulds and Garson without realizing the irrational hatreds that motivated these men. Innocently and in good faith they argued a theory Faulds had suggested to them. Collins' photographs showed discrepancies, they said, which were obvious to any careful eye and demonstrated irresponsible negligence on the part of Scotland Yard.

The discrepancies they made so much of were those small differences which must occur when fingerprints are taken because it is impossible always to roll the fingers over the paper with the same pressure. Muir and Collins met this with a dramatic demonstration. Collins took the thumbprints of the jurymen several times in succession. He then showed the jury that the prints contained the same "discrepancies" which the defence insisted invalidated the prosecution's case. Each juryman was able to convince himself with his own eyes that these differences had nothing to do with the characteristic patterns which alone mattered. The cavillings of the defence were shattered. Moreover, a violent altercation broke out between Booth and Dr Faulds, with the latter relapsing into grim silence.

Troubled and uncertain, their faith in their experts severely reduced, Booth and Bennett hesitated to call Dr Garson to the witness stand. Perhaps, too, they saw a spark in Muir's eyes that suggested he might have a surprise in store and was prepared to annihilate Garson in cross-examination. But at last, for lack of any other ammunition, the defence decided to call Garson after all.

That decision proved even more fatal than their reliance on Dr Faulds. Muir produced a letter. Had Dr Garson written this letter to him? he asked rhetorically. In this letter had not Dr Garson proposed to aid the prosecution as an expert in fingerprints, before he offered his services to the defence? How did Dr Garson wish to explain this duplicity?

Everyone understood Muir's unspoken charge: that Dr Garson had been prepared to testify the exact contrary of his testimony for the defence, if the prosecution had been willing to have him and feed his self-importance. Garson threw one nervous look around the courtroom. Then he replied defiantly: "I am an independent witness." He was not allowed to go on. "I would say," Judge Channell interposed, "a completely untrustworthy witness . . ." He ordered Garson to leave the stand.

That was Muir's victory. In his instructions to the jury, Judge Channell cautiously observed that the fingerprint should certainly be regarded as valid evidence to a certain measure. The jury retired for only two hours. When they filed back, another suspense-filled hush descended upon the courtroom. Then the spokesman pronounced the verdict: Guilty. Judge Channell condemned Alfred and Albert Stratton to death by hanging. And the torrent of mutual abuse that burst from the two of them proved that they richly deserved their punishment.

The Stratton trial was a first milestone on the road to full legal recognition of dactyloscopy. Henry's system spread through Great Britain, Scotland, Ireland, and the British dominions and colonies. Concurrently, it began to be adopted all over Europe and throughout the inhabited globe.

THE COPPOLINO CASE

(Dr Carl Coppolino, USA 1965)

James A. Brussel

Carmela Coppolino died suddenly, allegedly after receiving a fatal dose of the "undetectable" drug succinylcholine chloride at the hands of her husband, an anaesthetist. Dr Carl Coppolino had become infatuated with Marjorie Farber, the attractive middle-aged wife of a retired army colonel who also died suddenly after being attended by Dr Coppolino. The bodies of both the wife and the colonel were exhumed. A needle puncture was found on Carmela's body, and the colonel showed signs of having been strangled. Coppolino was tried for the murder of both, and after much confusing and conflicting forensic evidence was found guilty of second-degree murder and sentenced to life imprisonment. For Dr Milton Helpern, the chief medical examiner of the City of New York, it was "the most extraordinary case ever to come my way." Coppolino gambled on his chosen weapon of murder, succinylcholine chloride, being impossible to detect. But he overlooked the fact that science is constantly pushing back the frontiers of ignorance in the fight against crime. Coppolino's story is told by James A. Brussel, a psychiatrist and criminologist, described as "the Sherlock Holmes of the couch". He came to public attention in 1957 in the case of New York's notorious Mad Bomber. Author Gerold Frank believed that Dr Brussel's ability to study a crime and from it reconstruct the criminal gave him a charmed name in police circles.

It started, as most of my adventures seem to do, with a phone call. It came on a dismal gray morning in December, 1966. The caller was Teri Plaut, Lee Bailey's charming girl Friday. She said: "Doctor, get down here as soon as possible."

By "down here" she meant Freehold, New Jersey, where her boss was at that moment appearing as defence counsel in one of the most bizarre criminal trials of the 1960s. I knew from reading the papers that this new trial was now in its second day. Something unexpected must have happened to make Lee Bailey call on me so suddenly. Normally he is a man who plans ahead, outlines his trial strategy, and lines up his witnesses well in advance of any court appearance. I had learned this while working with him on the Boston Strangler case. What was going on? What did he need me for?

Intrigued, I hastily reviewed my day's schedule in my mind. There was nothing on my calendar that couldn't be postponed. "All right," I told Teri, "I'll be there by noon."

"Wonderful" she said. She sounded relieved. "Mr Bailey will be grateful."

"Maybe he won't be when he gets my bill," I said.

"Pardon?"

"Nothing. I'll see you later."

And thus I entered the strange, baffling, multifaceted case of Dr Carl Coppolino. By the time my part in it had ended, I wished my phone had been out of order on that December morning. The Coppolino case was one of very few I've come up against in which I never formed a clear idea of who the criminal was – or, indeed, precisely what crime or crimes, if any, had been committed. It was perhaps the most mystifying case of my career. It was a case made of shadowy half-truths and vague suppositions, a case involving many people behaved in devious, sometimes inexplicable ways. Many lies were told, but it was hard to expose them as such. Undoubtedly, some truths were also told, but they were impossible to prove. In the end, as still today, there were as many theories about the case as there were people trying to get to the bottom of it.

Some of the cases I've worked on have been relatively simple and straightforward. I tell the Coppolino story to show that it isn't always so, to demonstrate just how complicated human circumstances can become.

In the early 1960s a housing developer bought a large expanse of gently rolling woodland and meadowland in suburban Middletown, New Jersey. Planning with care in order to save as many of the larger trees as possible, he carved out roadways and mapped plots for houses in the $35,000 price range. He called the section Fox Run. It was to be a development for people in the upper-middle-income bracket.

Buyers came quickly, for Fox Run showed promise of maturing into an attractive neighbourhood. They were people from varying social and economic backgrounds. Many of the men were commuters to Manhattan. Perhaps the developer wondered, as he met them, how they would get along as neighbours.

One plot of land, at 35 Wallace Road, was bought by a family named Coppolino. The Coppolinos were both physicians. Dr Carl Coppolino was a lean, dark, intensely nervous man of thirty with heavy black eyebrows and a prominent beak of a nose; he was a full-time anaesthesiologist at a nearby hospital. Carmela Anne Coppolino, twenty-nine, was a slim, attractive, dark-haired woman with an outwardly calm, sunny disposition. She worked at a pharmaceutical laboratory in Nutley, New Jersey. The Coppolinos had two children.

While the Coppolinos' new colonial-style house was rising, another house was taking shape diagonally across the street. This house, at 50 Wallace Road, was being built for a somewhat older couple named Farber. Lieutenant Colonel William Farber, fifty, was a medalled war veteran who had recently retired from the Army. He was drawing disability pay because of a heart ailment. He now held an executive job in a New York insurance office. He was a stocky man with a square, good-humoured face. His wife, Marjorie, looked far younger than he, though she was in fact forty-seven. She was a former divorcée. She had a round, pretty face and a figure that any college girl would have been proud of. The Farbers had two daughters.

Fox Run gradually changed from a sea of mud to a well-tended neighbourhood. The houses were finished. Families moved in and began to turn the houses into homes. Terraced lawns and shrubs covered the bulldozed earth. Slowly, families got to know each other.

The Coppolinos and Farbers met at a neighbourhood party and took an immediate liking to one another. Through late 1962 and the winter and spring of 1963, the foursome got together almost every weekend. Sometimes with other couples and sometimes not, the four played cards, dined, and went to parties and the theater. They became the nucleus of a social clique typical of upper-middle-class suburban neighbourhoods. At least, for a while, it seemed typical.

But changes were taking place – some of them overt, some beneath the surface. Signs of dissatisfaction were beginning to show in the Farber household. Colonel Farber, who had seen enough action in World War II and Korea to last a lifetime, had hoped that his new life in Fox Run would give him peace and quiet. Though he was an affable man, he didn't want to spend every evening and weekend on a merry-go-round of social activity. For much of the time, he preferred to be left alone, puttering in the tranquil solitude of his garden. His wife, Marge, wanted to be out where the action was. She grew increasingly restless, took lessons in golf and interior decorating; joined a riding club, more and more often went to parties without her husband.

In the Coppolino household, there were more abrupt changes. Carl came home one day and announced to the neighbourhood that he had resigned his hospital post because of a heart ailment. The heart ailment may have been a partial cause of his resignation, but there was in fact another that he didn't tell the neighbours about (and that came out later in court); he had become involved in a bitter quarrel with a nurse anaesthetist, and had sent her a threatening letter. The contents of this letter and circumstances of the quarrel have never been revealed, but somehow the FBI became involved. Fearing unfavourable publicity, the hospital authorities decided to end their relationship with Coppolino.

He did not seek another post. Instead, he and his wife (Carm, he called her) went to work on a book about alcoholism, *The*

Billion Dollar Hangover. She kept her daytime laboratory job and helped Carl with the book each night.

During the days, with Carmela and Colonel Farber away at work, Carl Coppolino and Marge Farber saw each other frequently. They made an odd pair. Marge was vivacious, outgoing, a woman who loved to be where there were lots of people and lots of noise. Carl had always been a singularly quiet man. In fact, as *Newsweek* later reported, he had been so shy and retiring at Fordham University that the editors of his class yearbook could think of only one thing to say about him beyond the bare outline of his biography: "He specialized in chemistry." Yet the lively Marge Farber was strongly attracted to this darkly taciturn man.

One thing led to another. At first he used to go to her house, or she to his, to discuss his book. She was a former alcoholic and had belonged to Alcoholics Anonymous. She occasionally chauffeured him around town when he complained that his heart ailment made him feel too weak to drive. Marge was a heavy smoker; and one day – following a laughing suggestion from Carmela – Carl offered to help her break the habit through a series of treatments with hypnosis. He hypnotized her several times, and she did in fact stop smoking for a while. In repayment, Marge – an accomplished amateur artist – painted his portrait.

Carl and Marge became lovers. This much is known. Very little else about the subsequent events is known for sure.

Did Colonel Farber and Carmela Coppolino know what went on at Fox Run while they were away at work? Perhaps not. Perhaps, on the other hand, they did know – and didn't care. They certainly behaved with supreme nonchalance. One winter night, while the four were sitting around drinking coffee and chatting, Carl remarked that he'd like to go to Florida for a few weeks to hasten his convalescence and perhaps speed up work on his book. Since his wife couldn't leave her job, he said, wouldn't it be a good idea if Marge were to go with him and take care of him? Strangely, the suggestion carried both houses unanimously. And so, early in 1963, Carl and Marge went off to Florida while their spouses cheerfully stayed home in Fox Run. To some of the neighbours, this seemed to be carrying broad-mindedness to an extreme.

Suntanned and happy, the two lovers came home to Fox Run a few weeks later, and life went on more or less as before. Carl spoke in ecstatic tones of Florida. While there, he told neighbours, he had looked around at some properties with an idea of buying or building a home there one day. He particularly liked the idea of living on one of Florida's coastal islands or keys. The seclusion of island life appealed to him.

On July 30, 1963, Lieutenant Colonel William Farber suddenly died in his home.

Understandably, people panic at times like that; they become disoriented and confused, later cannot recall precisely what happened. Such was the case when Farber died. Nobody seemed quite sure, later, who had done what during the hour or so after the tragedy. All that is known for certain is that Carmela went to the Farbers' house and, in her capacity as a physician, made out the death certificate. She listed the cause of death as coronary thrombosis.

Now there were three. The trio stayed together, attended cocktail parties and even church as a group. The neighbours thought it was good of the Coppolinos thus to take Marge under their wing in her bereavement.

In the spring of 1965, Carl Coppolino finally realized his dream of living in Florida. He and Carmela sold their house in Fox Run and moved into a modest but pretty white stucco house on fashionable Longboat Key, near Sarasota. Marge Farber seemed unable to get along without them. Two months later, she, too, sold her house in Fox Run and with her two daughters moved into a house next door to the Coppolinos on Longboat Key.

On August 28, 1965, Carmela Coppolino abruptly died in her home at the age of thirty-two. Dr Juliette Karow, a Sarasota physician, was called in to complete the death certificate. She talked to Carl, who (she said later) told her Carmela had been suffering chest pains the day before. He said he had found her dead in bed that morning. Dr Karow examined the body and listed the cause of death as coronary occlusion.

Now there were two.

Or so Marge may have thought. Unhappily for her, however, Carl was no longer the ardent lover he had been in Fox Run. He and Carmela had been going out socially without Marge, and he had been looking appreciatively at other women. One, whom he had met at a bridge game, was a pretty, dark-haired, thirty-eight-year-old divorcée named Mary Gibson. Mary later testified in court that her income was a mere $8,000 to $10,000 a year, but she was rumoured to have won an enormous lump-sum divorce settlement and she owned an elegant villa in the wealthy Forest Lakes Country Club area of Sarasota. Six weeks after Carmela's death, Carl married Mary Gibson and moved into her villa.

Now there was only one: Marge Farber, lonely and stranded on Longboat Key. How did she feel? Angry, certainly. Full of hate for Carl, who had jilted her? Perhaps. The question of what went on in Marge Farber's mind later became an important one, but it was never answered completely.

What is known is that, late in 1965, she talked to Carmela's father and to Sarasota County Sheriff Ross Boyer. She said there was "something odd" about Carmela's death – and also about Colonel Farber's death two years before.

Boyer listened to her story. It seemed to him (as to others later) that she was highly confused; the story she told was internally inconsistent, full of holes and implausibilities. Moreover, when asked to repeat parts of the story, she told it a different way each time. All the same, Sheriff Boyer felt that some checking into the story was warranted. He couldn't just file the story and forget it. It was too shocking. Marge Farber was accusing Carl Coppolino of murder.

Sheriff Boyer began a discreet investigation that slowly widened and deepened until it included police authorities in both Florida and New Jersey. The bodies of Colonel Farber and Carmela Coppolino were disinterred. Physicians, chemists, and other experts examined the corpses and gave their opinions. The case exploded into the public news media. It was a sensational story that could be played large on page one – a story of sex and murder in a high-income suburb.

Murder? Well, possibly. It was hard to say for sure.

The main theme of Marge Farber's story was that her husband – and, she suspected, also Carmela – had been murdered with a drug called succinylcholine chloride. As an anaesthesiologist,

Carl Coppolino would have been well acquainted with this drug. According to Marge, he had talked several times about it as an ideal weapon for murder – one which, he said, would be impossible to trace in a dead body and would leave no outward evidence of its having been the cause of death. In one version of her story, Marge said that Carl had handed her a lethal dose of the drug and that she, acting on his instructions, had injected it into her husband. In another version, she said that she had stood by while Carl injected it. In still another version, she said the drug didn't kill her husband fast enough, and she and Carl had suffocated him with a pillow.

Which version, if any, was true? Nobody could find out. There is no doubt that succinylcholine chloride could be used for murder. It is a common drug, available to physicians under various trade names such as Sucostrin (Squibb) and Anectine (Burrough Wellcome). It is packaged as a white powder which when it is to be used, is introduced into a glass container of sterile fluid. It can be given either by hypodermic injection or intravenous drip. Its main effect is muscle relaxation. In psychiatry, we use light dosages of it during electric shock therapy. Heavier dosages are used in surgery, dosages that would be lethal if there were no anaesthesiologist present to counter their effects. In these dosages, the drug renders all the patient's muscles completely flaccid – including the muscles that are used for breathing. The patient can no longer breathe for himself; the anaesthesiologist keeps him alive by pumping gases in and out of his lungs. Without this artificial breathing aid the patient would die very quickly, looking relaxed and peaceful.

Did Colonel Farber and Carmela Coppolino die this way? Examining the body tissues, some experts thought they detected chemical residues of succinylcholine chloride. But other experts, equally eminent, thought they found evidence that both the colonel and Carmela had died of heart attacks, as the death certificates said.

There was circumstantial evidence against Carl Coppolino, however. He had had access to supplies of succinylcholine chloride before both deaths. He had been in the neighbourhood at the time of both deaths. Moreover, it turned out, Carmela had increased her life insurance coverage shortly before her death. It wasn't a big boost, from $50,000 to $65,000. But it was enough to add to the mounting suspicion.

In July 1966, a New Jersey grand jury returned an indictment against Carl Coppolino, charging that he had murdered Colonel Farber. A few days later, a Florida grand jury charged him with murdering his wife.

In December, 1966, his first trial opened at Freehold, New Jersey.

I'd been following this sensational and confusing case as it developed in the newspapers. As a psychiatrist, I'd been particularly interested in the question of motive.

Why would Carl Coppolino have wanted to kill Colonel Farber? Because Carl wanted to have Farber's wife for himself? This was the suggestion being offered in the newspapers; yet, to me, it didn't quite add up. Carl was having his way with Marge Farber even though Colonel Farber was alive. Why take the risk of committing murder? Even if Carl were passionately in love with Marge, would the risk have been necessary I wondered. And, as Carl later demonstrated by marrying Mary Gibson, he was not passionately in love with Marge. In what way, then, did he profit by the colonel's death?

And what of his wife? The alleged motive in this case seemed a little more clear-cut. It was suggested that he had killed her so that he could marry Mary Gibson, share Mary's wealth, and simultaneously collect Carmela's $65,000 life insurance benefit. But the evidence was circumstantial and leaky.

Marge Farber's motives were still harder to fathom. It was generally supposed that she felt bitterly vengeful toward Carl and that this was why she had blown the whistle on him. In fact, Lee Bailey's main strategy in defending Carl Coppolino was to portray Marge Farber as a woman scorned – a woman who would make up fantastic fictions in order to get revenge. Yet, in some versions of her ever-changing story, she implicated herself in the murder of her husband: told of injecting the lethal drug into him or of helping suffocate him with a pillow. If the story were fiction, why did she thus jeopardize herself?

Perhaps to make the story more believable? To give it an "I was-there" quality?

It seemed possible. Assume for a moment, as Lee Bailey hoped to show, that Marge had made up the whole story. Picture her being questioned over and over again by police officers. She is in a highly emotional state, bitterly angry at Carl, eager to punish him at almost any cost to herself. To make her accusation of murder seem like more than conjecture, she says, "All right, I'll admit it. I was in the room when he killed my husband. In fact, I *helped*."

Later, perhaps, she would regret having implicated herself thus. But, at the time, in her passionate eagerness to hurt the man who had jilted her, it may have seemed like the only thing to do.

This was merely conjecture on my part. Marge's story may have been wholly or partly true. And yet . . .

And yet, if it were true in part, why did she keep changing it? Her explanation was that she had been frightened and confused at the time of her husband's death – so much so that she couldn't remember sequences of events clearly nor separate fact from her own bewildered imaginings. Such a mental state is conceivable. People's recollections are seldom clear after some terrifying event – a fact that irritates the police when questioning witnesses to a crime. There are often as many diverse versions of the story as there are witnesses. Thus Marge could have been simply confused. On the other hand, as Lee Bailey hoped to show, she could have been lying deliberately in some versions of the story or in all versions.

Either way, it was impossible to know the truth. Had Carl alone murdered the colonel? Had Marge helped? Had Marge done the deed by herself? Or had Colonel Farber actually died of an ordinary heart attack?

These questions were in my mind as I drove to Freehold that December morning. I arrived at the courthouse shortly before the noon recess.

Freehold is an attractive suburban community. Once principally a farm town, it has been engulfed by the inexorable spreading-out of the New York metropolitan area and now it exists largely as a bedroom town for commuters and their

families. Its courthouse is an old brick structure that, under the
bleak winter skies, looked impenetrably mysterious. I felt pessi-
mistic. Would the mystery now housed in this building ever be
unravelled?

After a hurried lunch, Lee Bailey took me into the court library
and handed me a transcript of Marge Farber's testimony of the
day before. "When you read this," he said, "you'll see why I need
you on the stand. Marge Farber has changed her story one more
time."

I looked at him, puzzled. "A new version?"

"Right," said Bailey, "and it took everybody by surprise,
including the prosecution. Do you know what she's saying
now? She says she helped kill her husband because Coppolino
hypnotized her and made her do it."

"*Hypnotized* her?"

"That's what she says. She claims she was under his spell for a
year or more after he hypnotized her out of a smoking habit. She
says she had no free will, had to do whatever Coppolino told her
to do. Is it possible?"

"Not likely," I said.

"I didn't think so. And that's what I want you to testify on."

I settled down to skim through the transcript. I didn't have
much time, but I managed to digest the meat of Marge's testi-
nomy. She explained her entire part in the affair by reference to
an alleged hypnotic influence. Carl Coppolino had hypnotized
her to help her stop smoking, she said, and had then carried the
hypnosis into other areas of her life. She hadn't known what was
happening to her. She became a puppet, with Carl pulling the
strings. When he ordered her to help him murder her husband,
she claimed, she felt irresistibly compelled to obey without
knowing why.

The story seemed wild to me. And, I wondered, what was the
point of it? Why had Marge suddenly brought it up, after having
said nothing about the hypnosis through all the months before
the trial?

One possibility suggested itself. Perhaps, as I'd suspected
could happen, Marge was now sorry she had implicated herself
in the alleged murder of her husband. Perhaps this new hypnosis

story was designed to get her out of trouble – to lighten or remove the criminal responsibility of which she had accused herself.

Perhaps. On the other hand, perhaps she really believed she had been hypnotized into helping a murderer. The case seemed to be growing more complex by the hour. My pessimism increased. I had the baffled feeling that the truth was slipping out of sight, irretrievably lost like a jewel sinking in swirling, muddy waters.

I went into the courtroom and took my place as the afternoon session began. Lee Bailey was relying mainly only on medical men to clear Coppolino of the murder charge. First there were Drs Richard Ford and Joseph W. Spelman, medical examiners, respectively of Boston and Philadelphia. These two men produced evidence showing that William Farber had had a diseased heart and could have died of a heart attack. They doubted that he had died either of a fatal drug injection or of suffocation or strangulation with a pillow; at least, they showed that there was no reliable evidence to support either conclusion. The jury listened to these two men attentively. Prosecutor Vincent Keuper could not find any chinks in their professional armor.

Next on the witness stand were two men who knew about hypnosis. One was Dr Leo Wollman, an obstetrician and president of the New York Society of Clinical and Experimental Hypnosis. I was the other.

After having me qualify myself as a psychiatrist who knew how to use hypnosis, Lee Bailey asked me: "Is it possible for someone to be forced into a criminal act under hypnosis? I mean an act that he wouldn't otherwise be willing to perform?"

I answered flatly: "No. No amount of hypnosis could make him do it if he weren't at least unconsciously willing to begin with." I pointed out that, if hypnosis could compel people to do what they didn't want to do, despots like Hitler could have had whole populations hypnotized into slavish obedience. Troops could be hypnotized into a total disregard of their own safety. No such magic spell has ever been invented, except in science-fiction novels. "If Mrs Farber wanted to do something under hypnosis," I said, "she would do it. If she didn't want to, no amount of hypnosis could make her do it."

Prosecutor Keuper now tried to tear my testimony apart. He wanted me to concede that "anyone can be hypnotized into doing something." He began by getting me to concede one point, then went on to try to make me concede others.

Keuper: Mrs Farber said that she was, at times, under a compulsion to perform certain acts. At other times, though, shortly before or shortly after, she would have complete freedom from any compulsions. Doctor, is this consistent with what we know about the hypnotic state?

Brussel: Yes, it is.

Keuper: If I were a smoker and came to you because I wanted to stop smoking, could you implant a posthypnotic suggestion in my mind so that I wouldn't smoke for the rest the week?

Brussel: Yes – because you didn't want to continue smoking.

Keuper: If at the end of the week I wanted to continue not smoking, could you do something, like snapping your fingers, to prolong your posthypnotic suggestion?

Brussel: I can't answer that question. No two minds are the same.

Keuper: Could you plant a posthypnotic suggestion that would last a lifetime?

Brussel: Possibly, but all I can tell you honestly is that no one would know whether you were reacting to my hypnosis, or reacting to your own desire to stop smoking. I'm being as honest as I can.

Keuper: But the suggestion that I stop smoking came to me from a hypnotist?

Brussel: No, the suggestion really started with you. You wouldn't have consulted a hypnotist unless you wanted to stop smoking.

Keuper: Are you able to tell this jury what hypnosis actually is?

Brussel: No one can.

Keuper: If a posthypnotic suggestion lasts a lifetime,

couldn't you give some credit to the hypnosis – and not to the subject's willingness?

Brussel: There's no honest answer . . .

Prosecutor Keuper kept returning to the subject of smoking, no doubt because this is how Marge Farber's alleged compulsion to obey Carl Coppolino got started.

Keuper: Now, then, if I wanted to stop smoking and I came to you, could you hypnotize me out of the habit?

Brussel: If your conscious desire was backed up by an unconscious desire – that is, if your unconscious mind was fearful of smoking as a threat to life. In that case, I could. If this unconscious desire was absent, I could not.

Keuper: Oh, come, doctor! Could you or couldn't you hypnotize me out of smoking?

Brussel: If your unconscious wanted it, yes. If not, no.

Keuper: All right, we'll say you *did* succeed in hypnotizing me. How long would the spell last? Forever? A year? A month?

Brussel: As long as your unconscious feared smoking.

Prosecutor Keuper was getting nowhere. He grew increasingly irritable. Lee Bailey, who senses people's moods very quickly and seizes every opportunity to take advantage of them, deliberately added to Keuper's discomfort. Bailey kept turning around in his chair and looking at the prosecutor with a faint smile. As the tide of the trial swung ever more heavily against him, Keuper found this harder and harder to ignore. Finally he could stand it no longer.

"Judge," he shouted, "make him stop looking at me!"

The judge sighed. "Mr Bailey," he said, "please stop looking at Mr Keuper."

"Yes, Your Honour," said Bailey contritely, "I'm sorry."

This was one of the few points Prosecutor Keuper won. The jury deliberated for four and a half hours and returned with the fully expected verdict: Carl Coppolino was innocent of any complicity in Colonel William Farber's death.

Marge Farber looked angry. Carl Coppolino, neatly dressed in a dark suit, smiled as he was escorted from the courtroom under guard. He was taken immediately to Florida, where he next had to stand trial for the murder of his wife.

In May, 1967, a Florida jury found Carl Coppolino guilty of murdering his wife with succinylcholine chloride.

Oddly, the verdict was for second-degree murder – which under Florida law, means murder without premeditation. To many observers, the verdict seemed to contain a built in paradox. How can you obtain supplies of a drug and prepare an injection without premeditation?

That was the verdict, however. Carl Coppolino was sentenced to life imprisonment. Lee Bailey immediately appealed the verdict, and a new trial awaits Carl sometime in the future.

Did he really commit a murder? Were any murders, in fact committed? If so, who really killed Colonel Farber and Carmela Coppolino – or did they die a natural death?

Shortly after the close of Coppolino's New Jersey trial, Prosecutor Vincent Keuper tried to approach the mystery from a new angle. He asked a grand jury to indict Marge Faber for the murder of her husband. The jury refused on the ground of insufficient evidence.

Since then, I've often been asked for my opinion of the case. But I have no answers. I don't even have anything strong enough to be called a hunch.

The Coppolino–Farber episode remains my most baffling case. I puzzle over it sometimes, but I get nowhere. I assemble one group of facts into what seems like a workable hypothesis, but then another group of facts knocks it down. In the end I can only agree with Hamlet: there are more things in Heaven and earth, Jim Brussel, than are dreamt of in your philosophy. Or your psychiatry.

It may seem strange, in a way, for me to end this book with a failure. Or, if not a failure, certainly not a total success. I've ended the book thus for what I think is a good reason. I want to remain humble. Only a humble man can go on learning.

Perhaps, in some of these stories of my encounters with crime, I have made myself seem less than humble. I may have seemed too much impressed with my own deductive and intuitive victories. This last story is here to make amends. And to keep me lean and hungry ready for the next time my phone rings and a police officer says, "Dr Brussel, we've got a case here that's giving us some trouble—"

PARTICLE OF DOUBT

(Barry George, 1999)

S.C. Lomax

One of Britain's best-known television personalities, Jill Dando, was brutally shot dead on the doorstep of her London home in April 1999. The crime shocked the nation: with her blonde, girl-next-door good looks, she had been one of the most popular faces of the 1990s, reading the news and appearing on the BBC's Crimewatch *programme, appealing for the public's help in solving crimes. Who could have wanted her dead? One theory was that it was a criminal whom Dando had brought to book via her programme, another that she had been murdered in revenge for NATO bombing in Belgrade. Or, again, it may have been a jilted lover. Eventually, police arrested a local misfit, Barry George, and charged him with Dando's murder; in 2001, he was convicted by an Old Bailey jury and sentenced to life imprisonment. But since then, there have been growing doubts about the safety of George's conviction, based mainly on the forensic evidence in the case. This evidence is scrutinised here by S.C. Lomax (b. 1983), the youngest true crime writer represented in this collection. Scott Lomax started writing at the age of eight. After obtaining a degree in Archaeology and Prehistory at Sheffield University in 2004, he became a professional author, specializing in crime and, in particular, cases of suspected miscarriages of justice. He has campaigned for a number of individuals, two of whom, Graham Huckerby and James Power, had their convictions quashed by the Court of Appeal in December 2004. When he was 21, S.C. Lomax made his publishing debut with* The Case of Barry George *(2004); this book has since been updated to become* Who Killed Jill Dando? *The book discusses her murder, the investigation and subsequent controversial conviction of Barry George. Lomax was the first to document all the evidence, expose the weaknesses in the prosecution's argument and appraise the prosecution's case in light of evidence which was not heard in court.*

"You have deprived Miss Dando's fiancé, family and friends of a much loved and popular personality. You are unpredictable and dangerous . . ."

With these words Mr Justice Gage sent Barry George to prison, to serve a life sentence for murder, and opened up one of the most controversial criminal convictions in recent years. Almost everyone seated in Court Number One at the Old Bailey had expected the defendant to be acquitted and even the media, which had demonized George from the time of his arrest, expressed concern over the jury's verdict.

On 2 July 2001 George, then aged 41, was found guilty, by a majority of 10 to 1, of killing the popular television presenter Jill Dando who had been shot dead on the doorstep of her unlived-in house, in broad daylight, two years earlier. The evidence at trial was entirely circumstantial and relied heavily upon the testimony of one questionable eyewitness identification, made by a woman who saw a man near the scene of the crime four and a half hours before the shooting, and two microscopic pieces of forensic evidence, the credibility of which has been heavily disputed.

On Monday 26 April 1999 Dando had spent much of the morning in a local shopping centre in Hammersmith, south west London, before driving to her former home on Gowan Avenue in Fulham, stopping off en-route to buy some fish for the evening meal. Since Dando had moved in with her fiancé Alan Farthing, her visits to Gowan Avenue had become less frequent, with her using the large terraced house as an office. Dando arrived outside 29 Gowan Avenue at 11:30 that morning and, with carrier bags in her hands, approached the front door. Before she had time to unlock the door she realised she had been followed. She screamed briefly before being held to the ground. A 9mm semi automatic adapted handgun was thrust into the left side of her head, just above her left ear. Dando screamed again and the gunman pulled his trigger. One shot was enough and he walked calmly away, leaving Jill Dando dead on her doorstep.

There followed a massive police investigation, Operation Oxborough, the largest manhunt since the Yorkshire Ripper at that time. In total the police devoted up to 50 detectives working full time on the Dando case, for a period of two years, at a cost of approximately £2 million. Ex-boyfriends were questioned and eliminated. Convicted criminals, captured with the assistance of the programme Crimewatch UK during Dando's time as a co-presenter on the show, and their friends and families, each had to be investigated, as did the possibility that Dando was killed in revenge for the NATO bombing of a Belgrade television centre.

However, in May 2000 the police made a breakthrough and arrested Barry George, who lived half a mile from the scene of the crime. George was an epileptic with a variety of personality disorders. He had acted suspiciously two days after the murder, detectives had been told. George had, without doubt, demanded staff at an advice centre tell him at what time he had been present at the centre on the day of the murder. The woman who had dealt with him, Susan Bicknell, had been adamant that George was with her at 11.50 a.m. If this was true then George was indisputably innocent, the jury at his trial would later be told. But other members of staff suggested that George had arrived much later, some saying he only arrived at 1.30 p.m. which gave him plenty of time to commit the murder, wash and change his clothing and walk to the advice centre. The only problem with this was that from 1.00 p.m. George was at a taxi office and had already been to the advice centre. This was proven in court. However, the police and prosecution maintained George committed the murder before making his way to the advice centre and returned two days later in a desperate attempt to falsify an alibi. George had also revisited the taxi office on 28 April 1999. For this reason he emerged as a suspect and was questioned in April 2000, at his mother's home, in connection with the murder before being arrested the following month. The jury were never told that

George had been previously questioned in connection with the murder of Rachel Nickell on Wimbledon Common, and this had resulted in George fearing that whenever there was a murder he would become a suspect, even if he was innocent, and therefore he would have to determine his whereabouts to prove to the police that he had an alibi.

The Justice for Barry campaign, which was founded following George's conviction, believes George should never have been arrested let alone convicted: "It is simply shocking that a disabled, vulnerable man was railroaded through the justice system," they said. "We do not know who killed Jill Dando, or why. But we do know that there was no reliable evidence linking Barry George to the crime. We hope that this mockery of justice will be rectified as a matter of urgency."

George was held in police custody for four days before being charged. During questioning he maintained he had no involvement in the crime whatsoever. Why did he have eight articles in his flat that referred to Jill Dando? George told them he collected newspapers. Indeed he did; amongst the rubbish in his flat were over 800 newspapers and the articles that referred to Dando were not cut out or highlighted in any way. What was his interest in Jill Dando? He said he had no interest in Jill Dando, that he did not even know who she was until after her death. Had he ever owned a gun? No, George replied, though he had once owned two blank firing guns but they were stolen in the early 1980s. Did he murder Jill Dando? "No, Sir," was George's response.

More than a month prior to George's arrest, the police had raided his flat on Crookham Road, Fulham, and subjected it to a thorough search, removing many items for forensic examination. One of the items removed was a dark blue Cecil Gee jacket which George had purchased in 1988 for his wedding. It was in this jacket that the infamous particle of alleged firearms discharge residue was found. A firearms expert located the particle three weeks before police made their arrest and did not lay their winning hand for until the third day of questioning their prime suspect. Yet it was this evidence, the police would later claim, that was the key to charging George with the murder. It seems strange, therefore, that they did not act upon it sooner if it was the "compelling" evidence of proof that it would be described as at one of the highest-profile, and most contentious, trials of the century the following year.

The particle was microscopic at 11.5 microns in size, which is approximately 0.0125 millimetres. Compositional analysis showed that the particle was made up of three elements; barium, aluminium and lead, which matched compositionally with particles found in and around Dando's head wound. The microscopic particle of alleged Firearms Discharge Residue (FDR) was seen to be compelling proof of his guilt. One officer would later claim that once the particle had been found, "*We knew that we had enough evidence to arrest him*," though, as has been said, George was not arrested until three weeks later.

One of the problems relating to the particle was that it was found in a dark blue jacket which would be worn for formal occasions, whilst the crime was committed by someone wearing a dark (probably black) wax/Barbour style jacket that went down to the killer's knees. The Cecil Gee jacket was certainly not that worn by the gunman. A second difficulty with the particle was that it can never be said with any degree of certainty that it originated from a firearm, let alone the murder weapon, which has never been found. The alleged firearms discharge residue was only compositionally identical to those particles fired from the gun used to kill Jill Dando. At best, this indicates the particle came from a cartridge of a similar or same type as that used by Dando's executor. The prosecution's expert witness at trial, Robin Keeley, would never be able to rule out the possibility the particle came from a blank firing gun or even a firework and we know that George was in the habit of collecting old fireworks.

The major problem with the particle discussed at trial was the possibility that it found its way into the jacket pocket due to contamination, which would explain the total absence of other particles within George's flat. The defence scientist, Dr John Lloyd, a forensic scientist with over 30 years of experience, told the court that it was a "unique suggestion" to propose that a single particle could be the remnant of a crime committed one year previous to the particle being discovered:

The claims that it is so related are based on scientifically
unsupported assumptions. The evidence is dependent on flawed
police procedures. It is my view that this evidence is not reliable
as evidence of the defendant's involvement in the shooting. . . .
There is no particular reason why this particle can be so related
to the shooting of Miss Dando.

A series of flawed police procedures had taken place in relation to
the handling of the crucial exhibit, with the jacket being removed
from its sealed bag and placed on a table on which ammunition
had previously been photographed. The jacket was then placed
on a tailor's dummy, on top of a shirt belonging to a police officer
trained in using firearms. The jury at George's trial were informed that police officers who recovered the jacket had not been
wearing the correct forensic clothing; that the officer who put his
hand inside the jacket pocket, to check if it had any contents
before removing it from the flat, had been wearing the same
clothing he had worn when handling ammunition. The police
also admitted they had not taken samples of the van used to take
the jacket and other belongings for examination. Therefore it
could not be ruled out, it was acknowledged, that traces of
firearms discharge residue may have been in the van.

More recently multiple witnesses have said they saw armed
police officers inside George's flat on the day the jacket was
removed, though the police deny this. There were many ways in
which contamination could have occurred and as a result Mr
Justice Gage told the members of the jury that they could not be
allowed to consider the particle to be evidence in its own right. It
could, he warned, only be used to corroborate other evidence.

During police questioning George was asked about his interest
in guns. Had he ever owned a gun? Had he ever adapted a
firearm? Dando's killer had used a modified 9mm handgun. This
was known because there were no rifling marks on the bullet and
so the murder weapon must have been either been a blank firing
gun that had been altered so that it could fire bullets, a deacti-
vated gun which had been reactivated, or a gun with a long barrel
which had been shortened.

George can be described as a man who has fads. His interests change on a regular basis. During his adolescence and early adult years he was fascinated with rock music and would claim to be called Paul Gadd (based on the real name of the then popular musician Gary Glitter). During the early to mid 1980s George had become interested in guns, as many young adult males are, and it must be remembered George is quite immature. Whilst interested in guns he used the false name Thomas (or Tom) Palmer, after a member of the SAS who was involved in the Iranian Embassy siege. When George then became interested in stunts he changed his "name" from Tom Palmer to Steve Powers (an amalgamation of the real name and character name of the *Six Million Dollar Man*). In the 1990s George then turned to the name by which he was best known residents of Fulham even following Dando's murder: Barry Bulsara, the name George used when pretending to be the cousin of Freddie Mercury (Mercury's real surname was Bulsara). By the 1990s, when Barry Bulsara was the only false name George ever used, the name Tom Palmer had not been used for more than 15 years. The name was no longer used because George's fad with firearms had long ended.

George had fired rifles under supervision during a brief service with the Territorial Army in 1982, before he left after failing his basic training, and he had tried to join a gun club that same year although, contrary to what the jury were told at trial, George never fired a weapon during his visits to the club and he was not allowed to go onto the firing range. His membership was turned down because he was unemployed and could not find a suitable person to be his reference.

By April 1999 Barry no longer had the same level of interest in firearms that he had displayed in the mid 1980s. All the firearms magazines in George's flat (perfectly legal magazines that can be bought in any large newsagents) dated from the 1980s. The only reason they were still in the flat was the same as why lots of junk was present: Barry hoards rubbish. There was so much rubbish when the police entered the flat, during a search of the premises, that they could not see there was a bed in his bedroom. There was no evidence George had fired a real gun since 1982 and there was no evidence he had ever owned a real firearm. One particle of alleged firearms discharge residue amongst all of George's belongings can never be interpreted as proof of George's ownership of any gun, let alone the murder weapon.

The particle of alleged firearms discharge residue was not, contrary to popular belief, the only forensic evidence in the case of the Crown vs George.

Forensic examination of Dando's clothing revealed a single polyester textile fibre on her raincoat. The fibre was one half of a millimetre in length but, according to experts, it matched the fibres on a pair of trousers found at George's flat. This, the prosecution alleged, contributed to the compelling evidence against the defendant. However, like the particle of alleged firearms discharge residue, the fibre was not without its problems.

Garments or clothing, such as a pair of trousers, are produced in huge numbers. Although George was extravagant enough to spend a large sum of money on a Cecil Gee jacket for his wedding, the remainder of his clothes were ones widely available in High Street stores and through catalogues. Therefore if the fibre originated from the killer's clothing it only meant they had clothing with fibres of the same size, shape and material as those in George's trousers. Additionally there was nothing to say that the fibre on the victim's raincoat even originated from a pair of trousers. It could have come from any garment which happened to have polyester within it.

Furthermore, the fibre did not necessarily originate from the gunman. Dando had been shopping up to half an hour before her death and so the fibre could easily have transferred from an innocent shopper as they brushed up against her. Or it might conceivably have originated from a paramedic or member of the public who had tried to attend to Dando as she lay bleeding. Someone would later describe the scene as resembling "Piccadilly Circus" with all the people who had been present after the crime, trying their best to assist the television presenter, even though she was technically dead the second the bullet was fired.

Due to the small size of the fibre it could only be subjected to four of the five tests that are usually carried out to prove that two fibres are identical. Dye could not be extracted from the single fibre and therefore its true, specific colour could not be identified. The fibre was grey but this was insufficient information to compare it with the colour of the fibres in the trousers because the exact shade remained a mystery.

Mark Webster, giving evidence for the defence in relation to the fibre, told the court that: "A single grey polyester fibre is not in my view significant evidence. It is not something you should rely on."

Webster believed the evidence was so weak it should have been thrown out of court and it had no significance towards the crime. However, although the evidence was only just deemed admissible, the prosecution told the members of the jury that it contributed towards a significant chain of forensic evidence.

The forensic evidence in the Barry George case was, as has been shown, circumstantial in its entirety and so questionable that it could not, in any way, be deemed to be compelling by any stretch of the imagination. None of George's fingerprints, hairs or DNA were found at the scene of the crime and none of Dando's DNA was present on any of George's clothing, including the pair of trousers that the prosecution claimed the fibre originated from, despite the certainty that Dando's killer fled the crime scene with blood upon his clothing. The position in which he held his victim during the kill would have ensured, at the very least, a small but significant amount of backspatter.

The main evidence used to charge George with murder was the particle. However, the main evidence used to convict the man serving a life sentence in Whitemoor Prison, was eyewitness testimony that was unavailable to the police until four months after George was remanded into custody pending his trial.

In July 2002 the Court of Appeal ruled that without the evidence of Susan Mayes, evidence which the police only obtained in October 2000, it was unlikely any trial would have taken place. By the time the police had decided George was the most suitable candidate for the position of defendant in the Jill Dando murder trial, the only two witnesses who are known to have seen the killer failed to recognize George when he stood on an identity parade. In fact both eyewitnesses believed George was not the man they had seen on the day of the crime.

The evidence of a number of eyewitnesses (witnesses who saw a man in the area, not necessarily the man responsible for the shooting), including one who could not even estimate an age of the man she had seen and a second who failed to realize she had seen anyone on the day of the murder until one year later, failed to impress although the prosecution at trial managed to somehow convince the jury that the latter's evidence was compelling. Her description of the man she had seen one hour and forty minutes before the murder seemingly comprised of a collage of descriptions provided in the media in the weeks after the shooting, which has led to the suggestion that she might not have seen anyone and her memory of seeing a man was in reality a result of the media having influenced her recollection of events, due to an autistic condition she suffers from which means she cannot accurately remember when certain events took place.

Mayes claimed she was "very sure" she saw George across from 29 Gowan Avenue at 7.00 a.m. on the morning of 26 April 1999. Mayes looked at the man intermittently for a total of five to six seconds, she told the court at George's trial. During this time, she said, the man was covering his face for part of the time and had his face turned away for at least a second. He was wiping the windscreen of a car and looked agitated, the court heard. Mayes believed the man was responsible for the vehicle, which was unnecessarily double-parked. Barry George cannot drive due to his epilepsy and general inability to perform even the simplest of tasks.

In her statement to the police, Susan Mayes described the man as having a "short smart" haircut, whereas at trial she described the man as looking thuggish with long and untidy hair, going over his collar. It was a very different description. Yet in October 2000 Mayes was convinced the man on the video screen (Barry George) was the man she had seen eighteen months earlier even though in the video footage only George's face was visible and by this point in time he had grown a beard and moustache, whereas the killer was clean shaven.

All in all it was the evidence of Susan Mayes which allegedly placed George at the scene of the crime, albeit four and a half hours before the crime was committed, and it was the evidence of the particle and fibre which allegedly proved George's involvement in the crime. The jury were told that the eyewitness and forensic evidence together provided "compelling" proof of George's guilt, with the Court of Appeal adding justification, it has been claimed, for the police and prosecution's theories, and the jury's verdict when three appeal judges told a shocked Barry George that they had "no doubt" as to his guilt. The failure of his previous appeal is not a testament to his guilt, however. Indeed in July 2003 David Cooper and Michael McMahon had their murder convictions quashed after their five previous appeals had been dismissed. Each time Cooper and McMahon had been told that there was "no doubt" as to their guilt but new evidence showed otherwise.

George's conviction may have been upheld at the Court of Appeal but the growing disquiet surrounding his conviction, and the new evidence obtained by the campaign for justice, means the controversy surrounding this high-profile criminal case is unlikely to go away. Barry George has never wavered from his claim he did not murder Jill Dando. He has never confessed to the crime and has never provided incriminating evidence to anyone he has spoken to during the almost seven years he has spent in prison. Unusually, those who have served with him in prison believe him to be innocent, as do prison staff. The evidence against George was substantially weakened at trial, with claims that the infamous particle may have been the result of contamination, and has been eroded further since the conviction. It is hardly surprising, therefore, that an increasing number of notaries, including a small number of MPs, are beginning to believe that eight years after her untimely death, Jill Dando's murder remains unsolved with an innocent man having been incarcerated for a crime he did not commit and, more worryingly, that there may be a cold-blooded killer who is still on the loose.

THE VAMPIRE RAPIST

(Wayne Boden, Canada 1971)

Clifford L. Linedecker

The Canadian press dubbed Wayne Boden "The Vampire Rapist" because he sank his teeth into his victims' breasts with such force that his teeth-marks were plainly visible at the autopsies. Boden had a sadistic obsession with women's breasts, and killed and raped several times before being caught and convicted on the clinching evidence of an orthodontist. This expert identified the teeth-marks on one of the women's breasts as having twenty-nine points of similarity as Boden's. The assaults began in the summer of 1968 in Montreal and by early 1970 the killer was wanted for four rape-murders in and around that city. But despite massive publicity and a huge manhunt, Canada's most notorious killer remained at large. The next killing occurred 2,500 miles away in Calgary in May 1971. This time the killer was glimpsed at the wheel of his car and Boden was picked up the following day. He was sentenced to life imprisonment for the murder of the Calgary victim, and received three more life terms for three of the Montreal murders, always denying responsibility for the first killing. Clifford L. Linedecker (b. 1931) worked as a reporter and rewrite man for various American newspapers before switching to magazines in the 1970s. For much of the 1980s he was executive editor of the weekly tabloid National Examiner *and is now a full-time author and freelance writer. He has written nearly thirty books, most of them on true-life crime, and lives in Florida.*

Despite the serene expression on the face of the petite young schoolteacher who looked almost as if she had merely dropped off to sleep after a few pleasant moments of romance, homicide investigators realized as soon as they saw her that they were dealing with the grisly handiwork of a murderous sexual psychopath.

Attractive twenty-one-year-old Norma Vaillancourt was dead. And the peaceful expression on her face was spoiled by an ugly purple-and-red bruise that circled her throat – and by ragged, bloody marks left by human teeth that had savaged her bare breasts. She was nude.

The teacher's macabre death marked the beginning of a ghastly sex, mutilation, and murder spree that would make headlines throughout Canada and baffle the Montreal police department's top homicide investigators for nearly four years.

And ironically, the horror that began in Canada's largest city on a hot midsummer day in 1968 would not end until the psychopath that both journalists and police called the Vampire Rapist moved more than twenty-three hundred miles away to the western province of Alberta.

Homicide detectives summoned to Miss Vaillancourt's Montreal apartment a few minutes after 1 p.m. on July 23, however, could hardly have known that they would soon be looking for a perverted serial killer with an amazing ability to exert a hypnotic-like charm over trusting young women. Like Miss Vaillancourt, most of the victims would be lured into romantic trysts that ended not in the promised glamour and excitement of a love affair but in savage mutilation and violent death.

Except for clues collected from the body itself – semen, foreign pubic hairs, and the telltale bite marks – investigators were unable to collect much helpful evidence in the victim's apartment. There were no signs of a struggle, such as overturned furniture or torn flesh under her fingernails or bruises, to indicate she may have tried to scratch and fight off an assailant. Nor was there any indication that any of her personal property had been stolen.

Detectives quickly turned to the circle of acquaintances she had formed since moving from the small town of Ste Anne-des-

Monts, along the southeast shore of the St Lawrence Seaway, to taste the big-city life of Montreal. She had loved the excitement of the city and was as vivacious and popular as she was pretty. Investigators quickly put together a long list of boyfriends. They learned, in fact, that she was seen with three different men on the day before her death.

After an autopsy was performed, pathologists estimated the time of death at about 10 p.m. the night before the body was discovered.

But although investigators patiently tracked down her friends and acquaintances, paying special attention to the men she had known, their efforts didn't produce a single solid suspect. Contacts with other law-enforcement agencies in Canada and in the United States in efforts to turn up reports of similar crimes were also fruitless.

The popular young schoolteacher had been dead more than a year when twenty-year-old Shirley Audette died. Like Norma Vaillancourt, she had brown hair and was petite, weighing in at around one hundred pounds. She had also had sex with a man shortly before her death, her breasts were shredded and bloodied by a series of savage bite marks, and she had been strangled.

Unlike the other woman, she was almost fully clothed, except for her brassiere, which had been forcefully ripped off before her body was found in a courtyard at the rear of an apartment complex about a block from her own. But like Norma Vaillancourt, she was a small-town girl; she had moved to the city from suburban Longueuil.

Investigators theorized that the victim was strangled and raped in one of the hundreds of apartments in the neighbourhood, then dressed by her killer, carried to the courtyard, and dumped.

Questioning of acquaintances quickly turned up indications that the young woman not only had known her killer but had also suspected that he was dangerous. Detectives learned that she had confided her apprehension to a friend at the shop where she worked as a clerk. "I'm embarked on something which I'm not sure I'll be able to get out of," she had said.

The dead woman's boyfriend provided even stronger indications of her distress when he told police that he telephoned her at about 3 a.m., during his 7 p.m. to 7 a.m. shift at an area factory.

"I'm scared," she said.

When he asked her what she was frightened of, she replied that she was "just scared." She refused to elaborate.

The boyfriend was the last person known to have talked to her, except for her killer.

More than a year later, twenty-year-old Marielle Archambault was murdered. The body of the pretty jewellery-store clerk was found in her apartment at about 1 p.m. on November 24, 1969. She was sprawled on the living-room floor, partly covered with a blanket. Her panty hose were pulled down under her knees, and her brassiere had been ripped and torn down the middle.

The Vampire Rapist had left his macabre calling card on her breasts and neck. They were torn and bloodied with the marks of human teeth.

This time, however, there were signs that a minor struggle had occurred, and the killer had left behind what appeared to be a promising clue: a crumpled photograph of a handsome young man.

The photograph itself was too badly damaged to permit making reproductions with a camera, but a police artist provided a sketch that was quickly flashed to law-enforcement agencies and the news media throughout Canada. Other officers began contacting acquaintances and friends of the slain young woman for questioning and viewing of the sketch.

Her employer and other co-workers quickly agreed that the drawing resembled a young man who had twice stopped at the store to chat with Marielle on the last afternoon they had seen her alive. They said he first stopped in at about 4:30 p.m., then an hour later. She seemed to be pleased, and the second time she told him to wait, because she would be getting off work in a few minutes. He nodded in agreement, and the couple left the shop together at about 6 p.m.

The shopkeeper and his employees said that the first time Marielle talked with the young man she spoke French, then switched to English. She called him Bill.

Because her first language was French, the fact that she had called to him in English when she suggested he wait for her led investigators to believe that English was his primary language.

The mystery man was described as about twenty-five years old, five feet, nine inches tall, 160 to 165 pounds, and well dressed, with moderately long, carefully styled hair.

Delving further into Marielle's background, detectives learned that she had come to the big city from nearby Jolliette, and liked to party and have a good time with other fun-loving singles at popular local night spots.

Bill was also apparently a regular at many of the discotheques, and several young people pointed out that they frequently saw him around on the club, scene. But no one was able to provide a last name, address, place of employment, or any other information helpful in leading police to the slippery man-about-town. And despite his obvious fondness for nightclubs and pretty girls, he dropped abruptly from sight. He wasn't seen around at the discos anymore.

But he was a hot suspect in at least three grisly sex-and-mutilation murders, and investigators felt almost certain that it was only a matter of time and opportunity before the Vampire Rapist would strike again. They renewed the public warnings to young women to beware of strangers, no matter how charming they might appear to be.

A new year and new decade were ushered in without incident. Then, barely three weeks later, Jean Way died. The lovely twenty-four-year-old brokerage-firm secretary was apparently raped and strangled in her apartment while a boyfriend stood impatiently outside, ringing the doorbell to pick her up for a date.

The date had been set for 8:30 p.m., but the boy-friend arrived about fifteen minutes early and was surprised and disappointed when she didn't answer the bell. He later told investigators that he just couldn't believe she had broken their date without notifying him.

Disappointed but not yet ready to give up seeing the lovely secretary, he walked to a nearby tavern, where he had a couple of beers, then he tried to telephone her at about 9:15 p.m. When she failed to answer the phone, he returned to the apartment. This time when she didn't respond to the bell, he tried the door. It was unlocked, and he swung it open and walked in.

His girlfriend was stretched out naked on the front-room sofa with a leather belt knotted around her neck. Her clothes were lying all over the floor, where they had been thrown as they were ripped from her body. Her breasts were covered with bloody bite marks.

A window was open, leading police to speculate later that the killer had planned to leap from the second-floor apartment after the boyfriend's unexpected arrival interrupted the murder and rape.

Jean roomed with a nurse who worked a 4 p.m. to midnight shift at a local hospital. The room-mate told detectives that she telephoned her friend at about 7 p.m., and Jean said that she was with a male friend. Jean named him, but the nurse could remember only the first name, Bill.

Detectives also learned that on the afternoon of the day before she died, Jean had stopped in a photo studio to have some film developed. When she left she pleaded to use the back door. The proprietor said she told him that she was frightened of a man outside who had been annoying her.

"I'm scared," she said.

Of four victims, she was the third who had confided to friends or acquaintances shortly before their deaths that they were afraid of someone.

An autopsy confirmed evidence of sexual intercourse between the victim and a man shortly before or at about the same time of her death. And although she had died of strangulation, the weapon was the killer's hands. The belt had apparently been looped around her neck and tightened after she was killed, to make sure that she was dead.

But the age and appearance of the victim, including her petite build, as well as the location of the murder and the mutilated breasts, clearly marked the slaying as the handiwork of the same killer who had been terrorizing young Montreal women for nearly three years. And like the other women, Jean Way was not a native of the city. The second of three children of a surveyor and his wife, she was a native of Hare Bay, Newfoundland.

Some of the most experienced homicide detectives on the Montreal Police Department had devoted two years to the investigation of the sex stranglings, and yet it seemed there was nothing they could do to put a stop to the horror. They had few leads to work on, and one of the most promising – the crumpled photograph – had distintegrated when they learned that the man in the picture had died before the first murder in the series occurred. Police had spent hundreds of man-hours trying to match a suspect to the photograph.

And despite repeated warnings, naive and trusting young women continued to fall under the evil Svengali-like spell of the bloodthirsty killer. "If the fiend isn't a hypnotist, he has a hypnotic way about him," a frustrated police spokesman declared at a press conference. "He seduces and strangles with such a delicate touch that the victims show no agonized expression."

Among themselves, some investigators speculated that the killer might have selected young women he instinctively felt were a bit masochistic and would permit some delicate biting and strangling during sex. But sometimes their lover would get carried away, lose his gentle touch, and become homicidal.

Detective Lieutenant Marcel Allard, who was in charge of the special ten-man squad working almost full-time on the case, warned that investigators were certain the strangler would strike again. "We're dealing with a psychopath," he continued. "We've had dozens of psychiatrists tell us that he must hate women, or that he hated his mother, or sister, or wife, etc, etc. But that still doesn't help find him."

Although police weren't yet aware of it, the nightmare had in fact ended at last for the shaken citizens of Montreal. It hadn't yet started more than two thousand miles away, in Calgary.

Known worldwide for its famous rodeo, the annual Calgary Stampede, the city of nearly a half million people is broad-shouldered and brash, and peopled by citizens who pride themselves on self-reliance and minding their own business.

But the entire community was stunned when it was learned that one of the most sadistic and ghoulish killers in Canada's history had apparently shifted his nightmare activities from Montreal to their city.

The first hint of trouble surfaced when Elizabeth Anne Porteous, a skilled and well-liked business education teacher at Bowness High School, failed to show up for morning classes or to notify her principal that she was ill. She didn't answer telephone calls from other school employees, and she failed to respond after the manager of the high-rise apartment hotel she lived in was notified and knocked at her door.

Another teacher who lived in the same building had knocked at the door earlier on her way to work and had gotten the same results. There was no response.

By early afternoon, the concern of the thirty-three-year-old teacher's colleagues was turning to dread. She had a reputation for dependability and efficiency and wasn't the kind of person who would suddenly decide she needed an unscheduled day off or would leave town because of family problems without notifying her employers. The building manager was contacted again and was asked to enter her apartment to check on her.

The manager let himself in with a pass-key. The apartment was a shambles. Furniture was overturned, and papers were scattered over the floor. The manager quickly retreated and called for police.

The schoolteacher was lying on her back on the bedroom floor. Her dress was ripped open and her brassiere had been violently torn from her body. Her breasts and neck were smeared with blood and punctured with the imprints of human teeth.

It was May 18, 1971, nearly a year and a half since Jean Way died in Montreal. An alert news reporter quickly recognized the ghastly trademark of the Vampire Rapist, and after confirming his suspicions with a phone call to Montreal, he passed on his information to Calgary police.

Had Canada's most-sought-after serial slayer moved to Calgary from Montreal? The media wanted to know. Or were police looking at the work of a copycat killer?

Like three, possibly four of the Montreal victims, the schoolteacher had been slain in her own apartment, and like all four, her breasts had been mutilated with bites from human teeth. And like the others, she had grown up as a small-town girl. The only child of a banker and his wife, she was a native of Dundas, in Ontario.

But despite the similarities to the Vampire Rapist's dark deeds, there were also several glaring differences in the teacher's slaying. The condition of the apartment and of the body left no doubt that she had put up a fierce fight for her life. Not only was the front room a shambles, but the fight had apparently extended into the bathroom as well. A corner of the water closet on the toilet had been shattered, and the medicine cabinet was pulled from the wall. Bright red buttons from the victim's dress were scattered over the floors of both rooms, like malignant drops of blood. A woman's shoes, with the heel ripped off, lay on its side in the hallway.

And there was no sign of the serene expression on the teacher's face that had added such a bizarre dimension to the Montreal murders. Her agonized grimace showed clearly that she had died in terrible fear and pain.

After police technicians had photographed the body at the crime scene, and its location on the floor had been pinpointed as precisely as possible, the corpse was removed for autopsy to the morgue at Calgary General Hospital. As the body was being raised at the hospital to remove the shredded remains of the dress, a man's cufflink clattered onto the metal examining table. It would become a valuable piece of evidence.

As expected, the autopsy disclosed that the victim had been raped. And, true to the murder style of the Vampire Rapist, she had been strangled: either with the killer's hands, or from pressure applied to her throat with his forearm.

Pathologists also discovered five fresh burn marks on her back, which they believed were inflicted with the tip of a lighted cigarette.

As news of the tragedy flashed throughout Calgary, friends and acquaintances of the dead woman began to contact police with information. A man-and-wife pair of educators told police that the night before Elizabeth's body was discovered, they had seen her with a man who appeared to be in his mid-twenties. They said they were stopped at a traffic light when she and her well-dressed companion pulled up beside them. They recalled that the car was an older-model light blue Mercedes, and it had the small figure of a steer visible in the rear window.

A description of the vehicle was disseminated to all uniform and plain-clothes officers in Calgary, and they were told to be on the lookout for it. The owner, or driver, was wanted for questioning.

One of Elizabeth's friends told police that the teacher had talked to her about a date she had set up for the night of May 17. But, unfortunately, she hadn't named her escort or provided any other helpful background about him.

But another friend, a former teacher at the high school, informed detectives that they were in the nearby mountain resort town of Banff about a month earlier when Elizabeth met a handsome young man in a cocktail lounge. The good-looking stranger appeared to be in his mid-twenties, had stylishly long brown hair, and was well dressed.

While exchanging the usual cocktail banter, he had identified himself as a car salesman and said he drove a Mercedes. He said his name was Bill. Surprisingly, the couple learned, they had grown up in the same town, Dundas, Ontario.

Elizabeth was impressed with the smooth-talking stranger, and before leaving the lounge she scribbled her name, address, and telephone number on a piece of paper and suggested that he give her a call sometime.

The day after the grisly discovery of the teacher's body, a policeman spotted an older-model light blue Mercedes parked a few blocks from her high-rise apartment. A stakeout was set up, and after a brief wait a young man was apprehended as he approached the vehicle.

He readily admitted the car was his, but said he didn't know anything about the man called Bill, whom police were looking for. He said his name was Wayne Clifford Boden, he was twenty-three, and he had been in Calgary about eighteen months since leaving his native Ontario. He was a traveling salesman, and was originally from Dundas – Elizabeth Porteous's hometown.

Transported to police headquarters for interrogation, Boden conceded that he had dated the unfortunate schoolteacher, but insisted that he knew nothing about her murder. He said they had gone to a nightclub for a few drinks and dancing, and that he had her back at her apartment before midnight. She invited him in for coffee, he said, but explained that he declined because it was late and both of them had to work the next morning. He added that he heard her latch the door as he left.

"Elizabeth was alive when I saw her last," he declared.

When police interrogators showed him the cufflink that dropped from her dress, he admitted it was his but said he lost it at the apartment before they went out nightclubbing. They had looked all over the apartment for it, he claimed.

Despite Boden's smooth replies and repeated protestations of innocence, he was charged with first-degree murder in the teacher's slaying and lodged in jail.

But the investigation was still a long way from over. Police in Montreal were notified of the arrest and sent Criminal Investigation Bureau detectives to question Boden about the serial killings there.

Their difficulties with the bizarre case hadn't yet ended, however, and by a curious twist of fate, as the three detectives were returning to Montreal, their Air Canada jet was hijacked. They were eventually rescued, along with 115 other passengers and crewmen.

In Calgary, homicide officers spread out on a variety of assignments aimed at putting together an undeniable chain of evidence against the suspected sex strangler. Some detectives continued questioning acquaintances of the victim, and others began assembling information about Boden's background.

Checks with authorities in Dundas, and in the larger nearby city of Hamilton where Boden had also lived for a time, revealed that he had no record of trouble with police in either community. Police in Dundas, in fact, recalled him as a mild-mannered youth. He appeared to be well behaved and well liked.

A search warrant was also obtained from the Alberta courts, and police began a painstaking search of Boden's apartment. The search turned up a red button similar to those ripped from Elizabeth's dress. It had been discarded in a paper wastebasket. Detectives also confiscated a cartoon book filled with drawings of women, which someone had crudely sketched over with gross exaggerations of the breasts and nipples.

A young woman who had been living with Boden as his

common-law wife told investigators that they had come to Calgary from Montreal about eighteen months earlier. On the night the schoolteacher was murdered, he had told his sweetheart that he was going to a sales meeting. He returned about midnight, looking very tired.

The slender, soft-spoken salesman went on trial for the Porteous murder on Feburary 15, 1972, in the Alberta Supreme Court before Chief Justice J. V. H. Milvain. As anticipated, both the cufflink and the button recovered from the wastebasket figured as important pieces of physical evidence.

But some of the most sensational testimony was provided by a Calgary orthodontist who confirmed that the bite marks on the breasts and neck of the victim were inflicted by the teeth of the defendant. The unique character of Boden's teeth and bite matched the wounds on the victim.

Appearing as an expert witness, the orthodontist testified that an analysis of the wounds showed twenty-nine points of similarity to the formation of Boden's teeth. Thirteen points were matched on the right breast and sixteen on the left. The minimum total number of concordant points required by law for identification was thirteen, he told the court.

He added that his findings were confirmed by a skilled British orthodontist who was also an experienced consultant on similar wounds and a respected expert witness.

The dental expert's testimony made judicial history in Canada, where it marked the first time such evidence was admitted in court for the purpose of identifying a defendant.

A crime technician with the Royal Canadian Mounted Police crime-detection laboratory in Edmonton identified a pair of men's shorts, removed from Boden and found to be stained with seminal fluid. The technician testified that strands of hair found in the shorts were identical in color and texture to hairs taken from the body of the victim. He also identified hair taken from the rug in her apartment as matching hair taken from Boden.

But the most startling testimony of all dealt with a conversation Boden had at police headquarters with his live-in lover three days after the victim's body was discovered.

The chief of the Calgary Police Department's homicide squad

said he was present when Boden, in effect, confessed the murder to his girlfriend. Detective Sergeant Ernest Reimer testified that Boden told the woman he was going to plead not guilty by reason of insanity, then asked if she knew what he meant. He said Boden repeated the question, then declared:

"You understand? I am the one. That is why I am charged. I did it but I don't know why. It's not in my character to do something like that."

Boden's girlfriend also testified, confirming the homicide sergeant's statements about the conversation. She said that her boyfriend appeared to be "pretty shook up" when he told her about his plans for the insanity plea.

Boden did not testify, and his defence counsel did not call any witnesses.

At the conclusion of the trial, conducted without a jury, Boden was pronounced guilty by Chief Justice Milvain of non-capital murder. He was given the mandatory sentence: life in prison.

But the young sex strangler's troubles weren't yet over. He was still wanted in Montreal, where he was suspected as the Vampire Rapist who had terrorized the city for more than two years.

Although he had previously denied being the killer, he waived extradition to Ontario, then gave statements to police admitting three of the Montreal slayings. Police learned that he had known and dated Jean Way for about a year before she was killed. He had also lived in an apartment near Shirley Audette's home, and he hung around the same discotheques as Marielle Archambault.

When he appeared before Justice Jacques Ducros, in the Court of Queen's Bench in Montreal, Boden disregarded the advice of his court-appointed attorney and pleaded guilty to the three murders. He admitted that he had strangled Shirley Audette, Marielle Archambault, and Jean Way.

But he denied that he was responsible for murdering Norma Vaillancourt, the first victim in the shocking string of sex-and-mutilation slayings on Montreal's West End that had been blamed on the Vampire Rapist.

Despite the best efforts of the Montreal Police Department's homicide investigators, Crown prosecutors determined that there was insufficient evidence to convict Boden of the Archambault killing, so he was not charged and brought to trial in that case. Officially, the murder was left unsolved.

Boden, however, was sentenced to separate life prison terms for the other three slayings that he had confessed to.

The Canadian justice system hadn't yet heard the last of him, however.

Barely more than twelve years after he was sentenced to four life terms behind bars, he walked away from an unarmed guard in downtown Montreal while he was on an authorized strangler's day off from a federal maximum-security prison. The prison arts-and-crafts teacher assigned to accompany him on his daylong holiday gave him permission to go to the washroom in a hotel restaurant by himself – and he never returned.

Instead, the onetime Vampire Rapist who had held the city hostage to a nightmare more than a decade earlier not only left his escort without a prisoner to return with but also stuck him with the dinner bill as well. Then he looked up an old friend he had met in prison, and they went out on the town together.

Police caught up with Boden the next evening when patrons at a bar where he was drinking recognized him from the old days and turned him in. He was sitting quietly in the artificial twilight of the bar, wearing dark glasses, and casually sipping a beer.

According to his ex-convict pal, Boden had spent a good part of the previous evening drinking with a woman he met at another hotel bar in the same neighbourhood he roamed when he had held the city hostage to a nightmare of sexual assault, mutilation, and murder. He financed his spree with three hundred dollars in prison earnings and with a credit card he had been issued while behind bars in 1977.

Police and citizens were apprehensive and outraged when they learned that the Vampire Rapist had been allowed to so casually resume his old bar-hopping habits. When Louis Way, the father of one of the Montreal victims, was contacted by a newspaper reporter, he was shocked: "What's the world coming to when you have people like that prowling the streets?" he asked. "As far as I'm concerned, they should bring back the death penalty."

But the thirty-six-year-old killer was convinced that it was he who had been wronged, and when he appeared before Sessions

Court Judge André Chalous he complained that he pulled off the high-profile escape merely to get media attention. He was angry that he had been kept in prison so long without parole.

"I want someone to go to Ottawa and find out why I have been put off for thirteen years," he complained.

"You killed three people in Montreal," the judge sternly reminded him.

Boden was returned to the federal government's Laval Correctional Development Centre, with a new one-year prison sentence to serve for escape. He had fled the same prison during the second of two outings allowed outside the walls.

Asked about future security measures for the notorious Vampire Rapist, a corrections official told newsmen that it would be "a good while" before he was awarded another day on the town.

CONFLICT OF EVIDENCE

(Sidney Fox, UK 1930)

Sydney Smith

For Bernard Spilsbury, the Crippen case was a personal triumph, a turning-point. He was retained as a pathologist by the Home Office for the next thirty-seven years, and his appearance as an expert Crown witness in a series of important murder trials between the wars brought him celebrity status. "To the man in the street," explained Edgar Lustgarten, "he stood for pathology as Hobbs stood for cricket or Dempsey for boxing or Capablanca for chess." Spilsbury's good looks, easy courtroom manner and his knack of explaining complex forensic points in clear, simple language mesmerized juries. But in 1930 he found himself pitted against a younger, ambitious pathologist called Sydney Smith, who'd been retained by the defence in the sad and sordid case of Sidney Fox, a homosexual drifter accused of murdering his own white-haired mother. Fox was believed to have strangled her and set fire to her room in order to collect on her life insurance, which he had recently increased. Spilsbury, Smith and two other medical experts disagreed in court over the evidence of strangulation. Spilsbury (by now Sir Bernard), who conducted the post-mortem examination of Mrs Rosaline Fox, believed she had been strangled before the fire started, and that she had died from asphyxia due to manual strangulation. Sydney Smith, making his debut as an expert witness for the defence, gave it as his definite opinion that Mrs Fox had died of heart failure, brought on by exertion and fright, having woken to find her room full of smoke. Born in New Zealand, Sir Sydney Smith (1883–1969) was Regius professor of forensic medicine at Edinburgh University for twenty-

five years. The Fox case (Smith hyped it as "one of the causes célébres of the century") was the first of his frequent court clashes with Spilsbury. Although Fox's trial is said to have involved a direct conflict of medical evidence, the truth is less clear-cut. The evidence on which the two sets of expert witnesses (prosecution and defence) base their opinions is seldom the same: in this case, as in others, the pathologist summoned by the Crown was first in the field. Spilsbury saw the bruise on Mrs Fox's larynx, but Smith did not, because by the time he examined the larynx several months later, the bruise had disappeared.

Sidney Harry Fox was not a good citizen. He was in the hands of the police before he was twelve, and in prison at nineteen; and he was in and out of gaol throughout the remaining eleven years of his life.

He was a forger, a blackmailer, a swindler, and a thief. He was also a homosexual, although when he appeared at his last trial he had just been cited as a co-respondent in an action for divorce. He admitted the adultery but denied any pleasure in it. He was proud of his inversion, and claimed that he had never been with a woman except as a means to get her money.

Clever and plausible, and something of a charmer, he had lived by his wits all his life. Yet as a criminal he had not been a success. At the time of his final arrest, when he was thirty, he possessed nothing in the world but a long record of convictions and a number of debts. He had even been hard put to it to find two shillings for the premium on an accident insurance he took out on his mother's life.

They made a pretty picture, the dear old lady with the shuffling gait – she suffered from paralysis agitans – and the devoted son. She was undoubtedly fond of him, although hardly a model parent. Her husband was probably not Sidney's father, and she was a confederate in most of her son's crimes. When he was not in prison they lived mainly in hotels, moving round the country and leaving a trail of unpaid bills and dud cheques. It was a hand-to-mouth existence, and they had no luggage at all when they arrived at the Hotel Metropole, Margate, on October 16, 1929. Six days later Fox went to London and arranged for two accident insurances that he had taken out on his mother's life to be extended until midnight the following day. At 11.40 p.m. that day Mrs Fox was dead.

Fox himself had raised the alarm about ten minutes earlier. He ran down the hotel stairs, wearing only a shirt and shouting that there was a fire. It was in his mother's bedroom. A commercial traveller ran up with him, and succeeded in dragging her out of the smoke-filled room. Artificial respiration was applied, and two doctors were called. By the time the first of them – Dr Austin – arrived Mrs Fox was already dead. Dr Austin examined her, and certified her death as due to shock and suffocation. His colleague, Dr Nichol, arrived soon after, and did not question Dr Austin's opinion.

An inquest was held the next day. The proceedings were brief, and the expected verdict of accidental death was returned. Five days later Mrs Fox was buried in her native village of Great Fransham, in Norfolk. So far as the police were concerned the case was closed.

Fox put in for the insurance. His claims were investigated. An official of one of the insurance companies wired his head office, "Extremely muddy water in this business." Scotland Yard was informed. The case was re-opened, and eleven days after the funeral the body of Mrs Fox was exhumed. A post-mortem examination was performed by Sir Bernard Spilsbury, who said she had been strangled. Fox was charged with murder, and eventually committed for trial. I was asked by his solicitor to give evidence in his defence. After examining the medical part of the case for the Crown, I agreed to appear in the role of expert witness.

I had, of course, given evidence in this role hundreds of times before, but always for the prosecution. I was always available to the Crown in cases occurring in and around Edinburgh, and was commonly asked by them to investigate cases in other parts of the country; but I could also give expert evidence for the defence in cases outside Edinburgh.

It is, I think, to the credit of the British legal system that expert witnesses are made available to the defence by the Crown, and paid by them in cases in which the defendant is without means. Apart from this, I believe that any expert witness should be prepared at any time to place his special knowledge at the disposal of the defence, whether it is in a position to pay him a fee or not. The Crown has all possible resources at its disposal; it can afford to call in as many experts as it wishes, it has access to all records, and has control of the whole machinery of the police, including the Criminal Investigation Department and the police laboratories. The defence usually has only limited resources, is often short or entirely devoid of funds, and must depend to a great extent on a critical appraisement of the evidence produced by the Crown.

The attitude of a scientific witness should be the same whether he is called in by the Crown or by the defence. It is not for him to concern himself with the previous character of the accused or with other evidence in the case. As a scientist he should be completely detached: he must not let himself be influenced in any way by emotional considerations such as sympathy or antipathy. His sole function is to examine the facts which come to his knowledge in his special capacity, to decide what is the true or the most probable interpretation of them, and to indicate to the court that interpretation, along with the grounds on which it is based.

I have often been asked why I have given evidence for the defence in cases in which the accused seemed to be guilty or in which he seemed to be a scoundrel who was not worth saving. In a particular instance the life of the accused may not be worth saving, but the principles of justice always are. Once concede the possibility of conviction on insufficient evidence because the accused is a worthless scamp, and you open the way to flouting the fundamental proposition of our law that every man is innocent until he is proved guilty.

Fox was a bad hat, and he would be in every way, as an eminent Scottish judge said of another rogue, "nane the waur o' a hangin'." It was clear from the start of the case that the circumstantial evidence, especially that relating to the fire and to the insurance policies, might be strong enough to earn him one. That was no concern of mine. My interest was limited to the medical evidence, which I found remarkable.

It depended almost entirely on Spilsbury's post-mortem report. The surprising thing about this came at the end – "Cause of death: asphyxia due to manual strangulation."

A person being strangled fights like mad. Even if the victim is a feeble old woman, Nature will supply her with unsuspected additional strength to help her in her fight for life. She will struggle furiously to wrench the strangler's hands away from her throat. She may fail, but some marks of the struggle will remain. Nearly always there will be scratches about the neck.

There were none here. According to Spilsbury's report, there was no trace of external injury at all – no sign of injury about the mouth or nose or in the skin of the neck, no marks left by the indentation of finger-nails or pressure of finger-tips.

Nor were there any of the usual signs of manual strangulation under the skin or in the tissues, such as bruises in the muscles surrounding the neck and in the larynx where the fingers would grip. Most remarkable of all, there was no fracture of either the thyroid cartilage or the hyoid bone. In elderly persons the hyoid becomes brittle and is easily broken, and this is one of the most characteristic marks of strangling. Yet Mrs Fox's hyoid was unbroken – until Spilsbury broke it himself unintentionally while taking it out. For all his care he could not avoid breaking it in two places. It was as brittle as that.

A strangler's victim is usually not a pretty sight. Bluish or purple lips and ears, change of colour of the nails, froth and possibly blood-staining about the nose or mouth, the tongue forced outward, the hands clenched – these are the typical signs of death from asphyxia.

There were none on Mrs Fox.

There were none of the usual internal signs of asphyxia, either. Instead Spilsbury found, on opening the body, natural disorders that pointed to a different conclusion. Her kidneys were cirrhosed, her arteries diseased, and her heart was in an advanced state of degeneration. The state of the heart alone, as described in Spilsbury's report, seemed to me to have been bad enough to cause death at any time.

Spilsbury himself emphatically rejected this possibility. "Cause of death: asphyxia due to manual strangulation." The oracle had spoken. There was nothing more to be said.

At the trial, under cross-examination, Spilsbury agreed that he had never known of a case of strangulation with fewer signs. He agreed cheerfully, for by then the point was immaterial to him. Spilsbury, like the rest of us, could make mistakes. He was unique, I think, in that he never admitted a mistake. Once he had committed himself to an opinion he would never change it.

"The injuries could, in my opinion, only have been produced by strangulation by the hand." That was Spilsbury's opinion at the beginning and the end, in spite of all that went between.

This opinion was based on four signs. These were hæmorrhage in the epiglottis and three bruises – one on the tongue, one at the back of the larynx, and the third on the thyroid gland. On these he based his theory of strangulation, which he subsequently outlined to the court. Firm pressure, he said, between the thumb and fingers applied to the larynx could have produced the bruise on the thyroid and the hæmorrhage in the epiglottis; the bruise on the larynx might have been caused by forcibly pressing that organ upward; and this pressure could also have closed the victim's jaws and forced her to bite and thus bruise her tongue. With his use of tentative verbs like "could" and "might" the theory sounded so plausible that the unwary could forget it was only a theory, not hard fact.

Spilsbury gave evidence at the proceedings before the Margate magistrates, which began on January 9, 1930. As is usual in such cases, the defence was reserved and no witnesses were called, but Fox's solicitor, George Hindle, cross-examined the Crown witnesses very thoroughly. His purpose was to get them to commit themselves as far as possible – to make definite statements of which they might be reminded, if necessary, at the trial; and also to try to find out as much as possible about the prosecution's line without giving away any clue to the line of the defence.

Thus Hindle sent me an account of Dr Nichol's evidence with a request for any observations that might help him in cross-examination. In fact there was not much that could be asked, as Dr Nichol had neither examined Mrs Fox nor noticed anything

special about her appearance. I advised Hindle to ask Nichol to
confirm that he saw no signs of death from asphyxia, no marks of
violence of any kind, no signs of froth or blood-staining at the
mouth or nose; and that the appearances were quite consistent
with death from heart-failure. Hindle followed my advice, and in
cross-examining Dr Austin also he asked the same questions and
received similar answers; but while Dr Nichol thought the
appearances were not consistent with heart failure, Dr Austin
thought they were.

Spilsbury gave his evidence in his usual clear and definite way,
and he was too experienced in being cross-examined for Hindle to
get much out of him.

"Is it not extraordinary that there were no marks of violence on
the neck?" Hindle asked.

"It is not," Spilsbury replied. "It is unusual in a case of manual
strangulation, but that is another matter."

The case was transferred from Kent to the Sussex Assizes, and
the trial was fixed to begin at Lewes on Wednesday, March 12.
On the preceding Saturday I went to Spilsbury's laboratory at the
University College Hospital in London to look at the various
specimens he had removed at the exhumation.

It was my first professional encounter with the Honorary
Pathologist to the Home Office, a prelude to our first conflict
in court. He could not have been more courteous or helpful. He
showed me the whole of the exhibits.

Among the parts he had preserved was the larynx, which I was
particularly interested to see. Spilsbury regarded the bruise on
this as the main prop of his strangulation theory. I was inclined to
think it was the only prop, and not a very good one at that, for I
regarded the whole theory as flimsy. At the same time I was
intrigued by this bruise. Spilsbury had said in his report that it
was behind the larynx and about the size of a half-crown. I could
not imagine how such a large bruise could have been inflicted
there without damage to the tissues on the side of the larynx or
the neck.

Spilsbury said nothing while I examined the larynx. He just
stood beside me silently, while I looked – not at, but for, the
bruise.

There was none to be seen.

Putrefactive discoloration, yes. No doubt about that. But not even a sixpenny bruise, let alone one the size of half-a-crown.

With me in the laboratory was Dr R. M. Brontë, formerly Crown Pathologist for All Ireland, who had also been asked to appear for the defence. He had crossed swords with Spilsbury in court before. He also examined the larynx, and finally shook his head.

"I can't see any sign of a bruise, Spilsbury," I said at length.

"Nor can I," said Brontë.

"No," agreed Spilsbury. "You can't see it now. But it was there when I exhumed the body."

That fairly staggered me. The larynx had been preserved in formalin ever since the exhumation.

"Where's the bruise gone, then?" I asked.

"It became obscure," said Spilsbury, "before I put the larynx in formalin. That is why I did not take a section."

A microscopical section would have been of inestimable value in showing whether the patch of discoloration Spilsbury had seen was a bruise or not. Personally I was pretty sure it was not. A bruise is caused by the breaking of small vessels which allows blood to be forced out of the vessels into the tissues, where it clots. To get a bruise the size of a half-crown quite a lot of blood would have to be extruded. The blood remains in the tissues, and cannot be removed by post-mortem changes.

"I don't see how a bruise of that size could have just disappeared," I said.

"It became obscure," he repeated. "It was there. I saw it myself."

"Spilsbury, I don't doubt that you saw something," I said. "But I put it to you that it might not have been a bruise. It could have been a patch of discoloration from post-mortem staining or putrefaction." Brontë nodded agreement. "We all know how difficult it is to diagnose a bruise with the naked eye after partial putrefaction has occurred."

Spilsbury listened attentively and was very polite, but he would not argue the point. I had the feeling that nothing I said would make any difference, that his mind was closed. Had I known him then as well as I came to later I would have realized why I was wasting my time. He could not change his opinion now because he had already given it. He had described the alleged bruise in his report and given evidence about it before the magistrates. His belief in himself was so strong that he could not conceive the possibility of error either in his observation or interpretation.

We looked at the other signs of alleged injury. The haemorrhage in the epiglottis was there – a spot the size of the head of a pin, such as might be found on five out of six cases of death from natural causes. There was the bruise on the side of the tongue, which might well have been caused during strangulation – and, just as easily, by the old lady biting her tongue, as she could so easily have done with the badly fitting dentures she wore. Finally there was the alleged bruise on the thyroid gland, and this led to another difference of opinion. It consisted of a few stray red blood corpuscles such as might be found in a section of any ordinary thyroid.

"I cannot accept that as a bruise," I said emphatically.

"Nor can I," said Brontë.

Spilsbury said nothing, but we found an ally in Dr Henry Weir, a pathologist of standing whom the Crown had engaged to support Spilsbury's evidence for the prosecution. He also said it was not a bruise.

The four of us discussed it in the laboratory, and I thought Spilsbury yielded to our view. He said little himself, but I went away with the definite impression that he accepted that on this relatively small point we were right and he was wrong.

Brontë knew him better than I did.

"Not Spilsbury," he said as we left. "You wait till we're in court."

The case for the Crown was that Fox had strangled his mother and then set fire to the room to cover up his crime. Spilsbury had looked for soot on the linings of the air passages, and had tested the blood for carbon monoxide, with negative results in each case. He was therefore satisfied that Mrs Fox had not died through suffocation by smoke. So was I. In my opinion she had not died of asphyxia at all. I thought she might very well have died of heart failure brought on by sudden exertion or fright. The shock of waking up and finding the room full of smoke, and the effort to get out of bed and escape, might well have put a fatal additional strain on her already weakened heart.

One would have thought that any pathologist would have agreed that this was a possibility, but though Weir agreed Spilsbury would not.

The prosecution of Fox was led by the Attorney-General, Sir William (later Lord) Jowitt, and he seemed determined to hang Fox. It is, of course, not the proper function of the Crown counsel to press the case against the accused. An eminent authority, Mr Justice Crompton, once said that the duty of prosecuting counsel was to acquit themselves as ministers of justice, aiding in the administration of the criminal law, and not as advocates attempting to secure a conviction.

Jowitt's attitude was anything but judicial. His treatment of the medical evidence in his opening speech was open to criticism, especially the part dealing with the half-crown bruise. "It will be said, how could the inside bruise be done without an outside bruise? This much is plain: the inside bruise is there. It is there—"

It was not there. Spilsbury himself was to testify that it had vanished from sight four months before.

The first five days of the trial were taken up mainly with non-medical evidence, which was heavy against Fox. Of course, nothing was said about his criminal record, and when Chief-Inspector Hambrook of Scotland Yard gave evidence on his conduct of the case the jury had no inkling that he had arrested Fox for forgery thirteen years before. The evidence that could properly be brought, however, made it pretty clear how he normally obtained his living. There was adequate evidence of motive in the insurances he had taken out on his mother's life. His conduct on the night of her death was at least suspicious.

Dr Austin was the first medical witness. He repeated the evidence he had given at the proceedings before magistrates. Cross-examining for the defence, Mr J. D. Cassels asked him if he saw any signs of death by asphyxia.

"No, except that the face was very flushed, which you find in a case of asphyxia."

"Did you see any marks of violence?"

"No."

"Or appearances consistent with death by heart-failure?"

"Well, I should hardly think so."

Cassels' next question brought out the value of Hindle's careful cross-examination at the preliminary hearing.

"Did you say, in examination at the police court, 'I saw no signs of death from asphyxiation and no marks of violence. As far as I was able to see, the appearances were consistent with heart-failure'?"

"If I am reported to have done so I must have done," Dr Austin replied. "It is five months ago."

Dr Nichol also was cross-examined to good effect. He said that after death Mrs Fox's face was composed, pale, and presented no special significance, that he saw no marks of violence, and that "the woman did not give me the impression of having died from asphyxia."

But all this was of little consequence compared with Spilsbury's evidence, which was given clearly and with great sincerity – and complete conviction.

To explain his theory of how Mrs Fox died, Spilsbury produced a porcelain model of the human mouth and neck.

"At the back of the larynx," he said, pointing to the spot, "I found a large, recent bruise about the size of half-a-crown. It was then that I had the first indication of the conclusions to which I finally came, that death was due to strangulation."

Spilsbury repeated his previous evidence about the bruise on the tongue and the very small haemorrhages on the epiglottis. Then he came to the alleged bruise on the thyroid gland.

"I found a small dark area just on the surface which I thought might be a bruise," he said. "I made microscopical preparations of it which in my view confirmed the presence of a little bruising. I showed the preparations to Dr Weir, Professor Smith, and Dr Brontë, who, however, did not take the same view, and for that reason I prefer that the bruise shall not be considered as a possible injury caused at that time."

"Apart from the thyroid gland," he was then asked, "are we, in your view, outside the region of doubt?"

"Yes."

This answer implied that Spilsbury accepted that there was doubt about the bruise he claimed to have seen on the thyroid gland. With Weir against him as well as us he could hardly do otherwise. But when he was cross-examined he made it clear that he still thought that he was right and the rest of us wrong.

"Is your opinion upon this part of the case as definite as it is on the other parts of the case?" Cassels asked.

"Yes."

The judge asked, "Your opinion is still that the thyroid gland was bruised?"

"That is so."

Since he was still so sure of this, it was not surprising that he refused to admit even the possibility of doubt in the matter of the alleged bruise on the larynx, which only he had seen or would ever see.

Cassels suggested it might have been a mark of putrefaction.

"It was a bruise and nothing else," Spilsbury answered shortly. "There are no two opinions about it."

Certainly only he had seen it. This sort of thing is a common handicap to medical expert witnesses appearing for the defence. The Crown's experts are there from the start, and often there is nothing left to see when the experts for the defence come in. Spilsbury was scrupulously careful and painstaking in his work, but once he had given an opinion nothing would make him change it. The supposed bruise on the thyroid gland was a case in point. No doubt if he alone had seen it he would have put that also outside the region of doubt.

He was an excellent witness, especially for the Crown. I listened attentively while he gave evidence, making notes and passing them to Cassels whenever a fresh line of questioning occurred to me. But there was very little to be got out of Spilsbury, and as usual he made a good impression on the jury. Even the admission that this was the first exhumation he had done in a case of what he thought was manual strangulation did not detract from the effect of his undoubted reputation and complete assurance.

Spilsbury was followed by Dr Weir, who was pathologist to the National Hospital for Diseases of the Heart. He had not seen any more of the remains than I had, but he accepted Spilsbury's statement about the half-crown bruise. However, he did not share Spilsbury's view that death was caused by asphyxia, but agreed with us that it was due to heart-failure, and he was an expert on diseases of the heart. He attributed it to commencing strangulation – but "in my opinion, except for the bruises, there was sufficient disease in the heart to account for death from natural causes."

So the conflict of medical evidence was not only between the prosecution and the defence.

Weir was the last witness called by the Crown. Fox himself was the first witness for the defence, and probably he did himself much more harm than good. He made what was considered his worst mistake when Jowitt questioned him about his actions after discovering the fire in his mother's room.

"Can you explain to me why it was that you closed the door instead of flinging it wide open?" Jowitt asked.

"My explanation for that now is that the smoke should not spread into the hotel."

"Rather that your mother should suffocate in that room than that smoke should get about in the hotel?"

"Most certainly not, sir" – and then, realizing the implication of his answer, Fox half-denied that he had closed the door. But by then the damage was done.

I was called later the same day.

In the course of the years I had learnt a number of lessons about giving evidence in court. One was to confine one's answers to the questions asked; another was not to try to score off counsel. I had also found that it pays to be reticent, and to keep back a few odds and ends to release under cross-examination; this makes the opposing advocate more careful in his approach.

Until this case I had always been treated with consideration and courtesy, and my evidence had not been seriously challenged.

Over many years and in many different courts I had always tried
to give my evidence on the facts as I saw them without any regard
as to whether my opinions were helpful to the prosecution or the
defence. This was my first experience of the clashes between
counsel and expert witness that are a feature of British criminal
courts.

In my examination-in-chief I gave my opinion that there was
not sufficient medical evidence to support a charge of strangulation.

Jowitt began his cross-examination the next morning.

"You stated in your evidence-in-chief that you had a very long
experience in cases involving manual strangulation?"

"Yes."

"Were they cases of strangulation by a young man of an old
woman as the old woman lay in bed?"

"I have had many cases of strangulation of elderly men and
elderly women."

"Will you try to answer my question?"

"I will think of the special conditions for one moment. Yes, I
have had."

"Do you mean to tell us you had not considered that question
before you came to give evidence in this case?"

"I have considered the question."

"Then I take it you have brought your notes of a person being
strangled in bed."

"No, I have not."

"Was there one case, or more than one case?"

"I have had many cases of a somewhat similar nature. May I
explain?"

"Please answer my question. It may be difficult for a gentleman who gives lectures to answer questions, but I want you to
answer mine."

So it began, and so it went on: sharp, harsh, and somewhat
blustering. Jowitt had been well briefed. After a series of questions about the signs of asphyxia he read out a passage from
Taylor's *Medical Jurisprudence* and asked me if I agreed. As my
name was on the title-page of the book as the current editor I
could not have easily disowned it. In fact, however, it was not in

conflict with the opinions I had expressed in evidence, as I was able to explain.

Jowitt continued to press his questions in a rather hectoring way.

"Do you think that is being quite candid with me?" he asked once. Then, "If the answer is 'No' say 'No.' You are not trying to make it difficult for me, are you? I want you to try to help."

"I am, to the best of my ability," I replied, "but you won't give me an opportunity of putting you right. If I begin to explain you say, 'Please answer my question.' It makes it very difficult."

Jowitt went on to the matter of the half-crown bruise.

"You said yesterday that in training assistants you had to be careful in distinguishing in post-mortem examination between bruises and discoloration marks. Do you put Sir Bernard Spilsbury on a par with one of your assistants?"

This was a catch-question. Jowitt was trying to make me belittle Spilsbury.

"Do you suggest Sir Bernard would not know the difference between the two?" he persisted.

"Nobody can tell merely by looking," I replied. "I do not think anyone should say a bruise is a bruise until it has been proved that it is."

"Do you say that you would not say a bruise was a bruise until you put it under a microscope?"

"No, I should cut into it."

"If you saw a fellow with a black eye would you say, 'Let me put it under a microscope before I say it is a black eye'?"

This question surprised me. It was not the sort of thing I would have expected from the Attorney-General.

"Sir Bernard says there can be no two opinions about it," he went on.

"It is very obvious there can be," I pointed out.

"You are bound to accept the evidence of the man who saw the bruise?"

"I do not think so."

"How can you say there was not a bruise there?"

"Because if there was a bruise there it should be there now. It should be there for ever. The larynx is there to be examined by anybody."

With that Jowitt left the half-crown bruise, and the rest of his cross-examination was in a slightly milder tone.

He began pressing again when he cross-examined Brontë, who confirmed my evidence and went on to give the opinion that putrefactive changes "would magnify the bruise and make it easier to detect." He quoted a case in which Spilsbury himself had said the same thing.

Jowitt asked more pointed questions about Spilsbury and the half-crown bruise.

"Are you suggesting Sir Bernard did not see what he said he saw?"

"Far be it from me to make such a suggestion."

"Did you suggest that Sir Bernard Spilsbury was wrong, and that it was a post-mortem change? If Sir Bernard made this mistake it would be a very elementary mistake to make? It is a sort of mistake that every laboratory assistant is warned against?"

Cassels put the matter back into perspective in his closing speech. He recalled the two bruises on which Spilsbury based his theory of strangulation.

"There was, of course, another at one time," he reminded the jury. "Another pinpoint mark, which under a microscope was said to be a sign of bruising upon the thyroid gland – that mark which Sir Bernard Spilsbury still retains his opinion about, but does not desire to have as much importance attached to it as to the other two, because Dr Weir, Professor Smith, and Dr Brontë did not agree with him. If Sir Bernard Spilsbury is wrong about one thing might he not be wrong about something else? No one can say that an individual, whatever his position and skill, is never likely to be mistaken. No one can claim for anybody infallibility."

Mr Justice Rowlatt summed up with perfect fairness.

"There were no external indications of asphyxia. There were no external marks on the throat. Sir Bernard Spilsbury has said it was quite possible there would be none, but you and I might think it difficult to believe it. As regards the brittle bone in the throat known as the hyoid, it is a very curious coincidence that that bone was not broken in this case. That is a very strong point in favour of the accused. As to the mark at the back of the larynx, alleged by the prosecution to be a bruise, there is no doubt that

Sir Bernard Spilsbury saw some object there. It is unfortunate that those tissues could not have been preserved for others to see. The defence have said – and are justified in saying it – that that point rests on the testimony of what one skilled man observed, and observed at one moment only . . ."

Perhaps the judge did not quite appreciate the dangerously high esteem in which that one skilled man was held. Perhaps Spilsbury did not fully realize that fame brings responsibility as well as honour. I do not think the jury would have returned the verdict they did if his evidence had been given by anyone else but Spilsbury.

One hour and ten minutes was all they needed to find Fox guilty.

"My lord," he whispered, "I did not murder my mother. I am innocent."

I believe he was.

I certainly would not have put it past him to murder his mother. He was bad enough for any crime, and the evidence about the renewal of the insurances was heavy against him.

There were many suspicious circumstances in the case, but Fox was specifically charged with and was hanged for strangling his mother. I thought then – and I still think now – that he was innocent of that.

"ACT OF MERCY"

(Dr Hermann Sander, USA 1949)

David Rowan

The case of Dr Sander, the first to involve an act of so-called mercy killing, caused a sensation in the early months of 1950. It arose from Dr Sander's open admission that while treating a dying patient, Mrs Abbie Borroto, he had injected 40cc of air into her arm, causing an embolism. The injection had been witnessed by a nurse at Dr Sander's side, and although bowel cancer was given as the cause of death, the doctor declined to alter his written record of how he had treated Mrs Borroto, and he was widely applauded for his act of euthanasia. Dr Sander stood trial for murdering Mrs Borroto, and there was much evidential confusion over whether the patient was actually already dead when Dr Sander administered the injection of air. The doctor was acquitted and eventually resumed his career.

No place on earth can be so silent as a room of imminent death. Outside Hillsborough County Hospital, New Hampshire, a bitter wind moans relentlessly through the snow-laden trees. Inside, the noise is blanketed by the comfortable central heating and double windows; even the nurses chattering about Christmas to come are only a distant murmur. But in all the hospital on this December morning in 1949, no room is more still than that of one middle-aged patient, Mrs Abbie Borroto.

For over a year, Mrs Borroto has been ill with cancer. She has wasted away to little more than half her usual weight. Now the

dread disease has reached its climax. Death is only a matter of
hours, perhaps of minutes. Already it is almost impossible to
detect signs of life. A pretty, grave-faced nurse tries in vain to
find the pulse. White-clad shapes move soundlessly out of the
room. Finally one doctor and a lone nurse are left. The doctor
bends over the bed, syringe in hand. Then he straightens himself
and, with shock effect, speaks in his normal voice. It is all over . . .

To the medical profession, that scene may be a commonplace.
In large hospitals, it happens several times a day. This time,
however, the scene was to become the subject of tall headlines in
newspapers throughout the world – and was to rekindle a controversy that is likely to remain unsettled for many generations.

The first clue that the commonplace had a distinctly uncommon feature was detected by a young nurse-secretary, Miss
Josephine Connor, to whom the doctor in charge of Mrs Borroto
had dictated his notes on the case. The clue appeared amid the
welter of medical detail certifying the cause of death as cancer.
Meticulously, the doctor had recorded the fact that, on the
morning the patient died, he had injected a small amount of
air into her veins. It might have seemed insignificant, but it led
the young nurse to inform the hospital authorities immediately.
For injecting air into a victim's veins is one of the classic murder
methods beloved of the thriller writers. On reaching the heart,
the air bubble supposedly has the same effect as a blood clot,
causing an embolism, or blockage, which brings death within
minutes of the injection.

For the hospital authorities who opened an enquiry into the
strange entry, the inference was plain – Mrs Borroto had been
eased through death's door before her time. It might have been a
mere hour or so before, but there was still only one word for it.
Murder.

On December 29th, as the suspect walked into Goffstown
Hospital to attend another patient, two detectives stepped forward.

"Dr Hermann Sander?"

"Ah, yes, gentlemen. I've been expecting you."

The charge: first-degree murder. The maximum penalty:
death.

And the motive? Nothing like so clear cut. Material gain, revenge, or any other of the usual motives for murder were all out of the question. The prosecution's answer, provided at a preliminary court hearing the following day, had far wider implications. It emerged from an alleged statement by Dr Sander, denying that he had committed murder and saying: "I did it as an act of mercy. There was no malice on my part." It was further alleged that he told the county prosecutor, Mr William Craig: "Her family had asked me if anything could be done to end her agony."

From that moment on, it was certain that the trial of Dr Hermann Sander would arouse the strongest feelings throughout the US. In a country which calmly accepts such a phenomenon as the Forest Lawn cemetery (as dissected by Evelyn Waugh in *The Loved One*), and where the fear of pain often transcends even that of death itself, there are probably more protagonists of euthanasia than in any other nation in the world. These are the people who favour the "putting to sleep" of the incurably sick, to save them from terrible pain before their inevitable deaths. Resolutely entrenched against them, however, are millions of Church-goers, particularly the Roman Catholics, whose religious teaching is utterly opposed to such an idea. It is fair to say, therefore, that this case split the American nation violently in two – emotion versus Church discipline, "modern" thinking against twenty centuries of spiritual belief.

Nowhere was that general picture more acute than in the accused's own little New England community. At least two-thirds of the local population were Roman Catholics – many of them simple immigrant French-Canadians from over the border. On the other hand, within hours of Dr Sander's arrest, more than six hundred people in his home-village of Candia had signed a petition on his behalf, expressing their "unshakable faith" in his integrity. The petition added: "We respect him as a man of Christian virtue, devoted to the higher interests of human welfare at all times." To add bitter piquancy to the situation, the lawyer who was to lead for the prosecution, Attorney-General William Phinney, had been at school with the accused and was a lifelong friend and neighbour. Finally, although Phinney promised that he would show no leniency in pressing for a conviction, bail was set at $25,000 (nearly £9,000) – which, although a stiff sum, was just within Sander's reach and enabled him to remain at liberty until the Grand Jury hearing.

At first glance, the forty-one-year-old man who had inspired such a wealth of sentiment and bitter arguments seemed an unlikely figure for the role. A long, rather sallow face; dark hair, parted in the middle; a pencil moustache; spectacles; mild brown eyes; a slight, not very strong physique. Study of his career, however, showed that he had some of the stuff of which martyrs are made. Friends told of his long hours of selfless work, of how he usually "forgot" to send the bill to his poorer patients. He was evidently a man who knew his own mind, even if one might not always agree with his views. Earlier in the year, he had toured Great Britain to inspect the National Health Service. On his return, he expressed frank admiration for it (contrary to general American opinion at that time), but still said he opposed the idea for the US – on the somewhat dogmatic ground that "the Government should keep out of medicine".

It was characteristic of him that, when the question of a police charge arose, he told his secretary not to cancel any of his appointments. A few hours after his release on bail, he was helping to bring a baby into the world. He had been "booked" by a Mrs Louise Crocker and, though he had only just returned home, he did not fail her – duly delivering her of a 5 lb 12 oz daughter.

Great play was made with such details in the Press. There were long stories of how, on Sunday, New Year's Day, he had left his white-timbered home on the outskirts of Candia and gone to church with his wife, Alice, an ex-nurse, and their three young daughters. The following day, the newspapers reported faithfully, he had gone on his country rounds as usual, calling, first on Mrs Crocker and her baby, then on a young boy on whom he had performed a minor operation on New Year's Eve, and then on twelve more patients. The doctor was quoted as saying: "It is tremendous what people have said and done. I am rather overwhelmed. From every walk of life they have called to sympathise with me. I have never seen so much sentiment." When asked about the circumstances of Mrs Borroto's death, according to another report, he replied: "Doctors tell me these things have happened many times but have never been put in the records. They say I'm a couple of decades ahead of my time."

If the last report were accurate, it seemed pretty damning. For, despite the whipping up of mass emotion, nothing could get over the cold fact that, in law, there is no such thing as "mercy killing". It remains murder, pure and simple.

Pure it may have been, but simple, no. The complexities were typified by statements made by the victim's family. Her husband, sixty-five-year-old Mr Reginald Borroto, a retired oil salesman, might have been expected to appear as an injured party, yet he said openly that he was "terribly saddened" at the charge against Dr Sander, whom he described as the "biggest man I ever knew". One of Mrs Borroto's brothers, Louis Constantino, agreed: "I bear him absolutely no ill-will." But two other brothers strongly disagreed. The first, Bernard Constantino, declared: "My sister was at death's door, but she had great courage and refused to give up hope. I still insist that he had no right at all to take her life." The second, Thomas Constantino, denied that he had made any suggestion for ending Mrs Borroto's pain. "It should have been left to the will of God."

On Thursday, January 5th, 1950, Sander drove with his wife to the nearby town of Manchester to face the Grand Jury. Long before the couple climbed the stairs together to the second floor of the red brick courthouse, the building was crammed to overflowing. Outside was another big crowd, with newsreel cameras and a large jostle of Press photographers. The accused's cheeks were hollowed and his eyes black-ringed, but his voice was unexpectedly strong as he answered "not guilty" to the charge.

"Hark to the indictment," intoned the clerk, and Sander's hands clenched tight as the clerk went on: ". . . feloniously, wilfully and of his malice aforethought did inject ten cubic centimetres of air four times in close succession into the veins of Mrs Abbie Borroto, fifty-nine, his patient."

Four times. Most people in the room sat up with a jolt. That was a total of forty cc – far more than they had been led to believe by the early newspaper reports.

Nevertheless, at the end of the short hearing, Dr Sander was again granted bail in the sum of $25,000, although this time on condition that he treated no more patients before his trial.

Just over two weeks later, Mrs Borroto's body was exhumed and three pathologists made a post-mortem examination lasting ten hours. A month afterwards – on Monday, February 20th – the trial opened in Manchester.

By now, outside interest knew no bounds. Dr Sander had received some 3,000 letters from sympathizers all over the world, including Britain. Many Euthanasia Societies had offered to help pay for the defence – offers which were declined. Every hotel room in the town had been taken. Special writers sent to cover the trial included such personalities as John O'Hara and Fanny Hurst. Among the boilers in the courthouse cellar, space had been cleared for telegraphic equipment, tables for typewriters and even a broadcasting studio. It was uncomfortably hot in this makeshift news-centre, and the stifling atmosphere was aggravated by the fact that the temperature in the street outside was several degrees below zero.

The effect of all this on the people of Manchester was somewhat revealing. Feelings had run so high that for weeks past the local newspapers had refused to comment editorially on the case or to print readers' letters about it – a most unusual step in the US, where the strictures of *sub judice* do not apply as under British law. At the same time, the town could not quite get over its astonishment at finding itself the centre of world attention, whatever the cause. The presence of four correspondents from London newspapers was an item on the local radio, and the last-minute arrival of Nicholas Chatelaine, of the Paris *Le Figaro*, earned him a front-page picture in the *Manchester Evening Leader*.

That was superficial parochialism, however. Only two factors really counted: (1) In this tightly knit community, Dr Sander had been a familiar and respected figure all his adult life; and (2) Roughly 50,000 of Manchester's 80,000 population were Roman Catholics.

Clearly, the task of selecting an unbiased jury would be extremely difficult. Under American law, counsel are allowed to cross-examine prospective jurors and, if desired, to reject them. It is nearly always a tedious business, but this time it promised to take longer than ever.

When the accused arrived – wearing a heavy overcoat and a bright red scarf against the icy cold – he found a panel of no fewer than 145 candidates for the jury in the courtroom. Hour by hour, the slow process dragged on. A surprising number of the candidates immediately disqualified themselves by stating that they had already formed definite views which would not be changed by any evidence they might hear. By the end of the day, only nine of the thirteen necessary jurors (including a substitute) had been chosen. The following day was even worse. Still more jurors were dismissed from service after saying that they must put a "higher law" before the laws or evidence of the court. Another setback came when one of the jurors selected the previous day (a naturalized American of British birth, who had come to this little Manchester from the great Lancashire city of the same name) was successfully challenged by the prosecution – following a one-and-a-quarter-hour conference between the judge and prosecuting and defence counsel.

It was not until the third morning that an all-male jury satisfactory to both sides was at last completed. The jurors' average age was fifty-four, and they comprised nine Catholics, one Episcopalian, a Baptist and a Methodist.

Throughout the frustrating delay, Dr Sander and his wife, who had left a sick bed to attend court, had sat listening patiently. Sometimes they held hands. Between sessions they went for a stroll round the block. Every day a police car brought them to and from their home eleven miles away. Otherwise the doctor was a free man – an ironic situation for the unfortunate jurors, who had to remain locked up in their hotel.

Throughout this period, too, despite the somewhat premature objections of the dismissed jury candidates, there had been no official mention of the phrase "mercy killing". But now Attorney-General William Phinney, in his opening speech for the prosecution, underlined the unusual nature of the case by announcing that agreement had been reached under which the State would *not* ask for the death penalty. Although he did not elaborate, one possible explanation of this clemency lay in his use of a single word. Medical evidence would show, he said, that forty cc of air injected into a woman in Mrs Borroto's condition would *probably* cause death and that the air which Sander administered was in fact the cause of her death. "Probably" was a most unexpected qualification. Until this moment, it had been assumed that the State's assertion would be categorical. Now the lists were wide open for a conflict of expert opinion.

A minor clash occurred during cross-examination of the very first witness, Dr Harold Loverud, director of the Hillsborough Hospital, who had told of the discovery of the fateful entry in the victim's medical records. Rising to his feet, the chief defence counsel, Mr Louis Wyman, put a long but deceptively simple question. Had another member of the hospital staff, Dr Albert Snay, seen Mrs Borroto at 11.10 or 11.15 on the morning of her death, just before Dr Sander entered the room and just before any injection of air; and could Dr Loverud say, he concluded, "if Dr Snay at that time examined Mrs Borroto and pronounced her dead, would he be able to give pretty reliable information?"

Mr Phinney jumped up immediately and objected to the question. It should not be admitted, he insisted, unless evidence were to be produced to support the suggestion. A pronounced stir rippled along the two hundred and fifty public seats in the court as grey-haired Mr Wyman assured him: "In due course we expect evidence to that effect."

Behind the involved language, this was the first open sign by the defence that they intended to fight the case by arguing that Mrs Borroto was already dead when the air was injected – and that they believed they could prove the claim.

The hitherto rather bored reporters seized the news gleefully, correctly envisaging the largest possible headlines. From across the Atlantic, five hours ahead in time, the results of the British general election on the same day were flowing in. It was the election in which the Labour Party only just held on to power, with the barest majority. Most Americans, accustomed to "rooting" unabashedly for the team of their choice, no matter where its home ground, had been hoping for a Conservative victory. Yet even this close struggle had to take second place to reports of the Sander trial in the US popular Press.

The following day, Friday, February 24th, produced significant details of the notes with which Dr Sander had trapped
himself. Nurse Josephine Connor, to whom he had dictated
them, confirmed in evidence that he had said the patient was
"practically moribund" on the day before her death and that she
"expired within ten minutes" after he started injecting air on the
following day. She then described a conversation between the
accused and Dr Robert Biron, the county medical referee, after
she had drawn the hospital authorities' attention to the notes.
"Dr Biron asked if Dr Sander realised he had broken the law. Dr
Sander said, 'Yes, he had broken laws before – he had been
through stop signs.' Dr Biron said this was more serious; this was
murder. Dr Sander said he did realise he had broken the law but
the law should be changed. Dr Biron said, 'Why didn't you
change it first – before you did this?' "

When asked if he realized the seriousness of the situation, Miss
Connor said, Dr Sander replied that he assumed the Medical
Association would probably reprimand him for it, "tell him not to
do it again."

This had been damning evidence, and not least for the phrase
"the law should be changed", with its apparent acquiescence in
the principle of euthanasia. Moreover, the light-heartedness of
some of the alleged replies struck an unhappy note. Another blow
followed almost immediately, although this time the defence
parried it more successfully. It came when the prosecution tried
to squash once and for all the rumours, repeated in evidence, that
Mrs Borroto's husband had pleaded with Dr Sander to end her
suffering. A police witness, Sheriff O'Brien, took the stand to
testify that the prosecutor had obtained from Mr Borroto "a
signed, sworn statement . . . that he had nothing to do with Dr
Sander in this". This brought an immediate defence protest.
Justifiably, for Mr Borroto himself was on the list of witnesses.
The court, concurring, sustained the objection and ordered the
sheriff's remark to be struck out. To demonstrate that he had
nothing to hide, however, Mr Wyman told reporters later that the
defence would probably call Mr Borroto if the prosecution
decided not to do so.

Before that happened, there was vital evidence to hear from a twenty-four-year old, slim and attractive nurse who set necks craning as she walked forward. Her name, Elizabeth Rose, suited her blue eyes and blonde hair to perfection. But there was a macabre incongruity about the minor diversion caused by her appearance. For Miss Rose was the nurse who had been alone with Dr Sander at the time he made the injection.

It was not long before she caused a stir of another kind. Reading from the notes she had made at the bedside, she told the court that, shortly before Dr Sander entered the room, three people had been unable to detect Mrs Borroto's pulse.

Sensation! If this meant what it seemed to mean – that the patient was already dead – the case was virtually over. The Attorney-General, however, evidently had reason to think otherwise. Step by step, he took the witness through the events of the victim's last morning. When she went on duty at 7.00 a.m., Miss Rose said, the patient was asleep and her respiration was very shallow. A little later she sipped coffee and said she was uncomfortable. "At 11.00 a.m.," the young nurse went on calmly, "I was unable to get her pulse."

Another nurse, Miss Garrard, was also unable to find a pulse and Miss Rose then went into the corridor and met Dr Albert Snay. He, too, said he could not get any pulse. He asked for a stethoscope but could hear nothing.

Mr Phinney: "Did Dr Snay say the patient was dead?"

Miss Rose "No."

"There is no question of that in your mind?" – "No."

At this point, the witness continued, Dr Sander arrived and talked briefly to Dr Snay. She did not overhear the conversation.

Mr Phinney: "Did you notice Mrs Borroto after Dr Snay left?"

Miss Rose: "Yes. *There was some gasping.*"

So here was the goal for which the Attorney-General had been aiming. Firstly, he had established that, despite the failure to detect Mrs Borroto's pulse, no authoritative confirmation of the fact of death had been given at the time. Secondly, although Dr Snay might counter this when he gave evidence later, he would have to do so in the face of the nurse's testimony about the subsequent gasping. The prosecution had certainly turned the tables . . .

Miss Rose's description of the final scene enabled Mr Phinney to drive home his advantage still further. After Dr Snay left the room, she said, Dr Sander also tried to find Mrs Borroto's pulse. He made no comment about this, but asked her for a syringe. She saw him apply the syringe, which was empty, to the patient. Then, she asserted, "I heard a gasp from Mrs Borroto," and Dr Sander, turning to her, had said: "Air in the veins would act like an embolus."

The accused's face flushed as he listened from the defence table, only a few feet from the witness stand. It was a bad moment – the prosecution had now shown twice what appeared to be proof that the victim was alive when the injection was made. Moreover, what would the jury read into his alleged comment about an embolus?

Mr Phinney paused to give the witness' last words their full dramatic effect, before asking: "What happened next?"

Miss Rose: "I looked at the syringe. The plunger was down on the barrel. After two or three minutes, Dr Sander turned and handed me the syringe and needle. He said he would notify Mrs Borroto's people and call the undertaker."

Mr Phinney: "What did that indicate to you?" – "That the patient was dead."

For the defence, at this juncture, the sole hope seemed to lie in re-emphasising the first half of the young nurse's evidence. Cross-examining, Mr Wyman went straight to the point. "On January 2nd," he asked, "did you say Dr Sander did not kill her because she was dead before the injection was made?"

Miss Rose: "I couldn't get her pulse."

This failure to answer the question directly incurred its own penalty. Fishing a typewritten sheet of paper from the mass of documents on his table, the chief defence counsel read out, in a flat, dry voice, a statement made by Miss Rose during enquiries before the Grand Jury hearing. The key words of this statement were: "Dr Sander did not kill her because she was already dead."

One point retrieved for the defence . . . By itself it could hardly overcome the image in everyone's mind of a dying woman gasping, but – particularly since the judge admitted the statement as a defence exhibit – it had at least reopened the door to doubt.

Hitherto the conflict had been mainly on a medical plane, if at a minor level. Now, with the long-awaited appearance of Mr Reginald Borroto, the dead woman's husband, it swung back towards the latent euthanasia controversy and the by-play of mass sentiment. The Attorney-General, sticking to the guns which had been temporarily spiked when Sheriff O'Brien took the stand, asked at once: "Did you at anytime, directly or indirectly, ask Dr Sander to shorten your wife's life?"

"No."

Despite this denial – which anyway came as no surprise – Mr Borroto obviously disliked his position. The State had decided to call him as a prosecution witness after all, doubtless to Mr Wyman's disappointment. Yet, for the job of re-establishing public sympathy, the defence could hardly have asked for a better ally. Had the accused been his own brother, Mr Borroto said, he could not feel more kindly towards him. "If my wife had been Dr Sander's mother or sister, he could not have done more to minister to her." The doctor had made many gifts to her, he went on. "Once he brought her a canary in a cage, complete with all the fittings. She became very fond of the bird." And it had done much to distract her attention from her suffering . . .

All this gave abundant heart-rending material to the weepier writers at the trial. But a court of law is supposedly concerned only with the facts at issue before it – and the most important tests had yet to come.

As a first step, one vital point had to be cleared up. Of the three people who had failed to find Mrs Borroto's pulse, only one could say with authority whether she was dead – Dr Albert Snay, the staff doctor who had examined her only a few minutes before Dr Sander entered the room.

To the audible relief of the accused's sympathizers, Dr Snay seemed to have little doubt. On examining the patient, he said, he found no pulse, no reflex of the eyeball and no sound through the stethoscope. "I concluded then that she was dead. I remarked to Miss Rose that the patient appeared to be gone. Dr Sander walked in and I said something to the effect that there was nothing to be done." He did not make a report because he knew it was Dr Sander's case. Later he met the accused, who said: "She was dead." Dr Snay added: "From her appearance it was amazing to me that she had lived as long as she did. Nothing Dr Sander or anyone else could have done could have affected her condition."

On the surface, this was definite enough. It looked once more as though the defence had triumphed. Yet close observers noted that, despite his strong emphasis, Dr Snay had still not committed himself fully. He had *concluded* that the patient was dead . . . He had remarked that she *appeared* to be gone. Moreover, the stumbling-block remained: How was his evidence to be reconciled with that of Miss Rose – the nurse who said she heard Mrs Borroto gasp when the needle was applied?

Quick to widen any available loophole, the Attorney-General called Dr Robert Biron, the county medical referee who had first questioned Dr Sander. Wheezing stoutly from the heavy witness chair, Dr Biron quoted hospital records as stating: "Patient given ten cc of air, repeated four times, and expired ten minutes after this was started." He had asked Dr Sander if he realized that Mrs Borroto died of an air injection. Dr Sander had said he did. "I asked him if he knew he had broken the law. He stated that he had the permission of Mr Borroto and that he thought the law was not correct in this case, that he might have broken the law but that the law ought to be changed." Much of this was repetition, merely amplifying earlier evidence, but it was a reminder that came at a telling moment.

As a climax, the Attorney-General now produced his most powerful ammunition – impressive medical evidence from two experts who had attended the exhumation and post-mortem and who both asserted flatly that the air injection had led to death . . . And no quibbles about the possibility of Mrs Borroto being dead beforehand.

The first of the two, Dr Miller, said that, in his opinion, death was caused by a pulmonary embolism (a blood clot in the lungs) after air had been injected. The second expert, Dr Milton Helpern, Deputy Medical examiner for New York City, went into greater detail. Using a large black-board to explain to the jury how the air would travel through the veins to the heart, he said: "A big bubble of air would be just as effective in blocking circulation as a big clot of blood." The autopsy, of course, could not disclose the presence of air. But, he added, "it was significant that it did not reveal any other cause of death which would have caused as rapid a death." He concluded: "In my opinion, death was caused by an air embolism resulting from the injection of forty cc of air."

Dr Helpern's evidence ended the case for the prosecution. It seemed an effective case, with weighty answers to any doubts which the defence had succeeded in arousing. Inevitably, though, the defence immediately called for the charge to be dismissed, basing the plea on two grounds:

(a) Failure to establish that death was of a felonious nature; and

(b) Failure to show that air injections and not cancer killed Mrs Borroto.

Just as inevitably, the plea was rejected. Still, there was no harm in trying . . .

It was now Thursday, March 2nd, so it had taken more than a week, excluding the time for selecting the jury, to reach the half-way point of the trial. In most criminal cases, except those in which defending counsel has a major surprise up his sleeve, it is often possible at this stage to gauge the probable verdict. This time, however, it still looked anybody's guess. The fact that Dr Sander had made the injections was not in dispute. In effect, therefore, the issue boiled down to three questions: (1) Was Mrs Borroto already dead when the air was injected? (2) If so, why did the accused inject the air? (3) If not, was the air responsible for death?

The prosecution had claimed that the answer was "No" to the first question and "Yes" to the third. The defence had said that the answer to the first question was "Yes". Failing that, they could seek for a "No" to question No. 3, by trying to prove that, in any case, the amount of air was insufficient to cause death. But a really convincing answer to the second question would still be all-important. What possible reason could there be for an act which, by their own submissions, was completely pointless? Without a good explanation, it would be impossible to satisfy the jury over the other two questions.

The defence jumped straight into the deep end. Dr Sander,

counsel said, would admit making the air injections "on the impulse of the moment" and in spite of the fact that "he was satisfied she was already dead". To understand why, it was necessary to understand his background, his character, the tensions of everyday life. This information would be given.

In other words, as one cynical American reporter put it, the court was in for a psychological blood-bath . . . That may have been as inaccurate as it was cruel. But at least it was clear that, although the "mercy killing" theme was taboo, the defence would have to invoke much that would appeal to popular emotion – as demonstrated by their first witness, Mrs Borroto's pretty nineteen-year-old daughter, Elise. Wearing a grey suit with a black sweater and an incongruous little sailor hat, she told the court that Dr Sander "seemed to feel almost as badly" as she did about her mother's death. After it occurred, he had invited her and her father to stay at his home, "not overnight or for a day, but for a week or as long as we wanted".

Further tributes to the accused's humanitarian qualities were paid by his blonde medical secretary, Helen Maciolek, who testified: "He was not an ordinary doctor – he was a saint. He was a twenty-four-hour doctor and did not take a proper day off, so that he would be available when other doctors were not." Other witnesses told how he started a clinic for under-privileged children and had collected $6,000 for a new hospital wing. His poorer patients, it was stated, were often asked to stay at his home for their convalescence – and were never charged.

This picture of Dr Sander, as a dedicated, honourable physician, explained why nearly all his patients had already contributed a total of more than $11,000 (some £4,000) towards a fund for his defence. Yet, to acquit him of murder, character references were not enough. Quickly, therefore, the defence switched back to its first claim; that no crime could have been committed because the patient had already gone. Among witnesses who supported this view was Mrs Cecilia Smith, duty sister in the part of the hospital where Mrs Borroto died. A few minutes before the air was injected, she said, Mrs Borroto had a death pallor and was not breathing. "I thought she was dead."

Defending counsel had shown skilful timing throughout the

case and it was at this point, with the words of the last witness still
in the jury's ears, that they launched a frontal attack on their most
difficult obstacle . . . Just *why* had Dr Sander asked for that
syringe? From in front of the jury box, counsel nodded across at
him and said with slow emphasis: "He saw that Mrs Borroto was
lifeless. Her heart was not beating. He thought she was dead. A
doubt, however, did cross his mind. He was thinking of giving
assurance that the pain which she had conquered would not
return. He injected the needle." And with that, almost before
the spectators had time to murmur, Dr Sander was before the
witness stand, his right hand raised to take the oath.

The trial had now been in progress for two weeks. In that
time, the accused's composure had been remarkable. There were
dark rings under his eyes, betokening some sleepless nights, and
it was noted that he avoided looking at the Attorney-General
face to face, even when his old friend was pacing up and down
only a few feet in front of him. Outwardly, though, he had
betrayed no sign of nervousness and it was as if chatting with old
friends that he gave the requisite detailed account of his career,
recalling how a famous book about a doctor, *The Magnificent
Obsession*, had made him decide to become one himself. In
recent years, he said, his wife had felt that he was working
too hard.

Imperceptibly, something of that strain began to make itself
felt in court – and at last, as he told of Mrs Borroto's closing days,
Dr Sander's own calm was broken and his voice sometimes
choked with emotion. Two weeks before her death, he said,
"she could hardly move. She could not eat. All she ate during
the last month would not make a single normal meal. We had to
go by the expression on her face to tell if she was having pain." In
the final week, she "looked like a dead person". When she did die,
he believed the cause was cancer and had signed the death
certificate accordingly.

At the behest of the second defence counsel, Mr Ralph Langdell, he described what happened when he called for the syringe.
"It was my opinion then that she was dead. I can't explain exactly
what action I took then. Something snapped. Why I did it, I can't
tell. It doesn't make sense."

Mr Langdell: "Did you have any intention of killing Mrs Borroto?"

Dr Sander: "I never had any intention of killing Mrs Borroto."

"Did you ever agree to kill Mrs Borroto?" – "I never agreed to kill her."

"Did you know what you intended to do with the syringe?" – "I don't know what I intended to do. I remember trying to get into her vein."

"Was there blood on her arm?" – "There was never any blood anywhere. I tried to get into the vein. I did not use a tourniquet to bring up the vein. Her veins were collapsed."

Dr Sander said he had a ten cubic centimetre syringe. "I withdrew the plunger to make suction, but nothing came out – there was no blood."

Mr Langdell: "What did you do next?" – "I injected a couple of cubic centimetres and I injected a couple more – and nothing happened. There was a slight swelling around the needle. I continued to inject small amounts of air until the entire ten cubic centimetres was gone."

"Was there any change in her expression at any time?"

– "During this entire procedure there was no indication of life, no reaction."

Dr Sander went on: "I detached the syringe by holding the needle with my left hand and unscrewing the syringe. I repeated the process with five or six cubic centimetres, two cubic centimetres at a time, till the syringe was empty."

"Was there any change in her expression, appearance or reaction?" – "No, sir."

"You repeated the same procedure a third time?" – "I did."

"Did you note any change in her expression, any motion or activity at any time?" – "No, sir."

Altogether, Dr Sander said, he had injected a total of "between twenty-five and twenty-eight cc" of air – as compared with the prosecution claim that it was a full forty cc Asked why he had dictated the entry in the medical records which had trapped him, he explained: "I think it is the duty of every doctor to put down on the charts what he has done for every patient, whether it has any effect or not."

Why, then, had he said that the patient "died within ten minutes" of the injections?

"I probably was not being fair to myself. It was casual dictation. The fact that I say she expired at that time does not mean she died at that time. It is merely a means of closing out the case on the chart."

The atmosphere in court became tenser than ever as Attorney-General William Phinney rose to cross-examine, pressing yet again for an explanation of the injections. Looking at him squarely for the first time since the trial started, Dr Sander replied: "I was influenced by the expression on her face – the long suffering – also the suffering of her husband. The expression on her face touched me off. What I did does not make sense."

Mr Phinney: "Why did you put the needle into the vein?" – "I don't know."

"Do you want to tell the jury that?" – "That's right."

"You said something snapped in your mind?" – "What I was thinking at that time is hard to explain. I realized I had not taken a life. I told Craig (the county prosecutor) I had not committed a crime. I meant by that I had not taken a life. The whole behaviour was an irrational behaviour."

Once more Mr Phinney demanded a practical explanation and once more the accused insisted firmly: "I was terribly upset inwardly and I tried to preserve an outward calm. I knew I had not committed any sin. My conscience has been clear throughout the whole affair. I do not know why I did all these things. I was upset to do this and I do not know why I kept on nor why I stopped."

Mr Phinney: "You knew Mrs Borroto was unconscious?"

Dr Sander, emphatically: "I knew she was dead."

"Yet you had this obsession to pump air into this poor dead soul?" – "That's right."

"Have you ever been of the opinion that a patient might be better served by being dead?" – "I have never thought that."

"You said you knew you had broken the law?" – "I do not recall any such answer."

And that was that. After nearly four hours on the witness stand, the only reason Dr Sander had given for his action was that it was an "irrational behaviour" – that there was no reason. Nothing could have seemed weaker, yet in that might lie its very strength. Just as honest witnesses of the same incident almost always differ about what they see, so a jury might be more impressed by a confused mind than by one which thinks with complete clarity – particularly when, as here, evidence is provided to show how the confused mental state arose.

The following day, the defence rounded off this character evidence by calling Mrs Alice Sander, the accused's wife. Since February 20th, she had been away from his side only while he was on the witness stand. Now, wearing a quiet grey suit and speaking in a soft, pleasant voice, she told the court that she had first met her husband when they worked together at a New Jersey hospital. She had admired him because "he respected the poorest patients". The former nurse smiled at the jury as she confessed: "I never wanted to marry a doctor. I knew most doctors spend long hours at work and put that ahead of their families. After we were married, I was never allowed to say he was not in to any patient."

Mrs Sander was followed briefly by Nurse Gertrude Morency, who said that the doctor had given his own blood to a patient. "He told me: 'They need it more than I'."

At this climax of *vox humana*, the defence abruptly switched their line of attack again. They had elaborated their assertion that Mrs Borroto was dead before the injection occurred; they had built up a picture of the psychology which, they claimed, lay behind their client's strange deed. It was time to tackle the third outstanding question: Was the amount of air injected actually sufficient to cause death? The prosecution had produced two experts to answer "Yes" to this question. The defence called only one, although the balance had been made up a few days beforehand, in effect, by a widely publicised challenge from Dr Harry Robinson of the University of Maryland Medical School. From Baltimore, nearly four hundred miles away, Dr Robinson had boldly offered to receive an injection of forty cc of air to prove it would not be fatal, asserting: "Injections of air into the veins cannot cause death." He was quoted as saying that he had given such injections to patients and: "There are no results – good or bad."

The printing of such stories as this, even before the defence had broached the subject, is among the more surprising features of the American scene – particularly to people accustomed to the *sub judice* principle of British Law, under which, once a charge is preferred, no outside comment about a case may be published until the trial is over. Fortunately, it is the rule that all references to their case are cut out of the newspapers before the jurors, locked up in their hotel, are allowed to read them. Moreover, the defence expert whom they were invited to hear in the proper place, before them in court, did not need anyone else to help him. The name alone of Dr Richard Ford, head of the Department of Legal Medicine at Harvard University, was enough to bring a buzz of anticipation from the spectators. For here was one of the country's most celebrated pathologists, an American Spilsbury.

Dr Ford, who had performed the autopsy on Mrs Borroto at the defence request, declared roundly that the patient could not have died from the air injected. The argument between prosecution and defence, as to whether it was forty cc or only twenty-eight cc at the most, was immaterial. Forty cc of air – and he demonstrated – was the equivalent of a small whisky and was not enough to kill. During the past year. Dr Ford said, he had been engaged in the study of air embolism. In his opinion, between two hundred and three hundred cc, delivered within twenty-five seconds, would be required to cause death. "Forty cubic centimetres is not enough to block any appreciable part of the arterial system leading to the human lung." And, he concluded, the fact that a human being's heart action was poor at the time of injection would not make any difference.

Pity the poor jury that had to make up its mind between this authoritative evidence and the equally definite statement to the contrary by the prosecution's chief expert, Dr Helpern!

At last, on Thursday, March 9th, seventeen days after the trial opened, the jurors retired to consider their verdict. They were out for sixty-nine minutes. As they shuffled back into their box, Dr Sander stared intently across the court.

"What say you?" asked the clerk of the court. "Guilty of first-degree murder, guilty of second-degree murder, or not guilty?"

"Not guilty."

Immediately a hubbub that nothing could suppress. A burst of clapping, cheers – and above them, a man's voice crying: "Thank God!" Throughout it all, Dr Sander still stared, though now tears came to his eyes. Beside him, his wife bowed her head and wept unashamedly.

It is strange, at this distance of time, to note the way in which the character of the case had changed. At first, the tremendous controversy over "mercy killing", the sweeping assumption that this was the sole issue. Gradually, as the trial went on, the theme was pushed more and more into the background until it appeared to have been forgotten. In the final analysis, the defence fought and won on grounds of medical fact. No other way could have been successful. Yet the outburst of emotion after Dr Sander's acquittal showed that, under the surface, many people still regarded him in the light of what they had originally believed to have been his role.

Indeed, the doctor's ordeal was not over. His medical peers, as was their right, could still impose punishment for professional misconduct. A few days later, he was barred by a Roman Catholic hospital in Manchester. The following month, the State Board of Registration in Medicine revoked his licence. Even if the air injections were made after death, the Board said, they were "morally reprehensible". However, it was indicated that he could apply for reinstatement after June 19th.

Well-wishers had raised the amazing sum of $21,000 for Dr Sander, but all had gone to pay his legal expenses. For two months, he supported his family by working as a ploughman, using his own electrically-driven plough, for $4 an hour. Fortunately for him, the professional "sentence" imposed on him proved to be indulgent. On June 28th, the Board announced that his licence had been restored – and his first patient called just ten minutes later.

Whatever view one takes of euthanasia, and of Dr Sander's temporary, unwitting position as a hero of its supporters, three additional points emerge from the trial. The first is that, despite the partisan fervour which greeted his acquittal, no comparable case has since come to public notice in the United States. The second is best illustrated by a confession made to me some years ago by the late Sir James Purves-Stewart, the great British neurologist, who died in 1949 at the age of eighty. (Since he also told this story to a medical meeting, I am not breaking his confidence now.) Sir James said that he was once called to the bedside of a friend, "a charming, cultured woman", who was dying of an incurable disease. She asked him to kill her. "I cannot promise you anything," he replied, "but goodbye and God bless you." Sir James concluded: "I will not say what action I took, but the next day the sufferer failed to awake. Had I been placed in the dock, I might, perhaps, have been convicted and condemned."

The third and last point arises from the sad circumstance that, six months after his acquittal, Dr Sander's pretty young secretary, Helen Maciolek, committed suicide. The doctor, who led search parties all night until her body was found, said that she had recently been "emotionally upset". There is not the slightest evidence that her act resulted in any way from her employer's trial. Yet it may well serve as an indication of the dangerous strains – on people indirectly as well as directly involved – which might arise even if "mercy killing" one day has the full sanction of the law.

THE ACID-BATH VIRTUOSO

(John George Haigh, UK 1949)

Edgar Lustgarten

Haigh's was one of the most sensational murder trials in England, in which dental evidence clinched the the identity of the victim. Haigh's mistake was to believe that without a body, there could be no conviction. As he cheerfully told the police: "Mrs Durand Deacon no longer exists. She has disappeared completely and no trace of her can ever be found again. I have destroyed her with acid. Every trace has gone. How can you prove murder if there is no body?" But in spite of Haigh's boasts, a team of forensic scientists was able to prove that even after a lengthy immersion in sulphuric acid, enough of a human body would survive to provide conclusive evidence. In this case, Mrs Durand Deacon's new acrylic resin dentures were found, buried but intact, in several hundred pounds of greasy, oily sludge recovered from Haigh's premises in Crawley, Sussex. The dentures were conclusively identified by her dentist, and even though the question of his sanity loomed large at the trial, Haigh was hanged. Edgar Lustgarten (1907–78) was a prolific journalist and broadcaster, perhaps remembered best for hosting a series of black-and-white television programmes telling the stories of famous trials with the demeanour of a weary lizard. Lustgarten, a former president of the Oxford Union, came from a generation that scorned sympathy for the likes of Haigh, believing that (like many other notorious killers) he actively enjoyed murdering, being insensitive and indifferent. "I rejoice that they were executed," Lustgarten declared, "every one of them."

For many years I acted as commentator and narrator of a film
series with a self-explanatory title – *Scotland Yard*. During the
early fifties, in one of these films it was my privilege to be
associated with Sir Travers Humphreys, the famous High Court
judge, who had recently retired.

On the evening before his scenes were scheduled I was asked
whether I would call for him and escort him to the studio. On the
way you can tell him the form, suggested the producer.

I said I should be delighted, and inquired where Sir Travers
lived.

"He lives now," the producer said, "at the Onslow Court
Hotel."

A shiver shook my spine, as if some unrevealed and unac-
countable cosmic irony reposed in that impeccably respectable
establishment. I could not immediately construe my own reactions. Then, after a moment's reflection, understanding dawned.

Travers Humphreys was the judge, who, only a few years
earlier, almost at the close of his memorable career, had tried the
acid-bath multi-murderer Haigh, and had dispatched that chemical virtuoso to the gallows. And Haigh, although he had
committed his crimes elsewhere – a storeroom at Crawley, a
cellar on Gloucester Road – had latterly quartered himself in, and
involved himself with, and operated from, the Onslow Court
Hotel.

There are hotels and hotels; the term is now so wide that it has
ceased to be descriptive. Nor do I know whether the Onslow
Court Hotel, in particular, corresponds exactly with its earlier
image. It certainly could have served once as the prototype of
those hotels which do not desire to attract a floating clientele – in
contrast equally to international stop-offs and commercial taverns. With their discreet comfort, orderly routine, and close
resemblance to a well-conducted home, they form a communal
permanent retreat for unhoused members of the English upper-
middle class.

The preponderant characteristic of such hotels is Quiet. Lowered voices in the lounge. Soft footfalls in the corridors. Modest
entries and inconspicuous exits. Subdued greetings and sedate

farewells. A quietness of bearing, too, as well as of speech and movement: the formidable reserve of the consciously well-bred.

This austere tradition of calm correctitude was firmly established by the earliest residents, and ever since has been maintained by recruiting others like them. Ex-Army officers, pensioned civil servants, former Church dignitaries – and, of course, their relicts. Indeed, the female almost always outnumbers the male, though not to the same extent that the old outnumber the young. But sex and age are negligible elements in a relatively ageless and entirely sexless world. You are of it, or not of it. You belong, or you do not belong. It is a world painstakingly secured against the vulgar and the sordid and – above all – the violent; those notorious, lamentable, excesses of inappropriate parentage and indifferent education. It is a world conceived and born in the nineteenth century, jealously preserving its corporate exclusiveness against the social explosions of the twentieth.

Only if your individual personality – from which is deduced your birth and upbringing – stands up to the critical scrutiny of your fellows can you hope for more than temporary survival in such a dedicated bastion of good form. Their freezing disapproval – silently conveyed – has, within its narrow scope, finality.

Pass that test, and you are politely welcomed. Fail, and it is made clear that you do not fit in.

Olive Durand-Deacon – to the porter, One-One-Five – fitted in as perfectly and as harmoniously as anyone who has ever stayed at the Onslow Court Hotel.

She was a widow, once endowed with more than average good looks, and still possessing a certain mellow comeliness which – quite justifiably – she made the very most of. Her hair was nicely done. Her face was skilfully made up. She liked gay handbags and an orthodox show of jewellery: earrings, a string of pearls, a diamond wristlet watch. She had a taste for hats and her wardrobe included that acknowledged status symbol, a coat of Persian lamb. Her status, though, had deeper and more assured roots – in the fine set of her head, in the rich tones of her voice, in her unassuming and effortless good manners. No-one could doubt for a moment she belonged.

Mrs Durand-Deacon, none the less, had avoided the most dangerous pitfall of belonging. She had not allowed her mind to atrophy or rust. She relished leisure, but did not equate it with passivity. She cherished friends, but did not engage in vacant chatter. Within the permissible frontiers of her environment, she thought and talked to practical effect. Particularly she was inclined to ventilate ideas for minor business ventures in which she could participate; ventures ingeniously designed both to increase her income and occupy her time.

In 1949 – the year that she was to be murdered – Mrs Durand-Deacon was sixty-nine years old, and she had lived at the Onslow Court Hotel for the past six.

John George Haigh – to the porter, Four-Oh-Four – also fitted in at the Onslow Court Hotel, at least up to the point of gaining qualified acceptance. But whereas Mrs Durand-Deacon fitted in by nature, Haigh only did so by studious contrivance.

He was a bachelor, smooth, persuasive, charming; the type that Kensington mamas of bygone days would have considered – on first impressions – an eligible match. He was well-dressed (even to those with an eye for dressing) and well-spoken (even to those with an ear for speech). His small moustache was neatly trimmed, his dark hair neatly cut, his behaviour courteous, his smile agreeable. And yet . . . you couldn't quite put your finger on it, could you? . . . and yet, with all these marketable, assets, he didn't quite – did he? – he didn't quite belong.

The residents still adhered to that opinion after they had warily allowed him in their circle. But they were relying solely upon instinct. The manageress and book-keepers knew what they did not – that Haigh was a bad payer, a poor financial prospect; existing, apparently, from hand to mouth, from day to day. But that, in turn, marked the limits of their knowledge. That he had served several sentences for theft and fraud – including one of penal servitude – was then only known to a remote and scattered few. That he had done deeds so black and terrible that they would spread his evil fame across the earth was then not known to anyone at all.

In 1949 – the year that he was to be hanged – John George

Haigh was thirty-nine years old, and he had lived at the Onslow Court Hotel for the past four.

They sat at adjacent tables in the dining-room. Civilities were exchanged, and sometimes conversation. Mrs Durand-Deacon's estimate of Haigh remains conjectural; probably it coincided with that of her neighbours. He wasn't quite – not quite. But for her, unlike them, one aspect of him aroused interest. Haigh was an agent of sorts, active and in touch with contemporary business, who might on occasion prove a useful intermediary. That had always been the trouble: she hadn't – inevitably couldn't have – the contacts. Next time I devise a saleable project, this man – so Mrs Durand-Deacon hoped – can do the selling.

Once such a project had taken viable shape, like all enthusiastic amateurs she couldn't wait.

On 14th February, Mrs Durand-Deacon entertained a woman friend to lunch. Her name was Gwendoline Birin, and some may detect a mystical significance in the fact that she was an official of the Francis Bacon Society, and hence, through that great Stuart Chancellor, tenuously linked with the sanctions of the law. Although theirs was a regular lunch engagement between intimates, normally absorbed by each other's company, this time the hostess brought in a small box, which she placed beside herself in obvious readiness. It had nothing to do with Mrs Birin. It had to do with Haigh.

When presently the latter took his seat at the next table, Mrs Durand-Deacon begged her guest's pardon, and turned round.

"Mr Haigh, would you glance at those?"

She passed over the box. Haigh opened it and took a look inside.

"I see," he said. "Novel, aren't they?"

"They have a strong appeal to women," Mrs Durand-Deacon said.

"Possibly."

"For sure. All I need is a manufacturer." She exerted her considerable charm. "You know so many people. Now, think, Mr Haigh. Think hard, Mr Haigh. Please."

Haigh thought hard – harder than Mrs Durand-Deacon guessed.

"I know a chap in Crawley," he said. "I'm seeing him in the morning. If I could get him interested – just as a start – perhaps I could arrange for both of us to go and see him."

"That would be splendid. Thank you very much, Mr Haigh."

He passed back the box. Mrs Birin could not refrain from eyeing it. Mrs Durand-Deacon laughed at her friend's curiosity.

"Artificial fingernails," she said.

On 18th February – it won't surprise the superstitious that it was a Friday – Haigh drove Mrs Durand-Deacon down to Crawley. Ostensibly they were going there for discussions about the manufacture of artificial fingernails.

Haigh had spoken to the chap in Crawley – in view of what was brewing, it is not clear why. In any event, the chap wasn't enamoured of the notion. Fingernails – artificial fingernails? Technically it would be a most expensive process. No, not worth bringing along the other person.

Haigh did not argue, but continued with his plans.

The chap at Crawley was head of an engineering firm with premises in West Street and at Giles Yard, Leopold Road. Giles Yard was used almost solely as a storeroom, and Haigh – the firm's unpaid London representative – had made a practice of borrowing the keys from time to time. "For a conversion job," he said on one occasion, but generally he was not required to explain.

During the hours that mattered on 18th February, the keys of the storeroom were reposing in his pocket . . .

Between four and five o'clock that afternoon, Haigh called for a minute or two at the George Hotel in Crawley. He arrived with Mrs Durand-Deacon and he left with her.

At a quarter to seven that evening, Haigh called at the Ancient Prior's restaurant in Crawley and stayed for a quarter of an hour. He had an egg on toast, a cup of tea, and a chat with the proprietor.

He arrived and left alone.

"Do you know anything about Mrs Durand-Deacon? Is she ill? Do you know where she is?"

Mrs Lane – residing nine years at the Onslow Court Hotel – looked up from her breakfast almost angrily. She did not care for Haigh, and she was greatly worried at Mrs Durand-Deacon's unexpected absence.

"Do *I* know? Don't *you* know?" she retorted. "I understood from her that you wanted to take her to a factory."

"Yes, but I wasn't ready," Haigh parried Mrs Lane with his customary blandness. "I hadn't had lunch, and she wanted to go to the Army and Navy Stores, and asked me to pick her up. I waited there an hour, and she did not arrive."

Nobody would have felt, or need have felt, alarm, if Mrs Durand-Deacon had not been of such methodical habits. She hardly ever stayed a night away from the hotel, and certainly never without notifying the staff. And yet she had gone out early yesterday afternoon, and since then not a word, nor a message, nor a sign. Little wonder that as Saturday passed by, Mrs Lane's concern steadily increased.

At Sunday breakfast Haigh again came over.

"Have you had any news?"

"No," snapped Mrs Lane. It is in the highest degree improbable that, at this stage, she had even an inkling of the truth. A jumble of emotions fuelled her resentment: against Haigh as an Outsider with impermissible aspirations, against Mrs Durand-Deacon as a Lady with impermissible condescensions, against herself for connecting their innocuous relationship with the catastrophe she vaguely apprehended. "No, I have not had any news. This afternoon I shall go to the police-station and ask them to take the matter up at once."

Haigh nodded thoughtfully, and withdrew. After breakfast Mrs Lane went into the Tudor Room, and there Haigh approached her yet again.

"I think," he said, "that we had better go together to the police-station."

"I think so, too."

"I'll drive you there," said Haigh.

So it came about that her murderer went with her best friend to report Mrs Durand-Deacon's disappearance to the police.

*   *   *

In the days following – on the Monday and the Thursday – Haigh made two lengthy Statements. The gist of them, however, can be put into a sentence: when Mrs Durand-Deacon failed to keep her appointment on Friday afternoon at the Army and Navy Stores, he went by himself to Crawley, where he "attended to some business", returning to London in the evening on his own.

With the police, Haigh seemed neither reticent nor nervous. He exuded frankness as he exuded confidence: the frankness of a man who had nothing whatever to hide, the confidence of a man who had nothing whatever to fear. If the frankness was counterfeit, the confidence was authentic. Deceived by past experiences and lulled by present vanity, Haigh believed the precautions he had taken were cast-iron.

Police scepticism determined otherwise.

Both their professional *nous* and their professional records forbade them to accept a man like Haigh on trust. On Saturday – two days after Haigh's second Statement – with the owner's consent they forced the storeroom at Giles Yard. In this building – the keys of which Haigh still retained – a singular collection of objects greeted them.

Three acid carboys: full, half full and empty. A stirrup pump. A rubber apron. A pair of rubber gloves. A leather box, containing a revolver (lately fired), together with eight rounds of appropriate ammunition.

And – transforming baulked perplexity into sharp suspicion – a cleaning firm's receipt for a coat of Persian lamb.

The case that gradually built up from these beginnings was as formidable as any in the history of crime. Of course the Persian lamb coat was Mrs Durand-Deacon's. A watch that Haigh had sold on 19th February at a shop in Putney was Mrs Durand-Deacon's. Jewellery that Haigh had sold on 22nd February at a shop in Horsham was Mrs Durand-Deacon's. And a chain belonging to Mrs Durand-Deacon was found on 8th March beneath a hedge at Buxted, exactly where Haigh had said it would be.

More conclusive – and more grisly – evidence, however, came from an intensive search through Giles Yard itself. The least conclusive evidence lay in the bloodstains on the wall (as there were bloodstains on the rubber apron), and the hairpin embedded in a sea of grease coating the bottom of a forty-five-gallon tank. The most conclusive evidence lay in a quantity of sludge which had been deposited over the soil outside.

The sludge was removed to Scotland Yard, and for three days Dr Keith Simpson, the pathologist, accompanied by Dr Henry Holden, the Director of the Metropolitan Police Laboratory, sieved and sifted it in minutest detail. The principal fruits of this investigation were some fragmentary human remains (elderly female), the handle of a red plastic handbag (Mrs Durand-Deacon's), and – hardly less infallible than fingerprints – an upper and lower pair of dentures, both intact, which were identified by Mrs Durand-Deacon's dentist.

Many of these discoveries were still to be unearthed – in some instances quite literally unearthed – when the police reviewed their situation at the end of one full week's consistent work. But they were now seized of sufficient information to justify a further interview with Haigh; an interview at which they threw in what they had.

Haigh's statement of Monday, 28th February – his most veracious as well as his most macabre utterance – furnishes a lesson in criminal flexibility. Confident as he was, like any prudent general he had doubtless devised provisional measures to counter and cushion an unforeseen reverse.

Only under irresistible compulsion, though, would he drop the mask of innocence and bring them into play.

"I have continued my inquiries into the death of Mrs Durand-Deacon," said Detective Inspector Shelley Symes, as Haigh settled himself comfortably in a chair. "And I want you to answer some more questions."

"I'm quite willing," Haigh said amiably, "to answer anything I can and to help you all I can."

"Have you anything to say about a coat of Persian lamb?" The Inspector smoothed a crumpled ticket between his fingers. "Or about this jewellery?" He spread the items on the table. "I would like you to tell me about them, if you will."

Haigh preserved unaccustomed silence. They had got on the trail all right. His bluff was fairly called.

"How did you come by this property, and where is Mrs Durand-Deacon?"

The interposing of a formal caution granted Haigh a little time. He had hardly begun to speak when he was granted more; Inspector Symes was called out of the room.

Left waiting with another officer, Haigh had opportunity to deliberate. Plainly now they *knew* that he had done it. And, having got so far, they might conceivably *prove* that he had done it. But not necessarily – and even if they did there were ways and means of escaping from the worst.

Haigh's reactions at this crucial moment held important implications for the future. Certainly – to quote the Attorney-General at the trial – there was no sign of reason tottering on its throne.

"Tell me frankly," he said to Detective Inspector Webb, "what are the chances of anyone being released from Broadmoor?"

Haigh was not discouraged by Inspector Webb's refusal to enter into a discussion of that kind. He had now reorganized his dispositions, and was impelled to behave accordingly.

"If I told you the truth," he went on, "you would not believe me; it sounds too fantastic."

"You are not obliged to say anything," began Inspector Webb, but Haigh heard out this second caution with impatience.

"I understand all that. I will tell you all about it. Mrs Durand-Deacon no longer exists. She has disappeared completely, and no trace of her can ever be found again."

"What has happened to her?" asked Inspector Webb.

"I have destroyed her with acid. You will find the sludge that remains at Leopold Road."

But even as Haigh – for a rarity – told the truth, and thereby, in effect, committed himself to an insanity defence, he still cherished a modicum of hope that there might be no need for any defence at all. He did not know yet – not did the police themselves – that Mrs Durand-Deacon had not "disappeared completely";

that certain plastic substances – for example, dentures – resist erosion even by sulphuric acid; and that – perhaps because he had moved with too much haste – even certain perishable constituents had survived. And Haigh embraced a common delusion, still shared by many, despite an outstanding demonstration of its falsity in the Porthole murder trial of 1948.

His next question to Inspector Webb was thus half interrogatory and half rhetorical.

"How can you prove" – Haigh looked right and left and centre – "how can you prove murder if there is no body?"

We went to Crawley together in my car. She was inveigled into going by me in view of her interest in artificial fingernails. Having taken her into the storeroom at Leopold Road, I shot her in the back of the head while she was examining some paper for use as fingernails. Then I went out to the car and fetched in a drinking glass and made an incision, I think with a penknife, in the side of the throat, and collected a glass of blood, which I then drank. Following that, I removed the coat she was wearing, a Persian lamb, and the jewellery, rings, necklace, earrings, and crucifix, and put her in a forty-five-gallon tank. I then filled the tank up with sulphuric acid, by means of the stirrup pump, from the carboy.

That is the core of Haigh's Statement to Inspector Symes about the murder of Mrs Durand-Deacon – a Statement which also confirmed what was already known (that he had previously "fenced" about the matter), admitted what could no longer be denied (his abstraction and sale of her personal possessions), and factually reported on his calls at Giles Yard to observe the advance of acid dissolution. *Saturday* . . . "Not satisfactorily completed." *Monday* . . . "A piece of fat and bone still floating in the sludge. I emptied off the sludge with a bucket and tipped it on the ground opposite the shed, and pumped a further quantity of acid into the tank to decompose the remaining fat and bone." *Tuesday* . . . "I found decomposition complete and emptied the tank off." (What had seemed complete to him was not complete to eyes more expert.)

"I emptied the tank off" – those words marked the gruesome end of the lady with an interest in artificial fingernails. But they did not mark the end of all that Haigh desired to say. There had been a hint of nameless revelations yet to come in that remarkable allusion to a glass of blood. It suggested – and I think it was intended to suggest – that the murder of Mrs Durand-Deacon had resulted from a lunatic compulsion on Haigh's part. Such a compulsion, by its character, must, almost always, be repetitive. And sure enough, when he had dealt with the subject then in hand, and when he had no doubt that he would be detained, and when he had briefly scanned the hazards of detention, he insisted on widening the compass of his Statement; he laid to his own account several other murders, of which, up till that moment, the police had never heard.

"In 1944," Haigh declared, dictating, "I disposed of William McSwan in a similar manner in the basement of 79 Gloucester Road, SW 7. And of Donald McSwan, and of Amy McSwan, in 1946* at the same address. And in 1948, Dr Archibald Henderson and his wife Rosalie, also in a similar manner, at Leopold Road, Crawley."

The McSwans were a family Haigh had known for many years. William was the son, and they met one evening – Haigh told Inspector Symes – at a public-house in Kensington High Street called The Goat.

"From there we went to 79 Gloucester Road, where in the basement, which I had rented, I hit him on the head with a cosh, withdrew a glass of blood from his throat, and drank it. He was dead within five minutes or so. I put him in a forty-gallon tank and disposed of him with acid."

The War and its by-products had been handy as a cover; Haigh put William's parents off the scent by intimating that their son had gone away to dodge the call-up. Subsequently, from Scotland, he posted bogus letters to them (Haigh was a fluent and proficient forger). But the parents' turn, too, eventually came. "I took separately to the basement the father, Donald, and the

* That date was given by Haigh in error. He should have said 1945.

mother, Amy, disposing of them in exactly the same way as the son."

Inspector Symes continued to write it down as though taking particulars of a stolen bicycle. Training and discipline count on such occasions.

"I met the Hendersons by answering an advertisement offering for sale their property at Ladbroke Square. I went with them to Brighton where they stayed at the Metropole."

As a surgeon might recall his operations, so Haigh recalled how, one February morning, he had taken Dr Henderson to Crawley, where he shot him through the head and put him in a tank of acid; and how, that afternoon, by saying her husband had been taken ill, he tricked Mrs Henderson into making the same journey. "I shot her and put her in another tank. In each of the last four cases, I had my glass of blood, as before."

In every case – or so he *said* – he had his glass of blood. In every case – or so he *thought* – he had got rid of the corpse.

These two facts may not be disassociated from his – imperfect – understanding of the law.

I am not affirming, or insinuating, that Haigh's Statement of 28th February, taken in its broader aspects, was untrue. One may make a reservation in respect of "my glass of blood" without attacking the entire fabric. That he did kill, not only Mrs Durand-Deacon, but the McSwans and Hendersons, by the means described, does appear in retrospect a virtual certainty.

Less credence can be accorded to his Statement of 4th March – what may be described as the Haigh apocrypha.

Held in jail on a capital charge, with every waking hour devoted to a single theme, Haigh could refine and elaborate his plans. During that long session with Inspectors Symes and Webb, he had vaguely staked a claim – the term is used advisedly – to several further killings, then unspecified, which he did not choose to incorporate in his Statement. Four days' solitary reflection apparently convinced him that this was a mistake. At his own request, Inspector Webb visited him in custody, to hear and record whatever else he should impart.

There were three victims – more precisely, alleged victims –

that Haigh now added to his ample catalogue. A woman about thirty-five ("slim, dark"), casually encountered in the streets of Hammersmith, and "duly" destroyed (1945) at Gloucester Road. A "youngish" man ("about my height and build") persuaded from the Goat public house to Gloucester Road, where (1945) "the same thing happened". A girl ("Mary"), picked up on the front at Eastbourne, and put in an acid tank at Crawley (1948).

In one respect, these three supplementary murders – according to Haigh's considered narrative – followed the common pattern of the six for which he had earlier held himself responsible. Each time he had "tapped" his victim's blood. But in another respect, the six and the three were differentiated. Each of the six had meant financial gain to Haigh (secured, as he admitted, by forgery and fraud); none of the three had done, or ever looked like doing so. The slim woman "had next to nothing in her handbag". The youngish man "had no more than a pound". Mary "had little or no property". Such a complete absence of material inducement – so laboriously and clearly pointed out – conveniently left "my glass of blood" as the sole motive.

The police – who checked Haigh's Statements by their own inquiries, and had confirmed much in that of 28th February – could not find any confirmatory evidence for the assertions in his Statement of 4th March. Lord Dunboyne, a recognized authority on the case, wrote thus in his preface to the transcript of the trial: "Though not impossible, it is, in all the circumstances, highly improbable" that Haigh ever murdered anyone other than those whom he expressly named in full. I do not doubt that Lord Dunboyne is right, and that the Statement of 4th March is a cunning fraud.

Some may suppose that Haigh was merely getting it off his chest, that the Statements of 28th February and 4th March constitute an undesigned catharsis of confession. Others – of whom I am one – prefer to take the view that he had skilfully prepared his counsel's brief and given a useful lead to his psychiatrist.

The trial of Haigh took place at Lewes in July. From every point of view it was a memorable occasion: the greatest criminal judge in England on the bench, the greatest criminal in England in the dock, and the two most eminent members of the English Bar (Sir Hartley Shawcross and Sir David Maxwell Fyfe) appearing respectively to prosecute and defend.

Haigh was tried for the murder of Mrs Durand-Deacon only. Sir Hartley Shawcross – then, as Attorney-General, the senior Law Officer – scrupulously refrained from introducing any other. Nothing about the McSwans and Hendersons; nothing about the slim woman, the youngish man, and Mary. Those references were deliberately excluded when the Crown put Haigh's Statements in as evidence. It was Sir David Maxwell Fyfe who subsequently brought them to the notice of the jury. Actually they tended to support, not to prejudice, his case.

For there was no dispute at all upon the facts. Neither the murder nor the method was contested. Out of thirty-three prosecution witnesses, Sir David cross-examined only four, and never to mark a disagreement or a challenge. His questions, without exception, were designed to underline Haigh's mental abnormality. Sane or insane? That was the sole issue. Must Haigh bear responsibility for his deed according to the tests prescribed by the M'Naghten Rules?

Even those who most persistently attack the M'Naghten Rules would concede them one great merit: simplicity. They do not require the expert intervention of initiates; they can be grasped and applied by an ordinary group of citizens exercising their ordinary sense. Although formulated at a full conclave of judges – after a man named Daniel M'Naghten had shot the Premier's secretary in 1843 – the Rules are not an arbitrary innovation by that conclave, but a solemn and authoritative statement of the law as it was, and had been for centuries. This statement declared that an onus rested on every person raising an insanity defence – the onus of proving that *either* he did not know what he was doing, *or* that he did not know what he was doing was wrong.

Did Haigh know what he was doing when he killed Mrs Durand-Deacon at Giles Yard? And if he knew what he was doing, did he know that it was wrong?

It constitutes an essential feature of the M'Naghten Rules – without which they would lose much of their realism – that the prisoner's state of mind is only relevant as "at the time" when the act was committed. None-the-less, a moment cannot be judged in isolation; it demands recourse to what went before and to what came after.

Immediately prior to the murder of Mrs Durand-Deacon, Haigh was facing an acute financial crisis. He had no assured and regular source of income. He was overdrawn at the bank by £83 5s 10d. His hotel bills, accumulated over several weeks, totalled about £50 on 15th February, and he felt constrained to borrow that amount, out of which he pacified an insistent management. The loan, however, afforded him only the shortest breathing-space for it had been made conditional on repayment by the weekend, so that the lender could discharge a premium then due. (Part was, in fact, repaid on 22nd February.) Haigh, therefore, on the morning of the murder was more than ever impecunious and sorely pressed.

The murder, though, did not occur on sudden impulse. Very few in history have been so premeditated – or premeditated to such practical effect. During the two preceding days Haigh methodically assembled the necessary instruments to carry out his purpose. He ordered sulphuric acid from a firm in Clerkenwell. He arranged with a local mechanic to collect it. He bought the forty-five-gallon tank from a firm in Barking – a tank especially lined to resist corrosive chemicals. He took a stirrup pump to have the foot sawn off (which would make it possible to insert the body of the pump through the narrow neck of a sulphuric acid carboy). And lest anything should be overlooked or forgotten, Haigh, like a prudent housewife, made a shopping-list ("Stirrup Pump, Gloves, Apron, Rags", and so forth) which the police discovered later in his room. Nothing was left to improvisation or to chance.

Nor did his prudence vanish after the event. While he was making those solicitous inquiries, he was also paying those visits to Giles Yard; surveying his handiwork, pumping in fresh acid, and finally pouring away that residual sludge which yielded up its shocking mysteries at Scotland Yard. Simultaneously the spoils of his crime were turned into the cash he so desperately needed. He obtained £10 for Mrs Durand-Deacon's watch. He obtained

£100 for Mrs Durand-Deacon's jewellery. He took the loose coins from her bag and slipped them in his pocket. He had not realized the coat before arrest, but it needs no great flight of imagination to divine the reason for which it was being cleaned . . .

Didn't know what he was doing? Didn't know that it was wrong? It is against the background of these facts – all either stated by Haigh or else accepted by him – that his insanity defence should be examined.

An insanity defence is generally based on alleged abnormalities of behaviour observed by others (especially by experts). The best testimony, therefore, is that of such observers.

The case for Haigh's insanity, though, assumed a different character.

His alleged abnormalities had not been manifest; indeed, the persona he presented to the world might have passed for that lawyer's incarnation of plain sense, the reasonable man on the Clapham omnibus. The jury were asked to infer insanity, not from any overt and visible phenomena, but from what Haigh was supposed to have thought and felt and done in the recesses of his mind or in the secrecy of solitude. The best testimony, therefore, would be that of Haigh.

But Haigh did not go into the box. Had he done so he could have given, as no-one else could give, a first-hand, direct, immediate description of the thoughts and the feelings and the hidden acts on which his counsel was constrained to place reliance. Had he done so, he would have provided, as nothing else could provide, an opportunity for the court to study his mental composition. Had he done so, however, he would have also been liable, in both respects, to cross-examination.

That liability being declined, and Haigh holding fast to the sanctuary of the dock, the only witness called on his behalf was a Harley Street psychiatrist, Dr Henry Yellowlees. That witness's credentials and experience were – and are – impressive. He was a Fellow of the London Royal College of Physicians (where he held a Diploma in Psychological Medicine), a Fellow of the Edinburgh College of Physicians, and a Fellow of the Glasgow Royal

Faculty of Physicians and Surgeons. He had been honorary
Consulting Physician, Physician for Mental Diseases, and Lecturer in Psychological Medicine at St Thomas's Hospital. He had
been examiner in Mental Diseases and Psychology at the University of London. During the Second World War, as a colonel in
the Army Medical Service, he occupied the post of Consulting
Psychiatrist to the British Expeditionary Force in France. When
the judge subsequently referred to him as "a highly qualified
gentleman" and "a gentleman of position" he gave Dr Yellowlees
no more than his due.

Doubtless it was his misfortune rather than his fault that he
enacted two distinct roles at the trial of Haigh – roles which
neither complemented nor sustained each other. On the one
hand, the trained and impartial diagnostician; on the other,
the accused's sole channel of communication with those to whom
he must communicate. Dr Yellowlees had to tell Haigh's story
before he could submit his own assessment of it. That put him at
a grave disadvantage straightaway. The more effective he proved
as Haigh's expositor and spokesman, the more suspect he became
as Haigh's examiner and analyst.

The dilemma was inescapable – and so was the handicap of
being, in his prior capacity, a mere agent for an available principal. "Members of the jury," said Sir David Maxwell Fyfe in
opening the defence, "I am not going to detail it [Haigh's actions,
reactions, and accounts of them] because *it is much better that you
have it from Dr Yellowlees.*"

The jury cannot be blamed if they reflected, as Dr Yellowlees
stepped up and took the oath, that it would have been better still
if they had had it from Haigh.

Dr Yellowlees had seen Haigh on three occasions, in jail, within
three weeks of his impending trial. The time they spent together
totalled two hours and ten minutes, during which Haigh appears
to have unfolded a psychopathological conspectus of his life. Dr
Yellowlees now faithfully passed this on, interspersed, as oppor-
tune, with the conclusions that he drew.

The story reached right back into the roots of childhood. I was
brought up in a fanatic religious atmosphere (Haigh had said); my

parents were Plymouth Brethren, and the vengeance of God broke over my head for each trifling misdemeanour. My mother was given to telling the future from dreams (Haigh had said); books on the subject were always around for me to read. I was a solitary youngster (Haigh had said); no friends, no comrades, odd man out at school. In my teens, I became attached – first as chorister, then as organist – to Wakefield Cathedral, which was High Church (Haigh had said); the opposite extreme from the services I knew. "About that time I began to get recurring dreams in which I saw either the head or the whole body of Christ on the Cross with the blood pouring from His wounds."

From this data Dr Yellowlees deduced that the adolescent Haigh had "a paranoid constitution".

That is not a disease of the mind, Dr Yellowlees explained, but it can be a preliminary state in mental aberration. It makes the psychiatrist alert for further symptons – which, in this instance, the psychiatrist discovered. Or rather, Haigh reported, during those talks in jail, what had been to him (he said) mystical revelations, but were medical symptoms to Dr Yellowlees.

His first "revelation" occurred (Haigh had said) when he was only sixteen or seventeen years of age. "Divinely guided", he construed a phrase in the Old Testament as an instruction to drink his own urine. Haigh told Dr Yellowlees he had obeyed that instruction, and had continued to obey it ever since.

The second "revelation" came much later (Haigh had said), not until 1944 or 1945; another recurring dream in which a forest of what he thought were crucifixes, but found were trees, dripped with what he thought was rain or dew, but found was blood. One tree presently turned into a man, who invited Haigh to drink blood collected in a bowl; but before Haigh could reach it and satisfy himself, the man receded and the dream resolved. These dreams (Haigh had said) confirmed his belief that he was divinely guided; created a feeling of uneasiness and distress during their cycle; and often – or always – culminated in his killing.

The third "revelation" (Haigh had said) embraced the killings themselves. In these, he acted as the instrument of the outside power. They concerned – he could not be more definite – eternal life. He drank – Dr Yellowlees was "pretty sure" he at any rate tasted – the blood of his prey on every occasion. "I have a destiny," Haigh had asserted, "to fulfil."

From this data Dr Yellowlees deduced that the adult Haigh had developed paranoia.

What is paranoia?

Sir David Maxwell Fyfe had already apprised the jury. "Paranoia," he said, "brings a complete and permanent alteration of the entire personality which overwhelms the mental outlook and the character and the conduct. Broadly and fundamentally, it is the result of the patient's interest and energies being turned in upon himself and withdrawn from the real world around. It really amounts to, practically, self-worship, and that is commonly expressed by a conviction that he is in some mystic way under the control of a guiding spirit which means infinitely more to him and is of infinitely greater authority than any human laws or rules of society. The defect, and at the same time, the badge of this disorder is that the victim who suffers from it knows that his secret life of fantasy has got to be lived alongside the ordinary life of the world; and the paranoiac is, therefore, lucid, astute, and shrewd, when he is not actually acting under the influence of his fantasy. In such cases, he takes the steps which one would expect in order to avoid trouble."

That was an adroit and skilful definition which, while wholly unexceptionable from a general standpoint, corresponded closely with the particular facts. Dr Yellowlees qualified it only by limiting its application to "completely well-established paranoia". As he maintained that Haigh's paranoia had "gone over the line", this qualification had no practical significance.

But while "completely well-established paranoia" might count as insanity in a consulting-room, it did not necessarily do so in a court of law. Is a paranoiac spared by the M'Naghten Rules? Does a paranoiac not know what he is doing, or – in relevant circumstances – that what he is doing is wrong? Can this "self-worship", or this "guiding spirit", eliminate consciousness of ordinary values and ordinary sanctions?

"Taking the last question of the legal test," Maxwell Fyfe said finally to Dr Yellowlees, "would it be right to say at once that you are not prepared to express an opinion on whether he knew that what he was doing was wrong?"

It skipped the initial step, but with ample justification. Nobody himself in his right mind would be convinced that Haigh did not at least know what he was doing.

"You are not prepared to express an opinion on whether he knew what he was doing was wrong?"

"Yes," replied Dr Yellowlees. "That is so."

"In your view what amount of contact with the accused and what opportunities of observation would be necessary in order to answer that question?"

"I do not think," said Yellowlees, "that any psychiatrist could even attempt to answer that question unless he had lived with such a paranoid patient for years."

The Attorney-General began to cross-examine with a paramount target that all could plainly see.

Dr Yellowlees had given a physician's diagnosis; he had declined to comment on its implications. The question remained at present in the air: Did Haigh know what he was doing was wrong? The whole of the Attorney's admirably succinct interrogation, therefore, was designed to extract an affirmative reply.

After a short preliminary exchange which put the witness at initial disadvantage (he had confused the number of his interviews with Haigh), Sir Hartley Shawcross set about his task.

"You would agree, would you not, that the prisoner is a person on whose word it would be utterly unsafe to rely?"

"Yes," said Dr Yellowlees.

"But you have, as a matter of fact, relied on it entirely as the main basis of your opinion in this case?"

"No," said Dr Yellowlees.

"Have you not?"

"No."

"What *objective* signs of insanity are there in the prisoner?"

"I should have to repeat all my evidence to show you."

"Far be it from me to ask you to do that." The Attorney's gentle sarcasm followed on an examination-in-chief which had occupied the court for a full hour and a half. "What objective signs of insanity are there, apart from what the prisoner has said to you?"

Yellowlees replied.

"There are no such things as isolated objective signs of insanity. It is one of the oldest fallacies."

"Then you are relying in the main on what the prisoner said to you?"

Yellowlees was encountering a clear-headed and tenacious cross-examiner. But he continued to present his thesis with manifest sincerity.

"No, I am relying in the main upon my lifelong knowledge of such cases, and my observation of a *cumulative* series of symptoms, as I said."

"What symptoms are you referring to, apart from what the prisoner said to you? Mention one."

"I am relying on his verbosity, his egocentricity, the fact that he is unable to speak the truth, the fact that he has no shadow of shame or remorse for his deeds, the stories that he tells me about his dreams, and the fact that paranoia is, I think, the most difficult of all mental disorders to simulate, and I do not think – I may be wrong – but I do not think I would have been hoodwinked."

"That may be so," Shawcross said impassively, "but all the things you have mentioned are things the prisoner said to you?"

"He has not told me he is verbose," retorted Yellowlees.

"Of course not. But he has talked to you with verbosity?"

"Very well."

"All those symptoms" – there was an iron will behind that velvet voice – "arise, do they not, from what the prisoner has said – except the last one which is not a symptom at all?"

"I do not think," Yellowlees said, "that I can help you further."

Shawcross now proceeded to drive his point home with the minimum of words.

"Do you attach importance to the dreams?"

"Yes, great importance."

"Whether this man dreamed or not is a matter you can only judge by what he told you?"

"Yes."

"You said a moment ago that he is unable to speak the truth?"

"Yes."

Thus smartly was that outsize chicken sent back home to roost.

"You know, do you not, from the prisoner's statements in this case, that he is a man who, in connection with the various murders, has practised an elaborate system of forgery and false pretences in order to possess himself of his victims' property?"

"I don't know whether he did it in order to possess himself – that is not a question for me, but he has done so, I believe."

"With the *result* that he possessed himself of his victims' property?"

"Yes."

"Do you think it is an impossibility that he might have deceived you about his dreams and other symptoms?"

The doctor's answer was inconclusive.

"I will put it to you quite frankly," Shawcross said, "that this man has been inventing a defence and has been deceiving you in regard to these symptoms upon which you have relied for your opinion that he is a paranoiac."

Yellowlees, to his honour, refrained from dogmatism.

"I do not think I am likely to be deceived on this subject, but I may well be."

"You may well be deceived?"

"Undoubtedly."

Whatever possibilities of escape for Haigh had ever reposed in the evidence of Dr Yellowlees, these were receding as each moment passed. It says much for Maxwell Fyfe's professional aplomb that he gave no outward sign of pressure or anxiety as Shawcross pursued his devastating course.

"Did you ever ask the prisoner how much he realized in pounds, shillings and pence from the murders of the Hendersons and McSwans?"

"No, I do not regard that as my province."

This rejoinder may have fairly reflected psychiatric method. Those who were not psychiatrists, though, could perhaps be forgiven if they registered shock.

"Were you not considering it as part of your province to discover what the motives for these offences were – whether it was a motive which lay in the field of insanity or a motive which belonged to a more mercenary field?"

"It was quite obvious from the first interview with him that there was no question of motive in the popular sense at all."

Mr Justice Humphreys had been following closely. Now he intervened.

"Did you in fact inquire, or were you told, whether this man made large sums of money or not from the murder of the persons whom he said he murdered?"

Dr Yellowlees thought he had read as much in some of the statements, "but I do not remember inquiring specifically myself."

Mr Justice Humphreys rubbed his cheek with his bent knuckles.

"In your opinion, is it of any importance whatever in this case whether he made money or whether he did not?"

"In my opinion," Dr Yellowlees said, "no."

"That is what I thought you'd say," observed the judge.

The ground was crumbling under an honest – but, as I think, misled – witness when the Attorney-General moved in close for the finale.

"This man knew the nature and quality of what he was doing?"

"Perfectly."

"Did he know that what he was doing was wrong?"

Yellowlees maintained his previous position.

"I have no opinion to give on that," he said.

"You have given evidence in a great many cases where the defence has been insanity?"

"Yes."

"And you have not previously had difficulty, have you, in saying whether you thought the prisoner concerned knew or did not know that what he was doing was wrong?"

"It depends," said Yellowlees, "on what you mean by difficulty."

"You have given evidence upon the point, at all events?"

"Yes."

"This is the first case, is it not, in which you have been unable to say whether, in your view, the prisoner knew that what he was doing was wrong?"

"Yes," said Yellowlees, "I think that is true."

"Is your difficulty really this – that you realized from the preparations which the prisoner made that he *must* have known that it was wrong?"

"No." The rejection was categorical. "If that had been my difficulty I shouldn't have dreamed of coming to give evidence."

"Why do you think he procured sulphuric acid in advance in order to destroy the body?"

"You have answered the question, haven't you? In order to destroy the body."

"Why do you think he thought it necessary to destroy the body?"

"Because he wished to escape detection."

"Why do you think he wished to escape detection?"

"Because he did not wish to be punished."

Three short jabs. But deeply penetrating. And, moreover, opening wide the way – as Shawcross had intended – for the Crown case to be deployed at full strength.

"Does it not follow that he knew if he were detected he would be punished?"

"I think he certainly knew that murder is punishable by law, as a general proposition."

"Is it your opinion, then, that he was acting in obedience to a higher law?"

"Yes." Dr Yellowlees made his last stand. "He said so."

"Whether he believed he was acting under the guidance of a higher law or not, did he believe that, *according to the law of this country*, what he was doing was wrong?"

"He cannot have, if he believed he was acting under a power above the law."

Shawcross repeated and persisted.

"I asked you whether this man, thinking, as he may have done, according to you, that he was acting under the guidance of some higher power, still believed that what he was doing was wrong *according to our law*?"

"I don't know."

The Attorney only needed to ask a very few more questions. "Can you draw any other possible conclusion from the elaborate preparations he made in advance and the attempts made subsequently to conceal what he had done?"

"No, it looks like it." Dr Yellowlees might have been communing with himself. "On the other hand, I know, or I would not be here, how little this question of knowledge of right and wrong has to do with patients in the condition I believe this man to be. It is a difficulty with all disorders to express it satisfactorily in a legal way, and I can only say I do not know."

"I am not asking you" – Shawcross pressed with remorseless relevance – "whether this man decided in obedience to a higher power to do what he realized was wrong. I am asking you to look at the facts and tell the jury whether there is any doubt that he must have known that *according to English law* he was preparing to do, and subsequently had done, something which was wrong?"

Dr Yellowlees examined the situation.

"I will say 'Yes' to that if you say 'punishable by law' instead of 'wrong'."

It delayed the final thrust by seconds only.

"Punishable by law," said Shawcross, "and therefore wrong by the law of this country?"

"Yes, I think he knew that," said Dr Yellowlees.

The trial was virtually over.

In vain did Maxwell Fyfe, with all the eloquence and force at his command, plead that Haigh's "divine control" had operated so as to annul his sense of right and wrong. The defender was not merely asking the jury to say something that Dr Yellowlees would not say himself. He was asking them to say something in contradiction of what Dr Yellowlees had already said.

It is not surprising that they preferred to accept the Attorney-General's pithy phrase for Haigh – "Not mad, but bad." It is not surprising that they needed only seventeen minutes to reach their verdict – guilty, without qualification or proviso. It is not surprising that no appeal was launched (rare though that is when the sentence has been death). It is not surprising that a special medical inquiry – appointed under statute – pronounced that Haigh was simulating insanity, and that he was neither irresponsible by legal standards *nor insane by medical standards either*.

It is certainly not surprising that the Home Secretary found no sufficient ground to justify him in advising His Majesty to interfere with the process of the law.

A whole host of legends has collected around Haigh. That he was either sub- or super-human; a werewolf, a demon, a ghoul, an incubus. That he installed a mincing-machine at Gloucester Road, and expelled the sliced remnants of his corpses down the drains. That his victims numbered, not the six we know nor the nine he claimed, but many hundreds who have wholly disappeared.

Those, though, were the fancies or the fantasies of others. The legend Haigh devised himself has lasted best of all.

There are still people who believe that there was "something in it" – something in that second-best and second-hand defence; something in that dream of weeping crucifixes; something in that thirst for drinking human blood. They believe it because it is the solitary alternative to facing a stark and disagreeable fact.

That fact is easier to state than to digest. Occasionally human beings are begotten who combine a complete sanity of mind with an infinite capacity for evil. Their mental equipment is unexceptionable, but they are morally uninhibited and emotionally void. Haigh furnishes an excellent example.

He was intelligent, rational, sensible, and acute; even – though it doesn't bear on sanity – quite cultured. On any IQ test, Haigh was somewhere above average. I do not think he had any defect of reason whatsoever, nor that he had – as one writer has proclaimed – a lust for killing. If Haigh had any lust at all, it was a lust for money; and for money he would kill as readily as others might back a horse or take a job.

It is illuminating in this regard to note the profits he extracted from his earlier – authenticated – murders, and also the means that he adopted to extract them.

From the three McSwans, through forgery and personation, he realized securities, freehold properties, furniture, and personal belongings amounting in value to about £4000. From the two Hendersons, through forgery and theft, he realized a house, a motor-car, jewellery, and other possessions amounting in value to an even larger sum (during the twelve months after they were murdered his famished bank account was fed with over £7000). Fortunate indeed – as Sir Hartley Shawcross commented on the loot that Haigh derived from Mrs Durand-Deacon – fortunate indeed the man whose irresistible impulses and monetary interests lead to exactly the same result.

By comparison, of course, Haigh's murder of that lady harvested only modest dividends. But two considerations must not be overlooked. Beggars can't be choosers, and in February, 1949, even a hundred pounds to Haigh spelt temporary salvation. Moreover, detection followed too closely upon crime for anyone to gauge how far his schemes lay uncompleted.

It must have been galling – especially for a man with Haigh's high pride in his professional achievements – to forfeit all in an attempt to win so little. He did not waste time, though, on fruitless lamentation. He applied those quick wits to a revised purpose; if they failed at one level, they might prosper at another. So he set out to feign insanity ("What are the chances of anyone being released from Broadmoor?"), and it must be admitted that he did it very well. But not quite well enough.

None need regret his failure. The verdict did him absolute as well as instant justice. It assigned him his rightful place in criminal history – that of a passionless and calculating murderer for gain, who planned his killings with a chess-player's precision, executed them with a slaughterer's indifference, and exploited them with a usurer's rapacity.

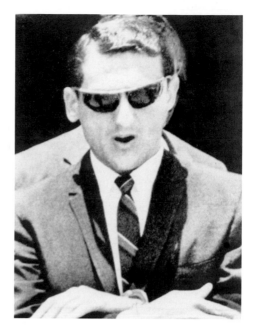

Carl Coppolino, sentenced for the murder of his first wife

The Fox case: the room at the Hotel Metropole, Margate, where Sidney Fox arranged the "accidental" death of his mother

The Acid Bath murder: Home Office pathologist Dr Keith Simpson sifts through soil and embers for evidence against John George Haigh, the killer of Mrs Durand Deacon

The Daily Mirror reports Haigh's arrest, 4 March 1949

Haigh arrives at Horsham magistrates' court
to hear the prosecution case against him

A policeman carries a vat, wrapped in canvas, into court

Kenneth Barlow, wife-killer

Rachel and Harry Dobkin on their wedding day

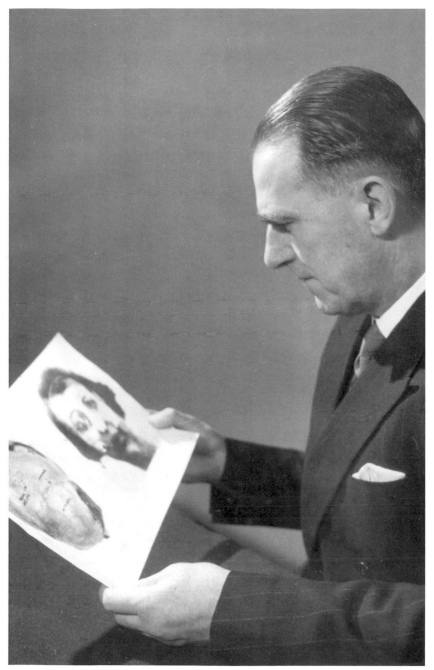

A detective compares photographs of Rachel Dobkin in life and in death

My Notes of appeal against
a sentence of Death

I did not kill my Wife
I did not take her to Kennington Lane
Why was I not alowed to Identify my wife
had my son Stanley Dobkin ~~been asked~~
been asked to Identify the elleged body
of his mother if so then where is his evidence

A Police Constable's evidence who saw me enter
302 Kennington Lane at 545 a m on the morning
of aug 4th could be disputed by several 3 witnesses
That were missing

The same Constable whom I have never seen nor
spoken to remarked that he knew me quite well
and had cautioned to me several times about my light
during the blackout could be disputed that there were
no lights whatever no running water as everything
was bombed through enemy action

That Constable should be requestioned
at my appeal

The evidence of an off Licence woman who stated
that she knew me quite well and heard me tell a
Police constable that on the morning of the fire
I Did Not Do It. I dont know Nothing about it is
entirely not true. Where is that Constables evidence

I have not been questioned by any Police Constable
or the fire Brigade of a fire weh did not concern me

Evidence of Mr Palmer a builder that after he repaired
the house at 302 Kennington Lane in april 1941 he
moved. It could be denied that mr palmer did not repair
302 Kennington Lane and did not ~~mak~~ till after november

SPECIMEN OF DOBKIN'S WRITING

Harry Dobkin's notes for his appeal against the death sentence

Dr Buck Ruxton, who chopped
up his wife and his servant

The ravine at Moffat
in Scotland where
the remains of
Ruxton's wife and
maid were found

The Peter Griffiths case: police guard the spot
where he murdered June Anne Devaney

Peter Griffiths

"IF—"

(Emile Gourbin, France 1912)

George Dilnot

Every contact leaves a trace. The French criminologist Edmond Locard (1877–1966) established one of the key precepts of forensic science while working at the University of Lyon in 1910. His theory was that a criminal will always take something away from the scene of his crime and leave something behind. Two years later, Locard was able to prove his theory while investigating the case of Emile Gourbin. Gourbin was suspected of having strangled his mistress, but detectives failed to shake his alibi. When Locard scraped beneath Gourbin's fingernails, he was able to analyze the resulting debris under a microscope. As expected, Locard found flakes of skin from the victim's neck. But crucially he saw that the flakes were coated with a fine powder, the same cosmetic she used as make-up. Gourbin confessed. George Dilnot (1883–1951) was general editor of the Famous Trials *series, and the author of a dozen factual books on crime. He was also a prolific writer of crime and detective fiction.*

The most significant word in the language is "if."

There are men and women who have died because of an "if" and this is the story of one of them. If Emile Gourbin had thought of visiting a manicurist – if he had been a better actor . . . Search, if you like, the archives of the principal detective bureaux in the world – in London, Paris, New York, Berlin, Vienna – and you will understand how frequently fate plays a grim game with an "if."

The fact of the matter is that, nowadays, the lady or gentleman who takes a step outside the criminal code often does not get a sporting chance. The law has no scruples in potting its game sitting. It has made a profound study of "ifs." It is rarely possible for any human being, however farseeing, to dodge them all. The detective has called to his service so many allies in the realms of science that "ifs" are multiplied beyond the conception of most criminals.

There was a time when the law-breaker knew to some extent the type of detective against whom he would be pitted, the methods that would be adopted in the hue and cry. Now he cannot be sure. He may have his guilt made manifest by some man he never sees. Some enthusiastic specialist working in a laboratory, not necessarily with test tubes, but even with so prosaic an instrument as a vacuum cleaner, may glean a story which nothing can controvert. The microscopist, the bacteriologist, the analyst, the photographer, and a score of other experts in the domain of science are mobilized in that search for "if." It will be found – almost to a certainty they will find it.

All this is preliminary to the case of Emile Gourbin. Now, Emile Gourbin was a clerk with a post at a bank in Lyons. It has been the fashion since the days of Lombroso to dwell on the abnormality of murderers – observe that I make no secret of the fact that Gourbin was a murderer. As a fact, murderers are much like other people. You and I, gentle reader, are quite capable in certain circumstances of killing someone. That is one of the difficulties of investigating cases of homicide.

Therefore, I regret that I cannot paint Gourbin as otherwise than a very ordinary young man to all external appearances. He was of a type familiar everywhere in the world – an amiable fellow of convivial disposition, perhaps a trifle neurotic, with plenty of friends, and ambitious of ultimate promotion in the bank.

There was, of course, the girl. Marie Latelle was as fragrant and piquant a piece of femininity as ever caused a bank clerk's heart to miss a beat. It is not to be supposed that this gay and debonair young lady was without her string of admirers. For

besides her personal attractions was a "dot," which would serve
to solve many of the difficulties of starting housekeeping for one
with the modest emoluments of a bank clerk. Her family if not
wealthy was at least well-to-do, and they had a neat little villa on
the outskirts of Lyons. Yet I would not do Gourbin an injustice.
He was very much in love, and if Marie Latelle had been without
a sou it would possibly have made little difference.

Here it will be noticed that I break all the rules of the detective
story-writer. I have given away my murderer instead of reserving
him for the last paragraph, and the astute reader will already have
gleaned some conception of motives. Things, outside fiction, do
not happen that way, and I am bound to my facts. Young
Gourbin and Marie fell in love. There came a day when they
were betrothed. Then it was that Gourbin touched the limits of
ecstasy. He swam in dizzy heights, no longer a bank clerk but a
silken prince of romance, the affianced of a princess of dreams.

Thus the days passed. Gourbin was an assiduous lover – too
assiduous it might have been for the little lady, who had hitherto
thrown her kerchief to any gallant as her butterfly whim dictated.
I would not be misunderstood. There was no harm in Marie. She
was young and volatile. Her dainty feet scarce touched the
ground. The inhibitions of her lover were a matter of jest –
but more than once of tears and passionate defiance.

The psychology of a man fiercely in love baffled even Solomon.
Why, therefore, should I attempt to define it? There were morose
brooding fits of sulky jealousy – futile outbursts of anger. He was
suspicious and contrite by turns, but always at the back of his
mind was the morbid fear that she was playing with him. Such a
frame of mind reacting on a temperament such as Gourbin's
might have been the subject of either comedy or tragedy. Destiny
decided that it should be tragedy.

The days grew into months. And one morning it befell that
they found little Marie dead in the parlour of her parents' home.
There were the marks of a man's fingers about her throat, but
beyond that there was no clue by which the crime might be
brought home to the assassin. The doctors said that she must
have been killed shortly before midnight. So far as any of the
family knew she had had no visitors that evening.

The house lay just outside the boundaries of the Lyons police district, but the local gendarmes felt that they were confronted with a mystery that was beyond their powers. They, therefore, turned the case over to the city authorities, and the complicated but highly efficient French system of criminal investigation began at once to work.

Unlike British procedure, a magistrate invariably takes a prominent part in the investigation of a crime in France. The detectives, the *police judiciare*, are apart from the police proper, are especially recruited, and have never worn a police uniform.

These, then, were the skilled and experienced officials who began to probe the mystery. The usual formulae were sedulously observed. Nothing that might be of moment in their search was overlooked. They probed relentlessly in every direction. Beyond the marks on the white neck of the girl, which on a superficial examination they took to be fingerprints too blurred to be of use, there was no tangible thing on which they could fasten. There was not a shadow or a shred of proof which might open some avenue of inquiry. They were baffled, against a blank wall.

That terrible snowball, the *process verbal*, which is unknown to British jurisprudence, but which is so formidable a weapon in the hands of Continental police, was commenced. Anyone and everyone who might have had any connection with the crime, or who conceivably might throw light upon it, was submitted to interrogation. All the tittle-tattle and gossip of fifty tongues was reduced to writing to be used – when there should be someone to use it against.

Even here there was nothing solid against which the detectives could lean. Suspicion there was, but an utterly unsubstantiated and flimsy suspicion.

In the wide cast that was taken, it was of course, inevitable that Emile Gourbin should be sought. Among the whispers that had been caught by the detectives was word of his jealousy. That might mean anything or nothing; but he, at least, had a possible motive. So they talked with him. They plied him with subtle questions. He was badgered and browbeaten and coaxed. They were seeking for an "if" – a little "if" – but the examining magistrate and his *confréres* were ready to snatch at the most tenuous trifle. In the beginning it had nothing to do with manicuring. Their methods were as old as crime itself. Gourbin was cunningly cross-examined; but he had expected that.

The young man was utterly grief-stricken, garrulously desolate. He was very ready to tell them anything he knew, anything that might aid them. Alas, it was very little. Through his streaming tears he answered brokenly. Yes, he had been foolishly, insanely in love with his beautiful Marie. There was now nothing in the world for him to look forward to but death. Ere that came, no doubt, messieurs would have found the dastard who had done this thing. With vengeance inflicted on the murderer of his heart's life he would die happy. Yes, it was true that he had been a little – the *Bon Dieu* forgive him – a little jealous. He had even – yes, messieurs – reproved his rosebud for little freedoms with other men. She was young. She did not understand that it was a censorious world. Messieurs would pardon his uncontrollable emotion. She was gone, the incomparable . . .

A wise man, it was once laid down by an eminent Persian philosopher, sometimes does not know when to begin; a fool never knows when to stop. So it was with Emile Gourbin. His grief was just a little too grievous; he was a shade too insistent on his emotions.

"That man," whispered one veteran police official to another, "is the murderer of Marie Latelle."

"True, friend," agreed his colleagues. "But how are we going to prove it?"

This may be an age of detective science, but science is not always necessary in certain aspects of human nature. These men knew a liar when they met one. But it is very difficult, even in France, to substantiate a charge of murder against a man because he has paraded a grief he has not felt.

Nothing that the young bank clerk had said in his examination was accepted. Every point was probed and tested. Again the officers ran against a blank wall. There is nothing more exasperating for a police officer than to feel a moral certainty of the guilt of a person, and yet to find that every fact he unearths bears apparent testimony to that person's innocence.

In practically every particular the story told by Gourbin was borne out. He had given what appeared to be an unassailable alibi. On the evening of the murder he had been entertained by friends at a house some miles away from that in which Marie Latelle had been found dead. These friends had been sought out. Not only did they assert that Gourbin had dined with them, but he had remained playing cards until about one o'clock in the morning, and then gone to his room.

Now if that was true, and the conclusion of the doctors that the girl had been killed before midnight was also true, the young bank clerk could not have been the assassin. It seemed pure madness to put Gourbin under arrest. That, however, was just what the police did. They were convinced that there was a nigger in the fence somewhere. There was nothing to go upon but an impression, and that impression had been utterly shattered by the alibi. British police officers would certainly and properly have hesitated at such a drastic step. It looked like courting trouble.

But the Lyons men played their hunch and took a chance. If the prisoner was innocent – why, so much the better for him. If he was guilty – well, certain of them held their own views. It could do no harm to put him under lock and key till they had decided the next step.

Gourbin, also, was no doubt quite content. They were fools, these detectives, if they thought to match their wits against his. And it was perfectly true that they were in a quandary. Any legal tribunal in the world would have laughed them out of court had they dared to take their case for trial.

We have now reached a point at which the story of Emile Gourbin becomes different from that of other murderers. Things had gone in some degree as he had expected. He had reckoned that his alibi was airtight – that it would place the police in just such a cul-de-sac as they had in fact reached. He had not thought of Dr Edmond Locard; it is doubtful if he even knew of his existence. What interest has the ordinary, obscure bank clerk in scientific matters?

Yet, all the same, Dr Locard was quite a well known person in circles of the world alien to those in which Gourbin moved, though perhaps not as well known as he has since become. His reputation as a criminological scientist was worldwide. He was, and is, among that select few which includes people like Hans Gross in Prague, Sir Bernard Spilsbury in London, and Dr Réné Faralicq in Paris. By a chance unfortunate for Gourbin, his efficiently equipped police laboratory was situated in Lyons itself.

It was not unnatural, therefore, that in their dilemma the Lyons officials should turn to this calm student, who, with his strong face, thick black hair, and dark moustache with a slightly aggressive little tilt at each corner, looked quite unlike a student or a professor, and least of all like Sherlock Holmes.

He listened thoughtfully to the story that was told to him. Quite frankly the police assured him that, unless he could find some way out, the man whom they were convinced was a brutal murderer would have to go free. He was their last hope.

"I had better look at this girl," he said.

So he was taken in a motor-car to where the still body of Marie Latelle lay. He studied it with close attention, and then proceeded to adjust a singular photographic microscope of his own invention.

This instrument, eight feet long, is capable of magnifying objects up to fifty thousand times their natural size. It was rather a pet of Locard's, for it had more than once been of service in simplifying many extraordinary cases when other methods had failed.

I step aside for the moment from the episode of Gourbin to recount that of Josef Holle, whom the police of Paris had good reason to suppose was doing a flourishing coining business by using nickel and an alloy to manufacture bogus franc pieces. Against him, however, they could get no positive evidence. They referred the matter to Locard, and on his advice Holle was arrested on a trumped up charge, which had nothing to do with coining. He was provided with a new suit of clothes and his own were taken away from him and sent to Locard, who had them beaten in a dust-proof bag – a vacuum cleaner is now used in similar cases – and then photographed the dust through his microscope. When the negatives were developed a large proportion of nickel and alloy particles were disclosed. The scientist followed this up with a chemical analysis. Those bits of metal were exactly similar to those which had been used in the false coins. That finished Holle.

Then there was the murder case which resulted from the quarrel of two men employed in a timber yard. One of them had been killed in a desperate struggle to and fro over the ground. There were no eyewitnesses, and the suspected man declared that he had not either quarrelled or fought. From his clothes, however, Locard extracted dust, among which, as well as sawdust and wood fibre, were infinitesmal fragments of soil which showed that he had at least been in contact with the soil of the timber yard. The dead man's clothes showed an exactly similar result. This evidence provided the missing link and convicted the prisoner.

As I have said, it was with this appliance that Dr Locard examined the body of Marie Latelle. He almost at once established beyond cavil or doubt that the marks on the neck were not blurred fingerprints, but superficial scratches that must have been inflicted by her assailant during the death struggle. The skin of the throat had in places been slightly scraped away.

The police glumly accepted his conclusion. Here, it seemed, was the last chance of a clue washed out. If the great criminologist, with his wealth of knowledge and resource, could not help them, where were they to turn? The case was at an end. Gourbin had beaten them after all.

Something of their feelings they conveyed to the black-haired scientist, who shrugged his shoulders and shook his head with a whimsical smile.

"Oh no," was the effect of his reply. "Give me an hour or two. Meanwhile I would like to see this young man."

They brought the prisoner to him. Gourbin was a little confused, a little doubtful of what it all meant. But he met the swift, first scrutiny of the scientist with confident self-possession. What harm could this keen-eyed, stern-faced man do to him? Had he not established an impregnable alibi?

"So you are Gourbin," said the scientist quietly. "Sit down, I want to see your hands."

The bank clerk silently obeyed. Locard drew his chair nearer to that of the prisoner and studied the hand that the other had thrust forward. Those who were present in the room beheld the strange sight of a great scientist acting with infinite care as manicurist to the nails of a suspected murderer.

"What are you doing?" demanded the mystified Gourbin.

"You will know in time," answered the absorbed scientist. "Keep your hand still."

Gourbin was not the only person who was mystified by the action of the scientist. The police officials themselves were puzzled to some extent. But they had enough confidence in Locard to be sure that there was profound significance in any action he took, however fantastic it might seem. He had some practical end in view, and it boded no good to the murderer of Marie Latelle.

"That will do," announced Locard. "I must get back to the laboratory. In a few hours I may be able to tell you something."

Back in the laboratory the scientist and his assistants set to work with businesslike zeal – for even a wizard of crime investigation has to be businesslike if he is to succeed. Also in matters of this kind speed is frequently of importance. Locard knew that he had obtained the clue which had hitherto been overlooked. A very short while would either demonstrate the guilt of Gourbin or his innocence.

There are many great scientists in the world; there are many great police detectives. In this case Locard displayed some of the qualities of both. Science had provided the instrument, but shrewd reasoning from effect to cause had really given the clue. Ninety-nine men out of a hundred had they made the discovery that the marks on the throat of the victim were scratches and not fingerprints would have left it at that. Not so Locard. He recognized that the scratches might be almost as infallible as fingerprints in bringing home the crime.

It is not fair to hold the reader longer in suspense. Locard had reasoned that the person who was responsible for the crime had carried away *beneath his fingernails* the chief evidence that was needed in the case. With that point fixed on his mind, he had seen his course clear. He had acted as a manicurist, and it was on the material he had found beneath Gourbin's nails that he set to work.

The first fact that the microscopic photographs revealed was that in the dirt taken from the nails there were unmistakable blood corpuscles. That, by itself, was enormously significant, but by no means conclusive. It was quite possible for an innocent man to have had his hands in contact with blood. A second discovery carried the case a step farther. Some very tiny fragments of flesh were found – just such fragments as the murderer must have carried away. Again there was the remote possibility of coincidence. These two things combined were of enormous value, and a strong case against Gourbin might have been built on them, notwithstanding the alibi to which he so resolutely held. All the same, there was not that precision of proof which Locard wanted. It was circumstantial evidence without absolute certainty. A jury might have preferred to believe the alibi of the accused man.

Once Locard had found the tiny pores of a murderer's hands clogged with blood, which he believed that he had washed away. With a remembrance of this case before him, he scanned the photographs again and again, seeking for he scarcely knew what. He asked the police to examine the personal belongings of the dead girl, and at long last he was able to put his finger on the point that was to send Gourbin to the guillotine.

The photographs disclosed traces of something that, on experiment, proved to be nothing else than the face powder which Marie Latelle had been in the habit of using. Coincidence could not stretch so far as that. The blood corpuscles, the fragments of flesh, and the face powder could not be explained away.

These facts were placed in the hands of the examining magistrate, and the confident Gourbin brought once more before him. Then one by one the proofs were stressed to him. For a time he held out, but when the damning fact of the face powder was made clear to him, in the dramatic style affected in French criminal procedure, he broke down and confessed.

It was all very simple. Those people who had substantiated the alibi had been perfectly sincere. Time flies fast during a convivial evening, and who would suspect a guest of altering a clock? Thus Gourbin had gone to his room much earlier than was supposed. He had slipped out while his companions imagined that he was in bed, had that fatal interview with Marie, returned, and put the clock right without rousing any suspicion.

He had luck – to a point. If he had thought of those fingernails the mystery of Marie Latelle would have remained a mystery and the guillotine would have been cheated after all. "If—"

A RIDDLE OF MAGGOTS

(William Brittle, UK 1965)

Keith Simpson

Fixing the time of death can be crucial in a murder investigation. In the case of William Brittle, accused of murdering Peter Thomas, the Home Office pathologist Professor Keith Simpson used some school-boy biology to establish this all-important fact. Having found blue-bottle maggots on Thomas's body, Simpson was able to show that the fact they had not pupated meant the victim had been dead for at least nine or ten days, a fact that destroyed Brittle's alibi. Simpson recalled the case in his memoirs Forty Years of Murder.

The police record for clearing up murders in England and Wales could hardly be better. Of the 150 or so real murders – not technical homicides – they hear about each year, only a handful have to be written off as unsolved. But how many more are unknown to the police? How many murdered persons are buried or, worse, cremated, as ordinary natural or accidental deaths? How many are hidden so successfully that their bodies are never found and recognized as human remains?

It's anybody's guess, of course. But it seems certain that some murders escape detection, for some come to light by pure chance. The body of Peter Thomas, for instance, could have remained for ever half buried in a Berkshire wood but for its unlikely discovery by two thirteen-year-old boys looking for bait for a Sunday fishing expedition.

The bait they were after was maggots, the larvae of flies that lay their eggs on the carcasses of dead animals. So off they went one Sunday, young Tony King and Paul Fay, to Bracknell Woods, in the hope of finding a dead pigeon or rabbit, as they had several times before. On this occasion, 28 June 1964, they found the maggots before the carcass – a seething mass of fat white maggots, on a mound of rough sods of turf loosely covered with beech cuttings lying a few feet off a forest path. The boys at once started to pull the turf away, and were so pleased that they hardly noticed the stench as they dragged the sods aside to get at the maggots – until they caught sight of a decomposing forearm with the remains of a hand at the end.

The fishing expedition ended before it had begun. Being sensible boys, they left everything, including the precious white maggots, and ran to the nearest police station.

"There's a dead body buried in the woods," they told the duty sergeant in their commendably matter-of-fact style.

Shortly after I was rung up out of my Sunday afternoon snooze in the garden at my cottage at Tring, and by 5 p.m. I had joined Detective Superintendent Arthur Lawson, chief of the Berkshire CID, at the scene, where I set about a more scientific disinterment of the lightly buried body. I stopped to allow photographs to be taken at every stage as I removed the turf cuttings and sprays of beech wood; looking around, I noticed there were no beeches in the vicinity. From Lawson I learnt there were none in Bracknell Woods. Had the body been brought there dead, then? The police searched very thoroughly but found no appropriate tyre tracks or footprints.

It was the body of a man, lying on his back, fully clothed, with his head wrapped in towelling. How long had he been there; or, rather, how long had he been dead? It was much too late to try to measure the loss of body temperature, and rigor mortis would certainly have come and passed off again long before. The body was disintegrating, and the police assumed it must have been dead for six or eight weeks.

"At least nine or ten days, but probably not more than twelve," I told Lawson, who stared at me in disbelief. "It's astonishing how quickly maggots will eat up the flesh," I reminded him. "I've seen a body reduced to this state in *as little as ten days*."

I thought it safe to assume the maggots were larvae of the bluebottle *Calliphora erythrocephalus*, but I preserved samples because the maggots of other flies of the calliphorine type, with slightly different hatching times, are not dissimilar to the naked eye. The ordinary life history of the bluebottle is quite simple. The eggs are laid in day-light, usually sunlight, and in warm weather they hatch on the first day. The tiny "first instar" maggot sheds its skin after eight to fourteen hours, and the second instar after a further two to three days. The third instar, the fisherman's maggot, feeds voraciously for five or six days before going into a pupa case. The larvae I was looking at were mature, indeed elderly, fat, indolent, third-stage maggots, but they were not in pupa cases. Therefore I estimated that the eggs had been laid nine or ten days earlier. Adding a little more time to allow for the bluebottles getting to the dead body, I reckoned death had occurred on 16 June or 17 June.

Lawson telephoned the Scotland Yard missing persons bureau and learnt that a Peter Thomas had disappeared from his home at Lydney, in Gloucestershire, on 16 June, and that Detective Superintendent Horace Faber of the Yard had been down there helping the local police in their investigation. Faber was so interested in the report of the body in Bracknell Woods, though it lay more than a hundred miles from Lydney, that he joined us at the scene the same afternoon.

Because of the extensive decomposition and maggot infestation I had decided to examine the exposed parts – head and neck and hands – as they lay. This was a fortunate decision, for as the neck came into view I saw a pool of liquid blood over the left side of the voice box – and not at any other site. (I found later it was the only pool anywhere in the body.) The small bones of the larynx were crushed on this side, and I picked them out loose.

"He received a blow across the throat," I said. "Not a violent constriction but a blow."

"What sort of a blow, doctor?" asked Superintendent Faber.

"A punch, a kick, a bottle—"

"What about a karate chop with the side of the hand?" Faber had been on Commando training in the war.

"That would do very well."

When I continued my examination in the mortuary I found blood in the main windpipe and bronchial passages and a few asphyxial haemorrhages on the surface of the heart. I saw no sign of any skull or other fracture, but the disintegrated liquid state of the brain made it impossible to discover whether unconsciousness might have been caused by some other blow. In the absence of any other positive finding I attributed death to bleeding into the windpipe from the blunt injury to the throat. This would have disabled the victim so that he would have been likely to inhale the blood and die in a few minutes.

But was he the missing Peter Thomas? I put his age between forty and fifty: Thomas was forty-two. When stretched out, the body measured 5 feet 3 inches: Thomas was said to have been 5 feet 3 inches or 5 feet 4 inches. He had neglected attentions to his teeth so the dental data were no use. But it was said he had broken his left arm in youth, and X-rays showed an old fracture of the left forearm. He had a criminal record, so his fingerprints were on the files: the experts succeeded in getting some impressions of the skin peeling off his finger-pads which were identical with both the records and prints found in his home at Lydney. A tailor's tab in the jacket of the dead man's suit also led to Thomas. Beyond doubt Superintendent Faber had been right in his hunch – it could hardly have been more – that the man who had disappeared from Lydney had ended up dead in Bracknell Woods. How?

Peter Thomas had been living very simply in a tumble-down wooden bungalow outside this little Welsh border town, alone except for his dog. He pretended poverty and drew unemployment pay although he had inherited about £5,000 from his father three years before. Letters found in his home revealed that he had recently lent £2,000 to William Brittle, a heating engineer salesman of Hook, Hampshire, and the loan was due for repayment in the month Thomas had disappeared. It was a strictly business loan. Brittle had advertised in a Cardiff newspaper offering a "quick return" on a loan for an "agricultural prospect". Thomas, against the advice of both his solicitor and his bank manager, had lent him the money at $12\frac{1}{2}$ per cent interest (a moneylender's rate in those days) for six months.

Questioned by Faber, Brittle said he had motored to Lydney
and repaid the debt on 16 June, the very day Thomas had
disappeared. But there seemed to be no proof that the money
had been received. Faber pressed Brittle to say how he got this
large sum. Not from agriculture, he admitted. "I got an accu-
mulator on a roll-up system at the races," he said. Faber asked
him for the names of the winning horses but he "could not
remember them", nor could any of the bookmakers or betting
shops in the district recognize his photograph. As evidence that
he had been to Lydney on 16 June Brittle mentioned that he had
given a hitch-hiker a lift on the way back home.

Brittle's car was "taken apart" at the Regional Forensic
Science Laboratory without yielding anything more suspicious
than a single beech leaf under the driver's mat. No beeches grew
anywhere near Brittle's Hampshire home. A few scattered bloodstains were found on the sleeve of Brittle's coat: group O, the
same as Peter Thomas's: but as it happened the same, too, as
Brittle's. The police found out that while in the Army Brittle had
attended a course in unarmed combat which would have included
the use of "the chop". Although the blow required training rather
than great strength, Brittle did not look like a man who could
commit murder with one bare hand. "What, killed by *this* man?"
his counsel, the redoubtable Quintin Hogg, asked scornfully at
his trial. "Felled like an ox at one blow?"

Meanwhile Brittle's hitch-hiker had been found from his
description. A golf caddy, he confirmed the truth of Brittle's
story that he had gone to Lydney that day. To repay Thomas or
to kill him? If Faber's suspicions were correct, Brittle had
stopped to pick up the hitch-hiker on his way back when he
had Thomas's body in the boot of his car. That would have been
very cool; and, as Quintin Hogg was to point out, the most
thorough and expert search of the vehicle had failed to produce
a trace of the body. Wrapped in cloth or a sack or bag, of course,
this might well be.

Faber had been working doggedly on the case for four months
when a man named Dennis Roberts, a nylon spinner, came
forward to say he had seen Peter Thomas at Gloucester bus
station, studying the timetable, on *20 June*. Roberts said they had

exchanged greetings (they had once worked together in a sawmill) and he was sure of the date because it was the only day in his life when he had been on strike.

If Thomas had been alive on 20 June, the whole case against Brittle collapsed. His day of opportunity to kill Thomas was 16 June, and if Thomas was alive on 20 June, he had been dead only eight days at the most when I saw his body (and the tell-tale maggots) in Bracknell Woods.

"Is that possible, doctor?" asked the anxious Faber, who had brought Roberts's statement to my laboratory at Guy's.

"No, it isn't," I answered immediately. "And I am ready to stand up to severe cross-examination on the point if it comes to trial."

Faber looked as if I had taken a great load off his mind. If I had answered that one could never be absolutely sure about such a matter, the case would have crumbled and Scotland Yard would have lost confidence in me – with good reason. Why, if I had not been really sure, had I pin-pointed the time of death with confidence at the start?

Faber asked me for a written statement that he could attach to his report for the Director of Public Prosecutions, and I dictated one on the spot to my secretary Jean Scott-Dunn. It was as unequivocal as the estimate that I had given in my original autopsy report:

Guy's Hospital, 21 October 1964

I have today been shown by Detective Superintendent Faber a copy of a statement made by Dennis John Roberts to the effect that on Saturday 20 June he saw a man whom he recognized as Peter Thomas at a bus station. The condition of the body when examined in the wood suggested in the first instance, while still at the scene – "some nine or ten days, possibly more" – was a minimum period. Nothing in the post-mortem state of the body suggested any special conditions likely to have accelerated the ordinary process of maggot infestation and disintegration of the body.

And to put a final "nail in the coffin" I added:

> I have had considerable experience in the timing of death
> and would regard Dennis Roberts's statement as being
> wholly inconsistent with my findings.

To prosecute or not to prosecute? The question was for the
Director of Public Prosecutions in London, and he considered it
for several weeks. He took the opinion of Senior Counsel, and
finally decided the case was not strong enough. He could not
ignore Roberts's statement, and it might well deter a jury.

All Faber could do then was to refer the case to the coroner at
Bracknell and let his jury hear the evidence; which they did, in an
inquest lasting seven days. Nobody expected a coroner's jury to
commit Brittle for murder after the DPP had declined to do so,
but to everyone's astonishment the jury found Thomas had been
murdered on or about 17 June and they named Brittle as the
person responsible. The coroner committed him into custody,
and he was tried at Gloucester at the Spring Assize of 1965.

His counsel, Quintin Hogg, QC – later Lord Hailsham, the
Lord Chancellor – was making a trial return to the Bar after a
distinguished career in the upper echelons of politics. Long
before that he had been a very promising young barrister, and
I expected a really testing cross-examination, especially when I
heard he had taken the trouble to consult another Home Office
pathologist, Dr David Bowen, and an entomologist, Professor
McKenny-Hughes. It was a good thing I had decided to bottle a
few maggots on that Sunday afternoon in the woods, for McKenny-Hughes wanted to see them and check if they really were the
larvae of *C. erythrocephalus*, as I had said.

When I was examined by the Crown counsel, Ralph Cusack, I
set out as clearly and briefly as I could the nature of the fat, third
instar maggot, not yet pupated, yet plainly having passed the
growing-up stages from the day the eggs hatched. I further set
out the several periods of time that (it was accepted, I said) eggs
took to hatch, and the three stages of maggot instar to develop
before pupation. I added up the times and said, as deliberately
and purposefully as I knew how:

"So, I had no doubt in my mind at the time" – I emphasized. that I had made up my mind at the outset – "that this man had been dead some ten days." Nine or ten was a minimum.

Cusack brought his examination to a quick finish. It was late in the afternoon, and he did not want to give the defence counsel the chance to discuss my evidence with his advisers before cross-examining me. But Quintin Hogg was an equally shrewd tactician.

"Doctor," he began, "may I assume" – counsel likes to use this phrase instead of "I am sure" – "that you made notes during the successive stages of uncovering that body in the woods?"

"Yes, I have them here in court." They were before me.

"My lord," he said, "I am going to ask that they be duplicated by photostat and handed to the members of the jury in the morning."

The judge agreed, and Quintin Hogg was able after all to consult his advisers before cross-examining me, and I expected them to supply him with an armful of questions, skilfully worded to probe any weaknesses in my evidence. Next morning I braced myself when he got to his feet and pulled at his gown.

"Doctor," he began, "I have only to say, of your notes, that the sketch which accompanies them is of more help to me in understanding the lie of the body than the police photographs!"

I was off the hook. He was not going to challenge me on my evidence.

But he still had Professor McKenny-Hughes, who was certainly more of an expert than I on the habits of the bluebottle and maggots. If anyone could pick holes in my evidence he was the man.

"Professor, you have heard the evidence given so far in this case," he began. "Will you kindly tell the court in what respects your views as to the times of egg-laying and hatching of the larvae differ from those of Professor Keith Simpson?"

The distinguished entomologist ran his fingers through his wispy hair and favoured me with a jovial beam. Was he going to enjoy himself cutting me up into little pieces?

"Well," he said, still smiling, "I'm not sure there's anything I really . . ."

"Professor," interrupted Quintin Hogg rather desperately, "can we agree about one thing?" His witness nodded and waited. "Let us suppose that the bluebottle lay its eggs on the dead body at midnight on the . . ."

"Oh, dear me, no!" exclaimed the entomologist. "No self-respecting bluebottle lays eggs at midnight. At midday, perhaps, but not at midnight."

There were stifled giggles in the public gallery, lawyers and reporters hid their smiles with their hands, and even the judge's face twitched. Poor Quintin Hogg tried again.

"At what period, then, Professor, would you expect the eggs to hatch?"

"Well, it all depends." The professor seemed oblivious of the effect he was creating. "You see, in warm weather—"

"Yes, Professor, we know it was June and quite warm," Counsel came in hastily. "How many hours would have elapsed before the first maggots were hatched?"

"Well, I agree with Dr Simpson," said McKenny-Hughes, looking as if he expected everyone to be pleased about that. "Say eight to fourteen hours for the first instar, and . . ."

"And these maggots would settle down on the dead tissues at once?"

"Well, maggots are curious little devils," the entomologist said engagingly. "Suppose this is a dead body." He had taken out a matchbox and placed it on the edge of the witness box. "And suppose you have a hundred maggots here." He indicated them with an expansive spread of his hands. "Ninety-nine will make their way towards the body, but the hundredth little devil" – the professor was back in the lecture hall, completely unmindful of his real surroundings – "he'll turn the other way."

Mr Justice Phillimore's face twitched again, the Crown lawyers hardly dared to exchange glances, the jury looked relaxed and almost happy, and Quintin Hogg's frown deepened into a furrow as he told the professor very frostily that he had no more questions for him.

But the defence had three more witnesses who were not at all as acceptable to the prosecution.

First, Dennis John Roberts told how he had seen and spoken to Peter Thomas at Gloucester bus station on 20 June. "Hello, Dennis," Thomas had greeted him, he said; and Ralph Cusack, QC, who led for the Crown, could not shake him in cross-examination.

Next Mrs Jane Charles, of Lydney, said she had seen Thomas walking along the road towards Blakeney village on 21 June. She knew the date because it was the longest day of the year. She had been a passenger in a car and could only have glimpsed him briefly, but she was sure it was Thomas whom she knew. Finally Mrs Gwendoline Padwick, of Blakeney Stores, also said she had seen Thomas on 21 June, in her shop, buying matches. He was a regular customer, and she knew the date because she had just made out a cheque for her mother, who was staying with her for the first time.

Cusack pressed both women hard in cross-examination. It was, as he pointed out, a long time ago – nearly nine months – and their memories could have played them false. He asked them what else they could remember of that day, and of the previous day. What else had happened? What had Thomas been wearing? And so on. All three witnesses seemed perfectly honest persons – they had been "found" by the defence but there was not a breath of suspicion about this – and the question was simply whether they had each made an honest mistake.

Quintin Hogg decided not to call Brittle, doubtless because he did not want his client exposed to cross-examination by the very skilful and penetrative Ralph Cusack. "He has already made three long statements," Hogg said, as if these rather contradictory accounts put his client in the clear. He went on to speak confidently of the three witnesses who said they had seen the dead man after 16 June; and since just one of them had been enough to raise sufficient doubt to stop the DPP from prosecuting, it seemed quite likely the jury would acquit Brittle. But, in the event, they decided my maggots were more reliable in their hatching habits than Quintin Hogg's three alibis, and found Brittle guilty of murder. He was given a life sentence.

The case was particularly satisfying to me. My insistence on

the timing of death had become pretty well known, to the police,
the Director of Public Prosecutions, the lawyers – and the Press,
who would have scented a public disgrace for me if I'd been
wrong.

A RAY OF SUNLIGHT UNMASKS A KILLER

(William Henry Podmore, UK 1930)

Tom Tullett

When the great pathologist Sir Bernard Spilsbury examined the hammer used to murder Vivian Messiter, he found a single hair adhering to the hammer head. It matched the hair from Messiter's eyebrows, proving that the hammer had indeed dealt the fatal blow. But Messiter's killer, William Podmore, was brought to book not by a single hair but a single piece of flimsy paper. It was, as one criminologist observed, a case of small clues and large inferences, which is why it remains of exceptional interest to the student of modern crime detection. Indentations were found on a page of a receipt book, produced by the pressure of the pencil through another sheet on which some figures and initials had been written. The initials – W. F. T. – were those of Podmore's alias, William F. Thomas. Photographs were taken of these tell-tale indentations using a strong light thrown on them from an oblique angle. This cast a shadow across the indentations, enabling the eye to read them quite clearly. Because this scrap of paper linked Podmore with his victim, and was a vital part of the evidence against him, the case is notable as a triumph for forensic photography. Tom Tullett (1915–91) was chief of the Daily Mirror's *crime bureau and the only journalist to have been a member of the Criminal Investigation Department at Scotland Yard. With Douglas G. Browne, Tullett wrote the standard biography of Spilsbury in the early 1950s.*

By the end of the 1920s, murder investigations had gained some sense of order, and the countrywide search for the killer of a man who had been dead for more than two months when his body was found shows how the use of technical aids and methods of record-keeping were paying off.

At 6.45 on the evening of 10 January 1929 a telegram from Mr McCormac, Chief Constable of Southampton, was received at Scotland Yard. It read: "A case of murder has occurred here. A man has been found shot dead in a room the door of which was padlocked. The body was found today and has probably been in the room for some eight or nine weeks. Will you please send an officer down to investigate the matter."

Detective Chief Inspector John Prothero was tall and commanding and his colleagues called him "Gentleman John". He was always immaculately dressed, and spoke in an accent thought then to be the mark of a university education. He wore spats and had his shirt cuffs showing, at that time a rich man's luxury. But he was not rich, nor had he been to university. He was a great detective, who decided he wanted to be better dressed than the rest of his colleagues. He never raised his voice, never appeared to be angry, but his quiet insistence got the facts he required.

Prothero took with him to Southampton Sergeant Hugh Young, a Scot from the Black Isle in Ross and Cromarty. Like others before him he was a country boy who rose to command the Squad, and the experience he gained on this particular case was a great stepping-stone in his distinguished career.

The detectives went first to the Southampton mortuary to see the body of the victim, Vivian Messiter. The local police surgeon said that the murder had taken place some weeks before, and Messiter had last been seen alive on 30 October 1928. The body was in a bad state of decomposition and the rats had been busy, so that the features of the dead man were unrecognizable.

Vivian Messiter had been found in a lock-up garage-cum-storeroom at 42 Grove Street, Southampton, where he carried on business as a local agent of the Wolf's Head Oil Company, whose head offices were in London. He had not been seen alive since he left his lodgings at 3 Carlton Road on the morning of 30 October. He was a quiet man of regular habits, and when he failed to return home as usual his landlord, Mr Parrott, an ex-police-man, informed the police he was missing.

An officer went to the garage, but on finding the place securely padlocked from the outside, concluded that wherever Messiter was, he was not in the garage.

Mr Parrott wrote to Messiter's employers, reporting his lodger's absence. They asked him to visit the garage and, by breaking a window and peering through the aperture with the help of a candle, he could see that Messiter's car was safe and that nothing appeared to be amiss. It was concluded that Messiter had simply walked out of his job and had, perhaps, returned to the United States, where he had spent many years of his life. The subsequent lack of interest in his whereabouts was one of the striking features of the case.

Messiter was a member of an old Somersetshire family, educated at a minor public school. As a young man he had gone to the States with his brother Edgar and together they started a horse-breeding ranch in New Mexico. When Edgar drifted into mining operations in Colorado, Vivian went into business in Denver. Later he went to New York City, where the new subway railroad under the Hudson River was in course of construction. Such was his energy and ability to handle men that he rose from a subordinate position to the office of Chief Engineering Constructor. He became so well-known in this capacity that engineers from England were invited to meet him.

At the outbreak of the First World War he was wealthy and generally prosperous. He came home and enlisted, was commissioned in the Northumberland Fusiliers and went to fight in France. He was shot through both thighs and he remained slightly lame for the rest of his life. In 1928 he was fifty-seven, a reserved, solitary man, divorced from his wife, and he returned to England that year from another long absence in the United States and Mexico. Yet he had relatives in this country, and he had a job, and the fact that he was lost to sight and knowledge for more than two months without any serious efforts being made to discover what had become of him throws a curious light on the casual attitude of his friends and family and of the firm which not only employed him, but had recently made him a director.

Messiter's job was that of local agent for the Wolf's Head Oil Company and the garage in Grove Street was his headquarters. It was not until 10 January that this firm sent a Mr Passmore to take over the agency. With a friend Passmore gained access to the outer yard of the garage via the roof of the Royal Exchange public house next door. The garage was a long, narrow building with white-washed walls. Along the right-hand side was a double row of oil drums upon which boxes were piled. More boxes were stacked at the end, and in a recess was the body of Messiter lying face upwards.

After moving the body to the mortuary local police searched the garage. On the back seat of Messiter's car they found a duplicate order book and a memorandum book, from both of which a number of pages had been torn out. On one page of the memorandum book was a receipt signed by a Mr H. H. Galton for 2s 6d commission on the sale of five gallons of oil, dated 30 October, the last day Messiter was seen alive. The next page had been torn out, but on the following page were the words: "Cromer & Bartlett, 25 Bold Street, 5 gallons heavy". In the duplicate order book there was no writing of any kind, but, tucked away at the end of it, were two sheets of carbon paper on which could be just seen some names and addresses. The first was "Cromer & Bartlett" of Bold Street, Southampton. Then there was a note, "Sold to Ben Baskerfield, Clayton Farm, Bentley Road, near Winchester" and a third entry, "Ben Jervis, Crescent Bassett, 5 gallons number 8 at 5s 6d".

When the Yard men went to the garage they were given these items by the local police and then began their own search for any clues which might help. But first, since nothing had been moved apart from the body, they decided to reconstruct the crime. The local detective inspector persuaded Mr Hall, the licensee of the pub next door, to play the part of the corpse and he was placed in the same position as the body was found. A trilby hat had been found near Messiter's head, and to give a touch of realism for photographic purposes, Sergeant Young placed his own hat beside the recumbent figure of Mr Hall. The detectives noted the position of several bloodstained boxes in relation to the body, some of which had been splashed to a height of several feet, an almost sure indication of blows by a heavy weapon used as a club.

John Prothero then ordered all the boxes to be moved. "Search every nook and cranny," he commanded. During this search three clues were found which played a vital part in the investigation.

The first was a rolled-up ball of paper, stained and begrimed with oil and dirt, lying between two oil drums near the garage door. It was a receipt for rent dated 20 October and bore the name "Horne" of Cranbury Avenue. On the back of this scrap of paper were some faint words which obviously referred to an order for "35 or 36 gals, Tuesday" and there was a signature – "W.F. Thomas" – the small "O" being crossed out.

A second piece of paper was found behind another oil drum and on that was a written message. It read: "Mr W.F. Thomas. I shall be at 42 Grove Street at 10 a.m. but not at noon. V. Messiter."

The third clue found in the garage was a hammer, lying at the back of more oil drums against the side wall. Both the shaft and the head of the hammer were stained with blood, and stuck in the blood there was a single eyebrow hair. This last discovery changed the whole complex of the killing, for the hammer was without doubt the murder weapon. Vivian Messiter had not been shot, as had at first been suspected, but battered to death, and the small wound in the dead man's forehead had not been caused by a bullet but by a ferocious blow from the pointed side of the hammer head.

The pathologist Sir Bernard Spilsbury was called in, and while the Yard men waited for him to arrive, they began to make inquiries about the other things they had found.

The landlady at Cranbury Avenue, Mrs Horne, established that she had recently had a quiet, well-behaved couple staying there for about two weeks. Their names were Mr and Mrs Thomas and they had left on 3 November, leaving an address care of Allied Transport Co., 38 High Road, Chiswick.

The Chiswick police checked and found there was no firm of that name and, moreover, there was no house in the High Road bearing that number. Further checks relating to names and addresses on the other scraps of paper found in the garage revealed there was no Bold Street in Southampton, nor any firm bearing the name Cromer & Bartlett. There was no such place as Clayton Farm anywhere near Winchester, while Ben Jervis had never been heard of at Crescent Bassett.

It began to look as though Mr W.F. Thomas was at least a liar and it did prove he had some connection with the murdered man. The only thing so far proved genuine was the signature of H.H. Galton, and it looked as though it had been deliberately left in the memorandum book to make him a suspect, for Mr Galton was traced and proved to be a genuine customer.

Messiter's lodgings were in Carlton Road, and among the papers he had left behind was a letter bearing the address of Cranbury Avenue and signed "W.F. Thomas". The writer was applying for an agency with Messiter in reply to an advertisement which the latter had inserted in the *Southern Daily Echo*. This was another link between Thomas and Messiter, but where was Thomas?

Prothero issued a full description of Thomas to the press, mentioning a small scar on his face. Newspapers always like a dramatic headline and so the hunt for Thomas became "Hunt for Man with a Scar".

Five days after the discovery of the crime Bernard Spilsbury went to Southampton and examined the body of the victim. He described his findings: "At least three blows on the head, any one producing immediate unconsciousness. The head of a large hammer, used with great violence, would account for injuries. Those across base and on right side produced when the head was on a hard surface. Position of injuries at back suggest that deceased was bending forwards. Puncture wounds on top of head – striking edge of tin box in fall."

The Yard men went over the information they had and came to the conclusion that the man they wanted was cunning enough to be no stranger to crime, as evinced by his inventing bogus orders to get commission; his flight from one place to another; the tearing out of what were probably incriminating pages from the books found in the garage; and the adroit way he had tried to cover his tracks. Sergeant Young suggested to his chief that the man might have a record.

"Send for Battley," Prothero said. A call to the Yard brought

Detective Inspector Harry Battley, then head of the Fingerprint Bureau, to Southampton and with him he brought all the files in the name of Thomas. There were eighty-three dossiers.

Battley examined the hammer and the shaft and all the other finds but there were no useful fingerprints. All the files holding photographs of men called Thomas were shown to the landlady, Mrs Horne, and to various other people who might have recognized him. But not one person was able to pair up a photograph and the missing man.

The investigation seemed to be running down when luck took a hand. The Wiltshire police, who had seen the circulated description of W.F. Thomas, sent a message that they were looking for a man with the same name. This man had worked for a building contractor named Mitchell at Downtown, near Salisbury. Thomas had entered the employ of Mr Mitchell on 3 November 1928 (the day Thomas had left his Cranbury Avenue lodgings) and had disappeared with more than £130 of his employer's money on 21 December. He had given as his previous employers the Allied Transport Road Association, Bold Street, Southampton.

A landlady in Downton told the police that a Mr and Mrs Thomas had lodged with her and, in a vase in the room they had occupied, was found yet another scrap of paper. It was a docket from an order book, headed: "A & R S".

Underneath was an address – 85 London Road, Manchester.

The piece of paper left at Downton was one piece of paper too many – it began to provide leads.

A swift inquiry was made to the Manchester police. They did not know a W.F. Thomas, but they did know Auto & Radio Services at London Road. A detective said, "We are looking for a man named Podmore who used to work for them. We want him for conversion of money he received for a car. His picture was in the *Police Gazette*."

Criminal Records now came into their own. William Henry Podmore had a file, and there was no question that he and Thomas were the same person. A check on his history was revealing and began to fill in the gaps. He was well known to the Staffordshire police, having been first arrested by them when he was only eleven. He was married but parted from his wife and had been living with a young woman in various parts of the country.

At one time he had lived with his parents at Greenly Road, Abbey Milton, Stoke-on-Trent. Near his home was Bold Street, the street name which kept cropping up in the Messiter case. He had known a Mr Baskeyfield whom he always called Baskerfield, the name of the person mentioned as living at the Clayton Farm address, while a Mr Albert Machen, who actually lived at Clayton Farm, Newcastle, Staffordshire, used to deliver milk to the Podmore family. He also knew a Mrs Lucy Jervis, although not personally.

Podmore had made the mistake common to petty criminals, that of mixing up familiar names and places in the faint hope of appearing to be honest. It is an error that has helped to trap many people. It began to look very much as though Podmore, alias Thomas, was the man who had murdered Vivian Messiter. But proof was still lacking. Prothero decided to concentrate his search for the woman companion who was called "Lil".

Inquiries at Podmore's home revealed that he had stayed there over Christmas and had left early in the New Year to take a job as a garage hand at the Stonebridge Hotel, Solihull, near Birmingham. He had arrived there on 5 January 1929 with his "wife", Lil, who was to work as a cook. Six days later, when the evening papers printed the reports of the Southampton garage murder, Podmore handed in his notice, saying he wanted to leave at once. Next day Podmore and Lil departed without even asking for their wages. Podmore obviously thought that Lil, called "Golden-haired Lil" in the Press, was an embarrassment, and that it was no longer safe for them to be seen together. The first signs of panic had set in, and he sent her back to her home at Stoke-on-Trent. There she was interviewed by the local detective inspector, Mr Diggle, who had been making all the inquiries in Staffordshire. She told him she thought it likely that Podmore would have gone to the Leicester Hotel in Vauxhall Bridge Road, near Victoria in London.

Two telephone calls, one to Southampton and one from there to the Yard, had Detective Charles Simmons with a sergeant casually leaning against the reception desk of the Leicester Hotel asking quietly for "Mr Thomas" or "Mr Podmore". He was in his room and agreed to accompany the officers to Southampton. Under the circumstances refusal would have been difficult although, in truth, there was little evidence of murder against him at the time.

On 18 January, just eight days after the finding of Messiter's body, Podmore met for the first time the two men who had been hunting him, Detective Chief Inspector John Prothero and Detective Sergeant Hugh Young. Podmore was nonchalant, almost cocksure. Prothero was his usual calm, gentlemanly self, and Young sat at a table, pen in hand and a pad of statement forms in front of him, the classic reception for all suspects.

It was clear that Podmore had been through this routine before and was fairly confident. It was also clear that he was not going to give in without a struggle. He admitted he was in trouble in Manchester and in Downton and that he had worked for Messiter. He had seen the report of the finding of Messiter's body. He was completely frank about using the names of Thomas and Podmore. He said he went to see Messiter on the morning of 30 October and that also there was an agent named Maxton or Baxton, a subtle suggestion that this was the man who had killed Messiter. He had only seen him once but he did not need pressing to give a description. Details of the man's height, build, hair, complexion and clothing rolled off his tongue in almost indecent haste.

Podmore said he had left Messiter's employ for a better job with Mr Mitchell at Salisbury. He admitted taking Messiter's car to go for the interview at Downton on 30 October, the last day on which Messiter was seen alive, and said that he had returned at 4.30 p.m. that day, parked the car in the garage and gone to his lodgings.

In its way this was a helpful admission. Unless someone else could be found who had seen Messiter later, Podmore was the last person to have seen him alive.

There was one obvious motive for the murder in Podmore's case – the bogus orders in equally bogus names and addresses – an easy way to get commission on non-existent sales of oil. And if Messiter had found out and challenged Podmore, what then?

Podmore was held in custody. This caused no problems to the Yard men, since he was already wanted for other offences. Meanwhile luck again turned in favour of the detectives. They had circulated a description of the hammer to the newspapers and a Mr Marsh came forward to say the hammer was his. He had bought it in France and was able to recognize it because it had been "touched up and filed down" by him. He remembered that at some time around 29 October a man with a scar on his face, who looked like a mechanic, had come to the motor works in Southampton where Marsh worked and asked to borrow a hammer. It was never returned.

Podmore blandly denied he had ever borrowed a hammer.

The case looked like breaking. Podmore was put up for identification with several other men of similar age, build and appearance and Mr Marsh walked quietly along the line. It is one of the nightmare moments in the life of a suspect. The parade was held in the yard of Bathgate police station with a uniformed inspector in charge. The Yard men stood well away. It was explained to Podmore, before the men formed themselves into line, that he could stand anywhere he chose.

It is a time for the mind to race. Which is the best place? Which of these men looks most like me? Which is wearing similar clothes? For the policemen it is slow, inexorable and ordinary. To the suspect it is mounting panic. "Will the expression on my face reveal my guilty knowledge?"

Mr Marsh tried hard. Three times he walked up and down the line and, in the end, shook his head.

"The man is not there," he said.

The volunteers departed and a relieved Podmore went back to the cells. Soon afterwards he was arrested by the Manchester police for theft of a car and he was sentenced to six months' imprisonment. For a while he was away from the attention of the Yard men, but he was not far away and not for long. Two months later he was brought from prison to attend the resumed inquest on Messiter, which had been formally opened and adjourned. He sat between two prison officers but was able to smile and wave at "Golden-haired Lil" who was also in court.

Only one red herring was trailed across the path of justice, when a man serving a sentence in Winchester prison was called as a witness. He had previously made a statement that a woman he knew had returned home at 2.30 p.m. on 30 October in Southampton with blood all over her face. But before the coroner he admitted his story was pure invention.

During the inquest the exercise book containing the receipt from Mr Galton for 2s 6d was produced and handed to the jury, as were the two sheets of carbon paper found in the duplicate order book. The jury returned an open verdict, Podmore went back to prison to serve the rest of his sentence, and the Yard men took away the exhibits to carry on the investigation. They went back to the Murder Room at Scotland Yard and analyzed every bit of information they had collected. Prothero, Young and Battley debated the case for hours. Then Prothero picked up the exercise book and sauntered across to the window overlooking the Thames. They had nothing in mind but it was as though they were willing this tatty, torn book to yield up its secret. They looked again at the pages they had scrutinized so many times before. Then, as Prothero held the book up in the light, a ray of sunlight, striking the paper slantwise, threw up in relief the shadowy outline of some writing. It was not the actual writing itself, only the faint impression left on the page underneath the one which had been torn out, and on which the message had been written.

When photographed the shadowy words read: "October 28, 1928. Received from Wolf Head Oil Company commission on Cromer and Bartlett, 5 gals 5/6 commission 2/6. W.F.T."

Comparison handwriting tests proved that this message had been written by Thomas, alias Podmore.

This now proved, beyond doubt, that Podmore had been swindling his employer, Mr Messiter. And it proved that the page from the exercise book had been torn out with Podmore's own hand. If he was the murderer he would have had good reason to destroy every bit of written evidence which connected him with Messiter. If, on the other hand, somebody other than Podmore was the murderer, what possible motive could he have had in tearing out the pages showing details of the transaction between himself and Messiter?

Still the authorities hesitated to bring a charge of murder and still Podmore remained in prison. When he finished the first sentence for the Manchester offence he received another six months for stealing money from Downton. This rather Micawberish attitude may have been influenced by the verdict of the coroner's jury. What would have happened had not Podmore been safely in custody is an interesting conjecture. But something more did turn up; two of Podmore's fellow-prisoners in Wandsworth reported statements made by him, and one of these amounted to a confession. The man's name was Cummings and he gave a statement to Prothero and Young. That was in October, and on 17 December 1929, the Yard men were waiting outside the gates of Wandsworth Prison.

In accordance with regulations, a prisoner must first be released and the new arrest made outside the prison gates. Podmore walked out with his usual jaunty air. Perhaps he felt confident he had covered all his tracks and that he had nothing to fear. Then a handcuff was locked round one of his wrists. The other handcuff was already round the wrist of Sergeant Young and Podmore was taken back to Southampton to be charged with murder.

He was tried at Winchester Assizes in March 1930, fifteen months after the crime, before the Lord Chief Justice, Lord Hewart. He was convicted, and his appeal against conviction was dismissed. An attempt to take the case to the House of Lords failed and Podmore was hanged on 22 April.

There was some agitation by well-meaning people to alter the course of the law because of the delay in bringing to trial and because two convicted criminals had been called to give evidence. They shared the common misunderstanding of the value of circumstantial evidence. In the volume on the case in the *Famous Trials* series the authors, one of them a lawyer, pointed out that the case against Podmore rested not only on what was found, but on what was not found.

Had the books been unmutilated, had the missing invoice and the missing receipt been there, they would have established a case of swindling against the prisoner, but it is more than doubtful whether any jury would have held that they established more – it is a very long step from false pretence to wilful murder. But they were not there, and there could have been but one hand that removed them – the hand of the man who had fabricated the orders and signed the receipt. And that removal must have taken place after Messiter's death, for before it would have been useless. That was the evidence that really convicted Podmore.

There can be no doubt that Messiter discovered the swindle and taxed Podmore with it, threatening to call the police. If it had been Podmore's first offence he would have had no cause for undue concern. But he was already wanted by the police in Manchester. Podmore, who had never before used violence, lost his temper. The hammer was there, maybe in Podmore's pocket, certainly to hand, and Messiter was struck down. The worst feature of the attack was that while the unconscious man lay on the concrete floor his assailant rained more blows on him. That callous behaviour must have told on the jury, and so must his actions immediately afterwards. For Podmore admitted that he had locked the garage and taken Messiter's car to give his lady friend, "Golden-haired Lil", a drive and "some fresh air".

THE POISONER

(Kenneth Barlow, UK 1957)

Percy Hoskins

*The first murder case in Britain in which the weapon was said to
be insulin, the drug used to treat diabetes. Kenneth Barlow was a
male nurse who claimed that insulin was the key to the perfect
murder, since once it dissolved in the bloodstream it was untrace-
able. When his wife Elizabeth was found dead in her bath, a
doctor noticed puncture marks on her skin. Samples from her
body, tested on mice, led to the detection of insulin. In a ground-
breaking experiment, a team of forensic scientists discovered that
lactic acid which had formed in Mrs Barlow's muscles after death
had prevented the breakdown of insulin. Barlow broke down while
being interviewed by detectives. While he denied injecting his wife
with insulin, he claimed he'd actually injected her with ergometrine in an effort to induce an abortion. In fact no abortifacient
drugs were found in Mrs Barlow's body. Doctors, scientists and
biochemists all gave conflicting evidence at Barlow's trial. The
defence theory was that Mrs Barlow had fainted in the bath,
causing a massive and fatal dose of insulin to be released into the
bloodstream. But the jury was not persuaded, and Barlow was
convicted and sentenced to life imprisonment. The legendary crime
reporter Percy Hoskins (1904–89) joined the* Daily Express *in
1928. He is best remembered for his work on the 1956 case of John
Bodkin Adams, the Eastbourne doctor accused of killing rich,
elderly patients in order to collect from their wills. Hoskins was
the only Fleet Street journalist convinced of Adams' innocence,
and reported accordingly to the* Express. *He also assisted in the*

doctor's defence. Adams was acquitted in 1957, the year in which the Barlow case occurred.

Poison lends itself most conveniently to the dream of perfect murder. Use a gun, and the commotion will bring every copper for miles around, and the tell-tale mark of the firing pin is as damning as any fingerprint.

Strangle, and the pathologist will find you out, even if you fake murder to look like suicide by hanging *and* bury the body afterwards.

Chop the victim into pieces, dismember, drop the segments in tightly wrapped parcels into the sea and still the Murder Squad will triumph: witness the human wild animal called Hume caged in his Swiss prison.

Do what you will to escape detection: burn the body; suffocate; rain blows on the skull from behind; electrocute; knife; destroy the whole human frame, bones and all, in a tank full of acid; hide the corpse so well no man will ever set eyes on it again; push it through a ship's porthole and feed it to the sharks (as James Camb did to "Gay" Gibson) and even then stand trial for murder.

But poison: there you have a chance to get off scot-free. It is so easy to administer. The victim is hungry or thirsty and, in any case, unsuspecting.

And, if you do your homework sufficiently well, you may hit upon a poison that leaves no trace at all. I know of one, not too difficult to obtain, where the apparent effect is one of heart failure . . . with no trace of poison left in the system. That is the great attraction of poison to the murderer: the protection afforded by its worm-like stealth.

There are others. It is a weapon well suited to the weak, hence its popularity with women. And it is a joy to possess and use if you hate someone enough: of all methods of murder, here is the most painful, sly, and cruel. Poisons like arsenic, the commonest and easiest to obtain, guarantee a monstrously agonizing end.

For all these reasons, poison has been a popular method of

killing since the time of the Borgias. What is rare is to find motiveless poisoning. It seems inconceivable that any man should plan murder this way merely to see if it can pass undetected – or does it?

Of all the cases that have come my way in this specialized field of poison, the Barlow case rates a mention on two counts. He committed the first known case of murder through injection of insulin – his wife was a non-diabetic, so it led to her collapse and drowning in the bath – and he did it for no reason anyone can discover. The only conclusion I can draw from the known facts is that he believed he could get away with murder by insulin and experimented accordingly.

Kenneth Barlow, aged thirty-eight, lived with his wife Elizabeth in a terraced two-up and two-down in Thornbury Crescent, Bradford, in Yorkshire. He was a male nurse and worked in St Luke's Hospital in the West Riding town of Huddersfield. She had a local job, in a laundry. They had been married less than a year. They seemed to be ideally happy. The neighbours found them a happy and apparently easy-going pair.

On the night of 3 May, 1957, between 11 p.m. and midnight, Kenneth Barlow hammered on his neighbour's door and shouted to them to call the doctor – *quickly*. He said his wife had passed out in the bath, and he had found her with her head under water; he had tried artificial respiration without success. Then he ran back indoors, to continue artificial respiration, until the doctor arrived.

Barlow had his story off pat when first the doctor and then an observant Detective Sergeant called Naylor from Bradford CID called round. His wife was tired that night, said Barlow, and had gone to bed early. He put the child (from his previous marriage) to bed himself, went round and locked up in the normal way, and went upstairs some time later.

About 10 p.m. Mrs Barlow, who had complained of the heat, said she now felt better and was going to take a bath. Right, said Kenneth Barlow, and promptly dozed off: came to about 11 p.m., found his wife had not come back to bed, then noticed the light still on in the bathroom. He went in to find her unconscious, with her head well under water. He pulled the plug out at once and

began to administer first aid. Now he stood in the hallway, cool
and composed although naturally sad, to greet doctor and detective as they arrived.

  Both of them noticed how the pupils of her eyes were dilated,
as though she were under the influence of some drug. Sergeant
Naylor also spotted one curious thing: Barlow's pyjamas were
bone dry, although – on his own admission – he was wearing
them when he tried to revive poor Elizabeth Barlow. The alarm
bells that ring to warn every good policeman things are not as
straightforward as they seem sounded that night in the house in
Thornbury Crescent, and Naylor called his superiors right
away.

  The Chief Constable of Bradford, Mr H. S. Price, went to the
house. He looked at the body. He too was baffled by those dry
pyjamas and another factor: lack of water on the walls and floor.
Curious, when the bath was full enough to drown Mrs Barlow,
that the attempts to lift her out and give artificial respiration had
not even left one puddle on the bathroom floor.

  He called in Dr David Price, the West Riding pathologist and
the senior inspector from the Harrogate laboratories. Dilation of
the pupils seemed a sure indication that Mrs Barlow was drugged
when she died. The police found syringes in the house, but
Barlow was a male nurse and his story that he had used one to
give himself penicillin for a carbuncle on the neck seemed
reasonable.

  The body was taken to the mortuary for post mortem and
extensive tests for poisons and drugs. More scientists were called
in next day but immediate tests again showed nothing traceable in
the system. What Dr Price did find, however, were four tiny red
dots in the buttocks similar to marks left by hypodermic injection. He cut away the flesh around and below both sets of
punctures and ascertained that they had been made shortly before
her collapse and death in the bath.

  More specialists were called in for consultation: Professor C. S.
Russell, a gynaecologist from Sheffield (Mrs Barlow was found to
be in the early stages of pregnancy); Professor Thompson, from
Guy's Hospital in London; and a senior chemist from Boots'
factory at Nottingham. They had to weigh the symptoms shown

by Mrs Barlow before death – including her collapse before sliding under the level of the bathwater.

Insulin, of course, is not a poison in the sense that arsenic is. It is extensively used in the treatment of diabetics to reduce the sugar content of the blood. If it is injected into a non-diabetic, that person goes into a state of shock and collapse. So, if the bath should be full enough, such a fainting fit could well prove fatal.

Insulin? There was no known case of injection by insulin in the course of murder. Here was a completely virgin field of research for the combined Murder Squad – police backed by the scientists. While Dr Price and his colleagues concentrated on laboratory experiments, the police stepped up their inquiries into Barlow's background.

In the laboratory, samples taken from the flesh cut away from Mrs Barlow's body were injected into mice. Other mice were injected with insulin. The results were identical. The creatures went into a state of collapse and died. Guinea pigs were used in the same way with the same result. The human tissues were then injected with anti-insulin compounds and used again on the mice and guinea pigs, but this time, with the insulin destroyed deliberately, there were no ill effects. So it *was* insulin that was used to murder Mrs Barlow.

In the CID headquarters at Bradford every precaution was taken not to forewarn Barlow of their line of inquiry. Discreet checks were made at the hospital where he worked to see what medicines and drugs he had access to, and how much – if any – was unaccounted for. There was professional evidence aplenty that he often gave injections of insulin to patients.

Barlow was charged with the murder of his wife. All through the period of arrest and trial he protested his innocence.

Sir Harry Hylton-Foster, then Solicitor-General, led the prosecution. It is not the easiest of cases to take through the court, in spite of the magnificent backroom work by Dr Price and his associates.

Here you had a man and wife, known to be happy together, married less than a year. No shred of evidence as to any quarrel or bad feeling between them, no sudden blazing row that could have ended in a resolve to murder. What could the motive have been? There was no suggestion of gain. There was no hint of jealousy, no rumour of another man or woman in the marital background.

Barlow's story of how those two syringes came to be found in his house was still convincing enough. Traces of penicillin *had* been found on the one he said he used for the boil on his neck, and he said both he and his wife had used the other. She had given her father injections of morphia, he said, to ease the pain of cancer; and he had used it on her for injections of a drug called ergometrine, to end her pregnancy – at her own request.

He also said she had had fainting fits before: once in the bath, and he described how he had rescued her just in time on that occasion.

Sir Harry called on three witnesses who had heard Barlow refer to insulin in the past as one means to the "perfect murder". There was male nurse Harry Stork, who had worked with Barlow in a sanatorium in the middle fifties. He recalled Barlow saying it would be difficult to detect afterwards as it dissolved in the bloodstream.

A former patient at the same sanatorium remembered a conversation with Barlow who said of insulin: "Get a load of this, and it's the quickest way out." Then there was a woman nurse who had tended diabetics with Barlow, and remembered him saying: "You could kill somebody with insulin as it can't be found very easily – unless you use a very large dose."

There was, however, a significant weakness implicit in this line of prosecution argument. Barlow had been married to Elizabeth less than one year. Was the jury to believe he was already contemplating the murder of a wife he had yet to meet?

The defence, led by Mr Bernard Gillies QC, called as their expert witness Dr Hobson, from St Luke's Hospital in London. He told the court that in moments of stress (like anger, for instance, *or fear*) the human body automatically releases and pumps adrenalin into the bloodstream. This in turn raises the sugar level – which could produce an increase of insulin as a natural reaction.

"If [Mrs Barlow] knew she was slipping down and drowning in the bath," he said, "and that she could not get out, she would be terrified and I think that would produce all the symptoms the chemists have described."

Against this was the amount of insulin found below those hypodermic syringe marks in the woman's body. Insulin produced naturally in the way Dr Hobson described would be evenly distributed over the body – and it would need a fantastic amount to reach the overall level found round those puncture marks.

The judge told the jury: "If you are satisfied he injected insulin into his wife and knowingly injected it, you will probably find no difficulty in reaching the decision that he did so with intent to kill."

Mr Justice Diplock told them to make up their minds, saying "This is murder or nothing". The jury found for murder. Barlow was sentenced to life imprisonment, and a new page had been written in British criminal history.

Apart from my constant checks through Scotland Yard, I took no part in the police investigation before Barlow was finally charged. This was a matter for my associates in the northern offices of the *Daily Express*. What fascinated me, and took me to the trial, was the knowledge that this was to be the first trial for murder by insulin injection in any murder investigation.

I have discussed the case many times since with many an expert and always our talks have ended with the one question: why did he do it?

Barlow's first wife had died in 1956 at the early age of thirty-three. Even after the inquest, doubt existed over the precise cause of her death, although it was found to be from natural causes. If his protestations of innocence at the time of his trial for the murder of Elizabeth, his second wife, were genuine, then here was someone who had been dealt a doubly cruel blow by Fate.

But if the verdict was just – that he committed "a cold, cruel and carefully premeditated murder" as the judge said – even though he was happily married, we are left with only one possible conclusion. Here was a man who really believed he had found the way to commit the "perfect murder" and so carried it out as a cold-blooded and clinical experiment. On his new wife, who unfortunately happened to be the most convenient human guinea pig.

If his method of murder was unique, it shows Barlow held at least one trait in common with all poisoners: a callous disregard for suffering. He would have done well in any Nazi wartime concentration camp.

THE JEKYLL AND HYDE OF NEW YORK

(Dr Arthur Waite, USA 1916)

John Laurence

Even on trial for his life, accused of double murder, Dr Arthur Warren Waite laughed at the law. It was, he agreed, all true. He had indeed murdered his mother-in-law by mixing germs in her food. He had also killed his wealthy father-in-law, but when the germs failed, and arsenic too, Waite had used chloroform, suffocating the old man with a pillow to finish him off. Why? "For the money" said Waite. His trial was the New York sensation of its day. The debonair young dentist cheerfully explained how he had poisoned his mother-in-law mixing pneumonia, diphtheria and influenza germs into her meals. Waite's father-in-law had been a hardier soul, resisting tuberculosis bacteria sprayed up his nose, chlorine gas, and various attempts to give him pneumonia, including dampening his sheets. Science caught up with Dr Waite when arsenic he'd poured into the old man's soup was detected at the autopsy.

Doctor Arthur Warren Waite, dentist and crack tennis player, to all outward seeming was a child of fortune. He had everything the normal man wants and envies in others, good looks, charm of manner, athletic abilities, a charming wife, and a millionaire father-in-law.

Let us particularize. In appearance Doctor Waite was the

typical athletic American, clean-shaven, clear-eyed, regular-featured and frankly healthy. He was popular with men and women alike, and all with whom he came in contact trusted him. He was always perfectly groomed and had that *savoir faire* which comes from wide travel. A witty conversationalist, he could talk entertainingly on most subjects, and he was much in demand by the hostesses of New York.

His father-in-law was John E. Peck, a retired millionaire druggist of Grand Rapids, Michigan, of which town Waite himself was a native. Waite's parents were not well-to-do, but their son showed such brilliance and promise that he was encouraged in every possible way to obtain the best education which they could afford. He went to the University of Michigan and there took a dental course.

From there the brilliant student went to London and afterwards to South Africa, where he did a certain amount of practice in the profession for which he had been trained. Shortly after the outbreak of the Great War he returned to the United States and to his native town. There he met Miss Clara Peck. In spite of the wide gulf between their financial positions, a gulf which might almost have made people suspect he was a fortune hunter, no suggestion of the kind was made when it became known that the two were engaged. Everyone who met the good-looking dentist predicted such a successful career for him that he would never be in any financial difficulties.

Clara Peck and Arthur Warren Waite were married at Grand Rapids in September, 1915. To the surprise of many, however, he did not begin practising there, but moved at once to New York on the plea that the opportunities for advancement were much greater in that town, and his newly-married wife would have greater chances of amusement.

Waite was in no hurry to begin practising. He had always shown a great interest in medicine, and within a few days of arriving in New York he had got in touch with a number of doctors whom he deluded into believing he was a fully-qualified man himself, wealthy, and interested in scientific research, especially the study of bacteriology.

A certain amount of verisimilitude was given to Waite's story

by the fact that he had a flat in the exclusive Riverside Drive
Apartments, a flat which was richly furnished. The doctor was
also well-known as a very good amateur tennis player who had
only recently taken part in a number of tournaments at Palm
Beach, Florida. He had, too, a considerable amount of medical
knowledge, partly acquired through his study of dentistry, and
partly learnt through an instinctive desire to acquire knowledge
which might prove of use to him in later years.

Through various influences Waite got in touch with Dr Percival L. de Nyce, who was in charge of the bacteriological
laboratory of the Flower Hospital, one of the best known in-
stitutions in New York. Dr Nyce was impressed with his new
pupil, and the extraordinarily keen interest he took in all germ
cultures. But it was only in the most virulent and deadly germs
that his pupil was really interested, and he actually complained to
Dr Nyce that the germs he was studying were not virulent enough
for the experiments he had in mind!

Clara Waite firmly believed her husband was in practice as a
doctor, and once or twice, in order to foster that belief and
account for the necessary income to keep up their expensive
style of living, he took her to the Flower Hospital and asked her to
stay in the waiting room for a while. After keeping her there
kicking her heels for half an hour or so, and reflecting on what he
might be doing, he would return and announce that he had just
finished an important operation. The deluded Clara, who understood not a single detail of the medical account her husband gave
her, was full of pride that his abilities were being recognized in
such an important institution.

It may well be asked at this stage, where was the comparatively
poor student of a year or two ago getting the large sums of money
which were necessary not only for his living expenses but for
those in connection with the bacteriological experiments he was
carrying out?

Waite had ingratiated himself so well with the Peck family that,
with one exception, they were intensely proud of the brilliant
addition to it. His wife's father helped financially so that his son-
in-law should not be handicapped in any of his research work
which he represented was necessary to advance in his profession.

He not only gave his daughter a very handsome dowry, out of which the Riverside apartments were so luxuriously furnished, but he allowed her £60 a month.

It must be admitted that Waite had an exceedingly great attraction for women, especially for women older than himself. Mrs Peck adored him. Nothing he could do was wrong, and her sister-in-law, Miss Catherine Peck, who had given her niece a cheque for nearly a thousand pounds as a wedding present, had even a higher opinion of him. So much did she value his advice, indeed, that she was easily persuaded to let him have £10,000 of her money to invest. It was on this money that Waite lived. Aunt Catherine was unwise enough to let it be known that on her death Waite would receive a very substantial legacy. It was also common knowledge in the family that Mr Peck's will left half his fortune to his daughter Clara. If Mr and Mrs Peck died, and Aunt Catherine died, and perhaps later on Clara Waite, Arthur Warren Waite would be a very rich and eligible widower!

A few weeks after their arrival in New York the devoted young husband – and there was not the slightest doubt that to all outward appearances he was infatuated with his young wife – suggested that her mother and father should be asked to stay with them for a while. Both parents were delighted to accept their son-in-law's invitation, but neither stayed very long on this first visit, for the air of New York did not seem to agree with Mr Peck. He felt run down almost as soon as he arrived. His son-in-law diagnosed a coming cold and sprayed his throat every evening. But that did not ward off the feeling of lassitude, any more than did the medicine which Waite had made up, and Mr Peck returned to Grand Rapids to be thoroughly overhauled there by his own doctors. They confessed themselves completely puzzled. However the air of Grand Rapids certainly suited old Mr Peck better than did that of New York and he was soon feeling as fit as ever.

Mrs Peck had found the visit to her beloved daughter and son-in-law all too short and as soon as she was satisfied that her husband was on the road to recovery and not likely to have a relapse, she paid them another visit – her last. Shortly after her arrival, she, too, began to feel ill, and a Doctor Porter was called in. He diagnosed that there was nothing very much the matter, though Dr Waite strongly disagreed, and asserted that he was sure his mother-in-law was seriously ill.

One night when Dr Waite was out ostensibly visiting his patients, a very remarkable incident occurred, though no one thought much about it at the time. Mrs Waite, who had gone to bed, detected a strong smell of gas and traced it as coming from her mother's room. When she entered it she found that the tap of the gas stove had been left on and if it had not been for the fact one of the windows was partly open there is no doubt her mother would have been asphyxiated.

From that day, however, Mrs Peck grew steadily worse, and on January 30th, 1916, she died. Doctor Porter, who had suspected nothing wrong, readily gave his certificate. Dr Waite, who seemed utterly grief-stricken by his mother-in-law's sudden death, accompanied her body to Grand Rapids, where he told various members of the family that her last dying wish was that she should be cremated. The ashes were buried in the family vault. The act of cremation had effectively destroyed all danger of anyone finding out the real cause of the old lady's death.

Mr Peck was overwhelmed by the loss of his wife and in February he accepted a second invitation to come to New York to visit his daughter. Both he and Clara had been very fond of Mrs Peck and both were eager to be together in their common sorrow. Old Mr Peck, too, liked his son-in-law, for the latter had been more sympathetic than even a devoted son-in-law might be expected to be. Waite was so charming, so anxious to make his father-in-law forget, so full of warmth on the old man's arrival, that for a few days Mr Peck really was cheered up and felt far less lonely than he had been feeling since his wife's death. There was a very strong bond of affection between his daughter and himself, for in her he saw again the mother as she was in the days when he first courted her and began his successful struggle for fortune.

During those early days of Mr Peck's second visit to the Riverside Apartment there occurred an incident which has a considerable bearing on the rest of the story. Dr Waite, as far as his devoted wife Clara knew, and her father knew, was an exceedingly busy man. He had to be out many evenings visiting his patients, and sometimes he was so hard-pressed that he did not return until the early hours of the morning. Actually Waite was very fond of wine, women and song. He had early discovered that he exercised a peculiar influence over women, and his life in New York was a continual round of gaiety. Although the delightful doctor distributed his favours on a fairly lavish scale, entertaining at the most expensive restaurants and dance cafés those whom he favoured, there was one lady in particular who proved more attractive than the rest, a Mrs Horton.

Margaret Horton, a beautiful young grass widow, had met Waite first at the Berlitz School of Languages. She was ambitious to become an opera singer. In a few days Waite had installed her in a suite of rooms at the Hotel Plaza. He himself was very fond of music and the two proved very congenial company for one another.

"Dr Waite had an extraordinary kind heart," she said some months after their first meeting. "He loved all the fine sentiments and the beautiful things of life. He used to say to me, 'Margaret, when you sing you make me weep, because you make me think of beautiful things'. He loved music. It was that love of music which drew us together."

It was while dining with Margaret Horton that Waite was seen by a Doctor Cornell, a relative of the Peck family, and a Miss Hardwicke. When Waite saw Cornell he made an excuse to his companion and walked across to the other table. He explained glibly that he had just completed an important operation.

"I have brought my own special nurse with me for dinner as I felt that she deserved something out of the ordinary for her skill and devotion to my work," he explained.

He told his story with easy confidence and all those at the table, with the exception of Miss Hardwicke, were inclined to believe it. But she had been watching Waite and Margaret Horton, and she was secretly convinced that there was a deeper relationship between the two than that of doctor and nurse. But she made no outward comment, though the time was soon to come when she was to crystallize her suspicions into such drastic action that Waite's name, in consequence, was to fill the front pages of the American newspapers for many a long day.

A few days after the incident in the restaurant Mr Peck was taken seriously ill and a Dr Moore was called in. He diagnosed digestive trouble and prescribed accordingly. Mr Peck's son-in-law was most attentive. The sick man did not like his medicine and Dr Waite soon found a way out of the difficulty. One evening Waite came into the kitchen and without any disguise poured some medicine into his father-in-law's soup. Later in the evening he came into the kitchen again when tea was being prepared for Mr Peck and poured some further medicine into the teapot.

"Dora," he explained to the servant, "father didn't like his soup, so I must put some more medicine in his tea."

Although Dr Moore had not considered the condition of his patient to be very serious, Dr Waite, as in the case of Mrs Peck, disagreed with him.

"He hasn't a very strong constitution," he declared, "and I should not be surprised if he did not live for long."

As with Mrs Peck, Waite's prophecy proved more accurate than had that of other doctors. On March 12th, but six weeks after his wife's death, Mr Peck died, and Clara Waite had lost both her parents. And as with the case of Mrs Peck, Waite declared that his father-in-law's last wish was that he should be cremated and his ashes placed beside those of his wife. Accordingly, the body, accompanied by the grief-stricken Clara and her sorrowing husband, was taken to Grand Rapids for that purpose. Before that journey, however, the body had been embalmed, a fact which should be borne in mind.

To Dr Waite's astonishment he found when he got to Grand Rapids that the family were not in favour of the old man being cremated. He was careful enough, however, not to raise any great objections, and after duly seeing his father-in-law buried he hurried back to New York – and Mrs Horton. Of late he had been spending money freely, too freely, but now, under his father-in-law's will, through Clara, he would have no cause to worry about money for some time. When he had, there was always Miss Catherine Peck, who had promised him a substantial legacy on her death.

There was one member of the Peck family who had never been very friendly with Dr Waite, who had always disliked him in fact, despite his great charm. That was Percival Peck, Clara's only brother. It was Percival Peck who had raised the greatest objections to his father being cremated. Just before the arrival of the body at Grand Rapids he had received a mysterious telegram from New York which read as follows: "Suspicions aroused. Demand autopsy. Keep telegram secret. – K. Adams."

The name of Adams was quite unknown to Percival Peck, but that fact did not influence him in the least. It transpired afterwards that K. Adams was the Miss Hardwicke who had seen Dr Waite and Mrs Horton dining together, and who had disbelieved the story the former told that the lady was his nurse. But the telegram, from whatever source it came, provided young Peck with an opportunity which he eagerly seized. He had a secret examination made of his father's body and at the same time employed private detectives to keep an eye on his brother-in-law and keep a record of his movements.

Clara, who had become seriously ill following upon the double shock of her mother's and father's deaths, had stayed behind at Grand Rapids, while her husband had hurried back to the gaieties of New York.

And then Waite received his first shock. He had left Grand Rapids fully satisfied that he had bluffed everyone, that he could now spend money just as freely as he wished, enjoy himself to the top of his bent. But a few days after his return Mr Peck's son-in-law received a shock. The undertaker who had arranged for the embalming of Mr Peck called upon him and asked that his bill should be paid.

"What's the hurry?" asked Waite. "You know the money is safe enough, don't you?"

He was surprised at the sudden demand for the bill, but he was more than surprised by the undertaker's reply. It worried him. It was the tiny black cloud on the edge of the horizon.

"It's really Mr Kane, sir, the embalmer," explained the undertaker. "He thinks he might not get his money."

"Why?" demanded Waite, struck by the uneasy look in the other's face.

"Well, there's some idea that arsenic had been used," explained the undertaker.

Waite was well aware that it was against the law for arsenic to be used in any embalming fluid, as he was also aware that arsenic would be found in Mr Peck's body if it were examined.

"I think I'd better see Mr Kane," he said evenly.

When the doctor saw Kane he did not beat about the bush.

"How much is it worth to you to say that you used arsenic?" he asked.

The embalmer named a sum, and after some haggling Waite agreed to pay him $9,000. But Kane's nerve broke at the last minute and he told a remarkable story to the police when questioned.

"Waite told me he was in a hole and asked me to put arsenic in the sample of embalming fluid I was to give the District Attorney. He said he would make me independent for life if I did what I was asked."

Waite by now suspected that his movements were being watched and he arranged for Kane to meet him casually in a cigar store.

"I met him there by a telephone booth," Kane related. "And he gave me a big roll of bills. I was so scared that I could hardly tell where I was. I stood there with the money in my hand.

" 'For God's sake get that stuff out of sight,' Dr Waite said, 'and get the sample down to the District Attorney's office.'

"I went right home; I was so nervous that I couldn't count the money. I tried afterwards and couldn't do it. I put it in a bureau drawer. I was so nervous about the money that my wife noticed it. She got to worrying me and at last made me go to a doctor to find out if I was sick. I knew all right, but I didn't tell her. I shook like a leaf every now and then when I got to thinking about the money in the bureau drawer. Then I took it down to Greenport and buried it. I didn't put anything into the sample of my embalming fluid. I made up the sample just as I always make the fluid."

Kane's own record wasn't of the best. He had been suspected on more than one occasion of helping clients "who were in a hole" out of it on the payment of a reasonably large sum. But for the fact that Percival Peck had brought pressure to bear with the authorities and had had his own private detectives following his brother-in-law, the interview between Kane and Waite and the handing over of a large sum of money in the cigar store might not have been known until too late. But within a very short time of the meeting, it had been reported to the police, and Kane was asked for the sample of his fluid. Rumours were flying about, and it was these rumours coming to his ears which made him break down. He had embalmed the body of Mr Peck before it had been conveyed to Grand Rapids and he was now beginning to realize that there was trouble ahead. And this wouldn't be the first time he had been in trouble.

The District Attorney's suspicions had been aroused on receiving a report from Professor Vaughan, of the University of Michigan, who had made an examination of Mr Peck's body. He had sent in a report to the effect that the millionaire had died from arsemic poisoning. There was just a possibility that the arsenic had been in the embalming fluid, but when he heard Kane's story he immediately issued a warrant for the arrest of Waite.

The iron nerve of the suspected man was breaking fast under the strain of waiting, and it broke a few hours before the detectives called at his Riverside Apartments with the warrant for his arrest. He was found unconscious in the room adjoining that in which Mr and Mrs Peck had died.

But Waite was not to evade the law so easily. He was rushed to the hospital and strong emetics administered. In the hands of skilful physicians he made a rapid recovery. While he was getting over the effect of the drugs he had taken, however, he was thinking out what story to tell. He was now fully aware of the likely evidence against him and only a miracle could save him. He decided to play the part of Dr Jekyll and Mr Hyde.

When questioned by the District Attorney in hospital Waite at once admitted that he had given his father-in-law arsenic.

"Have you any accomplices?"

"Only this other fellow," replied the accused man with claborate carelessness.

"What other fellow?"

"The man from Egypt. He's always been inside me ever since I can remember. He has made me do things against my will. He made me take up the study of germs, as if I used them I wouldn't be detected. I was compelled against my will to put them in my father-in-law's food. Try as I would I could not get rid of my murderous other self. Often I have gone for long walks and fought against the evil one, and tried to run away from him. But he was so fleet of foot that he always caught me up."

So earnestly did Waite tell his story that it was partly believed. "Did this Egyptian make you kill Mr Peck?" he was asked.

"When my father-in-law came to stay with us I wanted to help him all I could. Then the man from Egypt said Mr Peck was too old to live, that he ought to die, and if he did die I wouldn't have to worry about money. He brushed aside all my arguments. When Mr Peck had first visited us the Egyptian made me spray his throat with germs, but though they made him ill they did not kill him. I was ordered this time to use arsenic as it was quicker. I was told to put it in his soup and tea and egg nog. I did my best, but the Egyptian was in control. Try as I could I found it impossible to get rid of him. But now that he has forced me to do these things he has left me, and for the first time I felt that my soul is free. He seemed to leave me last night and he hasn't returned again to-day to torture me with his evil suggestions."

The story told by Waite had exactly the effect he foresaw. It was so wild that it seemed as though only a madman could tell it. Some of the leading alienists in America were called in by the prosecution as well as by the defence.

Dr Jeliffe, the leading alienist for the prosecution, said at the trial, "In my opinion the prisoner was sane and knew the nature and quality of his act. He was fully aware of all the phases of his crime. In my opinion he is an average man, somewhat superficial, inclined to be snobbish and of no great intellectual attainments."

With that a number of other leading doctors agreed and ultimately their opinion prevailed.

While he was waiting his trial an amazing story came to light. Some of this has already been told. A search of Waite's flat resulted in the discovery of a number of books on poisons and a hundred and eighty slides containing germs of tetanus (lockjaw), typhoid, diphtheria, cholera and other deadly diseases with which he had been experimenting. He had spent large sums on women and amusement and had given Mrs Horton jewellery which had been entrusted to him by Miss Catherine Peck. Practically all the money the latter had given him to invest had gone in riotous living. Only the death of his father-in-law, indeed, could save him from exposure and ruin. So cunningly had he disguised his various amours that until he was arrested his wife had no knowledge of them.

"I was so shocked and amazed that I could not believe them true," she declared after her husband's arrest. "It seems impossible that a man who has been so uniformly gentle and kind to me and apparently so loyal could be guilty of the crime with which he is charged."

Dozens of people who knew Waite well were as puzzled. Many believed that he really was a Jekyll and Hyde, that he had been obsessed by the man from Egypt, as he asserted. Others asserted that the story was told deliberately in an attempt to evade the law. There was one man who never believed for one single moment that the doctor was insane. That was Percival Peck, the man who had received the mysterious telegram and acted on it so promptly, the man who at once employed private detectives to follow his brother-in-law's movements, who never ceased his efforts to unearth everything he could to prove Waite's guilt.

"I know that Arthur is guilty," he declared shortly after Waite's arrest. "The electric chair will be too good for him. Even if he were tortured his death would never bring back my beloved parents or pay for his horrible deeds. I will do all in my power to see that he is found guilty and executed.

"He is surely entitled to no consideration whatever. I am convinced that Dr Waite married my sister Clara with but one idea, and that was to get her money. Even before her mother died he predicted an untimely death for us all. We believed him to be a surgeon, and when mother died we suspected nothing. Even when the news of father's death came we did not suspect until I got that telegram. I am sure if it had not been for that my sister and my aunt would have died next."

Percival Peck was adamant to the last. He approached the prosecution shortly before the trial and said:

"I have only one favour to ask, and that is that I have a seat through every minute of the trial near that man, so that I can see the last gleam of hope gradually fade from his face."

In the witness box Waite was perfectly cool, and he made no attempt to hide the appallingly evil personality of the man from Egypt who had compelled him to commit and contemplate crimes which shocked even New York. The more terrible his story, the more coolly it was told, the greater the chance the jury would believe that only a madman could do these things. His own counsel, by clever questions, brought out details of the murder of Mrs Peck and her husband which seemed to show that only a madman could have acted the way Waite did.

"What did you do after you had given your mother-in-law the fatal dose of poison?" asked his counsel.

"Why, I went to sleep, of course," answered the prisoner in the witness box. He added that in the morning he went along to his mother-in-law's bedroom and, finding her dead, quietly came out of the room again and waited for his wife to make the discovery her mother had died in the night. He told the jury of all the ways he had afterwards tried to kill Mr Peck before he finally succeeded.

"I gave him a throat spray and a nasal spray containing germs, and when that didn't work I got a lot of calomel which I administered to him in order to weaken him so that he could not resist the germs, but it failed. The man recovered every time. I would get him to go out and expose himself to draughts in the hope that he would catch cold, and I dampened his sheets for the same reason. Once I got some hydrochloric acid and put in the radiator in his room expecting the fumes would affect him. Finally I gave him arsenic. I sat up with him that night, as my wife was tired. He was in great pain, groaning. I gave him some chloroform and when he was unconscious I placed a pillow over his face and kept it there until he died."

Is that the evidence of a sane man or not?

"Waite has told you the truth. There is no part of his story that is not true," said the counsel for the defence in his final speech. "He has no moral sense whatever. What are we going to do with such a man as this? You would not send to the electric chair an idiot, a lunatic or a child. On the other hand we cannot permit such a man as Waite to be at large. We must remove him from society by placing him in an institution."

Mr Justice Shearn demolished the arguments of the counsel for the defence, in his address to the jury.

You are not concerned at all with the question of the punishment of this man. The question raised by defendant's counsel of what to do with such a man is not the question at all. The law determines what shall be done. Your function is to determine the facts so that the law may operate.

Don't get into your heads that you are called upon to determine anything but the facts. Juries have no right to set up standards of what constitutes right and wrong, and no right to discuss how the law shall deal with a man like this. You must not attempt to usurp the functions of the Legislature.

In this case no claim is made that the defendant did it in the heat of passion. On the contrary he himself admits premeditation, intent and a motive. No matter what the defendant has confessed you must remember the burden still rests upon the prosecution to establish his guilt beyond a reasonable doubt. The defendant is entitled to have the case determined on the facts and not on what he says.

Part of the remainder of the judge's summing up is so phrased that a copy of it should be handed to every jury in a murder case where the defence is one of insanity.

You might infer from arguments of counsel and some of the evidence that you are here to hold a medical clinic. That's not so at all. It would be absurd to ask twelve laymen to determine whether from the medical point of view a man is sane or insane, especially as men learned in the profession do not agree on the matter. The question is not whether he is sane but whether he was responsible under the tests prescribed by the law – that is, did he know the nature and quality of the act and know it was wrong. That's not a test for experts, but for men of commonsense. Moral indifference is not insanity.

The claim that the defendant was weak in will power and
that he was unable to resist suggestions like those from 'the
Man from Egypt' has also been passed on by the highest
courts, who have held that, no matter what medical authority there may be for such a claim, it cannot be assented to by
the courts. Indulgence in evil passions weakens the will
power and at the same time the sense of responsibility.

The trial was very much shorter than the great majority of
sensational murder trials in America, where money can hold
up justice for months. The trial only took five days and the jury
were only a little over an hour bringing in their verdict of
"Guilty."

To the last the condemned man showed that curious double
personality which puzzled all those with whom he came in
contact. He never wearied of talking about himself.

"My life consisted of lying, cheating, stealing and killing. My
personality was that of a gentleman and I went for music, art and
poetry."

He dedicated a long poem to himself, an address to his body by
his soul after death.

> And thou are dead, dear comrade,
> In whom I dwelt a time,
> With whom I strolled through star-kissed bowers
> Of fragrant jessamine.
> And thou wert weak, O comrade,
> Thyself in self did fail,
> And now the stars are turned to tears
> And sobs the nightingale.
> And though I now must leave you,
> The same old songs I'll sing,
> And o'er yon hill the same soft dew
> Will spread its silver wing.
> Across the fields, among the stars,
> I now must go alone,
> Your spirit now will roam afar,
> And leave you, friend, alone.

A few days before his execution, when he was reading the Bible, he remarked with his usual charming smile, "I was looking over the ten Commandments and found I had broken all but one – the one about profanity. I have never been profane."

He kept up his story about his two personalities until the last.

But it did not save him. He went to his death with that boyish smile and charming manner which had characterized him from the day he began his career.

THE TALKING SKULL

(Harry Dobkin, UK 1942)

Nigel Morland

A single female body unearthed amid the mass slaughter of the London Blitz was identified as a victim not of war but of a private, murderous act of mutilation – thanks to the evidence of the dead woman's dentist. Harry Dobkin, forty-nine, Russian by birth, bald, squat and bull-necked, killed his estranged wife Rachel who'd been pestering him to return to her. After crudely separating the head from the torso, Dobkin tried to remove all identifying marks, and concealed his wife's remains beneath the floor of a badly blitzed chapel. Finally, he set fire to the building under cover of enemy action, a singular deed for a man employed as a wartime fire-watcher. But the charred skeleton was discovered by chance more than a year later, and the Home Office pathologist Dr Keith Simpson reported that the unknown woman had been strangled. Her identity was established through the testimony of Mrs Dobkin's dentist, who recognized the curious shape of the upper jaw as well as other features of the teeth and gums. Dobkin was convicted of murdering her and duly hanged. Nigel Morland (1905–86), one of Britain's most prolific writers of crime fact and fiction, was a co-founder of the Crime Writers' Association. After a spell as a journalist in the Far East, he edited publications as diverse as Doctor *and the* Edgar Wallace Mystery Magazine. *He also ghosted a number of showbiz memoirs. Nigel Morland was the founder and editor of* The Criminologist *and other crime-related journals including* Forensic Photography, International Journal of Forensic Dentistry *and* Current Crime.

In the greater conflagration of war it is somehow remarkably incongruous that all the vast resources of detection and justice should be devoted to the seeking and condemnation of a civilian murderer with but a single victim notched to his credit.

While thousands die on the battlefields, there is a footnote to history in a nation's trivia of homicides, yet, clearly, it is the duty of the authorities to maintain law and detect transgressions of it even if the world is falling about their ears. The pen of the historian, then, had to turn aside from the horrors of World War I, in June 1915, to record the trial of that singularly revolting, utterly worthless creature, George Joseph Smith.

And in 1942, much in the same way, part of the country paused to watch the Baptist Church murderer stand his trial while Rommel was retreating in North Africa and the Germans receded like a spent wave from the rubble-fortress of Stalingrad.

Despite the chaos of World War II, Britain's aficionados of murder could still note with interest a trial that was indeed more distinguished for the medical work contributing to its solution than for its forensic colour.

The trial was a worthy occupant of the Central Criminal Court at Old Bailey, where so much legal drama has been played out, even if it failed to reach the heights of some of its predecessors.

Chance enabled me to be present at the hearing, though it was impossible to attend on the last day, for, and it may be of faintly ironic interest, I was receiving a reprimand for putting ideas into the heads of would-be murderers. It was a sound example of how officialdom sought to guard the innocent when, in a far larger way, the innocent were being slaughtered.

It happened I had written for a newspaper a short story involving an imaginary murder during an air raid. The plot concerned a man who slew his wife by means of a piece of flak, or anti-aircraft shell, fastened to a stick and used as an edged bludgeon. It contrived a death not attributable to himself but to the rain of shell fragments which were also London's protection. The scheme was foolproof except, like all fictional (and many real) murderers, he had made a mistake by leaving the fragment at his dead wife's side still bearing the string originally tying it to the bludgeon.

An over-conscientious features editor thought this just a bit too feasible and perhaps tempting; he mentioned it casually to a Ministry of Information official, who asked me to visit him, and suggested – and no more – that it was not the best of policies to make crime *too* easy. Could I not contrive something less likely to cause possible trouble for an over-worked detective force?

Thus it was I never heard Mr Justice Wrottesley's masterly summing-up on the final day of the Baptist Church murderer's trial, but the story of the case is a veritable marvel of the medical jurist excelling fiction by conjuring from little more than dust a recognizable human being whose gruesome end was finally avenged.

The July sunshine poured through the windows of the Gordon Museum at London's Guy's Hospital, making the room warm, a heat in no way improved by a tart chemical smell and the brittle, throat-catching aroma of ancient death.

There was a brown paper parcel containing remains for the attention of Dr (later professor) Cedric Keith Simpson, noted Home Office pathologist, a parcel already familiar to him.

Its contents were first seen on 17 July 1942, when a gang of demolition workers was clearing bombed premises at 302, Upper Kennington Lane, a short distance from south London's Kennington Oval cricket ground.

Raising a stone slab in what was the cellar of a now demolished Baptist church, human remains were revealed. According to the routine of such cases, the local coroner was informed. Dr Simpson, also according to routine, saw the remains in Southwark Mortuary the following morning and was not personally satisfied they were all that was left of an air-raid victim. He thought it wise to conduct a closer examination at Guy's Hospital because of the possibly long task of trying to get some sort of identification from an incomplete skeleton bearing decaying tissues. The poor fragments, the skull entirely separated from its trunk, were bundled into a prosaic paper parcel and transported for due attention on Monday morning.

The remains were transferred to a white dust sheet and these Dr Simpson pondered before commencing what was quite a considerable task in detective work at a time when his day was filled and his leisure almost non-existent.

The first thing was visual verification of his original surmise that death had taken place some twelve or eighteen months previously;* that the victim was female was easily discernable by the remains of the uterus being still present.

Using camel hair brushes and loosening the tissues, the doctor began slowly, and with extreme delicacy, gradually to clean the dirt from the almost mummified remains of the body. It was exacting and wearing, the adhering dirt being not easily removed; it required a combination of firmness and lightness, with special precautions to avoid damage to the soft tissues still remaining.

The following day saw progress add up to considerable results. It did not seem to Dr Simpson that this was an air-raid casualty. The skull had been severed cleanly from the trunk, the lower jaw was missing, and the skull also bore no scalp tissue other than a small fragment at the back – no bomb had the power to scalp and behead quite so selectively.

There were no lower portions to the arms or legs, which argued amputation. There were also marks of burning on the head, on the left side of the trunk and at the level of each knee – the left arm had been severed at the elbow joint and the right arm immediately above that joint, while the legs were separated on the left below the knee joint and at the joint on the right. The cut portions were all missing.

As a snap guess it was possible to wonder if the mutilation, and this included stripping the identifiable tissues, was the work of an unskilled person determined to hide a human identity by crude but effective methods even if, with careful disposal, she came to light some time after death.

It was without doubt a case of murder, for the small bones of the voice box bore an injury – with bruising showing it to have been sustained in life – which Dr Simpson knew was seen only when fingers had grasped the throat and strangulation had followed.

In the busy if pedestrian professional life of a great pathologist, it is only natural that the few real puzzles which stand out from the unhappily ordinary dead are challenges to his

* A deposit of yellowish powder over the whole was proved to be slaked lime.

ability and, after all, threads of colour in his more mundane daily round.

Dr Simpson knew he had before him a veritable mystery and wondered if his skill and knowledge would enable him to establish the identity of the victim, or at least sufficiently chart it for purposes of enquiry. He wanted science to give the police something sound to work on at the start of their enquiries.

The first thing to ascertain was the height of the dead woman in life. The weapon to be used was Pearson's formulae for the determination of stature, a process requiring the utmost knowledge and experience.

Reassembly of the body had revealed its stature to be about 5ft $0\frac{1}{4}$ in to 5ft $0\frac{3}{4}$ in, allowance being made for the missing lower legs, feet and soft tissue. Pearson's formulae, worked on the remaining long bone, the left humerus, gave height as 5ft $0\frac{1}{2}$ in to 5ft 1in.

The next step was to age the remains in life. This is done by checking the closure of the skull vault sutures (the zigzag markings or joints between the plates of bone in the skull vault). Here is an awkward gap from the anatomical point of view – till about twenty-five years of age the accuracy of age estimation can be achieved by several pointers in the human frame. Between that maximum and until roughly forty, there is little, except appearance, to help in closely estimating age.

But at about forty-years-old the skull vault sutures commence to close and other closures lend their aid to achieve reasonably accurate age estimates.

It was therefore possible from the skull sutures, and the closing of the palate suture (usual between 45 and 60), to settle on the approximate age of the corpse as 40 to 50; these bone fusions were remarkably helpful in Dr Simpson's reconstruction.

Colouring was proved by the fragment of scalp, to which some hairs were still attached; they were dark brown, ageing, and going grey.

There was a fibroid tumour of the uterus, a benign growth having nothing to do with death, but possibly of value in clinching identification. Finally, there were four teeth, and some roots, remaining in the upper jaw. These had received dental attention.

This initial data Dr Simpson gave to the police with his suggestion the remains might be those of a murdered person, a woman, aged 40 to 50; she was 5ft to 5ft 1in in height, with brown hair turning gray. She suffered from a fibroid tumour of the uterus, and had possibly received medical attention for it. She had met her death some twelve to eighteen months before and, if dental records could be found, there was an upper jaw with four teeth together with their details of dental repairs, fillings, and so on available for comparison or matching.

In the meantime police enquiries had followed *their* usual routine; Divisional Detective Inspector Frederick Hatton, of "M" Division, had caused to be checked the lists of women notified to the police as missing during the period in question, twelve or eighteen months previously.

A coincidence emerged and because detectives have frequently found that coincidences often lead to the discovery of important circumstantial evidence, Hatton's CID staff got a feeling they were on to something.

The coincidence was a missing woman named Dobkin, who had vanished some fifteen months before. Her husband had been a fire-watcher at 302, Upper Kennington Lane. He had looked after storage premises containing papers practically on the edge of the spot where the demolition workers had turned up the body. It was a pointer to a line of enquiry far too promising to be ignored.

Detective Inspector John Keeling, Hatton's second-in-command, obtained Dr Simpson's first findings and went to see Mrs Dobkin's sister (she had originally reported the disappearance to the police) in order to get a full description.

It was uncannily similar to the scientific reconstruction. The missing Mrs Rachel Dobkin had been 5ft 1in tall, with dark brown hair going gray. Her age had been forty-seven, and she had attended the London Hospital for a fibroid tumour of the uterus. Further enquiries began to turn up some very interesting facts.

The husband of the dead woman, Harry Dobkin, was a bald,

somewhat bull-like Jew of Russian birth* and just forty-nine
years old. Before the war he worked as a ship's steward and cook,
while, on shore, he managed to live by undertaking various jobs
in the tailoring trade.

On 3 April 1941, a firm of solicitors engaged him as a fire-
watcher to look after a small building belonging to them in which
were stored quantities of papers and documents.

This building stood well back from the street in a yard containing the Vauxhall Baptist Church and its adjoining school, both
places having been demolished by bombs. Two small houses
fronting Upper Kennington Lane – between the Lane and the
paper store – had also been bombed and were empty.

It was Dobkin's job to patrol round the paper store a prescribed number of times during the night in between which
activities he made himself comfortable in a chair in one of the
two small bombed houses. It would have been a pleasant life for a
reflective man though, for certainty, Dobkin must have preferred
to keep his mind strictly on the unforgiving minute and let the
past bury itself.

A fortnight after his duties began, and, it was of interest to
note, only very shortly after Mrs Dobkin's disappearance, there
was a fire in the cellar under the site of the ruined church vestry.
The fire brigade quickly put out the blaze, largely consisting of
burning straw from a mattress lying within yards of the slab
where later the scorched skeleton was to be found.

Dobkin at the time showed some agitation and made an odd,
and uncalled-for, observation to a police constable that: "I didn't
do it." The fire took place three days after Mrs Dobkin's sister
reported the disappearance.

Police records revealed that as soon as news of the woman

* It may be of no possible sociological significance but of some interest
that the origins of several people concerned in one way or another with
notable British murder trials are remarkably varied; a casual handful
picked haphazard from the headline names suggests the Island Race does
not always lead: Florence Maybrick, American; Adelaide Bartlett,
French; H. H. Crippen, American; George Chapman, Russian; Eugéne
Marie Chantrelle, French; Buck Ruxton, Parsee; Jean Pierre Vaquier,
French; Alma Rattenbury, Canadian; Oscar Slater, German; etc.

being missing was received, the husband was interviewed because, as I have mentioned before, police officers are inclined to go and talk lengthily to the husband when his wife vanishes – this is based on a simple, strictly sensible rule; frequently it pays dividends.

In this case Harry Dobkin made a statement which mentioned he had married a Rachel Dubinsky in 1920 at Bethnal Green Synagogue, a union that had failed from the beginning. A maintenance order for £1 weekly had been made against him a few months after the marriage, not that Mrs Dobkin ever succeeded in getting the stipulated amount from him. Becoming seriously in arrears over the payment landed Dobkin in jail for a brief term.

On 11 April 1941, Mrs Dobkin told her sister she was meeting her husband, apparently to try and coax some of the money due to her; as usual it was well behind. After lunch she set out and was seen in early evening by a waitress at a Dalston cafe having tea with Dobkin. That was the last of her so far as the world knew, though Dobkin was to swear he saw her off in an east-bound bus.

The following day her handbag, containing among other things an identity card and ration book, was found in a Guildford post office but never claimed. At five o'clock that afternoon Polly Dubinsky, the sister, gave information to the London police that Mrs Dobkin was missing. She bluntly accused the husband, who had physically attacked his wife in the past, of being the responsible party.

In the resulting police investigation it was suspected that Dobkin must have started the fire in the church himself. Searches were made there without any result, though detectives were within inches of the concealing flagstone; apropos, a trench – 6ft by $1\frac{1}{2}$ ft – recently dug *was* found under the main church floor but there was no body in it.

Nothing ever came of this or of photographs published in the newspapers and gradually, through the enormous pressure of wartime work, the matter was dropped. Dobkin remained at his fire-watching job until May 1942, when his employers removed their documents and no longer required his services.

Having been a sort of custodian of the secret grave for all those months, Dobkin probably left his situation with some relief. It must have been galling for him to be told that within two months of quitting the post, demolition workers had retrieved the body and the problem of Mrs Dobkin had returned to the inquisitive world.

Dr Keith Simpson had already formed the private opinion that Dobkin must have murdered his wife by strangling in order to rid himself of an incubus, concealing the remains after mutilating the body and trying to destroy it by fire. The missing parts, never found, could easily have been disposed of in the Thames or in some similar way. But this was far from being a sound basis for a murder charge: identity had first to be transformed from a high probability into a complete certainty.

A technique was tried which Professor John Glaister and his colleagues initiated in the Ruxton murder case. The police had got hold of a portrait of Mrs Dobkin. It was enlarged for Dr Simpson to life size and a life size photograph of the jawless skull was taken. Superimposition of one on the other showed they corresponded exactly, the bony facial architecture forming a perfect foundation for the features in the portrait, the eye shape, set and angle aligning with the eye orifices in the skull and so on.

This was still by no means final. The next thing was the all-important dental data. Mrs Dobkin's dentist, on being found, supplied valuable evidence. This gentleman, Barnett A. Kopkin of North London, produced his dental treatment record card concerning this patient and was able to draw a diagram of Mrs Dobkin's upper jaw as he had last seen it together with fillings he had made.

The treatment given to the teeth in the skull was Kopkin's and later, seeing the actual teeth and their fillings, he immediately identified his work. He also stated that in extracting two teeth on the left side of the upper jaw in 1941, residual roots had been left, a not unusual occurrence. Sir William Kelsey Fry, a leading Guy's dental surgeon, made X-ray films of the skull and revealed those same roots. Identity was no longer in doubt.

Lastly, there was the question of how Mrs Dobkin had met her death.

The sprinkling of slaked lime on the body (the action of a layman in the belief that such lime destroys*) had preserved certain tissues round the neck. The hyoid and thyroid cartilages of the voice box were thus preserved, showing, on microscopical examination, clear traces of dried bruising. The upper horn of the right wing of the voice box was fractured, this part of the bone being driven inwards towards the windpipe, and since the bruising surrounding the bone could only occur in life, Dr Simpson's view was that death resulted from manual strangulation, the only likely cause of such a fracture.

There was also found a blood-clot on the back of the head indicating heavy bruising which could have been inflicted by a backwards fall or the result of the head being dashed more than once against the ground by the violence of the strangler.

It was not a comfortable thought, the processes of that grim murder, the stripping of the tissues, the partial dismemberment and disposal of material, all to hide identity. The murderer's tenacity must have been remarkable, backed by a sort of malignant determination to destroy.

Not only is it hard work for the unskilled to hack up a dead body, but to remove tissue requires a steel-strong nerve, and an absolute lack of pity. As a practising crime novelist, I know only too well how glibly dismemberment can be written about, and how fictional licence can excuse or strengthen the criminal. In real life it is subject to a hundred hazards, quite apart from the physical repulsion felt by the ordinary person who undertakes such a deed.

At last Dr Simpson was satisfied, as far as any scientist ever can be satisfied, with his work that he had properly identified Mrs Rachel Dobkin after three months' steady probing into the mystery. He had given all his results to the police and in October Divisional Detective Inspector Hatton moved. Harry Dobkin was arrested and charged with the murder of his wife.

---

* From the wild inaccuracy laid down by a medical witness at the Manning trial in 1849 (and the belief existed earlier) that lime destroyed bodies, murderer after murderer has shown a pathetic devotion to lime as a decomposition agent, using it recklessly and time and again causing the victim's corpse to be properly *preserved* for subsequent investigations.

The Press, quite unaware of this impressive drama of detection going on behind the scenes, awoke to the case with much excitement by the time Dobkin appeared in Lambeth court for the preliminary hearing. Any time lost was made up by an elaborate coverage achieved against the vaster claims of war: as always one locally slaughtered female body was worth, in news value, a thousand dead soldiers overseas.

The trial at the Central Criminal Court took place before Mr Justice Wrottesley on 17 November 1942. It contained little drama and an enormous amount of detail.

Harry Dobkin was an uneasy captive in the dock. He seemed to glare a great deal at various people concerned with the prosecution side, and frowned heavily at times with the concentration of an empty mind. He was extremely fortunate in having his defence in the capable hands of Mr F. H. Lawton, a youthful barrister who was so highly regarded by the accused's solicitors that they did not brief a K C to lead him even though he had never before handled the defence in a trial for murder.

Dr Simpson was the last witness on the second day of the trial; he was taken carefully through his evidence by Mr L. A. (later Mr Justice) Byrne, for the Prosecution. To reproduce a part of the court examination is to show how every point was elaborated. The book frequently referred to was a volume of photographs, containing notes, for the enlightenment of the court, every photograph having been taken and prepared for the support of Dr Simpson's findings by Miss Newman, in charge of the Photographic Department at Guy's Hospital.

> *Mr Byrne:* As to the identification of the body, I want to deal with that. You told us first of all you were able to determine the sex. That was comparatively simple, was it not?
>
> *A.* Yes.
>
> *Q.* Then did you determine how tall the woman had been?
>
> *A.* Yes.
>
> *Q.* How did you arrive at that?

A. I did it by two methods, the first by reconstructing as
far as was possible the body as shown in Plate 2 and making
due allowance for the missing parts, the joints at the knee
and for the flesh and the feet, and by those means I
estimated the stature to be $59\frac{1}{4}$ inches – that is to say,
three-quarters of an inch short of five feet. I estimated the
height to be about five feet and a quarter of an inch to five
feet and three quarters of an inch.

Dr Simpson went on to explain his tables in the book which
showed how he had arrived at the height estimates:

. . . I did this by two methods: by using the Pearson's
formulae I estimated the height to be five foot and half
an inch to five foot one inch, using the left humerus, the left
upper-arm-bone, and by using the Rollet's tables, which are
not so accurate in my view, I estimated the height to be four
foot ten and a half inches to four foot ten inches. The mean
of those estimations from both methods give a height
estimation of about five foot and half an inch.

The question of the superimposition of the photographs on the
dead woman's skull was explained in Dr Simpson's answer:

. . . The general contour of the skull was the same, allowing
for scalp thickness; the contour of the cheeks, allowing for
flesh, was the same; the position and shape of the upper jaw
fitted the photograph well, was the same; the position, the
height, and the width of the nose space were the same, and
fitted perfectly.

On the following day the examination was resumed. Dr Simpson
taken detail by detail through his findings, while the prosecution
tested every fact and, indeed, re-tested it, so there could not be
the slightest possible doubt.

In the minds of the listeners it was clear how the medico-legal
case proved contentions offered by Dr Simpson, but in spite of it,
Mr Lawton made a brave showing for the defence.

He went through the facts with the same care as Mr Byrne but
sought to disprove them or find a weakness in Dr Simpson's
conclusions. The superimposed photograph received a great deal
of attention, pointed by Mr Lawton's remark that:

Is not the difficulty exaggerated in this way, that when
taking a photograph one is obviously taking something in
two dimensions, but when you are taking a photograph of a
skull you are taking a photograph of something in three
dimensions, and does not that tend to lead to inaccuracy in
the two photographs?
A. That is one of the objections. That is a difficulty we
had in this case; we had no measured portrait or anything by
which we could measure the portrait precisely.
Q. And in particular when dealing with the photograph of
a skull which in its three dimensions . . .
Mr Justice Wrottesley: I want to make sure that I follow
that. When you say "no means of measuring the portrait",
that means you have no means of reducing the portrait to
three dimensions?
A. No, it means that we do not know the precise width of
the head and the height of the head in life from a portrait;
we have nothing, as was so in the Ruxton case, by which the
portrait could be measured.

Mr Lawton then made use of references to *Gray's Anatomy*, the
standard medical work on the subject. He asked Dr Simpson:

Q. See if you can follow this passage: "In comparing the
shape of one skull with that of another it is necessary to
adopt some definite position in which the skulls should be
placed during the process of examination." Obviously, they
have both got to be placed in exactly the same position, have
they not?
A. Yes.
Q. In this case you have not got a skull, but a photograph,
and you cannot be certain, can you, that you had them in the
identical positions?

A. The answer to that is that it was possible to move the skull so as to place it in the same position as the photograph.

Q. And in the same plane?

A. That is in the same position.

Q. Not quite, is it? You could have it in the same horizontal position, but not necessarily in the same plane.

A. This was in the same vertical and the same horizontal position.

With item after item concerning the skull discussed, and not to the advantage of the defence, the cross-examination moved on to a check on the structure of the voice box and the question of manual strangulation. It was also the defence's last effort to try and discover holes in the expert findings.

It was established that Dr Simpson found the whole of the voice box in connection with the body.

Q. By voice box do you just mean the thyroid or the two bones that go top and bottom of the thyroid?

A. I mean the hyoid, which is the upper bone shown in this photograph on which the tongue is placed, and also the two wings shown below of the thyroid. Those two together compose the voice box.

Mr Justice Wrottesley: Those three together?

A. Yes; I am taking those two below as one; those three together, yes.

Mr Lawton: In addition to those three bones, the hyoid and the two branches of the thyroid, there are one or two tiny bones, besides, are there not?

A. Yes, there may be.

Q. Many tiny bones besides?

A. There may be, yes.

Q. In particular there are two rather important tiny bones called the arytenoids?

A. There may be.

Q. There are, are there not?

A. There may be; they are not always bony.

Q. If they are not bony, they are in the nature of cartilages, are they not?

A. Yes.

Q. In fact, I am right in saying, am I not, that it is not until late in life that those bones, the hyoid and the thyroid, become bony at all?

A. About in middle life.

Q. Did you find the arytenoid cartilages?

A. Yes.

Q. And just above the horns of the thyroid there are two tiny cartilages known as the triticia, or something like that?

A. Yes.

Q. Did you find those?

A. Yes.

Q. I want you to assume that this situation arises: somebody standing in the road, or on a piece of waste ground, with a lot of rubble about, parts of bricks, and so on, being thrown violently forward by blast from a high explosive bomb, and in falling catching the voice box on a kerb or a piece of brick or masonry, or something of that sort. Is not it possible – I do not put it any higher than that – that a fall under those circumstances might break the cornu of the right thyroid?

A. I have seen injuries under those circumstances on many occasions, and the injuries have never been confined to a fracture of the cornu, as is present here.

Q. That may be, but have you seen injuries under those circumstances which have in fact broken a wing of the thyroid?

A. Yes, but not broken the cornu; broken the thyroid wing, yes. That is not what I described here.

Q. No, I know that, Doctor. I confused the two. Have you seen injuries in the street which have broken a wing of the thyroid and a horn of the thyroid?

A. I have seen both broken together.

Mr Justice Wrottesley: The broken wing being, of course, the lower part?

A. Yes; I have seen the whole thyroid crushed, with both cornu and both wings crushed.

Q. Is your evidence "I have seen such injuries as are described by the throat hitting something"?

A. Yes.

Q. But they never occurred as here, that the thyroid was broken?

A. Yes. It is that which, in my view, is so significant.

Mr Lawton: Do you say it is impossible that a fall of the type I have described to you would break only the cornu of the thyroid?

A. I say that in fifteen years I have personally examined over 11,000 cases, and I have never seen this injury except in manual strangulation.

The defence had worked superbly against heavy odds. "Mr Lawton," one commentator rightly said, "did everything except the impossible" which was to get his client free. The patient medical evidence was too careful and too precise to be argued away.

Dobkin was put in the witness box. If the case against him was strong before he got there, the task was made much easier for the prosecution when Dobkin was to show himself a worse witness than anybody would have believed – it is ironic to think that the Criminal Evidence Act was meant as a privilege, and has often turned out to be the cause of many accused being convicted who, but for their showing in the box, might have got away with it.

Dobkin's eyes seemed to move sharply from point to point while his broad nostrils dilated continually during his destructive cross-examination by Mr Byrne. Most of the good work put in by pertinacious Mr Lawton was destroyed through Dobkin's reactions to certain questions.

In the end he was a sorry picture of panic and fear – I have seldom seen quite so grim a portrayal of a man betraying absolute guilt by a sort of gradual disintegration in which the shrivelled little soul was finally stripped bare of all pretence.

The steady hammering of the circumstantial evidence and Dr Simpson's work bore Dobkin down at every turn until he was accusing all the prosecution's witnesses of lying.

At some trials there always remains a feeling of doubt in the

minds of certain of the expert spectators but Dobkin's prosecution was notable for the steady piling of fact on fact until the
resulting edifice was as solid as the skills of science and detection
could make it; the conclusions could not be gainsaid. There never
was any question of Dobkin's guilt, and his protestations of
innocence were futile. The defence tried to show the head
bruising might have been a result of a fall by Mrs Dobkin after
a bomb blast, and that, as a last surmise, the horn fracture was
caused by a "tiny bomb splinter passing into the neck from the
rear and getting into the throat". Dr Simpson thought this
possible, but accepted it only as a remote chance. Granting such
an event, there still remained the ancillary medical evidence,
damning in itself.

For some there was the thought that perhaps, for all his
brutality, Dobkin might not have premeditated his crime, that
it was the result of overwhelming rage. Though he did what he
did to get rid of the body, and he was a large man and she a small
woman, it still might have been manslaughter. Yet, as he
admitted nothing and flatly denied everything, the verdict of
guilty was reached by the jury after only twenty minutes of
consideration. It was by no means unexpected except, it would
seem, by Dobkin. His features changed from white to red and
back again, and he made a brief, rambling protest signifying
nothing.

For Dr Keith Simpson, whose medical work had made the case
into a modern classic,* there was to be one more meeting with
Harry Dobkin.

It was on a foggy morning at Wandsworth Prison when, with
the coroner and police officials, he made the customary post-
mortem always held on the body of a hanged person. It is said that
Dobkin looked peaceful.

What Dr Simpson thought at the completion of this full circle

---

* The case has come to be quoted and written of in the standard
textbooks on medico-legal subjects, as a classic example of the rewards
of patient application of simple principles in identity reconstruction –
comparing with, even exceeding in detail, the cases of Dr Parkman and
Dr Ruxton. It happened also that it contained enough colour to achieve a
place in the literature of crime detection.

cannot be guessed, but at least he had the knowledge given to few men that his own reconstruction from poor fragments of a dead and dismembered woman had given her back an identity, with the result her murderer was caught and hanged, a just and rightful conclusion with which no fair man can possibly quarrel.

THE JIGSAW MURDER CASE

(Dr Buck Ruxton, UK 1935)

Jonathan Goodman

The problem facing investigators in the gruesome Ruxton case was how to identify the human remains which had been wrapped in a newspaper like so much butcher's offal and thrown into a Scottish stream. Two heads were found, but the killer had been at pains to mutilate all the recognizable features: in one, the eyes had been removed, in the other, not just the eyes but the nose, lips and ears. The police believed they knew the identity of the two victims, and brought in two experts to help them prove it. Their brief, unprecedented in medico-legal history at the time, was to show conclusively that the remains were those of two women who had gone missing from home 100 miles away in Lancaster. The great forensic achievement was to show the astonished jury at Ruxton's trial life-sized photographs of the women in life and pictures of the skulls found in Scotland. Superimposed one on top of the other, they fitted exactly. The tale is told by Britain's leading crime historian, Jonathan Goodman (b.1931). After a successful career in theatre and television production, in 1969 he published his classic re-examination of the Wallace murder case, the first of a series of true-crime books which established him as the pre-eminent investigator of past crimes. He has also written crime novels, verse, plays, television scripts, short stories and articles. Jonathan Goodman has most recently written and presented the Discovery Channel's series on historical crime, Tales from the Black Museum.

If you are old enough to remember the first croonings of a romantic song, *Red Sails in the Sunset* – which, had there been such a thing as a pop chart in the mid-1930s, would have been top of it for a good many weeks – you may also recall an illicit version of the lyric which went like this:

Red stains on the carpet,
Red stains on your knife,
Oh, Dr Buck Ruxton, you cut up your wife;
The nursemaid, she saw you, and threatened to tell—
So, Dr Buck Ruxton, you killed her as well.

The fact that this anonymous rhyme was recited and sung on innumerable occasions gives an idea of the interest and excitement caused by a double murder in a small northern county town.

So far as public awareness is concerned, the case began on the bright but chilly afternoon of Sunday, 29 September 1935, when Susan Johnson, a young Edinburgh woman holidaying with her brother at Moffatt, a picturesque village thirty-five or so miles across the Scottish border from Carlisle, took a stroll to the bridge over Gardenholme Linn, a stream running into the River Annan.

Glancing over the rough stone parapet, she saw . . .

No, it couldn't possibly be.

She looked again. Her heart was thumping by now.

The second look convinced her that she was staring at a human arm, protruding from some wrapping at the side of the ravine.

Susan Johnson rushed back to the hotel. When she told her brother Alfred why she was in such a state, he asked the landlord to give her some medicinal whisky, then raced to the bridge. Clambering down the heather-strewn embankment, he saw not only an arm just above the waterline, some ten yards from the bridge, but an oddly-shaped bundle wrapped in bed-sheeting and newspaper.

He timorously pulled apart the wrapping and saw that the parcel contained chunks of flesh and bone.

Deciding that he had seen enough – more than enough – Alfred went in search of the village policeman and told him how the beauty of Gardenholme Linn had been marred.

After confirming that this was no false alarm, Constable James Fairweather telephoned the headquarters of the Dumfriesshire Constabulary, then went back to the bridge. And waited.

Not for long. Dumfries is no more than twenty miles from Moffatt, and Sergeant Robert Sloan rarely needed to slow down on the gently curving road that Sunday afternoon.

One wonders what went through his mind as he drove. Did he perhaps think about the Brighton Trunk crimes that had caused such a stir the year before? Did he fear that something similar – parcelled remains rather than bodies as luggage – would create as much work, as many problems, for himself and his colleagues?

He parked near the bridge, and had a few words with Constable Fairweather and Alfred Johnson; then treading carefully so as not to disturb the ground, he lowered himself down the side of the gully.

Within a few minutes, he had observed four parcels. After an hour, he had carefully parted the paper and sheeting and made a rough inventory of the respective contents, which included parts of legs, hands (with the tips of fingers and thumbs lopped off), thigh-bones, miscellaneous pieces of flesh, the chest portion of a human trunk, and two heads, hideously mutilated so as to be unrecognizable.

By the time Sloan had completed his notes and marked the positions of the parcels, other policemen had arrived from Dumfries. It was starting to get dark. Constable Fairweather unlocked the diminutive mortuary in Moffatt Cemetery, and the parcels were transported there.

During the next few days, forensic experts from Edinburgh and Glasgow visited the mortuary and made preliminary examinations of the decomposing, maggoty remains. One of the experts was John Glaister, who had been appointed Professor of Forensic Medicine at the University of Glasgow four years before, following the retirement of his famous father.

Then the "bits and pieces," as John Glaister referred to the remains, were taken to the anatomy department at Edinburgh University. Between the time of their arrival there and 4 November, they were augmented by the contents of other parcels found by the police and the public close to Gardenholme Linn and along the River Annan. The parcel farthest removed from those that had started the investigation was discovered at Johnson Bridge, on the main Edinburgh–Carlisle road, nine miles from Moffatt.

The malformed, "Cyclops" eye of an animal was found among the remains. It was better preserved than the human flesh and tissues, suggesting that it had been immersed in formaldehyde, perhaps by someone interested in ophthalmology.

While the pathologists, an anatomist and a dentist tried to solve the two "jigsaw puzzles", and to find distinguishing marks to assist in identifying the victims, the police made inquiries about persons reported missing before 19 September, when there had been torrential rain in the area around Moffatt, filling streams and rivers; it seemed clear that the parcels had been left behind on the banks as the level of the water had fallen.

The police had one apparently important clue. A piece of newspaper that had helped to wrap one of the packages was recognized as being part of the *Sunday Graphic* of 15 September 1935: part of a special "slip" edition of 3,700 copies, carrying a report and pictures of the crowning of the Morecambe Carnival Queen, that had been distributed only around Morecambe and the nearby county town of Lancaster.

On the very same day that the Chief Constable of Dumfries got in touch with the Lancaster police, he happened to notice a report in the *Glasgow Daily Record*. Briefly tucked away on an inside page, the report referred to the disappearance, in mid-September, of Mary Jane Rogerson, the twenty-year-old nursemaid to the children of an Indian doctor named Buck Ruxton, who ministered to the sick at his home at 2 Dalton Square, Lancaster, 105 miles south of the bridge over Gardenholme Linn.

Struck by the Lancasterian coincidence, the Chief Constable initiated inquiries in that town. He soon learned that the disappearance of Mary Rogerson had been notified to the local police – also that there was a rumour that Dr Ruxton's wife had left him at about the time the nursemaid was last seen.

A detective was sent to get a detailed description of the missing girl from her stepmother, who lived in Morecambe, and as a result of the visit two further pieces of information came to light.

The human remains found at and near Moffatt had been wrapped mainly in newspaper and bed-linen – but a blouse and a child's romper suit had also been used. When the blouse was shown to Mrs Rogerson, she at once recognized it, saying that she had bought it at a jumble sale and given it to Mary just before Christmas 1934; she had no doubt that it was the same blouse, for she had sewn a patch under one of the arms.

Mrs Rogerson told the police that, during the summer, her stepdaughter and two of the Ruxtons' three children had spent a fortnight in a guesthouse at Grange-over-Sands, and that the landlady had given Mary some secondhand clothes.

A detective visited the landlady, Mrs Edith Holme, who instantly identified the romper suit as one of the things she had given the nursemaid: her own child had outgrown the suit; before parting with it, she had put new elastic in the waistband, tying the ends in a knot of her invention.

So far, the control and conduct of the investigation had been emphatically Scottish; but now, although the scientific work of piecing together the assortment of human remains continued in Edinburgh, overall responsibility for the case was passed to Captain Henry Vann, the Chief Constable of Lancaster.

Captain Vann and his subordinates already knew quite a lot about Dr Buck Ruxton – and in a few days, without having to put themselves out to any great extent, they learned much more.

When Ruxton was born in Bombay, in 1899, he was called Bukhtar Rustomji Ratanji Hakim, or Buck Hakim for short, but some thirty years later he anglicised his name by deed poll.

He was touchy about being referred to simply as an Indian, and would insist on the more specific designation of Parsee, pointing out that he was a descendant of the Zoroastrians who migrated from Persia to India in the eighth century.

He held three medical degrees, two from the University of Bombay and one (MB) from the University of London.

After gaining the first of those degrees, he served for about three years in the Indian Medical Corps and then travelled to Britain, where he lived first of all in London, working as a locum while pursuing his studies, and then in Edinburgh, preparing for the examinations for Fellowship of the Royal College of Surgeons of that city.

His failure in that examination may been due, at least in part, to the fact that his dedication to his studies was diminished by his infatuation for Isabella Van Ess, a woman two years younger than himself who, following her estrangement from her Dutch husband, was working as a waitress in a restaurant in Princes Street, Edinburgh.

Sharp-nosed, wide-mouthed, and with legs that did not narrow towards the ankles, Isabella was far less lovely than her name; but still, Ruxton was smitten from the moment she first took an order from him for tea and scones.

Presumably because he decided that Isabella would consider him more dashing if she thought he was an army officer, decently reticent about his many decorations for gallantry, he led her to believe that he was Captain Hakim.

He returned to London at the beginning of 1928, and Isabella joined him soon afterwards. Though she was now divorced, and though between 1929 and 1933 she gave birth to three children, she never married Ruxton.

In 1930, Dr and "Mrs" Ruxton, with their first child, Elizabeth, moved to 2 Dalton Square, a grey-stone terrace house of three storeys and a basement that stood next to a picture palace in the centre of Lancaster. Of the four rooms on the ground floor, two each side of a hall, Ruxton used three for his general medical practice, one as a waiting room, one for consultations, the third as a surgery; the fourth room, at the back, was a kitchen.

There were two living rooms and a dining room on the first floor, and at some time since the house had been built, towards the end of the nineteenth century, a bathroom had been squeezed in as a sort of addition to the first-floor landing. There was a master bedroom and three smaller ones on the top floor.

Ruxton soon had a large panel of patients. This was partly due to an insufficiency of doctors in the town, partly because his practice was very general indeed, including even dentistry and ophthalmology, and partly because he seemed invariably affable, worthy of the locals' descriptions of him as "that nice, obliging, young foreign doctor".

But Isabella did not consider him altogether nice. As the months, the years, went by, the couple quarrelled with increasing frequency and vehemence.

Sometimes the rows were over what Ruxton called "Belle's temporary sillinesses". Sometimes the cause was jealousy: Ruxton was particularly suspicious of a friend of Isabella's, a young man called Bobby Edmondson who worked in the solicitor's department at the town hall, just across the square from the doctor's house. And sometimes there was a sexual motive for the arguments, for both Ruxton and Isabella experienced enhanced pleasure from intimacy when it was part of "making-up".

By April 1935, Isabella was either tired of Ruxton's tantrums or terrified by his bad temper. As the result of a statement she made to a detective, Ruxton was invited to the police station. When he saw his "wife" there, he (in the detective's words) "flew into a violent passion and said, 'My wife has been unfaithful. I would be justified in murdering her'."

The detective pacified Ruxton (or thought so), reassured Isabella (or believed that he had), and put the incident out of his mind – until a month or so later, when he was called to 2 Dalton Square, again to act as peace-maker.

It would have been better for Isabella – and for the young nursemaid, Mary Rogerson – if, instead of seeking help from the police, she had waited until Buck Ruxton was answering a house-call and then escaped to a place where he might not find her or could not harm her.

Following the press reports of the gruesome discoveries at Moffatt – and long before the police suspected Ruxton of murder – a good many people in Lancaster, including the doctor's several charwomen and some of his patients and neighbours, wondered whether there was a connection between what they had read in the papers and the disappearance of Mrs Ruxton and the nurse-maid.

Both before and after the mutilated remains were found, Ruxton contended on various occasions and to various people that the two women had gone to Blackpool . . . that they were taking a holiday in Scotland . . . that the nursemaid was pregnant, so Isabella might have taken her away for an abortion . . . that Isabella had gone off with a lover . . . that she had returned to London.

When early newspaper accounts stated (wrongly, as it turned out) that some of the remains found at Moffatt were of a man, Ruxton was joyful. After giving one of the charwomen a rest from her chores while he read aloud a report of the "Ravine Murder," he chortled, "So you see, Mrs Oxley, it is a man and a woman – not our two," then burst into helpless laughter at Mrs Oxley's response that she sincerely hoped not.

But within a week of that incident he was distinctly unhappy about what the papers were saying. He turned up at the police station at half-past nine on the night of Friday, 11 October, and, waving a copy of the *Daily Express* in one hand and furiously gesticulating with the other, screamed at the Chief Constable that such publicity was ruining his practice.

While Captain Vann tried to get a word in edgeways, Ruxton sat on the desk, perched his feet on a visitor's chair, and banged the back of it with his free hand.

Abruptly changing the subject – and crying now – Ruxton accused a man of being Isabella's lover, claimed that he had tapped telephone conversations between them, and implored Captain Vann to intercept the alleged lover's mail.

Then, reverting to the press, he asked the Chief Constable to issue a statement that the remains found in and around Moffatt were not those of Isabella and Mary Rogerson. Captain Vann was still uming and ahing about that when the doctor stalked out.

Uming and ahing . . .? Well, yes. If only because Ruxton's arrival had interrupted a discussion between Captain Vann and a senior detective as to whether the time was ripe to charge the doctor with double murder.

Ever since the responsibility for the investigation had been passed to Lancaster from Dumfriesshire, the Lancaster Borough Police Force had been just as busy as the scientists gathered in the anatomy department at Edinburgh University, piecing together the incomplete jigsaws of flesh and bone, and drawing conclusions from what they found – and could not find.

The police knew, among many other things, that on Saturday, 14 September, Mrs Ruxton had driven to Blackpool in the doctor's Hillman car, registration number CP 8415, to see the illuminations with her two sisters, and that she had started the return journey just before midnight. Though she was never seen alive again, the presence of the car in Lancaster the next day indicated that she had arrived home.

Some of the strongest evidence against Ruxton came from his charwomen. At half-past six on the morning of Sunday, 15 September, Mrs Agnes Oxley was getting ready to go to the doctor's house when Ruxton drove up in his car and told her that she could have the day off as "Mrs Ruxton and Mary have gone away on a holiday to Edinburgh".

That afternoon, however, the doctor visited one of his patients, Mrs Mary Hampshire, and asked if she wanted to earn seven shillings and sixpence by scrubbing his staircase. He explained that he needed her help because Isabella was in Blackpool and Mary Rogerson in Edinburgh, and he had cut his hand badly in trying to open a tin of peaches for the children's breakfast. (He certainly had a severe wound on one of his fingers, and a subsequent remark to Mrs Hampshire that he had taken his children to stay with a dentist friend in Morecambe was true.)

When Mrs Hampshire arrived at 2 Dalton Square, she found that the place was far more messy and untidy than she had expected: the carpets had been taken from the stairs, which were scattered with straw; rolled-up carpets, stair-pads and a man's suit were lying in the waiting room, and in the back yard were other carpets, clothing and towels, all heavily stained with blood and showing signs that an attempt had been made to burn them.

Mrs Hampshire, a trusting soul, accepted the doctor's explanation that the carpets had been taken up because the house was to be decorated, and seems to have assumed that, though Ruxton did not look anaemic, the blood saturating the things in the yard had flowed from the cut on his finger.

She did not ask him to explain the straw protruding from beneath the doors to two of the bedrooms – or why those doors were locked and the keys removed.

Mrs Hampshire started tidying up, and, when her husband

came to the house a few hours later, got him to lend a hand. Ruxton gave the couple a load of soiled carpets and clothing, but presumably Mrs Hampshire was paid more than the promised seven shillings and sixpence for her labours, not only on the Sunday but on subsequent days, on some of which she was assisted by the doctor's regular chars.

The police had much more evidence against Ruxton, including the testimony of a cyclist who on Tuesday, 17 September, had been knocked over by the doctor's car on a road leading to Moffatt; Ruxton had not stopped but was caught by a policeman, who noted that he was as jumpy as a flea.

But all this evidence might be insufficient to convict Buck Ruxton if the scientists in Edinburgh were unable to establish that the bits and pieces of flesh and bone on their laboratory tables were the remains of Isabella Ruxton and Mary Rogerson.

It was vital that the separated, mutilated remains found in Dumfriesshire be identified as those of the doctor's common-law wife and his children's nursemaid. Admittedly, by the time of the Ruxton case there can have been few judges who wholly accepted Lord Halsbury's contention that "in the absence of evidence (that a body or part of a body has been found, which is proved to be that of the person alleged to have been killed) there is no onus upon the prisoner to account for the disappearance or non-production of the person."

Only the year before, a man named Davidson had been convicted of the murder of his small son though no body had been found, the presumption being that the body was consumed in a fire on a garbage tip.

But a clever defence lawyer might confuse less clever members of a jury about the meaning of "reasonable doubt" by speaking of ancient cases in which men had been hanged for the murder of people who had afterwards, like Mark Twain, complained of reports of their demise, and use any uncertainty concerning the fact of death to suggest uncertainty about the act of murder.

The team of experts at Edinburgh University not only used accepted methods but invented new techniques as they sorted out which of the remains belonged to one body, which to the other –

as they then searched for clues that might, singly or in relation to others, give more reality to the incomplete bodies than the original designations of "No 1" and "No 2" – as they sought indications of the cause, or causes of death.

Probably for the first time, an anatomist had been brought into a murder investigation. This was James Couper Brash, professor of anatomy at the University of Edinburgh – a city that, a hundred or so years before, had become associated, through the activities of Burke and Hare, with the unlawful aspects of the science.

Brash was able to get an exact fit between some of the dismembered remains and, using anatomical formulae and X-rays, classified other parts as belonging to one body or the other.

After weeks of work, two partially reconstructed bodies lay side by side on tables in the laboratory. "No 1" was less complete than "No 2", but Brash had gauged the living stature of the bodies as, respectively, five feet and five feet and three inches.

There was ample evidence that both bodies were female. If – a very large "if" at this stage – they were of the women from 2 Dalton Square Lancaster, then "No 1" was Mary Rogerson and "No 2" was Mrs Ruxton.

With help from an odontologist, Arthur Hutchinson, Brash estimated the age of "No 1" as 20 (as was the nursemaid) and that of "No 2" as being between 35 and 45 (Isabella Ruxton was 34).

Paradoxically, many of the mutilations of the remains assisted the pathologists in their search for evidence. The manner of dismemberment (without the use of a saw and with only slight damage to the separated parts), together with the fact that components that might have indicated cause of death had been removed, showed that the criminal was skilled in the use of surgical knives and that he had anatomical and medical knowledge.

The criminal had removed from both heads the eyes, ears, lips and nose – in all of which signs of asphyxia might be found – but so far as body "No 2" was concerned, there remained several indications that death was due to asphyxia by throttling.

The most iterated example of "negative evidence" comes from fiction – the dog that, as Sherlock Holmes noted, did not bark in the night. For a real-life example, it would be hard to better what the experts in the Ruxton investigation noted as being absent from the remains.

Virtually from the start, John Glaister and his colleagues supposed that the reason for many of the mutilations was to make identification more difficult, but it was not until the scientists knew some of the distinguishing features of the two missing women that they began to suspect answers to specific questions.

Perhaps the eyes of body "No 1" had been taken out because Mary Rogerson had a cast in one eye. Had the skin been removed from the upper part of the right forearm because Mary had a conspicuous birthmark there? Were the soft tissues shaved from the right thumb because the nursemaid had a scar there?

And had the nose of body "No 2" been cut off, and the teeth been extracted, because those were prominent features of Mrs Ruxton? Had the soft tissues of the legs been removed because Isabella's legs were the same thickness from the knees to the ankles? Were the toes lopped off because Isabella's were "humped"?

So many of the sites of the excisions and mutilations corresponded with those of distinguishing features of the missing women that there seemed only one answer. Added to the evidence already gathered, the "negative evidence" virtually proved that the bodies were those of Isabella Ruxton and Mary Rogerson.

But to make assurance double sure, James Brash did something that, so far as is known, had never been attempted in a criminal investigation. After obtaining photographs of the missing women, he arranged for the head and shoulders in each to be enlarged to life-size. He took immense care to ensure that the size of the enlargements was correct; for instance, a piece of jewellery worn by Mrs Ruxton in one of the photographs was located and measured to the nearest millimetre, so that the size could be used to establish the measurements of her head and features. The enlarged photographs were then superimposed on photographs, taken to the exact size, of the decapitated heads in the laboratory. The resulting "double exposures" showed a remarkable correspondence.

On Saturday, 12 October, after the evidence assembled by the Scottish scientists had been added to that gathered by the police, Chief Constable Vann invited Buck Ruxton to his office.

The doctor arrived at 9.30 in the evening and spent the next ten hours answering questions. Then he was charged with the murder of Mary Rogerson.

He looked flabbergasted. "Most emphatically not," he spluttered. "Of course not. The farthest thing from my mind. What motive and why? What are you talking about?"

Following Ruxton's arrest (on 5 November he was further charged with the murder of Isabella), the investigators searched the house in Dalton Square for more indications of his guilt.

They found a good many, of which the most important, perhaps, was a sheet that had precisely the same peculiar fault in the selvedge as did pieces of a sheet that had been used as wrapping for the hideous bundles found at Moffatt.

By the start of the new year, the investigators believed that the case against Buck Ruxton was complete, watertight.

But then they learned something that worried them greatly: the doctor was to be defended at the trial by the velvet-voiced Norman Birkett, who was thought of by some people as "the courtroom magician", by others as "the murderer's best friend".

If anyone could persuade the jury in the Ruxton case to return a nonsensical verdict, it was Birkett.

The trial started on Monday, 2 March 1936, at the old Manchester Assize Court in Great Ducie Street, with Mr Justice Singleton, a stickler for the niceties of courtroom behaviour, presiding.

J. C. Jackson, one of the best-known silks on the Northern circuit, led for the Crown, assisted by two barristers who would rise to high positions in government: one, a Socialist, was Hartley Shawcross, and the other, a Tory, inspired the couplet:

> The closest thing to death in life
> Is David Patrick Maxwell Fyfe.

Buck Ruxton's defender, the tall, bespectacled Norman Birkett, made few notes during the opening speech for the prosecution;

but right from the start, Ruxton, sitting in the dock behind Birkett, scribbled messages to his counsel.

According to Mr Jackson's view of what had happened in the house in Dalton Square, Lancaster, after Mrs Ruxton's trip to see the Blackpool illuminations: "When she went up to bed, a violent quarrel took place; Ruxton strangled his wife, and Mary Rogerson caught him in the act and had to die also."

There was, of course, much more to Mr Jackson's speech than that; he dealt with every aspect of the case, occasionally in greater detail than some observers thought necessary, starting with the discovery of the human remains at Moffatt and concluding with the arrest of the Indian doctor.

The speech went on till late in the afternoon, leaving only enough time for four prosecution witnesses to be called that day. Though the evidence of those witnesses was formal – to do with plans, photographs and the like – Norman Birkett cross-examined each of them in some depth.

And during the following seven days of the trial, hardly any of the prosecution witnesses – over a hundred of them – left the court without having been questioned by Birkett. At times, when there was a flurry of requests by counsel for the production of exhibits, the well of the court looked like an untidy jumble sale, with bottles, jewellery, books and kitchenware scattered over piles of clothing, carpets and bed-linen.

Mrs Mary Hampshire, one of the several women who had laboured to make the doctor's house presentable after the disappearance of Mrs Ruxton and the nursemaid, fainted in the witness box. Perhaps the sight of some bloodstained carpets, given to her by the generous doctor but taken from her by the police and now exhibits, made her feel queasy. As she was being carried from the court, the doctor peered from the dock at his former patient and gave his professional opinion that she would be all right. When she returned, he made a what-did-I-tell-you? gesture, then started scribbling again.

The last of the Crown's witnesses were the Scottish scientists who had made medico-legal history by their reconstruction and scrutiny of the bodies. They had done their work so thoroughly that Birkett scored few, and then only minor, successes in cross-examination.

Before the last of the scientists was called, Birkett wrote a memorandum for Ruxton's solicitor to show his client. It ended:

"In my clear and very strong view, if Dr Ruxton desires to give evidence, we should confine our evidence to him, and exercise our right of the last word to the jury . . . Any other course, in my view, would be absolutely fatal."

Ruxton agreed, and on the morning of the eighth day of the trial was escorted from the dock to be the sole witness in his own defence.

His solicitor had warned him that he must remain calm, listen carefully to each question, and restrict his answers to what had been asked, but the flashily handsome doctor soon forgot – or, believing that he knew best, ignored – the advice.

After asking a few "tuning-up" questions, Birkett inquired about Ruxton's relations with Isabella – and was made most unhappy by the reply: "If I may be permitted to put it in appropriate English, I can honestly say we were the kind of people who could not live with each other and could not live without each other."

Not finished yet, Ruxton said something that his counsel didn't understand.

"You have added something else," Birkett muttered irritably.

"Forgive me the interruption," said Ruxton, "but I just used the French proverb, 'Who loves most chastises most.' My mentality thinks in French, and I have to translate into English everything you are asking me."

No doubt feeling that his task was hard enough without the imposition of a language barrier, Birkett from now on tried to leap in with a question as soon as Ruxton had delivered the first sentence of his answer to the previous one.

But Birkett was rarely fast enough, and eventually snapped, "Perhaps you will just deal only with the questions I put to you."

No use: the words continued to tumble out, and every so often Ruxton burst into tears.

His answers to two successive questions are often quoted to exemplify how witnesses should not respond.

Birkett asked, "It is suggested here by the Crown that on the morning of the Sunday after your wife had come back, you killed her?"

"That is an absolute and deliberate and fantastic story," the doctor screamed, waving his arms about. "You might just as well say the sun was rising in the west and setting in the east."

Next question: "It is suggested also by the Crown that, upon that morning, you killed Mary Rogerson?"

"That is absolute bunkum, with a capital B, if I may say it. Why should I kill my poor Mary?"

It may be that the jury never made up their minds about that – or about the motive for Isabella's murder – but after another couple of days, which included the cross-examination of Ruxton, the closing speeches, and the judge's summing-up, the jury returned a verdict of Guilty.

Asked if he had anything to say why sentence of death should not be passed, Ruxton raised his right hand, the palm towards the judge, in what could have been a salute or a blessing, and uttered some flowery but irrelevant remarks. He made the same gesture as the judge spoke the final words of the death sentence, then bowed before being escorted from the dock.

Six weeks later, after the doctor's appeal was dismissed, something rather odd happened. In towns from one end of the country to the other, masses of people, few of them certifiably insane, signed petitions for a reprieve; in Lancaster alone, there were six thousand signatories.

But the Home Secretary had the good sense to ignore the petitions, and Ruxton was hanged at Strangeways Prison, Manchester, on the fine morning of Tuesday, 12 May.

The following Sunday, anyone who had signed a petition and was also a reader of the *News of the World* should have been a trifle embarrassed. There on the front page was a facsimile of a confession to the two murders that the good doctor had written the day after he was arrested.

A CASE OF "HIDEOUS FEROCITY"

(Peter Griffiths, UK 1948)

Norman Lucas

Peter Griffiths, the killer of little June Devaney, was caught by his fingerprints. Griffiths had crept into a hospital ward in Blackburn where the child was sleeping and taken her from her cot. The child's body was found in the hospital grounds. She had been brutally raped. The murderer's fingerprints were found on a bottle by the child's cot. Three days after the killing, the baffled police took an unprecedented step. They decided to fingerprint the entire male population of Blackburn. Every one of the town's 35,000 homes was visited, and every man and boy aged sixteen or over asked for his prints. It was a long, laborious task, and early results were not encouraging. The breakthrough came after three months and more than 46,000 sets of prints. Peter Griffiths thought he'd slipped through the net because his name didn't appear on the local electoral roll. But he'd reckoned without the records of wartime ration books. After Griffiths' execution, the prints taken in the course of the inquiry were publicly burned. Norman Lucas (1920–98) was the Sunday Mirror's *chief crime reporter. He exposed the Kray mob in London's East End and broke the story of the first child's body being uncovered by Lancashire police in the Moors murders of the 1960s. Norman Lucas's experiences enabled him to write seventeen books on crime, two of which were reprinted in seven languages including Czech and Japanese.*

On the night of 14–15 May 1948, little June Anne Devaney was sleeping soundly in her cot in the babies' ward of Queen's Park Hospital, Blackburn, Lancashire. She had been suffering from pneumonia, but after ten days in hospital had been pronounced well enough to return to her parents, Mr and Mrs Albert Devaney, who lived in Princess Street, in the Waterfall district of the town.

It had been arranged that her aunt, Mrs Ann Whalley, would collect her the following day because Mrs Devaney, in addition to two other children at home, had had a new baby – born 5 May, the day June had been taken to hospital.

June, a big girl for her age – three years and eleven months although she looked about six years old – was very bright and intelligent. That evening she had been chattering happily to the nurses, and to her new black doll, about going home to Mummy and Daddy and seeing the new baby.

She was the eldest of the six children in the ward and the only one who could talk.

At 11.30 that night Nurse Gwendoline Humphreys took over duty in the babies' ward and the adjoining toddlers' ward, in which there were several more older children. She looked round both wards and the sun room and a side room, then went into the kitchen to start preparations for the children's breakfast. While she was seeing to the porridge she heard a child crying and found it was Michael Tattersall, a baby in the next bed to June Devaney. In her rubber-soled shoes she tiptoed to Michael's side and remained with him for about twenty minutes. She noticed that little June was fast asleep, and returned to the kitchen. Just before 12.30 she thought she heard a girl's voice from the direction of the porch door and went to investigate. She looked out into the moonlit grounds but could not see anyone, then a little girl in the toddlers' ward began to cry and she spent about fifteen minutes with her.

At 1.15 a.m. Nurse Humphreys returned to the babies' ward and immediately noticed that June Devaney's cot was empty. She looked around the ward and in the toilet, but there was no sign of the child. The nurse also noticed that a Winchester bottle of sterile water, which had been on a trolley in the ward, was lying beneath June's cot. Then, to her horror, she saw what looked like the prints of large bare feet running the whole length of the highly polished ward floor and more footprints beside June's cot. Nurse Humphreys raised the alarm and the police were called.

June's father, a thirty-three-year-old foundry worker, joined in a search of the hospital and grounds, and he was with the police when at 3.15 a.m. they found the body of his little girl. She was lying in the grass near a stone wall encircling the hospital grounds and it was plain that she had been raped and battered to death.

Within an hour of their gruesome discovery the local police had called in the county police and the county police sought the aid of Scotland Yard, so that by noon of the day of the murder the Chief Constable of Blackburn, Mr C. G. Looms, was conferring with Detective Chief Inspector Robert McCartney, of the Lancashire Constabulary, and Detective Superintendent Jack ("Charlie Artful") Capstick, of the Yard's Murder Squad.

Only the previous evening Capstick had arrived back in London after two months of intensive inquiries into the murder of Jack Quentin Smith, an eleven-year-old schoolboy who had been found stabbed and battered to death in Farnworth – barely thirteen miles from Blackburn. The police had a description of his killer – thin, tall and youngish, with deep-set eyes and a pimply face – given by another boy, David Lee, who had been attacked at the same time but had managed to escape. All possible leads to the boy's killer had proved abortive and Capstick returned to London for a conference at the Yard.

He was more than usually concerned at the failure to capture little Jack Smith's murderer because four years earlier a six-year-old girl, Sheila Fox, had disappeared on her way home from school in Farnworth, and within less than two years another child in the same town – nine-year-old Patricia McKeon – had been attacked near her home.

Not unnaturally, parents in that area of Lancashire were beginning to be really frightened and the murder of baby June added to the rapidly growing rumours that a "moon maniac" was at large.

It was four o'clock in the morning of 15 May when Jack Capstick, after only an hour or two in bed, was woken by the phone and told by Chief Constable Looms about the murder of June Devaney. By 6.20 a.m. Capstick and the late Detective Sergeant John Stoneham were on their way back to Lancashire, arriving in Blackburn by lunchtime.

In the meantime Detective Inspector Colin Campbell, chief of the Lancashire County Constabulary Fingerprint Bureau, had found an enormous number of confused fingerprints on the Winchester bottle which had been found under June's bed, and among them were seemingly fresh thumb, index finger and palm prints. The footprints on the ward floor were photographed and were shown to have been made not by naked feet, but by large feet enclosed in socks. The pattern of the weave was clearly revealed and a few tiny fibres of wool from the socks were found adhering to the wax polish on the floor.

The prints on the bottle showed that the killer had big hands; those on the floor indicated large feet; the fact that there were no hand prints on June's cot meant that the child had probably been removed without the side of the cot being lowered – in other words the police had a picture of a killer who was tall enough to have leaned over the rail and lifted her out of her bed. They knew they were looking for a man with big hands and feet who was probably familiar with the layout of the hospital building and grounds.

Everyone who might legitimately have handled the Winchester bottle was fingerprinted – nurses, doctors, relief staff, patients' visitors, ambulance drivers, electricians who had worked in the ward, and tradesmen delivering goods. In three days 642 sets of prints were taken from people who might have handled the bottle in the preceding two years. This check eliminated many prints but still left the fresh prints believed to have been made by the killer.

Because the police were convinced that he was a local man familiar with the hospital routine, the finger-printing was extended to all men who had been patients in the last two years, all male visitors to the hospital, ex-members of the staff, husbands and boyfriends of nurses – bringing the total prints to more than 2,000. But still the vital prints remained unidentified.

Then Detective Superintendent Capstick put forward an idea

which was at first regarded as impractical and impossible to
implement – to fingerprint every male over the age of fourteen
in the whole town of Blackburn. There had never been a mass
fingerprinting of a town's population before and it was doubted if
the people would co-operate. The Mayor gave the lead by
volunteering to be first and the response of the town was very
wholehearted. An undertaking was given that all fingerprints
obtained in this great check-up would be destroyed when their
purpose had been served, and the 50,000 prints were in fact
ceremonially destroyed at a later date.

Every one of the 35,000 houses in the borough was visited, but
the check had necessarily to go further afield because some men
who had been in Blackburn on the night of the murder had
moved. Some had been visitors, others seamen who had rejoined
their ships or members of the armed forces who had returned to
their units. Eventually prints were forwarded to Blackburn from
places as far afield as South America, Sweden, Hong Kong,
South Africa and Canada.

But still, none matched the vital prints on the Winchester
bottle.

In the meantime the usual red herrings had been drawn across
the path of detection. Two parties of nurses returning to the
hospital on the night of the murder said they had been accosted
by a man near the gates and had experienced difficulty in evading
him while other nurses reported seeing a "Peeping Tom" peering
into a bedroom window of the nurses' home. When this man was
traced he was found to be the husband of a woman in the
maternity ward. He was quickly eliminated from the inquiry.

A youth then came forward and confessed to the murder, and
was found to be the same lad who had confessed to the murder of
Jack Quentin Smith a few weeks previously. It was proved
conclusively that he could have had nothing to do with either
of the killings.

At this point in the inquiry the police had their first lucky
break.

Food was still rationed in that post-war year of 1948 and in
August a new issue of books was due. Inspector Bill Barton, of the
Blackburn police, had the bright idea of checking the names on

the enormous pile of fingerprints with the list of new ration books to be issued – and it was found that 200 men and youths had either deliberately or involuntarily slipped through the net.

So the final search began. Among the missing 200 was a twenty-two-year-old ex-Guardsman named Peter Griffiths living in Birley Street, Blackburn, who was seen by Police Constable Joseph Calvert on 11 August. Griffiths, then working as a flour mill packer, had somehow evaded the fingerprinting team when they had called at his house during the first big check, but raised no objection to having his prints taken when the second call was made.

The prints were sent for examination by the experts – and were found to match exactly those on the Winchester bottle.

At nine-thirty in the evening of 13 August Jack Capstick and Inspector Barton stopped Griffiths as he left 31 Birley Street, where he lived with his father Peter Griffiths senior, his mother, Mrs Elizabeth Griffiths, and his half-brother, James Brennan.

Told that he was to be arrested for the murder of June Devaney, he said: "What is it to do with me? I have never been near the place." Later he asked: "Is it my fingerprints why you came to see me?" He was told that it was.

He then said, "Well if they are my fingerprints on the bottle, I will tell you all about it". He made a statement in which he said that on the night of the murder he intended to spend a quiet evening on his own.

He had five pints of bitter at the Dun Horse public house, then went on to Yates Wine Lodge where he had two glasses of Guinness and two double rums. He returned to the Dun Horse and had about six more pints of bitter, leaving at closing time. In Jubilee Street a man in a car asked him if he would like a "spin" and took him to the front of Queen's Park Hospital.

"The next thing I remember was being outside the ward where there was some children," he said. "I left my shoes outside a door . . . it opened to my touch and I went in. I heard a nurse humming and banging things . . . so I came out again and waited a few minutes. Then I went back in again. I picked up a biggish bottle off a shelf . . . I overbalanced and fell against a bed. I remember a child woke up and started to cry and I hushed her. I picked the girl up out of the cot and took her outside. She put her arms round my neck and I walked with her down the hospital field. I put her down on the grass. She started crying again and I tried to stop her, but she wouldn't do like . . . I just lost my temper and you know what happened. I banged her head against the wall. I then went back to the veranda outside the ward and put my shoes on. I went back to where the child was, I just glanced at her but did not go right up to her but went straight on down the field."

Griffiths added that when he got home he slept on a couch downstairs. The following day he had his breakfast, went for a walk and then to a cinema and later returned home to tea.

"I looked at the papers and read about the murder," he said. "It didn't shake me so I just carried on normally after that. That is all I can say and I'm sorry for both parents' sake and I hope I get what I deserve."

On the day following Griffiths' arrest the police recovered from a local pawnbroker the suit the accused man had worn on the night of the murder. Bloodstains on the jacket and trousers were found to be of Group "A" – the same as the dead child's blood group – and fibres from the suit matched some found on her nightdress and body. Tests on a pair of Griffiths' socks showed that the colour, method of weave and number of twists to the inch tallied with the socks worn by the murderer as he walked through the ward. His footprints, too, matched those on the waxed floor.

A Miss Rene Edge told the police that on Sunday, 16 May – the day after the murder – she had gone for a walk with Griffiths and he had shown her a bloodstained Soldiers' Song Book. She asked how the blood had got there and he told her he cut his hand during a fight when he was in the Army.

Griffiths had been "walking out" with Miss Edge, a quiet, religious girl, for some time, but she did not approve of his drinking and in April that year had told him that their friendship must end. Four days before the murder she told him quite definitely that she would not change her mind that there could be no question of a marriage.

Griffiths' familiarity with the hospital buildings and grounds was also established when it was discovered that he had spent two years there as a patient between the ages of ten and twelve. His hospital record showed that he was suffering at that time from incontinence of urine.

When Griffiths stood before Mr Justice Oliver and a jury at Lancaster Assizes on 15 October 1948, there was really only one issue to be decided – not whether he killed June Devaney but whether or not he was sane at the time.

Mr W. Gorman, KC, and Mr D. Brabin appeared for the Crown and Griffiths was defended by Mr Basil Nield, KC and Mr J. di V. Nahum.

Dr Gilbert Bailey, police surgeon for Blackburn, giving evidence for the prosecution, described the child's injuries and was cross-examined by Mr Nield.

"In the course of your thirty-four years in medical practice you have from time to time dealt with cases of violent death?" – "Yes, many."

"In your experience have you ever seen any injuries more consistent than those in this case with the outburst of a lunatic?" – "I certainly consider the man who did this act must have been in a state of maniacal frenzy."

"Does that mean in a condition of complete ferocity?" asked Mr Justice Oliver. Dr Bailey replied: "Yes".

The judge: "A man is not necessarily mad because he acts in a ferocious manner?" – "Not at all."

"All you can say is that this was done by someone acting in a ferocious manner?" – "At that time."

Further questioned by Mr Nield, Dr Bailey said that the man who had murdered the child would be, in normal life, quite a normal man, but would have sudden outbursts of frenzy or mania. He had the impression that the man might be a schizophrenic. The motive in this case was an uncontrollable sexual impulse.

Mr Justice Oliver commented: "There was a sexual motive here; whether sane or insane, the jury will decide".

Mr Gorman, further examining Dr Bailey: "You have been asked a number of theoretical considerations in this case; is it necessary before you can arrive at a proper view as to the condition of this man that you should have him for some time under observation?" – "Yes. In this particular case, I would like to say now that I have not had this man under observation.

"I am not prepared to say what his true mentality is. All I am prepared to say is that the act of murder and rape on this child could have been the act of a man with a 'split' mind."

Opening the case for the defence, Mr Nield said it was his submission that Griffiths, at the time of the murder, was mad and he added: "I say to you frankly at this early stage that I cannot ask for this man's liberty, but I do ask for his life."

There were, he said, six categories of evidence which would help the jury to decide whether Griffiths was sane or insane.

Firstly, there was his family history. In 1918, for a period of about nine months, his father had been in a mental hospital suffering from what was described at the time as "delusional insanity" – a condition which in the more technical term of modern times was described as "paranoid schizophrenia".

Secondly, Peter Griffiths' own personal history had to be considered. When he was six years old he fell from a milk-float upon his head, but a doctor was not called. Later he spent two years in hospital suffering from something about which there was little real information – incontinence of urine. Might there not have been some neurotic foundation for that long stay in hospital?

"Even at the age of seventeen this young man was childish in his habits," continued Mr Nield. "He would shut himself up in a room and play with corks, pretending they were trains. So noticeable was this that his mother rebuked him and said he was going mental. Thereafter there is a long history of solitary habits, always alone, depressed, and a typical picture of an incipient schizophrenic who might at any time fall under the blow of this disease in which, in a moment of maniacal frenzy, this sort of hideous happening can occur."

Griffiths had left job after job, never remaining for more than a short time; as a boy he was unstable and stole things; his Army category was bad or indifferent and he deserted twice.

The third category of evidence, said Mr Nield, related to

events immediately preceding the act – and one of these was the meeting with Miss Rene Edge, whom the young man wished to marry, when she told him for the second time that she was not prepared to go on with the friendship.

"You may have in the case of a schizophrenic a precipitating factor which may produce one of these frenzies," he added, "and an unhappy love affair is typical of such a disturbance."

It was also quite plain that the accused had had a great deal too much to drink on 14 May, and medical testimony was that excessive alcohol might induce the mental disturbance.

The fourth consideration related to the act itself. It was recognized that an act of gross and hideous ferocity might well be an indication of mental disorder. "Can you think of a case of more hideous ferocity than this?"

The events immediately after the act were to be considered in the fifth category.

"This man went away from that hospital, slept that night as if nothing had happened, and then went out with this young lady," continued counsel. "There was no effort to wash away any stains from his suit and there was that unnatural calm which goes with one who has had a mental breakdown of the nature I have suggested."

The sixth category of evidence was that of the medical experts, said Mr Nield, who then called Dr Alistair Grant, of Whittingham Mental Hospital and Dr Geoffrey Talbot, Medical Superintendent of Prestwich Hospital.

Dr Grant said that he had twice examined Griffiths and had formed the opinion that he was suffering from schizophrenia. One of his reasons for that belief was the question of heredity. The man's father had suffered from what was probably paranoid schizophrenia and in sixty per cent of schizophrenics heredity was given as a cause.

In reply to questions put by Mr Nield, Dr Grant said that solitary habits and childish behaviour were the sort of symptoms found in early schizophrenia. Constant changing of jobs was very typical. An unhappy or frustrated love affair could precipitate the condition and it was a well-known fact that schizophrenics reacted badly to alcohol.

Cross-examined by Mr Gorman about the statement Griffiths made after his arrest, Dr Grant said the man might not have recalled raping the child because he did not mention it.

Mr Justice Oliver: "Why should he forget that if he remembered every other detail?"

Dr Grant: "In a case of ordinary schizophrenia, I would be rather surprised to find that a man had remembered so much and yet forgotten such an important thing, but that is the sort of partial amnesia you would get in a drunk."

Mr Gorman: "Is it not quite clear that the whole of that statement, with its details, with its lies, with its concealments, is the statement of an active mind appreciating what was being done at the time?" – "Most of the points you have made I am in complete agreement with, but I do differ about the material time, the time when he murdered the child."

"Will you tell me what there is in this statement that enables you to take a portion of time and say that within that portion of time this man was in this mental state?" – "I am judging by my direct experience in these cases, and I again repeat that, in my opinion, it is quite possible for a man, having schizophrenia, to have a maniacal attack lasting a short time and to recover himself fairly quickly afterwards."

Mr Justice Oliver: "I want to ask you one thing. Do you regard the raping of even small children as evidence of insanity?" – "No."

"Is there anything mad in what he did – on the part of a man who had been brutal enough to ravish her – is there anything mad in beating her brains out to stop her screaming?" – "I think so, for this reason, that she was a child, she would have no evidence against him, and he could have got away."

Dr Talbot gave evidence relating to the detention of Peter Griffiths senior in Prestwich Hospital and said that he was sent there by the Army as a dangerous lunatic soldier. The medical note entered on the record was a very good description of the condition now known as paranoid schizophrenia, which was known to be hereditary. Griffiths Senior had been discharged in 1919, after nine months, but that did not mean that he had been completely cured.

"My conclusion was that the type of mental illness from which he, the father, was suffering may have been regarded as hereditary and likely to appear in any or other of subsequent generations." he concluded.

The fourth medical witness, Dr Francis Brisby, Principal Medical Officer at Liverpool Prison and former Assistant Medical Officer at a Lancaster county mental hospital appeared for the prosecution. He said that from observation and examination of the accused man he had found no evidence of any disease of the mind which would prevent him from either knowing what he was doing or that what he was doing was wrong. Cross-examined by Mr Nield, he said he did not think the evidence suggested a complete picture of schizophrenia. He would expect some alteration of character, some change in the man's personality occurring before the event, some history of conduct alien to his nature.

In his lengthy and detailed summing up to the jury, Mr Justice Oliver said it would seem to him a most amazing disease when the man could be perfectly sane right up to the moment he laid the child on the ground, then a schizophrenic maniac during the time he was raping her and beating her brains out, then perfectly sane afterwards and remain sane ever since.

"It does indeed seem to be a very odd sort of disease," he said. "We are only laymen, we have not got the knowledge of the experts. I do not know whether you find it difficult to envisage a man quite sane and knowing what he is doing when taking the child out of the hospital ward and walking with it into the grounds, and then suddenly becoming bereft of his senses and raping and killing, and then getting his senses back again. I do not know whether it seems to you to be more likely, if that is really true, that the man would have a blank and would say, 'All I remember is picking the child up and taking her out, and I cannot tell you what happened until I found myself at home.' That may, at any rate, seem more consistent with the facts here, but you are the judges, not I."

The jury of nine men and three women were out only twenty-five minutes before giving their verdict of Guilty.

Passing sentence of death, Mr Justice Oliver said to Griffiths: "The jury has found you guilty of a crime of the most brutal ferocity and I entirely agree with that verdict." June Devaney's murderer was hanged in Walton Prison, Liverpool, on 19 November 1948. On the day before the execution he was interviewed by Superintendent Capstick and Detective Superintendent Lindsay, of Lancashire CID, who asked him if he had also killed Jack Quentin Smith.

Griffiths replied, "No", but Capstick remained convinced that the ex-Guardsman was the "moon maniac" of Lancashire and had been guilty of more than the one murder of which he was convicted.

THE CLOSING OF THE RING

(Ronald Bennell, 1970)

Allen Andrews

This case, the rape and murder of an innocent young girl called Linda Stewart, became a small but important milestone in the history of forensic detection. It was cleared up in less than a week, thanks to the work of a forensic dentist, John Furness. He managed to match the killer's teeth not only with bite marks on the victim's body but also with the tooth impressions found on a meat pie abandoned just before the attack, thus providing an interesting development in forensic odontology. The case is recalled by the author Allen Andrews (1913–1984).

Mrs Rhianwen (Gwen) Hughes was a widow of seventy-two, and normally an early riser. But it was Saturday morning and she thought she deserved a little lie-in, particularly after a disturbance that she had undergone the night before. So it was nine o'clock before she got up and put on the kettle for a modest breakfast in the neat semi-detached Manchester Corporation house where she lived, at 285 Kingsway, Burnage. Then she began to tidy the house. She raked the fire and put the cold ashes in newspaper before taking them out to the dustbin. Then she opened the side door on to the tarmac garden path which had been re-surfaced only the previous day and stepped out a little gingerly, hoping that the path would not be so soft and tarry that it would mark her slippers.

She turned towards the dustbin with the bundle of ashes in her hand, and stopped very short. There was something on the path ahead of her – long red hair cascading from a jumble of fabric. She was looking at the body of a woman lying with her feet towards the garden, and naked except for the clothes pulled over her head.

Mrs Hughes turned and ran towards her front gate. She saw a neighbour passing, Miss Mellor from a few houses down Kingsway. She gasped out what she had seen. Miss Mellor, very concerned, brought her back into the house. She peeped out of the back to make sure that this was true and she hurried away to find a telephone and contact the police.

The telephone message to the police was immediately relayed to the divisional duty officer and the headquarters information room. Information located the nearest patrol car to the scene and radioed for it to go instantly to 285 Kingsway to establish and maintain radio contact. The nearest CID car was then diverted to the scene. Next, the news of the discovery of the body was passed to the Head of the CID, to the operational superintendent acting as his deputy and to the appropriate divisional detective chief inspector. Finally the information room officer arranged for the murder-scene bag to be collected and taken immediately to Kingsway.

The Head of Manchester and Salford CID, Detective Chief Superintendent Charles Horan, hurried to the scene with a very small team. His area detective superintendent, Roy Hartley, after a swift radio check with the patrol in the diverted CID car, gave instructions for the pathologist to be alerted at his home in Southport. He checked that the photographer and other specialists were being summoned, and drove to Longsight Police Station where the suite of offices permanently reserved there as Murder Headquarters had been opened up.

The body had been discovered soon after 10.30 a.m. on Saturday 28 November 1970. The first senior officer on the scene was the divisional detective chief inspector, Mr Joseph Wright. He had carefully approached the body to make sure that the woman was dead, and then left it severely alone for the moment. Taking a swift look around the scene Mr Wright saw that there was a break in the privet hedge separating the front garden from the footpath of the main thoroughfare of Kingsway; there were scuffle marks on the soil of the flower border inside the hedge, and drag marks were showing in the dew on the front lawn going round to the back of the house where the body lay. On the front lawn lay a tangle of women's tights and underwear and a black leather glove. Mr Wright pointed these out to Mr Horan when he arrived after being intercepted at a routine visit to a police station. Mr Horan turned to Detective Constable Jack Butler and appointed him exhibits officer to handle any object or sample collected at the scene, but according to Manchester and Salford practice no exhibits were at first even approached.

Mr Horan waited while his specialist officers opened the murder-scene bag. This is a small case packed with measuring tapes, plastic bags, foolscap paper and clip boards and pencils, labels and specimen bottles and swab tubes, a body sheet, rubber gloves – against contracting septicaemia from handling a decomposed body – and every "Sherlock Holmes" piece of equipment down to scissors, tweezers and magnifying glasses. There were even children's lolly sticks which were stuck into the ground, where any object was finally removed, and labelled with a notice like "Knife removed from here".

The scenes-of-crime men first waved in the air a clumsy-looking instrument with the appearance of a football rattle. This was a thermometer for recording the air temperature. Since it would be some time before the pathologist arrived, and from his own measurements of body temperature he would make an estimate of the time of death, it was necessary to record as quickly as possible the temperature of the air affecting the body. They then took some swift general shots of the scene and its outstanding features with a Polaroid camera as an emergency reserve before the official photographer arrived. Then, while Detective Constable Butler made a rough sketch of the scene, the specialist officers got busy with chalk and tape and ground pegs to mark off an approach lane to the body, the access route which they calculated would destroy least evidence when used and which all officers and the doctor and scientist had to observe. This precaution was especially important in the present instance because the soil of the garden border and the grass of the lawn preserved very clear marks of violent movements, and in addition the detectives noted that the tarmacadam of the garden path was soft after being recently re-laid.

Detective Chief Superintendent Horan had a firm policy to disturb the scene of crime as little as possible until the scientific experts arrived, for he laid great stress on the detailed findings of their examination. As he put it: "This is a job for trained forensic science officers working on the scene. We can't be experts at everything, so every man to his job. As detectives, our expertise consists in running the investigation, guiding the lines of inquiry, and questioning the prisoner once he is brought in. I don't want to go around all the time pulling out my tweezers and magnifying glass and saying, 'Have a look at that." If you're after finding blood, or semen, or fibres, there's no one better than the expert who's specially trained for this sort of thing – and the lab. men are first class. Of course I will do a little – have a quick look around, possibly move the body very slightly in the hope that the murderer had dropped his pay packet, which would clear up the job in two minutes. It would be silly not to do anything. But I like the doctor [the pathologist] and the forensic scientist to come down to the scene and do their own investigations on the spot."

Detective Constable Butler was, however, doing some discreet investigation on the perimeter of the scene. Reconnoitring in order to make sure what had to be preserved, he went into the road fronting the house. He examined the footpath outside the glaring gap in the front hedge, with the scuffled earth within. At the base of a tree on the footpath near this gap he found a half-eaten meat pie, and near it a white cardboard food tray. He carefully put these objects into plastic bags, labelled them with exhibit numbers, and marked the places on the ground from which he had taken them. On top of the hedge he found a piece of dark material. It was far too early yet to say whether it had been torn from clothing, but he preserved this also. Then he saw, lying within his reach on the flower border, a small printed card. It bore the words: "City of Manchester Welfare Services Department, Presented by . . ." and in writing there was filled in: "Miss Burroughs."

Had the card been dropped in a struggle, fallen from a pocket or handbag? Was Miss Burroughs the woman who lay so cruelly exposed on the path inside? Constable Butler showed the card to Mr Horan, gingerly holding it by the edge, and the Head of CID immediately had the details on it sent over to Superintendent Hartley at Longsight Police Station. Here was something to work on straight away.

In the Manchester and Salford Force the system of setting up *ad hoc* murder headquarters varying with the location of a specific investigation had been abandoned. A suite of rooms had been fitted up for permanent use at Longsight Police Station, where there was sufficient emergency car-parking space and the convenience of a twenty-four-hour canteen. An adequate number of reserved telephones was available so that there was never any need for emergency installations by the Post Office, and there was radio communication from the actual scene. All that the Murder Control Inspector had to do when notified of a major investigation was to unlock the suite, take the dial locks off the telephones, open the journal which already lay on the table – and he was in business. It was at Longsight that a team of some sixty detectives had already gathered, quite far from the location of the crime. The only men on general inquiries near the scene were those who had already been detailed for house-to-house investigation around 285 Kingsway, and these were already on the knocker.

It was the practice for the senior investigating officer, at the scene and later at the post mortem, to "feed" his deputy at murder control with the facts as they emerged demanding follow-up inquiries, so there was a smooth flow of activity rather than a tidal wave at the end of the post-mortem examination. For example, the clothes would be taken off a victim's body at the mortuary long before the pathological examination was completed, and if an old letter was found in a pocket showing an address that might be the victim's man-friend, the initiation of the follow-up inquiry would be telephoned immediately to Control. In the Kingsway murder the "quick look around the scene" which Mr Horan allowed for before the expert detailed examination threw up the Welfare Services card, and the CID were set to trace it back.

At 11.30 a.m. Mr Henry Martin, the official police photographer, arrived and took his first records of the scene. As he worked the senior detective officers gazed bleakly down at the body of the murdered woman. The victim lay on the tarmac path, face upwards but with the cape, the cardigan and the dress she had been wearing pulled over her head, leaving her naked from the shoulders but with her long reddish hair escaping from the tousled bundle over her face. There appeared to be bite-marks on her body, and across her breasts were what seemed to be the impressions of the toe and heel of a boot, as if she had been stepped on. "Cover her up," said Detective Chief Superintendent Horan, and his men rigged a protective screen above her, attached to the side of the house like a low tent.

Inside the house Mrs Hughes shakily related the events leading to her dreadful discovery of the body. No. 285 Kingsway was a corner house in that busy dual-carriageway main road, with one side of its garden running along Ferndale Gardens. Widowed Mrs Hughes had a nineteen-year-old student as a lodger, but he had left the house on the previous day, Friday, at ten in the morning on the understanding that he would not return that night but spend the week-end at his home in Widnes. All that Friday the Corporation workmen had been busy re-laying the tarmac paths of the house and garden, and when they left at about four o'clock they told Mrs Hughes to be careful over the week-end because the new path was in a soft and tarry condition and would take a day or two to set.

In the evening Mrs Hughes was visited by a friend, an elderly lady who lived near by. The friend left at eleven o'clock, and from the darkened window of her front room Mrs Hughes watched to see that she crossed Kingsway safely – not that it was a rough area, but the traffic at night went fast and there were often a few boisterous people walking home down the thoroughfare late at night on a week-end. Mrs Hughes went back to her living-room, knitted until, she thought, about midnight, and went to her bedroom above the living-room, with its window overlooking the back lawn. She peeped through her curtains and noticed that the lights were on both in the ground floor living-room and the water-closet of the house next door. This throwaway domestic detail, seemingly irrelevant to listen to or record, was important in fixing the time she went to bed. The next-door neighbours were firm that they had been in bed by midnight, soon after the television was switched off, that the water-closet had been used three times between 11.40 p.m. and midnight, and that the housewife deliberately checked that the lavatory light was out when she went upstairs, because it had more than once been left on all night by mistake.

Mrs Hughes got into bed, read for a little, turned out the lights and fell asleep. She was awakened at what she thought might have been one or two o'clock. What had disturbed her were thudding sounds, for all the world, she thought, like the thuds the workmen had made while they were flattening the new tarmac outside. The noise was so strong that Mrs Hughes got out of bed and looked through her window on to the back lawn, but she could see nothing. She walked out of her bedroom and looked through two other windows on that floor, facing down Kingsway and on to the front lawn, with no result. But although she could see nothing, the battering noise was still audible. Mrs Hughes had not put on any light, and shortly after she had gone back to her own bedroom the noise stopped. She went back to bed and to sleep, came downstairs at nine o'clock and was pottering about in the living-room for an hour and a half before she went outside to the dustbin and found the body.

While Mrs Hughes was talking to the senior detectives, others from the general inquiries team were interviewing neighbours all round. The people next door thought that their lights had probably been out by 11.45 p.m. Other neighbours heard a sound between 11.35 and 11.50 which they described as a muffled scream or whine. At first they thought it was a dog that had been hurt, then decided that it was human. "But living on this corner, we are quite used to youths making a noise and larking about, so we didn't pay any further attention." Another neighbour reading in bed at about 11.40 heard a short sharp female scream— "but people often scream and laugh loudly as they pass along Kingsway". No one else remembered having heard the thumping noise.

A message was passed to Detective Chief Superintendent

Horan that the pathologist and the forensic science officer had
arrived in Manchester, and the Head of the CID went to meet
them and escort them to Kingsway. These experts were Dr John
G. Benstead, Home Office pathologist attached to the North-
western Forensic Science Laboratory at Preston, and Dr Richard
P. G. Gregory, a specialist biologist at the laboratory. Detective
Chief Inspector Wright formally identified the body stretched
before them as that found on the site in the morning, and Dr
Benstead began a preliminary examination as the photographer
recorded every stage of uncovering or moving the body.

Dr Benstead took the body temperature and noted that rigor
mortis was fully developed. When the clothes were dislodged
from the girl's head it could be seen that she had been savagely
battered and this was the apparent cause of death. There were
split wounds and extensive bruises, some of them over two inches
long and suggesting that a boot had been used. There was a bite
mark on her cheek, two bite marks on the right breast and one on
the left. There were impressions of the heel and sole of a boot or
shoe across her breasts in the direction right to left. It appeared
that she had been raped. There was a black glove on the left hand
and the bare right hand was damaged, the middle finger later
being found to have been fractured. When the body was gently
turned over it was seen that there were extensive signs of grazing
on the shoulder blades, as if she had been dragged across rough
ground by her feet. Because the tarmac on which she lay was still
soft, and indeed warm, the tarry asphalt had discoloured the
whole of the back of her body.

Before the body was removed Dr Gregory had taken adhesive-
tape swabs from the exposed skin surfaces, applying the strips of
tape and removing them so that they preserved fibres which were
not always immediately visible to the naked eye. He also took
cotton wool swabs of the areas on the body where there appeared
to be bite marks, for later analysis to try and determine the blood
group of the biter. When the left arm of the body was raised it was
seen that there were three pieces of paper under it. One was a pink
receipt slip, one had a note of "Mam's works telephone number",
and the third had a note of "Terry's telephone number". The
details were immediately passed to Longsight for further inqui-

ries towards identification: it was small help that it was then Saturday afternoon when the most indicative of the clues, "Mam's works telephone number", could not be swiftly followed up by a call at a crowded factory, but lists of addresses of individual workers would need to be painstakingly made up and followed through.

After their preliminary examination of the body both Dr Benstead and Dr Gregory turned to the garden, still preserved behind the tapes of the approach area. The gap in the privet hedge in the front garden had been made by the hedge's having been pushed inwards from the pavement. The flower border and the adjacent lawn had been trodden down for a distance of six feet in what could have been a violent struggle, and the drag marks across the lawn began from this spot. In the earth of the flower border there was a heel impression, and Dr Gregory asked one of the detectives for a plaster cast to be made of this print after photography. At one end of the trampled area there was an amount of fresh blood staining, and Constable Butler scooped up a sample of the bloodstained earth to add to his exhibits. In the centre of the trampled area of the flower border, and not immediately obvious, Dr Gregory found a metal ring, flat and about half an inch broad, of the type that could be worn on a finger. The shiny condition of the metal and the impression it made in the earth suggested that it had only recently been trodden into the border.

The scientists moved carefully on to the lawn and began to examine the drag marks, seeking fibres, debris and any suggestion of footprints. The black leather right-hand glove was carefully lifted, examined for a note to be taken of the label, and bagged as an exhibit. The tangle of underclothing proved to be a pair of women's tights enmeshed in three pairs of knickers, and these were preserved for later analysis. Dr Gregory tested for semen stains on various areas of the lawn, patting down a white detector and treating it with water for the tell-tale red stain that might indicate that there had been a sexual attack in the front garden, before the body was dragged to the back. When the experts rose from their concentrated labour the exhibits officer was guarding samples of asphalt, hedge, soil and grass, besides all the specimens which had been passed over to him; many more were to be secured at the post mortem.

The police mortuary van was standing by to take the body to the mortuary. As one of the policemen carrying the stretcher raised himself to full height with his burden he lost his balance and grabbed a drainpipe to save himself. By this sheer accident he left a "clue" which misled the detectives for the first two days of the inquiry. For as the scenes-of-crime men took over they found a fingerprint on the pipe, three feet four inches from the ground, which it took them two days to eliminate. The occurrence only emphasized the justification of Mr Horan's principle that the fewer the people who attend a scene of crime, the less chance there is of even unwitting contamination.

Through the afternoon detectives had been busy in the city following up the Welfare Services card. They discovered without difficulty that Miss Burroughs was not the victim of the murder. She was a welfare officer concerned with visiting old folk and her description was nothing like that of the young woman in Kingsway. She had left her card with a number of senior citizens, and it was now the team's task to trace these persons individually.

Another officer, concerned with the immediate house-to-house inquiries round Kingsway, had been able to put in some very valuable information. He found an old pensioner who did the gardening for Mrs Hughes and one or two other old ladies: he was in fact the husband of the friend who had visited Mrs Hughes on the fatal night. This man had spent Wednesday and Thursday completely tidying up Mrs Hughes' garden. He had cleared all the lawns and hoed all the borders and filled seven bags with dead leaves. "When I left," he assured the detective, "the lawn was clear, all the borders were clear, there were no footprints in the soil and it was absolutely clean. I can safely say that there was no ring or clothing in the garden, not even a piece of paper in it. There was definitely no break in the hedge. I take pride in that hedge, as I have brought it on from what it was, looking very bad, to one which I am now proud of."

"That was an enormous help," Detective Chief Superintendent Horan said later. "We had seen all the scuffling inside the garden. We were quite certain that the murderer had dragged the girl through the hedge at that spot. But there could always be another explanation. Kingsway is not a rough area, but there are so many people going along there, and we have so many false leads with murders that we get a bit wary. To have someone say that the garden was absolutely tidy the day before was a fantastic relief. The tarmac, too: absolutely flat and new and sticky as fly-paper to hold any prints or debris or fibres. If some stage manager had wanted to set an uncontaminated scene for a crime we couldn't have asked for a single further detail."

At four o'clock the post-mortem examination began in the Manchester City Mortuary. It confirmed the first indications of horrific damage to the skull and recent forcible sexual inter-course. The victim was in a fairly advanced state of pregnancy. Dr Benstead gave it as his opinion that death had resulted from shock with cerebral haemorrhage and contusion in association with multiple fractures of the skull caused by blows to the head. He believed that there had been ten or more blows delivered with great force and consistent with blows from a fist or foot rather than a weapon, and that death had probably occurred between midnight and 2 a.m. that day, Saturday.

As soon as Mr Horan had had confirmation of the apparent bite marks on the girl's breasts and face he sent for Mr John Furness in Liverpool. Mr Furness was a dental surgeon and a Home Office lecturer in forensic dentistry who had made a specialist study of identification by teeth marks in cases of assault and homicide and had given evidence in several recent cases where identification rested on teeth marks. Mr Furness travelled to Manchester and arrived at the mortuary, where he had the teeth marks on the dead girl's body specially photographed for future reference.

Detective Chief Superintendent Horan wanted the fullest information about the dead girl in the fastest possible time, and that meant going immediately to the public. It was Saturday afternoon, and he could catch the first editions of the Sunday papers, but at his first Press conference he could give little priming. There was no identification: he could give the apparent age of the girl as twenty-five and her height as five feet six, and he could describe her clothes. "I am appealing," he said, "for anyone who has a girl of this description missing from home to contact me at police headquarters. I would also like any motorists who might have seen a struggle or anything suspicious on Kingsway between 1 a.m. and 2 a.m. to contact me." He gave these times because when he first saw the Press he had not had an opportunity to collate the statements of the Kingsway neighbours and was relying on Mrs Hughes' idea of the time when she was awoken: later he realized that Mrs Hughes could hardly have dropped off before she was alerted.

Mr Horan also caught the Saturday evening radio and television news with his first announcement. But he wanted to prompt public reaction at the scene of the crime. He therefore asked one of his constables, Fred Spender, an excellent artist who had done several murder posters for him in the past, to design something in a hurry for use that night. He sent a mobile police caravan to Kingsway and parked it with its blue light flashing in the gutter outside No. 285 and not ten yards from where the murder had taken place. A portable spotlight played on the poster on the side of the caravan, which was used as an office by detectives who stopped passers-by to ask if they had taken the same route the previous night. That caravan was in position by 7 p.m., and on either side of it police warnings flashed "SLOW DOWN" to motorists, who crawled past the poster and, if they had been there around the previous midnight, spoke to the detectives.

As the caravan went into position Mr Hartley's detectives radioed in to Murder Control the news that the victim was identified. She had been carrying a Welfare Services card which Miss Burroughs had left for her grandmother, and she was Linda Stewart, twenty-two years old and single, who lived with her large family in Burnage within a mile from where she died.

The immediate detective concentration was on her background, since four murders in five have a domestic setting, and on her movements the previous night. For her movements the investigators concerned were referred fairly swiftly to the girlfriend with whom Linda had gone out the previous night. This left the stricken family house clear for the steady, gentle, essential probing for information about employment, quarrels, troubles, boyfriends and the everyday tensions of everyday people who are *not* murdered every day.

Linda Stewart lived with her grandmother, her widowed mother, her married brother and his wife and baby daughter, her two sisters and her two brothers in a house off Kingsway which they had taken only a fortnight previously. Linda had a regular boyfriend and she was seven months pregnant by him. Because of her condition she had finished her work as a shop assistant and spent much of her time looking after her brother's two-year-old daughter. She was a quiet girl who did not bother with men apart from her boyfriend. It was difficult for the experienced detective who was culling this information to catch a feeling of any significant tension within this family apart from an understandable reticence about her pregnancy and some apparent uncertainty about her future with her boyfriend.

But she went out very frequently with her boyfriend. Why had she not done so on the previous night? "Well, better ask *him*, hadn't you? Or the girl she did go out with, Jennifer Earl."

Jennifer also lived in Burnage, about half a mile from Linda's new house. She said she and Linda had been friends for ten years and they always went out together except when Linda went out with her boyfriend. They used to walk a lot, and talk a lot, and go to a pub, but only during the last hour of opening time and only for one drink or two. This was indeed how the evening had gone on the previous night. Linda called on Jennifer at home at about half past eight. "Coming out?" she asked, and Jennifer said yes, but she meant to have her bath first. So the two girls walked together five houses down the road to where Linda's other married brother lived. Jennifer dashed back for her bath and called for Linda at half past nine. They walked for a bit up Mauldeth Road and then a bus came along and they caught it for the rest of the journey to Fallowfield. There they went into the Princess Hotel at about ten past ten. They nattered to each other until closing time at eleven, and during that period they each had two lager beers. They came out meaning to catch the last bus, but when they got to the stop it had gone, and they had to walk home all the way down Mauldeth Road again. They reached the junction with Kingsway at about half past eleven and they both went to the public lavatory there.

As they came out of the lavatory, though they were still talking Jennifer noticed a man who passed them and crossed the road and then looked back at them. On the other side of the road he stood looking into a lighted shop window displaying motor cycles. The girls had to go in opposite directions along Kingsway from this spot to go to their respective homes, and Jennifer, a little uneasy about the man waiting at the shop window, asked Linda if she would be all right walking alone that way, or would she like Jennifer to walk with her. Linda said she would be all right, and they said good night and she crossed the road and started down Kingsway. Jennifer noticed that as she passed the man at the shop window he looked towards her, and after she had gone a little way he started to follow her. And that was the last she saw of Linda.

Jennifer could describe the man very clearly. She said he looked about twenty years old and had blond hair growing down to the nape of the neck and long sideboards. She said he had good features and was of a smart appearance. He was of medium build and he was wearing a three-quarter-length car coat of a beige colour with a white fur collar and under it a beige-coloured suit. Linda was wearing the clothes she had been found in, but of course she had shoes and a handbag. The shoes were black patent leather with a gold buckle and they had thick block heels. She carried a black handbag with a gold clasp, and inside it Jennifer – again describing visual objects very clearly – reckoned there would have been some letters from a brother in London, from a sister in Australia and from her boyfriend; probably some photographs of her boy-friend and of her nieces and nephews in Australia; a Barclays Bank book in her name; a gold bangle made up from intertwined circles; a white and blue enlarger-viewer for photographs; some Bodymist deodorant; a packet of ten plain Park Drive cigarettes with a box of matches and a white plastic purse about four inches by five inches.

This invaluable information was rushed to Detective Chief Superintendent Horan in time for a second Press conference that evening. The investigating officers had been very puzzled by the absence of both shoes and handbag from the scene of the crime. They could accept that, even though the motive for the crime was apparently sexual, the assailant might be a thief as well and had taken the handbag because he thought there might be some money in it. But why should a murderer take a girl's shoes? Still taking the later time of the attack as between one and two o'clock in the morning, an explanation for the absence of shoes might have been that there had been an earlier meeting between the girl and her assailant, and even an initial attack elsewhere, perhaps in a motor vehicle, and the girl had perhaps left her handbag and shoes inside the car.

However, Mr Horan was not giving theories to the Press, but very explicit facts. "We believe," he said, "that this girl was attacked on Kingsway, dragged through the hedge of a front garden, was the subject of further attack in the front garden, was dragged unconscious across the garden to the rear of the house, laid on the tarmac path there, was raped there and finally kicked and battered to death. All this on a well-lighted main trunk road in a big city. It seems incredible that no passer-by saw something."

Mr Horan went on to give the Press the detailed description of the man Jennifer said she had seen, and he described the shoes and the handbag. "We must find them," he said. He also detailed the movements of the two girls on Friday night, named the pub they had been in and the route they had taken home. In addition he quickly had the poster on the police caravan in Kingsway amended to carry the description of the man he sought, had a blown-up photograph of Linda fixed to the caravan, added a description of the shoes and handbag, and kept the exhibition floodlit all night. Manchester Corporation replaced his generator and portable floodlights with a special illumination run off the street lighting circuit.

That night there was no rest at all for the main body of the Manchester and Salford detectives. House-to-house inquiries had to finish at a reasonable time, but the CID went on later with their initial turnover of all known criminals with a record of sex offences. All customers in the Princess Hotel that night were interviewed to discover if they had been there the night before and noticed anything significant. A squad went round the late-night clubs of the city, following up the possibility that Linda *had* been enticed into a car, taken for drinks, and perhaps assaulted when she thought she was being taken home. The caravan team stopped all the pedestrians making their way down the long sodium-lit avenue of Kingsway that night. Questionnaires for the house-to-house inquiries next morning had to be prepared. And there had to be time to reflect, consider, put up possibilities.

The very full Press and broadcasting coverage which Mr Horan had secured for the investigation brought in an enormous public response on the Sunday. The most promising item of information came from a Sunday-paper reader who said he had seen a grey Mini Traveller motor-car parked at the corner of Ferndale Gardens and Kingsway – by the very house where Linda was murdered – at about 12.30 a.m. on the Saturday morning. The occupants were a man and a woman and they had seemed to be arguing. Later they had been seen driving away, apparently still arguing. Mr Horan relayed this to the Press and said he was most anxious to trace this couple who had been arguing only some fifteen yards from where Linda was found. "The colour of the estate car may be in doubt," he said, "because the sodium-vapour lamps tend to alter colours." Mr Horan immediately diverted a squad of six men to trace the motor-car and alerted all his police cadets to be ready to go into the local motor-taxation office and root out details of all Mini Travellers.

A motorist reported that he had been driving his car along Kingsway in Burnage at 11.50 on the night of the murder when he saw a youth pulling a girl across the road in the path of his car. The driver had to brake in order to avoid an accident. He described the youth as five feet seven inches tall, with blond hair worn long, and wearing a fawn raincoat or camel-type coat. The girl had long hair and wore a cape. The descriptions were extremely suggestive of the appearance of the man Jennifer Earl had seen and of Linda, but the police had to remember that they could have been suggested by the details already printed in the newspapers. It was one of the dangers of releasing generous information.

At ten o'clock on the Sunday morning Detective Chief Inspector Wright had the melancholy task of escorting Linda's married brother, with whom she had lived, to the mortuary to identify her body. It was then his duty to re-interview both the mourning family and Jennifer Earl. But the most vital interview of the day had to be with Linda's boyfriend. He was completely innocent, and the CID was entirely satisfied after he had been seen, but he had to endure a necessarily searching interrogation before he could be eliminated.

He was a twenty-year-old skilled engineering worker, and he had known Linda for two and a half years. They met on a blind date and were "serious" within two months. They saw each other sometimes five nights a week. They went out either together or in company with Linda's sister and her boyfriend. She was not the girl to go out with a crowd, and the only other person she kept company with was her friend Jennifer. Although she was pregnant by her boyfriend he had lately had to tell her that because of the way his career was going he had decided that he could not afford to get married. He had no doubt that the decision had hit her hard, but they still went out together.

Ironically, it was because of the circumstances of the uncertainty of his career that he had not gone out with Linda on the fatal night. It is strange that the closing down of an engineering firm brought this among many lesser tragedies in its wake. The boyfriend's firm was going out of business that Friday, making him and all his fellow-workers redundant, and he wanted to have a final celebration with his mates. He travelled to Linda's home at noon on that Friday to tell her this, and though she tried to persuade him against it, she finally accepted his decision and they arranged to meet the next night instead. The lad then started a pub crawl which lasted, with one interval of an hour in the late afternoon to change his clothes, from one o'clock lunch-time until two the next morning. He could give full details of all the taverns he had visited and the dance hall where he had finally stayed drinking until the early morning. And fortunately for him he had witnesses to his alibi ranging from fifty engineers at 1 p.m. to two pals and a friendly car-driver who stayed with him, pretty dead drunk, until he collapsed in his own bed.

Meanwhile at the North-western Forensic Science Laboratory the analyses were going on that were to help the Manchester and Salford investigation. Among other findings, the stomach contents showed no indication of the digestion of anything resembling the meat pie found half-consumed in the road, and it was unlikely that Linda had been eating it. The blood grouping tests carried out on the swabs taken from the bite marks found on the body and from semen specimens were less conclusive, possibly being masked by Linda's own blood group, and indicating the blood groups which did *not* include the attacker rather than his precise group. Fibres found on the body were retained for comparison with those of the clothing of any man later brought in.

On Monday morning the Mini Traveller investigation fell to the ground. A man came forward after reading that morning's papers and said that it was his car that had been seen at the spot but that he had not had a woman with him, but a man with long hair. After careful checking the police accepted this story, and it was again a tribute to the Press coverage that this abortive line of inquiry could be abandoned with economical swiftness, releasing a number of officers who had been busy tracking down Mini Travellers and interviewing their drivers.

Mr Horan was now able to concentrate on his main line of inquiry, the search for the blond man who had been seen following Linda. But he still had to overcome the enigma of the missing shoes. The man had been seen on foot, and therefore it was likely that the once-attractive theory of an attack in a car should be jettisoned. But where were the shoes? Had the attacker taken them with him? Since he was walking it could be assumed that he was a local man. If he were local he might have dodged into familiar gardens nearby and dumped the shoes in a hedge or even in a dustbin. Again Detective Chief Superintendent Horan called on the communications media, and he appealed through the Press, radio and television that people in the Burnage area should search their gardens and dustbins for the missing shoes and handbag. To back up this search Mr Horan thought it would be necessary to have an organized police comb-out of all gardens and dustbins in the area. But for this to be effective a reversion to old-fashioned methods was necessary. Garbage collection in Burnage was undertaken by collecting disposable paper sacks and destroying their contents in the street by throwing them into a mobile machine which instantly ground and compressed them.

Mr Horan arranged with the Manchester Corporation Cleansing Department that they would suspend this clearance of the paper sacks for a week and substitute an old-type dustbin-emptying cart manned by a special team of dustmen. With the dustmen a squad of detectives were to travel, and it was the detectives who were to search the contents of each bag as it was brought out before emptying in the dustcart. Having made these delicate arrangements Mr Horan decided he could get his head down for his first sleep since the investigation started.

The dustcart manoeuvre had instant success. At eleven o'clock on Tuesday morning Constable Norman Croston, searching a garbage container of a house in Kingsway 150 yards from the scene of the crime, found a lady's left shoe half way down the bag. At the very bottom he found a bundle of papers, letters and photographs. The letters were addressed to Linda Stewart and one of the photographs was of her. The shoe was taken both to Linda's brother and sister by Mr Wright and was immediately identified. At eight o'clock that night – the police were not working normal dustmen's shifts – Constable Edward Higginson, working in a side street off Kingsway only 100 yards from the last find, unwrapped a newspaper screwed round an object and produced a black plastic bag containing a chain bracelet, a pencil and a few papers. This was also identified and handed to the fingerprint men.

This double discovery convinced Detective Chief Superintendent Horan that he was after a man who either lived or worked locally, and he decided on all-out psychological war against his quarry. He called an emergency Press conference to announce the dustbin finds and asked reporters to plug as hard as their editors would allow them his theme that the wanted man was local and it was certain that the police would catch up with him. At the same time Mr Horan brought up his reserve artillery, releasing to the Press news of the metal ring which had been found trodden into the soil of the garden border and issuing a photograph of it.

Because Mr Horan believed so strongly that his man had local connections he now authorized a mammoth operation to check the fingerprints of all males between the ages of fourteen and fifty living within the square mile around the scene of the crime. The check was against the finger- and palm-print found on the drainpipe above the spot where Linda had lain. "We will fingerprint 800 people a day until the district is covered," Mr Horan told the Press, not adding that he was proposing a seven weeks' operation. With his own men Mr Horan used the local search as a boost of morale as they reached for their second wind. He was using a number of uniformed branch men switched to plain clothes for his house-to-house inquiries widening out from the central point of 285 Kingsway. They were using a questionnaire based on "Where were you on the night of 27th November?" and they were highly enthusiastic workers since it was not such a routine operation for them as for regular detectives. There was a large wall map of the house-to-house area, and Mr Horan stood in front of it before his men. "Take it from me," he told them, "the killer either lives or works on this map, and all you've got to do is *pull him off the map*." The message got home in a useful personalization of the quest.

On Wednesday morning Mr Horan was gratified to find that the Press had done him proud. "I am more and more convinced that the man we're looking for is local," he was quoted as saying. "Someone travelling through would not stop at every street corner to drop things off." The photograph of the ring received its first publication, and in reproduction it seemed individual and identifiable, which is not always the case with more expensive rings in photographs. But Mr Horan had not yet finished menacing his wanted man with news of the ring. On the Wednesday morning he asked Detective Inspector Jack Ridgway to take it for analysis to the Department of Metallurgy at Manchester University.

The ring was of stainless steel, obviously made by an amateur but a skilled amateur using sophisticated machinery. "Our minds immediately sprang," said Mr Horan, "to engineering works, knowing as we do that the men there are wont to do the odd foreigner instead of the work they are so highly paid to do." And there were a number of engineering works in the Burnage area. Inspector Ridgway took the ring to Manchester's electron-optics lab, where Dr Muhsin Jabbar Nasir, a highly skilled metallurgist, analysed the metal with an electron-probe micro-analyser and produced a breakdown of the contents of the stainless steel, even suggesting the Yorkshire firm which had probably supplied it. Mr Ridgway then went to an engineering factory, showed the manager the ring and asked if workmen made them there. "Not if I'm looking," was the reply, "but I know some of the apprentices do." "Do you think you could sanction one of them to show me how the ring is made?" asked the Inspector. The demonstration was given, and the new ring had similar striations (vertical parallel marks on the inside of the ring) to the sample he was carrying. He asked the reason for this and was told that these striations occurred when the ring was made by wrapping the metal round an Allen bolt. Mr Ridgway therefore concentrated future inquiries on engineering firms using Allen bolts.

Next day the Head of Manchester and Salford CID increased his pressure on the unknown killer by making a further strong detailed appeal to the public, coupled with a hint of almost supernatural powers at the command of the investigating detectives. The Press co-operated magnificently, but it was not through charity: Horan was dishing out some good stuff. He was speaking direct to the people of Burnage, Manchester. "Ask yourself four vital questions," he told them. "The answers can possibly prevent another killing. If the answer to any of the following questions is yes, it is not only a public duty to tell the police, but it might be vital to the safety of your family and your friends. Here are the questions which paint a portrait of a man who could kill again. Ask yourself:

Do I know a man who is as the police describe – in his twenties with long fair hair and sideboards and who wears a beige car coat?

Is there any youth or man missing from home since last Saturday in my neighbourhood?

Do I know of any youth or man who hasn't been to work since last Saturday without good cause?

Have I seen any youth or man with blood- or tar-stained clothes?

"If you come forward you have my personal assurance that you will not be identified in any way.

"It is likely that the killer lives within a square mile of the scene of the killing. It is probable that someone living with him, or even a neighbour, may know or suspect something about him.

"That man's clothing must have been covered with tar from a newly laid path, and with blood which it would have been impossible to hide."

Then, turning to the subject of the ring, Mr Horan said, "It is of stainless steel and may have been a do-it-yourself job by a machine-minder at an engineering factory. It is now being analysed by Manchester University Department of Metallurgy.

"The scientist will certainly identify the metal and may, by analysis, be able to say where the metal was made." (This had, in fact, already been done.)

"As we are reasonably sure," Mr Horan added, at his most demonic, "that the ring came from an engineering shop, we could by this analysis even reach the man who fashioned it."

Mr Horan was soon to know how effective his war of nerves had been, for on the day after the publication of this last broadside the man under pressure cracked and ran.

On that Friday it had been decided to suspend temporarily house-to-house inquiries and all other routine inquiries, and to put every available man on the Murder Squad into the local engineering factories to check engineering workers, especially the apprentices. Mr Horan calculated that if the police theories were right the killer must now be in a state of near panic as a result of the pressure which the Press, television and radio were exerting. He twisted the screw for the last time that morning by boldly announcing in the newspapers that "the hunt for the killer has now spread to the factories."

That morning a team of detectives entered the factory of the Renold Engineering Works, which was within the square mile of Burnage where Horan had concentrated the hunt. The investigators began their long series of individual interviews.

Immediately after the lunch-break the factory welfare officer brought to the senior detective an apprentice carrying a note on the back of a job order card which he said he had found pushed into his locker. The note read:

Andy I want you to tell the firm to send my wages home to my parents, I think I killed that girl but I am not sure, but it's my ring they found, so it must be me, tell the cops not to look for me because I will kill myself

Ron

"Who wrote that?" the detective asked the apprentice.

"Ron Bennell."

"Please get his personal details," the detective asked the welfare officer, and made a swift call to Murder Control.

Ronald Bennell was an eighteen-year-old apprentice fitter living with his parents and four other children at Cheadle, Cheshire, about three miles from the scene of the killing.

Immediately it was confirmed that he had bolted, a large detachment of the Murder Squad was assigned to making a physical search for him, particularly on the banks of the River Mersey near by, on the chance that he contemplated suicide there.

Others were sent to visit his home, his relatives, friends and associates. A smaller team remained in the Renold factory questioning apprentices. But their inquiries no longer implied "Did you do this murder?" They were asking "What do you know of Ron Bennell?" What immediately emerged was that he had been to an apprentices' dance in Burnage on the night of the murder and that he was known to have made flat metal rings from stainless steel at work.

The search for Bennell continued. At 9.15 that night Detective Sergeant John Reed, with Detective Constable Waring, knocked at the door of a house in the Manchester suburb of Benchill. It was opened by a frightened or shocked girl of sixteen and she said they could come in. The sergeant looked around the main rooms of the ground floor while the constable went upstairs. The sergeant checked that the back door leading from the kitchen was securely shut by two bolts. He came back to the living-room and then heard scuffling in the kitchen. He ran through and saw a young man trying to draw the top bolt. He took his arm, calling to his colleague upstairs, but there was no resistance. The sergeant asked the youth, "Are you Ronald Bennell?" "Yes," he answered, "I was hiding in the pantry." "I want you to accompany us to Longsight Police Station," said the sergeant, "where a senior police officer wishes to interview you about a certain matter." "O.K.," said Bennell, "can I say goodbye to my girlfriend?" He was told, "You will no doubt be able to see her later." They began to walk to the door of the living-room where the white-faced girl was standing. Detective Constable Waring was looking at her hand. "Where did you get that ring from?" he asked. "I got it off him," she said. "May I have it?" asked the detective, and she gave it to him. It was a stainless steel flat ring similar to the one found in the garden at Kingsway, but it had the word Ron inscribed on it.

At 9.45 that night Ronald Bennell was shown into a room in Longsight Police Station where Detective Superintendent Hartley introduced himself and Detective Chief Superintendent Horan, and formally cautioned him. Mr Hartley went on: "About 10.30 a.m. on Saturday 28 November this year, the body of Linda Stewart was found on a tarmac path in the rear garden of the house 285 Kingsway, Burnage. The girl had severe head and face injuries. She had also apparently been raped. You answer the description of a youth seen in the near vicinity of the scene."

Bennell said, "I can't remember what happened that night."

"It's not long ago," observed Mr Hartley. "Where did you go that evening?"

"To an apprentices' dance at Selnec on Slade Lane and got drunk."

"Did you leave the dance alone?"

"No." And Bennell named a fellow apprentice and his wife.

"Where did you go?"

"We went to a chip shop and then I walked along Kingsway."

"Did you speak to anyone on Kingsway?"

"My mind is a complete blank as to what happened on Kingsway."

"Take your boots off."

The detectives examined the brown leather boots he was wearing. Mr Hartley said, "The heels have tips which are identical to footprints found in the garden where the dead girl was found."

Bennell said, "I can't remember going into any garden."

Mr Hartley said, "You left this note at work," and showed him the card to Andy signed "Ron". "Did you in fact write that note?" he asked.

"Yes."

"Is it true? And do you remember where you were?"

There was a pause of some length, and Bennell continued in an entirely different tone: "Well, I'll tell you what I remember. It all started last Thursday night when I finished with my girlfriend . . ."

With little more prompting except to maintain the sequence, Bennell gave an account of what had happened that night which accorded with all the detectives knew, except that he denied having kicked the girl, only "thumped" her. Later he made a statement. In summary he told the detectives that after he had quarrelled with his girlfriend he was in an angry mood, and everything was building up on Friday. He went to an apprentices' dance and drank too much. On leaving the dance he bought a pie and chips and walked along Kingsway. He saw Linda Stewart and accosted her with a "Hallo, love," and she told him to get lost. He could not control his temper and he grabbed her and pushed her through the hedge. The girl started screaming and he told her to be quiet, but she continued to scream and he put his hands round her throat. There was a struggle in which his ring must have come off. The girl went quiet and still, and he dragged her on to the tarmac path by her feet. He stripped her clothes off and had sexual intercourse while she was unconscious, at that time biting her on the breasts. She then started mumbling again. He told her to shut up and started "thumping" her again in the face. He realized what he had done, and stood up and walked over to the hedge where he picked up the shoes and handbag which she had dropped as she fell through. He then saw that her tights and knickers were dangling from his coat, and he detached them and left them on the grass. He ran off, stepping on the body as he passed, and took a route through some gardens. In one garden he stopped, opened the dustbin, took out some paper, wrapped one of the girl's shoes in it and put it back in the bin. Later he dropped the handbag and some papers in another bin. He walked home and as he was crossing the River Mersey realized that he still had one shoe and some miscellaneous items from the handbag in his pocket. He threw these into the river. Afterwards he cleaned his clothes as best he could and told his mother he had been in a fight at the dance through breaking up another fight, for which the manager had thanked him.

His remarks on his reaction to the "war of nerves" were revealing. On the Monday he had gone to a technical sandwich course, having read the newspapers, and a lad there said he looked like the man suspected of the murder. On the Tuesday he went back to the factory where everyone was talking of the murder, and he was very worried by the prominence of the newspaper stories. On the Wednesday he read the repeated description of himself in the papers with the addition that the beige-coloured coat must be marked with tar, and "I just didn't know what to do." On the Thursday he read that from the metallurgists' analysis it would be possible to trace the man who had made the ring. On the Friday, when the apprentices began to be interviewed, one lad joked that Bennell fitted the description given, and that anyway he was just the sort of chap to be gazing into a motor-cycle window since motor bikes were his craze. Another apprentice asked him, "Is that your ring they found?" and he mumbled no, he had given that to his sister. As he realized that his interview was imminent he bolted.

Although Bennell had confessed to the killing it was necessary to corroborate this confession with all the available evidence, just as the case would have to be proved had he denied the attack. There were eight salient points:

The police proved that the metal from which the ring was made had been supplied to the Renold Engineering Company. They also proved that a similar type of ring could have been made on Bennell's machine by shaping metal round the head of an Allen bolt, producing similar striations. The police also proved that Bennell had given an identical ring to his girl-friend a week or two previously.

The bite marks on the girl's breast had been photographed. Mr Furness, the forensic dentist, saw Bennell after his arrest and took plaster casts of his teeth in much the same way as a cast is made for fitting a dental plate. He then marked the cutting edges of the plaster cast with black ink. He made photographic transparencies of the cutting edges and compared them with the marks on the girl's breasts in much the same manner as comparison is made of fingerprints, making points of identification.

The meat pie which had been found near the scene of the

killing (and which Bennell said he had dropped during the attack) had also been photographed, and Mr Furness matched the bite marks on the pie with the plaster cast of Bennell's teeth.

Dr Gregory was able to say that the heel of Bennell's left boot was similar in shape and size to the heel impression found in the garden border, of which a plaster cast had been made.

Dr Gregory was also able to say that there was tar staining on the clothing of Bennell which could have been made by the tarmac on the path of 285 Kingsway.

Fibres taken from the skin surfaces and clothing of Linda Stewart were similar to fibres taken from the trousers and jacket of Bennell.

Small particles of asphalt similar to that from the garden path of 285 Kingsway were found in the pockets of Bennell's jacket.

There were small blood stains on Bennell's jacket of the girl's blood group, which was different from his.

At the Crown Court at Manchester on 1 March 1971 Bennell pleaded guilty to murder and was sentenced to life imprisonment.

THE MURDERER WHO GOT AWAY WITH IT

(John Donald Merrett, UK 1926)

Macdonald Hastings

*This case presents one of the few occasions in which a human ear —
that of a murder victim — was produced in court as evidence. John
Donald Merrett was only eighteen when he was tried for the murder
of his mother. Mrs Merrett had been found in her sitting-room with a
bullet hole above her right ear. Her son, who inherited a fortune on
her death, claimed she had shot herself. At the young man's trial, the
Crown's ballistics experts claimed that the wound could not have
been self-inflicted. For one thing, Mrs Merrett could not have
mustered the strength needed to pull the trigger, and for another,
there were no powder burns around the bullet hole. The opinion of the
experts was that such burns would have been there if the gun had been
fired at close range by Mrs Merrett herself. The celebrated pathologist Sir Bernard Spilsbury, appearing for once for the defence,
disagreed. He testified that it was quite possible for the wound to have
been self-inflicted, explaining the absence of powder burns by pointing out that they would have been washed away by bleeding and in
the course of cleaning the wound. Although the case against young
Merrett was strong — he had also forged his mother's signature on
several hundred pounds'-worth of cheques — the jury felt unable to
disregard the sworn evidence of the great Spilsbury. Because the case
was tried in Scotland, they were able to return a verdict of Not
Proven on the murder charge. (Merrett was convicted of forgery and
was jailed for a year). Merrett resurfaced as Ronald Chesney more*

than a quarter of a century later, when he killed his wife and mother-in-law and finally himself. The Merrett case was told by the writer and broadcaster Macdonald Hastings (1909–82) in his biography of Robert Churchill, the ballistics expert whose evidence featured in many British murder trials in the 1920s and 1930s.

The newspaper headline, "Now It Can Be Told," on February 17, 1954, announced that a controversy of the criminal courts which had been the cause of debate, often bitter debate, for twenty-eight years was at last resolved. Churchill and Spilsbury were two of the central figures in the argument. The case was essentially a conflict between experts, one which subsequently lent weight to murmurings of doubt as to what value could be reposed on the evidence of specialist witnesses. To make a cool assessment of it, the story of the nefarious career of John Donald Merrett is one which is best considered, not from its beginning, but from its end.

On February 16, 1954, Ronald John Chesney, one of several aliases which John Donald Merrett adopted during his life, was found shot dead through the mouth in a wood on the outskirts of Cologne. A Colt automatic, an ugly weapon which blew off the top of his head, lay at his side. He had committed suicide; and none too soon. He was wanted for the murder of his wife and mother-in-law, who ran an Old Folks' Home in the normally safe respectability of the London suburb of Ealing.

He killed his wife with the intention of obtaining a sum of money he had settled on her many years before which he himself had inherited from his mother after she too had had a violent end. He killed his mother-in-law because she had the misfortune to discover him when he was faking the appearance that his wife's death was accidental.

It was a disappointing outcome for him, because he had put himself to some trouble to prove that he could not have had any part in the affair. He had previously made a visit to England from Germany, a country where he had business interests and a girlfriend, during which he stole a passport from a man he

met in a pub, and made a sufficient exhibition of himself at the
port of departure to secure that he had an alibi. He subsequently
returned on the stolen passport. His wife's murder – he sank her
body in a bath – might possibly have passed as an accident if his
mother-in-law hadn't interrupted him.

Thereafter it was only a matter of time before the police were
on his trail. Merrett, alias Chesney, had a criminal record which
identified him all over Europe. He shot himself because he
recognized that his number was up.

At the age of seventeen and a half, on March 17, 1926, he had
shot his mother through the side of the head. His reason was that
he had been forging her signature on cheques, and was afraid that
he was going to be found out. His history has become famous for
the fact that, when he was tried in Edinburgh for matricide, the
Scottish jury of ten men and five women brought in a majority
verdict of "Not proven." He was merely sent to prison for twelve
months for uttering forged cheques.

In his autobiography, Sir Sydney Smith, Emeritus Professor of
Forensic Medicine at Edinburgh University, expresses the feeling that the verdict aroused among experts at the time:

> The slackness of the police and the credit given to the
> misleading evidence of Spilsbury and Churchill, who had
> made a mistake and were too stubborn to admit it, allowed
> Merrett to live – and to kill again. A worthless life was
> saved, and two innocent women were thereby condemned
> to die.

In retrospect, no one can fairly disagree with Sir Sydney's
summing up of the case, except perhaps with the justice of his
comment that Churchill and Spilsbury "made a mistake and were
too stubborn to admit it." That opinion rests on what I believe to
be a delicate and still unresolved point of professional conduct –
the question as to how far the expert witness, especially when he
appears for the defence, should volunteer evidence of value to the
other side.

Churchill always insisted that he gave his evidence irrespective
of whether it helped the prosecution or the defence. He refused

on principle to support Marshall Hall's plea in the Green Bicycle Case. On several occasions, when he was called for the Crown, his evidence destroyed the Crown's case. During the Merrett trial, when a newspaper reporter asked him, "Do you think the prisoner is guilty?" he replied: "I don't know. I am only interested in the firearms side of the case."

With the knowledge that Merrett was certainly guilty, it is interesting to imagine oneself as a juryman in the trial before the Lord Justice-Clerk (Lord Alness) which began at Edinburgh on February 1, 1927, when what had previously passed as a suicide case had been transformed into a charge of murder.

It is so perilously easy to be wise after the event that, on the facts of the case, one wonders that the jury were ever in doubt. The defence made scarcely an effort to clear Merrett of the charge that he had forged his mother's signature on her cheques. The evidence was overwhelming that, while he was supposed to be a student at Edinburgh University, he was playing the Casanova at cheap dance halls. He had purchased for £1 15s, after obtaining a firearms' certificate from the police (on what grounds heaven knows), a .25 automatic pistol of Spanish make with fifty rounds of ammunition from Hardy Brothers in Princes Street. He was alone in the room with his mother when she was shot. He had the motive, the opportunity, and the means. The case rested on whether it could be proved, without possibility of doubt, that he did indeed shoot his mother, and that she didn't shoot herself.

Merrett had the inestimable advantage as a murderer that he didn't run away. When he shot his mother, through the lobe of her ear shortly after breakfast, he reported the event to the daily maid. When the police came they never questioned that it was a case of attempted suicide. Poor Mrs Merrett was detained at the Royal Infirmary, Edinburgh, in a cell with barred windows in the shadow that on her discharge arrangements would be made for taking her into custody for attempted *felo de se*.

With a bullet in her head, she lived astonishingly for a fortnight. She told her nurses that she had heard "a kind of explosion." She was surprised that a pistol was involved. "Did Donald do it?" she asked. "He is such a naughty boy." Before he shot her she remembered that she said: "Go away, Donald, and don't annoy me." Up to her death she never accused him. At the trial the judge described the failure of the police to take a dying deposition from her as "an almost criminal neglect of an obvious and imperative duty."

From the beginning the police and the doctors were at fault. The police, believing that it was a suicide case, failed to make a conclusive record of the position of the weapon and the body, and produced a witness in the daily maid who contradicted her story twice. Professor Harvey Littlejohn, the eminent pathologist of Edinburgh University, concluded from the post-mortem examination that the case was consistent with suicide. It was only later that it was discovered that Mrs Merrett's son had "uttered as genuine" twenty-nine cheques upon her bank account. Only then was he charged with murder and forgery.

Mrs Merrett believed that her husband, who had deserted her many years earlier, was dead. It emerged in the trial that he wasn't. There is reason to suppose that John Alfred Merrett had associations with the Secret Service.* Otherwise, it is difficult to understand how such a formidable, expensive, and determined defence was organised on his son's behalf. Mr Craigie M. Aitchison, KC, was briefed to represent him. Even more remarkable, Bernard Spilsbury, who had never appeared in any case except for the Crown, and Churchill, who himself normally gave evidence for the Director of Public Prosecutions, were called for Merrett's defence. It is one of those trials, like Mrs Barney's five years later, in which the circumstances are charged with question-marks.

Churchill himself said that he had never worked so hard on any case in which he had been called: "I took my wife with me to Edinburgh during the ten days I was there with the idea of making some visits to friends after Court hours, but counsel for the defence was indefatigable. We had conferences each evening

---

* Major Hugh B. C. Pollard writes: "Informed gossip at the time held that Merrett's father was a rather important figure in Intelligence in South America; not necessarily under the same name. Mrs Merrett was dead and 'reasons of State' are sometimes more important than the conviction of a horrible adolescent."

after dinner in which we went right through the transcript of the shorthand notes of the day's proceedings and prepared the next day's work as well."

The trial settled into a conflict between experts; and nine of them were called. The choice was to decide whether the shot which killed Mrs Merrett was sufficiently close to be self-inflicted or at a range sufficiently far to establish that the gun must have been fired by her son. It is important to remember that, at the time, the prejudice of the jury was in favour of suicide; and that the men and women on it were reluctant to convict a youth of the unnatural crime of murdering his own mother. Further, the evidence for the prosecution was inconclusive.

Professor Harvey Littlejohn, the chief medical witness for the Crown, had asserted after the post-mortem examination in April 1926 that:

> there is nothing to indicate the distance at which the discharge of the weapon took place, whether from a few inches or a greater distance. So far as the position of the wound is concerned, the case is consistent with suicide. There is some difficulty in attributing it to accident, although such a view cannot wholly be excluded.

When Sir Sydney Smith suggested to him that it was murder Professor Littlejohn, after various experiments, made a new report with a different conclusion, over a month after Merrett had been charged with the murder of his mother. Counsel for the defence didn't let him forget that he had changed his mind.

In fact, there wasn't a large difference in the factual evidence, although there was an important difference in conclusion, given by the experts on both sides. Merrett would have hanged if it could have been established that the bullet which killed his mother was fired at more than three inches' range. At a lesser range there was a reasonable doubt as between suicide and murder. It was that matter of inches which saved Merrett's neck.

Not the least difficulty of the nine experts on both sides was that there was no evidence of scorching or tattooing – or if there had been it had been swabbed away – round the wound through the lobe of Mrs Merrett's ear. If evidence of scorching from the powder in the cartridge could have been established it would have materially assisted the case for the defence because it would have shown that the pistol was fired from a range close enough to admit that the possibility of suicide couldn't be discounted.

The experts for the prosecution, led by Professor Harvey Littlejohn, waffled. Littlejohn, after reporting that the case was "consistent with suicide," changed his mind and made his second report that there was no indication of blackening or tattooing by ingrained particles of powder to suggest a near shot; "i.e. within 3″ of head." Professor Glaister said in evidence: "I am unable to exclude absolutely the production of such a wound as in this case by self-infliction." Mr McNaughten, the Edinburgh gunmaker, stated that the explosive in the pistol was "a modified form of cordite, called smokeless powder, which caused less discolouration than gunpowder."

By contrast, Churchill and Spilsbury commanded the court. Sir Sydney Smith, who had no love for either of them, makes in his autobiography a notable back-handed compliment:

To counter Littlejohn's expert evidence they put up Sir Bernard Spilsbury, the Home Office pathologist, who was very brilliant and very famous, but fallible like the rest of us – and very, very obstinate. In England, where he always appeared for the Crown, many murderers were justly convicted on his evidence. Now he was making one of his rare appearances for the defence. With him was Robert Churchill, often described as the expert on ballistics. Robert Churchill was famous, too, and I am sure he was an excellent gunsmith. He also was stubborn and dogmatic. He and Spilsbury often appeared together in shooting cases, and they were indeed a formidable team – terrifying when they made a mistake, as they did here.

But did they? Merrett, as subsequent events proved, was guilty. But Spilsbury and Churchill were called to show that it was *possible*, on the existing evidence, that Mrs Merrett committed suicide. At the time nobody except Merrett himself knew any more. In that knowledge it is difficult to accept that Churchill's and Spilsbury's evidence was "mistaken." Churchill's own opinion was that the other side made a mess of the case. The prosecution insisted that it was impossible for Mrs Merrett's wound to have been self-inflicted, although their own expert witnesses were uncertain in the matter. Churchill and Spilsbury did no more than demonstrate that suicide was, in fact, a possibility.

Together they had worked hard on the case. Churchill maintained that the absence of scorching or blackening round Mrs Merrett's wound wasn't significant. "Smokeless powder will mark paper or cardboard but it will not indelibly mark skin. Experiments with animal skin are not satisfactory; it doesn't respond like live human flesh. Superficial powder blackening round a wound may be washed away by the flow of blood. This was especially true," Churchill added, "in the Merrett case where the weapon was a little .25 automatic pistol. The cartridge, with a two-grain charge of nitrocellulose powder, consumed itself within an inch of leaving the barrel. Our London experiments with a similar pistol confirmed this view."

Bernard Spilsbury insisted on the experiment. When Churchill told him that shooting at inanimate targets would prove nothing Spilsbury sent the word round the London hospitals that he wanted a lump of human flesh. In due course the amputated leg of an elderly woman patient was provided. Wrapped in a brown-paper parcel, the two experts took the macabre object in the train to Churchill's shooting grounds in Kent. They hadn't got the pistol in the case, but they used a weapon of the same calibre and ammunition from the same shop that Merrett had bought his own gun. At varying distances, firing at the amputated leg, they established that there was no trace of a powder-mark on the skin.

Churchill himself wasn't entirely happy with the experiment. He said to me years later that, if it had been any other than Spilsbury, counsel would have challenged his evidence by pointing out that the reaction of dead flesh is quite different from living flesh. But Churchill himself was in no doubt that the evidence of the experiment, such as it was, was of no significance.

Curiously enough, Professor Harvey Littlejohn, for the prosecution, had been experimenting with shots into human flesh himself.

Littlejohn, using Merrett's pistol, found that at three inches the automatic "left very definite powder and burning marks round the wound in the skin area. Further, the discoloration on the skin couldn't be readily washed off." Later Churchill and Spilsbury attended a demonstration in Edinburgh of test shots at white cardboard with the same pistol with similar results. Churchill believed that neither the results on cardboard on that occasion nor the dead flesh in his experiments with Spilsbury in London were conclusive.

He knew that Hugh Pollard, behind the scenes, had constructed ear membranes of a glycerine and gelatine substance which he had tested to see if any confidence could be reposed in the absence, or otherwise, of blackening. There was no decisive information to be drawn from that experiment either.

In his evidence Churchill described the scorching effect that a small automatic at close range would have on live human skin. But he advanced an explanation of Mrs Merrett's death, subsequently supported by Spilsbury, and the judge too, which transformed the case. Examining him, Mr Craigie Aitchison asked:

"Have you in your experience had a case of a suicidal wound behind the right ear?"

"Yes."

"Was that the case of a man or woman?"

"The case of a woman."

"Who shot herself behind the right ear?"

"Yes."

"Was the weapon directed forwards or backwards?"

"Forwards."

"Did it roughly correspond to the direction of the wound in this case?"

"Yes, roughly."

"And was that an undoubted case of suicide?"

"It was brought in as suicide."

"It has been suggested, but I do not think persisted in, that, in order to get the weapon into such a position as to produce a wound of the kind we have here, the hand would need to be put into a strained position. What do you say to that?"

"I say that it is quite possible to reproduce that wound without any movement of the arm at all – just a movement of the head. I teach shooting, and I find that women flinch from the discharge at first, by closing their eyes and by turning the head away from the discharge instinctively."

"Does it come to this, that supposing the weapon were pointed at the side of the temple, an instinctive movement of the head, without any movement of the arm, might get the pistol into the position that would give you the direction we have in this case?"

"You could reproduce this wound exactly by doing that."

"In your view, can the angle be easily accounted for on the view that the pistol was pointed at the temple, but there was an instinctive aversion of the head at the moment the trigger was pulled?"

"It is possible to reproduce this wound in that way."

"And, if this was a case of suicide, would you, from your experience of instinctive movements of the head when firearms are fired, think it a likely thing to occur?"

"Yes. I have also considered the wound from the point of view of accident."

"In your view, could a wound of this kind, having regard to all the facts, direction and so on, have been accidentally caused?"

"I could reproduce that wound by holding the pistol with the thumb on the trigger-guard and the fingers of the hand at the butt of the pistol."

"Assume that Mrs Merrett – she seeing the pistol in the bureau – had picked it up in that position, and assuming that she over-balanced and fell, is there any difficulty at all in getting an accidental discharge that would produce a wound in the head such as you find here?"

"No."

Churchill demonstrated his theory by putting his thumb on the trigger, with the butt of the pistol in the palm of the hand, and jarring the back of the hand on the ledge of the witness-box, the muzzle being pointed towards the head and the face averted from the pistol.

"Accordingly, are the facts in your view consistent with accident?"

"Accident is possible."

"Similarly, supposing that, having lost her balance at the moment the pistol was in her hand, she instinctively raised her hand to her head to protect her head in the fall, is there any difficulty in getting the pistol into a position that is consistent with accident?"

"There is no difficulty in getting the pistol into position, but I should not expect it to happen that way. I think I have given the two most likely ways that this could happen. I think the most likely way is to pick the pistol up with the thumb on the trigger guard and to fall on it."

"Which might happen if Mrs Merrett had her chair tilted up at the time?"

"It is possible to reproduce the wound in that way."

"Is it in accordance with your knowledge and experience of firearms that accidents occur which it is sometimes impossible to explain?"

"It is impossible to explain some of them."

"In the case of gunshot wounds where you are using a gun – I mean suicidal wounds where you are using a gun – where do you usually find them, or where do you often find them?"

"Usually in the mouth."

"Where you have a suicidal wounds from a long-barrelled revolver, where do you frequently find them?"

"Usually in the temple. I am saying usually, because sometimes they are in the mouth."

"But when you find a wound inflicted with a short-barrelled firearm, such as the automatic pistol you hold in your hand, where do you usually find them?"

"Usually in the side of the head. A shotgun, on account of its very long barrel, naturally can only be placed in the mouth. A long-barrelled revolver can be placed in the mouth, because there is something you can put in; and also it can be put, on account of its length, at the side of the head. But with an automatic pistol, such as I have in my hand, it is natural to do it at the side."

"Taking all the facts as you have them in this case, do you find anything in the position or the direction of the wound to exclude either suicide or accident?"

"No."

He was cross-examined by the Lord Advocate:

"Take first of all your suggested possible method, that of suicide, which you have demonstrated, are you assuming that this is a woman who is not skilled in firing pistols?"

"A woman who is nervous of firearms, and I find that every woman is nervous at first."

"Is it a very uncommon thing for a woman to commit suicide with a pistol?"

"I have had a few cases. Naturally, it is not common."

"And still more uncommon for women who are ignorant of the use of such weapons?"

"I would say that."

"Among these few cases, was there any one of a woman committing suicide with a pistol in the presence of a near relative, such as a son?"

"In one case a woman committed suicide for no apparent reason. The shot was behind the ear, and no action was taken against the husband, who was asleep in a chair alongside. That is the only case I can cite near to this."

"Assuming that sitting in the chair Mrs Merrett put her elbow at the angle you have suggested, it would come in contact, or risk coming into contact, with the bureau. Does not that exclude the possibility of your theory?"

"No."

"If it did come in contact, it would upset it. If there was a risk it would render it doubtful?"

"Yes."

"Come now to your suggestion of accident. The only suggestion you make, as I understand, is that the thumb goes into the trigger guard with the hand grasping the butt of the pistol?"

"Yes."

"But, surely, the person so grasping it must have known the pistol was there?"

"That is right."

"You could not put any papers between, or the thumb would not go into the trigger guard, would it?"

"No."

"Were you assuming that the pistol was picked up off the bureau?"

"I am simply assuming that the lady was sitting in the chair and was stretching out."

"You do not know whether she needed to tip the chair or not in order to reach the pigeon-holes?"

"No."

"Or whether it would be possible for her to tilt the chair?"

"I expect that in the case of accident she would have to tip the chair to fall."

"Are you assuming that she is sitting at an angle to the bureau, with her back half towards it?"

"Yes, falling back on the right hand against the bureau."

"The effect of that would be to jerk the pistol out of her hand, probably, would it not?"

"I am assuming that she falls on to the pistol."

"You are assuming that she stretched towards the pigeon-hole to get the pistol out of it?"

"Yes."

"Are you aware that there are some 20 inches between the pigeon-hole and the edge of the writing slab on the bureau?"

"No, I do not know."

"So that the pit of her arm would be touching the writing slab as she reached for the pistol?"

"I do not know that."

"That would rather affect the theory that you are putting forward?"

"It would, if the body were stopped by this bureau."

"You made certain experiments in London. It was you who actually did the firing?"

"Yes."

"Were those experiments made with a different pistol and different cartridges and gunpowder to those which we know were used in this case?"

"Yes, a pistol of similar make, of Spanish manufacture, and the ammunition supposedly of similar but of later make."

"It was a different maker, was it not?"

"It was Nobel's ammunition. They are all one combine."

"Do I understand that you experimented on both skin and cardboard in London and in Edinburgh?"

"Yes."

"Did the powder used in London produce more of a yellowish colour and not so black as in Edinburgh?"

"The powder used in London produced more tattooing."

"But was not the colour more of a yellowish tinge?"

"Slightly flame."

"You would agree, in view of your experience, that the advisable thing in every case is to carry out tests with the actual weapon, and with as identical powder and ammunition as you can get?"

"Yes."

"On the Sunday, 30th January, eight days ago, was it you who actually fired the pistol?"

"Yes."

"Was the pistol in good working order?"

"Yes."

He was re-examined by Mr Aitchison:

"You were asked whether you knew of any case in which a mother had shot herself in the presence of her son. You do recollect a case in which a wife shot herself in the presence of her husband?"

"Yes."

"And there was a Home Office investigation?"

"Yes."

"Was that established as a case of suicide?"

"Yes."

"And did the investigations reveal any motive of any kind?"

"No motive."

Churchill was followed into the box by Sir Bernard Spilsbury. Spilsbury added the opinion that women, through the lifelong habit of putting up their hair, had a great extension of the shoulder-joint and, as a consequence, it was possible to imagine that Mrs Merrett could hold a small pistol in a position to point it at the back of her skull. He insisted that her wound could not be considered as definitely inflicted by another person. Spilsbury said that he thought it was suicide.

The assuredness of the two expert witnesses for the defence undoubtedly carried the jury. The judge was equally impressed. In his summing up, in Scotland called "the charge to the jury," Lord Alness said that the chief objection suggested to the theory of suicide from the direction of the wound was that it would involve a constrained position of the arm on firing. "Well, you will consider whether that objection was not met, or invalidated, by the exceptionally simple suggestion made by the London gun expert, Mr Churchill, that a sudden and instinctive aversion of the head by the person who was going to fire the pistol would naturally account for the position of the wound, without any constrained position of the arm."

The jury brought in the middle verdict of "Not Proven" on the murder charge. While Scottish law is often criticised in England, it meant exactly what it said. Merrett wasn't proved guilty, but the jury thought he was. Further, it is unarguable that Spilsbury and Churchill between them saved his unworthy neck, although Churchill himself gave all the credit to the counsel for the defence.

"Mr Craigie Aitchison, afterwards Lord Aitchison, was in my opinion the best cross-examiner I ever heard. The way he used the Scottish phrase 'come awa' with it' to a witness until the witness did indeed 'come awa' with it' was wonderful. I was very tickled when, in examination, he waved his fingers prettily at Sir Bernard Spilsbury and said, more phonetically than I can write it: 'Now tell me, Saint Berr-nard!' In court, it passed unnoticed.

"The book of the case in the 'Notable British Trials' series does not reveal the skill with which Craigie Aitchison conducted his defence, how he threw quick-fire questions at one witness until he had conceded his point; how he played with another, not so intelligent, until he had got the evidence he wanted. Craigie Aitchison and his junior got Merrett off. In that case, counsel was the Scottish Marshall Hall, Muir and Norman Birkett rolled into one."

History has placed the blame for Merrett's acquittal firmly on the shoulders of Churchill and Spilsbury. It is undeniable that the evidence of the two best witnesses in the land influenced the judge and the jury. It is probably true that neither Spilsbury nor Churchill believed that Merrett was innocent. The heart of the affair is simply whether they thought, as they did, that Mrs Merrett's death could possibly have been caused by suicide or accident. It is a matter of conscience to decide whether it was right for Spilsbury and Churchill to advance the best argument that they could for the defence, or whether they should have refused to appear at all. Myself, I don't know the answer.

PICTURE A MURDERER

(Edwin Bush, UK 1961)

Richard Jackson

Identifying a suspect in a murder case can be a hazardous business. Witnesses are often confused, sometimes frightened, occasionally mistaken. But their ability to recall facial characteristics can be crucial. In the late 1950s, new techniques were developed to improve the likeness achieved by a combination of witness descriptions and artists' impressions. The first of these facial assembly techniques was known as "Identikit". Guided by an eye-witness, a skilled operator assembled transparencies of the suspect's key facial features into a two-dimensional composite. The picture could then be circulated by the police. In 1961, Edwin Bush became the first murder suspect in Britain to be brought to book by the Identikit method of compiling a picture of a suspect's face. Bush was arrested within four days of the Identikit's publication by a policeman on patrol. Richard Jackson (1902–75) was assistant commissioner (CID) at New Scotland Yard. But by training and temperament he was a criminal lawyer rather than a policeman, and an excellent raconteur, a trait that endeared him to the press. He held and expressed trenchant views of a range of subjects, including the need for tough sentences for violent criminals and a detestation of liberal reformers. When he retired in 1963, Richard Jackson received a knighthood and wrote his memoirs, in which he recalled how the new-fangled Identikit technique resulted in the arrest and conviction of a killer.

"If this paper remains blue," Sherlock Holmes told Watson, "all is well. If it turns red, it means a man's life." He dipped the litmus paper into a test tube and it flushed into a dull, dirty crimson . . .

Conan Doyle's stories may have had some influence in showing the police how science can be used as an aid to detection, and even more influence in leading the public to think of forensic science as a kind of magic. It is a very useful aid; it isn't a kind of magic. Criminals are caught by men, not by gadgets.

Forensic science has, of course, tremendously advanced since Sherlock Holmes's day, particularly in its ability to show, by matching minute particles of soil or dust or thread or cellulose, that a suspect must have been at the scene of the crime. As well as the laboratory techniques which support them, as it were, behind the lines, the police have acquired a number of gadgets to help both in their preventive and in their investigative work. Rapidly coming into use now are personal two-way radios carried by constables on the beat, hidden television cameras to keep a watch on vulnerable streets and markets and car parks, and an infra-red spotlight for use at night.

One device which we acquired during my period at the Yard caught the public imagination more than any other – the Identi-kit.

I first heard about it on July 30th, 1959. At a lunch that day in the Café Royal I met a huge genial giant of a man, called Pete Pitchess. He had been in the FBI and was now Sheriff of Los Angeles County. After lunch he came back to the Yard to see the Black Museum and the Information Room. When we were having a drink in my room afterwards, with a few senior officers whom I'd invited to meet him, he showed us a piece of equipment which had been invented by his Deputy, Hugh McDonald. It was a book of interchangeable transparent flaps, each with a drawing of some part of a face – eyes, eyebrows, hairline, nose, mouth, and so on; rather like those books in which children put the head of a giraffe on to the body of a lion and the legs of an ostrich. With this range of possible parts, Pitchess said, a useful picture of a wanted man could be built up from the selection made by a witness who had seen him.

There was nothing new, of course, about constructing pictures from eyewitnesses' descriptions. As long ago as 1935, when I was prosecuting in the Grierson case, I was struck by what a good likeness the police drawing had been of the man who eventually appeared in the dock; it was a profile, I remember, with a hooked nose and glasses. But in Britain (contrary to the practice in some other countries) the artist didn't normally work with the witness; he merely followed a description which was handed to him. And a witness who is shown a completed drawing is too apt to accept it, whereas an Identikit picture can be continually altered until the witness really does feel satisfied that it represents the face he saw.

I showed the Identikit to the Commissioner, and we both expressed interest in the possibility of acquiring it. A week or so later I received a letter from the American company which manufactured the equipment. (If the company had been British I dare say I should never have heard any more about it, not for months or years anyway.) Pitchess had told them of our interest, they said; they were willing to consider leasing it to us, and they invited us to send an officer to California for a course of training. I replied that I couldn't spare a man. There was further correspondence, during which they asked me, among other things, for a list of every police force in Britain with more than a hundred officers. I sent it to them. They pondered on the size of the potential market, and, the following spring, offered to send their representative to Scotland Yard, to run a course of instruction here.

After clearing this proposal with the Commissioner, the Receiver, and the Home Office I circulated it to all provincial forces through the Chief Officers Association and the Chief Constables of Scotland Association. The response was gratifying. We finally arranged a three-day course for the beginning of March 1961.

The class consisted of thirty-one officers – ten detective sergeants from the Metropolitan Police, twenty provincial officers, and one officer from the United States Air Force. Superintendent Du Rose of C1 was in charge, and the instruction was given by Deputy Sheriff Hugh McDonald himself, who proved to be extremely good.

The course ended on Friday, March 3rd. A detective sergeant

from "H" Division went back to his duties next day, and, using the Identikit, was immediately able to catch three men who had committed a robbery. But a more serious crime had been reported in "E" Division.

At 12.15 p.m. that Friday, before the Identikit course was even ended, I heard that a woman had been found stabbed to death in an antique shop in Cecil Court, off the Charing Cross Road. The body had been discovered by the proprietor, Louis Meier. A wireless car from Bow Street arrived, and the officers found the dead woman lying on her back with an antique dagger stuck in her breast and another in her neck.

She was Mrs Elsie May Batten, and she had been an assistant in the shop. The daggers, which had evidently been taken from the stock, still had their price tickets on them.

At 12.30 Detective Superintendent Pollard arrived. In those first few hours his chances of success seemed steadily to dwindle. There was no reason to suppose – and, since the weapons were clearly impromptu, it seemed unlikely – that Mrs Batten had been killed by a personal enemy; nor had she been sexually assaulted. Robbery was the likeliest motive, but her handbag and the box used as a till both appeared to be untouched; Mr Meier couldn't say if anything had been removed from his stock. Local inquiries elicited nothing. A hairdresser opposite had seen Mrs Batten open the shop at 9.15, but since then nobody had been observed going in or out. The only clue Pollard found was a piece of wood under the dead woman's legs, bearing the impression of a heel and faint sole marks.

When the pathologist, Dr Keith Simpson, arrived halfway through the afternoon he found a third dagger underneath the body and a third stab wound in the back. He said the woman had also been struck on the head with a heavy stone ornament, and he confirmed that there had been no sexual interference.

Then things began to move. A fifteen-year-old boy, an apprentice sign-writer, was brought to the police by his uncle. The boy had told his uncle, and now told us, that he had gone into Meier's shop at about half-past eleven that morning to buy a billiard cue, and had seen what he thought was a dummy lying on the floor at the back. When he realized it was a woman he assumed she had fainted – and promptly left the shop. Which doesn't seem a very chivalrous act. Perhaps he was a timid boy.

Meanwhile Meier recalled that a young man who said he was half-Indian and half-English had been in the shop during Mrs Batten's lunch hour on the previous day. This Eurasian had spent some time examining the antique daggers, but had left without buying anything. He had returned later, accompanied by a girl, and asked the price of a dress sword. Mrs Batten had remarked to Meier afterwards that it was odd for a man so poorly dressed to be interested in a sword costing £15. Meier gave us a description of the young man, and said he thought that he would be able to recognize him. All he could remember about the girl was that she looked somewhere between seventeen and twenty, and was fair-haired. There were several dress swords in the shop, and he couldn't say if any of them were missing.

A team of twenty detectives, under Superintendent Pollard, began working their way through all the other antique shops and jewellers. But they found what they wanted, next morning, only a few yards away.

Opposite Meier's shop was a gunmaker. His nineteen-year-old son had been alone there on the morning of the murder when, soon after 10 a.m., a young Indian walked in and tried to sell him a dress sword. The sword had been wrapped in a sheet of brown paper. When he was asked how much he wanted for it the Indian replied, "I paid fifteen pounds, but I'll take ten." The gun-maker's son rightly thought this a suspicious remark. He asked the Indian to come back at 11.15, when his father would be in. The Indian agreed and left the sword, but never returned.

The gunmaker himself now added a piece of information. A dark young man – he couldn't remember much else about his looks – had called at the shop on the previous afternoon, and asked, "Do you buy swords?" The gunmaker said he might, but he would need to see the article. The young man replied that this sword had an engraving on it, and he promised to bring it in.

So we now had the sword. It was immediately identified by another woman who worked part-time in Meier's shop, and who remembered having shown it to a customer the week before. The brown paper had gone, having been used to wrap up a pair of gun-barrels, but Pollard's men traced it to a customer in Kilburn, and sent it, together with the sword, to the fingerprint department at the Yard.

Meier and the gunmaker's son were each able to give a clear and detailed description of the young Eurasian; so, less than twenty-four hours after the course had ended, we had an ideal opportunity for giving Identikit a trial run. On March 4th one of the officers who had been on the course, Detective Sergeant Dagg, interviewed Meier and the gunmaker's son – separately – and built up pictures matching the descriptions they gave him. The two pictures proved strikingly similar, except for one detail: the hair style was quite different.

I was shown photographs of these two Identikit reconstructions. They looked good enough to be useful and close enough to one another not to cause confusion. I decided that not only should they both be circulated to all police forces, but they should also be published in the Press and shown on television. At the same time we released Meier's much vaguer description of the girl.

Four days later, at 1.40 p.m., a certain PC Cole was on duty in Old Compton Street, Soho, when he spotted a young man who seemed to match the picture. And the young man was accompanied by a girl of about seventeen with blonde hair. Cole stopped them, and told the man that he fitted the description of someone wanted for questioning in connection with the Cecil Court murder.

"Yes, I saw the photo in the paper," said the young man casually. "It did look a bit like me."

The accent – Cockney, not Peter Sellers-type Indian – also matched the police circulation. Cole asked them both to come with him to the police station.

"I'd rather not," said the man. "We're going to buy a ring."

Cole insisted, and, since this was a murder case, he took no chances. He searched the man, there and then. Finding no weapons, he marched the couple off towards a police telephone box in Cambridge Circus. An off-duty constable in civilian clothes saw what was happening and telephoned for a police car while Cole stood guard over his prisoners. Both the man and the girl repeatedly asked to be allowed to go; they were in a hurry, they said. Which merely intensified Cole's suspicions. Then a car arrived and whisked them away to Bow Street.

The young man was half-Indian, half-English, and gave his name as Edwin Bush. He was just twenty-one years old. As soon as he arrived at Bow Street impressions were taken of the soles and heels of his shoes. While these were being compared with the marks found under the body Pollard questioned the girl.

She was seventeen and had known Bush for about two months, and had come into the West End with him that day to choose an engagement ring. As it was also his twenty-first birthday, they were going to have a double celebration at an Indian restaurant.

She denied ever having been to the antique shop in Cecil Court, and, oddly enough, she was telling the truth. As we discovered later, the girl who had accompanied Bush was his sister, aged eighteen and not blonde at all but very dark. It was sheer luck that, because Meier wrongly thought she had been fair, the description happened to fit the couple whom Cole picked out from the crowd in Old Compton Street.

While Pollard questioned the girl, detectives called at Bush's home. His mother said he had left the house at 7.30 am on March 3rd, presumably for work. When in due course Pollard asked him about his movements on March 3rd he immediately said that he had spent the whole of that morning at home with his mother. The shoe-prints matched.

Pollard told the duty officer at Bow Street that he wanted to hold an identification parade. This was easier said than done, since it involved collecting nine men of similar age and colour who could speak English without a foreign accent. Eventually a group was assembled, and the parade was held at 10.25 p.m. Meier walked down the line first. He stood for some time in front of Bush, then said, "I'm not positive, but I think this is the man." The gunmaker's son was brought in. He picked Bush with no hesitation at all.

Pollard then charged Edwin Bush with the murder of Mrs Batten. After a moment's silence Bush said, "The girl is nothing to do with it. I did it alone." And he went on to make a statement admitting that he had killed Mrs Batten in order to steal the sword. Just to clinch matters, there was blood on some of his clothes, and his palm-print and two of his fingerprints were found on the brown paper in which the sword had been wrapped.

When he came up for trial at the Old Bailey in May he pleaded not guilty to capital murder. He now said that he killed Mrs Batten, not to get the sword, but after she had made an offensive remark about the colour of his skin. Cross-examined by Mervyn Griffith-Jones, Bush didn't deny that he had in fact stolen the sword.

"You admit that you went into the shop in order to steal it, and admit that having stolen it you killed the lady with these three daggers?"

"Yes, sir."

"You lost your temper simply because she passed the remark, 'You niggers are all the same, you come in and never buy anything'?"

"Yes, sir."

In his summing up the judge instructed the jury that, if they believed this was the true cause of Bush's attack on Mrs Batten, they ought not to convict him of capital murder. They didn't believe it. After two hours' deliberation they found him guilty – which, the judge said afterwards, was the only possible verdict. Bush was hanged.

The result was a great deal of publicity for Identikit. The newspapers hailed it as a marvellous new aid to criminal investigation; and, sure as a Pavlovian reflex, some people expressed alarm at this new danger to civil liberties. How risky it would be, they said, to use composite pictures as evidence against an accused man! No-one, of course, had ever suggested using them as evidence. If an arrest was made as a result of circulating an Identikit picture the witnesses would then have to identify the suspect in the ordinary way. "If hopes were dupes, fears may be liars" – and *vice versa*. The apprehensions about Identikit were wholly unjustified, and the enthusiasm too was exaggerated. Identikit is simply a way – one way among several – of fixing, illustrating, and making permanent a witness's recollection, so as to help in the hunt for a wanted man when no photograph is available.

Its spectacular success in the Batten case proved a considerable embarrassment. Too much was then expected of it. As people saw more Identikit pictures, enthusiasm turned to ridicule. How odd, they said, that all wanted men should look just the same! But to policemen they don't look just the same; Identikit puts into visible form what a police description is supposed to provide – a catalogue of the few distinguishing marks which divide the wanted face from all the other human faces.

In his report to me after the course Superintendent Du Rose pointed out that one of the advantages, if Identikit were widely adopted, would be that a telephone call to a central index – the Criminal Record Office, perhaps – could by using a code of numbers and figures pass a likeness to other forces without any need to transmit the actual picture. It could be useful internationally, he suggested; and he arranged a demonstration for the Chief Superintendents of C1, which includes the Interpol Office, C9, and the Criminal Record Office. Identikit requires trained operators, and he recommended that a phased scheme for its introduction should be adopted as soon as possible.

The arrangement we eventually made was that the apparatus itself remained the property of the American company, which would lease the sets to the forces which wanted them. The Receiver of the Metropolitan Police District agreed to act as the hiring agent for all British forces. Whereupon we immediately ran into a bureaucratic snag. We became liable for import dues, assessed by the Customs at an exorbitant figure. Not without difficulty, we obtained special exemption.

The possibility of using Identikit internationally was debated at length during the Interpol General Assembly in 1962. I realized then for the first time how many comparable systems were already in use. The Canadians, for example, had been using cut-up photographs of their own criminals for years; and there were several rival systems in the States. Advocates of these other systems objected to the use of the word "Identikit" as though it were a generic, instead of a brand, name. The Assembly did not, in the end, recommend its international adoption, chiefly because it wasn't applicable at the moment to non-Caucasian faces.

That anyone could genuinely have objected, on principle, to the use of Identikit remains, to me, a great puzzle – or, at least, an example of the attitude of mind which is incorrigibly and irrationally suspicious of the police. British courts and our rules of evidence provide the most scrupulous protection for the accused. To extend this proper care and start complaining that the police weren't "sporting" in the way they acquired the evidence is to tilt the whole balance of the law in favour of criminals, who aren't "sporting" at all. In some ways the Americans have gone even further in this direction than we have, declaring inadmissible any evidence, however damning, which wasn't acquired in strict accordance with the rules – with the ludicrous result that confessed murderers have had to be released because their confessions weren't taken in quite the proper form.

Telephone-tapping is another example. On both sides of the Atlantic this aid to investigation has roused strongly hostile feelings and has now been forbidden except in very special circumstances. The Metropolitan Police are allowed to intercept telephone calls only on the signed authority of the Secretary of State after application has been made by the Assistant Commissioner. Such nice regard for privacy no doubt does us credit, but is it really necessary? Innocent people have much more to fear from the unimpeded activities of criminals than from the remote possibility that the privacy of their telephone calls might one day be unobtrusively infringed by the police – an infringement far less embarrassing to their domestic secrets than the crossed lines which our beloved telephone system is for ever mischievously providing.

THE BITER BIT

(Gordon Hay, 1968)

George Saunders

The case of teenager Gordon Hay was remarkable because he was convicted on the evidence of the teeth-marks found on the body of his victim. Expert medical evidence clearly showed that the characteristics of the bite-marks were consistent in every detail with a dental impression taken from Hay. The trial judge, Lord Grant, described forensic dentistry as a relatively new science, "but there must, of course, always be a first time." George Saunders (1923–95) reported Hay's trial for The Scotsman, *the newspaper on which he worked as law reporter for some thirty years. He included this account in a collection of Scottish cases published shortly after his retirement in 1991.*

The science of forensic odontology was still in its infancy in March 1968 when Scottish legal history was made by the conviction of an eighteen-year-old approved schoolboy, Gordon Hay, known as "Gags", for the murder of a fifteen-year-old Biggar schoolgirl, Linda Peacock. The successful use of odontology to identify Hay as the murderer by the bite mark he left on the young girl's breast was hailed as "a forensic triumph." Scottish courts had always been slow to accept the latest advances in science but, surprisingly, showed a new receptiveness on this occasion to careful scientific evidence in what became a classic case of circumstantial evidence.

Even the presiding judge, Lord Grant, the late Lord Justice Clerk of Scotland, described the case as "unique, difficult and puzzling."

The eminent pathologist, Professor Keith Simpson, then head of the Department of Forensic Medicine at Guy's Hospital, London, and leading expert on odontology, gave evidence at the trial. He had the highest praise for the Scottish team, who produced crucial evidence and showed infinite patience and attention to detail. They produced, he said, the finest "bite mark" photography and dentition-matching that had yet been brought to court.

Both the Scottish experts, Detective-Inspector Osborne Butler and Dr Warren Harvey, who later became honorary consultant Forensic Odontologist to the Glasgow Police, were aware that their work on the case was vital. The only proof of the murderer's identity, their evidence survived a most searching cross-examination at the trial.

Linda Peacock, who was only 5ft 1in tall, was the youngest of eight children. She was a bright and lively girl, interested in ponies, records and, naturally at her age, boys. She spent the afternoon of Sunday, 6 August 1967 at a farm busy with her favourite pastime, exercising ponies.

Linda then spent the evening in the Lanarkshire market town of Biggar. Normally, she would have gone to her sister's home in Main Street to wait for one of her brothers to take her home.

But, on that fateful evening, her sister was on holiday. Linda set off to walk more than a mile to her home at Swaire Cottage. She was last seen talking to friends in the town about 9.30 p.m. Next morning, she was found strangled under a yew tree in St Mary's Cemetery, only 269 yards away from where she was last seen alive. The police said there were sadistic touches to the murder and a massive manhunt began. The cemetery in unlit Carwood Road was screened from the narrow road by a 5-foot-high wall. It was not locked at night and was often used by courting couples.

The murder hunt was led by Detective Chief Superintendent William Muncie, the head of Lanarkshire CID who had successfully led investigations into fifty murders, including those com-

mitted by mass murderer, Peter Manuel. He later became Assistant Chief Constable of Strathclyde before his well-earned
retirement. Muncie's patience, clever reasoning and dogged
determination had made him a legend in the force.

More than 100 officers from the Lanarkshire force and the
Regional Crime Squad began a house-to-house search in the
vicinity immediately after Linda was found. Tracker dogs were
used in the surrounding fields and every male over fourteen in the
area was interviewed. A young couple had been seen on the road
near the cemetery at about 10.15 p.m., just after Linda, on her
own, was seen by two men who knew her and waved to her as they
drove home. A woman told the police she heard a scream coming
from the cemetery late on the Sunday evening.

Police began compiling reports on the movements of inmates
and ex-inmates of nearby Loaningdale Approved School. The
small town itself was in the grip of fear lest the killer would strike
again. A petition calling for the return of capital punishment was
signed by 20,000 people.

Nine days after the crime, the police returned to the scene of
the murder to comb the area inch-by-inch. The bereaved parents,
George Peacock, a retired electrician, and his wife, Mary, made
an impassioned plea to the public for information.

But the investigation into their daughter's death would prove
to be a slow and painstaking forensic exercise, and Hay would not
be arrested and charged with the murder until 110 days after the
crime. The police interviewed more than 300 people, drawing up
a short list of 29 who could possibly have been involved. All of the
short-listed individuals agreed to dental impressions being taken.
After these were compared with transparencies of the bite marks
on the girl's breast, the list was reduced to five.

Second impressions were then taken of these five. Six weeks
after the murder, the team of four dental experts told the
authorities they had eliminated everyone on the list except for
No 11. It was only at this stage that it was revealed to them, in
confidence, that No 11 was in fact Gordon Hay.

A further impression was still required in order for the dental
experts to be absolutely certain. The Crown then took the unique
step of applying to Sheriff-Substitute Gordon Gillies, QC at

Lanark for a warrant to authorise a third impression of Hay's teeth. The warrant was granted.

Hay, by then, was the principal suspect but had not yet been arrested. For this reason, the legality of taking a third impression of his teeth would be fiercely contested at his trial.

Largely on the strength of the odontological evidence, Hay was charged with the murder of Linda Peacock. Appearing at a pleading diet at Lanark, he lodged a special defence of alibi. When his trial opened in the High Court in Edinburgh on Monday, 26 February 1968, before a jury of six women and nine men, the Crown listed 105 witnesses, including Professor Simpson and other dental and medical experts.

Hay pleaded not guilty to murdering Linda by striking her on the head with an instrument, biting her on the breast, tying a ligature round her wrist and her neck and strangling her. His special defence of alibi claimed that between 9 p.m. and midnight, when the crime was alleged to have been committed, he was in the approved school.

Prosecuting for the Crown was Mr Ewan Stewart, QC, then Solicitor-General for Scotland who had already established a reputation as a terrier of a prosecutor – probably the best prosecutor in Scotland for many years. His patient and sometimes aggressive cross-examinations had proved the downfall of many criminals. He was assisted by Mr Hugh Morton (later Lord Morton of Shuna, a judge in the Court of Session). For the defence there was an equally tenacious Stewart, Mr Ian Stewart, QC (later Lord Allanbridge), who was assisted by Mr James Law. Their battle over the medical evidence was to prove the highlight of the trial.

Lord Grant immediately ruled that no witnesses under seventeen should be named, adding that inmates of the approved school who were over seventeen should be treated in the same way.

Five local girls, all aged 15 or 16, told the court that girls had dates with boys from the school and that a pre-arranged signal – an owl hoot – was used to attract the attention of the boys when they were not meant to be out of the school. The boys, they said, got out of the school through the gymnasium.

One girl said Linda had a boyfriend in the school but he had left. Another girl recalled Linda speaking to Hay and another boy on Saturday, 5 August 1967 – the day before she was murdered – at a fun fair at Biggar.

The girls all said the boys at the school could come and go as they pleased, especially at weekends. One girl said she met boys from the school at the pictures on Saturday nights and went to dances at the school.

A sixteen-year-old boy who was a pupil at the school at the time said he was with Hay when they met Linda at the fun fair. Linda spoke to the boy but he walked on. Hay stayed behind, but his schoolmate did not know if he said anything to Linda. Afterwards, however, Hay told him he would not mind a night with her. Hay's schoolmate also described how some of the boys from the school had attended a camp at Montrose. After a beach barbecue on Friday, 4 August, the night before they returned, he saw one of the boys pick up a metal hook on the beach. On the evening of Linda's murder, at about 9 p.m. he saw Hay wearing pyjamas, a dressing gown and boots in his dormitory. He did not see Hay again that night.

But a fifteen-year-old boy who was also a pupil at the time said that when, after the murder, the police arrived at the school, Hay told him something like, "We were in the dorm all last night". He understood that this was what he was to tell the police, although it was not true.

Mr Ewan Stewart asked, "Were you invited by Hay to tell a lie?" The boy replied, "That was what it sounded like but I wasn't sure."

The boy remembered Hay going to the toilet in his pyjamas. Afterwards he fell asleep and woke up with the wireless playing. He did not know how long he had been asleep.

Cross-examined by Mr Ian Stewart, the boy said he had tried to get a date with Linda but failed. He also had written letters to her. Because of this he was a little bit worried. The police took away his clothes as well as those of Hay.

Two separate witnesses recalled hearing a scream from the cemetery about 10 p.m. A farmer's wife testified that she saw a couple standing in the cemetery, and had remarked to her husband that she had heard of courting couples in many places but not in a churchyard. A local farmer who had known Linda all her life stated that while passing Carwood Road in his van he had seen Linda. He had dogs in the back of his van and could not offer anyone in good clothes a lift; otherwise, he would have picked her up and taken her home.

Linda's father testified that on the day before her murder his daughter went to Huntfield to help with exercising ponies, returning home at about 4 p.m. The following day, Linda again went to Huntfield. He and his wife spent the day in Carluke. When they returned they found that their daughter was not at home. Worried, they contacted the police and a full-scale search began. Two constables found their daughter's body in the cemetery at 6.40 a.m.

She was lying partly under a yew tree beside a grave. A purse was near her head. There were bloodstains on the grass and blood on her head and cheek. A piece of string was found hanging from a nearby tree. Linda was lying on her back and her clothing was displaced. There was a deep weal round her neck which had broken the skin. Her anorak was bunched up under her head.

Detective-Sgt John Paton, who photographed the body, said there was bruising on the girl's breast which looked like bite marks. A doctor who examined the body said she was fully clothed but her upper garments had been drawn up, exposing the upper part of her body. Her lower garments were also drawn up. It appeared that a cord or string had been tightly tied round her neck.

Bank manager, Thomas Aitken, testified that while driving home he saw a young couple in his headlights near the cemetery. At home, he put on the television and heard Dickie Henderson introducing Frank Sinatra, Jun. on the *Blackpool Show*. He was later taken to Scottish Television's Glasgow studio where he saw a re-run of the programme, using a stop-watch to indicate the precise moment he first saw the programme. It showed that he first saw the programme about 10.20 p.m. It took 20 minutes to drive from the point where he had seen the young couple.

On the second day of the trial, a fifteen-year-old boy from Fife said he saw Hay in pyjamas, dressing gown and boots on the night of the murder. Later he saw the dressing gown and pyjamas lying on Hay's bed in the dormitory they shared. He fell asleep and was awakened by the door slamming. Hay was there with all his clothes on. His face was dirty and there was dirt on the knees of his jeans. His hair was dishevelled.

Another boy, who slept in the same dormitory, recalled finding a metal fishhook on the beach at Montrose. He brought it back to the school and put it on top of a wardrobe. He showed the hook to Hay, who said something about using it for fighting in Biggar.

He saw Hay that night taking part in a whilst drive. Later, he watched *The Untouchables* on the television until about 9.55 p.m. He then went back to his dormitory but there was no one there. Because of something he had been told he looked for the hook but could not find it. The last time he saw it was the day before, when he had shown it to Hay.

He saw Hay's dressing gown and pyjamas on his bed. Feeling worried, and anxious to find the hook, he searched for Hay. He went through the dormitories, the games room, sitting room and dining room but Hay was not there.

Returning with another boy from his dormitory at about 10.15, he saw that Hay's dressing gown and pyjamas were still on his bed. Roughly ten minutes later, the two boys went to sleep.

The boy's most dramatic evidence described how he was woken up by the sound of the door slamming: "I saw Gordon was there. He had his clothing on, light-coloured jeans and a school jersey. He had nothing on his feet but his socks. I don't think he knew I was awake.

"His face was dirty. His hair was as if he had been out in the wind. It was blown all over the place. It was just like he had been out working in the garden and sweating and he drew his hand across his face. His knees were a bit dirty, just like he had been kneeling down."

Hay put on his pyjamas and washed at the sink. He was acting quite normally. Just as he was getting into bed a member of the staff turned out the lights and said "Goodnight". Hay said "Goodnight" back. Hay's room-mate awoke later when a car arrived bringing back their housemother. The three boys in the dormitory went to the window and spoke to her.

Hay's room-mate asked him where he had been; Hay denied he had been anywhere. The boy told Hay he had been looking for him; Hay asked him where he had looked and then said he had been in the bathroom. The next day, the boy found the metal hook in the bottom of the wardrobe and put it back on top.

When he was cross-examined, the boy admitted he had told lies to Hay's solicitor and to the police but said he was now telling the truth. Immediately after the murder he was not prepared to say anything that would implicate Hay but he later changed his mind.

A twenty-three-year-old student, William Bennett, who was acting as temporary housemaster at the school that night, had been in charge of Hay's dormitory. He told the court how Hay had won a prize that night at a whist drive. Not later than 10.35 p.m. Bennett went to the dormitory to turn out the lights. Hay had said "Goodnight". After 9.20 p.m. the staff were patrolling to see that the boys were getting ready for bed.

The deputy headmaster, Clifford Davies, who was in charge that night, said he saw Hay in his dressing gown about 9.45 p.m. There was usually a check on the boys at 10 p.m. but there was no check that night because of the whist drive.

Three days after the crime, Hay was transferred to Rossie Farm Approved School, Montrose where, four days later, the police arrived to interview him. The headmaster, Mr John Henderson, insisted on being present as the police questioned Hay from 10 p.m. until 3.30 a.m. He was prepared to intervene, he told the court, if Hay were treated unfairly.

Asked if he had occasion to intervene, Mr Henderson replied "The boot was on the other foot. The boy was impertinent to the police. He was truculent and aggressive."

The boy was later taken away to Lanark and was brought back to Rossie Farm, the following evening. Hay claimed his nose had been injured but Henderson saw no sign of an injury. It was not unusual for approved schoolboys to hint that they had been mishandled by the police. Henderson found nothing to merit investigation.

Dr James Imrie, a lecturer in forensic medicine at Glasgow University who examined Linda Peacock's body at the cemetery and also carried out the post-mortem, told the court there was a ligature mark round her neck as well as bruising and the mark of a ligature on the left wrist. There was an area of bruising over the left breast. He thought it was caused by a bite.

There were white spots in the centre of the bruising on the breast. Asked what form of tooth would cause such a mark, Dr Imrie replied, "A tooth with a hollow in its cutting edge."

In the doctor's opinion, Linda had died between 10 p.m. and midnight. She was a virgin. On her left wrist there was blackening due to scorching as well as a blister. There were also two lacerations and bruising on her head. The doctor had found bloodstains on a grey shirt and trousers belonging to Hay. He said he had seen many bites in connection with sexual assaults and had tested for saliva with varying results. No saliva test was taken in this case. Even if it had been taken it might not have helped. There was no sign of wetness on the skin.

He had not considered the possibility of identifying the assailant as a result of the bite. If he had seen obvious teeth marks he would have considered it possible to identify the assailant. At the time, he said, they did not have it in mind to use the bite as a means of identification. If he had thought of this, he would have sent for a dentist to look at the breast.

When he was shown a metal hook, he agreed it could have caused the girl's injuries, although there were many other blunt instruments which could have done so.

On the third day of the trial, Lord Grant was accompanied on the Bench by Lords Walker and Milligan. The proceedings were interrupted by a three-hour debate on the question of whether evidence arising from the warrant to take impressions of Hay's teeth for the third time was admissible or not. Retiring for only five minutes following the debate, the judges returned to announce that the evidence was indeed admissible.

A week after Hay's conviction, Lord Grant issued a written judgment on this important ruling, which depended upon the judges' finding that the warrant authorizing the Crown to take impressions of Hay's teeth was valid. It had been argued that, since Hay was not present at the hearing of the petition for the warrant before the sheriff, it had been incompetently granted.

Given that the Crown did not ask Hay's permission to take the third impression, the warrant would be illegal if it had not been competently granted. Had Hay been under arrest at the time, different considerations would have applied.

There was no doubt that a warrant to search premises was not illegal merely because the person concerned had not been apprehended or charged. The defence position, however, was that a search of premises was a very different matter from the possibly forcible invasion of the privacy of the person. Nor were there any reported cases of a warrant being granted to search the person.

Lord Grant said that although he was not persuaded that the difference was a matter of principle rather than degree a warrant to search the person should be granted only in very exceptional circumstances. Even if he was wrong in holding the warrant to be competent, he would have admitted the evidence, for in this case, by his committal to an approved school, Hay had largely ceased to be the master of his movements. In these very special circumstances, the Sheriff-Substitute was, in Lord Grant's opinion, justified in granting the warrant.

By the fourth day of the trial, the Crown had clearly shown that Hay was not around the school at the time of Linda Peacock's death. There was, however, little other evidence pointing to Hay as the assailant – until Professor Simpson electrified the court by confidently asserting that it was Hay's teeth which had caused the bite mark on the girl's breast.

Professor Simpson testified that he had thirty years' experience in forensic medicine and was consultant to New Scotland Yard. He had no dental qualifications but he had lectured all over the world on forensic odontology, had published articles on the subject, and was currently head of the Department of Forensic Medicine at London University: impressive credentials to support the crucial evidence he was about to give.

The marks on the girl's breast. Professor Simpson stated, were undoubtedly human bite marks. There were four marks which he regarded as quite characteristic of the points of pressure of teeth.

A firm hold had been made and the teeth had made a very distinct impression. There was some degree of suction; the bite must have been a painful one. In more than thirty years' practice the professor had seen many bite marks, both in his own cases and in others shown to him. He had never seen a bite mark with better defined detail than this.

It was accepted and orthodox practice to make transparencies and superimpose them over photographs of the injuries printed to the same scale in order to see to what extent exact matching took place. The methods in the Hay case followed the usual pattern. Professor Simpson was shown photographs taken from plaster casts of Hay's teeth as well as transparencies superimposed on photographs of the bite marks. He told the court: "I have looked at these with the greatest of care, as I commonly have to do with instruments of any kind in relation to marks on the skin.

"I see on this couple of superimposed transparencies a number of points of comparison, two of which, in my experience, are quite remarkable and quite unique.

"I would say that these two marks, in their position and in their character, and the other kind of mark which shows a scraping of the skin surface, for which I would require some explanation, are three quite exceptionally detailed marks.

"The presence of these three in this position and with those details would carry me a long way towards feeling that this was an exact comparison. I would be satisfied that this set of teeth – whichever it was – was the set that caused those marks".

He was satisfied that Hay's teeth caused the bite marks on the girl's breast. Under cross-examination the professor said a saliva test was another test that could be applied in such cases. Some people excreted blood in their saliva and it might be possible to group the blood.

Mr Stewart said it was agreed by experts that it was easier to prove that bite marks were *not* caused by a particular suspect than to prove that they *were*. Professor Simpson replied that less trouble was entailed in excluding certain teeth. Others had to be studied more closely.

The court was told that in fingerprints sixteen points of comparison were required to conclusively identify a particular suspect. Asked if a similar claim could be made for forensic odontology, Professor Simpson replied that the number of points of comparison was not as great as in fingerprinting. There had been, for example, eight to ten points in an English case.

Detective Inspector Osborne Butler, of the Identification Bureau of Glasgow City Police, told the court that he went through the twenty casts of impressions of teeth taken from pupils and staff at Loaningdale and found that only No 11, belonging to Hay, fitted the marks found on the girl's breast. When he superimposed transparencies of Hay's teeth on the bite mark he found "a demonstrable matching." Hollows on the upper and lower canines, he said, corresponded with the bite mark.

During cross-examination, Detective Inspector Butler stated that the teeth marks were "probably unique." Asked if there would be any other teeth in Great Britain which could have made the marks, he replied, "I would be surprised to find that." Mr Stewart asked, "Are you going as far as to say this is conclusive?" Inspector Butler indicated no doubt when he replied, "In my view, due to the characteristics in the teeth, this is conclusive."

Evidence was then given by other dental experts, who described how plaster casts had been taken from teeth impressions at Glasgow Dental Hospital. Hay's dental record card was produced, showing he required four fillings. Large diagrams of his teeth were used in court to ensure the jury understood the technical aspects of the evidence.

Two policemen who timed a run from the yew tree in the cemetery back to the school said it took one minute 43 seconds.

Detective Superintendent James Weir said that Hay's attitude was "one of resentment" when he saw him at Rossie School. When he was asked to account for his movements, Hay said he had watched television, had a game of cards and then went up to the dormitory at about 10.15 p.m. Two boys were in the "dorm" when he went in. Weir told Hay that his statement was in conflict with other statements. Later, when he asked Hay if he had left the school that night, the boy replied, "No, I never left the school. I can't change my story now, sir."

The most dramatic evidence in the case came to light on the fifth day of the trial when Dr John Warren Harvey, lecturer in dental surgery at Glasgow University, entered the witness box.

He told the court how he had examined the canine teeth of no fewer than 342 junior soldiers two months after the murder. He was trying to ascertain whether any of their teeth compared with the bite marks on the dead girl.

He looked at more than 1,000 canine teeth in the mouths of the soldiers. Only two had pitted eye teeth and none had pits in opposite canine teeth. He spent more than 200 painstaking hours studying the 29 teeth impressions taken. Only the canine teeth of Hay corresponded with the peculiarly-shaped bite marks on the girl's breast.

Using himself as a guinea pig, Dr Harvey demonstrated to the jury various bite marks. By pressing a copper impression of Hay's canine teeth against his finger he produced the peculiar pale-centred mark which was found on the girl's body. Using a small stick he produced from his pocket, he showed the jury the mark left by a solid object. Then, using a ball-point pen, he showed the court the mark left by a hollow-ended object.

Using Hay's upper right canine tooth, he showed that it left a mark on his finger which was pale in the centre and reddened round about.

When asked by the Solicitor-General if he could go any further than saying it was *possible* that Hay's mouth caused the bite marks, Dr Harvey said, "I find it extremely difficult to conceive that another mouth would have this number of extraordinary characteristics."

He said there was a broken edge on one tooth and a hook effect where part of a filling was missing. These were remarkable characteristics when taken together. The mark just below the nipple was quite unlike any mark he had ever seen described in forensic literature.

Dr Harvey described how he had been contacted by Inspector Butler while on holiday in Ireland. Returning to Scotland, he was given twenty-nine plaster models of teeth from impressions. They were identified by number only.

He was able to eliminate 24, leaving 5, including, as it was later revealed, the impression of Hay's teeth. A second set of impressions was taken. From these, Dr Harvey was able to exclude another four – leaving only No 11. The small pits he found in the tips of the upper and lower canines were "quite dramatic and extraordinary." He had never seen marks made by teeth which left a pale centre. It was something quite unusual.

Re-examining all twenty-nine of the impressions taken, Dr Harvey found one set which answered the problem of the gaps and the abrasions or tears in the skin. The set which made these extraordinary marks was No 11.

It was at this stage that he decided to make perfectly certain by using different materials and techniques to obtain a third, more finely-detailed impression. A warrant to take the final impression of Hay's teeth was subsequently granted.

Under cross-examination, Dr Harvey told the court that 80 per cent of the people in court might have hollows in their teeth but these were completely different from the strange pits in Hay's teeth. Asked if he could exclude the possibility of another mouth in Great Britain making the bite marks, he said he would find it extremely difficult to believe that such a mouth existed.

After more than five hours in the witness box, the doctor was unshaken in his conviction that the bite marks on Linda Peacock's body were made by Hay.

On the sixth day of the trial, Gordon Hay spent more than two hours in the witness box. Looking perfectly cool, calm and collected, he strongly denied that he was out of the school on the night Linda Peacock was murdered. He did agree, however, that he had left the school a few times to meet girls when he was not supposed to be out. He also agreed that he told lies in several of the statements he made to the police. He denied that his two room-mates were his alibi. The two boys he claimed, were telling lies and Mr Davies, the deputy headmaster, must be mistaken if he said he last saw him at 9.45 p.m. that night. Hay told the court he had been convicted of breaking and entering at Aberdeen Sheriff Court in December 1966 and arrived at Loaningdale Approved School in January 1967. He said he had never been convicted of assault.

He had seen Linda Peacock in Biggar a couple of times but had never spoken to her. The day before she was murdered, he went with two other boys and a master to the pictures in Biggar; that evening, they went to a fair. A girl came across and spoke to one of the boys. He did not know her at the time but he now knew it was Linda Peacock. He did not speak to her at all. Asked if he had said he would not mind going out with Linda, Hay replied, "Yes."

Hay said that he remembered another boy producing a metal hook and saying he was going to get someone with it. He told the boy he would only get into trouble and took the hook from him and threw it on top of a cupboard. The next time he saw the hook was in court.

He also denied saying to anyone that he intended going to Biggar, and claimed never to have left the school at all that evening. He had won a prize at a whist drive in the school and, before supper, changed into a white shirt with his pyjama bottoms. He did not think he had a dressing gown on. He was wearing his boots as he did not like the school sandals. After supper, he watched *The Untouchables* on television, which finished at 9.55 p.m. He then went to the dining room to watch a game of cards. At 10.02 p.m. he spoke to another boy and they checked their watches. He spoke to another boy for ten or fifteen minutes, returning to his dormitory between 10.15 and 10.30 p.m. One of his room-mates was already there; the second came in afterwards.

They got into bed and a member of the staff turned out the lights. Later the boys spoke to the housemother when she arrived back by car and then listened to the radio, which was switched off about midnight. Hay denied having had a conversation the next day with one of the boys about what they would tell the police concerning the murder.

Hay recalled being visited by detectives at Rossie School after he had been transferred there. They greeted him: "Hello, Gordon. You weren't expecting to see us again, were you?"

They said to him in the presence of the headmaster: "We know you did it, Gordon. Why not admit it?"

When the detectives went out, Hay was left alone with the headmaster, who told him: "They know you did it. I know you did it. Why not admit it?"

After being taken to Lanark, he was returned to Rossie, where he told the headmaster, "My nose was skinned." The headmaster asked him what had happened and he told him a detective had hit him. He also told the headmaster the police banged his head against a wall a couple of times and put him in a cell. They kept trying to get him to admit it.

Mr Ewan Stewart, cross-examining, said, "You are just lying to try to blacken everyone?" But Hay denied this.

Hay agreed he had sneaked out of the school and back again without the staff finding out. But he denied he had his eye on Linda. He admitted he had not always told the same story about his movements that night.

During the rigorous cross-examination, Hay remained completely unruffled, putting on an altogether calm and convincing performance. Re-examined by his own counsel, he again denied he was out of the school that night and denied killing Linda.

On the final day of the hearing of evidence, a dental expert called for the defence threw a small spanner in the works when he cast doubt on the significance of the bite marks. Professor George Beagrie, Professor of Restorative Dentistry at Edinburgh University, said he found it difficult to determine what the Crown experts meant by their statements that defects in canine teeth were rare.

He had carried out an experiment with fifty teeth impressions from his own department and found teeth with pits similar to those which the Crown said Hay's teeth showed. He accepted that the bite mark could have been made by Hay but he did not feel it was beyond reasonable doubt. The incidence of defective canine teeth was greater than the Crown experts said. He felt that there could be other mouths in Great Britain that could have caused the bite marks.

Addressing the jury, the Solicitor-General said the case had "some unusual features". A certain amount of evidence against Hay was dental and pathological evidence concerning the bite marks. It was clear from the dental evidence, he said, that the only set of teeth out of the twenty-nine that could have made the bite was Hay's.

He said there was no criticism of Linda Peacock of a sexual character. She was not sexually promiscuous. The jury might think it was highly unlikely that she would go voluntarily into the graveyard with some stray tramp who just chanced to meet her on the road. She would only have accompanied someone she knew to that place.

Hay, he said, must have "worn the cloak of invisibility" for he had not been seen after 9.50 p.m. by six of the masters at his school. His alibi should thus be rejected, root and branch.

When he came to deal with forensic odontology, Mr Stewart said: "We are not dabbling in some kind of experimental matter. There have been cases on the Continent and in England in which this form of identification has been used. But even supposing there were other people with this kind of mouth existing in the world or even in Britain, how many of these people had on August 5 been expressing a sexual interest in Linda Peacock? How many were living within two minutes of the cemetery? How many were sneaking back into their beds about ten minutes after the murder with their hair blown about and dirt on their faces and clothing? How many had in their possession an instrument such as a hook? How many of these people were next day trying to get their friends to tell lies? There is only one verdict here which an objective and just appraisal and evaluation of the evidence can lead to – a verdict of guilty."

Mr Ian Stewart, for the defence, said this was the first case of its kind in Scotland in which forensic odontology had been used. In Britain this science was in its infancy. Sixteen characteristics were required in fingerprints but that was not the case here. In Britain, he said, the experience of the dental profession was very limited in this type of case. Only one dentist had said it was beyond reasonable doubt that Hay's teeth caused the bite marks.

The fact that Hay had lied on occasion and may have lied in evidence did not make him the murderer, Mr Stewart argued. If the Crown broke Hay's alibi that still did not make him the murderer. The evidence for the Crown was circumstantial; the case was balanced "on a knife edge." The only evidence that connected Hay with the crime and, moreover, with the scene of the crime, was related to bite marks.

In his two-hour charge to the jury, gravel-voiced Lord Grant warned that circumstantial evidence was not enough to convict Hay. "For that reason," he said, "the dental and pathological evidence is of paramount importance. This forensic odontology, as it is called, is a relatively new science but there must, of course, always be a first time."

Lord Grant reminded the jury that scientific and medical knowledge advanced as the years went on. It was only comparatively recently that fingerprints had come to be accepted as infallible. It was only in 1945 that palm prints had been recognized. It was of importance that the law should keep pace with science.

Lord Grant said that the case was, as well as a grave one, in some ways unique, difficult and puzzling. But he thought it right to say that he and the jury had been assisted in their task by the way in which it had been prepared and also by the admirable presentation by the Solicitor-General, Mr Ewan Stewart and his colleague, Mr Ian Stewart, for the defence.

Lord Grant pointed out to the jury that even if Hay had told lies that was not sufficient to establish his guilt. They must therefore examine the evidence on the bite marks with care and in the light of their assessment of the expert witnesses. In assessing the evidence, he continued, the jury should keep in mind that the Crown experts had both made a special study of forensic odontology. The two experts for the defence, on the other hand, were being pushed rather beyond the field where their own expert knowledge lay.

The judge's dismissal of the defence experts' evidence was probably a crucial factor in the jury's deliberations and must have removed any doubts in their minds about the strength and weight of the scientific evidence for the Crown.

After an absence of two and a half hours, the jury returned a majority verdict of Guilty. The judge ordered Hay to be detained during Her Majesty's pleasure as he was under eighteen when he committed the crime.

Hay showed no emotion as he was led away. Sitting in court were his grey-haired mother, Mrs Hannah Hay, and the mother of his victim, Mrs Mary Peacock.

Mrs Hay said afterwards that her husband, Robert, a farm labourer, died on the day after Gordon's sixteenth birthday. "Up till then, Gordon was fairly happy and content but I think his dad's death had an effect on him. After that, I saw an awful change in my boy. He seemed to go completely off the rails.''

Gordon wrote to his mother twice a week while he was awaiting trial. His mother said: "I always looked forward to his letters. He's my son and I can forgive him although I can never believe he did this terrible thing. I will stand by him."

Gordon Hay was a country-born boy who loved cars and often boasted about girlfriends. His love of cars got him into trouble and led to him being sent to an approved school. He danced well and was admired by the girls but friends said he was basically a loner.

Linda's parents, however, could never forget or forgive. Her father said afterwards the school should never have been in Biggar at all and that he would support any move to have it closed down.

Mrs Peacock spoke of her ordeal and her bitterness. "Linda was a lovely young girl whose life was cut short viciously by a boy from that school," she said.

It was the third time that tragedy had struck the Peacock family. Two years earlier, Linda's elder sister died after an illness and a year before that her uncle, a ship's cook, drowned in a dockside accident in England.

Hay's appeal two months later in the Court of Criminal Appeal in Edinburgh was heard by a bench of five judges because of the important legal question of whether the sheriff had the right to issue the warrant to take further teeth impressions from Hay before he was charged.

Lord Clyde, Lord Justice General, presided with Lords Guthrie, Migdale, Cameron and Johnston.

Mr Ian Stewart, in a strong argument, contended that the dental evidence obtained under the warrant was inadmissible and was prejudicial to Hay. The police were not entitled to search the person of a suspect before arrest, he claimed. His argument was particularly concerned with the search of a person as a means of identification rather than to find objects in his possession.

Police powers on identification were limited to such observation as was possible without interfering with the person. Interference with the person without consent and before the individual's arrest was technically as assault. It was a principle of Scottish criminal law that you could not search a person before arresting him.

Mr Stewart argued that there is always a conflict between the rights of an individual and the rights of the state. The right of the state to override the rights of the individual was a matter on which Parliament alone should legislate; it was not for the court to overrule a principle of personal liberty established for many years.

The Solicitor-General argued for the Crown that although the warrant in question was unique there was nothing unlawful about it. If the court could not accept that proposition, the circumstances in the case were such that an irregularity fell to be excused.

Moreover, there was a general power for magistrates to grant warrants for the advancement of the course of justice. In the present case, there had been insufficient evidence to put Hay on trial and the Crown wished to confirm further evidence. The warrant, the Solicitor-General argued, was perfectly valid in the special circumstances. There was no unfairness. Everything was done in the public interest and in the interests of the accused.

The five judges rejected the appeal and on 30 May 1968 gave their reasons. Lord Clyde said that although Hay was not present or legally represented at the hearing for the warrant, the presence of an independent judicial officer, such as the sheriff, afforded the basis for a fair reconciliation of the interests of the public in the suppression of crime and of the individual, who was entitled not to have the liberty of his person or premises unduly jeopardised.

The hearing before the sheriff was by no means a formality; the court had to be satisfied that the circumstances justified the unusual course that had been taken and that the warrant was not too wide or oppressive. The sheriff was the safeguard against the granting of too general a warrant. A warrant of this limited kind would, however, be granted only in special circumstances.

The judge held that the warrant was quite legal and the resulting evidence therefore admissible. Apart from anything else, there was in this case an element of urgency; a visit to the dentist or an injury to Hay's teeth could have destroyed the evidence.

After the conviction, there was a public outcry against the approved school. Biggar Town Council demanded it should be closed immediately or, at least, that the whole staff from the headmaster down should be changed. Provost James Telfer said that since 1963, when Loaningdale opened, the town had wanted a public inquiry into the running of the school. "We got it during the trial. The security there was terrible," he said.

In 1965, the Town Council, worried by a spate of petty crimes, demanded a meeting with the school's board of managers. It was an experimental school set up to rehabilitate young boys. A spokesman for the Scottish Education Department said at the time that it was not a penal institution to keep children permanently out of the community. Only boys who were thought capable of returning to society in a matter of months were to be admitted to the school.

Security at Loaningdale was tightened in January 1968, after the council met Mr Bruce Millan, the Under-Secretary of State responsible for education. A night alarm system was installed to alert staff to any break-out. If any boy left the school without permission he was immediately sent to a stricter establishment. But Councillor James Stephen summed up the feelings of local people when he said, "There is no doubt that this experiment has failed. You cannot cure a bad boy by permissiveness. And when prizes of cigarettes are given out at whist drives and thirteen-year-olds are allowed to smoke, the whole thing is ridiculous."

The headmaster, who was on holiday at the time of the murder, was in favour of trying to rehabilitate young offenders. He allowed smoking in the school and allowed the boys to call masters by their Christian names. He recommended Hay's transfer to another school because he did not think he was suitable for Loaningdale.

Provost Telfer, who joined the board of the school in 1965 after the first row, said, "If it was left to the people of Biggar, it would be closed immediately. There is a tremendous amount of ill-feeling in the town about it. Since the murder, there has been a fantastic amount of complaints by people who have not voiced them before."

Councillor Stephen, who canvassed more than 20,000 signatures for his petition calling for the return of the death penalty, said the Loaningdale experiment – it was the first "open" type of school in Scotland – had failed lamentably. The petty dictators of St Andrews House, he said, had decreed it would be sited at Biggar regardless of local feeling.

A spokesman for the Social Work Services Group at the Scottish Office said: "There have been, and always will be, enormous difficulties in rehabilitating young people who have been out of step with society. It is difficult to talk about success or failure in a social education context."

At the time, there were 36 boys in Loaningdale: 31 for theft, 3 for truancy and 2 for road traffic offences. This did not suggest the school was harbouring would-be killers.

After the meeting with Mr Millan, two more local people, a doctor and a minister, were added to the board of the school, of which Lord Birsay was chairman.

A Government spokesman summed up the difficulties of rehabilitation when he said: "Selection is a basic part of the experiment. A boy's record, IQ, family history and condition are all considered. In addition, great weight is given to an assessment of the willingness of a family to co-operate in treatment and of inter-family relationships."

Linda Peacock's parents at first considered suing the Scottish Education Department, who were responsible for selection of the boys sent to the school. Eventually, however, they accepted £2,000 compensation from the Criminal Injuries Board.

Mrs Peacock said:

> The money is no compensation for Linda's life. We are more interested in punishment for all those responsible for the negligent system that led to her death. We had considered a civil action but have now dropped that as the only measure a civil court might take would be to award damages, which is little comfort to us.

Writing in the Glasgow Police magazine some time later, Dr Warren Harvey, in an article called "The Tooth, the Whole

Truth and the Police" revealed that twenty-five dentists were now linked with the police in Aberdeen, Dundee, Edinburgh and Glasgow to help in criminal cases. When a victim is bitten, Harvey wrote, the marks must be seen at the first possible moment by a dentist, a police photographer and a pathologist. He pointed out that the Biggar murder trial verdict was by a majority of 14 to 1 and that about one third of the 1,100 foolscap pages in the transcript of the evidence consisted of dental and medical evidence.

But, a few years later, allegations by an internationally known expert on forensic odontology, Dr Soren Keiser-Nielsen of the Department of Forensic Odontology at the Royal Dental College in Copenhagen, cast a slight shadow over the new science. He alleged that he came to Scotland before the trial but his evidence had been "hushed up" and he had been hurriedly got out of the way. In a letter to the Forensic Society's journal, he said he concluded there was nothing in the mark on the victim's breast to indicate it was a bite mark. Even if it were, he added, there were too few points of similarity to warrant a dental identification of the originator. He had explained his reasoning and conclusions, and asked whether the fact he had drawn conclusions adverse to the Crown case would come to the notice of the defence.

But the Crown revealed that the doctor had considered the evidence insufficient to justify a firm conclusion on identification and had declined to give evidence. Counsel for the defence had accordingly been informed by the Crown that Dr Keiser-Nielsen was not willing to give evidence.

The Crown also said the doctor's views expressed at the time did not match the views he expressed later. He had undoubtedly withdrawn, declining to give evidence. Mr Alistair R. Brownlie, Secretary of the Society of Solicitors in the Supreme Courts of Scotland, strongly denied the doctor's allegations. The doctor, Mr Brownlie maintained, had indicated he wanted nothing more to do with the case and was therefore not called as a witness. The police who drove him to the airport were merely exercising the customary courtesies. The doctor was not, as he later claimed, hurriedly got out of the way.

But the controversy still did not die down. Keiser-Nielsen

insisted in 1972 that the mark on Linda Peacock's breast was not a human bite mark. Hay's counsel, Mr Ian Stewart, recalled being told the doctor was not prepared to come and give evidence and that there was no point in calling him as a witness if he was unwilling to come.

While there is little likelihood of compulsory dental examination becoming a standard feature of Scottish pre-trial criminal procedure, the courts clearly recognised the exceptional nature of the case in approving the warrant to take the vital third impression of Hay's teeth. The power given to the prosecution to secure that important evidence from the previously inviolable person of the suspect might well be used again if the course of justice demands it.

Had genetic fingerprinting, which has been hailed as the greatest breakthrough in forensic science this century, been available at that time, even more conclusive proof might well have been provided by the scientists.

ACKNOWLEDGEMENTS AND SOURCES

The editor is grateful to Jonathan Goodman and Wilf Gregg for putting at his disposal their encyclopaedic collections of crime books containing many of the cases featured. He also wishes to thank the following people and organizations for their kind permission to reprint the following:

Albert Borowitz for *The Medea of Kew Gardens Hills* from *The Lady Killers*, ed. Jonathan Goodman (Piatkus, London 1990, © Albert I. Borowitz 1990). Reproduced by permission of the author;

Jonathan Goodman for *The Jigsaw Murder Case* from *Medical Murders* (Piatkus, London 1992, © Jonathan Goodman 1992). Reproduced by permission of the author;

Miss Lois Gribble for Leonard Gribble (writing as Leo Grex), *The Mystery of the Flying Blood* from *Mystery Stranger Than Fiction* (Robert Hale Ltd., London 1979, © Leonard Gribble 1979);

Sir Max Hastings for Macdonald Hastings, *The Murderer Who Got Away With It* from *The Other Mr Churchill* (Harrap, London 1963, © Macdonald Hastings 1963);

Sir Ludovic Kennedy for *The Birmingham Six* from *Truth To Tell* (Bantam Press, London 1991, © Sir Ludovic Kennedy 1991). Reproduced by permission of the author;

Clifford L. Linedecker for *The Vampire Rapist* from *Serial Thrill Killers* (Knightsbridge Publishing Company, New York 1990, © Clifford L. Linedecker 1990). Reproduced by permission of the author;

S. C. Lomax for *Particle of Doubt* © S. C. Lomax 2007;

Mrs Shirley Lucas for Norman Lucas, *A Case of "Hideous Ferocity"* from *The Child Killers* (Arthur Barker Ltd., London 1970, © Norman Lucas 1970);

The Trustees of the Estate of Edgar Lustgarten for Edgar Lustgarten, *The Acid-Bath Virtuoso* from *The Business of Murder* (Harrap, London 1968, © Edgar Lustgarten 1968);

James McClure for *Picking Up The Pieces*, originally published as *The Crumbles Murder* in *Killers* (Fontana, London 1976) © Estate of James McClure 2007;

Terry Morland for Nigel Morland, *The Talking Skull* from *Pattern of Murder* (Elek Books, London 1966);

Winifred Robinson for *Sweet Baby James* © Winifred Robinson 2007;

Mrs Margaret Saunders for George Saunders, *The Biter Bit* from *Casebook of the Bizarre* (John Donald Publishers Ltd 1991, © Estate of George Saunders 1999);

Jim Shelley for *Who Killed Bambi?* from *Weekend Guardian* 1993 © Jim Shelley 1993. Reproduced by permission of the author;

Linda Stratmann for *Blood In The Basement* © Linda Stratmann 2007;

Jurgen Thorwald for *Murder In Deptford* from *The Marks of Cain* (Thames and Hudson, London 1966, © Jurgen Thorwald 1966). Reproduced by permission of the author;

Joseph Wambaugh for *Unguarded Moment* from *The Blooding* (Bantam Press, London 1989, © Joseph Wambaugh 1989). Reproduced by permission of the author;

Dr Philip Willcox for *The Hilldrop Crescent Mystery* from *The Detective-Physician* (William Heinemann Medical Books Ltd., London 1970, © Philip Willcox 1970). Reproduced by permission of the author;

Colin Wilson for *The Dingo Baby Case* from *Unsolved Murders and Mysteries* ed. John Canning (Michael O'Mara Books, London 1987, © Colin Wilson 1987). Reproduced by permission of the author;

Gaby Wood for *The Death of a Pageant Queen*. Originally published as *Getting Away With Murder* in *The Observer* (London) © Guardian News & Media Ltd 2006;

Tom Zito for *Did The Evidence Fit The Crime?* Originally in *Life* Magazine, March 1982 © Tom Zito 1982. Reproduced by permission of the author;

Every effort has been made to trace the original copyright holders of the following, without success; the editor and publishers would be pleased to hear from any claimants to legal copyright of:

Allen Andrews, *The Closing of the Ring* in *Intensive Inquiries* (Harrap, London 1973);

James A. Brussel, *The Coppolino Case* in *Casebook of a Crime Psychiatrist* (Mayflower, New York 1969);

George Dilnot, *"If–"* in *Great Detectives and Their Methods* (Bles, London 1927);

Mike Gier, *The Man Who Could Read Thoughts* in *Crime Omnibus*, ed. Kurt Singer (W. H. Allen, London 1961);

Percy Hoskins, *The Poisoner* from *The Sound of Murder* (John Long, London 1973);

Sir Richard Jackson, *Picture A Murderer* in *Occupied With Crime* (Harrap, London 1967);

Robert Jackson, *A Welsh Mummy* in *The Crime Doctors* (Frederick Muller, London 1966);

John Laurence, *The Jekyll and Hyde of New York* in *Extraordinary Crimes* (Sampson Low, Marston & Co. Ltd, London nd);

David Rowan, *Act of Mercy* in *Famous American Crimes* (Panther, New York 1957);

Professor Keith Simpson, *A Riddle of Maggots* in *Forty Years of Murder* (Harrap, London 1978);

Sir Sydney Smith, *The Case of Sidney Fox* in *Mostly Murder* (Harrap, London 1959);

Tom Tullett, *A Ray of Sunlight Unmasks A Killer* in *Strictly Murder* (The Bodley Head, London 1979)

ILLUSTRATION ACKNOWLEDGEMENTS

Barry George/Bulsara at Bow Street Magistrates after being committed to trial for the murder of Jill Dando.
Copyright © TopFoto/National News

Enhanced video of two youths that police would like to question in connection with the murder of James Bulger, 18th February 1993. Jon Venables and Robert Thompson.
Copyright © TopFoto/PA

Lord Lucan pictured outside his London home on the occasion of the announcement of his engagement to Veronica Duncan, 14 October 1963.
Copyright © TopFoto/UPPA

The Coastguards Cottage, The Crumbles, the scene of the crime, 1924.
Copyright © TopFoto

Guilty of five murders Jeremy Bamber, 25, leaves Chelmsford Crown Court in a prison vehicle after receiving a life sentence of at least 25 years, for murdering five members of his family. He was found guilty of killing his adoptive parents, Neville and June, both 61, his ex-model sister Sheila "Bambi" Caffell, and her six-year-old twin sons Nicholas and Daniel last year. 28th October 1986.
Copyright © TopFoto/AP

Edmund Crimmins puts his arm around his wife Alice after she tripped and fell on stairs leaving Queens Supreme Court in New York. Mrs Crimmins was arraigned on first degree murder charge of her 4-year-old daughter, 13th September 1968.
Copyright © TopFoto/AP

The remains of Belle Elmore in the cellar of No 39 Hilldrop Crescent.
Copyright © TopFoto

The Crippen case, the first use of wireless telegraphy in the arrest of criminals.
Copyright © TopFoto

A detective leads Doctor Hawley Harvey Crippen from the SS *Megantic*, upon her arrival in England, August 1910. He had attempted to flee the country after murdering his wife, but was apprehended with the use of radio communication, tried and executed. (Photo by Hulton Archive/Getty Images).
Copyright © Getty Images

Lindy Chamberlain, the mother who was jailed for the murder of her daughter, "Azaria" pictured arriving at court in Darwin, Australia, to attend the inquiry into her conviction. She claims a wild Australian dog of the desert (a dingo) dragged her baby out of the family tent when they were camping at Ayers Rock in the centre of Australia in August 1980.
Copyright © TopFoto/AP

Bruno Richard Hauptmann, later convicted of kidnapping and murdering Charles Lindbergh Jr, takes the stand in his own defence in his extortion trial, 15th October 1934. (Photo by Hulton Archive/Getty Images).
Copyright © Getty Images

Investigators with baby clothing belonging to Charles Lindbergh Jr.
Copyright © TopFoto

Dr Samuel Sheppard wears an orthopaedic collar for an injury he said he received when battling with a mysterious bushy-haired man who beat Mrs Sheppard to death July 4th 1954.
Copyright © TopFoto

Harry Dobkin, was hanged for the murder of his wife Rachel Dobkin. In this picture can be seen the notes of Harry Dobkin for his appeal against the death sentence. Dobkin murdered his wife in April 1941 and as there were so many fatalities with bombing victims at that time tried to conceal his wife as a bomb victim under the ruins of Vauxhall Baptist Chapel.
Copyright © popperfoto.com

Dr Buck Ruxton (Bukhtyar Rustomji Ratanji Hakim), who was convicted of the murder of his wife, Isabella Ruxton, and his housemaid, Mary Jane Rogerson at his home in Lancaster. Ruxton was hanged for the murders at Strangeways Prison on 12th May 1936. (Photo by Topical Press Agency/Getty Images).
Copyright © Getty Images

Dr Buck Ruxton murdered his wife and and their nursemaid at Lancaster, and Mrs Ruxton's cut up body parts were found at Moffat, Dumfries. In this picture police are searching a ravine alongside a waterfall at Moffat. Dr Ruxton was found guilty and hanged in 1936.
Copyright © popperfoto.com

The spot where June Anne Devaney was found murdered. The white sheet marks the exact location. Peter Griffiths, 22 who was charged with the murder of 3-year-old June Anne Devaney, was found guilty and hanged at Walton Gaol in 1948.
Copyright © popperfoto.com

Former guardsman Peter Griffiths who was hanged at Walton prison, Liverpoool, for abducting, assaulting and murdering three year old June Devaney in 1948. The forensic evidence against Griffiths was overwhelming after 47,000 men in Blackburn had their fingerprints taken. (Photo by Keystone/Hulton Archive/Getty Images).
Copyright © Getty Images